American Legal Records

Edited for THE AMERICAN HISTORICAL ASSOCIATION by the
Committee on the Littleton-Griswold Fund

THE BURLINGTON COURT BOOK OF WEST NEW JERSEY
1680–1709

The Littleton-Griswold Fund of the American Historical Association was established in 1927 by Mrs. Frank T. Griswold in memory of William E. Littleton and Frank Tracy Griswold

COMMITTEE ON THE LITTLETON-GRISWOLD FUND

FRANCIS S. PHILBRICK, *Chairman*
CARROLL T. BOND
JOHN DICKINSON
LAWRENCE A. HARPER
MARK DeWOLFE HOWE
LEONARD W. LABAREE
RICHARD B. MORRIS

American Legal Records—Volume 5

THE
BURLINGTON COURT BOOK

A RECORD OF QUAKER JURISPRUDENCE
IN WEST NEW JERSEY
1680-1709

EDITED BY

H. CLAY REED
ASSOCIATE PROFESSOR OF HISTORY
UNIVERSITY OF DELAWARE

AND

GEORGE J. MILLER
COUNSELLOR AT LAW
PERTH AMBOY, NEW JERSEY

Originally published by the American Historical Association,
Washington, D.C., 1944
Reprinted, 1998, by Genealogical Publishing Co., Inc.
1001 N. Calvert St., Baltimore, Md. 21202
Library of Congress Catalogue Card Number 98-70093
International Standard Book Number 0-8063-1558-X

TABLE OF CONTENTS

	PAGE
Editorial Note	vii
Historical Introduction, *by H. Clay Reed*	ix
The Quakers of West Jersey	x
Swedish, Dutch, and English Predecessors	xii
Fenwick's Colony	xiv
The Burlington Settlement, 1677–1680	xxv
Government in West Jersey, 1680–1708	xxxi
The Courts and their Work, 1680–1709	xl
Burlington Court Minutes, 1680	1
The Burlington Court Book, 1681–1709	5
Index	347

EDITORIAL NOTE

The translation of a seventeenth-century manuscript court record into twentieth-century type, in a form both economical to print and easy to read, is not so simple a task as it might seem. The result of our efforts with the Burlington Court Book probably will not be wholly satisfactory to any reader of this volume. They are not to us; if we were starting anew we would do certain things differently. However, nothing, it is said, is done in vain. If the imperfections discovered in the editing of the Burlington minutes are of service to preparers of future publications of this kind, our labor on the Burlington book will be sufficiently repaid.

The principle guiding the editors in preparing this volume was that it must *read* like the original manuscript, but not necessarily *look* like it; that is, the exact meaning and content of what the successive scribes wrote down in the Burlington minutes should be faithfully reproduced, but in a form presenting a minimum of labor to the printer in manufacturing the book and to the reader in perusing its contents.

With this objective in view, some liberties have been taken, not with the matter, but with the manner, of the manuscript minutes. Contractions and symbols of words or parts of words, habitually used in those days to save paper and time, have been expanded, and spelled according to the writer's preference, or when that could not be ascertained, the usage of the time. A few abbreviations in present use, such as Mr. and Jr., have been kept, and in these cases raised letters have been lowered and the abbreviations followed by periods. The scribes' capitalization and punctuation (or lack of them) have been reproduced, with a few exceptions. Sentences have been regularly begun with capitals and closed with periods. To save space tabular or columnar material in the manuscript has been run on horizontally in the printed text. In such cases items in a series, such as names of jurors, have been separated by commas. Elsewhere, when the scribe used extra space instead of punctuation to set off words or phrases from each other, we have followed him: for example, *Smith v. Jones   Case   Continued.*

Marginal material has been brought into the body of the text, set in italics, and enclosed in brackets. Manuscript page headings, which usually consist only of page number and date, are set in bold face and enclosed in brackets. Missing dates have been supplied.

The English still used the old-style calendar, in which the new year began on March 25; but they frequently double-dated the interval from January 1 to March 24 inclusive. These dates have not been modernized in this volume. The reader therefore should remember that, for example, the day after December 31 1701 was January 1 1701 or 1701/2, and likewise the day preceding March 25 1702 was March 24 1701 or 1701/2.

Those who wish to consult the originals of the records printed herein will find the Court Record of 1680 (pages 1–4 of the present work) in a thin volume of Burlington Records in the Secretary of State's office in Trenton. The Burlington Court Book, which constitutes the bulk of this publication, is a folio volume, 11¼ by 16½ inches, in an excellent state of preservation. It is kept in the office of the Clerk of the Supreme Court, also in Trenton. Photostatic copies of it are deposited in the State Library, Trenton, and the office of the County Clerk of Burlington County, Mount Holly. Both of these manuscript volumes have been microfilmed, along with many other early New Jersey records, by the New Jersey Historical Records Survey.[1] Copies may be purchased from the American Documentation Institute, 1719 N. St., N.W., Washington, D. C. The libraries of Princeton University, the College of the City of New York, and the University of Delaware have copies of the Burlington Court Book film.

The editors are glad to make the following acknowledgements of assistance rendered: to the Committee on Legal History of the American Historical Association, and especially to its Chairman and its Secretary, who have borne the burden of supervision and criticism in the preparation of this volume; to Messrs. Charles S. Aitkin and L. Byron Atkins of the Secretary of State's office, Mr. Rue B. Brearly, Assistant Clerk of the Supreme Court, and Miss Dorothy Lucas, of the State Library, for facilitating our use of the historical material in their custody; to Mrs. Eleanor Melson, Department of Records, Philadelphia Friends Yearly Meeting (302 Arch St.), for invaluable aid in identifying the Quaker *dramatis personae* in this volume; to Mr. Frank H. Stewart, President of the Gloucester County Historical Society, Mr. Joseph S. Sickler, Postmaster of Salem, and Miss Edna L. Jacobsen, of the New York State Library, for help on various points; to Mr. James Walsh, who made the first typewritten transcript of the Burlington Court Book for the New Jersey Historical Records Survey, and to Miss Anne Koller, who prepared the copy for the printer; and finally to the Vail-Ballou Press, not forgetting the proofreaders who wrestled valiantly with the eccentricities of a seventeenth-century text.

H. C. R.
G. J. M.

[1] Listed on pp. 94–96 of the April 1943 edition of *Check List of Historical Records Survey Publications (W. P. A. Technical Series, Research and Records Bibliography No. 7)*, published by the Federal Works Agency, Works Project Administration, Division of Service Projects, Washington, D. C.

HISTORICAL INTRODUCTION *

Although the Burlington Court Book is the most important judicial record of proprietary West Jersey, it has never hitherto been printed. Its legislative counterpart was assembled and published nearly two centuries ago by two public-spirited West-Jerseymen.[1] Leaming and Spicer's *Grants* was a propaganda document, material for a study in comparative law by which patriots of that day could, the compilers hoped, readily discover how much better the old proprietary government had been than the royal rule under which they were then living.[2] Unfortunately for the historian, Leaming and Spicer did not consider it necessary for their purpose to print the Burlington Court Book, in which the laws and constitutions which they admired were enforced and applied. These judicial records have remained in manuscript, inaccessible except to those within travelling distance of Trenton. In 1938 they were microfilmed by the New Jersey Historical Records Survey,[3] and now at last, through inclusion in the American Historical Association's *American Legal Records Series*, they become as available to the student as the corresponding laws have been since 1758.

Like most of our earliest judicial records, the Burlington Court Book is a mine of historical ore of many kinds besides the strictly legal or judicial. The editors have not attempted to separate and refine these by-products, considering this a more proper task for specialists in the various branches of social and economic history.[4] The detailed index which is provided will, it is hoped, be a sufficient guide to the varied contents of the volume. The purpose of this historical introduction is to place the Burlington Court Book in its historical setting, rather than to describe its contents in detail.

To do so, it is necessary to recall, first, that West Jersey was a Quaker colony (the first, antedating its more famous neighbor, Pennsylvania, by six

---

* The legal introduction which was planned to follow this historical introduction was not completed in time for publication.

[1] Aaron Leaming and Jacob Spicer, *The Grants, Concessions, and Original Constitutions of the Province of New Jersey, the Acts passed during the Proprietary Governments, and other Material Transactions before the Surrender thereof to Queen Anne* . . . (Philadelphia, [1758]; Somerville, 1881). Citations are from the reprint.

[2] "If our present system of government should not be judged so equal to the natural rights of a reasonable creature, as the one that raised us to the dignity of a colony, let it serve as a caution to guard the cause of liberty" (Preface).

[3] See Editorial Note, above.

[4] *The Princeton History of New Jersey*, several volumes of which have already appeared under the editorship of T. J. Wertenbaker, will cover the various aspects of New Jersey's history more thoroughly than has yet been attempted for any other state. A volume in this series on West Jersey, by J. E. Pomfret, is almost ready for publication.

years), but that, second, the Quaker proprietorship was not the first white government in West Jersey, and the new owners therefore had to dispose of certain embarrassing situations created by earlier regimes before they could proceed unhampered with their own particular experiment in government.

THE QUAKERS OF WEST JERSEY

The religious background and history of Quakerism on both sides of the Atlantic have been studied with industry and insight by their own historians, and need not detain us here.[5] It is enough to observe that, in West Jersey at least, the Friends' migration was motivated by two purposes: first, to found a colony where they could practice their religion and govern themselves in the way they deemed best; and second, to reap a profit from their investment in this enterprise.[6] These two objectives were not at all incompatible, for without a certain degree of material well-being among Friends as individuals the Society could hardly hope to flourish as a religious entity. Spiritual and material prosperity went hand in hand. The English Quakers of the earlier period were, it is true, rather less abundantly endowed with this world's goods than their descendants.[7] Their membership none the less came from the middle and lower-middle economic brackets rather than from the poverty-stricken, while their doctrine and discipline encouraged industry and thrift, helped needy members of the group, and restrained the reckless. The Quaker founders of West Jersey were definitely men of means: few wealthy, among whom Penn was an outstanding example; some whose designs exceeded their resources, such as Byllynge and Fenwick; and scores of others who could spend a few pounds or hundreds of pounds for a tract of land and still have enough money left to bring their families and perhaps a few servants over to settle it.[8] They were either plain farmers ("yeomen") or craftsmen and tradesmen,

---

[5] See especially W. C. Braithwaite, *The Beginnings of Quakerism* (London, 1912), and *The Second Period of Quakerism* (London, 1919), and R. M. Jones, *The Quakers in the American Colonies* (London, 1911).

[6] R. G. Johnson, the first historian of Fenwick's colony, says of the first proprietors, Fenwick included: "They were, every one of them, speculators in these western lands, and . . . their sole object was to accumulate fortunes; and although they were all men of high character and distinction, yet it must be apparent to every observer that self-interest was at the bottom of all their schemes and manoeuvres" (J. S. Sickler, *The History of Salem County, New Jersey* (Salem, 1937), p. 32). Johnson was a descendant of Fenwick (T. Shourds, *History and Genealogy of Fenwick's Colony* (Bridgeton, 1876), p. 15), but a Presbyterian (Sickler, p. 200).

[7] For a comparison see W. Beck and T. F. Ball, *London Friends Meetings* (London, 1869), p. 90. On Quaker economic progress in general, see I. Grubb, *Quakerism and Industry before 1800* (London, 1930).

[8] For some examples see E. P. Tanner, *The Province of New Jersey, 1664–1738* (New York, 1908), p. 15. Among those who came in the service of their more affluent coreligionists were William Matlack and George Elkinton, servants for four years to Daniel Wills (J. Clement, *The Proprietary Towns of West Jersey. Read before the Surveyors' Association of West New Jersey, August 8th, 1882*; J. Whitney, *John Woolman* (Boston, 1942), p. 445).

rather than gentry.[9] Over here the emphasis was on agriculture, and while many continued to be known by the occupation they had formerly pursued, especially in the simpler crafts, such as carpentry or smithing,[10] which could be followed in a new country, they tended to become planters, yeomen, or husbandmen.[11] Those with good business judgment were likely to become merchants, if they had not been already. Thus Thomas Ollive, an outstanding early Quaker leader, was a haberdasher in Northamptonshire and a merchant in Burlington, where "his talents for business were considerable, and were highly appreciated by his fellow-settlers." [12] William Biddle, for many years a justice of Burlington court and a pillar of Quaker society, was a shoemaker in London; in West Jersey he bought and sold much land, and is designated first as "yeoman" and later as "merchant." [13] When a settler achieved economic success he might rise in the social scale too and become a self-made "gentleman"—a metamorphosis not entirely unknown even to the democratic Quakers.[14]

While the communal aspects of Quaker life were important, and their doctrine and discipline required a high degree of subordination of individual interests to the will of the group, nevertheless economic life in West Jersey was intense and competitive, as it had been in England. It was by no means overshadowed by religious preoccupations, as the voluminous and well-kept "meeting" records might otherwise suggest. The Burlington court minutes are a corrective to any such misapprehension. They contain the *minutiae* of Quaker temporal activities, just as the meeting records illuminate the Friends' spiritual life. The Quaker discipline recognized man as an economic as well as a religious being, and guarded against overtrading and enjoined punctuality in the payment of debts.[15] The Friends were also at first discouraged and

[9] Among those who purchased shares in West Jersey before emigrating were Thomas Ollive and William Peachee, haberdashers; Daniel Wills, "practicioner in chymistry;" John Lambert, joiner; William Biddle, shoemaker; John Cripps and William Hewlings, woolcombers; George Hutcheson, distiller; Thomas Hooton, chandler; Elias Farr, cheesemonger; Mahlon and Robert Stacy and Thomas Lambert, tanners; John Hooton, husbandman; William Snowden, Thomas Hutchinson, Thomas Pearson, Joseph Helmsley, Michael Newbold, and James Harrison, yeomen. See *New Jersey Archives*, first series (cited hereafter as *NJA*), xxi, 400–500.

[10] *Ibid.*, index, Occupations.

[11] "Walter Humphries alias Powell, formerly of Painswick, Co. of Gloucester, England, broad weaver, now of Burlington Co., yeoman" (*ibid.*, p. 496).

[12] J. Bowden, *The History of the Society of Friends in America*, ii (London, 1854), 114.

[13] His many land transactions may be followed in *NJA*, xxi, using index; see also *Pennsylvania Magazine of History*, vii, 263.

[14] Thus Richard Basnett, innkeeper and justice, by 1691 is a gentleman (*NJA*, xxi, 452, 489, 515). Likewise Daniel Leeds, by trade a cooper, became a man of large affairs and graduated from yeoman to gentleman (*ibid.*, index), after he had broken with the Quakers, however (see Jones, pp. 370, 388). In the Burlington minutes the title gentleman occurs first in 1689, applied to Edward Hunloke, merchant. "Esquire" is still higher, being reserved for dignitaries such as proprietor Daniel Coxe.

[15] Yearly Meeting, 1695: "Advised, that none trade, by sea or land, beyond their abilities; and that Friends keep to a word in their dealings, as much as may be; and if any are indebted,

later prohibited from going to law with one another, except amicably. The meeting, not the court, was the place where disputes between Friends should be threshed out.[16] That this rule was strictly observed is apparent from the Burlington records; after the first few years, Quakers rarely let their disagreements get as far as the court room.[17] But there was plenty of other litigation in which neither or but one of the parties was a Quaker.[18] It has often been remarked by students of our early judicial records that our ancestors were a litigious lot. The Burlington records bear out the general truth of this observation. The docket abounds in suits, some of them obviously trivial and exceedingly wearisome to the Quaker judges.[19] However, those who went to law merely in a fit of anger were still in the minority. The bulk of the civil business of the court was taken up with serious matters, with scores of suits entered by habitual drinkers at the fountain of justice, merchant Edward Hunloke for example; and this business originated usually from the most controversial phases of the economic life of the time, the acquisition of land and the collection of debts.

Swedish, Dutch, and English Predecessors

Turning to the historical setting of Quaker West Jersey, we may note first that it forms the eastern half of the drainage basin of the Delaware River. The

---

at home or abroad, and answer not the same in due time, that such be admonished thereof, that Truth may not be reproached, and people, whether rich or poor, kept out of their just debts." There was a similar admonition in 1701, and in 1710 steps were taken to advise with members "going backward in their worldly estate." See E. Michener, *A Retrospect of Early Quakerism* (Philadelphia, 1860), p. 263.

[16] Burlington Monthly Meeting, 1681: "It is generally agreed and ordered, that if anything fall out, by way of controversy, betwixt Friend and Friend, that if they cannot end the matter between themselves, then to refer it to two Friends, or more, to see if they can end it; then, if not, to bring it to the Monthly meeting, there to be ended." Yearly Meeting, 1681: "It is ordered that if any differences do arise betwixt any two persons that profess Truth, that they do not go to law before they first lay it before the particular Monthly Meeting that they do belong unto." Yearly Meeting, 1710: "As to Friends going to law one with another, it is the sense of this meeting that such things may not be admitted among us," except that, on the authorization of the Monthly Meeting, "when both parties are agreed," recourse might be had to the court when "a judgment of law" was needed "for the legal security of one or both" (*ibid.*, 267). Numerous examples could be cited from the monthly meeting minutes; *e. g.*, Burlington M. M. (MS Minutes, 3rd and Arch sts., Philadelphia), 7 mo. 10 1683: it was the "sense of the meeting" that the arbitration award between William Cooper and Daniel Wills should be performed; two were appointed to arbitrate between Samuel Jenings and Daniel Leeds.

[17] Some early Quaker suits are: *French v. Leeds, Shinn v. Arnold, Hollinshead v. Warner, Cripps, Budd, Jones,* and *Ollive v. Potts, French v. Basnett* (below, pp. 15–16, 20, 41, 42, 49). Later ones are *Pope v. Hancock, Calowe v. Wright, Hewlings v. French* (pp. 81, 132, 191).

[18] Of 13 civil suits in May 1689 (below, pp. 99–100) two had Quaker plaintiffs, two Quaker defendants, none were Quaker v. Quaker. William Biddle, Quaker justice for twenty years, in that time was plaintiff in but one suit.

[19] Arbitrators in an early Gloucester court case made a report "for the ending of all differences from the beginning of the world to the date hereof" (F. H. Stewart, *Gloucester County under the Proprietors* (Woodbury, 1942), p. 34).

INTRODUCTION   xiii

Delaware Valley region was an economic and cultural unit in colonial times, as it is to a considerable degree today. For a generation it was a political unit also. So it was under the Swedes and the Dutch, and under the English it successfully resisted dismemberment until 1680. In fact the Burlington Court Book marks the beginning of the career of West Jersey as a political entity separate from the rest of the region.

The first permanent settlement [20] in the valley was made by the Swedes in 1638 at Fort Christina (now Wilmington), on the western or Delaware-Pennsylvania side of the river. The Swedes quickly spread up the river, but except for a transitory establishment near the present Salem, New Jersey, stayed on the western side. So likewise did the Dutch, who conquered the Swedes in 1655 and remained in control until 1664, when they in turn yielded to the superior force of a naval expedition dispatched by the English James Duke of York (later James II). His brother, King Charles II, had granted him (March 12 1663/4) the land between the Connecticut and Delaware rivers, roughly the territory of Dutch occupation on the Atlantic coast.[21] It was left to the Duke to wrest the territory from the Dutch, and he did. New Amsterdam became New York. A side expedition from the Hudson conquered the Dutch settlements on the South or Delaware River, which were henceforth ruled by the Duke by right of conquest alone, since they lay to the west of the royal grant.[22]

During the Dutch regime on the Delaware Fort Christina had been superseded as the metropolis of the river by a newer settlement farther down the river called New Amstel, renamed New Castle by the English, which became the principal seat of local government and justice in the Delaware. Under both the Dutch and the Duke of York, however, the Delaware settlements were never more than an appendage of the more flourishing colony on the Hudson. Manhattan was really the capital of the Delaware region during this period, and to the governors and their councils there, Dutch and English in turn, the Delaware officials looked for authority and guidance until 1680–1682, when the Duke made over the territory to the Quakers of West Jersey and Pennsylvania.

Most of the known materials for the judicial history of this pre-Quaker era of Delaware River history are already in print. For the Swedish period, during which justice was administered chiefly by the governors in person, we have only their reports to Sweden.[23] For the Dutch and the Duke of York regimes most of the original records in the State Library at Albany have been

[20] Unless the Dutch trading post on the present site of Gloucester, N. J. (abandoned after a few years) be considered a permanent settlement.
[21] *Documents relating to the Colonial History of the State of New York*, ii (ed. E. B. O'Callaghan—Albany, 1858), 295.
[22] See A. Johnson, *The Swedish Settlements on the Delaware* (New York, 1911) and the histories of New Netherland by J. R. Brodhead (New York, 1853, 1871) and E. B. O'Callaghan (New York, 1848).
[23] A. Johnson, *The Instruction for Johan Printz* (Philadelphia, 1930).

printed or at least calendared.[24] For the period of English rule the local court minutes have been printed (usually without benefit of editorial comment), beginning in 1676 and extending on into the period of William Penn's proprietorship.[25] These judicial records pertain to the whole valley—to West Jersey as well as Delaware and Pennsylvania—down to 1680, when, as will be explained, the right of government over the eastern half of the area was finally confirmed to the Quakers. However, few if any of the first generation of Swedish and Dutch settlers occupied the Jersey side; a Swedish historian states that at the time of the Duke's conquest "there were as yet no residents upon the east side of the river, . . . which was a poor, sandy, and abominable country."[26] But there were a few by the time the Quakers began to arrive, as the censuses of 1677 show,[27] and the early lists of landholders in the Burlington Court Book[28] indicate an increasing influx from across the river in the next few years. These people, although retaining their language and customs, had of course been under English rule since 1664. Their ruler, the Duke of York, also claimed jurisdiction over the Quaker newcomers—not merely claimed it, but, as will be seen, exercised it for several years. Consequently, for the history of government in West Jersey, particularly of its judicial side, we must begin with the Duke of York and his representatives in New York and New Castle.

Fenwick's Colony

Conventional accounts of the English in New Jersey, West and East, open with the grant by Duke James of the area between the Hudson and the Dela-

[24] E. B. O'Callaghan, ed., *Calendar of Historical Manuscripts*, 2 v. (Albany, 1865, 1866); *N. Y. Col. Docs.*, especially xii (ed. B. Fernow—Albany, 1877), relating entirely to the Delaware settlements; *Calendar of Council Minutes, 1668–1783* (New York State Library, *Bulletin 58*, March 1902, History 6—Albany, 1902).

[25] *Records of the Court of New Castle on Delaware, 1676–1681* (Lancaster, 1904). A second volume, 1681–1699, contains land and probate matters only (Meadville, 1935). *The Record of the Court at Upland, in Pennsylvania, 1676 to 1681*, ed. E. Armstrong (Philadelphia, 1860). *Record of the Courts of Chester County, Pennsylvania, 1681–1699* (Philadelphia, 1910), a continuation of Upland court. The first extant volume of Sussex County, Delaware, court records, beginning 1681/2, is in the Historical Society of Pennsylvania at Philadelphia. Extracts from it are in C. H. B. Turner, *Some Records of Sussex County Delaware* (Philadelphia, 1909). The earliest minutes of Kent County, Delaware, and Bucks County, Pennsylvania, are now being edited for publication in the present series.

The laws enforced were naturally those of the mother country, modified as local circumstances might require. In New Sweden dictatorial powers were entrusted to the governor, he being instructed to judge according to Swedish law and custom as far as possible (Johnson, *Swedish Settlements*, ii, 450, 499). The local enactments of the Dutch are collected in E. B. O'Callaghan, ed., *Laws and Ordinances of New Netherlands, 1638–1674* (Albany, 1868). Upon the English conquest in 1664 the Duke's representatives compiled a code, "the Duke of York's laws," but it was not applied to the Delaware settlements until 1676, and even then it took the New Castle magistrates two years more to get a copy (*N. C. Recs.*, pp. 6, 22, 66, 98, 100, 112, 232, 242, 323). The Duke's Laws were printed for the first time in *Charter . . . and Laws of . . . Pennsylvania*, . . . preceded by *Duke of York's Laws* (Harrisburg, 1879), and again in *The Colonial Laws of New York*, i (Albany, 1894).

[26] Israel Acrelius, *A History of New Sweden* (Philadelphia, 1874), p. 106.

[27] *N. C. Recs.*, p. 161; *Upland Rec.*, p. 80.

[28] Below, pp. 25–28.

INTRODUCTION

ware to Lord John Berkeley and Sir George Carteret, June 24 1664.[29] This hasty gift was lamented by the Duke's servants, who, faithful to their master's interests, realized better than apparently he did the strategic disadvantage of driving a wedge, in the shape of New Jersey, between his main holdings in New York and the feeble but potentially important settlements on the western shore of the Delaware; and they did what they could to keep his original grant intact. Their efforts amounted to a delaying or rear-guard action which postponed, rather than prevented, the final surrender, but caused the West Jersey Quakers much embarrassment in the meantime. Another source of difficulty was the fact that the Duke's grant was limited, and to the Quakers seriously defective, in that, as was later contended, it conveyed the title to the land but no rights of government.[30] This was a point of law which was not apparent to the new proprietors, who thought their grant included governmental rights similar to those which other proprietors of colonies in America enjoyed. Otherwise the Quakers would never have undertaken the purchase, which was not merely a business venture but a prospective Quaker commonwealth where they would be free from the religious disabilities imposed upon them in the mother country.

Berkeley and Carteret proceeded to develop their new acquisition as if they had powers of government, issuing a "Concession and Agreement"[31] which provided for representative government and dispatching a governor who took up his residence in the eastern part of the province in 1665. However, in March 1673/4 Berkeley sold his half interest in New Jersey to Major John Fenwick, an old Cromwellian soldier turned Friend,[32] thus beginning the proprietorial interest of the Quakers in New Jersey,[33] and also necessitating the division of the province into two parts,[34] East Jersey, where English (including some Quaker) migration had already begun, and West Jersey, which

---

[29] Leaming and Spicer, 8. The story of this grant and the ensuing political complications in New Jersey's early history has been told many times. The latest analysis is in C. M. Andrews, *The Colonial Period of American History*, iii (New Haven, 1937), ch. 4. For greater detail see Tanner, *op. cit.*, and H. L. Osgood, *The American Colonies in the Seventeenth Century*, ii (New York, 1904), ch. 8. Samuel Smith, *A History of the Province of Nova-Caesaria or New-Jersey* (Burlington, 1765) is an important Quaker account. For the documents see *NJA*, i.

[30] "Technically speaking, he [the Duke] alone had governmental authority over the Jerseys and . . . could part with it only by consent of the crown"—which he never made any effort to obtain (Andrews, 140). However, the Quakers' practical problem was that the Duke's government in New York was exercising jurisdiction over them in West Jersey. When the Duke made his confirmatory grant in 1680 (below, p. xxxii) New York ceased its pretensions and the Quakers were free to run their own affairs. In other words, the grant of 1680 was accepted at its face value by the parties concerned.

[31] Leaming and Spicer, pp. 12–27.

[32] On Fenwick and his colony see F. H. Stewart, *Major John Fenwick* (Woodbury, 1939), which contains most of the old and some new material; R. G. Johnson, *An Historical Account of the First Settlement of Salem* (Philadelphia, 1839); Sickler, *op. cit.*

[33] The possibilities of a new world colony were weighed by the Friends as early as 1660. They were familiar with the territory here, for their founder, George Fox, had travelled extensively along the Atlantic seaboard, passing through New Jersey in 1672. See Jones, pp. 357–361, 418.

[34] By the so-called Quintipartite Deed of July 1 1676 (*NJA*, i, 205–219). The official names were East and West *New* Jersey, but except in official documents the "New" was dropped.

became the special goal of the Quaker emigrants. Before Berkeley's sale, however, the Dutch had made a short-lived reconquest of their former possession, which abrogated the royal grant to the Duke and the transfers following it, requiring a renewal or confirmation of all these instruments after the return of the territory to English possession. The Duke made the necessary grant to Carteret promptly (this time of the eastern half only), but kept the West Jersey Quakers waiting until 1680 before he finally signed an indenture "more firmly" conveying the territory to them.[35] Until that time, therefore, although the exodus of Quakers from the British Isles went on briskly, they had no better title to their new homeland than a deed from Berkeley to Fenwick which had been executed before the King issued his charter of renewal to the Duke, and so had no standing in law.[36]

As if this were not enough trouble for the new venture, Fenwick's purchase became a subject of controversy among the Friends themselves. It was claimed that Fenwick had bought in trust for Edward Byllynge,[37] a prominent coreligionist of London, and when the two quarrelled over their respective rights in the new purchase, the dispute was submitted to arbitration, a normal procedure among Friends. The umpire, William Penn, awarded nine-tenths of West Jersey to Byllynge and only one-tenth to Fenwick, who, after strong pressure from Penn, accepted the award.[38] For what lay behind this one-sided division we have only an explanation which was current gossip in West Jersey. The story, as picked up and recorded by a Dutch traveller in 1679,[39] was that Byllynge was a "great friend" of Berkeley and other courtiers who frequented Byllynge's brewery. At a time when Byllynge was in financial straits,[40] Berkeley suggested that he could recover his fortune by buying "a tract of land which the king had given him." Byllynge raised the money from his friends but since his own affairs were involved acted through Fenwick, who was to

---

[35] Andrews, pp. 152-163; *NJA*, i, 324.

[36] Berkeley's deed was dated March 18 1673/4; the King's new grant, June 29 1674. Between 1677 and 1681 1400 went to New Jersey (Braithwaite, *Second Period*, 403).

[37] For this we have Penn's own published statement (Smith, p. 89). Byllynge is not mentioned in Berkeley's deed to Fenwick (as recorded in Salem No. 1, Sec. of State's office, Trenton), but it hardly would have been, under the circumstances. Fenwick later declared (Sickler, p. 43) that the purchase had been made with his own money—a statement not necessarily contradictory of Penn's, but rather indicating Fenwick's dissatisfaction with the amount he was awarded.

[38] See the correspondence between Penn and Fenwick, Jan.-Feb. 1674/5, in Stewart, pp. 24-25. References to "my two parts" and "the 8 p'tes added" hint that it may possibly have been intended at first to allot Fenwick only 2/100 instead of 1/10.

[39] *Journal of Jasper Danckaerts, 1679-1680*, ed. B. B. James and J. F. Jameson (New York, 1913), p. 154.

[40] Byllynge issued a statement March 22 1673/4 (four days after the date of the deed to Fenwick) repenting his and his late wife's running into debt, and hoping that no one would charge his "miscarriage upon the principal people of God called Quakers" (Historical Manuscripts Commission, *Report on the Pepys Manuscripts* (London, 1911), p. 268). This suggests that other Friends may already have taken Byllynge's financial involvements in hand, with an eye on the territory so providentially offered to them through his instrumentality.

Pepys knew Byllynge, mentioning him four times in the famous diary, and apparently respecting his shrewdness and perspicacity—"a cunning fellow I find him to be" (Oct. 31 1660).

have a tenth of the purchase for his trouble. Thus, if we may credit this narrative, by a sudden stroke of good fortune the Quakers, already interested in an overseas refuge, got an opportunity to acquire one at a bargain price through Byllynge's fortunate acquaintance with Lord Berkeley.[41] Management of the affair was taken out of the hands of both Byllynge and Fenwick and lodged in a larger group, by a "tripartite indenture,"[42] February 10 1674/5, in which Byllynge, claiming an equitable interest, and Fenwick, retaining ten "equal and undivided hundred parts," conveyed West Jersey to Penn, Gawen Lawrie, and Nicholas Lucas, all Quakers, as trustees for Byllynge's creditors.

The plans which Penn and his associates were formulating for the development of West Jersey were upset by Fenwick's insistence upon settling his share without waiting for anyone else. Having yielded up nine-tenths of the worm, he was determined to be an early bird for the fragment that remained to him. In a printed proposal dated 1 mo. (March) 8 1674/5 [43] he offered land in West Jersey for £5 per thousand acres, and to non-purchasing emigrants, free land subject to an annual quitrent to him.[44] The London Quakers were unable to deter Fenwick, even by a printed broadside (July 1675) denying that "we as a people have advised Councelled and approved of the manner of his undertakings," and predicting that "the issue would prove Evil and Confused."[45] By that time Fenwick was ready to embark for America. Between February 25 and July 12 he had sold 150,000 acres in his colony.[46] Soon afterwards he set sail in the ship *Griffin* with 150 settlers on board. He arrived in the Dela-

---

[41] The price paid was £1000 (Stewart, p. 16).

[42] Recorded in Salem No. 1, Sec. of State's office, Trenton. Cf. *NJA*, xxi, 559.

[43] Reprinted in *Pa. Mag.*, vi, 86–90. -

[44] Of 1d. per acre. Masters of families were to have 100 acres for each member over fourteen. Those carried at his or others' expense were to serve four years and have 100 acres each, besides the customary freedom dues.

[45] *A Testimony against John Fenwick, concerning his Proceeding about New-Cesaria or New Jersey* . . . dated July 6 1675 and signed "From the People of God, called Quakers, in London," reprinted in F. Mood, "English Publicity Broadsides for West Jersey, 1675–6," in New Jersey Historical Society, *Proceedings*, liv (1936), 1–11. The broadside appends a letter by Fenwick "given by his own hand to Friends" in May, in which Fenwick profusely repents of some sin ("O! Wo is me; it is I that have Sinned Against Him;" "the Enemy blinded my Eyes, and deceived me," etc.) but omits to state what it was. Mood's assumption that Fenwick first published this letter himself is unwarranted. The ordinary way for a Quaker to make satisfaction to the group for a misdeed was to read or send a paper of self-condemnation to his "meeting," upon whose minutes it was then spread—but not published to the world at large. The fact that the London Quakers published Fenwick's letter shows how exasperated they were with him. They may also have been unfair. I suspect that this confession relates to the proceedings of about Jan. 1674/5, when Fenwick balked at giving up nine-tenths of West Jersey (he said later (Sickler, p. 43) that he did so more "for the sake of God's own blessed truth" than for reasons of law or equity), and not to the prospectus he published in March. For one thing, March to May would hardly have been time enough to extract a confession from him through proceedings in the monthly meeting; again, he gives no other evidence of having regretted going ahead with his own plans to colonize his tenth. Fenwick was a pious man. His public utterances abound in references to the Deity along with excoriations of his opponents. His and his associates' engagements of office in the Salem colony render fervent allegiance to the Supreme Ruler, before all earthly ones (see Salem Surveys, 1676, in Sec. of State's office, Trenton).

[46] See deeds calendared in *NJA*, xxi, 556–565; *Pennsylvania Archives*, i, 57.

ware in November and landed well to the south on the eastern shore, opposite from New Castle, where he established the town of Salem (originally New Salem)—the first Quaker settlement in West Jersey.[47]

Unfortunately Fenwick was to find no peace in Salem. At his departure he had had some debts outstanding. Two of his Quaker creditors, John Edridge and Edmond Warner,[48] exacted from him before he sailed an indenture of "lease, bargain and sale" conveying to them for a thousand years the unsold part of his tenth, as security for his debts.[49] It is a fair assumption that this conveyance was extorted from Fenwick under the threat of arresting him for debt and thus preventing his sailing. He could now depart with the comforting thought that the debts he was leaving behind would be taken care of, even though the title to his new possession was also left behind. However, his expectations were not realized. At first Edridge and Warner claimed that they could not sell any land at the price agreed on, and asked for their money.[50] No doubt Fenwick could not have paid them, but it would have been well for him had he been able to, for they subsequently joined the Penn-Byllynge forces against him and conveyed their rights in his tenth to the three trustees.[51] When he learned that Edridge and Warner had "confederated themselves together with certain persons" still unknown to him, and "gave out in speeches" that the conveyance was and was intended to be "an Absolute Lease and estate," he tendered them payment in full, August 1676, demanding the reconveyance of his property. When they refused to accept, he brought suit against them in the Court of Chancery in England, October 1676. But Chancery suits could be strung out for a long time, and Fenwick's resources were unequal to the luxury of protracted litigation. He had to act through the reluctant agency of his wife, and after two years of inconclusive proceedings he seems to have abandoned the effort to force a reconveyance from Edridge and Warner.[52]

[47] Stewart, *Fenwick*, pp. 7-10, 33.

[48] Edridge was a tanner, of Middlesex; Warner, of London, "citizen and poulterer" (*NJA*, xxi, 562).

[49] Including some, Fenwick later charged, that he gave them money to pay (Stewart, p. 43). The conveyance empowered Edridge and Warner to sell land to reimburse themselves with interest, made Fenwick responsible for payment if they were not so reimbursed within two years, and authorized but did not require them to pay certain other small debts of his, a schedule of which was annexed. When the two creditors were satisfied they were to reconvey the territory or part remaining unsold. This was dated July 17 1675. On the 19th Fenwick signed a release for the territory. These documents, a legal opinion on them, and Fenwick's subsequent suit in the Chancery court against Edridge and Warner are all in Stewart, pp. 12-22, 28-33. See also Fenwick's comments in his "Remonstrance," Sickler, p. 45.

[50] So Fenwick stated (Stewart, p. 31). "They sold not one foot" (Sickler, p. 45).

[51] Leaming and Spicer, p. 414. "By a fraudulent deed," Fenwick says, "in consideration of twenty shillings, to cheat me" (Sickler, p. 45). But this was only a nominal transfer, for Edridge and Warner later sold their shares (below, p. xx).

[52] The appeal and a résumé of the proceedings in Chancery are in Stewart, pp. 28-32. His wife in England was pessimistic about his suit ("I much fear thou wilt not get them to re-convey it") and urged him to end it, "though to thy loss." She was unwilling to use any more of her

INTRODUCTION

Meanwhile, having delimited the bounds between their and Carteret's half of New Jersey, the trustees were ready to embark on their plan of colonization. With Byllynge cooperating, and now Edridge and Warner, they could make short shrift of Fenwick's opposition. They instructed their agents in New Jersey [53] "to get a meeting with John Fenwick, and the people that went with him, . . . read the deed of partition with George Carteret; also the transactions between William Penn, Nicholas Lucas, Gawen Lawrie, John Edridge and Edmond Warner, and shew . . . John Fenwick he hath no power to sell any land there, without the consent of John Edridge and Edmond Warner." [54] Fenwick and his people were to be invited to join in the new plan, "according to our and his agreement in England," and if they refused, "you may let the country know . . . that he hath no power over the persons or estates of any man or woman more than any other person." All this was true, of course, so long as the conveyance to Edridge and Warner stood. As has been stated, they had been giving out that the sale was absolute, and they may have persuaded themselves that it was.[55] The trustees adopted this interpretation too, at least in their public statements, which recite the fact of the conveyance without indicating that its meaning was in dispute.[56] But Fenwick defied the trustee group, acted as proprietor in his colony, and went on selling land.[57] Justice may have been on his side, but until he obtained a reconveyance of his tenth his legal titles were necessarily imperfect. No wonder that many settlers in his colony saw this and supported the other side. The *coup de grâce* was administered to his pretensions by the Duke of York's confirmatory grant of West Jersey in 1680.[58] Reciting merely that Fenwick had conveyed his tenth to Edridge and Warner, it left him out entirely, and the new grant was made to the three trustees and Byllynge, Edridge, and Warner. Thereafter the interest of the latter two rested not only on Fenwick's indenture but also on a direct grant from the original proprietor of New Jersey. Before his death Fenwick made his peace with Penn and designated him one of his executors. But he never forgave Eldridge and Warner, "the cause of his trouble;" he stipulated in

---

own money and begged him to pay some poor men to whom he owed small sums (Johnson, pp. 50–51). She never came to America. Fenwick did not mention her in his will.

[53] In a letter signed by the trustees, Byllynge, Edridge, and Warner, Aug. 1676 (Smith, pp. 80–87).

[54] So far as the Salem deed records disclose, Fenwick sold no more land after he left England until the following spring, by which time probably he had got wind of what his two creditors were doing. He sold 1000 acres April 14 1676, 1000 on May 31, and numerous smaller lots during the summer and fall (*NJA*, xxi, 564–565).

[55] Mary Fenwick to John: "They both told me that they had the opinion of two counsellors, that they had an absolute estate in thy imposts; and though they can't for shame insist upon it now, they endeavor all they can to hinder thee from having any benefit by it" (Johnson, p. 51).

[56] See the *Proposals*, 1676, in N. J. H. S., *Proceedings*, liv, 8, and their letter in Smith, p. 88.

[57] *NJA*, xxi, 564–569.

[58] Leaming and Spicer, pp. 412–419.

his will (1683) that they be "Brought to an accompt in order to the Recovering of the Lease." [59]

* * *

Like the other proprietors, Fenwick assumed that their acquisition of Berkeley's half of New Jersey included the right to govern as well as title to the land. This was a personal adventure with the Berkshire squire, not just a business proposition, as it apparently was with Byllynge, the bankrupt brewer of London. Fenwick planned to come over with his settlers and act as a "Lord or Chief Proprietor" in his little colony in person, not by proxy, just as Penn did later in his. Fenwick was so determined to come, in fact, that in order to get away he surrendered the title on which his authority rested. This fact seems to have made little difference to him.[60]

Moreover, he seems to have given little thought to the problem of government. In comparison with the elaborate machinery devised by his fellow Quaker, William Penn, for Pennsylvania,[61] and the "Concessions and Agreements" of 1676/7 which formed the basis of the government later instituted at Burlington,[62] Fenwick's ideas were rudimentary. The proposal for his intended colony published March 8 1674/5 merely assured prospective "Proprietors" that they should "be made capable of Government," with a council of rotating membership.[63] In an agreement [64] made with his purchasers shortly before the embarkation of his colonizing expedition he was somewhat more specific. "The governor and magistrates shall be chosen each year by the advice and consent of the said proprietors and freeholders," and also a council of ten or twelve, half to be chosen annually, which should have

[59] Stewart, p. 43. A word on the subsequent history of Fenwick's claims. Both Edridge and Warner disposed of their interest in 1682. In July Edridge sold out to Warner, who in August sold this half interest to James Wasse, who in turn sold to Byllynge. After subsequent transfers to the Daniel Coxes, father and son, this half was finally acquired by Penn in 1707. In September 1682 Warner sold his own half to Penn. March 1682/3 Fenwick conveyed all his remaining interest in New Jersey to Penn, reserving 150,000 acres which he proposed to erect into a manor, with privilege of holding courts leet and baron (which, however, he probably never exercised—see *Pa. Mag.*, v, 327–328, and below, p. xxi). Thus Penn became the "chief proprietor" of Fenwick's colony, and all uncertainties of title to the land therein were removed.

[60] But it is characteristic of Fenwick—hot-headed, rather than clear-headed. His wife saw the difference. She wrote (1678/9): "I insist thou wouldst forbear to act as a lord proprietor, and to make orders and summon the people, till thou hast thy deed, and authority to it" (Johnson, p. 54).

[61] *Charter and Laws of Pa.*, p. 90.

[62] Leaming and Spicer, p. 382.

[63] "Whoever is minded to Purchase to them and their Heirs for ever, may for Five Pound have a Thousand Acres, and so Ten Thousand Acres; and thereby be made Proprietors or Free-Holders . . .

"The Government is to be, by a Governor and 12 Council to be Chosen every year, 6 of the Council to go out, and 6 to come in; whereby every Proprietor may be made capable of Government, and know the Affairs of the Country, and Privileges of the People.

"The Government to stand upon these two Basis, or Leges, *viz.* 1. The Defence of the Royal Law of God, his Name and true Worship, which is in Spirit and in Truth. 2. The Good, Peace and Welfare, of every individual Person." See *Pa. Mag.*, vi, 86–88.

[64] Dated June 28 1675, signed by 32 purchasers (Stewart, p. 57).

"full power to make such laws and customs for the good of the colony and suppression of vice as to them shall seem most necessary and convenient." What further plans of government Fenwick had, if any (once later, he declared his intention "to call an assembly"), came to naught, through the hostility of the Duke of York's agents and his own fellow proprietors.[65]

* * *

Sheriff Edmund Cantwell represented the Duke's authority in the Delaware River area, and he reported Fenwick's arrival "by a post" to the Duke's governor, Major (later Sir) Edmund Andros, at New York. That capable official acted with his characteristic forthrightness to protect his master's interests. The New York Council, observing that Fenwick had no "Order,"[66] and that if he had had, he should have brought it first to New York to be recorded, commanded that Fenwick "be used civilly" and that any of the newcomers who might "desire land to the westward" (as some of them later did) should be accommodated; but forbade any recognition of him "as Owner or Proprietor of any land whatsoever in Delaware" and required the existing duties on imports to be strictly collected.[67] Then ensued a spirited contest between the two resolute majors. Fenwick made the first move, in the summer following his arrival, when "the Proprietors, purchasers and freeholders now Resident in Fenwick's Coloney" chose him as their governor "for this present year 1676,"[68] and soon afterwards he took pledges of allegiance to himself from a number of the inhabitants, Swedes and Dutch as well as English.[69] Andros countered in September with a warrant to the Sheriff of Delaware to bring Fenwick to New York for trial before the Council.[70] Fenwick refused to obey the summons but was seized by a detachment of soldiers from New Castle and conveyed to New York, where he was tried January 1676/7 and convicted of having "Possessed himselfe of a large tract or Parcel of Land" within the Duke's patent "and assuming to himselfe to

---

[65] When Fenwick sold out to Penn he retained 150,000 acres which he proposed to erect into a manor in the feudal style, with courts leet and baron (see n. 59 above). To that end he commissioned Erick Yearnens of Finnstown Hook as "reve or bailiff" for "the hundred and manor of West Fenwick" (Johnson, p. 66); but there is no evidence that Fenwick ever exercised such jurisdiction. Penn's agent warned him against the danger of allowing Fenwick to do so (*Pa. Arch.*, i, 55–56).

[66] "Hee acknowledges to have no originall deed or grant here butt was left in Engl." (*N. Y. Col. Docs.*, xii, 568).

[67] *N. Y. Col. Docs.*, xii, 542.

[68] Sickler, p. 34. His attestation of office is dated June 21.

[69] *NJA*, xxi, 555–558.

[70] Sickler, p. 34; *N. Y. Col. Docs.*, xii, 559; *NJA*, i, 186. The charge was "That Major John Fenwick, now living at the East side of Delaware River doth pretend and give himselfe out to bee Proprietor of that side of the River and hath presumed to act accordingly, graunted Land extravagantly, dispossessed persons in those parts, sold their land, arrogating to himselfe a power of judicature, and hath given out Lycences for distilling contrary to the order settled in the River; By which means hee hath inveigled some persons from other parts, and distracts the mindes of the inhabitants, thorow out the whole River and Bay, not having any Lawfull Power or Authority."

bee Lord Cheife Proprietour etc. of the same." A fine of £40 was imposed, which he declined to pay, and he was detained at New York. In the following August (1677) the *Kent* touched at New York with the first contingent of the Burlington emigrants on their way to West Jersey.[71] Fenwick was released on parole to accompany them, on condition that he return by October 6, which he did. This time he was told by Andros to go back to Salem and "go about his lawful business." [72]

Fenwick did not long remain idle. In May 1678 we find the New Castle court meeting to consider "some new alterations on the East syde of this River" that he had made. It seems that he had called a meeting of the inhabitants (April 30) at which he appointed a surveyor, a register, and other officials, read his title deeds, and demanded the "submission of the People" to his authority.[73] The Delaware Sheriff was an interested observer at this meeting and he challenged Fenwick's authority. When Cantwell reminded Fenwick of a "small Levy" laid by the New Castle court "upon the People on that syde," [74] Fenwick answered that "the Court had no power to Lay no Levy on that syde." "Whoesoever did pay any Levy should forfeit their Lands and priviledges," and "the People should stand in their owne defehce if any Boddy Came to demand itt." He further forbade "Mr. Fopp Outhout," a resident of the eastern side and a justice of the New Castle court, who was also present, "to act any thing in the behalfe" of that court, on pain of forfeiting his estate. Fenwick declared that "he was subject to noe man but God and the King," and "that hee would doe or act nothing without the advyce of his Counsill which hee would nominate verry suddenly." [75] This he apparently did; [76] and if we may believe the New Castle justices, he not

---

[71] See below, p. xxviii.
[72] Sickler, pp. 34–36; *NJA*, i, 185–192; *N. Y. Col. Docs.*, xii, 545, 559, 565–569.
[73] Sickler, p. 38; *NJA*, xxi, 558; *N. C. Recs.*, pp. 206–208.
[74] This was a poll tax of 12½ guilders upon all "tydables" within the court's jurisdiction, laid in Nov. 1677. There were 307 such tithables, including 64 on the "Easterne Shore." Most of the latter were Swedes, but some of Fenwick's Quakers were included, Richard Guy, Edward Chamneys, John Pledger, and others (*N. C. Recs.*, pp. 158–161). At the same time the Upland court imposed a similar tax in its jurisdiction, which comprised the rest of the valley northward. The recently-arrived Quakers at Burlington, which was a considerable distance farther up the river, were not included in the Upland tax list, which had only ten persons from the eastern side (*Upland Rec.*, p. 80).
[75] *N. C. Recs.*, p. 207; *N. Y. Col. Docs.*, xii, 592.
[76] See, in Johnson, pp. 21–23, an order by "a council and consultation held at the town of New Salem, for Fenwick's colony," attended by Fenwick as "Lord or chief proprietor," Samuel Hedge, Surveyor General, James Nevill, Secretary, and John Smith, Edward Bradway, John Pledger, and William Malster, "four of the Council, besides the other two." This was May 16 1678. But Fenwick apparently allowed this council to lapse, perhaps because in October (as noted below) Andros took some of its members into camp by appointing them to a town court under his jurisdiction. At any rate we hear nothing further about Fenwick's council until March 1678/9, when he declared that he would assume his "lawful and absolute power and authority," and would "forthwith choose a council, and issue forth my precept (with their advice) to call an assembly, to set within my colony" (*ibid.*, pp. 37–45; Sickler, pp. 43–46). The only other reference to a council in the Salem records (as calendared in *NJA*, xxi, 554) is Richard Guy's subscription,

INTRODUCTION   xxiii

only forbade payment of their levy but countered with a tax of his own.[77]
The New York government thereupon ordered Fenwick again to "forbeare, the Assuming any power of Government . . . unlesse he can produce more Authentick power out of England than hee hath yett done;" if he refused, he was to be taken, by force if necessary, to New York. He went, though reluctantly, and was tried and convicted again. He was detained for a time, until Andros could take new steps to checkmate the stubborn Quaker.[78] Andros' next move was a shrewd and logical one. He set up, October 26 1678, a "Towne or Corporation" court for "Salem or Swamp Towne, and parts adjacent," to meet quarterly or oftener. Six of the English settlers, including Nevill, Fenwick's Secretary, and Bradway and Malster, members of Fenwick's own recently-appointed council, were made "Overseers, Select men or Commissioners" for the "new Commers" at Salem.[79] In case of any difference between them and the "Old Inhabitants of those parts," Fopp Outhout, an "antient Inhabitant there" and a justice of the New Castle court, was to be one of the court and to preside over it. The court could appoint one or more constables, lay out land, and determine all matters not extending to life or limb or exceeding £5, above which an appeal was to lie to the court at New Castle.[80]

Thus Fenwick's colony was formally incorporated into the judicial and administrative system of the government of New York, not by coercion from Andros, but by the acceptance of the leading Quaker inhabitants themselves.[81] In establishing this court Andros exhibited a practical statesmanship

---

June 21 1676, as one of the council. He was chosen by Fenwick and the proprietors, purchasers, and freeholders (Salem Surveys, 1676, in Sec. of State's office, Trenton, p. 1). The item following this, calendared as a minute of council, June 11, is actually an order by Fenwick, with the consent of all his purchasers and freeholders present (*ibid.*, p. 2).

[77] The court therefore desired "to know whether the People there shall pay any of the said tax, and how for the future this Court Shall act and behave them selves towards the said East syde" (*N. Y. Col. Docs.*, xii, 607).

[78] *N. Y. Col. Docs.*, xii, 594–607; *NJA*, i, 193–204; Johnson, p. 37; Sickler, p. 39.

[79] The others were William Penton, Richard Guy, and Edward "Ward" (Wade). All were selected from a list of a dozen names furnished by Malster. All but two of the nominees, Penton and Malster, have "quaker" after their names in this list (*N. Y. Col. Docs.*, xii, 608).

[80] At the same time the New Castle justices were instructed to take care that the east side people be not disturbed in their possessions by Fenwick or any others (*ibid.*, p. 610).

[81] All of the new commissioners except Penton had come over with Fenwick (Sickler, p. 25). He charged that "James Wasse and Richard Guy began vigorously to seize upon my said colony, causing the same to be surveyed by Richard Hancock, (my sworn surveyor-general) without my knowledge," and that Guy, Wade, Bradway, and Nevill had "done what they could to promote the same (under the pretext of the Governor's [Andros'] commission)" (Sickler, p. 44; Johnson, pp. 39, 40, 46). All the commissioners except Penton and Nevill had bought land from Fenwick, from 1000 to 10,000 acres, before coming. Of the four whom Fenwick specially accused, Wade was a London clothworker, Nevill a weaver (he became interested in law and government here), Guy a cheesemonger, and Bradway a lighterman, the last three of Middlesex (*NJA*, xxi, 342, 549, 559–561). Their membership on Salem Friends Meeting committees to choose a site for a meeting house (1679) (see J. Clement, *Sketches of the First Emigrant Settlers in Newton Township* (Camden, 1877), p. 215) indicates that they had the confidence of the Quaker group and it is fair to assume that they were representative of current Quaker opinion on the Fenwick issue.

conspicuously lacking in his opponent. Andros acted, while Fenwick blustered. True, his harassments were enough to unnerve anyone; but the fact still remained that he had now been in Salem three years without setting up anything which could be called a systematic and continuing governmental organization beyond his own personal rule. Andros was master of the situation, and he demanded only recognition of the Duke's overlordship pending the final settlement of the question of sovereignty. He showed no disposition to interfere in the local concerns of the Quaker newcomers,[82] save to protect the old Swedish property holders. From the Quaker settlers' viewpoint it was better to have a court of their own in Salem than to be subject to the direct rule of the New Castle court across the river. Under the circumstances they can hardly be condemned for finding it expedient, if not desirable, to submit to the authority of New York, as Burlington had already done.

James Nevill seems to have been the leader in cooperating with Andros against Fenwick.[83] The Salem court's commission was for a year, and when it was renewed [84] Nevill headed the commission instead of Penton, and Malster was replaced by Richard Hancock, Fenwick's Deputy Surveyor General, an original purchaser who had come to America with him.[85] However much it may have been opposed by Fenwick, the Salem court seems to have functioned as it was authorized to do, so far as can be determined from the scattered references to it, mostly about land matters, which have been preserved. In June 1679 the New Castle justices ordered a land dispute referred to "the Court att Salem, and that Justice outhout Endeauor to make an End of itt," which that magistrate failed to do, for the case came back to them from the Salem court in the following February.[86] In a Salem book of surveys the

---

Malster, "late of the City of Westminster, England, gentleman," though he furnished Andros with the list of names for commissioners, had the previous year been in England and testified in Fenwick's favor (*The State of the case between John Fenwick, Esqr and John Edridge and Edmund Warner*, in Stewart, pp. 32–33). He was dropped from the court in 1679. In 1680 Nevill reported to Andros that Malster and some others, hearing of a wrecked shallop, hastened to the scene and secretly conveyed away some of the gear to sell it "without being accountable to any" (*N. Y. Col. Docs.*, xii, 635, 650). Penton, the other non-Quaker commissioner, came with the first settlers of Burlington in 1677 (Smith, p. 99) but settled in Salem (*NJA*, xxi, 547). In 1678 he was appointed a churchwarden by the New Castle court, doubtless to uphold the dignity of the Church of England on the Quaker side of the river. He was illiterate, as were some others of the earliest settlers (*N. C. Recs.*, pp. 264, 363).

[82] See *ibid.*, p. 318, where the New Castle court non-suited the plaintiff in a suit brought against Mahlon Stacy, Burlington County Quaker, by a purchaser of a share in "New Beverly" (Burlington) (1679).

[83] Just as he was with Penn a few years later. See his letters to Penn, 1 mo. 1682/3 and 3 mo. 1683, urging Penn to remove Fenwick to Pennsylvania and warning against his projected courts leet and baron (*Pa. Arch.*, i, 55).

[84] *N. Y. Col. Docs.*, xii, 635.

[85] Sickler, p. 25; *NJA*, xxi, 547, 561. Surveyor Hancock had been a Middlesex upholsterer and bought 500 acres.

[86] *N. C. Recs.*, pp. 336, 387. For another undated case in which Outhout officiated see *Pa. Arch.*, i, 37, the granting of 100 acres of land. Penton, Bradway, Wade, and Nevill were also present.

minutes are recorded of a "special Court," September 13 1680, Nevill, Penton, Guy, Bradway, and Wade, commissioners.[87] They ordered a warrant to Hancock to survey a tract of land, which he did,[88] and accepted an acknowledgement of some unnamed "fault" from John Adams, of New Salem, planter, and his wife (a daughter of Fenwick's), with promises of future good behavior. An award of the Salem court of October 11, in an action about land in "Cohansey Creeke," was appealed to the Court of Assizes at New York.[89] The Salem court was also entrusted with the responsibility of keeping the peace, and while its duties along that line were probably not onerous in a Quaker community, Nevill, as first commissioner, seems to have been a vigilant defender of law and order. In 1680 he wrote Andros of several runaway servants from Virginia who had landed in West Jersey in a stolen shallop. He said he had apprehended the runaways and also recovered some tackle taken from the boat by ex-Commissioner William Malster and several other men, and asked the Governor for further instructions.[90] Besides these duties, the services of the commissioners were also required occasionally in settling the estate of a decedent, usually in connection with the New Castle court.[91] All in all, it appears, from the fragmentary information we have about it, that the court operated successfully under the New York–New Castle jurisdiction. With the prestige and power of the Duke's government behind them the magistrates may have found it difficult to be strictly impartial toward Fenwick's adherents; the hotter the fight, the less discrimination in the choice of weapons. But even Fenwick in his bitter quarrel with Edridge and Warner once forgot himself so far as to swear out a warrant in New York for the arrest of Edridge in New Jersey, in spite of his insistence that the Duke's government had no jurisdiction there.[92]

THE BURLINGTON SETTLEMENT, 1677–1680

Thus Fenwick succeeded no better in his contest with Andros over government than with the Quaker proprietors over division of the land.

[87] *NJA*, xxi, 549, 550.
[88] After this defection he was dismissed by Fenwick, who charged that Guy, Nevill, and "his followers" threatened to send Richard Tindall, Fenwick's Surveyor General, to prison, "unlesse he would engage to act no more for me" (Johnson, p. 45).
[89] *N. C. Recs.*, p. 430. The land in controversy had been sold first, June 8 1675, by two Delaware men, acting as agents for Fenwick before his arrival in West Jersey; and afterwards, apparently, sold again by Fenwick to others.
[90] *N. Y. Col. Docs.*, xii, 650.
[91] See a little volume entitled Salem Wills, 1679, in Sec. of State's office, Trenton, pp. 1–29. Nevill and Penton, commissioners, and Henry Jenings, "Counstable," took the inventory of the estate of Henry Salter, who died intestate in 1679. The Salem commissioners also recorded Richard Hunter's will. In both cases the proceedings were approved and recorded at New Castle (*N. C. Recs.*, pp. 346, 360). But in the death of William Hancock, 1680, the commissioners appointed an executrix and granted probate themselves.
[92] O'Callaghan, *Calendar*, ii, 66: March 22 1678, "Warrant to Ed. Cantwell, sheriff of Delaware, to arrest John Edridge of West Jersey, for debt, at the suit of John Fenwyck."

Meanwhile the latter had established the second and major focus of Quaker infiltration into New Jersey at Burlington, some sixty miles up the river from Salem. Fenwick was so close to New Castle that, had he been the most tactful of men, he would have had difficulty in avoiding friction with his Delaware neighbors; whereas Burlington was well to the north of the old Swedish-Dutch limits of settlement.[93]

The Burlington colony was planned on a more liberal basis both as to land and to government than Fenwick's colony at Salem. It will be recalled that by the tripartite indenture of February 10 1674/5 Fenwick accepted as his share one-tenth of West Jersey—ten "equal and undivided hundred parts" of the whole territory. These were assigned by lot; he drew numbers for his ten parts and the trustees took the other ninety.[94] This agreement formed the basis for the colonizing enterprises of both Salem and Burlington, but they have little else in common. Fenwick sold definite parcels of land, some 150,000 acres, in blocks of from 500 to 10,000 acres (one was 20,000), before he left England; after he arrived he disposed of a few thousand acres more in much smaller lots.[95] All this activity was repudiated by the other proprietors, who, as noted above, contended that his interest had passed to Edridge and Warner, and they had joined forces with the Penn-Byllynge group, who had a quite different scheme for the exploitation of West Jersey. By their plan it was "to be divided by Lot into one hundred Shares, or Proprieties," as in the currently-popular joint-stock company. Purchasers of shares, "several" of which, the prospectus said, were "to be sold," would receive dividends of land as the territory was bought from the Indians and surveyed. The promoters encouraged people to club together, six, eight, twelve, or more, to buy a share, since the total amount of land was thought to be very large.[96] Thus, the expectation was, a large number of small investor-settlers would be recruited. For those who wished to settle without becoming shareholders, small amounts of land (twenty to seventy acres) were offered to each person coming or transporting a servant, subject to a quitrent.[97]

Having perfected their arrangements the Quaker proprietors in Eng-

---

[93] "Takany, a village of Swedes and Finns" (Tacony, now part of Philadelphia) was the northernmost white settlement on the west side in 1679 (*Danckaerts' Journal*, p. 100). The Upland court's census of 1677 lists only ten tithables in their jurisdiction on the Jersey side (*Upland Rec.*, p. 80).

[94] Sickler, pp. 19–21; *NJA*, xxi, 559. For the whole subject of land title and distribution see Tanner, chs. 1 and 6.

[95] See the deeds calendared in *NJA*, xxi, 559–565, and a list in *Pa. Arch.*, i, 57.

[96] *The Description of the Province of West-Jersey in America; as also, Proposals to such as desire to have any Propriety therein* (July 1676), in N. J. H. S., *Proceedings*, liv, 8–11; Leaming and Spicer, pp. 382–383; Smith, pp. 82–87.

[97] Leaming and Spicer, pp. 386–387. Or masters of servants might give them land. Thus two sisters, binding themselves to go as servants for four years in 1681, were promised 40 acres each by their respective masters; Anthony Woodhouse got 40 acres for his services from his English employer, and so did William Lee and Nathaniel Sykes (*NJA*, xxi, 414, 417, 401; below, p. 7).

land offered their lands for sale, and between January and April 1676/7 disposed of twenty-four shares.[98] A block of ten, a whole tenth of the province, was taken by five Yorkshiremen, Byllynge's principal creditors, in settlement of debts amounting to £3500.[99] The rest went singly. John Kinsey, Thomas Budd, John Penford, and Andrew Robinson each bought a whole share; Thomas Ollive, Daniel Wills, and William Biddle, two shares among the three of them.[100] Two shares went to twelve Irishmen, who located in the so-called "Irish tenth," later Gloucester County.[1] The remaining five were bought by groups totalling twenty-one individuals.[2] Many of these original purchasers quickly subdivided their holdings into fractions as small as 1/64 of a share. Within a year the Yorkshire proprietors had sold at least half of their ten shares, mostly in fractions, to some twenty-six persons, all but six of whom emigrated.[3] Shares were similarly split by other purchasers, even by Ollive, Kinsey, and others who were emigrating themselves, thus adding eighteen more small proprietors, thirteen of whom came to West Jersey.[4] In short, within a year or two under the trustees' plan of colonization a quarter of the province had been parceled out to perhaps a hundred small proprietors. Absenteeism was discouraged by requiring land taken up to be settled within three years, and on conditions more favorable to emigrating proprietors than to absentee owners.[5] In 1680 about a third of the "Freeholders and Inhabitants" within the jurisdiction of the Burlington court were proprietors.[6] In its earliest stage West Jersey as Penn and his

[98] Or more. This many are recorded in the West Jersey deed books (*NJA*, xxi, 394-441).

[99] *Ibid.*, p. 418; Smith, p. 92. Of the five men, Mahlon Stacy and George Hutcheson are familiar names in the Burlington Court Book; Thomas Hutchinson emigrated but in 1687 was living in Maryland; Joseph Helmsley came on the first ship to Burlington (Smith, 92) but probably returned soon; while Thomas Pearson remained in England (*NJA*, xxi, 454). The last, it was charged, fraudulently tried to sell the land (*ibid.*), but apparently was stopped by court action (see below, p. 59).

[100] *NJA*, xxi, 394, 396, 397, 400, 405, 441. All emigrated, though Penford soon returned to England. He was present at the laying out of the town of Burlington (see Smith, p. 98; Clement, *Proprietary Towns*) and he bought land along with the other commissioners from the Indians in September 1677; but a trust deed he executed in October suggests that he was about to leave then; deeds of 1681 and 1682 place him in England, where he died, 1692 or before (*NJA*, xxi, see index).

[1] *Ibid.*, pp. 400, 405; Tanner, p. 102. Among them were Richard Hunter, who died at Salem in 1679, and William Clarke, who moved to Sussex County, Delaware (*NJA*, xxi, 401).

[2] *Ibid.*, pp. 394, 398, 408, 414. Of these William Peachee, John Cripps, Henry Stacy, William Roydon, Samuel Coles, Francis Collins, and Percival Towle are found in the Burlington colony.

[3] Samuel Barker, Thomas Farnsworth, Elias Farr, Thomas Folke, Godfrey Hancock, James Harrison, Samuel Jenings, John and Thomas Lambert, Robert Murfin, Michael Newbold, George Nicholson, Joseph Pope, George Porter, Edward Taylor (gentleman in London, merchant in Burlington), Samuel Taylor, William Warner, John Wood, and Joshua and Thomas Wright. See indexes to *ibid.* and to this volume.

[4] Bernard Devonish, Anthony Elton, Thomas Eves, Thomas Harding, John and Thomas Hooton, William Hewlings, Thomas Howell, Robert Powell, Benjamin Scott, John Stokes, William Snowden, and John Woolman.

[5] Leaming and Spicer, 387-388. On headright land there were to be two "able men servants" or three "weaker" ones per 100 acres, but for proprietors who emigrated, only one person per 200 acres.

[6] I count 22 on the list on p. 1, below.

xxviii   INTRODUCTION

associates planned it was a colony of small proprietors, who were not merely *free*holders but *share*holders in the enterprise. This was in the best democratic tradition of the Quakers, and more liberal than Penn's future colony of Pennsylvania, in which, although he shared the government with the people, he reserved the land to himself.[7]

The "Concessions and Agreements"[8] issued by the proprietors in London for the projected colony, March 3 1676/7, provided for a "general free and supream assembly" of a hundred members (one for each propriety) to be elected as soon as divisions of the territory should be made. This body, as its description indicates, was to have absolute control of the province.[9] Members were required to be proprietors or freeholders, but were to be chosen by all the inhabitants. Elections were to be annual, and voting by ballot. Pending the establishment of this legislature, the affairs of the new colony were to be managed by ten commissioners appointed by the proprietors, until 1680, when they were to be chosen by a general meeting of the inhabitants—unless, presumably, the assembly had been instituted in the meantime. In either event, as the Quakers planned it, the people were to rule in West Jersey without any restrictions or reservations whatever. That their expectations were not entirely realized was due to the interference of the Duke's government and to a change of heart on part of Byllynge himself.

* * *

The first shipload of colonists under the Concessions reached the Delaware in August 1677,[10] in charge of nine commissioners appointed by the proprietors (and all but two of them proprietors themselves),[11] with power "to order and manage the estate and affairs" of the province according to the Concessions. The commissioners, no doubt aware of the difficulties Fenwick had been encountering with New York, took the precaution on reaching this side of the Atlantic of calling first on Andros, "to acquaint him with their design; for [as Samuel Smith puts it] tho' they had concluded the powers they had from the proprietors, were sufficient to their purpose; they thought it a proper respect to the duke of York's commission, to wait on his governor upon the occasion." It was well they did. When they started to

---

[7] Penn had no proprietary or financial interest in West Jersey at this time. He was "every way unconcerned" when Byllynge asked him to be a trustee (Smith, p. 89).

[8] Leaming and Spicer, pp. 382-411.

[9] Subject to the provisions of the Concessions. There was no governor, but instead ten commissioners, to be elected by the assembly, as a sort of executive committee between sessions of the legislature.

[10] See Smith, pp. 92 ff.

[11] Thomas Ollive and Daniel Wills of Northampton, John Kinsey of Hertford, John Penford of Leicester, Thomas Folke of Derby, Joseph Helmsley and Robert Stacy, York, Benjamin Scott, Essex, and Richard Guy, Middlesex County. Guy was already here and had bought 10,000 acres from Fenwick. Stacy, though perhaps not a proprietor himself, must have represented the family interest.

argue with him Andros, "clapping his hand on his sword, told them, that [he] should defend the government from them, till he received orders from the duke, his master, to surrender it; he however softened, and told them, he would do what was in his power, to make them easy, till they could send home to get redress; and in order thereto, would commissionate the same persons mentioned in the commission they produced. This they accepted, and undertook to act as magistrates under him, till further orders came from England, and proceed in relation to their land affairs, according to the methods prescribed by the proprietors." Thus the Burlington commissioners made a discreet detour around the "unexpected and disagreable" problem of sovereignty.[12] Thereby they saved themselves the years of bickering and confusion that had frustrated Fenwick, and they could proceed at once to their more immediate business, the distribution and settlement of the land, while the other matter was being negotiated in England.

The commissioners [13] were probably all Quakers. Thomas Ollive, who headed the list, seems to have been the leader of the first group of emigrants, and was an outstanding figure in the early years of the Burlington colony. His name and that of Daniel Wills, second on the list, appear constantly in the records printed in this volume, as do, to a lesser extent, most of the others.[14] We do not know how far they considered themselves morally obligated to act in the name of the Duke. They failed to pass on to posterity any record of their magisterial proceedings during what we may call the "Andros period"—an omission which it is difficult to believe was purely accidental.[15] It is clear, however, that others, if not the Burlington Quakers themselves, looked upon them as being definitely under the judicial jurisdiction of New York. A traveller through the Delaware River region in 1679 mentions three "minor courts," at Salem, Upland (on the west side), and Burlington, as subordinate to the "high court of the South River" at New Castle, the "capital of justice." Nor did the Burlingtonians deny this subordination. In the same year a suit involving the ownership of Lessa Point, which had come before "the magestrates of Burlington" without their making an "End of itt," was with their consent removed to the court at Upland.[16]

The Burlington people were indeed disappointed to find themselves under another jurisdiction. As one proprietor wrote, "The place I like very well . . . But if it be not made free, I mean as to the customs and govern-

[12] Smith, pp. 92–94, 105.
[13] Andros named only eight, omitting Thomas Folke (*N. Y. Col. Docs.*, xii, 579, 635).
[14] Of the others, Guy was already on the Salem court. He moved to Burlington about 1690. Kinsey died soon after coming (Smith, p. 93). Penford is the only commissioner who does not figure later in the Burlington Court Book, and he, as noted, returned soon to England.
[15] No court minute book has been found antedating the records printed in this volume, nor are there even occasional minutes of court actions entered among the Burlington land records, like those cited above from Salem.
[16] *Danckaerts' Journal*, pp. 143, 156; *Upland Rec.*, p. 142.

ment, then it will not be so well."[17] But the policy of the commissioners was to maintain amicable relations with Andros while Penn and his friends in England used their influence with the Duke to perfect their title. The commissioners succeeded so well that there is only one instance of friction to record. It was specified in the proprietors' Concessions that the commissioners appointed by them were to govern the province until March 25 1680, when the resident "Proprietors, freeholders, and inhabitants" were to meet and elect ten men to be commissioners for the ensuing year, and so annually until a "general free Assembly" should be instituted.[18] Free elections had no place in the Duke's authoritarian regime on the Delaware, but this election nevertheless took place at the appointed time. This is known not from any mention of it in the West Jersey records, but from the unfavorable notice taken of it by the New York government, whose Council minutes of May 21 1680 record:

> Thomas Budd committed yesterday to the sheriff for writing and signing and sending abroad writings at Burlington and meeting together according to appointment March 25 and the signing to a paper.
> A special warrant to the sheriff to keepe the above Bud in Custody, untill he shall produce those papers signed and disperst, etc.*
> *—by summoning the Kings subjects and disturbing them in their peaceable Enjoyment.
> To bee of the good behavior.
> Samuel Cole did not signe though present. Every one else did.
> Hee was committed by another [   ].
> At Burlington they refuse to shew any authority or produce Copys. . . .
> The Commissioners at Burlingtons returne being 8:—5 of them to bee in Commission.
> The Clause for land to bee left out—and to act according to Law.
> An order against selling strong liquors to the Indyans to [   ] for [   ].[19]

It appears therefore that popular government began in West Jersey on schedule—government by a compact or agreement to which all concerned "voluntarily and freely set our hands."[20] We may reasonably infer that at

---

[17] Thomas Hooten to his wife, 1677 (Smith, p. 105). Andros was collecting duties on imports and exports in the River (*ibid.*, 116).

[18] Leaming and Spicer, p. 385.

[19] New York Colonial MSS. (State Library, Albany), xxix, 99, printed in part in *N. Y. Col. Docs.*, xii, 650. Brackets indicate illegible words.

[20] Leaming and Spicer, p. 409. That the signing of the Concessions was deemed important is evident from an order of the Burlington court (below, p. 8) requiring all within its jurisdiction to sign or "shew their reasons for their refusall." It is possible that the "signing to a paper" referred to by the New York Council was of the Concessions; Samuel Coles said he did not sign, and his name is not among the 200-odd appended to the document, either as printed in Leaming and Spicer or the copy in the MS. volume, Concessions Etc. 1681–1699 (Sec. of State's office, Trenton), which contains some additional names. It is curious to find, sandwiched in among some Salem signers, the names of three Delaware officials, New Castle court justices Fopp Outhout and Casparus Herman, and Sheriff Edmund Cantwell. Two of them had land in West Jersey bought from the Indians in the pre-Quaker period and perhaps signed in order to protect these interests. See, on these purchases, F. H. Stewart, *Indians of Southern New Jersey* (Woodbury, 1932), 71, 73.

the meeting which Thomas Budd promoted commissioners were elected in conformity with the requirements of the Concessions, and that the old commissioners then sent the names to New York as nominations for a new commission. That Andros was not too seriously offended by these proceedings is evident from his willingness to name five of the eight recommended to a new commission for the Burlington court. These five were, beyond any reasonable doubt, the five listed in the court proceedings of June 1680, on page one of this book. That court therefore was held by the authority of the Duke, although the record carefully refrains from saying so. Neither is any mention made of the Concessions. Instead, to indicate the popular basis of the proceedings, the names were recorded of all the inhabitants who were to "doe their sute"—that is, to be in attendance, as the ancient custom of English local courts required.[21] In this way the Burlington Quakers took a step forward toward self-government without repudiating the authority of the Duke. The absence of Salem names from this list indicates that Fenwick's colony was not included within the Burlington jurisdiction, and the Salem court continued to function under the ducal authority.[22] The continued deference of the Burlington immigrants to New York is illustrated by "the inhabitants of the new seated Towne nere the falls of Delaware (called Crewcorne)," who, April 12 1680, petitioned Andros to suppress the sale of strong liquor to the Indians. In September, when the official he appointed would not enforce the Council's order, the Crewcorne people suggested that the "Elected Commissioner"—that is, Mahlon Stacy, one of those elected at Burlington and commissioned by the New York government—be allowed to do so.[23] There was no response to this suggestion, but news was already on its way across the Atlantic which put an end of New York authority in New Jersey. The claims of the Quakers were finally confirmed by the Duke of York.[24]

Government in West Jersey, 1680–1708

Through the efforts of Penn and others the Duke of York was finally persuaded to relinquish his claim to customs duties in West Jersey,[25] and with it all his rights to the territory, in a deed of confirmation or release dated August 6 1680.[26] Most of the Quakers' troubles were over, but not all. A new but smaller fly was introduced into the ointment. By this deed James

---

[21] See S. and B. Webb, *English Local Government . . . The Manor and the Borough*, i (London, 1908), chs. 1, 2; . . . *The Parish and the County* (London, 1906), p. 296.
[22] See above, pp. xxiv–xxv.
[23] See *N. Y. Col. Docs.*, xii, 645–660. Quakers Richard Ridgway and Robert and Thomas Scholey were among the petitioners. The person complained against, Gilbert Wheeler, was fined for liquor selling by the Upland court June 1681 (*Upland Rec.*, p. 194), and again at Burlington in 1682.
[24] Smith, p. 124.
[25] Smith, pp. 116–124.
[26] *NJA*, i, 323–333.

eliminated himself from the scene, and by his granting West Jersey to the three trustees and Byllynge, Edridge, and Warner, Fenwick was eliminated too; but the government unexpectedly was settled upon Byllynge in person, not upon the group, and thus the Quakers in West Jersey found that they had merely exchanged one master for another. True, they could cope with Byllynge on a more equal footing, as they proceeded to do, but in the end he won out, retaining his right of proprietorial sovereignty over the province. The fact is important not because Byllynge or his successors tyrannized over West Jersey people but because it was a contributing cause of the subsequent surrender of the proprietorial government to the Crown.

Byllynge, living up to his contemporary reputation for shrewdness,[27] seems to have engineered this startling innovation himself, by tendering James a deed already drawn up for him to sign. To the objection that the Duke's legal counsel had neither drawn nor signed the document, Byllynge "urged the necessity of it now," as a ship with emigrants was ready to sail to West Jersey with it; and so the Duke signed.[28] Byllynge's master stroke was in the nature of a *fait accompli*, and there was not much the Quaker leaders could do about it except to urge moderation upon both sides—that is, upon the new lord proprietor in England and his angry subjects on this side of the ocean—and in this they were, on the whole, successful. The West Jersey people were persuaded to choose Byllynge as governor; and he designated as his deputy Samuel Jenings, who had been sent over with a new commission from the whole group of trustees and owners shortly before the issuing of James' grant.[29]

There was nothing in the Concessions about a governor of any sort; but legally speaking self-government under the Concessions ended August 6 1680—that is, before it could get under way—with the bestowal of the government upon Byllynge. Jenings called an assembly which met November 1681, drew up some "fundamentals" protecting its constituents against possible tyranny by governors, and then upon his acceptance of these provisions "accepted and received" Jenings as "Deputy Governor," after which they enacted a mass of legislation.[30] During its session of May 1683 the assembly elected Jenings governor, and sponsored a meeting of all the freeholders of the province, which resolved "that the purchase at first made, was of land and government together;" that Byllynge and the trustees were bound "to make good the former contract of the land and government to the purchasers;" that the assembly would stand by the Concessions; and that an

---

[27] "A close sutle witte man" (Stewart, *Fenwick*, p. 53). See Pepys' comment, above.

[28] *NJA*, i, 323.

[29] Strictly speaking, this appointment of new commissioners was not in accordance with the Concessions, for in 1680 the people were to begin choosing their own commissioners, and they did so, March 25, as noted above. Possibly word of this election did not reach England before the departure of Jenings, who reached West Jersey about Sept. 1 1680.

[30] Leaming and Spicer, pp. 423-437.

instrument should be drawn up and sent to "some trusty friends in London" (including George Fox) for Byllynge to sign, "whereby to confirm his first bargain and sale he made to the freeholders of this Province, of land and government together."[31] In 1684 they sent Jenings and Thomas Budd to England to press their case, electing Thomas Ollive governor after Jenings' departure.[32] The matter was thoroughly discussed among the English Quaker leaders, George Fox himself attending a dozen conferences on the "New Jarcey business."[33] The result was a defeat for the West Jersey people: Byllynge, they decided, was entitled to the government by the grant of 1680 and could not legally divide it; but he should confirm the Concessions.[34]

It is a tribute to the Quaker spirit of discipline that they acquiesced in this award, even though Byllynge did not confirm the Concessions.[35] The assembly continued Ollive as governor, rejecting a Byllynge appointee named William Welch.[36] In 1685 Byllynge appointed a new deputy governor in the person of John Skene, a resident of some prominence in the colony, having been elected to the Council in 1683.[37] His new dignity weighing heavily upon him, Skene made a dramatic entrance into the Burlington court, November 1685, read his commission, shooed Governor Ollive and the magistrates off the bench, and adjourned the court till next morning. He may have intended to appoint new justices, but if so he was disappointed. The court met not next day but six weeks later. In the meantime the assembly had met, bowed to the new commission (but "reserving their just rights and privileges"), appointed a committee to inspect Byllynge's new charter, and elected a new slate of justices, as was their annual custom. However, at the ensuing session of court (December 15 1685) it was definitely declared that the court was held by Byllynge's "power and Authority."[38] Skene continued as governor, the court minutes show, until August 1688—in November he is merely a justice. In April of that year James, now king, had annexed the Jerseys to New England and New York in a new "Dominion of New England,"[39] with their old nemesis, Andros, as governor. He did not bother the Jerseys much, appearing in West Jersey August 18 only to take over the province officially. Skene was authorized to distribute new

---

[31] Leaming and Spicer, pp. 468–472; cf. *NJA*, i, 421.
[32] Leaming and Spicer, pp. 483–490.
[33] Sept. 1684 to July 1685 (see *The Short Journal and Itinerary Journals of George Fox*, ed. N. Penny (Cambridge, 1925), index, Byllynge).
[34] Tanner, p. 119.
[35] *Ibid.*, p. 120.
[36] Smith, p. 190. In 1683 he was chosen register of immigrants, and a member of the Governor's Council (Leaming and Spicer, pp. 480, 481).
[37] *Ibid.*, p. 472.
[38] *Ibid.*, p. 503; below, p. 48.
[39] On this see C. E. Godfrey, "When Boston was New Jersey's Capital," reprinted from N. J. H. S., *Proceedings*, Jan. 1933.

commissions (with accompanying charges) for all incumbent officers and to have them deliver their records to him to be sent to Andros; but he seems to have collected neither fees nor records.

James' "Dominion" eliminated West Jersey's Assembly for the time being. But the Glorious Revolution of 1688 soon drove James from the throne in England and Andros from his post in America. From the departure of Andros' lieutenant in June 1689 until 1692 West Jersey seems to have been without either legislature or governor.[40] The only local government during this period was exercised through the courts, whose mill of justice ground on unperturbed, governor or no governor, assembly or no assembly, as the court minutes show. The lineup of justices on the Burlington bench during this interregnum remains unchanged. The local head of government, so far as there could be said to be any, was still John Skene, who though no longer governor continued to preside over the court.[41] But his colleagues were not overawed, judging from the alacrity with which they slapped him down whenever his name was called from the other side of the bench.[42]

Meanwhile the death of Byllynge had changed the proprietorial picture. Future governor-proprietors were destined to be non-Quakers. In 1687 Byllynge's heirs sold their inheritance to Dr. Daniel Coxe, court physician and dabbler in colonial enterprises.[44] The question of sovereignty was no longer debatable, he told West Jersey people, but he would abide by their "fundamentals," unless contrary to the laws of England, which, in his opinion, "extend to our colony." But Coxe's enthusiasm waned and in 1691 he conveyed most of his twenty-two proprieties and the government to a group of forty-eight men, mostly London merchants, who were not prospective immigrants but merely land speculators.[45] This "West Jersey Society" in 1692 appointed as their "Commissioner and Deputy Governor" Andrew Hamilton, a Scotch merchant of East Jersey, who was already governor of that province, and a man of prudence and tact, the best-liked governor, perhaps, that colonial New Jersey ever had.[46] Under Hamilton the legislature was revived, but on a bicameral basis with a council and a house of representatives.[47] Hamilton, who spent most of his time in East Jersey and seldom found time to preside over West Jersey court sessions, was authorized by his commission to appoint a deputy of his own in the western province. This he did, in the person of Edward Hunloke, a prominent Burlington merchant. During Skene's regime Hunloke had been second on the

---

[40] Godfrey, p. 14.
[41] His name heads the list of justices in sessions, and he is judge of common pleas.
[42] See below, pp. 98, 102.
[44] Tanner, p. 121; Smith, pp. 190–194.
[45] NJA, ii, 41, 64.
[46] Tanner, pp. 92, 122. His commission, dated April 11, is in NJA, ii, 87.
[47] Leaming and Spicer, pp. 507 ff.

INTRODUCTION xxxv

list of justices, and when the ex-Governor died in 1690 Hunloke moved up to first place. At first he was designated as "Deputy Governor," and as such he presided over the Gloucester court also;[48] and though this title was soon dropped in the court minutes, he continued to head the bench as long as he remained on it.[49]

In 1697 the West Jersey Society in an ill-advised moment decided to replace Hamilton with Jeremiah Basse, an Anabaptist preacher turned adventurer, who had been acting as their land agent. Basse arrived in Burlington in his gubernatorial capacity April 1698. Hamilton and the Quaker assembly refused to recognize him as governor, but he appointed a council (including John Tatham, Thomas Revell, John Jewell, and Edward Randolph, none of them Quakers) and magistrates.[50] The latter were at first prevented by violence from holding court, but at length, with the governor at their head, effected an entrance into the court house and began their duties.[51] The sessions recorded in the Burlington minutes between August 1698 and November 1699 were held under Basse's authority, he being present at three. Fourteen justices appeared on the bench at various times during this period, most of them non-Quakers or ex-Quakers.[52] The court

[48] Stewart, *Gloucester County under the Proprietors*, pp. 26, 27.

[49] Hunloke is one of the few local non-Quakers prominent in Burlington affairs during the proprietary period. That he was not a Quaker may be inferred from the absence of any reference to him as such in the Quaker meeting records. He was not among the earliest settlers and may have come to West Jersey through the Langfords, John and Ebenezer, who were merchants and landowners in Burlington County, the latter as early as 1684. Hunloke was a brother-in-law of John (*NJA*, xxi, 356, 419, 425). He is first noted in 1686/7, as an attorney in a suit and a member (probably foreman) of the Burlington grand jury. Soon afterwards he was indicted for selling rum to the Indians, for which, despite his plea of ignorance of the law, he was fined the full amount, £3 (Leaming and Spicer, p. 435). From this we gather that he was a newcomer and at the time interested in the Indian trade. Under such inauspicious circumstances Hunloke entered West Jersey public life. But the very next session of court (July) he was on the bench, where he remained till 1696—the first non-Quaker, with negligible exceptions, to sit there. He was plaintiff in 35 suits, mostly for debt. In one of them he was accused of keeping false books; in another the jury intervened to protect the defendant; in a third a witness declared she would give two servants their time before Hunloke should have them (below, pp. 81, 83, 180, 111). Hunloke prospered and in spite of local unpopularity enjoyed the confidence of the non-Quaker ruling element. He acted as land agent for Dr. Coxe, 1691-2 (*NJA*, xxi, 432; below, pp. 134-143). When Hamilton became governor of both the Jerseys Hunloke became his deputy for the western province. His commission as such was read in the court in Nov. 1692 and the last time he was noted under that title was in Oct. 1693. He was commissioned Collector of the Port of Burlington in 1695 (*NJA*, xxi, 499, and see below, pp. 183, 200). Unlike Thomas Revell (see below, p. xxxix), during the Basse controversy Hunloke supported the Hamilton-Quaker party, on the return of which to power he became clerk and recorder for the Burlington jurisdiction, 1699, and so remained until his death in 1702. He was also clerk of the council, 1700, 1701 (Leaming and Spicer, pp. 566, 569, 577, 579, 587; below, p. 265). He was named on Cornbury's provincial council upon the surrender in 1702 but died before that body convened (*NJA*, iii, 1). Between 1691 and 1694 he married (doubtless a second wife) Mary daughter of the Quaker Richard Basnett (*NJA*, xxi, 489). His widow and Margaret Hunloke his executrix were early benefactors of St. Mary's Anglican church in Burlington (G. B. Hills, *History of the Church in Burlington* (Trenton, 1876), pp. 215, 218).

[50] Tanner, p. 122; *NJA*, ii, 208, 401-402.

[51] *Ibid.*, pp. 381-382.

[52] Tatham, Revell, and Jewell, who as noted above were members of Basse's council, and

seems to have had an anti-Quaker bias, as was to be expected. Thus Daniel England fared badly in a suit brought against him by a French resident.[53] Henry Beck was apparently violently dissatisfied with the new order and was committed.[54] John Hollinshead boycotted the court and lost a case the decision on which a later Quaker court refused to enforce against him.[55] Burlington Constable James Satterthwait was also fined £10 for searching a house with no more authorization than that of Burgess Hollinshead.[56] Treasurer Peter Fretwell refused to acknowledge the court's authority and was committed, while the redoubtable Samuel Jenings was presented by the grand jury for saying that the governor's commission was unlawful.[57]

However, Basse's day was a short one. The only reason that the West Jersey Society had changed governors was because of doubt whether Hamilton, as a Scotchman, was eligible. Being now informed that he was, they reappointed him, August 1699, and at the February 1699/1700 court a general housecleaning took place, Basse and his adherents were swept out, and the familiar faces of Mahlon Stacy, Francis Davenport, Daniel Wills, and other good Quakers reappeared on the bench.[58]

The return of Hamilton restored the Quaker ascendancy in West Jersey, but it also sharpened the line of cleavage which had developed between the Quaker and anti-Quaker elements in the population. Though the validity of Hamilton's new commission was questioned, the Quaker court would brook no criticism of him. When Benjamin Borden, a violent anti-Hamiltonian of East Jersey,[59] appeared in the western province and "defamed" the governor by "supposing" that he "was run away," the court, with Hamilton on the bench, fined Borden £100.[60] The anti-Quaker faction made trouble wherever they could. They encouraged the "beliefe that no Act of Government could be done under the present Administration." In March 1700/1 a mob invaded Burlington, broke into the prison, and

---

Nathaniel Westland, John Test, Thomas Bibb, and Anthony Elton were non-Quakers. Michael and Joshua Newbold were originally Quakers but (probably during the Keithian controversy) left the Society and (with Westland and Jewell) became Anglicans (Hills, p. 215). William Emley, George Deacon, and Joshua Ely were Quakers.

[53] *Resnier v. England*, below, p. 206.
[54] Below, pp. 207–208.
[55] Below, p. 209; *Ogborn v. Hollinshead*, pp. 214–251.
[56] Below, p. 217.
[57] Below, pp. 219, 220. Jenings himself relates: "Upon his [Basse's] telling me, He believed I would use my endeavours to remove him from the Government, and bring in Coll. Hamilton again; I did tell him, That he had a shrewd hand at guessing, and that he might depend upon it" (S. Jenings, *Truth Rescued from Forgery* (Philadelphia, 1699, reprinted 1881), p. 23). Jenings was the *bête noire* of unworthy governors. Even the graceless Lord Cornbury quailed before his sharp tongue and steely stare (D. L. Kemmerer, *Path to Freedom: the Struggle for Self-Government in Colonial New Jersey* (Princeton, 1940), p. 70).
[58] *NJA*, ii, 257, 276, 299, 301; below, p. 226.
[59] See *NJA*, ii, 363, 396.
[60] This was no idle gesture. When Nicholas Brown allowed Borden to escape on Brown's horse from the sheriff, the cost of Borden's prosecution was saddled upon him (below, pp. 241–249).

rescued two fomenters of discord confined there because they would not find sureties for good behavior. The peaceful Quakers were at a disadvantage in dealing with mobs.[61] Some of the ringleaders were presented at the next court but nothing was done to them.[62] The anti-Quakers also encouraged the people not to pay the provincial tax which had recently been levied, and judging from entries in the Burlington record they achieved great success in this endeavor.[63]

These disorders caused, or at least hastened, the doom of proprietary rule in West Jersey. The West Jersey Society was neither pro- nor anti-Quaker; its members, like business men in every age, wanted peace and prosperity. Conditions in West Jersey were less disturbed than in East, but there was steady pressure from the Crown to surrender the government, which the Society was unwilling or unable to resist. At length it joined with the East Jersey proprietors in yielding up the government, attempting only to preserve some of the popular rights of the inhabitants, and in particular to keep Hamilton as governor. These efforts failed. There were no reservations in the surrender, and Hamilton's job was given to a cousin of the Queen, Lord Cornbury.[64]

* * *

"The surrender," wrote William Penn, "was knavishly contrived to betray the people."[65] It need not have taken place, had James been in less of a hurry to sign Byllynge's draft of the grant, back in 1680.[66] The Quakers were disappointed to lose their rights of government, but they were inured to disappointment and could take this calamity in their stride. The surrender was dated April 15 1702, but Cornbury's commission and instructions as governor of the united Province of New Jersey were not issued till the latter part of the year, and he did not publish his commission in Burlington until August 13 1703.[67] In the meantime the Quaker justices continued to hold court at Burlington up to May 1703, when they adjourned because of the death of "Coll: Andrew Hamilton Our Governour."[68]

[61] *NJA*, ii, 379. "Takeing advantage of the Governor being unprovided to Suppresse them because many of the Inhabitants of that Towne are such whose Religious Perswasions will not suffer them to bear Armes." It appears that the mob included several Quakers (*Pa. Mag.*, vii, 367).

[62] Below, p. 252. Of the eleven presented, three (Andrews, Woolston, Ogborn) may possibly have been Quakers, and two (Langstaff, Fisher) Anglicans.

[63] *NJA*, ii, 378, 382; below, p. 259.

[64] See Kemmerer, chs. 1–3, for an excellent account of the surrender and Cornbury's administration.

[65] Kemmerer, p. 20.

[66] See above, p. xxxii. In that case (to indulge in a bit of historical day-dreaming), East Jersey might have surrendered by itself, and become annexed to New York; and then Quaker West Jersey, left by itself, might have cast its lot with Quaker Pennsylvania; and thus there would be no New Jersey today.

[67] *NJA*, ii, 459, 500, 506; iii, 1.

[68] Below, p. 291.

The accession of Cornbury marks not only the end of the Quakers' judicial supremacy in Burlington but also their complete withdrawal from the court. The Burlington Court Book itself is silent on the events of this period, "Severall Minutes of Court and other things done" from Cornbury's arrival to December 1704 not being entered in the record.[69] Shortly after his arrival in Burlington, and while his ordinance establishing courts was being formulated, he appointed a "High Sheriff," a coroner, and a clerk for Burlington, all of them Anglicans.[70] Under date of August 20 he issued a commission of the peace to Samuel Jenings and eighteen others. Seven of the nineteen justices thus appointed were Quakers, probably fewer than their population in the county entitled them to, and a sad come-down from the virtual judicial monopoly which they had hitherto enjoyed.[71] Three days later Cornbury commissioned Jenings as judge of common pleas, to be assisted by any two of seven named justices, two of whom were Quakers.[72] So in the pleas also the Quakers were in the minority, three to five. Whether the Friends, thus outnumbered, attended any of the unrecorded sessions during "Captaine Jewells time" it is impossible to say, but they certainly did not appear at any session subsequently recorded in this volume. In this policy of noncooperation it seems that Samuel Jenings took the lead. On March 2 1703/4 Cornbury, reciting that Jenings "being a quaker does not thinke Convenient to Sit as Judge" of pleas, and that "the Execution of Justice hath been very much delayed" thereby, issued a new pleas commission for Revell as judge, to act with any two justices. The commission of the peace, however, was not renewed until November 6 1705, and even the new one was not wholly devoid of Quakers, Jenings, Davenport, and Deacon being included by virtue of their membership in the council. It is clear therefore that the Quakers' retirement from the Burlington court was voluntary; when control passed from their hands, they chose to get out entirely rather than to continue as a minority.

The new head of the Burlington judiciary, Thomas Revell, was the outstanding "career man" in the West Jersey proprietary government. An early settler and a protégé of the Quakers though not one himself, he had,

[69] Below, p. 291.

[70] These and other appointments are recorded in MS. Commissions, AAA, Sec. of State's office, Trenton. William Fisher was commissioned sheriff Aug. 14, John Ward coroner Aug. 20, and John Jewell clerk Aug. 23. Hugh Huddy succeeded Jewell as clerk Sept. 28 1704, after the latter had become clerk for Salem. All these men were identified with St. Mary's Church (Hills, pp. 45, 53, 214, 215). For the ordinance establishing courts see below, p. xlviii. Cornbury's comments are in *NJA*, iii, 3 ff.

[71] Thomas Revell was second on the list and Francis Davenport, Quaker, third. Five more old-line Quakers were included, Deacon, Emly, W. Wood, Biddle (jr.), and R. Ridgway. The others on the commission were Attorney General Alexander Griffith, Basse, and ten local ex- or non-Quakers who had been on the bench during the Basse regime. On Burlington population see below, p. li.

[72] These were Davenport and Deacon; the others were Revell, Leeds, Westland, Wheeler, and J. Newbold.

after many years of governmental service, broken with his Quaker employers during Basse's governorship.[73] He now passed into the Cornbury camp, and henceforth presided over Burlington judicial sessions, in company with other local men who had come to the fore in the Basse era: Nathaniel Westland, a warden of St. Mary's Church, and several apostate Quakers turned Anglican, William Budd, Daniel Leeds, Robert Wheeler, William Hewlings, and Michael and Joshua Newbold.[74] Under Cornbury the Quakers remained a power in the assembly but lost the courts to the Anglican party, which, by cooperating with Cornbury, sought to dominate West Jersey politics. St. Mary's, as a recent writer observes, became a sort of Tammany Hall of West Jersey.[75]

[73] Revell emigrated to Burlington with his family and servants in 1678. There is nothing in the Quaker records to indicate that he was a member of the Society, but he had Quaker connections, his wife being a sister of Thomas Potts, who with his family came on the same ship (Smith, p. 109; R. D., W. S., and D. B. Ely, *An Historical Narrative of the Ely, Revell and Stacye Families* (New York, 1910), pp. 109, 75). In the early years Revell made his living by his pen, rather than by the usual occupations of merchandizing, farming, or land speculating. He describes himself as a "scrivener"—the only one in early West Jersey (below, p. 39; *NJA*, xxi, 408, 728), and the neat and literate script in which he recorded the Burlington court minutes to 1696 (below, pp. 1, 12, 154, 187) evidences his competence in his chosen occupation. He seems to have acquired no land in the province until 1682, and little thereafter until near the end of the century (*NJA*, xxi, 396, 749; iii, 290, 301). He is clerk of the Burlington court at its first recorded meeting in 1680, continuing to be elected to that position, and likewise that of "register" of the Burlington jurisdiction and clerk to the assembly (below, pp. 1, 6; Leaming and Spicer, pp. 425–568). He was also clerk of the Chester County, Pennsylvania, court during the first two years of Penn's proprietorship (*Chester Co. Rec.*, pp. 3–28). In 1692, when the West Jersey Society commissioned Hamilton as governor, they made Revell the provincial literary factotum—"Secretary, Register and Keeper of the Rolls, and Clerk of the Council" (*NJA*, xxi, 434). He was a member of Hamilton's council in 1697 (*ibid.*, ii, 146), and probably had been from its beginning, for during 1693–1695, when he was clerk of the court, we find him occasionally on the bench or otherwise acting as a justice (below, pp. 157–184), a combination of duties which could be explained by his being a councillor and therefore a justice *ex officio*. He continued as clerk and recorder till 1696. He broke with the Quakers during the Basse regime. When the West Jersey Society appointed Basse governor they made him and Revell their agents (*NJA*, xxi, 504). He accepted membership on Basse's council (*NJA*, ii, 209) and sat regularly in the Burlington court, second to John Tatham, the presiding justice, as long as the Basse interlude lasted (below, pp. 205–226). Naturally, when Basse was ousted, Revell was out too. Thereafter he worked against Hamilton and the Quakers for the surrender of West Jersey to the Crown, and in due season got his reward, being a member of the council and president of the Burlington court under Cornbury and becoming one of that unworthy governor's tools (*NJA*, ii, 384; iii, 301; xiii, 301; below, p. 292). He became third judge of the provincial supreme court in 1708 (Commissions, AAA, p. 85). St. Mary's Church was organized in 1702, but Revell made no subscription to it until 1705 (Hills, pp. 215, 222); his conversion to Anglicanism may have been as much political as religious.

[74] See below, pp. 291 ff., and for Anglican connections, Hills, pp. 45, 53, 215 ff. Later occupants of the Burlington bench included John Bainbridge, originally a Quaker but apparently not in 1705, when he took an oath, which was contrary to Quaker principles; Roger Parkes, Quaker but later Anglican; John Rudroe, William Bustill, and Hugh Huddy, Anglicans; and Daniel Coxe, jr., Enoch Andrews, and Peter Sonmans, who were not identified with St. Mary's at the time but had no Quaker connections.

[75] See Kemmerer, pp. 50–57.

The Courts and Their Work, 1680–1709

Having sketched the political background of the Burlington Court Book, we must turn to a more systematic consideration of the judicial organization of West Jersey. As we have seen,[76] the commissioners appointed by the proprietors in 1677 to manage the affairs of the infant colony until government under the Concessions could be instituted, actually were obliged to act as magistrates under the authority of the Duke of York; and the commissioners chosen by popular vote in 1680 also functioned under the ducal authority. What officers the court had before 1680 we do not know, but at that time, besides the magistrates, there were a clerk, a constable, and (as the Concessions required)[77] a trial jury of twelve. In March 1681, after the Duke had yielded the government to Byllynge, another popular election took place. Ten commissioners, who were magistrates, were elected, and a sheriff, two constables, a register, and a surveyor, for the Burlington jurisdiction, besides certain officers for Salem. Since there was as yet no assembly, the court issued several orders which amounted to legislation, regarding such matters as the sale of liquor, the rate of exchange for money, and the taking up of lands.[78] We also find the Burlington court confronted with that perennial problem of colonial courts, how to secure the proper respect for its authority; and a person is bound over "for affronting the Constable."[79]

From the time the assembly began to meet, in November 1681, judicial officers were elected by that body rather than by direct popular vote.[80] The commissioners became a council, whose members were justices *ex officio*. In addition to the ten councillor-justices there were from six to eleven additional justices for the Burlington jurisdiction. Three could hold court.[81] Attendance varied; it was usually from five to seven, seldom fewer than four or more than nine. A trial for rape in 1686 produced a record attendance—thirteen, including Governor Skene.[82] The labor turnover on the bench was small. Some justices were seldom seen there, but the faces of others appeared regularly year after year; the most familiar was that of Quaker Justice William Biddle, whose span of service, 1682–1702, covers almost the entire proprietorial period, during which time he sat at seventy

---

[76] Above, p. xxix.
[77] Leaming and Spicer, pp. 395, 396, 428.
[78] Legislation on these subjects was enacted soon afterwards by the first assembly (Leaming and Spicer, pp. 434, 435, 437).
[79] Below, pp. 1–8.
[80] This was at variance with the Concessions, which stipulated that justices and constables be elected by the people, except the chief justice, who was to be named by the assembly (Leaming and Spicer, p. 408).
[81] Leaming and Spicer, pp. 443, 451, 457, 473, 491, 499, 504, 428.
[82] Below, p. 54.

INTRODUCTION xli

sessions of court. Thomas Revell was clerk from 1680 to 1696.[83] The sheriff's office changed more frequently,[84] and that of constable, annually. From 1682 to May 1685 the constables were included among the officers of government named by the omnipotent assembly.[85] In the following December, in the first court under Skene, a list of "Constables Chosen" (including, for the first and only time, a "High Constable"), appears on the minutes, and the names of constables are entered regularly thereafter.[86] The minutes are silent as to how these constables were selected during Skene's governorship, but from the early 1690's, at the latest, they were chosen by the townships or towns. The hiring of substitutes was not uncommon. The burden of presenting a successor lay upon the retiring constable, and failing therein he was liable to be continued in office himself.[87] As in England, the con-

[83] Later clerks were Thomas Bibb, 1697 (Leaming and Spicer, p. 552), and Edward Hunloke, 1699–1702 (*ibid.*, pp. 569, 579; below, pp. 231, 251–269). After this the minutes are less well kept, and there is a succession of clerks or scribes. Hugh Huddy succeeded Hunloke Sept. 1702 (below, p. 265). The handwriting changes again in November and in the following February, and in both sessions the declarations are entered *in extenso* in the minutes (below, pp. 272–281). The first clerk appointed by Cornbury was John Jewell, Aug. 1703 (Commissions, AAA, p. 10). None of his minutes are entered in the court book. In Sept. 1704 his place was taken by Hugh Huddy, who was succeeded by Charles Huddy in Nov. 1706 (*ibid.*, pp. 28, 55, 73). In these latter years there were frequent changes of scribes (below, pp. 300, 315, 336, 337).

[84] William Emley was the first sheriff (below, p. 5). John White was sheriff in 1682, Benjamin Wheat in 1683–1685, and James Hill in 1685 (Leaming and Spicer, pp. 444, 458, 492, 500, 504) and again in 1693 (below, pp. 157, 162). From 1695 to 1703 the sheriffs were (as mentioned in Leaming and Spicer, pp. 536–579, or below) Thomas Bibb, Henry Grubb, Samuel Furnis, Joseph Cross, Christopher Wetherill, Isaac Marriott, Thomas Rapier (with Henry Grubb subsheriff). Cornbury's appointees were William Fisher, Aug. 1703, John Kible, Nov. 1705, and Hugh Huddy, April 1706 (Commissions, AAA, pp. 6, 29, 55, 67, 73, 83, 93).

[85] Leaming and Spicer, pp. 444–500.

[86] Below, pp. 49, 62, 65, 81, etc.

[87] See "Town Dockets of Chesterfield Township," in *Pa. Mag.*, xxxv, 211–222; MS. Northampton Township Minutes, 1697–1803 (State Library, Trenton); below, pp. 159, 191, 212, 261; *cf.* below, p. liv.

In England at this time constables of hundreds ("head," "chief," or "high" constables) were "in the great majority of cases" chosen by the justices in county quarter sessions. "Petty" constables of parishes, townships, or manors were originally appointed at the court leet and so continued in parts of the country, especially in the north; but elsewhere, particularly throughout the southern counties, they too were appointed by quarter sessions. "The inhabitants of the parish never acquired any legal right to interfere with his [the petty constable's] selection or appointment" (S. and B. Webb, *op. cit.*, 489, 27–28). Both kinds were chosen by quarter sessions in Oxfordshire in 1687, when several chief and petty constables petitioned to be relieved. Each petitioner nominated two or three persons as successors, the first named of which is marked *"electus"* in the record. Apparently they were appointed for and were obliged to serve only one year. See M. S. Gretton, *Oxfordshire Justices of the Peace in the Seventeenth Century* (Oxford, 1934), 32, 48. There is nothing in the Oxfordshire record to indicate why the lightning happened to strike these particular nominees, whether they were the constable's own choice or whether the local unit which he served determined them. According to the Webbs (*op. cit.*, 27 n.), there was a "persistent belief in the right of the inhabitants of each tithing to nominate their own tithingmen" (as petty constables frequently were called).

When Cornbury took over in New Jersey his council agreed (Aug. 21 1703) "that all Constables be Chosen Yearly at the Quarter Sessions by the Justices then present" (*NJA*, xiii, 306). If this

stable's office was an unattractive one, without prestige and occasionally hazardous. In Burlington, however, cases of "affronting" the constable seem to have been comparatively few.[88]

As the business of the court expanded with the increase of population, its organization kept pace. Trial juries were required by the Concessions but no need of a grand jury was felt until 1684.[89] It is not until 1686, under Skene, that there is any mention of a prosecuting or king's attorney.[90]

The Quaker founders of the Burlington colony were determined that justice should be open, easy, and cheap, and all were free to plead their own causes without necessity "to fee any attorney or councillor." [91] In those days some legal knowledge was more likely to be part of a man's polite education than it is now; [92] and Burlington seems to have managed till the end of the seventeenth century with but one local professional lawyer.[92a] From that time on, however, the services of men skilled in the law were in greater request. By 1705/6, when a plaintiff appeared in court with *two* lawyers, we may feel confident that the modern era had arrived.[93]

In a burst of generosity the proprietors also in the Concessions exempted everyone imprisoned "upon any account whatsoever" from paying any fees to the "officers of said prison, either when committed or discharged." But the settlers would not go that far, and the first assembly omitted this pro-

---

meant literally that the courts were to select constables, rather than accepting choices of the townships, the practice did not continue in Burlington County very long. Chesterfield did indeed fail to note the choice of a constable among its township officers in 1703, but its choices are entered most of the time thereafter (see minutes cited above). In December 1704, the first recorded Burlington minutes of the Cornbury era, the constables appeared and made their "return of new constables," just as they had done under proprietary rule. A year later they "presented" the new constables; later lists are given of new constables "chosen," and the last of such lists in this volume says "appointed," suggesting that the court's appointment, not the township's election, was the determining factor (below, pp. 281, 292, 306, 319, 330, 336). Among the new constables chosen in 1706 was William Watson for Nottingham. When he did not appear at the next session the court fined him, and the township for not choosing a "fitt man" for constable. But the court did not remove Watson; it just kept on fining him for non-attendance (below, pp. 319, 321, 325). Nor do there seem to have been double nominations during this period. In 1709 Northampton began to "nominate" two persons, the second moving up to first place the following year; but Chesterfield continued to "choose" one man only (see minutes, as above).

[88] For examples, see below, pp. 8–9, 34, 207, 301, 303. Even the sheriff did not invariably meet with the respect and cooperation due an important servant of the king; see, *e. g.*, the passage between Sheriff Bibb and Jacob Perkins, below, p. 176.

[89] Leaming and Spicer, pp. 398, 429; below, p. 32. Juries were to be summoned by the sheriff. They probably had to be freeholders (see p. 317, where a juror summoned is noted "no Freeholder") and of mature age (see p. 70, where objection is made against the youth of the jury empanelled).

[90] This innovation seems to have been introduced by Skene or the court itself, as there is no law for it in Leaming and Spicer.

[91] Leaming and Spicer, pp. 398, 429.

[92] See C. T. Bond and R. B. Morris, eds., *Proceedings of the Maryland Court of Appeals, 1695–1729* (Washington, 1933), p. xix.

[92a] This was Thomas Clark. He is referred to as "the Lawyer" in 1700/1, appears in many suits from about this time, and is the first to be formally commissioned to practice as an attorney (1709) (below, pp. 249, 341).

[93] *Manners v. Abbot*, below, p. 312.

hibition from their laws confirming various provisions of the Concessions.[94] The judiciary was expected to pay its own way as far as possible. In the simple but effective procedure of the early Quaker court, a person whose prosecution on a criminal charge was actually begun was likely to be convicted. However, in 1696 and again in 1702 persons bound to court and then cleared by proclamation nevertheless paid their fees, and from 1701 it was a regular practice, when a person was held for court and nothing appeared against him, to dismiss him, "paying his fees."[95] After the surrender, when the Burlington grand jury was not seeing eye to eye with the provincial attorney general and returned several of his presentments *ignoramus*, the bench nevertheless assessed costs upon the defendants.[96] Against this last practice the provincial house of representatives remonstrated with Cornbury, and was upheld by the English legal authorities: "the Person accused not being properly in Court till arraigned before the Petty Jury, no fees till then can be demanded."[97]

While the internal workings of the Burlington court were growing more intricate and expensive,[98] the whole judicial system of West Jersey was also expanding. In the Burlington democracy of the Concessions, the people were to rule through their elected assembly, which was also the supreme executive and the court of last resort as well.[99] However, appeals from Burlington decisions were infrequent. The first was made in 1684 by the otherwise-minded Samuel Coles. The verdict in a land suit having gone against him he "requires an Appeale for England," which the court for what would seem to be sufficient reasons refused.[100] No other litigant had the temerity to look overseas for justice, but there were several who invoked the higher authority of the assembly. In 1686 a defendant, assessed £25 damages for pulling down a house, was refused an appeal because he could give no security to prosecute it.[1] In 1690 ex-Governor Skene was ordered by the court to

[94] Leaming and Spicer, pp. 398, 429.
[95] Below, pp. 187, 267, and *cf.* 311; 222–334.
[96] Below, pp. 307, 341, 343.
[97] To the governor's contention that accused persons had always paid fees in England "notwithstanding the grand jury have not found the Bill," the representatives replied that they were governed not by English practice but by "the unreasonableness of the thing." See *Journal and Votes of the House of Representatives of* . . . *New Jersey*, 1703–1709 (Jersey City, 1872), pp. 100, 105, 111; *NJA*, iii, 175, 182, 246; iv, 5.
[98] Court fees were increased in 1700 (Leaming and Spicer, p. 571).
[99] The Concessions empowered the commissioners to reprieve and suspend execution of sentences for reference to "the next General Assembly, who may accordingly either pardon, or command execution" (Leaming and Spicer, pp. 391, 426). They also reserved punishment for treason and murder to the assembly (*ibid.*, p. 404), but this was not reenacted by the first assembly and was therefore not binding upon the courts. The Burlington court never attempted to apply the bloody penal code of contemporary England. Down to 1693, when oyer and terminer was provided for capital cases, only one death sentence was passed by the Burlington justices, and it was not executed (below, pp. 142–148).
[100] *Cole v. Allen*, below, pp. 22, 25.
[1] *Whitehead v. Sife*, below, p. 62.

give his servant fifty acres of land due him by contract, whereupon he "offers an Appeal from this Session but the Bench take noe notice of it." [2] To whom Skene wished to appeal is problematical, in this interval between the downfall of the second Andros regime and the resumption of proprietorial government in 1692. Failure to specify "to the assembly" suggests rather definitely that in 1690 that body was not meeting; but it was by May 1692, and on the 11th of that month we find a defendant asking for an appeal to the assembly, which the court, "though they find noe Law for it in the book of Assemblies Acts," were not unwilling to grant.[3]

In the following November a similar request was granted,[4] but this was the last. West Jersey was now under the guidance of the popular and politic Hamilton. The assembly had just voted to meet only once instead of twice a year,[5] thus adding to the delay litigants could expect in taking their cases to the legislature. An act of October 1693, citing the inconvenience of the lack of a court "into which all appeals in law may be made," established a "Supreme Court of Appeals," to meet semiannually with "power of hearing and determining all appeals in law from any of the inferior courts in all civil actions of the value of five pounds and upwards." It was to consist of one or more of the justices of each county and of the governor's council, any three, one being of the council, to be a quorum.[6]

At first there was a tendency for litigants to rush to the new tribunal, and the court saved hotheads from themselves by subjecting them to a cooling-off period. In two cases [7] the court's action on requests for appeal was postponed till the next day, by which time the appellants had changed their minds. In another [8] the appeal was granted but the parties were induced to refer the case, which was then agreed, and both were "satisfyed and discharged." Of the five requests for appeals (including one "to Equity") from 1693/4 through 1695, only two were persisted in. In one of these [9] the provincial court successfully employed the same kind of delaying action that the lower court had used. When the case came up the court adjourned for six days, "the Appeallant and the Appealee agree," and the appeal was withdrawn. In the remaining six appeals to the Burlington court, 1697–1699, the bench allowed matters to take their course except in one instance, where appeal was refused because the case was under value.[10] In the one case among these of which we know the result, the judgment of the lower court was confirmed.[11]

[2] Below, p. 102.
[3] *Dicks v. Righton*, below, p. 140.
[4] *Cripps v. Stacy et. al.*, below, p. 147.
[5] Leaming and Spicer, p. 510.
[6] Leaming and Spicer, p. 517.
[7] *French v. Finimore*, below, p. 161; *Tatham and Leeds v. Myers*, p. 170.
[8] *Heath v. Crosse*, below, p. 181.
[9] *Stacy v. Croft*, below, p. 166.
[10] See index, Appeal.
[11] *England v. Resnier*, below, p. 226.

INTRODUCTION   xlv

At the same time that the court of appeals was established, "An Act for a Court of Oyer and Terminer" was also passed. The preamble described the "great inconveniency" hitherto experienced for the want of such a court "for the tryal of capital crimes, by reason whereof such offenders have and may be of great burden and charge to the Province during their imprisonment." Accordingly the court was declared erected, with a judge to be appointed by the governor with advice of his council, to be assisted by "two or more justices of that county where the fact may arise." [12] The need of a high criminal court had been strikingly illustrated by a murder which had been committed in Salem County, November 1691, during the interregnum before the resumption of legislative government under Hamilton. The murderer was convicted before the county court of Salem, which had no authority to sentence him but did so anyway on petition of the juries and many other responsible local residents.[13] Salem County seems to have been more afflicted with desperate characters than Burlington, requiring several special commissions of oyer and terminer during the next few years.[14] Only one such court is recorded in the Burlington minutes, in 1694, when a servant girl was accused of murdering her bastard child. An attempt was made to apply the English statute requiring that, when the mother secreted the fact of the birth, she must prove the child born dead; but Hamilton and the others on the bench brushed this aside with *ad terrorem* and the woman was acquitted.[15]

The establishment of convenient and conventional higher courts was the most important judicial reform of Hamilton's administration. There was still no recognition of any right to take an appeal to the king, but that was coming. The contest with Basse had drawn Hamilton and the Quakers closer together, and after he was restored to the governorship an act was passed in which concessions were made both to Quaker peculiarities [16] and

[12] Leaming and Spicer, p. 520.
[13] "Justices of the Peace, by the Commission of the Peace, are not impowered to pass Sentence of Death, where there are superiour Courts, but seeing we have no superiour Court in this Province, we must apply our selves to you [the county court] for Justice" (*Blood will out, or, an Example of Justice in the Tryal, Condemnation, Confession and Execution of Thomas Lutherland, Who Barbarously Murthered the Body of John Clark of Philadelphia, And was Executed at Salem in VVest-Jarsey the 23d of February, 1691/2* (Philadelphia, 1692), New York Public Library, copy in Princeton University Library.
[14] Two in 1696 for house burning and robbing and for child murder; another in 1697/8 for killing a servant (*NJA*, xxi, 491, 503). The county court minutes for this period are not extant.
[15] Below, p. 166. The only other trial for infanticide in these minutes, 1687, had a similar outcome (p. 69).
[16] One embarrassing religious tenet of the Friends was their objection to judicial as well as profane oaths. Quakers solemnly promised or deposed or averred (below, pp. 6, 18, 36) but they would not swear or require others to do so. The Concessions and the laws of 1681 required officers of government to "subscribe . . . that they will truly and faithfully discharge their respective trusts," and so they did, without any reference to the Deity (Leaming and Spicer, pp. 392, 427; below, pp. 5, 146). The Concessions further stipulated "that in all matters and causes, civil and criminal, proof is to be made by the solemn and plain averment" of the witnesses ("evidences," as they are called in the Burlington minutes). The first assembly did not enact this clause, and there was no specific

xlvi   INTRODUCTION

to conventional English ideas of judicial propriety. One provincial "Superior Court of Appeals" was set up, having both civil and criminal jurisdiction, with three judges to go on circuit when necessary, instead of sitting only in Burlington. The house of representatives was to choose the judges but the governor was to commission them. And finally, appeals above £20 could now go from this provincial court to the assembly, and from there also, the Quaker legislators grudgingly acknowledged, to the king.[16a] Thus, on the eve of the surrender of the Jerseys to the Crown, the Quakers of West Jersey at last cleared a judicial path from the subject to the king—but too late to be of much use to Samuel Coles.

---

law covering the point until an act of 1696 provided that no one "not having freedom to take oaths" should thereby be incapacitated for any office or excluded "from any right or priviledge which any of his Majesty's subjects are capable to enjoy" (Leaming and Spicer, pp. 397, 548). However, no such law was needed in the Burlington court, where for over a decade no oath was ever administered to any witness, juror, or official of government. Such persons instead took an "attestation" to tell the whole truth or perform their proper duties (below, pp. 40, 45, 64, 66, 151, etc.) The first oath recorded in the minutes was in 1692, in the course of a homicide trial, when the jury were "attested" as usual but the witnesses, none apparently Quakers, were all sworn and gave their testimony on oaths which doubtless were administered by Justice Edward Hunloke, the only non-Quaker on the bench (below, p. 137). In 1695 William Atkinson, originally a Quaker but not one in 1705 when he took an oath, was fined for refusing "to take Attest on the Traverse Jury" (below, p. 182); but it is not clear whether he was insisting on an oath or refusing to serve at all. The next Burlington oath-taking came in 1698 during the Basse anti-Quaker regime, when several witnesses were sworn (below, p. 210). After the restoration of Quaker control witnesses were permitted but seemingly not encouraged to swear, for only two did. They were Thomas Clark, the lawyer, and Daniel Leeds (below, pp. 230, 233). Poetic justice overtook Clark later when a Burlington constable presented him "for Swearing by his Maker in Vaine" (below, p. 304). Leeds was deserting the Quaker fold and by way, no doubt, of publicly confirming his defection desired to take the oath "according to the Law of England." It was so administered "by order of" Justice Joshua Newbold, another ex-Quaker—and, we may infer from this circumstance, without the blessing of the other sitting justices, who were all old-line Quakers. But with these few exceptions local non-Quakers forbore to grate upon the sensibilities of Burlington Friends by insisting upon "swearing strange oaths" in their court. For example, Hunloke, though he promised "to Swear before Some Magistrate" to the truth of an account, took the usual attestation as a witness, and so did George Willis, the Anglican inn-keeper (below, pp. 222, 231, 241).

Upon the inauguration of royal rule under Cornbury in 1703 witnesses were either sworn or attested (below, pp. 294 ff.), and so were juries, until almost the end of this volume. Cornbury's instructions were so specific in allowing Quakers to serve in "places of trust or profit" that he did not try to get around them (*NJA*, iii, 2–3). But under Ingoldsby the Burlington anti-Quakers began to eliminate Friends from juries, as the last pages of this record show. The court required oaths from all whose religious beliefs were not repugnant thereto, and Quakers had to present proof of membership (below, pp. 339, 342). These were reasonable requirements. But when the oath was demanded of the September 1709 grand jury the Quaker majority refused to swear, and then the court ordered the sheriff to make up another panel of non-Quakers (below, p. 341). This he seems to have done, for the next jury were all sworn except one, according to the minutes (below, p. 342). Here our volume ends, and the lack of further Burlington records till 1733 prevents the tracing of the dispute from this point in the Burlington court. But the Quakers lost out. In 1716 Governor Robert Hunter complained of their exclusion from juries, even though they were "Almost the Only men of Substance Sence and probity" in the county (*NJA*, iv, 234; on this subject further see the references cited in Kemmerer, *op. cit.*, pp. 91, 101, 134).

[16a] Act of Dec. 1699, Leaming and Spicer, p. 563. There was to be a separate clerk for this court, appointed by the judges. I have not seen any of its proceedings. There are only two references to it (as "the Provincial Court") in the Burlington minutes (below, p. 248).

INTRODUCTION xlvii

The Quakers were more concerned to keep down the cost and number of lawsuits than to prolong them by appeals. By arbitration within their own religious organization they kept their own members out of the courts to a great extent,[17] and the Burlington minutes reveal a few cases in which this device was used to end suits already begun before the secular tribunal.[18] For those who were resolved to have their law, the courts met frequently. An act of 1682 provided, besides the regular quarterly courts of sessions, "for smaller courts oftener, (if need require) both at Burlington, and at Salem, to be appointed by the justices, as they judge fit." Special courts could also be had, the party requesting them paying three shillings for each justice sitting and the regular fees for the other officials.[19] In 1685, under Skene, monthly courts were ordered, but this practice was of brief duration.[20] However, what with special and private sessions, the Burlington court doubtless met as frequently as the needs of the people required. In 1692, to avoid the trouble and expense of "petty actions," single justices were empowered to hear and determine actions of debt under forty shillings, with right of appeal to the county courts, and in 1694 this authority was extended to the burgesses of Burlington and Salem.[21]

By the end of the proprietorial period therefore West Jersey had developed an elaborate judicial system based on its own legislative enactments. The assumption of the government by the Crown revolutionized the constitutional basis of government. The Concessions and the laws passed in accordance with their provisions and spirit went by the board, and henceforth the constitution of the united Province of New Jersey was in actuality the instructions to and commissions of the royal governors. However, the existing judicial framework was not greatly changed.[22] Cornbury's "Ordinance for Establishing Courts of Judicature"[23] of 1703 gave single jus-

[17] See above, p. xii.
[18] See index, Arbitration.
[19] Leaming and Spicer, pp. 448–449.
[20] Below, pp. 49 ff.
[21] Leaming and Spicer, pp. 509, 542. The Burlington town records, 1693–1780, are available in microfilm.
[22] See Tanner, pp. 461–466. Cornbury's instructions forbade him to erect any court not previously in existence.
[23] The text was printed in New York in 1704 and reprinted in R. S. Field, *The Provincial Courts of New Jersey* (New York, 1849), pp. 50, 256. The ordinance was formulated during the meetings of Cornbury and his council in Burlington, Aug. 14-21 1703, and is referred to in his commission to Jenings as judge of common pleas for Burlington, Aug. 23 (*NJA*, xiii, 301–306; iii, 4; Commissions, AAA, p. 12). Judge Field's guess that the ordinance was the handiwork of Roger Mompesson has been accepted respectfully by later writers (Field, p. 50; Tanner, p. 171; Kemmerer, p. 64), but it is still only a guess. Mompesson arrived in Philadelphia from England early in July 1703, and so it would have been possible for Cornbury to consult with him, although there is no contemporary evidence that he did so. Neither is there evidence of Mompesson's having been in Burlington during the August council meetings; it is more likely that he was in Boston at that time (see *Correspondence between William Penn and James Logan*, ed. E. Armstrong (Philadelphia, 1870), i, 200, 220–223). Cornbury made him chief justice of New York in July and of New Jersey in October 1704 (*N. Y. Col. Docs.*, v, 423; Commissions, AAA, p. 23).

xlviii   INTRODUCTION

tices cognizance of debt and trespass up to forty shillings, provided for courts of common pleas to follow each county general sessions,[24] and established a provincial supreme court. The assembly was replaced by the governor and council as an appeal tribunal above the supreme court. But more important than any of these alterations in form was the fact that henceforth the personnel of all the courts was beyond popular control. The king appointed the governor, and he named the judges and justices and "other necessary Officers and Ministers."[25] The difference is at once apparent in the Burlington court; the Quaker justices depart, and Anglicans and Quaker-baiters succeed them.

* * *

There was also an important change in the substantive law applied. When New Jersey became a royal province the penal practices[26] of the Quakers were supplanted as a matter of course by the harsh English criminal law. Quaker penological views were representative of the most liberal thought of the time, and they had their first application in West Jersey. The most important Quaker variation from the English norm was in the punishment for crimes against property. Instead of hanging people for grand larceny and certain special categories of theft such as robbery, burglary, and horse stealing, the Quaker laws imposed punishment in kind—four-fold restitution out of the offender's estate or by his labor.[27] This penalty was regularly meted out for stealing throughout the proprietary period, except in a few cases, chicken- or hog-stealing or thefts by Negroes, in which whipping or fines were imposed.[28] The Concessions forbade imprisonment for

[24] A distinction between civil and criminal business which was of no practical significance so long as the personnel of the two courts was identical. In the Burlington court the distinction between pleas and sessions had been made regularly from 1694 on, but only rarely before that (see below, pp. 91, 100, 167).

[25] *NJA*, ii, 495.

[26] I say practices rather than laws, because the founding fathers in West Jersey did not enact an elaborate criminal code such as Penn put through in Pennsylvania (*Charter and Laws of Pa.*, pp. 107 ff.). The omission (not necessarily inadvertent) had the effect of allowing the courts wide discretion in imposing punishment. The decisions of Burlington court therefore throw more light on Quaker penal philosophy in West Jersey than the enactments of the assembly.

[27] Leaming and Spicer, p. 434.

[28] See below, index, Restitution; also pp. 11, 51–53, 224. The thrifty Quakers also required that persons committed to prison for criminal causes be required to "work for their bread" during the time of their commitment (Leaming and Spicer, p. 434). I have seen no evidence of prison labor in the records, and if there was any it must have had only casual supervision. The first reference to a prison is in 1682, when a "Convenient Logg house for a Prison" was ordered built; but the lack of a prison or jail was regularly complained of, 1687–1692. In 1691 the "house" used for a prison seems to have been without supervision (below, p. 127). Taxes were levied for building a court house and prison, which was finally accomplished, but the insufficiency of the latter was presented by the sheriff in 1705 and 1707/8. See index, Prison, Court house. Imprisonment was not used for punishment, and with no incarcerated debtors the prison population must rarely have been large enough for a foursome at whist, or "whisk," as the ancestor of modern bridge was "vulgarly" called in those days (Mrs. J. K. Van Rensselaer, *Prophetical, Educational and Playing*

debt, if the debtor yielded up all his estate; and while this clause was not confirmed by the first assembly, throwing debtors into prison seems to have been contrary to the established *mores* of the Burlington community.[29]

In other respects the Quakers' punishments were conventional, and against sexual irregularities, severe. Fines and the lash were the lot of fornicators and adulterers.[30] West Jersey justices hesitated to impose the death penalty for infanticide, but it was prescribed (although not carried out) against a Negro bugger in 1692.[31] Personal dishonesty was frowned upon. The only instance of mutilation as a punishment was decreed against a forger, who was to be pilloried and have an ear cut off.[32] The pillory was also employed at first for perjury and slander, especially of a scandalous nature.[33]

* * *

"The town of Burlington," the Assembly of 1681 decreed, "is and shall be the chief town and the head of this Province; in which town from time to time shall be held the Provincial courts, and the General Free Assembly."[34] Not unnaturally therefore the Burlington court tended to view itself as at least *primus inter pares* among West Jersey judicial institutions, if not a little higher, although in fact it was never anything more than a county court. Even under Andros, as we have seen,[35] Salem had its own court, and when the two rival settlements were united in government the people of Fenwick's Colony insisted upon maintaining their own local administration. Separate justices, sheriffs, registers, and clerks were chosen for the "jurisdictions" of Burlington and Salem from 1682 on,[36] and so far as we know the administration of justice proceeded there unhampered by interference from the court at Burlington.[37]

Cards (Philadelphia, 1912), 263; W. A. Chatto, *Facts and Speculations on the Origin of Playing Cards* (London, 1848), 163–166).

In 1700 the assembly gave ground slightly on the restitution principle, making burglary punishable by whipping, branding, and (for third offenders) imprisonment, with transportation optional (Leaming and Spicer, p. 573).

[29] Leaming and Spicer, p. 396. The only recorded instance occurred in 1695. Judgment was granted against the defendant but the bench, sheriff, clerk, and jury then gave him "all their perquisits of the tryall" (below, p. 184).

[30] See index, Adultery, Fornication, Immorality, Incest, Miscegenation, Rape. From 1691 fornication (including antenuptial indulgence by subsequently-married couples) either increased or the court took more notice of it. An act of 1694, declaring that "the sin of uncleanness is one of the greatest in the eyes of a pure God," specified penalties of £5–10 or 20–39 lashes (Leaming and Spicer, p. 527).

[31] Below, pp. 142–148.

[32] Below, p. 75.

[33] Below, pp. 58, 65, 125, and see index, Slander.

[34] Leaming and Spicer, p. 432.

[35] Above, p. xxiii.

[36] Leaming and Spicer, pp. 443, 457, 491, 499, 504.

[37] The earliest extant Salem County court minute book begins 1706. All we know about

INTRODUCTION

The territorial jurisdiction of the Burlington court was further limited by the assembly in 1686, at the request of the members from the Third and Fourth tenths for authority to "keep Courts" for those tenths. Permission was granted, and a sheriff and a clerk named. The inhabitants then met and (extraordinarily enough) adopted several rules of court, and from September on sessions were regularly held by justices already appointed for this area, which was henceforth known as Gloucester County.[38] At first some of the officials of the new court seemed to feel that it was inferior in status to the older court at Burlington, but this notion met with energetic resistance in Gloucester. In 1687 the Gloucester grand jury presented the sheriff and one of the justices "as betrayers of the Rights and privillidges belonging to the County of Gloucester by being concerned and assisting in the conveyance of Henry Treadway a notorious criminal of this County (where he was obliged to appear and receive his tryall) unto the Court at Burlington Contrary to the Trust in them reposed to the perverting of justice to the ill example of others etc." But the Burlington court in a special session had already punished Treadway and his daughter-in-law for carnal copulation, and the wrathful Gloucester grand jury could do no more than vent its spleen upon the apologetic justice who apparently had delivered the offenders to the Burlington authorities.[39] Some years later the Burlington court tried, though not very successfully, to take another morals case out of the Gloucester court's hands. That body from 1691 had had trouble with William Lovejoy and Anne Penston, who were living together in alleged adultery, Anne's husband Stephen apparently being out of the country. The court imposed penalties but could not separate the fond couple and their illegitimate child.[40] So in 1695 the Burlington court had them indicted, possibly at the instigation of Governor Hamilton, who was then on the bench. But the King's witnesses from Gloucester failed to answer subpoenas, except one who sent a "pregmaticall answer by a Letter," which drew a fine of £5. At the next court William and Anne were ready for trial, but by this time the Burlington justices' enthusiasm had waned, perhaps because the governor was no longer there to inspire them, and they quashed the indictment as insufficient.[41] Thus the prosecution ended, and with it all efforts by the up-river court to encroach upon Gloucester's judicial independence.

---

earlier proceedings is from a few entries, 1687, 1688, in a book of Salem surveys (see *NJA*, xxi, 552-553) and the trial described in *Blood will out*.

[38] See C. E. Godfrey, "The True Origin of Old Gloucester County" (Camden Historical Society, *Camden History*, i, no. 4, 1922); F. H. Stewart, *The Organization and Minutes of the Gloucester County Court, 1686/7* (Gloucester County Historical Society, 1930). Francis Collins, Andrew Robeson, Thomas Thackera, and John Wood, all Quakers, were on the bench at the earliest sessions.

[39] Below, p. 72; Stewart, *op. cit.*, pp. 21, 24, 25, 30.

[40] Gloucester County Court Minutes, March 1691–Dec. 1693.

[41] Below, pp. 182-185.

INTRODUCTION

One more subtraction from the extent of Burlington jurisdiction remains to be recorded. The inhabitants of the distant fishing settlement at Cape May at first had to repair to Burlington for their judicial business. In 1685 a justice for Cape May was appointed by the Assembly,[42] but it was not until 1692 that the district was erected into a county, with a court for causes under forty shillings, and actions "where any declaration or indictment shall be on traverse" to be tried at the Salem quarterly sessions. In 1693 regular quarter sessions were instituted, but with jurisdiction only to £20. In 1697 this limitation was removed and the Cape May court placed on equal footing with the others in the province.[43]

* * *

The Quaker pioneers and their descendants dominated West Jersey public affairs much longer than their relative numbers warranted. Their immigration was heavy for several years,[44] but then slackened off, while non-Quaker settlers continued to stream in from Europe and the older American colonies. By 1699, according to a computation in Daniel Leeds' almanac, only a third of West Jersey's population was Quaker 266 freeholders out of a total of 832, representing 4 to 5,000 souls.[45] Burlington was the only county to hold its own against the rising non-Quaker tide. In 1699 the Quakers were more numerous there than in "all the other Countys," possibly constituting a majority, although it could not have been very large.

However, where wealth counted as well as numbers, the older settlers with a stake in the country could retain control of government for a long time, and in the Burlington court they unquestionably did. Up to 1687, when the title to government passed from Byllynge's heirs to non-Quaker ownership, thirty justices had sat at one time or another on the Burlington bench, all but two of whom can be identified as Quakers.[46] The new owners could hardly be expected to continue the Quaker judicial monopoly unbroken, if there were any non-Quaker Burlingtonians of sufficient merit and prominence to be put into governmental positions. But such persons seem to have been few. The first non-Quaker justice to serve any length of

[42] Leaming and Spicer, p. 504. The appointee was Caleb Carman, who is a litigant in this book.

[43] *Ibid.*, pp. 508, 514, 553. The earliest Cape May minutes are printed in *Cape May Magazine of History and Genealogy*, 1937 and 1938.

[44] According to Bowden (i, 399) about 800 Friends, a large number of them "persons of property," emigrated to West Jersey in 1677 and 1678, and up to 1681, at least 1400. Some of these spread to the western side of the river, which after the founding of Pennsylvania was the superior attraction. The English Toleration Act of 1689 checked religious persecution and thus removed a major incentive to Quaker emigration.

[45] Burlington, 302; Gloucester, 134; Salem, 326; Cape May, 70 (*NJA*, ii, 305). In 1716 Governor Hunter, friendly to the Quakers, said they were "Almost the Only men of Substance Sence and probity" in Burlington County (*ibid.*, iv, 234).

[46] Henry Stacy, member of Council, sat twice in 1683; Richard Lawrence, of the Fourth Tenth (lower Gloucester County—see Leaming and Spicer, p. 504), once in 1686.

time was Edward Hunloke, who first appeared on the bench in 1687, and from then till his death figured prominently in Burlington and West Jersey affairs. More came in Hamilton's time. John Tatham, a wealthy Burlington merchant, locally suspected of being a Roman Catholic, served as a justice 1692–1696 and (as president) 1698–1699.[47] Nathaniel Westland was another merchant, who first appears in the Burlington record in 1693/4 as a justice.[48]

Hunloke, Tatham, and Westland joined in 1695 to buy land in Burlington for a burial ground for themselves and "all other Christian people" who might wish to use it—meaning non-Quakers, for the latter of course already had such a place.[49] Politically Hunloke stuck with the Quakers, but Tatham and Westland, with Thomas Revell, became the spearhead of the anti-Quaker party which later wrested control of the court from the Quakers. The movement against them was facilitated by an unfortunate doctrinal dispute among the Quakers caused by George Keith, which divided the Society in 1692 and led to the secession of a number of members who formed a separate group of "Christian" or "Keithian" Quakers. Some later returned to the orthodox fold, for example, Richard Fenimore, whose acknowledgement is entered in the Burlington Monthly Meeting minutes in 1704. Others, such as Thomas Budd, died in separation.[50] Still others who lived through the end of the century in West Jersey joined local Anglicans to establish St. Mary's Church in Burlington in 1702.[51] Among them were Daniel Leeds, William Budd, Robert Wheeler, Roger Parkes, the Hewlings's, and the Newbolds, people who had been long in the colony, and whose defection was both a loss and an embarrassment to the Quakers, as they seem to have been especially favored by anti-Quaker administrations in appointing justices. Anglicans and ex-Quakers united to support the Basse administration against Hamilton and the regular Quaker party. Besides former non-Quaker incumbents, Tatham and Westland, and new ones, Revell, John Test, Anthony Elton (all early settlers), Thomas Bibb, and Captain John Jewell, Basse commissioned as justices for Burlington several apostate Quakers: Leeds (who had been on the bench, 1692–1694), William Hewlings, and Michael and Joshua Newbold. Along with them sat a few orthodox [52] Quakers, George Deacon, William Emley, and Joshua Ely. But the Burlington court, for the

---

[47] See below, p. 209; *NJA*, ii, 43. Tatham died in 1700, leaving what was a large estate for the time (*ibid.*, xxiii, 453).

[48] Another non-Quaker, John Worlidge of Salem, attended a "Private Session" in 1693 (*ibid.*, 525; below, p. 156). (Special or "private" sessions of court for the accommodation of individuals were not uncommon; see index, and above, p. xlvii.)

[49] Hills, p. 15.

[50] He was one of Keith's leading protagonists. He died in 1697 and was interred, though not a Quaker, in the Quaker burying ground in Philadelphia, according to an early list of such burials (W. W. Hinshaw, *Encyclopedia of Quaker Genealogy*, ii (Ann Arbor, 1938), 441 ff.) Other West Jersey names in this list, who may have been Keithians, are Peter Boss (1709), John Budd (1704), and John Callow (1699).

[51] See Hills, pp. 214 ff.

[52] So far as I have discovered.

INTRODUCTION

first time in its existence, was in the control of the anti-Quakers, and so it remained until the return of Hamilton to the governorship. Then, at the close of 1699, all these justices were turned out, and the old Quaker leaders returned for an Indian summer of Quaker supremacy which lasted until Cornbury took over in 1703. Under him winter began in earnest for the Quakers; henceforth only non- or ex-Quakers administered justice in Burlington court.

The Burlington sheriffs were important judicial officers because they were the chief executive agents of the courts and empanelled the juries. They are not always mentioned by name in the Burlington minutes. Known Burlington sheriffs down to 1694 were Quakers, but the list is incomplete.[53] Thomas Bibb, though elected by the Assembly, seems not to have been a Quaker,[54] but his successors were, until Cornbury appointed William Fisher in 1703. Despite his membership in St. Mary's Church Fisher apparently was no slavish tool of Cornbury's ring, for he had a violent altercation with the court and either quit or was removed from his office.[55] Fisher was replaced temporarily (from November 1705 to April 1706) by John Kible. Hugh Huddy then became sheriff. He was an Anglican and his relations with the justices were amicable, so far as the court minutes disclose.

During most of the proprietorial era the juries, grand and petty, were overwhelmingly Quaker in composition. They were entirely so in 1680, and in the years 1680–1685 two-thirds of all those listed had no non-Quaker members and the rest usually one or two, out of twelve or (for grand juries) thirteen men. In the following decade all-Quaker juries become a rarity, there usually being from one to four non-Quakers in each group. Under Basse the non-Quakers increased, and on some juries the old-line Friends were in a minority. This was caused at least in part by Quaker boycotting of the Basse court. Thus in November 1698 three Quakers refused to serve, and the resulting grand jury of thirteen included only four Quakers. Again, in August 1699 too few jurors appeared to make full juries, and the court "Could not proceed in businesse" until November, when it operated with seventeen non-Quaker and only eight Quaker jurors. When Hamilton returned in 1699 the pendulum swung too far the other way, considering that by that time little more than half of the freeholders in the county could have been Friends. There were several all-Quaker juries in 1700 and 1701, although the average group included from one to five non- or ex-Friends, until the beginning of royal rule in 1703.

Under Cornbury, with non-Quaker justices and sheriffs, the same kind of juries could have been expected also, but such was not the case. Larger grand juries were used, eighteen to twenty-six in number, making it more

---

[53] See above, p. xli.
[54] He was buried as a non-Quaker in Philadelphia (Hinshaw, ii, 441).
[55] Below, pp. 298–306.

difficult to fill the panels with qualified non-Quakers. There was trouble with a few Friends who insisted on keeping their hats on while being attested.[56] The makeup of juries fluctuated greatly, perhaps reflecting confusion and uncertainty introduced into Burlington judicial affairs by the scheming Cornbury. At the session of December 1704 one-third of the jurors were Quakers; at the next, five-sixths;[57] and so it went, to the end of this volume.[58]

The duties of constable were avoided rather than sought. As late as 1686 all the constables in the county were Quakers. In 1691, however, only half of them were, and thereafter the Friends were frequently in the minority.[59] Except at first the office was elective by the various townships, but persons upon whom this unwanted honor was conferred were allowed to secure substitutes, and so the office would tend to be filled by persons in the lower economic brackets. Thus Quaker John Lambert got non-Quaker Thomas Tindall to take his place as constable of Nottingham in 1702. Tindall had already discharged his civil obligation in that office some years before, but he seems to have liked it, and served still a third year.[60] Various other instances of securing substitutes could be cited.[61]

On the whole, however, the Quakers took their civic duties seriously. In the throes of political controversy they might indulge in some effective boycotting, but in normal times they took their turns as constable or highway overseer and did jury service or were fined.[62] The Burlington Court Book paints a revealing portrait of the judicial Quaker. In the court room he exhibits a combination of sternness and humanity characteristic of his sect. Even among Friends individuals violated established rules of conduct and had to be punished; but when the penalty was paid the offense was forgotten, and the offender resumed his normal place in the political and social order.[63] In estimating the Quaker judiciary as a whole we may borrow the phrases in which a contemporary of Samuel Jenings characterized that great

---

[56] Below, pp. 293, 299.

[57] Below, pp. 292-293.

[58] In June 1705 and twice in 1706 the grand jury was wholly Quaker (below, pp. 297, 313, 316). In June 1709 it was 17 Quaker to 6 non, but thereafter the Quakers were excluded (see above, p. xlvi.

[59] Below, pp. 65, 131. In 1692/3, 6 Quakers, 5 non; 1694/5, 4 Quakers, 1 apostate, 4 non; 1696/7, 10 Quakers, 4 non; 1700/1, 7-5; 1701/2, 5-7; 1702/3, 4-5 (below, pp. 150, 176, 191, 247, 281).

[60] Below, pp. 150, 261, 281. On constables see above, p. xli.

[61] E. g., pp. 159, 191; Pa. Mag., xxxv, 213.

[62] James Wills was fined for his "peremtory refuseing" to serve on the jury which tried Negro Harry for buggery. This may have been a case of conscience, as the death penalty was imposed—although Wills himself had once beaten a slave so badly that she died. Quaker aversion to capital punishment is suggested by the makeup of an infanticide trial jury in 1694, which contained an unusually small proportion of Friends: 5 Quakers, 2 ex-, and 5 non- (below, pp. 142, 56, 166).

[63] Thus Henry Beck, guilty of fornication in 1691, served afterwards as constable and juror (see index under name).

Quaker leader: "of worthy memory, endued with both spiritual and temporal wisdom; . . . a suppressor of vice, and an encourager of virtue;—sharp towards evil doers, but tender and loving to them that did well." [64]

H. CLAY REED

---

[64] Quoted in R. Proud, *The History of Pennsylvania*, i (Philadelphia, 1797), 158.

THE BURLINGTON COURT BOOK

The Court Record   June 14th 1680.[1]

1680   The Proceedings of Court at Bur[lington][2] Thomas Olive, Daniell Wills, Robert Stacy and Mah[lon Stacy   Commissioners].

The Names of all the Freeholders and Inhabittants [   ] of the Court at Burlington, who are to doe their sute and [   ] Thomas Olive, Daniell Wills, Robert Stacy, Mahlon Stacy, William Emley Commissioners, Thomas Revell Clerke, Joshua Wright Constable, Samuell Wright, Andrew Smith, Thomas Lambert, John Wood, Thomas Woods, James Pharowe, John Rogers, Robert Mirfin, William Black, Anthony Woodhouse, John Hooton, William Beard, John Snowden, Thomas Budde, Thomas Wright, William Cooper, Thomas Gardner Constable, John Cripps, John Lambert, John Hollingshead, John Woolston, John Roberts, William Brightwell, William Peachee, Robert Powell, Thomas Eves, Samuell Lovett, James Wills, John Dewsberry, John Anthram, Jonathan Eldridge, George Bartlemew, Richard Dungworth, Seath Smith, Mathew Allen, John Kinsey, Richard Arnall, Godfrey Hancock, Thomas Potts, Thomas Ellis, Samuel Oldale, Henry Jacobs, Roger Hawkins, Francis [   ], Thomas [   ], William Hodg[   ], John Burton, John Petty, John Woodhouse, Henry [   ][3], Barnett Devonish, William Hillards, John Shenn, Clement Shenn, Jonas Keen, Capt. Hance Monse, Frederick Fred[?], Samuel Coales, Henry T[redway].

The Jurours[4] names   Thomas Lambert, Thomas Wright, Thomas Harding, John Cripps, John Woolleston, John Boarton, Samuell Lovett, Samuell Wright, Thomas Palmer, Walter Pomfrey, Robert Powell, William Cooper.

John Mifflin Indicted for Felloniously taking away one paire of Shoes and Five small Box Locks, late the Goods of Robert Hodgkins Deceased:

---

[1] This is the cover title of a thin volume, originally bound in vellum and now rebound and silked, in the Secretary of State's office in Trenton. Only the first four pages of this volume are printed here. At the bottom of page four is written: "Booke C Containing the Records of Probate of Wills, Administrations Bonds Specialties." The rest of the book is filled with such matters until near the end, where, in reverse pagination, several pages of marriage records are entered.

An earlier transcription of the whole record, in J. E. Stillwell's *Historical and Genealogical Miscellany*, II (New York, 1906), contains somewhat more than meets the eye in the original in its present state. Stillwell has "Be" after "Francis" and "Hod" after Thomas.

[2] Corner of page gone. Material in brackets supplied.

[3] Space left for last name, but it was not inserted.

[4] "Jurors" in MS.

1

whereof hee was formerly Convicted before Thomas Olive and Daniell Wills, Commissioners: And by them bound over to this Court: [5] The Prisoner Mifflin pleads not Guilty to the Indictment and putts himself upon the Jury: The Indictment being not proved the Jury (by Thomas Lambert their foreman) bring him in not Guilty, whereupon the Court Cleares him.

One Gelding of John Tests formerly Attached by William Byles (upon Tests not Appeareing) called forfeit: William Clarke haveing given in Evidence that the said Test was indebted to the said Byles about 10l. and Daniel Wills declared that the said Test had notice given to make his defence. The said Gelding was alsoe Apprized by Daniell Wills Mahlon Stacy Thomas Lambert to 7l. whereof the Court Charges and Apprizing was [   ].[6]

Ordered by the Court that if any person or persons shall hereafter directly or indirectly sell any Rumme or other strong liquor to any Indian or Indians either by great or small measure without order from the Court [   ] such person or persons soe offending shall forfeit and pay for every such offense 50s. And upon refuseall neglect or nonpayment of the same it shall be Levyed upon any of the Goods and Chattells of said person or persons [   ] by Distresse and Sale of the same: This to Continue till further order.

[2 1680] [Ordered] [7] That if any person or persons shall take away a Boat [from the] Landing where the owner shall leave the same, without [permission] shall forfeit and pay for every such offence—20s.

[Ordered t]hat if any person or persons within the Jurisdiction of the Court [   ]may for selling Ale Beere or strong liquors without [Lycence] the Court shall for every Moneth wherein hee or they shall [   ] contrary to order aforesaid forfeit and pay 5l.

[It is] further ordered That all persons within the Jurisdiction of the Court [bri]ng in to the next Court the marks and earemarks wherewith they have [marked] or intend to mark their Cattle Horses Sheep and Swine, to the intent that [each] persons mark may be entered and inrolled and their Cattle Horses Sheepe and [Swine] may be knowne each from other.

[168]o At the Court at Burlington August 3d. Thomas Olive, Daniell Wills, Robert Stacy, Mahlon Stacy and William Emley Commissioners. The Jurours Names William Peachee, William Cooper, Thomas Budde, Thomas Harding, Godfrey Hancock, Thomas Wright, John Rogers, John Lambert, William Hewland, Thomas Lambert, John Shinne, James Pharrowe.

Samuell Cliffe Complaines against Thomas Olive for takeing and unjustly detayning a Gunne of the said Samuells, to which the Defendant

---

[5] "Cort" in MS.
[6] Mutilated.
[7] Corner of page gone. Material in brackets supplied.

pleads not guilty: whereupon Issue is Joyned: But before the Jury bring in their Virdict the Plaintiff and Defendant referre it; and agreed.[8]

[3 1680] 1680 At the Court at Burlington September 6th. See more in Page 9.[9] Thomas Olive, Daniell Wills, Robert Stacy, Mahlon Stacy and William Emley Commissioners.

It is ordered that the persons concerned in William Peachees Propriety who have noe Meadowe belonging to them, shall have meadowe, at the Point of Rankokus Creek belonging to the same Lott proportionable to each mans purchase.

It is further ordered that noe Person or persons shall hereafter sell any Rumme or other strong Liquor to any Indian or Indians by any measure or measures smaller than by the halfe Anchor. And that all such persons as shall sell the same by the halfe Anchor, shall take speciall care that such Indian and Indians as shall buy the same Liquors in manner aforesaid shall speedily depart with the same Liquors apart into the Woods to drinke the same there; that soe the people may not bee disturbed by them; upon paine to forfeit for every such offence Fifty shillings: And upon refuseall or nonpayment thereof, to be levyed upon any of the Goods or Chattels of the Person or persons soe offending by distresse and sale of the same 2l. 10s. The former order about selling Rumme or other strong Liquors being this day and yeare above written Repealed.

Capt. Hance Permitt being Viewed this Court, beares date in February 1674.

The Court same day demanded of Jonas Keene to shew his Tytle to the Land hee holds; whose Answer was that hee holds it under Peter Peterson, which (Peterson) had it of Capt. Hance and after sold his Right therein to the said Jonas.

John Cripps and John Hollingshead Lycenced by the Court to keep (each of them) an Ordnary for selling Ale Beere and other Liquors and for the entertaining of Travellers: untill 29th September 1681.

[4 1680] [   ]ers An Action of Trespasse upon the Case against [John? Woo?]lston agreed.

[   ] enters an Action of Trespasse upon the Case against Thomas Potts agreed.

[Mathew] Allen enters an Action of Trespasse upon the Case against George Bartlemew and Mary his wife goes by.

Henry Jacobs enters an Action of Trespasse upon the Case against Daniell Wills and Robert Stacy:

October 4th 1680. Thomas Olive, Daniell Wills and William Emley Commissioners. The Jury William Peachee, John Cripps, Thomas Ellis, John Woollston, Bernard Devonish, John Shinne, Thomas Eves, Samuell

---
[8] The rest of this page and the first half of the next are filled with earmarks.
[9] A note by the clerk evidently referring to another list of earmarks on pages 9-12.

Lovett, Thomas Harding, William Brightwell, Godfrey Hancocke, John Kinzey.

Mathew Allen against George Bartlemew and Mary his wife. the Defendant pleads not but lets the Action goe by default; Plaintiff proves his Debt and has judgment awarded.

Henry Jacobs against Daniell Wills and Robert Stacy the Jury finde for the Plaintiff and give him his Debt and Costs of Suite.

Ephraim Warwin Indicted for breaking the stocks, found Guilty by the Jury, and Fyned 5l. which the Court mittigates to 50s.

Elizabeth Kinzey Enters an Action of Slaunder against Samuell Cole.

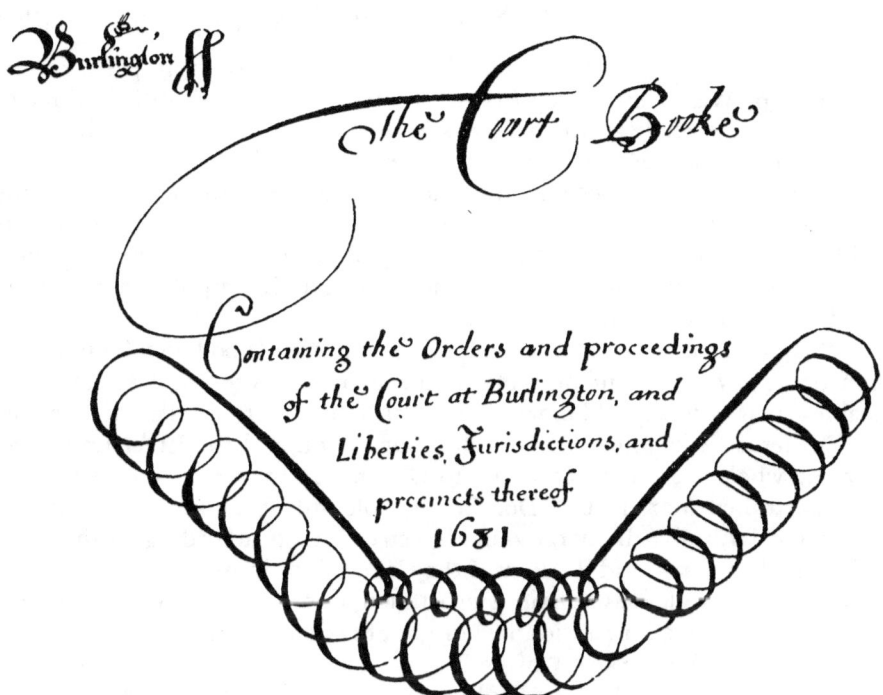

TITLE PAGE OF BURLINGTON COURT BOOK, REDUCED ONE-HALF

Com. Burlington to wit

The Court Booke
Containing the Orders and proceedings
of the Court at Burlington, and
Liberties, Jurisdictions, and
precincts thereof
1681

[1 1681] At the Court March 25th 1681. [*March 25th 1681*] Wee whose names are hereunder written (being Chosen Commissioners for the Province of, West Jersey from the 25th of the 1st Moneth called March 1681 for one whole year next ensueing by the Common Vote of the People) Doe hereby solemnly promise that wee will truly and faithfully discharge our Respective trusts according to the Lawe of the said Province and Tenour of the Concessions thereof in our Respective offices and duties   And doe equall Justice and Right to all men according to our best skill and Judgment without corruption favour or affection. [*Commissioners*]   By us   Robert Stacy, Tho: Ollive, Samll: Jenings, Thomas Budde, John Thompson, Thomas Lambert, Mahlon Stacy, Richard Guy, Edward Bradway.

[*March 25th 1681   Sheriffe*]   I William Emley being (by the Common

Vote of the People) Elected and Chosen Sheriffe for that parte of the Province of West New Jersey from St. Pinck to the Creek called Oldmans Creek for one whole yeare next ensueing to begin from the 25th of the 1st Moneth called March 1681 Doe hereby solemnly promise that I will truly and faithfully discharge the trust in mee reposed according to the Lawe of the said Province and Tenour of the Concessions thereof in my said office of Sheriffe And alsoe to doe equall Justice and Right to all men according to my best skill and Judgment without Corruption favour or affection: By mee William Emley.

[*March 25th 1681 Constables*] Wee Thomas Wood and John Woolston being (by the Common Vote of the People) chosen and elected Constables (that is to say) Thomas Wood Constable for the Falls and the Liberties thereof And John Woolston for Burlington and the Liberties thereof for one whole yeare next ensueing to Commence from the 25th of the first Moneth called March 1681 Doe hereby solemnly promise That wee will truly and faithfully discharge our respective Trusts according to the Lawe of the said Province and Tenour of the Concessions in our Respective offices and Duties And doe equall right to all men according to our best skill and Judgment without Corruption favoure or affection. By us

The marke J of John Woolston   The marke T of Thomas Wood

[*March 25th 1681 Register*] I Thomas Revell being (by the Common consent of the People) Elected and Chosen Register for that part of the Province of West Jersey from St. Pinck to Oldmans Creek for one whole yeare next ensueing to Commence from the 25th of the 1st Moneth called March 1681 Doe hereby solemnly promise That I will truly and faithfully discharge the Trust in mee reposed according to the Lawe of the said Province and Tenour of the Concessions in my said Office and Duty And doe equall right to all men according to my best skill and Judgment without Corruption favour or affection. By me Thomas Revell.

[2 1681] [*March 25th 1681 Register at Salem*] I James Nevill being (by the Common consent of the People) Elected and Chosen Register for that Parte of the Province of West Jersey from Oldmans Creek to Cohanzey and places adjacent for one whole yeare next ensueing to Comence from the 25th of the 1st Moneth called March 1681 Doe hereby solemnly promise That I will truly and faithfully discharge the trust in mee reposed according to the Lawe of the said Province and Tenour of the Concessions in my said Office and Duty And doe equall Right to all men according to my best skill and Judgment without Corruption favour or affection. James Nevill.

[*March 25th 1681 Surveyour*][1] I Daniell Leeds being (by the Commissioners for the tyme being) Elected and Chosen Surveyour for that part

---

[1] "Surveyor" in MS.

of the Province of West Jersey from St. Pinck to the Creeke called Oldmans Creek for one whole yeare next ensueing to Comence from the 25th of the 1st Moneth called March 1681 Doe hereby solemnly promise That I will truly and faithfully discharge the trust in mee Reposed according to the Tenour of the Concessions of the said Province in my said Office and Duty: And doe equall right to all men according to my best skill and Judgment without Corruption favour or affection.   By mee   Daniel Leeds.

[*March 26th 1681   Surveyours Fees*]   It is then ordered by the Commissioners that the Surveyours Fees from henceforward shall be as followeth (vizt)

	l.	s.	d.
For laying out the first Hundred Acres	00	10	00
For the second Hundred Acres	00	05	00
For the third Hundred and soe forward which shall bee taken up in one parcell	00	02	06
And for laying out Lands for the Publique for each and every day hee shall bee soe imployed:	00	10	00

And that if the Surveyour shall bee occasioned for the laying out of Lands to goe above the space of 12 myles from his place of aboad; That hee shall bee reasonably satisfyed for the same over and above the rates before mentioned:

[*Nathaniell Sykes May 3d 1681*]   It is then ordered by the Commissioners That Nathaniell Sykes (according to agreement by Indenture dated July the 9th 1677 with Edward Taylor his master shall take up Forty Acres of Land, in any place, not before taken up out of the Townes bounds of Burlington, in the first Setlement of the said Edward Taylor, to hold by him the said Nathaniell his Heires and Assignes forever, according to the said Agreement by his Indenture being under the yearly Rent of one penny per Acre to the said Edward Taylor and his Heires.

[*May 3d 1681   For Recording Deeds*]   It is then further ordered That all persons Concerned bring in their Principall Deeds at or before the next Court which will bee on Tuesday the Seaventh of the fourth Moneth called June next ensueing; or at the said Court to give in sufficient and satisfactory reasons for their omission thereof: That such Deeds may bee recorded according to the purport of the Concessions.

[*May 3d 1681   The Order for Rates of English money*]   It is then further agreed and ordered That English Silver money shall from henceforth passe at the rates following (Vizt)   The Shilling to passe at one Shilling Sixpence; And soe proportionably at the same rate for greater and lesser peeces of money; And further, That the Kings Copper farthings shall passe for one halfe penny a peece, And the Copper halfe pence of the same Coyne shall passe for one penny a peece; Provided that noe person or persons bee hereby compelled or compellable to take above Six pence of the said Copper coyne in one payment: This to continue till further order.

[*May 3d 1681 To prevent Illegall takeing up Land*] It is then further ordered That noe person or persons from henceforth shall take up survey or setle any Lott or Lotts of Land untill they obtain an order from the Commissioners or any two of them to appoint the Surveyour (Elected for that purpose) to lay out the same.

[*May 3d 1681*   ][2] It is then further ordered That all Freeholders and Inhabittants within the Jurisdiction of the Court [2a] appeare at the next Court, then and there to signe the Concessions; or shew their reasons for their refusall.

William Cooper and John Cripps were summoned to appear the next Court, to answer the Court for their illegall takeing up Land.

[3 1681] [   ] John Hollinshead enters an Action of Defamation against George Bartlemew and Mary his wife. [   ] Samuel Cole enters an Action against Henry Tradway in an Action Trespasse and Summons issued forth for him to appeare the next Court being on the Seaventeenth of August next.

[*August 17th 1681*] John Hollinshead versus George Bartholemew and wife drawing the Action withdrawn.

[*August 17th 1681*] Samuell Cole versus Henry Tradway, Tryall by Consent, The Action being an Action of Trespasse for takeing and killing a hogge of Samuells and for his owne use: which was proved by Edward Clement servant to Samuell Cole, And Alsoe the Defendant Henry confessed it: whereupon the Jury (vizt) Thomas Wright, Thomas Gardner, John Cripps, Bernard Devonish, Thomas Harding, John Barton, Daniell Leeds, Isaac Marriott, John Hollinshead, Thomas Stokes, Richard Fennimore, John Pane Finde for the Plaintiff and give him 3l. Dammage and 2d. Cost Suit.

[*August 17th 1681*] John Hance upon the Complaint of Richard Beach haveing found certaine goods in the possession of the said Hance which were formerly felloniously taken from him, was by one Bond Dated 21st June 81 bound over to this Court with Henrick Jacobs and John White his Sureties: And at this Court for valueable reasons haveing passt his word and Henry Jacobs with him to appeare at the next Court: was dismist: till then.

[*August 17 1681*] Thomas Wright enters an Action of Trespasse against John Cripps for his entring upon and surveying the Land before taken up and seated by the said Thomas.

[*August 17th 81*] Henry Jones by John White and Walter Pumphrey bound to appeare at the next Court being September 27 1681 for affronting the Constable.

[*Court Day September 27th 1681*] Robert Stacy, Thomas Budd, Thomas Lambert, Samuell Jennings, Thomas Ollive Commissioners. Daniell Leeds, Thomas Barton, John Newbold, John Pankhurst, Eleazor Fenton,

---
[2] Mutilated.
[2a] "Cort" in MS.

Samuell Wills,[3] John Rogers, Robert Scholey, William Black, Robert Murfin, John Snowden, Anthony Woodhouse, William Beard   Jurors.

Thomas Wright against John Cripps: Action Trespasse: Issue joyned. Witnesse: Robert Durham, Godfrey Hancock, Samuell Cliffe. The Jury before they agreed of a verdict, parte of them withdrawe their attendance (that is to say)   John Newbold, Eleazer Fenton, Anthony Woodhouse   and were Fyned 5s. a peece. And Thomas Eves the under Sheriffe for departing from the Court before the Jury agree, Fyned 40s.

Henry Jones appeared by John White his Attourney[4] and for his affront was fyned 50s. To bee paid by John White And the Recognizance withdrawne.

John Hance to appear next Court.

Israell Helme to appeare the next Court being November the 8th 81 to answer the matters laid against him.

John Cripps enters an Action of Trespasse against Thomas Wright.

John Cripps enters an Action of Trespasse against Daniell Leeds.

Register Fees

	s.	d.
A Conveyance in Parchment	15	0
The same in paper	10	0
A Conveyance Recording	5	0
Parcells and Lotts of Land each	5	0
a Bond Recording	0	6

Court Fees to the Clerke

	s.	d.
warrant to the Sheriffe	2	6
entring	1	6
Entrd and drawn and declard	2	6
Coppy thereof	1	0
Takeing and giveing the Jury the obligation	3	0
every witnesse	1	0
Takeing the Verdict	1	6
Recording the Verdict	1	0
Judgment and entring Execution 3s.	1	4

Edmond Stuart Enters an Action of Trespasse upon the Case against Samuell Wills   1s. draw decl[aration] 2s. 6d. Cop[py] decl[aration] 1s. Summond 1s.

[6[5] 1682] Samuell Jenings Governour[6] and Commissioners against Gibb Wheeler Defendant for selling Rum etc. in this Province. Thomas Wright, Godfrey Hancock, Thomas Gardner, Bernard Devonish, Thomas Harding, John Pancosts, John Woolston senr., John Roberts, Robert Powell,

---

[3] This name crossed out in MS.
[4] "Attorney" in MS.
[5] There is a blank page between pages 3 and 6.
[6] "Gov'no'" in MS.

Daniell Leeds, Isaac Marriot, Thomas Stokes Jury. Evidence Anthony Woodhouse, Marmaduke Hausman both prove the fact. Verdict The Jury finde the Defendant Guilty his Fyne by Act of Assembly is 5l.

Governour Samuell Jenings Plaintiff Francis Stephens Defendant Action withdrawne.

John Cripps Plaintiff Mathew Smith Defendant Action withdrawne.

Samuell Willis Plaintiff Nathaniell Allen and Nehemiah his sonne Defendants Action continued.

John Champion Plaintiff John Roberts Defendant nonsuite against the Plaintiff.

John Champion Plaintiff Henry Jacobs Defendant nonsuit against the Plaintiff.

Francis Stephens Plaintiff Benjamin Scott Defendant Continued.

Samuell Thrumball Plaintiff Francis Stephens Defendant Action withdrawne.

Mathew Allen Plaintiff Samuell Cole Defendant Action Continued.

William Dunks [Plaintiff] William Lee and William Matilock Defendants Action Continued.

Samuell Willis Plaintiff John Dewsbury Defendant Action withdrawne.

Daniell Brenson Plaintiff John Johnson Defendant The Defendant appeares not and his goods Attached called forfeit, the debt being 2l. 1s. to dammages and Court charges.

John White Plaintiff Joseph Stubbs Defendant The Defendant appeares not and his goods Attached called forfeit.

Edward Evarett Plaintiff Joseph Stubbs Defendant.

John Hollinshead Plaintiff Joseph Stubbs Defendant The Defendant appeares not, and his goods Attached called forfeit.

Benjamin Scott Plaintiff Thomas Ollive Defendant Action withdrawne.

Francis Stephens Plaintiff Richard Whittaker Defendant Action Continued.

Francis Stephens Plaintiff Thomas Allen Defendant Action withdrawne.

John Cripps Plaintiff Richard Coates Defendant Action withdrawne.

Jonas Keene in Court Produced a Receipt from Governour Markhams servant for 3625 foot of Bords delivered upon the Accompt of Joseph Stubbs etc. Amounting to 16l. 18s. 4d. at 9s. 4d. per hundred; And deposed that 7l. 16s. 5d. thereof belongs to him the said Jonas And John Hance and Elias Johnson prove 4l. 4s. due to them from Joseph Stubbs And Jacob Cozens proves 3l. 3s. due to him from Joseph Stubbs in all is 15l. 3s. 5d. and reste due towards satisfying John White, Edward Everett and John

White [7] 1l. 14s. 11d. The Court thereupon gave an order for payment thereof, unto Jonas Keene to receive the 15l. 3s. 5d. for himselfe and the rest due as above; and the 1l. 14s. 11d. to be received by John White, towards payment of him and Edward Evarett and John Hollinshead. of Governour William Markham, as per order is desired.

William Twyning, Indicted for stealeing Hennes, and was by his Jury found Guilty; And by the Court ordered to bee whipt betwixt the markett place in Burlington to the Landing place and to receive Twenty Lashes.

Jury Thomas Ollive, Thomas Barton, William Cooper, William Hewling, Seth Smith, Robert Scholey, Daniel Leeds, Jonas Keene, John Wood, Henry Jacobs, Francis Collins, Henry Grubb.

[*August 8 and 9th 1682*] ordered by the Court that noe Person or Persons, keeping or that shall keep an ordnary or Inne; within the Jurisdiction of this Court, shall from and after the Tenth day of August instant, take more than two pence for an Ale Quart (Winchester measure) of good wholesome Ale, or strong beere. And Benjamin Wheat and Henry Grubb are by the Court appointed, to bee Ale Tasters; And to see to the measures for Ale and beere, according to the order above, untill the next Generall Assembly, or further order.

[*August 8 and 9th 1682*] Ordered by the Court, that the Bridges called London Bridge and Yorkshire Bridge in Burlington, bee repayred, as farre as Tenne pounds will repayre the same, And that Thomas Budd and Thomas Gardner shall procure the repayrations thereof, on this syde or before the last day of the Moneth called August instant; And disburse the moneyes for the same; which is promised to bee repayed.

[7 1682] [*August 8 and 9th 1682*] Alsoe ordered by the Court, That if any servant, or servants, within the Jurisdiction of this Court, shall at any tyme or tymes hereafter, willfully or negligently leave, or depart from his, her, or their service, such servant or servants shall for each and every day whereon hee, shee, or they shall soe offend, serve one weeke, And for every weeke soe offending Two moneths, And for every moneth soe offending one yeare.

[*August 8 and 9th 1682*] Alsoe ordered by the Court, That Daniell Leeds Surveyour, with Convenient Assistance, shall at or before the Tenth day of the seaventh moneth next begin to Lay forth the severall Tenths, within this Province, That is to say, to take the extent of the River from St. Pinck to Cape May, And the same to Divide into Tenne Equall parts or shares.

[*August 8th and 9th 1682*] Alsoe ordered by the Court, That there shall bee a Convenient Logg house for a Prison Built in Burlington for the service of this Province, with all Convenient speed; And Samuell Jenings Gover-

---

[7] Apparently an error for Hollinshead.

nour, togeather with Thomas Gardner at the request of the Court, are to procure the same to bee built, and are to be reimbursed their charges therein.

[*Burlington at the Court held September 26th 1682*] Samuell Jenings Governour. Thomas Ollive, Robert Stacy, John Chaffen, William Biddle, Thomas Budd, John Cripps, Benjamin Scott, Justices present. John White Sheriffe. Thomas Revell Recorder.

Ordered by the Court that if any of the Justices shall be absent at the Courts hereafter to be held at Burlington after the nyneth hower in the morning upon the dayes appointed or to be appointed for the holding the Courts there, soe that there shall not bee a full Court, that then such Justice or Justices as shall be wanting shall bee fyned according to the discretion of the Justices who shall be then present to attend the Court not exceeding 5s. Alsoe further ordered That if any Person or Persons Legally Summoned to attend the Courts as Jury men, shall fayle in their Appeareance at the respective Courts whereunto they shall bee soe summoned to appeare shall (after they have been Twice called in the Court) bee fyned according to the discretion of the Court not exceeding 2s. 6d.

Samuell Willis Plaintiff   Nathaniel Allen and Nehemiah his sonne Defendants. An Action of the case.

The Defendants appeare not, and the Court haveing put by the Plaintiff last Court day upon the Accompt of the Defendants absence; and the Plaintiff requireing Justice to be done. The Action goes by default and Judgment is awarded for Costs and dammages the declaration being for 8l. 14s. 8d.

Edmond Stuart Plaintiff   Francis Beswick Defendant   An Action Trespasse. Jury   Henry Stacy, Thomas Barton, Thomas French, John Pancras, Bernard Devonish, Thomas Wright, Jonas Keene, Seth Smith, Henry Grubb, Fredrick Fredrickson, John Hollinshead, Samuell Lovett. Witnesse Thomas Stokes. Verdict   The Jury finde for the Plaintiff and give him 2d. damages and Cost suite. Thomas Stokes declares that the Defendants mare within the tyme in the Declaration mentioned did Eat the Grasse in the said Plaintiffs ground, And further sayth the Plaintiffs Fence is good.

Benjamin Scott Plaintiff   Daniel Furley Defendant   an Action of the Case. Henry Stacy, Thomas Barton, Thomas French, John Pancras, Bernard Devonish, Thomas Wright, Jonas Keene, Seth Smith, Henry Grubb, Fredrick Fredrickson, John Hollinshead, Samuel Lovett Jury. Evidence Sarah Curtice, Anne Snowden, Thomas Ollive, Daniel Wills, Samuel Cliffe. Verdict   The Jury finde for the Defendant and give him his Cost suite. Sarah Curtice declares That the Defendant sayd to the Plaintiff, hee would either serve the Plaintiff his master or pay him satisfaction for his tyme. Anne Snowden sayth That the Defendant sayd to the Plaintiff hee would serve the said Plaintiff for the tyme hee had to serve or give the Plaintiff his Master reasonable satisfaction.

[8 1682]   Thomas Ollive Deposeth, That hee and Daniel Wills agreed

with the Plaintiff for the Defendants service one yeare, and that after the Defendants tyme of service was out with him and Daniell, there came an order from the Plaintiff Benjamin, concerning the Defendant. Daniel Wills senr., Deposeth That the Defendant was the last of his tyme of service with him the said Daniell, and that hee the said Daniell might have kept him longer if hee would, but that hee looked upon the Defendant as a burden; And alsoe that the Plaintiffs order concerning the Defendant came after the tyme that the Defendants yeare of service as aforesaid was expired; And both Thomas Ollive and Daniel Wills say, they Defendant was very much out of Clothes when hee came to them. Samuel Cliffe sayeth That the Defendant paid his wife something for mending his the Defendants Clothes but how much knowes not.

Mathew Allen Plaintiff Samuell Cole Defendant. Action of the Case. Henry Stacey, Thomas Barton, Thomas French, John Pancras, Bernard Devonish, Thomas Wright, John Boarton, Robert Scholey, Thomas Lambert, Daniel Leeds, Walter Pumphrey, Samuell Lovett Jury. Witnesses William Beard, Samuell Cliffe, Jonathan Eldridge. Verdict The Jury finde for the Plaintiff and give him his bargayne, that hee shall have the Lands Confirmed, and his Costs of suite; And that the Defendant in Consideration of Interest for his want of purchase money shall have seaven pounds.

William Beard Deposeth that hee the said William bargained for the Land that is to say 1000 Acres certaine or $\frac{1}{16}$th parte of propriety in the Declaration mentioned, on the behalfe of the Plaintiff, and gave the Defendant Earnest of it; And further sayeth that Joseph Helmsley was to draw the writeings for assurance thereof, but had not Conveniency for it. Samuell Cliffe Deposeth, That hee was present when the Plaintiff and Defendant Reckoned for worke by the Plaintiff done for the Defendant, and that there was due to the Plaintiff 4l. odd money, which was agreed between them to remayne in the Defendants hands towards the Bargayne of Land, if hee the Plaintiff had the Land; or otherwise that the Defendant would pay back to the Plaintiff the 4l. odd money. Jonathan Eldridge Testimony not materiall.

Francis Stephens Plaintiff Benjamin Scott Defendant an Action of the Case withdrawne.

William Duncks Plaintiff William Lee and William Matlock Defendants an Action of the Case Continued.

Francis Stephens Plaintiff Richard Whittaker Defendant withdrawne.

John Cripps Plaintiff Thomas Allen Defendant withdrawne.

Edmond Stuart Plaintiff Elizabeth Boarton Defendant an Action of defamation withdrawne.

Thomas Wright Plaintiff Henry Bowman Defendant an Action of Debt Continued.

Thomas Wright Plaintiff Henry Bowman Defendant Attachment Continued.

Thomas Wright Plaintiff   Jonathan Eldridge Defendant   Attachment withdrawne.

Walter Pumphrey Plaintiff   William Brightwen Defendant   Action of the case   withdrawne.

Thomas Gardner Plaintiff   John Cornish Defendant   withdrawne.

John Hollinghead Plaintiff   John Wright Defendant   an Action of the case   Attachment   the goods of the Defendant Attached called forfeit.

Henry Ballenger for Walter Humphrey his master moved the Court for a peece of Land, which he hath before taken up, and now is taken up by widdow Perkins; The Court discharged the said Henry from further molesting the widdow Perkins in her possession of the Land.

[9 1682] Burlington at the Court held November 7th 1682. Samuel Jenings Governour   Robert Stacy, Thomas Budd, Benjamin Scott, John Cripps   Justices and Commissioners present. Thomas Revell Recorder. John White Sheriffe. Francis Collins, Henry Stacy, Isaac Marriott, John Roberts, Benjamin Wheat, Robert Powell, Thomas Hooton, Godfrey Hancock, Thomas Wright, John Woolston, John Boarton, Richard Basnett   Jury Returned.

William Duncks plaintiff   William Lee and William Matlock Defendants   Withdrawne.

Thomas Wright Plaintiff, Henry Bowman Defendant   An Action of Debt. The Defendant appeares not, And the Plaintiff proved Bill in the Declaration mentioned by William Clayton, who attested the same before Robert Stacy; The Court haveing Continued the Action last Court upon the Defendants Accompt; Therefore the Court award Judgment against the Defendant for the 32s. being the obligatory parte or summe penall from the Defendant to the Plaintiff and Costs suite.

Thomas Wright Plaintiff   Henry Bowman Defendant   An Action of the Case   Continued.

Anthony Woodhouse Plaintiff   John Stanbanck Defendant   Continued.
John Stanbanck plaintiff   Anthony Woodhouse Defendant   Continued.
Robert Young Plaintiff   Captain John Adye Defendant   withdrawne.
Hance Ustason Plaintiff   Anderson Coleman Defendant   withdrawne.
George Bartholmew Plaintiff   Samuell Willis Defendant   Continued.
Henry Grubb Indictment versus John Petty   Continued.
Thomas Budd, William Brightwen and Henry Grubb Plaintiffs   John Petty Defendant   an Action of Assault   Continued.

Edward Brookes Indictment, confessed, and submitted to the Bench and fyned 10s. 00d. and upon his refusall of payment Committed, untill hee pay it, and his Fees.

[*Thomas Wheatly*] Thomas Wheatly one of the shipmen belonging to Captain John Adye, being taken up by a mittimus, sent out at the request of the said Captain Adye, upon Edward Evaretts Ingageing that the said Thomas

Wheatly shall be ready to appeare and answer the said Captain Adye at Burlington for what hee shall object against him, was by the Court Dismist paying his Fees.

[*Samuel Abbott*] Samuell Abbotts Indictment, confessed, and hee submitted himselfe to the Bench, and was Fyned 3l. 00s. 00 and Dismist by the Court paying his Fees.

Ordered by the Court that the Acts and Lawes of the Generall Assembly shall bee read on the 18th of November instant at Burlington being the markett day there.

The next Court appointed to be held on Tuesday the 19th December next.

[10 1682] Burlington at the Court held December 19th 1682. Robert Stacy, Thomas Budd, John Chaffen, William Biddle, Elias Farre, John Cripps Justices Commissioners present. Thomas Revell Recorder. John White Sheriffe.

Anthony Woodhouse plaintiff John Standbanck Defendant withdrawne.

John Standbanck Plaintiff Anthony Woodhouse Defendant withdrawne.

George Bartholmew Plaintiff Samuell Willis Defendant Rests.

John Petty upon Indictment by Henry Grubb Rests.

Thomas Budd, William Brightwen and Henry Grubb Plaintiffs John Petty Defendants. Rests.

Thomas Wright Plaintiff Henry Bowman Defendant Action case goes by default.

Thomas Wright Plaintiff William Duncks Defendant action Case. Francis Collins, Henry Stacy, John Woolston, John Shinn, Daniel Wills senr., William Peachee, John Boarton, Thomas Barton, John Pancras, John Newbold, Thomas Stokes, John Payne Jury. Witnesses Robert Durham, Richard Ramsdell, Thomas Allen, Jane Abbett, Elizabeth Garner, Richard Coates. Verdict Jury finde for the Plaintiff and give him Six skipps Rye to be paid at John Hollinsheads within one moneth next and his Cost suite and the Girle to be cleare of her service. Robert Durham proves the Agreement for the Defendants daughter for 5 yeares in the declaration mentioned. Richard Ramsdale alsoe proves the same Contract. Thomas Allen sayth that hee heard the Plaintiff say to the Girle of the Defendant mentioned in the Declaration, that shee might goe her way home if shee pleased. Jane Abbott sayth that the Girle aforesaid to her knowledge used to weare little more then the old shift or bratt then shewed in Court, for the summer tyme. Richard Coates sayth hee hath seene the maid at severall tymes goe in the Cold of winter, with shooes and stockings not worth the takeing up.

Thomas French Plaintiff Daniel Leeds Defendant an Action Case. Francis Collins, Henry Stacy, John Woolston, John Shinn, Daniel Wills senr.,

William Peachee, John Boarton, Thomas Barton, John Pancras, Godfrey Hancock, John Newbold, Thomas Stokes   Jury. The declaration was soe farre acknowledged by the Defendant that the Jury finde for the Plaintiff and give him 2d. dammage and his Costs of suite.

Robert Durham Plaintiff   John Wood Defendant   action case   Withdrawne   3 supenas.

John Wood Plaintiff   Robert Durham Defendant   action of Case withdrawne.

Seth Smith Plaintiff   Thomas Allen Defendant   withdrawne.

Thomas Stokes Plaintiff   John Petty Defendant   Continued.

Burlington at the Court held February 20th 1682. Samuell Jenings Governour   Robert Stacy, William Biddle, John Chaffen, Elias Farre, Mahlon Stacy, Thomas Budd, John Cripps   Justices present. Thomas Revell Recorder. John White Sheriffe. Thomas French, John Lambert, Thomas Wright, John Hooton, William Evans, John Roberts, Thomas Harding, Walter Pumphary, Richard Basnett, Francis Collins, John Hollinshead, Isaac Marriott Jury summoned.

John Petty upon Indictment per Henry Grubb   Rests.

Thomas Budd, William Brightwen and Henry Grubb against John Petty Rests.

Thomas Stokes plaintiff   John Petty Defendant   action case   Declaration drawne and withdrawne.

George Guest plaintiff   Samuell Willis Defendant   withdrawne.

Neals of Upland plaintiff   Lassy Coleman Defendant   Continued.

George Bartholmew plaintiff   Howel Loyd Defendant   Continued.

Morgan Drewit plaintiff   Daniel Linzey Defendant   withdrawne.

Walter Pumphary plaintiff   Joseph Browne Defendant   Declaration drawne and withdrawne.

Richard Burgesse plaintiff   Martin Hoult Defendant   withdrawne.

Martin Hoult plaintiff   Richard Burgesse Defendant   withdrawne.

John Shin Plaintiff   Richard Arnold Defendant   withdrawne.

John Hollinshead plaintiff   Edmund Warner Defendant   withdrawne.

[11 1682] [*February 20th 1682   The order for Robert Wilson.*] Ordered then by the Governour and Commissioners That Robert Wilson shall have liberty to take up and Possesse Two Hundred and Fifty Acres of Land in the first Tenth, that is to say, one Hundred Acres thereof upon the Accompt of Mathew Watson, which hee the said Robert hath bought of the said Mathew; And the remaining one Hundred and Fifty Acres upon the Accompt of George Ward, which said George Ward (as the said Robert Wilson saith) hath a right in a Two and Thirtieth parte paid for to Thomas Hutcheson and is to have a Deed thereof from the said Thomas Hutcheson; Which last mentioned one Hundred and Fifty Acres, It is ordered by the Authority

aforesaid that the said Robert Wilson shall have liberty to take up and possesse; Provided nevertheless That if the said Robert Wilson doe not or shall not within one yeare next ensueing the date of this order, Procure and gett a Legall Deed from the said Thomas Hutcheson of and for the said Two and Thirtieth parte of the propriety paid for by the said George Ward as aforesaid, to and for the use of the said George Ward or his Assignes, or otherwise doe not or shall not purchase or Legally Indent for the said one Hundred and Fifty Acres at or before the expiration of the said Terme of one yeare of and from some person or persons as shall appeare to have a Legall right therein, That then hee the said Robert Wilson and his Executors and Assignes shall leave and yeild up the same one Hundred and Fifty Acres.

[*February 20th 1682   The order for Meadowe Land to be taken up at Northampton River.*] Ordered then by the Governour and Commissioners, That those Purchasers who have taken up Land at or neare Rancokus Creek alias Northampton River, who have not Meadowe for their Tracts or shares there; shall have liberty to take up meadowe on either side the said Creek or River; Provided hee or they who shall take up such meadowe, take not up more then four Acres to each and every Hundred Acres which hee or they have taken up there; The said Meadowe to be taken up at or upon the Forke there, at the discretion and approbation of the Commissioners.

[*February 20th 1682   The order concerning the Land for the Widdow Perkins Children.*] Ordered then by the Governour and Commissioners, That the Five Hundred Acres in the Second Tenth Adjoyning to Arthur Cookes Land, and allready taken up by the late Widdow Perkins deceased shall Continue and remaine to and for the use and behoofe of the Children of the said Widdowe Perkins; The said Children, or their Trustees paying to Enoch Chore for his improvements made upon the same Land at the discretion of Two men indifferently to be chosen betwixt the said parties.

[*February 20th 1682   The order about the Land taken up by John Newbold at the Falls*] Ordered then by the Governour and Commissioners, Concerning the Land at the Falls formerly taken up by John Newbold; That the said John Newbold shall reap and take away his Cropp, which hee hath Plowed and Sowne there, And alsoe that John Lambert shall reap and take his Croppe which hee hath plowed and Sowne there; And that the said John Newbold shall be paid for his improvements by the persons to be concerned in that Land, taken up and improved by the said John Newbold, which improvements shall be viewed and vallued by four persons indifferently to be nominated for that purpose; And then shall leave and yeild up the same Land, which is to be devided by agreement amongst the partyes Concerned therein.

[*February 20th 1682   Cyder 4d. per quart and Rum 18d. per quart*] Ordered then by the Court That from and after the first day of March next ensueing Cyder shall not be sold for more then four pence the Quart, And that Rumme from and after the tyme aforesaid shall not Be sold for more then one shilling six pence the Quart, this to continue in force untill further order.

[*March 14th 1682.*] John Carter of Elizabeth Towne in the Province of East Jersey being examined before John Cripps Justice, Deposeth, that hee lives at Elizabeth Towne aforesaid, And that hee the said Carter, and a woeman with whom hee is in Company (who hee calls Lydia Mosse, by the name of her Father) are marryed.

The said Lydia being then Examined before John Cripps, Deposeth, That the aforesaid Carter and shee the said Lydia were Marryed at Elizabeth Towne aforesaid, before the People called Quakers, at the House wherein one Samuell Groome Inhabitteth; And being then accused to be the wife of one John Toe of Elizabeth Towne aforesaid, Deposeth, and sayth that shee disownes the said Toe to bee her Husband.

One Alexander Callman being then examined conserning the premisses, solemnly Deposeth [12 1682] That hee knowes the said Carter, and the said Lydia, And that the said Lydia to his knowledge hath beene reputed and owned to bee the wife of the said John Toe for a Considerable tyme; And alsoe that hee the said Alexander the 4th instant was at the house of the said John Toe at Elizabeth Towne; And the said Lydia was then at home with her said Husband Toe. The said Carter thereupon deposeth, That hee knowes not that the said Lydia is the Wife of the said John Toe: But afterwards Confest it, And wished that the said Lydia was at home with her said husband.

Whereupon the said John Carter, and the said Lydia Mosse, alias Toe, were by Mittimus under the hand and Seale of the said John Cripps Justice Committed to the Custody of the sheriffe untill further order.

[*March 22d.*] The said John Carter and Lydia Mosse alias Toe, were had before Governour Samuell Jenings, and Robert Stacy and John Cripps Justices, And were (by them) ordered the next day by the Tenth hower in the Morning to be whipt on their naked bodies the said Carter to receive Thirty stripes, and the said Lydia Thirty Five stripes. And that the said Lydia should the same day be forthwith sent back by a passe to the next Constable homewards; And the said Carter should remaine in Custody one day after the said Lydia, and then to bee dismist, paying the Fees.   per Thomas Revell Recorder.

[*1683*] At a Court appointed by the Governour and Councell and held at Burlington the 22th of the 3d' mo. called May Anno 1683. The Jury called Daniell Wills, Bernard Devonish, John Hollinshead, Thomas Gladwin, Thomas Bartin, James Wills, James Hill, Richard Fenimore, Godfrey Hancock, Henry Grubb, Robert Powell, John Woolston.

John Ingram, Francis Griffis, Roger Symonds, and Walter Cheesley Indicted at the Court, and Ingram, Griffis, and Cheesley appeared, but Symonds appeared not, The said Ingram, Griffis and Cheesley plead Guilty to their Indictment, And submitt themselves to the Governour and Bench.

Whereupon the Court Considering the Ingenious Confession and submission of the Criminalls Fyne John Ingram 5l. as principall offender and Walter Chisley 50s. And for Francis Griffis finding him not soe Culpable as the rest—upon his promise of amendment for the future, Remitt the offence, and dismisse him and Ingram and Chisley paying their charges and Fees. their Fees being 3s. a peece to the Clerke and 2s. a peece to the Sheriffe.

Overseers Chosen for the Highwayes   For the first Tenth: John Woolston, John Shinn. For the second Tenth: John Cripps, Thomas Mathews, Benjamin Scott, Daniel Wills.

Overseers for lookeing after the Size of Bricks   Francis Collins, Richard Fenimore.

Officers for searching and Sealing Leather, for Regulateing waights and measures and Ale Tasters   Benjamin Wheat and James Hill. Jonathan Eldridge and Thomas Farnsworth.[8]

[13 1683] Ordered at the Court aforesaid That the Commissioners and Freeholders meet the Governour at Burlington the next Seaventh day being the 26th instant to make an Assessment for the Highwayes.

The second of the 4th Moneth called June the Governour, with Thomas Budd, John Gosling, Thomas Gardner and Henry Stacy Justices called Roger Symonds (formerly Indicted at the last Court) before them, who pleaded Guilty to his Indictment and Submitted to the Bench; And is Fyned 50s. and dismissed paying his Charges and Fees.

The 4th Moneth called June 1683. The Governour and Councell then sitting granted Lycence to John Cripps, Richard Basnett, and Thomas Potts to keep Common victualling houses and to sell Ale and Beere and other Liquours for one yeare next ensueing, under the Condition of their Recognizance then agreed to bee taken.

Burlington at the Court held the 8th of the 6th mo. 1683. Samuell Jenings Governour. Thomas Budd, John Gosling, John Skeen, Thomas Gardner, Henry Stacy, Thomas Ollive, Mahlon Stacy, William Emley   Justices on the Bench.

Henry Parker Plaintiff, Daniell England Defendant. Jury   William Peachee, John Boarton, William Brightwen, Thomas Bartin, William Budd, Bernard Devonish, John Daye, Robert Young, Daniell Leeds, Henry Grubb, John Hollinshead, Seth Smith.

Evidence   Daniell Wills sayth the Plaintiff was willing at the sealing the Bill to take the Defendants owne security, though hee then knew of the defendants removeall, and that Anna Salter did then offer to pay the Debt, in certaine goods, in behalfe of the Defendant.

[8] Apparently the first two for the first Tenth and the other two for the second Tenth.

Verdict   The Jury find for the Defendant and give him 2d. Dammages and Costs of suite and Judgment Awarded.

John Newbold, John Woolston junr., Michaell Buffin, Thomas Revell servant to John Newbold, William Wayt, Michaell Newbold junr., being formerly by mittimus Committed to custody by Mahlon Stacy and William Emley, Justices, upon the Complaint of John Lambert, appeared, And was Indicted; And upon Indictment all pleaded not guilty, and referre themselves to the Countrey for Tryall, The Indictment being that the aforesaid persons the second of July 1683 did in Riotous and forciable manner Enter upon the Lands of the said John Lambert and then and there Cutt downe the Corne of the said John Lambert. John Lambert the Complaint. The Justices Mahlon Stacy and William Emley set forth in the Indictment that they did in their persons Convict the said persons of the offence according to the statute in that case provided. John Boarton, William Brightwen, Thomas Bartin, William Budd, Bernard Devonish, Robert Young, Daniell Leeds, Francis Collins, Robert Powell, James Wills, James Hill, Thomas Harding   Jury. Their Verdict   The Jury bring in their verdict, That they finde the Prisoners Guilty for their Contempt of Authority in not obeying the magistrates. Whereupon the Bench Fyned the aforesaid John Newbold Five pounds, and the sayd John Woolston, Michaell Buffin, Thomas Revell, and William Wayt Fifty shillings a peece, and bound them all to their good behaviour, And aquitt Michaell Newbold—being but a youth.

Richard Basnett plaintiff   William Lotter Defendant   action Case withdrawne.

Joseph Knight plaintiff   Thomas Wheatley Defendant   action case withdrawne.

Daniel Linzey plaintiff   Powell Lawson defendant   action case   warrant not served.

John White Plaintiff   William Laswell Defendant   action case   withdrawne.

Marcus Lawrence plaintiff   Casper Fish Defendant   Action Battery withdrawne.

Thomas Budd plaintiff   Walter Pumphary defendant   action case Rests.

John Cripps plaintiff   Thomas Potts Defendant   Action case   Continued.

John White plaintiff, Samuell Reap defendant by John Walker Attourney for the plaintiff   the Court order him to seize the premisses formerly appraised.

William Guest plaintiff   Martin Hoult defendant   action case   Rests.

William Lee plaintiff   Mathew Allen   action of the case   Continued.

[14 1683]   Upon the request of Mathew Allen the Court order Execution to be taken out for the sayd Mathew against Samuell Cole upon the ver-

dict and Judgment formerly past against him the sayd Samuell Cole. Att the same Court before Execution was taken out, came the sayd Samuell Cole, and declared that hee haveing other Evidence then what hee produced at the Tryall formerly had wherein the verdict past against him, whereupon the said Samuell haveing paid the Costs of the said former tryall desires an Arrest of Judgment for staying Execution untill it bee tryed againe—whereupon the Court order the said Samuell to give bond for his prosecuting and trying the same at the next Court, and grant an Arrest of Judgment.

Burlington at the Court held the 3th of the 9th Moneth 1683. Samuell Jenings Governour and president   Thomas Budd, John Gosling, Thomas Ollive, William Biddle, William Emley, Elias Farre, Mahlon Stacy   Justices present.

John Petty upon Indictment Rests   Rests.
Thomas Budd Plaintiff   Walter Pumphary Defendant   Continued.
William Lee Plaintiff   Mathew Allen Defendant   withdrawne.
Thomas Budd, William Brightwen and Henry Grubb against John Petty Rests.
John Cripps Plaintiff   Thomas Potts Defendant   Rests.
Thomas Budd Plaintiff   Charles Pickering Defendant   withdrawne.
William Guest Plaintiff   Martin Hoult Defendant   The Plaintiff declares; The Defendant appears not, and soe letts the Action goe by default, Benjamin Wheat the Sheriffe deposeth that hee heard Martin Hoult acknowledge the debt (being 5l. 10s. English money and 23s. Boston money declared for). The Court thereupon Award Judgment against the said Defendant for the 5l. 10s. English money and 23s. Boston money, and Costs of suite to and for the said Plaintiff.

Thomas Graves Plaintiff   Martin Hoult Defendant   The Plaintiff Declares: And the Defendant appeares not; The Plaintiff acknowledges the Receipt of 1ol. parte of the summe declared for: And in regard the Declaration was not given in tyme, And the Defendant being sick and not able to appeare the Action is Continued.

Richard Basnet versus Samuell Thrumball   continued.
Samuell Cole Plaintiff   Mathew Allen Defendant. Jury   Thomas Mathewes, John Hollinshead, Thomas Curtice, Anthony Morris, John Daye, John Woolston senr., Robert Powell, Joshua Wright, Isaac Marriott, Robert Young, John Shin, William Peachee. Evidence   William Emley, Henry Grubb, John Roberts, William Beard. Verdict   see at the end of the Tryall, after the deposition of the Evidences. William Emley Deposeth, That about four yeares agoe Mathew Allen the Defendant sayd severall tymes to him the said William Emley, that hee the sayd Mathew had made a bargayne with Samuell Cole for a Tract of Land: but further sayd that (Land being litle or nothing worth) hee would not have it; but would have goods of Samuell the Plaintiff for what was due to him.

Henry Grub, Deposeth that about three yeares agoe hee the sayd Henry bought of Mathew the Defendant a parcell of Land, And that after the sayd bargayne, Mathew told him the sayd Henry hee would release him of the sayd bargayne.

[15 1683] John Roberts Deposeth That hee was present when the bargayne of Land betwixt the Plaintiff and Defendant was made, But hath nothing hee can remember materiall; But sayth that afterwards hee heard the Plaintiff Complayne against the sayd Defendant about the bargayne of Land, as that hee the Defendant had noe minde to stand to it; But that hee the sayd Plaintiff would make him stand to it.

William Beard Deposeth, that hee knowes of the bargayne that was made betweene the Plaintiff and Defendant for a Thousand Acres of Land, And that the sayd Mathew the Defendant was to pay 20l. for it, and sayth the bargaine was made neare Sixe yeares agoe.

[*The Juryes Verdict*] In the Action of Samuell Cole Plaintiff against Mathew Allen Defendant the Jury finde for the Defendant And give him his Sixteenth parte of a propriety according to bargaine; Hee the sayd Defendant makeing up to the Plaintiff what hee hath allready paid him the sayd Plaintiff the Summe of Twenty pounds, And alsoe paying to the sayd Plaintiff Eight Pounds more for interest of the money; And that Samuell the Plaintiff shall seale to the sayd Mathew a Legall Conveyance of the sayd Land, and pay Costs of suite.

Joseph Browne Plaintiff   Martin Hoult Defendant   The last Jury impannelled in the Tryall betweene Samuell Cole and Mathew Allen alsoe impanelled upon this Tryall. Evidence   William Higgins, Archibald Silver, Joseph Knight, Richard Coates, William Budd. The Verdict   see at the end of the Tryall after the Depositions of the Witnesses.

William Higgins, Deposeth that hee knowes there was great losse to the Plaintiff for want of Cover to the Bricks, and as hee thinks there might bee about Twelve Thousand Bricks lost thereby.

Archibald Silver, Deposeth That hee knowes there was great losse to the Plaintiff for want of Cover to the Bricks.

Joseph Knight, Deposeth, That (as hee remembers the tyme that the Plaintiff was put of from the worke of the Defendant is about 14, or 15 weekes agoe.

Richard Coates, Deposeth, That about two monethes agoe Martin Hoult was willing to give the Plaintiff five pounds upon the Accompt of the Plaintiffs losse in the worke, and that the Plaintiff was willing to accept it; And that the Plaintiff asked the Defendant to Accompt and the Defendant sayd hee was willing to it; But the Plaintiff said hee had not then his Accompts about him.

William Budd Deposeth, That hee asked Joseph the Plaintiff, concerning the difference betweene him and the Defendant, And hee the said Plaintiff sayd, that hee had made an Agreement with the sayd Martin the Defendant to take 5l. of him and to Burne his Bonds.

[*The Juryes Verdict*] The Jury in the Action of Browne and Hoult finde for the Plaintiff, that is to say, that the Bill now given in by the Plaintiff of his worke amounting to Nyneteene pounds Eight shillings Seaven pence shall bee paid to the Plaintiff, And that what the Defendant can make appeare is payd thereof, bee discounted by the Plaintiff; And that the Defendant alsoe pay to the Plaintiff Eight pounds Dammage and his Costs of Suite.

The next Court is the 20th of the 12th moneth.

[**16 1683**] Burlington at the Court held the 20th of the 12th moneth 1683. Present there Samuell Jenings Governour Thomas Ollive, Thomas Budd, Thomas Ollive [*sic*], John Gosling, Thomas Gardner, Francis Collins Justices. The Jury Robert Stacy, Robert Dimsdale, Thomas Mathewes, John Budd, John Dewsbury, James Hill, Seth Smith, John Burre, Thomas Gilberthorpe, Christopher Weatherill, John Browne, Mathew Allen.

Thomas Budd Plaintiff Walter Pumphary Defendant Rests.
Henry Grub Indictment against John Petty Rests.
Henry Grub etc. Plaintiffs John Petty Defendant Rests.
John Cripps Plaintiff Thomas Potts Defendant Rests.
Thomas Graves Plaintiff Martin Hoult Defendant Continued.
Richard Basnett Plaintiff Samuell Thrumball Defendant withdrawne.
Robert Stacy Plaintiff Peter Jegou Defendant withdrawne.
Thomas Wright Plaintiff Walter Reeves Defendant declaration and Coppy Continued The Court order that the Defendant shall pay to the Plaintiff his necessary Charges for Attending the Action, And grant a Reference untill next Court in regard the said Walter the Defendant is not able to appeare by Reason of a wound hee hath received.

Walter Reeves Plaintiff Thomas Wright Defendant Continued. The Court upon the same Accompt abovewritten grant a Reference till next Court.

John Walker Plaintiff Samuell Reap Defendant Continued. The Defendant agrees with the Plaintiff before the Court to secure the Debt of 2l. 11s. 6d. with Court charges to the Plaintiff by makeing over his the Defendants Sloope to the Plaintiff to pay the same in 6 weeks next after this Court.

John Wood Plaintiff Godfrey Hancock Defendant Declared Continued upon the Plaintiff and Defendants agreement to Referre it.

John Newbold, John Woolston junr., Michael Buffin, Thomas Revell junr., William Wayt formerly bound over to their Good behaviour; Quitted by proclamation paying their Fees.

Thomas Gardner and Richard Basnett Appointed Administrators of the Goods and Chattells of Alexander Glenn lately drowned; there being noe Relation to take care thereof in the Province; And upon the said Administrators giveing in a true Inventory of the said Estate and their giveing security to the Court to dispose thereof Lycenced to take a Letter of Administration.

[17 1684] Burlington at the Court held the 8th of the 3d moneth 1684. Thomas Ollive Deputy Governour a[nd] president there And Elias Farre and Thomas Gardner Justices. The Jury Returned Thomas Mathewes, John Shinne, John Woolston senr., Samuell Lovett, Bernard Devonish, Daniell Leeds, John Dewsbury, John Budd, Anthony Morris, Richard Basnett, Phillip Creek, James Hill.

Daniell England plaintiff Anna Salter Defendant an Action of Case withdrawne.

Seth Smith plaintiff Samuell Reap Defendant an Action of Case Rests.

Richard Basnett plaintiff John Newman Defendant Action of Case withdrawne.

Samuell Barker plaintiff John Tuely Defendant an Action of Debt withdrawne.

Robert Carter plaintiff John Allen and Mary his wife Defendants Action of Debt Evidence Thomas Budd, William Budd. Thomas Budd and William Budd by their Testimony in writing declare, That to the best of their Knowledge, or understanding, John Allen did agree to pay unto Robert Carter in Consideration of the Freeing of him and his wife from their service the Summe of Thirteen pounds sterling money of old England in Testimony whereof they put their hands to the said writing Thomas Budd William Budd. [Juryes Verdict] The Jury finde for the Plaintiff and give him the 13l. sterling aforesaid being the Debt and 2d. damages and Costs of suite and Judgment is thereupon Awarded by the Court.

William Pickering plaintiff Samuell Reap Defendant An Action of Case The Plaintiff appears not to prosecute, and thereupon, at the request of the Defendant the Court grant a nonsuit for the Defendant against the Plaintiff.

John Wood Plaintiff Godfrey Hancock Defendant Continued.

William Byles plaintiff Nicholas Young Defendant Action of Slander withdrawne.

Upon the Complaynt of Thomas Revell against William Lasswell for a Debt of 4l. appearing due to said Thomas, the said Lasswell not appeareing, nor haveing any personall estate visible in the Province, ordered that the said Thomas Revell Seize upon the Land of said Lasswell for discharge of the same Debt Judgment being then Awarded for said Debt and costs of suite.

Thomas Wright plaintiff Walter Reeves Defendant Action of Case Evidence John Walker and Sarah Walker Both give Evidence for the payment of twenty five shillings by the Defendant to the Plaintiff which the Plaintiff Acknowledgeth. Juryes Verdict The Jury finde for the Plaintiff and give him 19s. 11d. being the remainder of his Debt Declared for and 6d. Dammages and Costs of suite; And Judgment is thereupon Awarded by the Court.

Walter Reeve Plaintiff Thomas Wright Defendant The Plaintiff proceeds not, and the Court haveing given one Court before, doe now at the request of the Defendant grant a nonsuite for the Defendant against the Plaintiff and Judgment awarded for Costs of suite.

Samuell Cole at this Court requires an Appeale for England: And in regard Mathew Allen at the same Court tenders the said Samuell Cole a Bill upon Governour Penn for his money, or to bring the said Samuell the money, or pay Equivalent to the house of the said Samuell for the discharge of what the Court formerly ordered the said Mathew to pay the said Samuell, which the said Samuell refuseth: Alsoe the said Mathew then offers the Land (which hee had a Verdict for) to Release the same to the said Samuell for 50l. this Countrey money, which Samuell alsoe refuseth: And the Court thereupon refuse to grant an Appeale.

[18 1684] Att a Court appointed at Burlington for the Jurisdiction thereof the 3d of the 4th moneth Anno 1684. Thomas Ollive Governour and president there Robert Stacy, William Biddle, Elias Farre, Robert Dimsdale, Daniell Wills, Robert Turner, Thomas Gardner, Francis Collins Justices present.

The persons Summoned to appear at this Court by vertue of a Warrant to Hance Hopman, Constable, being Inhabittants or occupyers of Land within the Tenths from the Third Tenth as lowe as Oldmans Creeke: To make appeare at the same Court what Quantities of Land they hold and by what right or Tytle they hold the same.

Mons Jenson, Hance Hopman, Peter Jonson hold a parcell or Tract of Land about a myle in breadth or front, being betweene, or extending from Oldmans Creek and a small Runn upward; which they hold by a permitt from Governour Cartrett dated 25th June 1668; But did not produce the permitt, nor know they how much it contaynes, not haveing surveyed it. Acres certaine 450 Charles Jenson, Hance Woolston, Daniell Linzey Guessed to be about 450 Acres: Daniell Linzey purchased James Saunderlands Interest thereof, who had it by vertue of the same permitt abovewritten, And the said Daniell sold parte of the same to the other two partners; But noe survey thereof.

certaine 300 James Ustason alias Hance[?] Lassey Coleman and Neales Matson alias Lawson by John Anderson in possession Guessed to be about 300 Acres the said Neales had the same by vertue of the permitt above, and sold to the other two partners, but noe survey thereof. certaine 100 Peter Erickson and Woolley Derickson 100 Acres bought of Thomas Budd; But noe deed thereof appeares, or any survey thereof. certaine 200 James Saunderland 200 Acres purchased of Samuell Jenings and Thomas Budd and the Deed Recorded: on the publick Accompt. certaine 200 And Hance Hopman more 200 Acres purchased of Richard Basnett, and the Deed thereof to be made and executed by Richard Basnett. certaine 100 Paule Curvon Guessed to be about 100 Acres, formerly in two settlements, and now turned to one; But taken up of his owne accord, without any face of a Tytle. Undevided 650 Peter Rambo senr. 650 Acres of an undevided share purchased of Thomas Bowman and the Deed Recorded. certaine 200 Peter Dalboe and Woolley Dalboe 200 Acres from Thomas Budd and Samuell Jenings on the Publick Accompt and the Deed Recorded. certaine 100 Anthony Nealson 100 Acres purchased from Samuell Jenings and Thomas Budd on the Publick Accompt and the Deed Recorded. certaine 600 Israell Helme about 600 Acres, holden by permitt from Governour Cartrett, but noe Survey thereof.

The Governour and Bench have ordered and hereby laid a Fyne of 20s. a peece upon each and every of the persons concerned in the Lower Tenths, who were Summoned to appear at this Court, and did not appeare, according to the warrant; unlesse they can give a satisfactory Accompt of their Absence.

[19 1684] The persons absent and Fyned are Peter Ponyon alias Erickson, Woolley Derickson, Mattis Hoemanson, Andreas Hoeman, Hance Peterson, John Browne and Benjamin his sonne in Lawe, Neales Matson, Peter Dalboe, John Wood, Henry Tradway, William Warner, Richard Lawrence, Samuell Carpenter, Thomas Winn, William Frampton, John Songhurst.

And a warrant is then drawne and Signed by Thomas Revell per order of Court and given into the hands of Hance Hopman Constable, for the persons above who have not made their Appearance, strickly warning them to appeare at Burlington the seaventeenth day of the fourth moneth Instant by the nyneth hower in the morning, then and there to make appeare what Lands they hold and by what Tytle as they will Answer the Contrary at their perill.

And ordered then by the Court that the rest of the magistrates, Commissioners and officers who have not signed to their Engagement as such officers, shall appeare, to signe to the same, on the said 17th of the 4th moneth Instant.

[*upon the Complaynt of John Griffin*] John Newman (by Robert Stacy Justice) bound over to this Court to answer our Lord the King for his breach of the Peace, upon the body of John Griffin.

John Newman, then appeares; And upon his Indictment pleads not Guilty; which hee haveing before the said Robert Stacy Acknowledged; and now saith hee knowes not whether hee struck the said Griffin, or not; because (as himselfe acknowledged) hee was in Drinke; and did then at Court acknowledge that at two other tymes, (not mentioned in his Indictment) hee did stryke and abuse the said Griffin; but sayth it was because hee was in drinke, the Court therefore give the said Griffin tyme to prepare and bring in his witness at the Court to be held the 17th of the 4th Moneth next: And require the said Newman to Finde suretyes of his appeareing at the same Court to answer the premisses, and alsoe for his good behaviour towards the Kings subjects and alsoe towards the said Griffin, which the said Newman refuseing, the Court by Mittimus Committ him to the Sheriffs Custody untill the said Court, or untill hee shall give sufficient security as afore required.

Ordered then by the Court that Lycences, and bonds be drawne for the Innholders or ordinarye Keepers, to take, and to Signe and seale to, with sufficient securities. the next Court as aforesaid.

[*1st Tenth*] Further ordered by the Court that the First Tenth Chuse and appoint their overseers for the Highwayes, and that with as much speed as may be, they begin to repayre the Highwayes within the said first Tenth, and that such who shall refuse, or neglect to performe their worke at the said Highwayes according to the appointment of the overseers, shall pay, every person that keeps a Teame, for every day refuseing or neglecting to performe their said worke Tenne shillings, and every other person, refuseing or neglecting as aforesaid for every day Three shillings.

[*2d Tenth Daniell Wills and William Peachee overseers*] Further ordered, that the second Tenth begin to repayre the Highwayes within the said second Tenth, the next Second day, and that such as shall refuse, or neglect to performe their Four dayes worke, according to the appointment of the overseers, shall pay, every person keeping a Teame and soe neglecting Tenne shillings for every day soe neglecting, and every other person soe neglecting Three shillings per day.

[20 1684] Att a Court appointed at Burlington for the Jurisdiction thereof the 17th of the 4th mo. 1684. Thomas Ollive Governour and president there. Robert Stacy, William Biddle, Elias Farre, Robert Dimsdale, Daniell Wills, Robert Turner, Thomas Gardner, Francis Collins Justices present.

The names of the persons who appeared at this Court by vertue of a warrant; being Inhabittants, or Occupyers of Land within the Tenths from the Third Tenth as lowe as Oldmans Creek, with a particular Accompt of what quantities of Land they hold, and by what right or Tytle they hold the same, as the same is given in at the same Court.

Certaine 100	Peter Erickson and Woolley Derickson	100 Acres certaine from Thomas Budd on the publick Accompt but yet have noe Deed.
Certaine 150	Andreas Hoeman	150 Acres bought of Thomas Budd on the publick Accompt.
Certaine 050	Hance Peterson	50 Acres from Thomas Budd etc. on the same Accompt.

Certaine	100	Benjamin Bramma	100 Acres in the 4th Tenth from Thomas Matthewes.

Neales Matson appeares not.

Certaine	100	John Wood	100 Acres by Deed from Edward Byllinge.
Certaine	300	Henry Tradway 200	Acres by Deed on the publick Accompt.
		William Warner 100	
Undevided	500	Richard Lawrence	650 Acres by Deed from Edward Bylling.

Neales Lawson Land given in before per John Anderson.

Second Tenth

Undevided Certaine

500	Captaine Hance Jonas Keene and Fredrickson	500 Acres purchased on publick Accompt.
100	Jonas Keene	100 Acres from Samuell Jenings.
400	John Hance and Fredrick	400 Acres from Anna Saltar.

The names of the persons within the Third Tenth Summoned to appeare with an Accompt of their Lands in possession.

Undevided	Certaine			
250			Thomas Thackeray	250 Acres per Deed
250			Thomas Sharpe	250 Acres per Deed
400			And reserved for the	Towne bounds for the purchasers there
500			Robert Zane	500 Acres per Deed
	500		John Hogge	500 Acres per Deed from Robert Zane certaine
	200		Richard Arnold	200 Acres purchased on publick Accompt certaine
1000			Henry Stacy	500 Acres per Deed
			and more	500 Acres per Deed—in R. Mathewes tenure
500			Daniell Walton	500 Acres per warrant on William Hunt Accompt

But the said Daniell appeared not

[21 1684]

250	300		Hannah Newbie	250 Acres of an undevided parte, and 300 Acres certaine from the publick
2150			Robert Turner	2150 Acres an undevided parte
	650		Samuell Carpenter	650 Acres certaine
260			William Bates	260 Acres an undevided parte and hath noe parte of Towne bounds
250			William Albertson	250 Acres an undevided parte
250			Thomas Carelton	250 Acres an undevided parte
	500		Jeremiah Richards	500 Acres certaine
500			Samuell Cole	500 Acres an undevided parte
650			Thomas Howell	650 Acres an undevided parte in 2 setlements
250	100		Henry Wood	250 Acres an undevided parte and 100 Acres certaine
500			John Ithell	500 Acres an undevided parte

Undevided	Certaine		
	200	Marcus Lawrence	200 Acres certaine
	120	Casper Fisk	120 Acres certaine
	300	Richard Russell	300 Acres certaine
1400		Francis Collins	1400 Acres an undevided share
	100	John Kea	100 Acres certaine of Francis Collins
550		William Frampton	550 Acres an undevided parte
400	50	Edward Everett for himselfe	50 Acres certaine, and on William Roydens Accompt 400 Acres uncertaine.

Upon the Complaynt of John Griffith against John Newman

John Newman upon the Indictment acknowledgeth the Fact, And referres himselfe to the Judgment of the Bench; And not to the Verdict of a Jury. Evidence George Porter and Elleanor Hunter.

George Porter averres and sayth that hee sawe John Newman stryke the said John Griffith, and that hee sawe the said Newman and Griffith fall togeather on the ground, and (as hee the said George thinkes) the said Griffith was cast downe by the blowes that the said Newman gave him.

Ellener Hunter alsoe declares to the same effect with George Porter, onely shee thinks the reason of their falling downe was their stumbling upon a stoole, And further that shee heard the said Griffith say in the house that hee would not fight with the said Newman.

The Bench give Judgment against the said John Newman, and for his breach of the Peace Fyne him 40 Shillings: and order him to pay the Court charges And alsoe order him to pay to the said Griffith for his abuse and losse of tyme 30 shillings, And for his being three tymes drunk by his owne Confession, fyne him 9 shillings.

William Biddle (at the request of the said Newman who alsoe promiseth to save harmlesse and discharge the said William) Engageth for the payment of the respective Fynes and charges aforesaid, on the behalfe of the said Newman, that is to say the Fynes of 40s. and 9s. within 3 monethes next, the said 30s. to said Griffith within one moneth next, and the Court Charges, on demand.

And John Newman Quitt by proclamation.

Richard Arnold Indicted upon the Complaynt of Bethell Langstaffe, and to the Indictment pleads Guilty in parte:

And the said Arnold and Langstaffe referre the matter to Arbitration.

[22 1684] Bethnell Langstaffe Indicted upon the Complaynt of Richard Arnold, And the said Langstaffe and Arnold referre the Matter to Arbitration.

The Arbitratours chosen are Robert Stacy, Richard Basnett, William Biddle, Francis Davenport.

There Award is that all quarrells etc. between the said partyes to this day cease, And that both partyes be and beare the one halfe of Court Charges and other expences, etc.

The names of those within the Third Tenth who appeared not at the Court   William Cooper, Daniell Walton, the Accompt of his land is taken before, John Ashton, Timothy Hancock, John Roberts, William Matlock, Thomas Wallis, Jeremiah Richards, the Accompt of his Land is taken before.

Overseers for the Highwayes in the First Tenth   Godfrey Hancock, John Woolston.

Overseers for the third Tenth   William Cooper, Thomas Howell.

And overseers to doe the remainder of the worke at Yorkshire bridge Thomas Mathewes and John Cripps.

John Boarton Fyned 20 shillings by the Court upon the Complaynt of Daniell Wills overseer for the Highwayes in the second tenth for his the said Johns neglect of doeing his worke, and Contempt of the Authority of the overseers concerning the same worke at the Highwayes.

Att a meeting of the Proprietors and Freeholders in the first Tenth the 24th of the 4th moneth 1684 by vertue of a warrant to them directed, for the Chuseing their Assessours [9] and Receivers for the Assessment or rate Enacted by the Generall Assembly; And alsoe for the giveing in each persons quantity of Land in the said Tenth, both of undevided shares, and Certaine Tracts.

Assessours Chosen

From the Falls to Crosswicks Creek.   William Emley, Joshua Wright. From Crosswicks Creek vizt Chesterfield and Mansfield and places adjacent   John Hooton, Francis Davenport. From Mansfield or to Assiscunck and parts adjacent   Daniell Leeds, Percifall Towle. Robert Stacy and Thomas Revell Receivers.

The names of the Proprietors and Freeholders and the number of Acres they possesse.

Undevided	Certaine		
270		Robert Stacy	270 Acres
	150	Thomas Revell	150 Acres
		Seth Smith	
		The 3 brothers wheelwrights	
	200	Thomas Bowman	200 Acres
		Thomas Budd	200 Acres
		Richard Guy	
	100	Nathaniell West	100 Acres
325		Thomas Singleton	325 Acres
	50	Thomas Terry	50 Acres
	200	Mordecay Bowden	200 Acres
		John Goslinge and partners	445
100		John Cripps	100 Acres
	150	Joseph Blowers	150 Acres

[9] "Assessors" in MS.

1684]   THE BURLINGTON COURT BOOK   31

Undevided	Certaine		
500		Thomas Wright	500 Acres
	50	Edmund Stuart	50 Acres
	91	John Long	91 Acres
100		Samuell Oldale	100 Acres
150	300	Elias Farre	450 Acres
[23 1684]			
200		Francis Beswick	200 Acres
	200	Daniell Leeds	200 Acres
	50	Robert Young	50 Acres
	100	John Daye	100 Acres
200		Eleazer Fenton	200 Acres
300	100	John Shinn	400 Acres
500		Thomas Budd	500 Acres
	100	Thomas Curtice	100 Acres
650		John Butcher	650 Acres
1000		Samuel Barker	1000 Acres
300		John Curtice	300 Acres
	100	John Browne	100 Acres
400		Michael Newbold	400 Acres
500		Percifall Towle	500 Acres
		John Antram	150 Acres
400	100	John Woolston	500 Acres
300	100	Godfrey Hancock	400 Acres
	550	Henry Stacy	550 Acres
500		William Biddle	500 Acres
	500	John Underhill	500 Acres
	500	Samuell Andrewes	500 Acres
200		Samuell Borden	200 Acres
100		William Beard	100 Acres
200		John Snoden	200 Acres
380		John Hooton	380 Acres
	100	Henry Stacy	100 Acres
	200	John Horner	200 Acres
	120	William Barnes	120 Acres
350		Daniell Bacon	350 Acres
200		George Goforth	200 Acres
	50	Marmaduke Hawsman	50 Acres
130		Anthony Woodhouse	130 Acres
200		William Black	200 Acres
246		Thomas Farnsworth	246 Acres
	50	Peter Harrison	50 Acres
		Bryan Morehouse late surveyed	
	200	John Theakes late surveyed	200 Acres
200		Mathew Watson	200 Acres
300		Thomas Wood	300 Acres
100		John Wood	100 Acres
260		Robert Wilson	260 Acres
100		William Hickson on Jenkins Land	100 Acres
	200	Roger Parke	200 Acres
350		Thomas Fouke	350 Acres

Undevided	Certaine		
160		Francis Davenport	160 Acres
285		Samuell Wright	285 Acres
500		Thomas Wright	500 Acres
350		Joseph Stones	350 Acres
400		Thomas Lambert	400 Acres
	50	Thomas Tindall	50 Acres
220		George Hutcheson	220 Acres
140		John Pattison	140 Acres
160		William Lasswell	160 Acres
300	100	Robert and John Murfin	400 Acres
	100	Robert Pearson	100 Acres
	40	Thomas Sharman	40 Acres
200		Robert and Tomas Scholey	200 Acres
100		John Rogers	100 Ackers
60	100	James Pharoe	160 Acres
200		George Hutcheson	200 Acres
100	100	John Fullwood	200 Acres
	200	Andrew Smith	200 Acres
	100	Peter Fretwell	100 Acres
	100	Hugh Staniland	100 Acres
700		Mahlon Stacy	700 Acres
300		John Lambert	300 Acres
400		Joshua Wright	400 Acres
400		Thomas Lambert	400 Acres
400		William Emley	400 Acres
75	100	Thomas Bartin	175 Acres
160		John Pancras	160 Acres

[24 1684] Burlington Court 8th 6th moneth 1684. Thomas Ollive Governour and President. Robert Stacy, William Biddle, Daniell Wills, Francis Davenport   Justices.

Grand Jury   John Goslinge, John Payne, Thomas French, John Hollinshead, Daniell Leeds, Thomas Stokes, Freedome Leppincote, John Daye, John Butcher, John Borton, Thomas Barton, Godfrey Hancock, William Brightwen, Samuell Lovett, John Roberts. Petty Jury   William Peachee, William Myers, Walter Pumphary, Phillip Creek, John Wills, Thomas Kendall, John Dewsbury, James Wills, Daniell Wills junr., James Hill, Bernard Devonish, Casper Fish.

Upon the Indictment of Henry Tradway on the Complaint of Robert Holgate. The partyes agreed.

In the Indictment of Henry Tradway on the Complaint of Robert Zanes Constable. The Jury finde the Bill of Indictment whereupon Henry Tradway refuseth to Traverse; and Submitts to the Bench: and by the Bench Fyned Forty shillings for breach of the Kings Peace, and Three pounds to the Constable for the abuse to him: and alsoe ordered that Henry Tradway shall pay the charge of the officers and others goeing downe with a warrant to Fetch him up, and all other Court charges.

Samuell Coles plaintiff William Evans Defendant An Action of Trover The Jury John Goslinge, Godfrey Hancock, William Peachee, John Daye, John Boarton, William Myers, Freedome Leppincote, John Payne, John Butcher, Walter Pumphary, Daniell Leeds, Thomas Stokes. Plaintiffs Evidence Casper Fish, Fredrick Fredrickson, John Hance. Defendants Evidence John Woolston senr., John Roberts, Timothy Hancock, Thomas Wilkinson, Thomas French. Casper Fish: Declares that to the best of his understanding the Horse in the Declaration mentioned and which is in the Defendants possession is the Plaintiffs, and further sayth that the Plaintiffs horse was three yeares old last spring and that hee hath knowne the Horse since hee was 3 or 4 Moneths old.

Fredrick Fredrickson. Declares that hee hath knowne the Plaintiffs horse in question, and that hee haveing formerly and now seene the Horse that is in the Defendants Possession, sayth that hee lookes, or seemes to the best of his Judgment to be the Plaintiffs horse.

John Hance. Not admitted in Evidence because it appears by the Testimony of John Furnice, that hee the said Hance hath bought the horse in question, of the Plaintiff.

John Woolston senr. sayth hee hath seene and knowne a Horse which Thomas Ollive brought up, and Sold to the Defendant which horse is Turnd 5 yeares old, and to the best of his knowledge hee thinks the horse in question is the same horse.

John Roberts, Sayth that the horse in question is very like the horse that the Defendant bought of Thomas Ollive, and sayth that the horse that the said Defendant bought of Thomas Ollive is now turned 5 yeares old.

Timothy Hancock, Sayth that hee hath knowne a Horse which Thomas Ollive had, which hee hath seene since the Defendant bought him, and to the best of his knowledge the horse now in the Defendants possession being the horse in question is the same horse bought of Thomas Ollive.

[25 1684] Thomas Wilkinson; Sayth hee hath knowne a Horse of Thomas Ollives ever since hee was halfe a yeare old, and that hee hath used to looke after him, and that William Evans the Defendant bought the same horse of Thomas Ollive, and that the horse in question now in the Defendants possession by all markes and shapes to the best of his understanding hee thinks is the same horse.

Thomas French, Sayth hee hath knowne the horse that Thomas Ollive sold to the Defendant a considerable tyme, and that hee beleeves the horse in question now in the Defendants hands is the same horse which the Defendant bought of Thomas Ollive.

The Verdict. The Jury bring in a special verdict in regard they have noe positive Evidence either for the Plaintiff or the Defendant And thereupon the Jury request the Bench to propose a reference: Whereupon the Bench make this proposall to the Plaintiff and Defendant (vizt) That the

Defendant Evans take the Horse or Gelding into his possession and pay Fifty shillings to Cole the Plaintiff And if hereafter the said Horse appeare by his Mouth, or other playne demonstration that the horse is not the Defendants by his age, Then the Defendant to returne the Horse to the Plaintiff and the said Plaintiff then to pay back to the Defendant the 50s. And Plaintiff and Defendant, to pay equall share of Costs and Charges of Suite. To which proposall, Plaintiff and Defendant agree.

John Browne Preferred a Petition for buying the Land hee is upon: [Order of Court] whereupon the Court order that Israel Helme, concerned therein, and the said Browne appeare face to face before they determine the matter: And order in the meane tyme that the same Land be not disposed of to any other.

Israel Helme and Daniell Linzey both Summoned by warrant to appeare next Court.

Thomas Mathewes on the behalfe of the Province Requests that the Court will take order against the spoyle of Timber upon Lands not taken up: The Court thereupon order that a Proclamation be issued forth from Governour and Commissioners that noe person etc. fell or cutt downe any Timber Trees upon Lands untaken up, or take or carry away the same etc. under the penalty of being Fyned, and punished according to the nature of the offence not exceeding   per tree.

John Saunders on his Complaynt against Francis Collins his Master for the want of his Trade to which he was bound, The Court order that the matter be determined by the Governour and two or more Magistrates within 14 dayes next, and that the master and servant, shall be called before them in regard the master is not now present.

[26 1684] John Otter and Edmund Bennett Complaynants versus Thomas White Defendant   withdrawne.

John Antram Plaintiff   Thomas Potts Defendant   withdrawne.

Walter Pumphary plaintiff   John Antram Defendant   Declaration drawne. withdrawne.

Michaell Buffin and George Shin, called before this Court and for their breach of Peace in wounding an Indian Contrary to Lawe Fyned 5l. being formerly Convict thereof. The Indians name is Shocollawanghon.

Burlington at a Special Court held the 16th. 7th. mo. 1684: called at the Request of Peter Jegou against John Anderson in an Action of Debt. The partyes agreed.

Hannah Newbie appeared and desired Administration of the goods and Chattells of Marke Newbie her late Husband deceased, And upon her Attesting an Inventory thereof, given in, and giveing sufficient bond and security according to Lawe had a Letter Administration granted by Governour Thomas Ollive, Robert Stacy, William Biddle and Thomas Gardner Justices.

Burlington at the Court held the 3d of 9th moneth 1684.

John Walker plaintiff Samuell Reap Defendant an Action of the case The Plaintiff declares, and the Defendant appears not, the Plaintiff prooves his Debt by a former Record of Court, Thereupon the Defendants goods Attached are called Forfeit, namely 3 Loads of Stones 3l. 200 foot of Boards 10s. 6 peeces of Chuncks of old Roap 5s. a stemme and sterne post and a Keele of a Boate 20s. the whole apraisd at 4l. 15s. ood. And Judgment Awarded thereupon for Debt and charges: and the remainder to be returned to the Defendant being 12s. 2d.

Walter Pumphary Plaintiff, Samuell Gibson and Lydia his wife Defendants. The Plaintiff Declares, and the Defendants neither of them appeare; The Debt declared for, proved per Thomas Gardner: and for goods the plaintiff charges the Defendants with, The Constable James Hill Testifyes that some part was found with the Defendants Thereupon the goods Attached were called forfeit: And Judgment Awarded for Walters Debt being 49s. and charges to be paid out and the rest to remayne till further order being 10l. 14s. 11d.

John Hollinshead Plaintiff Samuel Thrumball Defendant An Action of the case The Plaintiff Declares, and the Defendant appears and promises in Court to worke out the Debt being 6l. 10s. with or for the Plaintiff.

Henry Grubb plaintiff Daniell England Defendant Continued.

[27 1684] Roger Walden Indicted for Felony upon the Complaint of Governour Ollive John Bradbury and Thomas Wilkinson The said Waldren, pleads Guilty to the Indictment and referres himselfe to the Bench: The Indictment is for money and goods appraised to 1l. 9s. 3d. which are restored in Court. The Bench according to the Lawe of the Province give Judgment for the Fellon to restore four fould which is 5l. 17s. ood. Soe that the goods being restored, there rests: 4l. 7s. 9d. which the said Waldren submitts to, and promises to deliver his Cow for payment And gives an order to John Hollinshead to receive her from Richard Ridgeway at the Falls in Pennsylvania.

Burlington Court held the 18th 9th Moneth 1684 appointed espetially for the publishing of Surveyes and none appeares.[10] Present there Governour Ollive William Biddle, Elias Farre, Daniell Wills Justices etc.

George Meales per Daniell Wills his Attorney Complaynes against Henry Jacobs in an Action of Debt: The Plaintiff declares Action withdrawne.

Burlington at a spetiall Court held from the 11th of the 10th Moneth 1684 and by Adjournments continued to the 16th of the same moneth And called particularly upon the Accompt of the goods brought to shore at

---

[10] onely one Survey of Thomas Revells of 130 Acres published and appointed to be recorded [marginal note by clerk].

Burlington lately run aground on the shore of this Province in the sloop called Beaverwick: Governour Ollive there present   And Robert Dimsdale, Thomas Gardner, Robert Stacy and Elias Farre, Justices. Alsoe   William Biddle, John Goslinge, Daniell Wills, Francis Davenport   Justices.

William Wood being asked by what Authority, or upon what Accompt they seized and secured the goods late in the Sloope called Beaverwick run a shore on this Province; Averres that hee seized and secured the same in obedience to and by vertue of the Authority of the Province.

Freedome Leppincoate, John Stacy, Godfrey Hancock, Henry Jacobs, Walter Pumphary, Eleazer Fenton and Zebulun Thorpe being all particularly asked the same question above doe each and every of them particularly averre that they seized and secured the premisses in obedience and submission to the Authority of this Province.

John Peake (owner of the sloope called the Hopewell) and Fredrick France Master thereof upon their Examination, Attest and averre that the Master and Marriners late belonging to the sloope called Beaverwick that was run a shore, did Bargaine with the said John Peake to goe in [28 1684] search of the said Sloope that was run on Shore, for the gaining the Rigging thereof and what goods they could finde, and that they agreed for Twenty Five pounds sterlinge to bring what they could gett to Appaquinamy Creek: [11] And that when the said John Peake tooke the Goods a board, hee tooke them on the Accompt of the Authority of this Province which was then produced; and agreed with the parties Commissionated by the Authority aforesaid to bring the goods to Salem for Twenty pounds, and afterwards agreed to bring the same up to Burlington for five pounds more all of Current spanish money: And alsoe further Averres that John Moll [12] master of the said Sloope run a shore, said hee expected there would be some persons at the place where the goods were left a shore, and that hee should therefore be forced to give each owner his owne.

Elizabeth Stacy on her Examination averres that shee was on Board the sloope when shee run a ground which was about 10 or 11 at night: And next morning shee and two other woemen went a shore: And that after the Master and Marriners gott severall goods a shore, And that they (the Master and marriners found Keyes and opened severall Chests, and that they pulled of Brasse hinges and a board at the bottome of a Chest of Drawers and looked what was therein, And alsoe that they opened one Hogshead with fruit therein and some Iron ware, And that they tooke a bagg of Wampam forth of another Chest: And that they opened one other parte of the Chest of Drawers and shee sawe therein a Silver Tankard, and three Silver

---

[11] Appoquinimink Creek, in Delaware.

[12] No doubt the John Moll who was a justice of the court of New Castle County, Delaware, or his son. See *Records of the Court of New Castle on Delaware*, ii (1681–1689) (Meadville, Pa.), 67, 106, 177.

Spoones; And alsoe that shee seeing severall neat Linnings, said it was pitty but the owner should have them againe, to which one of the Seamen called Symon replyed, but shee is never like to have them: And sayth that they ordnarily spake in Dutch one to another, which shee well understood not; And that shee heard them say they intended to procure a Sloope at Chrisparus Harmons[13] and to gett the goods thither, And further shee heard them say they should live well this winter haveing gott good Beere and victualls store, and that they should make Chrisparus fatt. And further sayth that the Master came to her when at Burlington, and desired her not to say any thing concerning what shee had seene and heard in the matter aforesaid, and shee should fare never the worse, and moreover they told her after the Sloope was cast away all the Goods they cold save were their owne.

Matthias Vanderhoyden on his Examination averres, That Chrisparus Harmon told him that John Moll and partners had made an Agreement with John Peake (owner of the Sloope called Hopewell) to Sayle with them to the Sloope run a Shore and to bring what they could finde to Appaquinamy Creeke, and that hee the said Chrisparus had drawne the agreement; But being more nearly required to declare the naked truth, whether Chrisparus did not tell him that they was to bring the Goods to his House, sayth, to the best of his remembrance hee did tell him soe, but cannot possitively affirm it.

Eleazer Fenton and John Smith Averre that they heard Matthias Vanderhoyden tell John Goslinge that Chrisparus Harmon told him that John Peake, and Master were by agreement to bring the Goods etc. to his the said Chrisparus house.

Matthias Vanderhoyden, being required to declare if hee knowes or hath any thing to say against any of the persons comissionated to seize and secure the goods; Averres that hee neither knowes or hath any accusation against all or any of the said persons concerning their proceedings therein.

[29 1684] [*12th 10th mo. 1684*] Elizabeth Stacy being further Examined what shee remembers more concerning the premisses, Averrs that shee sawe one of the Seemen open two Letters and burne them, And further, that shee sawe a paper written in English which concerned some goods to a person of Philadelphia, and that the Master (John Moll) seeing her reading it snatcht it from her and tore it, saying what did shee reading those? they were now of noe concerne. And that at another tyme the said Master and Marriners sayd none of the writings signifyed any thing now they were cast away.

Thomas Launce, averres hee was on board the Sloope when shee run a shore, and sayth that when they tooke the Goods a shore, hee sawe a Chest opened, and that the Master and marriners tooke out some Goods and put some in againe, and that hee sawe some Gloves taken away, and that a young

---

[13] Casparus Herman, a justice of the same court (*ibid.*, 94, 104).

woeman (related to Chrisparus Harmon) gave him one of those payre of Gloves: And further (being asked the reason) why hee did not declare (when they came first to Burlington, And publickly reported all was lost) That the goods or most of them were saved; Sayth the reason was because the Master and Marriners desired him hee would say nothing that might doe them injury; And further sayth hee was troubled, not knowing how hee should gett up his goods, in regard the Master and Marriners designed to Land the Goods at Chrisparus Harmons And further being asked if hee did not receive a Gun from the Marriners, sayth they gave him a Gun, and bid him take it for his owne defence, and being asked where the Gun is, sayth hee hath parted with it.

[16th 10 mo.] Thomas Launce being then required to showe the reason why hee tooke the aforesaid Gloves, sayth that hee seeing some Gloves laid by on Board, and haveing worne out his owne Gloves with pulling at the Ropes and Rolling goods a shore, was complayning for want of Gloves, being cold, and that Chrisparus Harmons Sister bid him take them, but hee replying, said hee had noe minde to meddle with them, they being not his owne, whereupon the same young woman tooke them up, and said take them, I give them to you, Alsoe the sayd Thomas sayth hee had a payre of Wosted Stockings, and an old shirt which hee desired to borrowe of John Vanderlenden, one of the marriners, which he sayth the said Vanderlenden tooke forth of his owne Chest, and Leant him, And the said Thomas further sayth that on the 14th of this instant 10th Moneth hee heard the Master and Marriners say they had resolved the day before they came with the Sloope Hopewell to the place where the goods were left on shore, that each owner should have his owne: And alsoe sayth that Symon Burden, one of the marriners, tooke away from the goods a Black hatt.

An Accompt of what goods the persons Comissionated had occasion to make use of, late in the said sloope run a shore, Upon their severall Attestations being all they had thereof, or all they knowe of in the possession of the rest according as is given in (vizt)   William Wood, a payre of Shooes, a payre stockings of course Iseland, 2 handkerchiffs, one marking Iron and a furr cap. Fredome Leppincote, a small Ivory combe. John Stacy, 3 pockett handkerchiffs, and a knife. Godfrey Hancock 2 pockett handkerchiffs, a knife thats broke, and a payre of shooes. Henry Jacobs, a payre stockings, an old shirt, and a handkerchiffe. Walter Pumphary, an old shirt, an old handerchiffe, a payre of Gloves and a knife. [30 1684] Eleazer Fenton, 2 handkerchiffs, a knife, a Combe and case and a payre of Gloves. Zebulun Thorpe, 2 handkerchiffs, a payre of Gloves, a Combe, a payre of Shooes and stockings, an old shirt, and a hatt. John Smith sayth hee hath nothing nor knowes of any thing further in the possession of the rest. Elizabeth Stacy sayth shee hath nothing, nor knowes of any thing further in the possession of the rest.

Thomas Launce being againe called and required to declare if hee had any thing else of the Goods late in the said Sloope belonging to the owners, more than his owne, and alsoe that if hee knew, or could remember any thing further concerning the passages amongst the said Marriners, matteriall to this Tryall: Averres that hee hath nothing more than what hee hath before given an Accompt of before the Magistrates. And as concerning the said Master and Marriners sayth that after the Sloop was run a ground hee remembers the sea Men would not worke, but after some tyme that they had discoursed things, they were then willing to worke: For which reason hee beleeves the Master promised something to them, but what, hee knowes not.

Thomas Launce being called to Answer, the Complaynt of the owners, for his fact, or fault in receiving or takeing the aforesaid Gloves and Gun, Humbly Acknowledgeth the same, and desires there may be noe Jury called for the same, but Submitts himselfe to the Judgment of the Bench: Which the owner is satisfyed with. The Bench order the said Thomas Launce shall restore four Fould, either the Gun and Three tymes its value, or four fould its value, unlesse the Complaynant Cornelius Bom please to mitigate it: The said Cornelius, upon the publishing the same order, declares hee is and shall be satisfyed if the said Thomas Launce deliver him the Gun cleare of charges, or its value, cleare of the same.

Thomas Launce cleared and Quitt by proclamation paying his Fees.

The owners, or Fraighters for themselves and the rest concerned, and the Persons Comissionated to seize and secure the Goods, mutually agree in open Court to referre their Matter (relating to the Charge in Seizing, securing, and bringing the Goods to Burlington) to Six persons each partye to chuse three: Thereupon the owners nominate and chuse, John Goslinge, Robert Dimsdale, and Thomas Bowman, And the Seazers, William Biddle, Richard Basnett and Thomas Revell. And if they end not the same, the aforesaid partyes agree to stand to the Umpirage of the Governour therein.

Thomas Budd merchant plaintiff John Yeo Defendant of Baltimore County in Mary Land Gent. by Nihil Dicit

Action Debt for 60l. 00s. 00d. Thomas Revell of Burlington Scrivener by vertue of a warrant of Attorney from the Defendant Yeo appeares to the said Action and Confest Judgment upon the said Accompt of Debt for Sixty pounds Lawfull money of old England for the non payment of Thirty one pounds fourteene Shillings Six pence of like lawfull English money on the Thirteenth day of October last past; whereupon Judgment is Awarded and entred against the said John Yeo for the realle Debt which is Thirty one pounds fourteene shillings Six pence lawfull English money with Costs of suite, Amounting to Twelve Shillings Six pence.

[31 1684] The Grand Jury Returned and Attested Thomas Bow-

man, William Peachee, William Budd, Daniell Leeds, John Shin, John Day, Christopher Weatherill, Robert Powell, John Bunting, James Wills, Anthony Morris, Nathaniel Ible, John Clarke.

Upon the Complaynt of Anthony Tompkins Matthias Vanderhoyden, William Cole and Cornelius Bom, upon the Accompt of themselves and the rest of the Fraighters or owners of the Goods late Cast on Shore in the Sloope Beaverwick, By Indictment against John Moll, Master of the said Sloope and Symon Burden and John Vanderlenden Marriners therein.

The Indictment found by the Grand Jury.

The Jury for Tryall Returned and Attested   Thomas Mathewes, John Woolston, senr., Thomas Bartin, Seth Smith, Henry Grubb, James Hill, John Hollinshead, Isaac Marriott, John Budd, Thomas Gladwin, Richard Love, Thomas Potts.

The said John Moll, Symon Burden and John Vanderlenden Arraigned, upon the Indictment And particularly plead Not Guilty and referre themselves to God and the Countrey for Tryall.

Matthias Vanderhoyden being Attested, Averres that the Goods delivered on Board the aforesaid Sloope to the best of his Judgment might amount to Six Hundred pounds.

The Prisoners confesse that they hid and secured parte of the Goods, after the Sloope run a Shore, and something thereof they brought away, as each of them a Blankett, Seaventy Eight Gilders and Six Stivers in Wampam, each of them a Gun, and one black hatt and a white hatt.

And alsoe confesse they opened a Chest, but say they did not breake any open, but acknowledge they opened it with a Key of their owne, and that they did take out some things, but say they put them in againe.

The Proofe of the Indictment insisted upon; That they run the Sloope a Shore Carelessly and negligently, prooved by their owne confession, that is to say, both Symon Burden and John Vanderlenden, say the Wind and Weather was well enough, only they Sayled too neare the Shore.

Alsoe proved they did hide and secure parte of the goods and Merchandize and opened some Chests and tooke some things forth and brought some things away; And alsoe their intent to secure and Convert the Goods and Merchandize to their owne use appeares by their publique reporting at Burlington that all was lost, when they had before seized and Secured a Considerable parte thereof, And afterwards hyre a Sloope to bring them to Chrisparus Harmons without acquainting the owners therewith.

John Vanderlenden confesseth hee did hide the wampam before mentioned under the Sayles which was left on Shore, which seems to appeare otherwise; For that Walter Pumphary on his Attestation Averres that when hee and the rest came to the place where the Goods were on Shore, they had occasion to remove the aforesaid Sayles, but found noe wampam there, [32 1684]   And further Averrs that the said Vanderlenden did never discover that hee had the wampam untill hee the said Walter was speaking of the danger of Concealeing it.

The said John Moll, Symon Burden and John Vanderlenden being asked the reason why they burned some Letters, as was Testifyed by Elizabeth Stacy, all Denye it: And John Moll denyes that hee snatcht any paper from the said Elizabeth Stacy, or that hee or any of them said that the Letters or writings signifyed nothing now they were cast, away. They alsoe denye that they told the said Elizabeth, or that any of them said, after they were run aground that all the Goods they could save were their owne. Whereupon the said Elizabeth Stacy was called and againe Attested it before them in the Court.

The Jury (after some tyme of Consideration) bring in their Verdict as followes, Vizt, That after the Sloope was Run a Ground, the within mentioned did enter into a Combination to defraud the owners of part of the Goods, which now being proved against them, Wee finde them Guilty, by concealing and secureing to themselves the aforesaid Goods after they had brought them on shore, and for a satisfaction to the owners in what of the said Goods is wanting they shall restore double the vallew thereof.

Att a Speciall Court called and held upon the request and at the suite of Griffith Jones against Thomas Potts at Burlington the 26th of the 11th Moneth 1684. Robert Stacy, William Biddle, Robert Dimsdale, Thomas Gardner and John Goslinge Justices present.

Griffith Jones Plaintiff Thomas Potts Defendant an Action of the Case. Plaintiff Declares, and the plaintiff and Defendant referre the matter to the Bench without a Jury. The Sumes declared for are 22l. 14s. 6d. on bond and 18l. 18s. 4d. on accompt which the defendant acknowledges in Court And the Interest for the Summe by bond 2l. 03s. 10d. Total is 43l. 16s. 08d. For which Summe the Court give Judgment with Costs of Suite. And for Execution, It is ordered by the Court that the Sheriffe serve Execution the 27th Instant upon the Personall and Reall Estate of the Defendant And that the Leather and Goods shall within three Moneths next be appraised by two honest substantiall men of the neighbourhood to be appointed by the Magistrates soe farre as to make up the aforesaid Debt and Costs of suite; And in case the said personall Estate shall not be by the same appraisure sufficient to discharge the same, Then the Reall Estate of the said Defendant to make up the same to be paid within Three Moneths next.

William Budd Plaintiff Thomas Potts Defendant Action case. At the Court above Thomas Potts appeares to the Action of William Budd and acknowledges the Debt of 19l. 15s. 8d. to the said William Budd due.

[33 1684] Att the Court held at Burlington the 20th of the 12th Moneth 1684. Thomas Ollive Governour Robert Stacy, Thomas Gardner, Robert Dimsdale, John Gosling Justices present. The jury Returned Richard Basnett, William Myers, William Brightwen, Percifall Towle, Wil-

liam Clarke, John Hollinshead, Richard Love, William Budd, John Budd, Thomas Gladwin, William Wood, Walter Pumphary, John Woolston.

Anne Clarke Widdowe against John Dewsbury   Action of case   Rests.

Governour Ollive against Thomas Potts   Action of Case   Rests.

Thomas Terry to answer the Complaynt of John Walker, Terry bound by Recognizance to Answer. Walker proceeds not against him   rests.

Thomas Revell against Thomas Potts   Action debt   Rests.

William Budd against Thomas Potts   Action of case   Rests.

Robert Stacy against Jonathan Stephenson and Mary his wife   declaration drawne etc. The Summe due is 3l. 11s. Jonathan promises to pay 540 foot plank in a Moneth next and the rest in the 2d Moneth next with costs of Suite.

Thomas Potts against Thomas Litchfield   an Action of case, warrant not served.

John Newman to appear on the Complaynt of Thomas Gardner, bound by Recognizance to answer, hee appeares not and forfeits.

Roger Pinnick and Thomas Fowler to Answer the Complaynt of Henry Patrick   An Indictment Fyled against them, To which Pinnick and Fowler plead not guilty, and referre themselves to God and the Country. The Court require of the Prisoners, whether they are sorry for their fault: To which they reply they are sorry. The Court alsoe require of the Prisoners, whether they will ask the Master forgivenesse, or not, before the Jury goe togeather: and wayt a while for their answer, they appeare a while unwilling to ask forgivenesse, but at last, they both desire the Master may forgive them, and that the Jury may be withdrawne, And the master forgiveing them, and assenting thereunto the Jury is withdrawne And the Prisoners cleared by Proclamation paying their Fees.

Daniell Wills, senr. makes Application to the Court for his proportion of Meadowe to make up his quantity after the rate of 5 Acres per hundred. Ordered by the Court that Daniell Wills have his quantity of Meadowe.

[34 1684/5] Att the Court held at Burlington the 10th 1st Moneth 1684/5. Governor Ollive   Robert Dimsdale, Daniell Wills, Thomas Gardner, Francis Collins, Elias Farre   Justices present. The Jury   Richard Basnett, John Shin, Isaac Marriott, Daniell Leeds, Joseph Blowers, John Long, George Elkington, William Myers, William Peachee, John Ogbourne. James Wills, James Hill, Thomas Gladwin, Anthony Morris, William Budd, William Clarke, William Peachee, George Elkington, Anthony Morris, Joseph Blowers not appearing fyned 3s. a peece.

Richard Lawrence plaintiff   William Warner Defendant   Richard Lawrence versus William Warner   Action Debt.

Anne Clarke Widdowe   versus John Dewsbury   Action Case   agreed and withdrawne.

John Newman Peter Jenings and John Flockna to answer Our Lord the

King upon the forfeiture of their Recognizance. They submitt to the Bench and desire the Jury may be withdrawne. The Jury withdrawne and the Bench understanding their non appeareing was through a mistake in the day the Action remitted paying the Court Fees.

Peter Jenings and John Flockna versus John Newman an Action debt rests.

Thomas Gardner by his verball complaynt against John Newman for his abuse of Authority. John Newman Submitts to the Bench and desires the Jury may be withdrawne. Thomas Gardner and alsoe the Bench remitt the offence and withdrawe the Jury Newman paying Court Fees.

Susanna Budd on the behalfe of Thomas Budd her Husband Complaynes of Thomas Bowman for his Felling wood and molesting them in their Towne Lott on Lessa Poynt syde. Whereupon the Court give Thomas Bowman a discharge from molesting any person or persons who have Land Legally Surveyed to them on Lessa Poynt.

21st 2 Mo. 1685 Att a speciall Court called on the Accompt and request of Luke Watson [14] Defendant at the Suite and Complaint of Thomas Taylor Trustee on the behalfe of Charles Jones Merchant and Company. Governour Ollive Daniell Wills senr., Thomas Gardner Justices present. Jury Summoned and Empanelled James Budd, Richard Basnett, John Budd, Thomas Mathewes, Martin Hoult, Richard Woodnutt, James Wills, Thomas Gladwin, Thomas French, Richard Love, Anthony Morris, James Hill. Thomas Taylor plaintiff Luke Watson defendant Plaintiff and Defendant agree and Court withdrawne.

Att the Court held the 8th 3 moneth 1685. Governour Ollive Robert Stacy, William Biddle, Elias Farre, Robert Dimsdale, Thomas Gardner, Daniel Wills Justices present. Grand Jury Percivall Towle, John Day, Samuell Anderson, Daniel Leeds, Thomas Butcher, Thomas Harding, John Payne, Bernard Devonish, John Woolman, Isaac Marriott, William Peachee, Thomas Gardner junr., Thomas Snowden. Petty Jury John Boarton, Robert Young, Thomas Bartin, John Shin senr., John Woolston senr., John Haynes, Henry Grubb, Seth Smith, Thomas Gladwin, Thomas French, Thomas Scholey.

William Jeanes and John Keene on Indictment. The Grand Jury finde the Bill. William Jeanes pleads not guilty and referres himselfe to God and the Kings Lawfull subjects. John Keene pleads guilty and submitts to the Bench. Evidences against Jeanes William Edwards, John Gosling, John Budd, Richard Davisse who prove the matter of Fact in the Indictment and the Jury finde them Guilty. And the Bench and Jury agree on this Judgment following which is pronounced. That whereas the Jury have found thee William Jeanes Guilty of the Indictment, wee doe therefore agree and appoint that thou shalt be forthwith sent from hence and shalt be stript from thy wast upwards to thy

---

[14] Probably Luke Watson, a justice of the Sussex County Court, in Delaware, or his son. See C. H. B. Turner, *Some Records of Sussex County, Delaware* (Phila. 1909), 40, 82, 116, 123.

naked body and whipt till thy body be bloody from the house of Henry Grubbs in Burlington to the market place, and back againe from the market place to the said house of Henry Grubb not exceeding Thirty stripes and alsoe finde Sureties for thy goode behaviour. [35 1685] And John Keene who referred himselfe to the Bench Fyned Five pounds the Court charges included therein, and to finde suretyes of the good behaviour, James Budd and James Hill to become bound for him.

Robert Stacy versus Jonathan Stephenson. The Court grant Judgment against the defendant for the Summe of 3l. 11s. and Costs of suite hee haveing fayled in performance of his promise heretofore made in Court.

Gerrardus Wessells by Thomas Litchfield his Attourney Complaynes against John Stephens in an Action of Debt, noe returne.

John Ithell desires a Caveat may be entered against Recording of 15 Acres of Meadowe in Steeles branch to John Reading. The Court order John Ithell and John Reading to appeare before 2 Commissioners in the 3d Tenth, and if the Commissioners agree them not: Then both to appeare next Court.

William Hunt versus John Renshawe   action of the Case   agreed and withdrawne.

Michael Huffe plaintiff versus Robert Pearson defendant   action case agreed and withdrawne.

Mordecay Bowden plaintiff versus Charles Pickering defendant   agreed and withdrawne.

John Chamnis plaintiff versus John Cornish defendant neither plaintiff nor defendant appeare.

William Budd requires Judgment and Execution against Thomas Potts for the Debt of 19l. 15s. 08d. and it's granted.

Att the Court held 26th 3d Mo. 1685.

Robert Wade by Thomas Revell his Attourney Complaynt against Joseph Helmsley in an Action of the Case   Defendant appeares not   rests.

John Hollinshead versus Henry Jacobs upon Attachment Defendant appeares not   John Wills Attested proves the Bill declared for. The goods Attached being one payre oxen, one Bull, 3 milch Cowes, 2 yearlings and 2 Calves called forfeit.

John Chamnis versus John Cornish, the plaintiff appeares not   The Defendant desires a nonsuite and it's granted, and the Defendant promises that if the Plaintiff will chuse a man, hee will chuse another to Arbitrate the matter in difference and what they two finde the Defendant indebted to the Plaintiff, hee the said Defendant will forthwith pay it, And the Defendant Promises to pay the suite charges.

John Reeves and Thomas Cleverley upon Indictment on the Complaynt of Governour Ollive. Grand Jury   William Peachee, Thomas Lambert, John Lambert, Thomas Barton, Anthony Morris, John Payne, William Bates, Thomas French, Daniel Leeds, Robert Hudson, William Hunt, William

Fleetwood, William Wood. The Bill of Indictment not found The said Reeves and Cleverley Continue bound to the next Court.

Rangers Chosen Freedome Leppincoate and John Shin Junr.

[36 1685] Burlington Court 8th 6th Moneth 1685. Thomas Ollive Governour Robert Stacy, Robert Dimsdale, Daniell Wills, Francis Davenport, William Peachee, Thomas Gardner, James Budd, George Hutcheson Justices Present.

A Jury Summoned and appeared but there being noe businesse for them were not Attested.

The Sheriffe upon the Returne of the Execution against Thomas Potts at Suite of Griffith Jones declares the Execution is discharged.

Upon the Returne of the Execution against John Allen at suite of Robert Carter the Sheriff hath served the same and hath certaine goods in Custody, and hath alsoe the Body of the said Allen in Execution.

John Allen for his Threatning the Sheriffe Fyned 40s. but mitigated to 10s. provided hee finde Sureties for the good behaviour: George Hutcheson and the Sheriffe to be bound for his good behaviour.

Henry Grubb Plaintiff Robert Pearce Defendant Action Case agreed and withdrawne Declaration drawne and Copy.

Thomas Mathews Complaynes on Summones against Robert Turner.

Thomas Budd Plaintiff Walter Pumphary Defendant Action Debt agreed and withdrawne Declaration drawne and Copy.

Walter Reeves Complaynes on Summones against Thomas Howell, Plaintiff appeares not, and therefore at the request of the defendant a Non suite is granted against the Plaintiff.

Robert Wade Plaintiff Joseph Helmsley Defendant Plaintiff declares and produced the Bill and protest in Court the Action Continued for that the Defendant appeares not. The Bill and protest proved in Court.

John Haynes Attested at this Court sayth, That on the 6th Instant hee being neare the house of Walter Reeves sawe an Indian goe into the said Reeves house with an Empty Bottle and that hee sawe the same Indian returne from thence in halfe a quarter of an Hower with the same Bottle filled with Rum: And further that hee hath heard that the said Walter Reeves hath threatned such as should discover him for selling Rum to the Indians. Bernard Devonish alsoe Attested sayth That an Indian went with an Empty Bottle from his House and said hee could have Rum at Walter Reeves house, and that the same Indian presently returned back againe with the Bottle filled with Rum (as the said Bernard perceived by his smelling thereat) and that the said Indian at his returne had Walter Reeves wife hatt on his head and her Coat on his Shoulder in regard it rayned. Walter Reeves called to Answer and give Accompt why the boards hee Cutt on the Publick Land and which are seized on shall not be Condemned to the Publick Use. To all which premisses the Court order said Walter to be Summoned to appeare next Court.

John Anderson and Peter Erickson To be Summoned to be Summoned to appear next Court to show their Right to certain Loggs Seized, and lyeing at or neare Redbanck. Summoned alsoe—Daniell Linzey to appear next Court to answer what the Court shall object against him.

[37 1685] on the Complaynt of Thomas French the Court order that William Biddle be Summoned to appear next Court.

Alsoe Summoned William Cooper junr. to appeare next Court to answer what shall be objected against him.

Ordered per Court That Robert Turner may take up 500 Acres of Land which George Goldsmith tooke up: George Goldsmith haveing by writing satisfyed the Court that hee holds the Land on the Accompt of the said Robert Turner.

Burlington Court held the 4th of the 7th moneth 1685. Walter Reeves called 3 tymes uppon the Accompt of certaine Loggs seized: That hee might prove his Tytle to them, and hee appeares not, whereupon the Loggs are Condemned to the Publique Use.

John Anderson and Peter Errickson called on the same Accompt ordered that the land they clayme be measured that it may be known whether the Timber be Cutt on their land or not.

[*Fyned 10s.*] Daniel Linzey called on the same Accompt sayth hee hath had the Land whereon hee Cutt Timber Seaven yeares in quiet possession and hee desires to purchase it: ordered that the land be measured alsoe And Daniell Fyned 10s. for his unhansome language in Court.

Thomas French versus William Biddle on Summons Agreed by plaintiff and Defendant to referre the matter being about the possession of Land, to four men to be chosen between them if they agree it not, the Arbitrators to chuse an Umpire.

William Cooper junr. to appeare on Summons about the Indian, the Summons not given by the Sheriffe, Summons yet in his hand.

Thomas Revell Labourer Complaynt against Walter Pumphary Action of Battery the Warrant not served: Thomas Revell desires Walter may be bound to the Peace, and deposeth he is afraid of bodily harme from said Walter, whereupon Walter with James Budd and Daniel Wills senr. hee is bound to his good behaviour and his appearance next Court to answer Thomas Revell.

Thomas Potts Fyled a Bill of Indictment Against Benjamin Wheat Sheriffe On the behalfe of the King Against next Court.

Caleb Carman and John Carmens Indictment for our Lord the King against Evan Davids Indictment Fyled: A Summons hath been sent to Davis, but hee disobeyed it. Edward Pyner Attested in Court deposeth That about the second moneth last hee being at the Plantation of said Evan Davis, the said Davis told this deponent that hee the said Davis had bought a fish of an

Indian cally [15] Nummy, and further that if this Deponent would goe with him to it, hee should have a share thereof whereupon this deponent went with said Davis, and comeing to the said Fish sayth it was a whale Fish and that hee sawe an Iron (with warp thereat) in the said whale Fish which Iron and warp the said deponent knowing them [38 1685] to belong to said Caleb Carman and Company told the said Davis thereof, who then swore if there was an Iron it was the better for himselfe. Thereupon the said Deponent would medle noe further therewith: But sayth the said Davis seized upon the said whale Fish and Tackling, and hid the same from said Carmans and Company.

Whereupon Caleb Carman in open Court binding himselfe in the Summe of 40l. to presente the said Complaynt A warrant was issued forth impowering Alexander Humfreys to be deputy Sheriffe or Undersheriffe, and to take into Custody the body of said Evan Davis and him to secure and bring to Burlington with all Convenient Speed to answer the said Indictment and such other things as shall be objected against him, and alsoe to answer for his Contempt of Authority: And the said Alexander is by said warrant impowered to take any to his assistance: And said Alexander is alsoe thereby required to Take Abraham Weston and his wife and their children and bring them up to Burlington to Answer such things as shall be objected against them, wherein hee is alsoe required to Summons Margrett the servant of said Davis to come up to Testifye what shee knowes in the premisses, or any others that hee shall know or heare of that can give information concerning the said Westons abuse of the Children.

[*Order for 3d tenth for their Towne and Towne Bounds*] Ordered by the Court That the Freeholders within the third Tenth in the Province aforesaid shall or may take up and lay forth 2000 Acres of Land for their Towne Bounds and 400 Acres for their Towne, And that each person and persons who are allready seated in the said tenth shall or may take up their respective proportions thereof according to their purchase, And that every such purchaser shall take forth a warrant for the takeing up of his particular proportion thereof, which is to be returnable at the next Court following the Survey thereof, and is to be Accompted as parte of their share or quantity of Land to them apperteyning within the said Tenth: of which order above said all persons concerned in the said third tenth are required to take notice, and to forbear to offer or make any obstruction or disturbance in the said premisses.

Burlington Court the 3d 9th moneth 1685. [*John Skene Deputy Governour Skene*] [16] The Court Called: And then John Skene came into Court and produced his Deputation or Commission, for Deputy Governour of the Province from Edward Byllinge, which was Read: And immediately after Reading the same, the said John Skene required the Magistrates Then upon

[15] Called.
[16] Written along the margin, in a different hand.

the Bench to forbeare further Acting, whereupon Thomas Ollive (the former Governour and Magistrates left the Bench: And by the order of the said John Skene the Court adjourned to the Tenth hower in the Forenoone of the next day.

Actions Depending, for the said Court etc.
Onesiphorus Austwick versus Walter Pumphary: on Indictment.
Walter Pumphary versus Godfrey Hancock   Action Case   withdrawne.
Thomas Potts versus Benjamin Wheaton   Indictment.
Walter Pumphary versus Isaac Marriott   Action Case   withdrawne.
James Budd versus Edward Randall   Action Debt.
John Ogbourne versus Joseph Blowers   Action Debt   withdrawne.
[39 1685] Mathew Allen versus John Davison   Action Debt.
John Hollinshead versus Samuell Abett.
John Allen   John Gray   Action Case.
Peter Erickson versus Thomas Mathewes   Action   Trover.
Joanna Pryor versus Henry Parker   Action Debt.
John Ithell versus Thomas Bishop and John Browne.
Nothing proceeded in the Court aforesaid.

    Burlington Court held the 15th 10th Moneth 1685. John Skene Deputy Governour Present. The Court called in this Forme following. After proclamation. All Persons that have beene Summoned to appeare or have any business at the Court held here this day for our Lord King James the Second of Great Brittaine and France and Ireland, by the power and Authority of Edward Bylling (Governour and Chiefe Proprietour [17] of this Province) Derived from the King are required to drawe neare and Give Attendance and they shall be heard.

    Then—These are in the name and Authority of the King, and of Edward Byllinge Governour and Proprietour of this Province, strictly to charge and Command all persons to keep silence in the Court: And to forbear offering any disturbance, or to take Liberty of speech without Lycence from the Bench, upon payne of being Fyned.

    James Budd, George Hutcheson, William Biddle, Richard Guy, Elias Farre, Thomas Gardner   Magistrates Present. The Grand Jury   William Peachee, John Daye, Robert Young, Thomas Barton, Eleazer Fenton, Bernard Devonish, Thomas Butcher, John Woolston senr., John Payne, John Shin, John Browne, Samuell Lovett, Christopher Weatherill. The Petty Jury Daniell Wills, Isaac Marriott, William Budd, John Budd, James Wills, Charles Read, Peter Basse, Symon Charles, John Hollinshead, John Lambert, James Satterthwayt, George Elkington.

    Thomas Potts versus Benjamin Wheat   on Indictment   The Grand Jury finde the Bill of Complaynt. The Complaynt being that Benjamin when Sheriffe tooke 4l. of Thomas Potts for Serveing the Execution and charges of

[17] "Proprietor" in MS.

1685]   THE BURLINGTON COURT BOOK   49

Execution [40 1685] in the Suite of Griffith Jones the Debt being 43l. 16s. 8d. which Thomas Compleyned of as unlawfull: The Petty Jury bring in their Verdict for the Defendant   only Robert Stacy was Evidence that Thomas was occasion of bringing charge on himself.

James Satterthwayt   William Satterthwayt Presented by the Grand Jury for entering on other persons Land Surveyed, and Cutting Timber without leave.

London Bridge also presented by them being spoyled by Hoggs.

George Hutcheson versus John Allen   withdrawne.

William Hunter versus Samuell Oldale   Withdrawne.

Thomas French versus Richard Basnett   Plaintiff (for not presenting his Action against the Defendant at the request of the defendant, is nonsuited.

Henry Parker Verbally Complaynes against Benjamin Wheat for stryking him the said Complaynant when hee the said Benjamin was Sheriffe after Arrest: Both referre themselves to the Bench. Benjamin Confest hee struck the Complaynant and by the Bench Fyned 10s.

James Budd versus Edward Randall   At request of the Defendant Rests till next Court by Consent of the Plaintiff.

Robert Wade versus Joseph Helmsley   rests.

Walter Pumphary versus Henry Bowman   Action Case   Rests.

Constables Chosen   John Budd High Constable, Joshua Eley for Falls, John Snowden Mansfield, John Butcher Birch Creek, Lawrence Morris and Thomas Gladwyn Burlington, John Wills John Payne   Rancokus.

Overseers for Highways   1st Tenth   Robert Stacy, Robert Young, John Daye. 2d Tenth   Richard Basnett, Symon Charles, John Boarton. Rangers 1st and 2d Tenth Eleazer Fenton, John Shin junr., Godfrey Hancock junr. Ranger and Overseer for preserveing Timber from upper end of 3d Tenth to Cape May (Salem excepted) Thomas Mathews.

Ordered   That a Court bee held every first Fryday (or 6th day) of every Moneth at Burlington, besides the Quarterly Courts.

Att a Court held the 1st day of the 11th Moneth 1685. Present there John Skene Deputy Governour   George Hutcheson, Francis Davenport, James Budd, William Biddle, Thomas Gardner, Elias Farre   Magistrates.

The Jury   Thomas Budd, Thomas Gilberthorpe, X William Beard, Robert Wilson, Mathew Watson, X Benjamin Wheat, Daniell Leeds, John Pancost, James Wills, John Chamnis, John Daye, John Crosby, Thomas Ollive, John Woolston senr. Daniell Wills objected against. William Budd objected against. William Beard and Benjamin Wheat appeared not.

Thomas French Plaintiff   Richard Basnett Defendant   on Tresspasse. The Case opened, the Defendant requires the Plaintiff to make out his Tytle to the Land in question. Two deeds of the Plaintiffs one from John Woolston senr., the other from Anthony Morris, shewing a Tytle to such a quantity of land as is in question. The Defendant Declares his Right to the Quantity of

Land in question in the London Tenth by virtue of his purchase from Isaac Marriott. Witnesses   Daniell Wills, Daniell Leeds, Bernard Devonish, Mathew Allen.

[41 1685]   Daniell Wills Attested Sayth Thomas French declared to him when hee required a warrant for takeing up the Land, That hee the said Thomas had given bond for building in Legall tyme to Thomas Budd And therefor the said Daniell knowing the said bond to be forfeit, Therefore hee gave a warrant to the Defendant for the Land.

Daniell Leeds Attested, Sayth hee received a warrant from Commissioners (then being) for laying forth the Land in question to the Defendant and accordingly did lay it forth.

Bernard Devonish Attested Sayth that Thomas Budd and Thomas Gardner was content to take the Plaintiffs Engagement for building according to Lawe instead of a bond, And that the said Bernard and Mathew Allen were Evidences to it.

Mathew Allen Attested Sayth the same with Bernard as above, and further Sayth that as for building within 6 Monethes after the Engagement, the said Plaintiff did begin, and that the building according to the declaration is ready. Juryes Verdict   The Jury finde for the Defendant and give him his Costs of suite and 2d. Dammages.

Arthur Cooke and Company versus William Cole   Action Debt.

Court Dissolved, the next Court to be the quarterly Court being the 20th of 12th Mo. next.

The Court of Session at Burlington held the 20th of 12th Mo. 85 and by adjournment continued to the 22d of the same. John Skene deputy Governour present   George Hutcheson, James Budd, William Biddle, Thomas Gardner, Francis Davenport, Francis Collins   Magistrates.

Robert Wade Plaintiff   Joseph Helmsley Defendant   Action Case Defendant appeares not   Robert Stacy Attested Sayth that Joseph Helmsley promised to pay the Plaintiff 10l. English money by Bill in England, being the debt declared for.

William Biddle and George Hutcheson upon the Bench alsoe averre that they have heard the same summe acknowledged to be due from the Defendant as aforesaid.

Where upon at the request of the Plaintiff, the Bench give Judgment for the Plaintiff against the said Defendant for the said Debt of Tenne pounds and Twenty Five pounds per cent dammages with Costs of suite: And the Defendant having noe personall Estate to Levy the same upon, The Court order the Plaintiff 250 Acres of the Defendants land in the Province to hold to the Plaintiff his heires and Assignes forever and to be Levyed by Execution upon the share of Land of the said Defendant in this Province with all mines mineralls woods fishings hawkings huntings and fowlings royaltyes forts franchises harbours profitts Comodities [?] and app[urtenances?] belonging.

James Budd plaintiff Edward Randall defendant Action Debt. The Jury Robert Stacy, Jonathan Wood, John Bunting, John Horner, Bernard Devonish, William Evans, Robert Styles, John Boarton, Nathaniell West, John Browne, Richard Heritage, John Hollinshead.

The Deed or Indenture of agreement betweene Plaintiff and Defendant Read and proved and alsoe the bond of Two Hundred pounds from the Defendant to the Plaintiff for performance alsoe read and proved.

Mary Budd, Attested sayth that shee being at London before the Defendant came away shee was told by an honest woman there who had some concerne amongst the Potters at London that she feared the Pott worke here would come to nothing for that the said Defendant Randall and the other persons who were to come to manage the same worke had not skill to perfect it.

[42 1685] William Winn, Attested sayth that hee can finde noe Clay in the Country that will make white ware, And further sayth that Edward Randall the Defendant is as good a work man as James Budd the Plaintiff can finde in England.

The Jury bring in this determination (vizt) wee can Give noe fynall Determination of the matter untill materialls requisite shall come from England to prove the skill of the Defendant. Whereupon the Bench order that the said Edward Randall mind the Concerne of the said James Budd untill fitt materialls be sent for from such place in England as the said Edward Randall shall appoint.

James Harrison plaintiff John Allen Defendant Action case. The declaration Read for 6500 good well burnt bricks in Consideration of Two Negroes The Defendant Confesses Judgment Luke Brunsley Attested, sayth that John Allen himselfe made the bargaine in the declaration mentioned, but that the said Allen did say the bargaine was on his and Thomas Bowmans Accompt. Samuell Bunting, Attested sayth hee was not by when the bargaine was made but heard the paper read of the bargaine and that plaintiff and defendant agreed thereto: Judgment Awarded.

Walter Pumphary Plaintiff Henry Bowman Defendant The Action called but noe determination made in it.

[Indictment] Daniell Howell and Mordecay Howell Indicted for the King on the Complaynt of William Cooper.

Charles Millard and Anne the reputed wife of Thomas Wright Indicted for the King on the Complaynt of Francis Davenport [*Anne appeares not*].

The Grand Jury Symon Charles, Thomas French, Samuell Cole, William Alberson, Thomas Farnsworth, John Hooton, John Key, Anthony Woodhouse, Walter Pumphary, Richard Love, Thomas Potts, John Chamnis, William Black Attested The Bills of Indictment found both Billa vera.

The Prisoners Arraigned, and plead not guilty to the Indictment, and referre themselves to God and the Countrey. The Traverse Jury Robert Stacy, John Buntinge, Bernard Devonish, William Evans, William Myers,

John Curtis, Robert Styles, John Boarton, Nathaniell West, John Browne, Richard Heritage, John Hollinshead   Attested.

Joseph Cooper and Daniell Cooper   Evidence   Attested, Joseph sayth they found the great Sowe mentioned in the Indictment newly shott which was the Complaynants Sowe and that they found the gutts of another Swyne within lese then fower Polls from the other, both being warme, And that being a Snow Daniell Cooper followed the Track from the said Gutts untill hee overtooke Daniell Howell and Mordecay Howell, with the Hogg carrying him away.

Daniell Cooper sayth hee followed the said Daniell Howell and Mordecay Howell from the Gutts aforesaid, and when hee overtooke them hee saw them with the Hogg, and that they then threatened but yet they bid him come and see the Hogg, whereupon hee did, and sayth that the Hogg was unmarked.

Joseph further sayth hee beleeves if hee and his brother had not hollered one to the other they might have taken them in the Act killing the Hoggs.

[43 1685]   Daniell Cooper further sayth the said Daniell Howell and Mordecay Howell had each of them a Gun when hee overtooke them.

John Borrowes Attested by the Magistrates belowe declared that Daniell Howell and another that wrought with him brought in a Hogg and that the Eares were cutt of, and that as they were boyling a peece thereof Howells sister coming in to the house, they hid the Kettle or Pott from her.

Samuell Cole Attested sayth that hee did sell Thomas Howell fower Hoggs and about Twelve shoits. Thomas Channders Attested, but Evidences nothing materiall either way.

Verdict The Jury finde the Prisoners guilty of killing Hoggs Contrary to Lawe, And further say, they beleeve the said prisoners did kill the other, but in regard the Evidence is not cleare they know nothing of that.

The Jury therefore lay a Fyne of Five pounds for the King to bee by them paid, And that they shall be kept in Custody untill they pay the Fyne and finde Suretyes for the good behaviour, and alsoe pay all Charges of Court.

[*this taken the last of 11th Mo. 1685*]   Further John Ladd Attested before Thomas Thackeray a Magistrate belowe Sayth that Daniell Howell told this Deponent when they were at worke togeather that hee the said Daniell helpt his father Thomas Howell to kill Twelve Wild Hoggs and Bores that was not his owne. John Hugg   Mathew Medcolfe, Joseph Weds and Samuell Taylor being witnesses to the said Attestation.

Adjourned to the 22nd day.

Charles Millard brought to the Barre and Arraigned pleades not guilty and referres himselfe for Tryall to God and the Countrey.

The Traverse Jury   Robert Stacy, Bernard Devonish, William Myers, John Boarton, Nathaniel West, John Browne, John Hollinshead, Henry Grub, William Peachee, John Woolston senr., James Wills, Richard Bassnett.

The said Charles Confesses hee did help to dresse two white Hoggs one cropt on the Farre Eare, and the other Hogg unmarked, and that Anne the reputed wife of said Thomas Wright promised to stand betweene the said Millard and danger.

The Attestation of Mary Horsman taken before William Emley produced in Court and read.

Richard Harrison Attested sayth that Richard Berry (one of the partyes told him that said Charles Millard Shott Two Hoggs one marked as is mentioned of the first Hogg specified in the Indictment, and the other sandee which hee told not the markes of, and that the said Berry at the Comand of the said Anne in the Indictment mentioned did help to Carry the Hoggs to Thomas Wrights house to dresse them and said that the said Anne gave powder and Shott to said Charles to shoot the said Hoggs when they came neare the doore, And that Charles was unwilling to shoot at first. John Snowden Constable Attested saith that hee went to serve a warrant on Thomas Wright and said reputed wife of Thomas Wright, and that said Thomas Wright said the Justices are all fooles to send for him and that the Province stood in [44 1685] need of better Government, and that hee would not obey the warrant, and said Snowden went for another warrant; And when hee came again hee heard the said Anne say that one of the Hoggs they had killed was a white Hogg, cropt of Left eare and peece cutt out of the right. John Cripps Attested sayth the aforesaid Richard Berry said hee had found many Wild Hoggs in the woods and that Charles Millard had killed two Hoggs; And the said Berry bid the said Deponent come to Thomas Wrights and it might happen hee might eat some of his owne Hoggs, and when the said John Cripps went to Thomas Wrights hee asked for the Eare markes of the Hoggs and that the said Anne said a dogg had run away with them.

The Juryes Verdict The[y] finde the said Charles Guilty of hoggstealing. But Anne in the Indictment mentioned not appeareing they have nothing in charge.

Therefore they give their Verdict that the said Charles shall be tyed to a Cart and whipt upon his bare back from the house of John Cripps in Burlington to Henry Grubbs at the Townes Landing and shall receive thirty nyne stripes.

The Bench upon Consideration Mittigate the punishment to Twenty stripes the tyme to bee tomorrowe betwixt the howers of 9 and 11 in the forenoone of the same day.

Arthur Cooke and Company Plaintiffs against Thomas Bowman Defendant   Declaration Read but noe further proceedings is therein but referred to the next Court.

Next Court appointed 26th 1st mo. next.

Court held 26th 1st Mo. 1686   Deputy Governour   George Hutcheson, Andrew Robinson, William Biddle, James Budd, Thomas Gardner, Francis Davenport   Magistrates Present.

Daniell Howell plaintiff   John Ashton Defendant   Neither Plaintiff nor Defendant appeared   Continued.

Walter Pumphary Plaintiff   Henry Bowman Defendant   Plaintiff appeares and declaration read and the 20l. declared for proved paid by the Plaintiff But deferred this Court till Evidence be given it was paid on the Defendants Accompt.

Arthur Cooke and Company Plaintiffs   Thomas Bowman Defendant   The Plaintiffs appeare not.

Robert Gano plaintiff   Henry Tradway defendant.

Daniell Wills plaintiff   Robert Chinton defendant   withdrawne.

Edward Eglinton plaintiff   Peter Matson defendant   defendant appeares not   Rests.

Jury   Walter Pumphary, Symon Charles, William Myers, Thomas Gladwyn, Hinry Grub, John Boarton, Bernard Devonish, Thomas Raper, John Woolman, Daniell Leeds, John Snowden, Benjamin Holt.

[45 1686]   Att the Court held the 12th 3d Moneth 1686. The Governour Present   George Hutcheson president   William Biddle, Elias Farre, Andrew Robinson, Thomas Gardner, James Budd, Richard Guy, Mahlon Stacy, Richard Lawrence, George Deacon, Francis Davenport, Francis Collins Magistrates present.

The Grand Jury   Thomas Mathewes, Israell Helme, Martin Holt, Freedome Lippincote, William Brightwen, John Budd, Mordecay Bowden, Daniell Leeds, William Beard, Symon Charles, Christopher White, William Budd, Bernard Devonish Attested. The[y] Present London Bridge for being out of repayre.

Evan Davis by his and Daniell Englands bond bound to appeare at this Court to Answer our Lord the King on the Complaint of Caleb Carman and John Carman, Evan Davis appeares not: And forfeits his Recognizance.

Anne the Reputed wife of Thomas Wright upon the Indictment of Our Lord the King, on the Complaynt of Francis Davenport Appeares at this Court. The Grand Jury finde the Bill of Indictment And thereupon the Traverse Jury called.

The Traverse Jury   Pete Basse, Daniell Wills, senr., John Day, John Wood, Christopher Snowden, Isaac Marriott, John Hollinshead, John Pancost, Daniell Bacon, Samuell Cole, John Reading, Abraham Senior   Attested.

The said Anne pleads not guilty and referrs her tryall to God and the Countrey.

Evidences   Charles Millard his Confession at his Tryall Read.   Mary Horsman her Attestation taken before the Magistrates also read. John Cripps attestation at Millards Tryall also read: And the said John also appeares in Court and againe Attests the same. The Jury finde the said Anne Guilty of Receiveing and dressing Hoggs Contrary to a Lawe of this Province made for which they Fyne her five pounds, which is with the Concurrence of the Bench.

Thomas Wright the reputed Husband of said Anne for his abuse of John Snowden Constable, and his affront of Authority, Fyned Thirty shillings to the Constable for his charges and abuse, And also Fyned more to the Publique Thirty Shillings. Thomas being Demanded to pay the aforesaid Fynes or secure the same And hee refuseing the same, is Comitted.

John Stanbanck upon Indictment for our Lord the King on the Complaint of Maudlin Walter bound over to this Court appeares. The Grand Jury finde the Bill of Indictment, And the said Stanbanck called to the Barre pleads not Guilty and referres the Tryall to God and the Countrey.

The Traverse Jury last above Impannelled Attested. [46 1686] Evidence: Maudlin Walter Aged about Twelve yeares Attested Testyfyes to the Truth of the Indictment. Richard Russell Attested declares that the Evidence of Maudlin Walter formerly taken from her mouth and now read in Court, Testifying to the Truth of the Indictment was truly taken, And is the same that was then taken.

Hance Walter age about Eleaven yeares Attested sayth, The said Stanbanck did throw downe the said Maudlin Walter, in the house in the Indictment mentioned, And that hee also after heareing the said Maudlin Cry out aloud Severall tymes for helpe came to the windowe of the said house, And did then see the said Stanbanck lye upon the Belly of the said Maudlin with his Breeches downe, and his yard out, But did not see his yard in the said Maudlins Body.

George Lawrence aged about Twelve yeares Testifyes the truth thereof being also with the said Hance Walter.

The Sheriffe for bringing his Prisoner Stanbanck into Court without Irons Contrary to the Command of the Magistrates Fyned Five pounds.

The Jury bring in their Verdict and finde the said Stanbanck Guilty of severall misdemeanours and abuses in Attempting the Ravishment of the said Maudlin Walter.

And the Jury with the Concurrence of the Bench Conclude upon this Judgment which is pronounced by the President, as followes.

Whereas the said John Stanbanck hath beene Indicted, and hath pleaded not guilty and referred himselfe for Tryall to God and the Countrey; And whereas the Jury have found the said Stanbanck Guilty of severall Misdemeanours and abuses in Attempting the Ravishing of the said Maudlin Walter. The Judgment of the Court therefore is That the said John Stanbanck shall be whipt on his bare back at a Carts Tayle, and that hee shall have Thirty Nyne lashes well laid on, betwixt the howers of Nyne and Twelve upon the next Sixth day; And that the said Stanbanck shall pay all Court charges, and other charges expended and accrueing by meanes thereof; And alsoe that hee give bond of one Hundred pounds for his good behaviour dureing life: And that hee shall remayne Prisoner untill hee performe the same.

Edward Eglington against Peter Matson   Matson appeares not: Haveing refused to appeare.

Daniell Howell and Mordecay Howell appeare and desire to be dismist; but refuseing to pay the Court Charges and Fyne, are ordered to be bound to good behaviour unless they pay the same.

Arthur Cooke and Company against Thomas Bowman   James Budd ordered it to be withdrawne.

Court dissolved next Court to be the 8th of the 6th Moneth next.

[47 1686]   Att the Court held the 9th of the 6th Moneth 1686. The Governour present   George Hutcheson present   James Budd, Elias Farre, William Biddle, Thomas Gardner, Francis Davenport   Justices.

The Grand Jury Attested   Symon Charles, John Shin senr., John Pancost, Joshua Humfreys, Thomas Butcher, William Budd, William Atkinson, John Crosby, John Day, Thomas Barton, Robert Young, Isaac Marriott, John Woolston senr. The Traverse Jury   Godfrey Hancock, Richard Bassnett, William Hunt, Michael Newbold, Henry Grubb, John Boarton, John Hollinshead, Bernard Devonish, Martin Holt, Daniell Leeds, William Brightwen, Daniel Bacon.

Attorney Generall for the King Christopher Snowden.

James Wills by Recognizance Bound over to appeare at this Court, and Indictment Fyled on the behalfe of our Lord the King called and appeares.

The Evidence for the King Attested   Katherine Greene, Thomas Greene, William Myers, George Lambert, Mary Grubb, William Peachee, James Hill, Thomas Gladwyn.   The Grand Jury finde the Bill.

The Prisoner Arraigned: And to the Indictment pleads not guilty as to giving the woman Negro any blowes that occasioned her death, but sayth hee caused her to be buryed, not knowing that the Lawe required there should have beene an Inquest touching the cause of her death.

And for Tryall referres himself to God and the Countrey. whereupon the Traverse Jury above is Attested, the Prisoner objecting against none of them.

Katharine Greene Attested. Deposeth, that the Negro woman Servant being by said James Wills sent to be a while at the house of the said Katharine, in regard the said negro had some distemper upon her, that shee might have conference with a Negro that belongs to the said Katharine: The said Katharine found that the Negro woman of the said James had her back very sore, and that the Negro woman told her it was with Fum, fum, which is (beating) and that further shee the said Katharine found a small Scarr upon her Belly which was sore, which the Negro told her came on the account aforesaid, But sayth that shee did not perceive any blowes that in her judgment might be the cause of her death.

Thomas Greene Attested, Deposeth the same in substance.

William Myers Attested, deposeth that hee heard at a Considerable distance many blowes or stripes and walking onward as hee thought hee heard a Negro Cry out many tymes, and, soe heard stripes or lashes continued till hee gott home, and then he supposed it to be James Wills beating his Negro woman, and heard still many Lashes more and Crying out, untill hee was greevd and went into his owne house and shut the dore, and said to his wife oh! yond cruell man, and sayth hee beleeves hee heard full a hundred stripes or lashes, but did not see James Wills beat his Negro.

William Peachee Attested, sayth that hee with Thomas Gladwyn being in the Smithy of Thomas Gladwyn at worke and heareing severall stripes or lashings and one crying out, went forth, and sawe James Wills beat his Negro Servant and give her many stripes which greeved both him and Thomas Gladwyn, whereupon they went againe into the Smithy to worke.

[48 1686] Thomas Gladwyn, Attested deposeth to the same effect. James Hill, Attested sayth hee sawe the said James Wills Beat his said Negro and tye her hands, and hang her up, but that her feet reached the ground and might sustaine the weight of her body, but hee beleeves it was painfull to her and that hee (this deponent, tooke her downe, but sayth the Negro was soe stubborne and willfull that might well provoke any Master to use her sharply: But sayth hee sawe nothing done to the Negro that in his Judgment might be the cause of her death; But that hee this Deponent beleeves she was unsound.

The Jury bring in their verdict: And finde the said James Wills not guilty. But in regard it appeares the said Negro was unsound, it was a fault, that hee did not therefore be the more spareing; And for that hee buryed her without a Jury or Inquest: Therefore they appoint (with the approbation of the Bench) that hee pay all Court charges. which is assented to by the Bench.

James Wills cleared by Proclamation. paying the same.

Thomas French by appointment to appeare at this Court, on Indictment fyled on the behalfe of our Lord the King—called and appeares.

The Indictment found by the Grand Jury: The Prisoner called to the Barre and to the Indictment being read pleads not guilty, according to the Indictment But refuses Tryall and Excepts against Bench and Jury, refuseing tryall in the Province.

[*The traverse Jury being the same as in the last except only William Wood, is put in instead of John Boarton because John Boarton is one of the Generall Assembly.*] The Prisoner sayth his case is determined before hand. The Governour and Bench, Answer if hee can make it appeare by any of the Jury who are to be his Judges, or any thing to object against them, they shall be put by. But in regard hee makes noe such thing appeare, nor makes any particular objections of the Jury, then as aforesaid the[y] proceed to Tryall, and the Letter of the Prisoners to Governour and Councell whereby hee accuses and Impeaches them and the Generall Assembly of the Province, is shewed to the Prisoner which hee ownes, and thereupon it is read in open Court: The Governour and Bench in favour to the Prisoner desire him to waigh the same, and the nature of the Crime and to acknowledge it: which hee refuses: The Jury after goe togeather and bring in their verdict, And finde the Prisoner Guilty of Contempt of Authority, and propose it to the Bench that his fyne may not exceed Five pounds: The Prisoner being asked by the Bench if hee be satisfyed in the Juryes Verdict and proposall of: Hee answers hee cannot pay it if it was but Two pence. Whereupon the Bench Fyne him Tenne pounds to be Levyed on his Goods and Chattells forthwith.

Edward Eglington Complaynes against Peter Matson The Plaintiff appeares: the Defendant appeares not, and therefore this being the Third Court the Plaintiff hath Attended hee desires Judgment upon his declaration [*Judgment Awarded*] and is Awarded which is for 7l. 17s. 6d. only hee acknowledgeth the receipt of   And for the remainder being   and Costs of Suite, with   for his losse of tyme in coming about 30 myles four tymes and Attending three Courts, and his expences in the same as hee gives in his Bill is accepted and allowed: The Court appoint the Sheriffe to put his Bayle Bond in Execution against the said Matson for 40l. and to pay the aforesaid Judgment forth of the same.

John Allen and Mary his wife Complaynes against Walter Pumphary an Action of Tresspasse. The Complaynants appeare not; And forfeit their Recognizance   The defendant Walter appeares and produces a paper in Court: wherein the said Mary declares that what shee charged and accused the said Walter of, touching his reputation, is altogeather falce, and that shee is sorry shee had soe wronged him; The Bench heareing the same read, and alsoe Attested by sufficient witnesses to be the free Act and deed of the said Mary: Forthwith sent to bring her to the Court   Mary Allen brought to the Court And it manifestly appeareing the said Mary had taken a false Attestation before the Magistrates, against the said Walter: And thereby Caused him to be bound to appeare at the Court: And haveing framed a great and infamous Complaynt against Walter which tended to the reproach and Shame of the said Walter: And shee haveing indeavoured [49 1686] to subborne others to beare false witnesse against the said Walter: as appeares in Court; It is demanded whether shee be willing to referre her selfe to a Jury or Committ her selfe to the Judgment of the Bench: Shee Submitts to the Judgment of the Bench: The Bench give Judgment That the said Mary Allen bee forthwith taken and sett in the Pillory and there to stand halfe an hower, as a perjured person: And order the Recorder to signe and Seale a warrant to the Sheriffe for Execution accordingly: And to write a paper in Capitall Letters (A falce perjured infamous woman) to sett upon the Pillory with her.

[*John Allen and Richard Lundy*]   John Allen and Richard Lundy: Indicted, Allen made his escape out of Court and Flees: Richard Lundy called, appeares. The Indictment being by the Grand Jury found: And Richard Arraigned: Pleades Guilty: and submitts to the Judgment of the Bench: The Bench in regard of Richards ingenious confession, and upon the good report given of him, and finding hee was threatned and drawne in by Allen through feare, to marke the Cowe for which they are Indicted they Fyne him but Twenty Shillings: And Richard (paying the same) is Quit by Proclamation.

And a Warrant is signed and Sealed by the Recorder, by order of the Governour and Justices to seize and secure the Goods and Chattells in the possession of said Allen: Directed to the Sheriffe.

The next Court appointed to be held the 29th September next.

Att a Speciall Court held the 10th of the 7th Mo. 1686. Called upon the Speciall request of George Masters and John Parker in their respective Actions against Richard Bassnett. John Skene Governour George Hutcheson President William Biddle, Mahlon Stacy, Elias Farre Justices.

George Masters plaintiff Richard Bassnett defendant in an Action of Debt. The Jury Godfrey Hancock, Joseph Pope, Martin Holt, Benjamin Wheat, Thomas Gardner junr., James Wills, Henry Grubb, Seth Smith, John Langford, Richard Woodnutt, Abraham Senior, William Clark Attested.

The Bond of Richard Bassnett and Edward Greene to George Masters for 29l. 19s. 06d. owned in Court by Richard Bassnett to be his owne hand and Seale. A Certifficate Read under the Attestation of William Frampton and John King that the above named Edward Greene (the person bound with Richard Bassnett) was by them seene since the 14th of the 6th Moneth last past in the Territories of Pennsylvania.

The Jury finde for the Plaintiff and give him the Money due by said Bond.

Judgment is thereupon Awarded by the Court upon the bond soe farre as to indempnifye the Plaintiff his Debt Costs of suite and charges: And Execution made out accordingly.

Richard Burgesse versus Robert Dove Action case agreed.

[50 1686] John Parker Plaintiff Richard Bassnett defendant in an action of debt The same Jury in the last case also Attested in this.

The bond read of Richard Bassnett and Edward Greene to John Parker for 74l. 1s. 8d. and owned in Court by Richard Bassnett to be his owne hand and seale: And alsoe upon the Certificate Attested by William Frampton and John King in the aforesaid Tryall.

The Jury finde for the Plaintiff and give him the money due by the said bond. And Judgment is thereupon Awarded by the Court upon the bond soe Farre as to indempnifye the Plaintiff his debt, Costs of suite and charges.

Upon the Complaynt and Petition of Thomas Hutchinson on the behalfe of Edward Bylling, Against Thomas Pearsons Executor.

The Court order that the money in the hands of George Hutcheson for Land by the Attourney of Thomas Pearsons Executor bee Legally Seized and Secured on the behalfe of Edward Bylling; And that all other moneyes in the hands of others for Such Lands Sold by the said Attourney of Thomas Pearsons Executor be alsoe Seized and secured on the behalfe of Edward Bylling untill the said Executor of Thomas Pearson can make appeare the payment for the said Land to Edward Bylling.

Att the Court held at Burlington the 6th of the 8th Moneth 1686 by adjournment from the 29th 7ber last.

Then Present   John Skene, Governour   Elias Farr, James Budd, Thomas Gardner   Justices.

Jury Summoned   Daniell Wills Senr., Samuell Andrews, William Hunter, Bernard Devonish, Thomas Curtis, Thomas Folke, Thomas Harding, John Hooton, Abraham Hewlings, Henry Grubb, John Bunting, Joseph Pope Attested in the Action betweene John Henryes and Thomas Wright his Attourney versus John Chamnis. William Brightwen, William Evans, William Budd   Sumoned but appeared not.

John Allen upon the Indictment of him and Richard Lundy, for felloniously markeing and keeping the Cowe, Confesses hee is guilty and Submitts to the Bench; The Court Fyne him the said Allen 40s. And require him to give security for his good behaviour and give him one weekes tyme to procure the same.

John Henryes and Thomas Wright his Attorney versus John Chamnis Action of the Case. John Henries Bill for 8l. 16s. produced and proved being owned by said John Chamnis: And John Chamnis produced an order of said Henries in Court dated first April 1683 for said Chamnis to pay the remainder of the money due to him the said Henries, unto Joseph Parker: And alsoe said Chamnis then produced said Joseph Parkers receipt in Court dated 27th April 1683 for the whole debt declared for: which receipt being shewed to Thomas Ollive and William Myers, who being Attested in Court declare that they have been acquainted with the said Joseph Parkers hand writing, And doe depose they verily beleeve the said receipt and Joseph Parkers name thereto to be the hand writing of Joseph Parker. Thereupon the Jury finde for the Defendant and give him his charge and Costs Suite.

[51 1686]   Action Case   Henry Parker versus Thomas Wright   Rests.

Henry Parker versus John Naylor   Action of Slander. The Plaintiff declares not, and called in Court to prosecute his Action which hee not doeing, at the request of the Defendant a non Suite called against the plaintiff.

Action Case   Henry Parker versus Robert Pearsey   Rests.

Seth Smith versus Godfrey Hancock Junr.   rests.

Action Trespasse   Michaell Huff versus Henry Parker   rests.

James Hill, Sheriffe versus Peter Matson   rests.

Action Debt   Joseph Knight versus Ralph Milner   case withdrawne.

[*Petition*]   Thomas Bowman came into Court, And desired to have his bookes and Concernes into his hands and Custody: The Governour thereupon declared, that as hee had (in the tyme of the said Thomas his weaknesse, or Lunatick State) Seized what hee could finde appertayning to the said Thomas Bowman, for secureing the same for and on the behalfe of the said Thomas, while hee soe continued, Soe alsoe hee should now as readily redeliver the same goods into the possession of the said Thomas, Provided an honest and able Jury upon their discourse with the said Thomas Bowman, and enquiry of his deportment of late, togeather with the Concurrence of the Bench and other persons then in Court, shall finde hee the said Thomas Capeable of Mannageing his owne affaires: Whereupon a Jury is called and Empannelled namely Daniell Wills senr., Samuell Andrews, William Hunter, Bernard Devonish, Joseph Pope, Thomas Folke, Thomas Harding, John Hooton, Henry Grubb, Thomas Wright, Robert Stacy, John Cripps, William Myers, John Hollinshead Attested.

The Jury abovesaid bring in their Verdict, that they are agreed unanimously that upon their Examination of said Thomas Bowman, and inquiry into the state and deportment of him of late, that to the best of their Judgments hee said Thomas Bowman is Capeable of Manageing his owne affaires and Concernes himselfe:

The Bench thereupon order that an Instrument or order be made out, To deliver to said Thomas Bowman his Goods and Concernes.

Bernard Lane is required to make appeare before next Court that when the Surveyors of the Highwayes charged him to come to worke at the said Highwayes, hee was before and at the same tyme the Hyred Servant of Francis Davenport and William Myers.

The Attestation of Henry Jacobs concerning Godfrey Hancock Senr. was this Court day taken before James Budd and Elias Farr. which Attestation is in the Minuits or Rolls of this Court.

[52 1686] Att the Court held at Burlington the 3d of the 9th Moneth 1686. John Skene Governour James Budd, Francis Davenport, Thomas Gardner, Richard Guy, William Emley, William Biddle, Elias Farr Justices present.

The Jury Returned Godfrey Hancock, Bernard Devonish, John Day, Isaac Horner, John Woolston senr., Joseph Pope, John Chamnis, Peter Harvey, William Ellis, Christopher Snoden, John Browne, John Shin junr. Attested.

Henry Parker versus Thomas Wright.
Henry Parker versus Robert Pearson withdrawne.
Seth Smith versus Godfrey Hancock junr. withdrawne.
James Hill versus Peter Matson withdrawne.
Governour John Skene versus Joseph Knight Action Case withdrawne.
John Snoden versus William Ellis Action Trover withdrawne.
Henry Parker versus John Cornish Action Slander withdrawne ordered the Defendant to pay Court charges declaration drawne.

Henry Parker versus Richard Davis   Action Slander   Withdrawne ordered the Defendant to pay Court charges   declaration drawne.

William Say moves the Court for what belongs to him from Anthony Elton his master as the Custome of the Countrey to which said Say his Indenture relates; The Court order him to have the same according to the Act of Assembly, which his master Assents to   (being Tenne Bushells of Corne, necessary Apparrell, Two Howes and one Axe).

Michael Huffe versus Henry Parker. Tryed by the Jury above Evidences John Bainbridge, William Myers, James Hill   Attested.

John Bainbridge Deposeth that hee borrowed a Canooe of the Indians, which hee (to the best of his knowledge) beleeves is the Canooe in question And that hee found the same Canooe in the Plaintiffs possession, and bid him keep it untill hee the said Bainbridge should call for it.

William Myers deposeth that hee heard the Plaintiffs wife desire the Defendant to Fetch the Canooe in question, which shee espyed driving on the River, whereupon said Defendant fetcht the Canooe with the Plaintiffs Canooe.

James Hill Attested sayth that to the best of his remembrance the Plaintiff was willing the Defendant should have the use of the Canooe of him the said Plaintiff in and about the Ferry (only the Plaintiff was to have Portage of his owne goods over the same Ferry and his owne passage Free).

The Jury Finde for the Plaintiff and give him Two pence dammage and Costs of suite.

Joshua Eley and John Snoden late Constables present John Carter and William Beard for new Constables   who are accepted by the Court.

The next Court ordered to be on the 15th 10th Mo. next.

[53 1686]   Att the Court att Burlington the 15th 10th Moneth 1686. John Skene Governour   James Budd, Elias Farre, Francis Collins, Thomas Gardner   Magistrates present.

Benjamin Whitehead plaintiff   Henry Sife Defendant   Action of Trespasse. The Jury   John Woolston senr., Richard Bassnett, John Shin senr., Joseph Pope, John Chamnis, William Brightwen, William Myers, Walter Pumphary, James Wills, William Roydon, Daniel Wills junr., Bernard Devonish   Attested.

The declaration being read the Defendant Sife Confest hee pulled downe the Frame of the House in the declaration mentioned: And further sayth that Thomas Chanders (then being in court) assisted him in pulling the same.

Whereupon it appeareing that the Plaintiff was then peaceably possest of the Land whereon the Frame stood, The Jury goe togeather and bring in their Verdict for the Plaintiff and give him 25l. dammages with his Costs of suite; And Judgment is thereupon awarded.

Henry Sife the defendant desires an Appeale may be granted and Entred to the Generall Assembly of this Province:

The Court required the said Sife to give sufficient security for his prosecuting his Appeale with effect and his appeale should then be Entred: The said Sife answer thereto is, hee can give noe Security and therefore the appeale could not be granted.

Henry Sife acknowledges hee hath noe deed from Robert Turner of the Land whereon the Trespasse was Committed: And that the said Robert Turner advised him the said Sife to pull downe the Frame of the said House on the Land aforesaid.

The Court require of the said Sife if hee will discharge the said 25l. damages and Costs Suite; which hee saith hee cannot, thereupon the Court order the Sheriffe to take him into Custody.

John Hollinshead versus John Allen   Action of Debt   rests.

Seth Smith versus Godfrey Hancock Junr. Action of Trespasse—Rests.

Court dissolved, next Court to be the 20th of 12th Mo. next.

[54 1686] Burlington   Att a speciall Court held 25th 11th mo. 1686 called at the request of Samuell Leonard, on the Accompt of one John Tulley who was taken for felloniously takeing certaine goods of said Leonards.

George Hutcheson president   James Budd, Thomas Gardner   Justices present.

Samuell Leonard on the behalfe of our Lord the King Indicts John Tulley. Grand Jury Thomas Budd, Robert Stacy, Godfrey Hancock, Thomas French, John Ogbourne, Benjamin Holt, Henry Grubb, William Stanley, Richard Love, James Sherwin, John Smith, Daniell England, John Ingram   Attested. The Jury finde the Bill. John Tulley Arraigned and Pleads guilty and referrs himselfe to the Bench. Samuell Leonards Attested—And Deposes that the goods produced in Court which were found with Tulley are the goods of him the said Leonards. The Bench order the said Tulley to pay Three fold the Goods proved, and by Tulley confest to be taken away, which by Godfrey Hancock, Thomas French, Richard Basnett, Bernard Devonish, James Sherwin, and Henry Grub are Praised to—7l. 7s. 6d. which 3 fold is—22l. 2s. 6d. whereof—7l. 7s. 6d. is one third parte returned soe rests for Tulley to pay—14l. 15s. 00d.

Burlington at the Quarterly Court held the 20th 12th Mo. falling by reason of the 1st day 21st 1686.

John Skene Governour present   George Hutcheson, William Biddle, Thomas Gardner, James Budd, Richard Guy   Justices on the Bench.

Robert Turner a Caveat entred against Recording 200 Acres Land in the 3d tenth adjoyning to Coopers Creeke on Newton side, Surveyed for said Robert to Henry Sife, and laid clayme to by Benjamin Whitehead, that noe further procedure be in Recording the same untill a fair heareing be had.

The Grand Jury   Edward Hunloke, Symon Charles, Joseph Pope, Thomas Butcher, John Budd, Jonathan Fox, Thomas Raper, James Marshall, Benjamin Holt, John Ogbourne, James Wills, Thomas Stokes, Edward Ruckhill, Thomas Bartin   Attested in the forme hereunder written.

[*The forme of the Grand Jurys Attestation*]   You shall dillingently enquire, and true presentment make, of all such Articles matters and things as shall be given you in charge: And of all other matters and things as shall come to your owne knowledge, touching this present service: The Kings Councell, your fellowes, and your owne, you shall keep secrett: You shall present noe person for hatred, or malice, neither shall you leave any unpresented for favor or affection, for Love, or gaine or any hopes thereof, But in all things you shall present the truth, the whole truth, and nothing but the truth, to the best of your knowledge—or otherwise bee accounted and prosecuted as perjured in Lawe. [*Oath of Grand Jurors*] [18]

[55 1686]   The Traverse Jury Returned   Robert Stacy, John Woolston senr., Henry Grubb, Richard Basnett, William Brightwen, William Myers, Samuell Furnis, John Kinsey, Joseph Adams, William Evans, John Bunting, Robert Young.

Anne the wife of Thomas Potts came into Court and acknowledged that shee hath taken away from the persons undernamed the particular goods mentioned, Vizt, from George Hutcheson a Bedtick and bolster, 1l. of browne thread, ½l. of whited browne, 3l. Coulored thread, 1 Buckeram Teaster, a botle of Elixer.   from James Budd one Dowlas shirt: from Thomas Budd, a Remnant of Serge, Two Remnants of Ribbon, a Remnant of Linnen Cloth, one brasse Cock: from Richard a small Bottom of Cotton: from James Marshall, one payr of Sisers and a Grosse of buttons: from Mary Grub a childs shirt and biggin and about 1l. and ½ of Tallowe, from Edward Slade about 3l. of beefe and some feathers about 5l: from John Budd about 3 yards Ribbon, from James Creek in money 8s.   from Mary Gosling a holland shift, a Towell, 2 pockett handkerchiffs, one payr Cotton Stockings, 1 white hud and blew apron, and from her maid a Combe. from Joseph Pope a payr Stockings Cost 4d.½ in England.

Susanna Reeves brought into Court on the Complaynt of John Woolston junr. John Woolston verbally Complaynes that the said Susanna hath slandered him and his wife in these following words, vizt, upon the examination of said Susanna taken the 15th of the 12th Moneth 1686. Shee the said Susanna sayd that her Dame Alice Huggins told her on fryday about 2 clock in the afternoone about a moneth past, that John Woolston junr. had turned away his wife, and that shee had beene at her Mothers a weeke, and the cause was because hee found her naught with an East Jersey man, and that shee had taken one of the Children, and that John might take the other two:

The said Susanna Came into Court and there Testifyed the same againe And afterwards came into Court againe, And there openly declared that

---
[18] Written in different hand, along margin.

what shee had before spoken and Testifyed against the said John Woolston and his wife is utterly false, and that shee hath therein wronged them, and that the other things shee hath declared Concerning Branford being burnt is alsoe false.

John Woolston junr. upon his Attestation averrs that Walter Reeve about eight dayes agoe in the jurisdiction of this Court Swore Seaven oaths, Vizt, (by God) Seaven tymes over.

The Grand Jurys verdict   In the case of Anne Pott, They haveing noe Indictment, and the said Anne haveing openly confest her facts in Court: They referre her to the Bench, And said Anne alsoe submitts to the Bench.

In the Case of Susanna Reeve; They haveing noe Indictment They finde not themselves concerned to medle further in the matter, seeing it appears to their Judgments to be rather a matter of slander then any other matter wherein they ought to medle; And therefore they referre it to the Bench.

In the Case of Anne Pott the Bench order the Lawe of the Province for Theft to be read which is to restore fower fold; which Thomas Pott the husband of said Anne declares hee is willing to restore: The Bench require said Thomas to secure the payment thereof; And give Judgment that Thomas Pott (according to the Lawe of the Province) the said Thomas and Anne shall restore fower fold the goods before acknowledged to be stollen; And give security for the same.

[56 1686]   In the Case of Susanna Reeve The Bench give Judgment That tomorrow being the 22d of the 12th Moneth instant betweene the howers of Nine and Tenne in the forenoone the said Susanna shall be sett in the Pillory in this Towne, and there to stand not exceeding one hower.

[*Order of Court   Edward Ruckhill the Master and Benjamin More the Servant*]   Edward Ruckhill brought a boy named Benjamin More, which hee brought from England and paid his passage, and hath found him meat drinke and clothes about one yeare,   the Boy is Twelve yeares of age the last 25th of the tenth Moneth 1686:   Whereupon by order of Court the said Benjamin More is appointed to serve his said Master Edward Ruckhill untill hee be twenty and one yeares old: and at the expiration of the said service the Servant to receive of his Master the Custome of the Countrey.

Lawrence Morris and Thomas Gladwyn Constables for the Precincts of Burlington present for new Constables   Joseph Pope and Richard Love. John Wills and John Payne Constables in the 2d tenth present for new Constables   Thomas Kendall and John Woolman. John Butcher Constable for Birch Creeke Presents for Constable in his stead   John Shin senr.   all accepted by the Court   Attested. Joseph Pope, Richard Love and Thomas Kendall, John Woolman   Attested as belowe. William Myers, Isaac Marriott and Thomas French   supervisours [19] in the 2nd tenth.

[19] "Suprvisors" in MS.

[*Constables Attestation*]   You shall well and faithfully serve our Lord the King in the office of a Constable; you shall see the Kings Peace well and duely kept and preserved, to the Utmost of your power; you shall Arrest all such persons as in your presence shall ride or goe Armed offensively, or shall comitt or make any Ryott, affray, or other breach of the Kings Peace; you shall doe your best endeavour that hue and cry, and the statutes for punishment of sturdy beggars Rogues, vagabonds, night walkers, and other idle and wandring persons within your Liberties be duely put in Execution; you shall doe your best endeavour upon Complaynt to you made to apprehend all Fellons, Barratours, Riottours [20] and persons makeing affrayes, and if any such persons shall make resistance, with force you shall Levy hue and Cry, and shall pursue them till they be taken; you shall have a watchfull Eye to such persons as shall maintayne, or keep any Common house, or place where any unlawfull games or playes are, or shall be used; As alsoe to such persons as shall frequent or use such places, or shall exercise or use any unlawfull Games or Playes there, or elsewhere contrary to the Statute: Att your Assises or Sessions you shall present all and every the offences comitted or done contrary to the Statutes made and provided for the restraint of inordinate haunting and tipling in Tavernes, Innes and Alehouses and for repressing of drunkenness and prophane swearing; you shall true Presentment make of all bloud shedding, affrayes, outcryes, Rescues and other offences committed or done against the Peace, within your limits; you shall well and truely execute all precepts and warrants to you directed from the Justices of the Peace and others in Authority in this Province; And you shall well and duely according to your knowledge power and ability doe and execute all other things belonging to the office of a Constable soe long as you continue in the said office; or otherwise be Accounted and prosecuted as perjured in Lawe.

Seth Smith versus Godfrey Hancock junr.   referred.

Henry Parker versus Thomas Wright   referred agreed and withdrawne.

Thomas Budd versus William Cole   Trespass   Rests because the Defendant pleades hee had not a Coppy of the declaration in tyme. Thereupon at the request of Thomas Budd plaintiff as Special Court is granted which is appointed to be the first day of the next Moneth being the third day of the weeke.

Thomas Revell Labourer versus John Allen.

[*see Joshuas Accompt in Court 12th 3 mo. 1687*]   The Accompts of Enoch Chore and Joshua Humphreys in the Concerne of Walter Humphreys their father are produced and Read in Court: And the Court have nothing against them.

The Court dissolve the next Court to be the 1st of the next moneth being the third day of the weeke.

---

[20] "Barrators, Riottors" in MS.

[57 1686] [*Thomas Budd Plaintiff versus William Cole Defendant*]
Att a speciall Court held the 1st of the 1st Mo. 1686 called by the desire of Thomas Budd Plaintiff against William Cole Defendant in an Action of Trespass. John Skene Governour present. George Hutcheson, James Budd, Richard Guy, Andrew Robinson   Justices then present.

Jury Empannelled: Symon Charles, Richard Bassnett, William Roydon, James Wills, Benjamin Wheat, William Brightwen, Hanniah Gaunt, John Daye, Robert Young, Isaac Horner, William Hunt, Samuell Furnis, John Browne   Attested.

William Cole the Defendant called three tymes to defend his cause and appeares not: The Court in favour to the Defendant suspend entring default: William Cole Defendant afterwards appeares.

The Declaration Read: And Thomas Budd produced his Survey of the Land whereon the Defendant had made the Trespasse being 216 Acres Surveyed to Thomas by Daniell Leeds   Surveyour.

Daniell Leeds Attested sayth hee Surveyed the Land in question being 216 Acres, And sayth that when hee came to Survey it, William Cole the defendant warned him from Surveying the same. Thomas Budd had his 3 deeds, one from George Hutcheson of 100 Acres one from John Butcher for 50 Acres and one from John Yeo and also smse [21] from George Porter for 66 Acres in the Towne bounds.

William Cole by Edward Hunloke his Attourney sayth hee hath done what hee hath done there by order of Thomas Bowman.

Robert Stacy Attested sayth that hee heard William Cole say that the Land in question hee the said William Cole said hee held it by vertue of Thomas Bowmans right; And that the said William Cole said if said Thomas Bowmans Tytle was not good, hee the said Thomas Bowman must make it good to him.

Richard Guy Attested sayth that hee hath severall tymes talked with William Cole about the Land in question and that hee allwayes (as this Deponent understood made Accompt of it as his owne Land. William Cole himselfe ownes that hee holds the Land in question, and that hee bought of Thomas Bowman. The deed from Peter Jegou to Thomas Bowman Read Alsoe then read a Certificate under the hand and Seale of Governour Philip Carterett intimateing that hee promised a Tytle to the predecessors of Jegou.

Samuell Oldale Attested sayth that hee (being with Governour Carterett in East Jersey) the said Governour enquired of him of Peter Jegou: And said that he the said Jegou promised him to keep an ordnary, and that upon that Accompt hee granted him a permitt to take up Land at Lessa Poynt, but noe certaine quantity, and that in regard said Jegou did not keep an ordnary there, hee the said Governour sent downe some Cattle, that is to say seaven

[21] *I. e.*, mise.

Cowes and a Bull to Lessa Poynt, with intent to keep possession there for himselfe and to live there himselfe in regard Jegou had deserted it: this the Deponent heard the said Governour Carterett speake about the Moneth of January 1676.

The Permitt from Governour Carterett alsoe Read in Court.

Peter Aldridge Attested Sayt[h] that there was in the yeare 68 or 69 some Dutch men, vizt, Cornelius Joris[?] and Joris Marcellus then lived on Lessa Poynt: And that as hee the said Peter [58 1686] was comeing that way from New Yorke found that the said Dutch men had beene out with the Indians marking Trees: and that hee heard it was called Leazy Poynt, because the persons there had lived such a Lazy life there: Peter Aldridge further sayth in the yeare :70 the Indians robbed Jegou at Lazy Poynt, and that they tooke him the said Jegou prisoner and that in :71: hee the said Peter Aldridge placed two men on Matinicunck Island to keep possession who was in the same yeare killed by the Indians.

[*Peter Aldridge Deposition*] Also a Deposition of said Peter Aldridge then read and owned againe by the said Peter, (vizt) Peter Aldridge aged 50 yeares or thereabouts Testifies and sayth that about the yeare :68: or :69: hee being at Leza Poynt (now in the Province of West Jersey) in Company of the Dutch men that were then Inhabitants there, they the said Dutch men told this Deponent that they had purchased of the Indians upon the said Poynt, as they had bounded by marked Trees, or to that effect, and further sayth not. Attested the 28th of the 12th Mo. 1686 before Thomas Gardner Justice.

Then read also Jegous Declaration and the Judgment of the Court at Upland in the case with[?] Thomas Wright and Godfrey Hancock. Read also another paper witnessed by John White and Henry Jacobs.

Thomas Revell Attested Sayth that Peter Jegou when hee preferred his Petition to the Assembly, and it was Read, The Assembly asked the said Jegou, if hee would wholly referre himselfe (as to his Tytle to Land in this Province) to the Assembly: And the said Peter Jegou then answered hee would wholly abide by and stand to their agreement and determination.

Richard Guy before Attested As to the Trespasse, deposeth that hee see the Defendant William Cole Cutt and burne Severall Trees upon the premisses.

John Allen Attested Sayth, William Cole hath severall tymes imployed him said Allen and others to Cutt downe Timber and paid him for soe doeing, and hath seene the said Cole burne the same wood: This was done about beginning of Last Winter but one.

The Court adjourne for an hower and halfe and then appeare and call the Court.

The Jury then bring in their Verdict And finde for the Plaintiffe, allowing for the Dammage and Trespasse forty Shillings six pence, besides Costs of suite and Court charges.

Att the Court of Session held the 12th of 3th Moneth 1687.

Governour John Skene George Hutcheson, James Budd, Francis Davenport, Elias Farr, Thomas Gardner Justices. The Grand Jury Symon Charles, Anthony Elton, William Brightwen, John Hooton, Nathaniel West, Thomas Butcher, Thomas Harding, Peter Bosse, Jonathan Fox, Benjamin More, Daniel Leeds, Samuell Furnis, William Hewlings Attested. The Traverse Jury Returned William Myers, Thomas Barton, John Woolston senr., John Day, Samuell Ogbourne, Seth Smith, Thomas Gladwin, Thomas Rapier, Edward Rockhill, James Sherwin, William Stayner, William Evans.

[59 1687] Clause Johnson and Derick Johnson verbally Complayne against Walter Pumphary Jonathan West and John Smith for an Assault.

James Boyden and John Johnson Attested in the Case and sent to the Grand Jury. The Jury present the Defendant the Complaynants declare they are willing to agree with the Defendants.

Court order the Plaintiffs and Defendants to pay Court Charges.

Bernard Lane Plaintiff John Chamnis Defendant Agreed Court Drawne.

Thomas Wright Plaintiff George Hutcheson defendant Action of the Case the Defendant declares hee had not his declaration in tyme and Therefore craves a nonsuit the Court order it.

[*Joan Heath*] Upon the Information of the Justices from Nottingham, Concerning a Bastard Child being Borne of the body of Joan Heath and found dead at the house of Hugh Staniland; The Bill or Information by the Grand Jury found presentable. Hugh Staniland and Mathew Clayton bound for the appearance of the said Joan Heath next Session.

A Complaynt being brought against Edward Hunloke for selling Rum, upon the Evidence of James Hill, James Wills, James Satterthwait and Richard Haynes.

Edward Hunloke presented by the Grand Jury: Edward Hunloke declares hee knew not the Lawe against selling Rum: But referrs himselfe to the Bench, The Bench order him to pay the Fyne of three pounds. See it discharged at Sessions Septis 5th 1689 per Evidence.

The Ballance of the Accompt due to Joshua Humphries from his Father as per Accompt 29th January 1686, and produced in Court 21st 12th Mo. 1686 and after drawne up by James Budd Amounts to 41l. 10s. 00d.

Court dissolved.

Att a Speciall Court held the 15th 5th Mo. 1687. Governour Skene present. Robert Stacy, Edward Hunloke, James Marshall, William Myers, Richard Basnett Magistrates present.

Jury Francis Davenport, Walter Pumphary, William Stanley, Abraham Senior, William Cole, Samuell Furnis, Samuell Houghton, Benjamin

Wheat, Richard Love, William Crues, George Goforth, Robert Engle Attested.

John Ingram Plaintiff Thomas French Defendant Action Debt The Declaration Read by the defendant The bond of the Defendant to the Plaintiff read and owned The Award read.

William Evans and Thomas Kendall the Arbitrators appeare and owne the Award to be their Act. And say that by the residue (mentioned in the Award) they meant that the plaintiff should have the Summe 5l. 6 per Thousand, except what hee had before received thereof in parte.

Thomas Kendall further sayth that hee and said William Evans tooke noe notice of the 50s. mentioned in the former Award because (sayth hee) the Articles (as they were informed) was out of doores. Anthony Fryor Attested sayth that the Defendant had 3 thousand of bricks from the plaintiff to end differences, and after sayth it was to pay John Sharps wages: Further sayth Thomas French was then satisfyed with the size of bricks to the best of his Knowledge, for that hee heard him say nothing against the size.

[60 1687] The Jury agree of their Verdict and finde for the Plaintiff and give him 5l. 11s. 8d. Debt; and dammages 1l. 10s. 0d. with all other Costs and charges of suite, in Compensation of the whole bond. Thereupon Judgment is awarded.

Mathew Allen disturbed the Court in speaking without Lycence, declareing the Jury Empanelled, are too young to be Jurors.

Att the Court held the 8th 6th Mo. 1687. John Skene Governour present. Elias Farr, Edward Hunloke, James Marshall, Richard Basnett, William Myers Magistrates present.

Grand Jury Godfrey Hancock senr., John Payne, John Sharp, Freedome Lippincot, Thomas Barton, Daniell Leeds, Eleazer Fenton, Richard Woodnutt, Henry Grubb, Christopher Weatherill, Robert Engle, Thomas Shinn, George Shinn Attested.

Traverse Jury John Shinn senr., James Saterthwait, Benjamin Hoult, Seth Smith, Joseph Adams, William Hunt, John Budd, Abraham Senior, William Evans, Thomas Stokes, Thomas Gladwin, Samuell Furnis Attested.

Joan Heath according to the Recognizance given 12th 3d Mo. last appeares upon Indictment And by the Grand Jury the Indictment found. Joan Heath Arraigned and to the Indictment pleads that Shee is guilty of beareing a bastard child, but not guilty of Murdering it: And referrs the Tryall to God and the Countrey.

The Traverse Jury haveing the Judgment and verdict of the Inquest taken upon the same by the Magistrates at the Falls: Bring in their Verdict, that the said Joan Heath they finde her guilty of bearing a bastard child contrary to the Lawe, but not Guilty of Murdering it.

William Fleetwood presented by the Grand Jury for begetting a basterd child on the body of Mary Reading Fleetwood appeares, and alsoe the said Mary Reading. The Court order said Fleetwood to give sufficient Security for the maintenance of the bastard child; And for said Mary Reading, for her offence, either to be whipt from John Cripps house to the River: And to have twenty and one stripes on the naked back: on the next Sixth day betweene the howers of 11 and 12 or pay 5l. William Fleetwood offers to engage the payment of the 5l.

And for Joane Heath the Court order That shee shall be whipt at the tyme above said on the bare back betweene the places aforesaid And to have Thirty nyne lashes or stripes severely laid on. or that shee shall serve five yeares service or pay Tenne pounds.

Richard Basnett plaintiff John Chamnis Defendant Action of the Case The Bill for 9l. 17s. 6d. Read and owned by John Chamnis: And alsoe the Accompt of 1l. 7s. 2d. produced And Richard Basnett Attests to the truth thereof as it is in the particulers in his booke Chamnis produced a receipt dated May 12th 1687 for the receipt of nyne pounds in parte of the Bill, with Richard Basnetts name thereto which Richard Basnett denyes: and alsoe sayth hee never had penny of the said Debt and denyes that name (Richard Basnett) to be his hand writing. Court adjournes for 1 hower and halfe.

[61 1687] John Fleckna Attested sayth that hee heard Richard Basnett ask Chamnis for his Debt, and said Chamnis then owned that his Bill to Richard Basnett had then beene due a Considerable while, saying to Richard, it hath not beene due past some 12 Monethes: said John Fleckna deposeth that hee heard this from Chamnis within 5 weeks last.

The Jury finde for the Plaintiff and give him his Debt of 11l. 4s. 7d. with 2d. damage and Costs of suite.

Elizabeth Clinton appeared in Court but none appeares to prosecute her, but shee owned some goods stollen by her: which the Court order shee shall restore four fold, or doe service untill 4 fould be discharged. The Grand Jury finde said Elizabeth Clinton Guilty for stealing goods according to her owne confession, and Shee referrs herselfe to the bench.[22]

The Returne of the warrant against Thomas French, by the Sheriffe is that the Wife of Thomas French did forcibly take away the goods which hee had seized by vertue of his warrant: The Court order to take fresh order and more strength.

A Survey of Freedome Lippincot being published in Court for 288 Acres and ⅝: Francis Collins Enters a Caveat against it.

[*Richard Basnetts returne upon the death of Samuell Binge*] The Returne of Richard Basnett appointed as Coronour [23] for the present Immirgencie to sitt upon and view the dead body of Samuell Binge:

---

[22] This sentence is in the margin.
[23] "Coronor" in MS.

The Second of the 6th Moneth 1687: The Jury or Inquest returned and appeareing James Marshall, Thomas Raper, Christopher Weatherill, Thomas Gladwin, Lawrence Morris, Anthony Burgesse, James Wills, John Budd, William Crues, John Kinsey, Isaac Smith, James Silver Attested. It is the Judgment of the Jury Upon Viewing the body and examination of such as were present or neare at hand, when the said Samuell Binge fell of from the Roofe of the house of Samuell Jenings: And the said Jury doe mutuall agree and give it as their Judgment that the death of the said Samuell Binge came by Accident, Testyfyed under their hands the day and year above written: Taken by Richard Basnett Coronour the day and yeare above written.

[62 1687] Att a Special Court called and held on the Accompt of Henry Tradway the 23th 6th Mo. 1687. Robert Stacy, Edward Hunloke, James Marshall, Richard Basnett, John Wood, James Martin, William Myers Justices Present.

Henry Tradway Indicted for haveing Carnall Copulation with his wifes daughter named Mary Driver.

Grand Jury Thomas Bowman, John Willis, William Stanley, Peter Jenings, Samuell OldAle, Thomas Gladwyn, Thomas Raper, Daniel England, John Kinsey, Abraham Senior, William Brightwen, Samuell Houghton, John Browne Attested.

Howard Ward and Elizabeth Salsbury Attested and sent to the Grand Jury. Alsoe the examination and Confession of Mary Driver taken before the Justices belowe, sent to the Grand Jury And Mary Driver alsoe Attested and sent to them.

The Grand Jury finde the Bill. And alsoe the Grand Jury present the County for want of a Prison, upon the Complaynt of the Sheriff. Alsoe the Grand Jury returne a Bill which is preferred to them concerning Henry Tradways uncivill actions with one Phillice Richards.

The Grand Jury returne Ignoramus upon the bill.

upon the first bill being found by the Grand Jury Henry Tradway Arraigned pleads Guilty.[24] And referrs himselfe to God and the Countrey.

Traverse Jury Thomas Gardner senr., Henry Grubb, Seth Smith, Seth Hill, James Satterthwait, Johosaphat Legrave, Samuell Herrott, Francis Isley, John Herrott, John Smith, John Cornish, Benjamin Holt Attested.

The Jury finde Henry Tradway Guilty upon the Evidence above.

And further the businesse and fact of said Mary Driver with Henry Tradway her father in Lawe appeareing by her owne Testimony and the Evidence above: The Grand Jury goe togeather againe, And present her, for that it appeares by her keeping her said fact secrett that Shee was willing and assented thereunto.

[24] Sic.

Whereupon said Mary Driver pleads Guilty And the Traverse Jury above said bring her in Guilty.

Thurla Sena preferrs a Bill of Complaynt against Henry Tradway on his owne behalfe, for the said Henryes abuse of him and declares and Attests in Court that hee is afraid of his life.

Elizabeth Salesbury upon her Attestation sayth that Henry Tradway said if hee could meet with the said Thurla that night (after hee had attempted to drawe up the said Thurla by the neck with a Rope) hee would either put him in the Creek or drowne him.

John Wood Attested sayth that to the best of his remembrance on the 19th of the 5th Mo. last Henry Tradway said that if the said Thurla came to his house, hee would scarr, or affright him.

The Court adjourne to the 5th day next at the 10th hower in the forenoone.

[63 1687] [5th day being 25th 6th Mo.] Henry Tradway and Mary Driver brought to the Barre.

The sentence of Court.

Henry Tradway! The Bench have Considered of the wickednesse of the Fact whereof by thy Jury thou hast been found guilty: And for the same doe fyne thee Fifty pounds: And also order thee to pay and discharge all Court charges and all other reasonable expenses and charges that are occasioned by reason of thy fact. And alsoe that thou be kept in prison untill the same shall be paid and discharged.

Mary Driver! The Bench have Considered of thy Lewdnesse in defyleing thy Mothers bed, of which thou hast beene found guilty: And for the same doe order that tomorrowe being the 26th instant betweene the howers of Eleaven and Twelve in the forenoone, thou shall be severely whipt on thy naked back at a Carts Tayle from the house of John Cripps in this Towne to the River side and that thou shall have thirty Nyne stripes well laid on.

The Bench further order that as Concerning the Complaynt made by Thurla Sena against Henry Tradway, The said Henry Tradway shall remayne prisoner untill hee give sufficient security for his good behaviour: And for the abuse of the said boy and losse of tyme said Henry shall pay him twenty Shillings.

Burlington Court held the 3th 9th Mo. 1687. Justices then present Robert Stacy, Richard Basnett, James Marshall, William Myers Justices present.

Jury Summoned and Empannelled Godfrey Hancock, John Day, John Hilliard, Peter Harvey, William Strayner, Edmond Stuart, John Crosby, Mathew Allen, William Evans, Daniel England, Joseph Pope, John Antram Attested.

John Chamnis upon Indictment of Forgery to answer our Lord the King on the Complaynt of Richard Basnett: Chamnis appears not, And according to the Courts order the forfeiture of his Recognizance entred.

Bernard Devonish plaintiff   John Ingram Defendant   Action of the Case. Defendant appeares not, The Plaintiff thereupon proves his Debt and it goes against the Defendant by default and Judgment awarded for debt and Costs of suite.

Henry Grubb Plaintiff   Samuell Abbot Defendant   Plaintiff nor defendant appeare   the Plaintiff at last appeares and gives order to withdraw the Court; but in regard the Jury appeares before order was given to withdrawe the Action the Jury to have Halfe Fees.

Jonathan West Plaintiff   Walter Pumphary Defendant   Action Case   Evidences   Eliakim Higgins Attested sayth that the Defendant Walter, said hee gave the Plaintiff Jonathan for his worke 4l. per Moneth this was the Defendant spoke about May last.

Joshua Newbold Attested sayth that at the same time that Eliakim Higgins mentions, Walter said hee gave the said Plaintiff 4l. per moneth and if it had beene 5l. the said Plaintiff deserved it in regard hee minded his worke soe close.

[64 1687]   William Huntley sayth that the Plaintiff said to him hee was to have the 4th parte of the wage for his worke.

Peter Jenings Attested, but his Evidence is nothing to purpose.

Juryes Verdict   The Jury finde for the Plaintiff and give him his Debt declared for and costs of suite.

John Pancost and Eleazer Fenton Presented for overseers for highways in that Division.

1687 Burlington Court 20th 12th Moneth.

Daniell Coxe Esqr. Governour   John Skene, Deputy Governour   Robert Stacy, Elias Farr, Richard Guy, William Emley, Edward Hunloke, Thomas Lambert, James Marshall, William Myers, Daniell Wills   Justices present.

The Grand Jury   Thomas Gardner, James Pharoe, Robert Scholey, Robert Murfin, John Hollinshead, Daniell Leeds, William Brightwen, Samuell Andrews, John Appleton, Joshua Humphreys, John Smith, John Hyllyard, Anthony Elton.

The Traverse Jury   Thomas Budd, Thomas Harding, John Rogers, Thomas Wood, Robert Wilson, George Smith, Thomas Scholey, John Hooton, William Hickson, William Matlock, John Roberts, Thomas Stokes.

[*Tryed*]   Joseph Burgin Plaintiff   Joseph Wood Defendant   Action of Trespasse.

Thomas Revell,   Richard Basnett   Evidences   Attested prove the Defendants opening and burning the Letter mentioned in the declaration, by the Defendants owne acknowledgment thereof to them. Verdict   The Jury finde for the Plaintiff and give him 2d. Damages and Costs of suite and thereupon Judgment is awarded.

Thomas Revell labourer Plaintiff Alice Griffith Defendant on Attachment. The goods Attached being a Canooe: The Plaintiff Proved his declaration by 2 Evidences as belowe.

Thomas Brock, Joseph Burgin Evidences Attested.

Thomas Brock sayth that the Defendant owned shee had the Goods declared for of the Plaintiff, and that shee owed the Plaintiff for the same 24s. and that this was about latter end of July last.

Joseph Burgin sayth that hee heard the bargaine made betweene the Plaintiff and the defendants husband and that the defendants husband was to pay for the weareing Clothes 34s.

Whereupon the goods Attached were called forfeit the Defendant being called 3 tymes to appear and answered not.

Indictment of John Chamnis for the King on the Complaynt of Richard Basnett.

After the Indictment found by the Grand Jury Chamnis Arraigned and Indictment Read Chamnis pleads not guilty and for Tryall referrs himselfe to God and the Countrey.

The Traverse Jury abovesaid being impanelled and accepted by Chamnis, upon the Judgment and verdict at the Tryall of Richard Basnett against said Chamnis for debt finding thereby Chamnis Convict of Forgeing an Acquittance with Richard Basnetts name thereto They finde him Guilty of Forgery.

[65 1687] [*The Sentence of the Bench against Chamnis*]

The Court give sentence upon John Chamnis, that the next Seaventh day betweene the Howers of Tenne and Twelve of the same day the said John Chamnis shall be taken to the Markett House in this Towne, and there be sett in the Pillory and shall have one of his Eares Cutt of, according to the Statute.

The Indictment of Charles Sheepey for the King upon the Complaynt and accusation of Elizabeth Hutcheson.

The Indictment found by the Grand Jury: Charles Sheepey being sett to the Barre and Arraigned, the Indictment being read, Sheepey pleads not Guilty, And referres himselfe for Tryall to God and the Countrey. Whereupon the Traverse Jury aforenamed are called and being all accepted by the Prisoner are Attested.

[*Elizabeth Hutchesons Deposition*] Elizabeth Hutcheson Attested deposeth, That when shee was in bedd at her Fathers house at Oneanickon in a Chamber, where the whole family used to lye, the said Charles Sheepey came to her bed side and putt his hand into the Bed to the Knee of her the said Elizabeth and from thence to her Elbowe, and that shee caught hold of his hand, and thereupon cryed out to the maid belowe in the house, to-bring up a Candle for shee had gott some body by the hand, and the maid and the rest in the house said Shee did only dreame soe, and therefore delayed to come; But when shee the said Elizabeth Continued calling more earnestly, a candle was brought up, but Sheepey perceiveing the Candle snatched away his hand and slipt away to his owne bedd; And that Shee intended to complayne thereof to her father; but Shee understanding that most of them in the House were of opinion shee only dreamed soe shee concluded they would persuade her Father it was but her dreame, and that shee should but then have his anger by it, and therefore did not speake of it.

alsoe further Shee the said Elizabeth deposeth that the said Sheepey made her and her Sister Martha beleeve hee could conjure, or tell fortunes, and by that meanes at severall tymes gott money from them.

Alsoe further that afterwards, when shee the said Elizabeth and her Sister Martha lived at the Falls, the said Charles Sheepey alsoe then living there, shee the said Elizabeth and Martha went to Thomas Lamberts house about a myle and halfe of, and desired Thomas Lamberts wife to give leave to her daughter Betty to goe and lye with them, in regard all the rest of the family was gone from home, but they two, and the said Charles Sheepey; but in regard Thomas Lamberts wife understood there was one man at home, shee said it was needlesse and therefore said shee could not then well spare her; And that therefore they went home themselves; And when they went to bed they thrust in some apron or clothes betweene the sneck (there being noe Lock or bolt on the doore of the roome where they lay) to keep it fast, And that in the night the said Charles Sheepey gott in and came into the bedd to her the said Elizabeth and her Sister, and that the said Sheepey when said Elizabeth endeavoured to resist him held her hands, and Shee then struggling and crying out awaked her sister Martha, and that notwithstanding they did both with all their strength strive to resist and repulse the said Sheepey, yet hee did then against the will of her the said Elizabeth force the said Elizabeth and with his yard had the use of her body by carnall Copulation; And that since that tyme hee never had to doe with her, or attempted it further.

[*Martha Hutchesons Deposition*] Alsoe Martha Hutcheson upon her Attestation Deposeth and Sayth that the tenour of her Sisters deposition above is true.

[*John Tomlinsons Deposition*] John Tomlinson Attested Deposeth, That hee heard Elizabeth Hutcheson call out for a Candel at her Fathers house at Oneanickon, and that hee stept up into the Chamber, and as hee came hee heard the feet of one passe by goeing from Elizabeth Hutchesons bed side, to the bed side where Charles Sheepey used to lye, and that the maid came after with a Light and that then Charles was gott into his bedd, And further sayth that afterwards when hee heard what said Charles Sheepey had done to Elizabeth when they lived at [66 1687] the Falls, hee the said

Deponent was greatly troubled, And Examined Elizabeth very closely of it; whereupon Elizabeth told him of her and her Sisters goeing to Thomas Lamberts to gett his daughter to come lye with them; according as Elizabeth hath before deposed: And alsoe of the said Charles Sheepeys getting into the Roome and comeing into the Bed and forceing her the said Elizabeth the same night after they went to Thomas Lamberts as aforesaid in Bettyes Deposition And that the said Elizabeth then told this deponent that the said Sheepey had never before that tyme or after that tyme to doe with her.

[*Charles Sheepey:*] Charles Sheepey declares, That hee never went to bed to Elizabeth Hutcheson nor shee to him, and sayth hee never put his hand to bed to her, as shee averrs, and further sayth that hee never had any money of theirs, and denyes hee told Elizabeth and Martha hee could tell them their fortunes and by that meanes gott money from them: But sayth that Elizabeth was desiring him to tell her her fortune, and sayd shee would doe any thing for him, if hee would; And that hee the said Charles said to her, if shee would let him kisse her, hee would tell her, her fortune, And Further sayth that hee had Carnall knowledge of the body of the said Elizabeth severall tymes: That the first tyme hee had to doe with her was out of doores under an Oake about a stones cast from the house, the second tyme by the water side, at which tyme hee sayth Shee followed him and asked him to doe it, a Third tyme in the house, a fourth tyme in the Parlour on the Bed: and sayth that hee never forced her, but Shee was alwayes as willing as hee.

Att Sheepeys request Jonathan Fox and Samuell Houghton are called and heard who say as followes. [*Jonathan Fox Testimony*] Jonathan Fox sayth that hee examined Charles Sheepey about the premises, And that Charles told him hee had to doe with Elizabeth Hutcheson once at the riseing of the Hill, and once in the house, and once that Morning that hee the said Jonathan and John Tomlinson went to George Hutchesons Plantation at the Falls; Further the said Jonathan saith that Elizabeth was unwilling to be at either Plantation without her Sister, And that Samuell Sykes informed him that Elizabeth had told the maid that Charles Sheepey had Ravished her, and that Shee then feared her selfe to be with Child: And alsoe that hee the said Jonathan acquainted John Tomlinson therewith, and that afterwards John Tomlinson told the said Jonathan hee had spoke with Elizabeth concerning the same, telling her hee had dreamed Sheepey had to doe with her five tymes, to which shee answered hee had dreamed too true and John Tomlinson then told him the said Jonathan that Betty had informed him the said John that Sheepey had to doe with her twice;

[*John Tomlinson*] But John Tomlinson upon his Attestation sayth that Betty never said to him that Sheepey had to doe with her more than once, And that hee did not tell Jonathan Fox that Betty ever said to him that Sheepey had to doe with her more than once.

[*Samuell Houghton Testimony*] Samuell Houghton saith that Charles Sheepey told him that Betty Hutcheson was desirous to knowe her fortune, whether shee must have John Dimsdale or goe to England, and that hee the said Charles replyed if shee would let him lye with her hee would tell her, and that shee said shee would, and that shee was willingly to lye downe, onely that shee feared to spoyle her Gowne, hee then put of his Coate and laid it under her, and that hee then had to doe with her, which was at the top of the Hill above the House, and that hee had to doe with her another tyme downe towards the water, and another tyme in the House, and that the said Charles told him that hee was once goeing to have to doe with her the said Elizabeth in the Parlour on the Bedd but the woman of the House came in and prevented it, And alsoe that Charles said further hee had to doe with her twice by the oven under an oake that stands there; And that hee asked Charles if hee had gott any money of the said Elizabeth or her Sister Martha, and Charles answered hee never had gott any money either from Elizabeth or her Sister.

[*Thomas Lamberts Deposition*] Thomas Lambert Attested deposeth that Elizabeth Hutcheson and Martha Came to his house to gett his daughter to lye with them, and that his wife understanding there was a man in the house, said in regard there is one of the men in the House there is noe need for her daughter at present to lye with them, And sayth that the Children went out where Thomas Lamberts maid was out of doores and desired the maid Shee would beg leave for Betty Lambert to lye with them, saying that if Charles Sheepey had beene from home, they durst lye by themselves without feare, and Thomas Lambert alsoe saith that his daughter went parte of the way home with the Children and that the said Children Betty and Martha cryed when they parted with Betty Lambert and that Betty Lambert was then troubled, that shee could not goe on to lye with them, not having her Mothers consent.

[67 1687] [*Charles Sheepey*] Sheepey being againe asked if hee gott any money of the said Children, Denyes that hee ever gott any of them, And that hee never tould them hee could conjure or tell them or either of them their fortune; Though hee said in his examination before in the Court hee would tell Elizabeth her fortune if shee would let him kisse her; But further replyes againe, that hee never had the use of the Body of the said Elizabeth, but by her owne consent.

[*Lewis Carpenter Deposition*] Lewis Carpenter Attested Sayth that Betty Hutcheson asked Charles Sheepey to tell her, her fortune, and Charles said if shee would let him kisse her, hee would, this Lewis sayth Charles told him. Severall women being then in Court, namely the wife of Samuell Jenings, the wife of John Budd, the wife of Edward Hunloke, the wife of William Emley and the wife of Richard Guy, doe before the Court Solemnly declare that they have made it their businesse to search Elizabeth Hutcheson, And that they finde it soe with relation to the state of her body; That whereas the said Sheepey declares hee hath had the use of her body severall tymes, The said Sheepey hath greatly wronged her in saying soe, As to them plainly appeares according to the naturall course of women, And that to the best of their understandings, What hath beene done, by the said Sheepey hath beene forcibly: And further they desire they make knowne the matter (for modestys sake) to some particular modest person, who may give the Jury a more particular relation thereof: which the Court approve of.

Sheepey being further required if hee have anything to say for himselfe before the Jury goe togeather; Sayth hee hath noe more to say, but as before, hee never had the use of her body, but with her owne consent.

After the Charge given to the Jury and it being somewhat late at night they are required to go togeather; and if they agree of their Verdict before the Court come togeather on the Morrow morning, to Seale up their Verdict in writing, and then to bring it into the Court; And the Sheriffe required to Attend them. And then the Court adjourned to the Eighth hower in the morning.

And according to the desire of the said women, the reasons for their asserting in Court as abovesaid, being made knowne, First to such modest person or persons as was judged requisite to impart the same to, was accordingly made knowne to the Jury.

[*21st of the 12th Mo. Juryes Verdict*] The Court comeing togeather and being sett, the Prisoner Sheepey is brought to the barr, And the Jury called over; And required whether they are agreed of their Verdict or noe, Answers they are agreed; And thereupon at the appointment of the rest the Foreman delivered their Verdict in writing Sealed to the Clerke; which the Clerke reads, vizt, Wee find Charles Sheepey Guilty according as hee stands Indicted. The Bench after some tyme to consider of the sentence, by an Unanimous Consent agree and appoint the Clerke to read their Sentence, past upon the Prisoner; Which accordingly the Clerke read, As followeth.

[*The Sentence*] Charles Sheepey, The Grand Jury and Traverse Jury haveing found thee Guilty according as thou hast beene Indicted, The Bench have required mee to read thy Sentence, which is, That thou shall be whipt this day betwixt the howers of Two and three in the afternoone upon thy naked Body at a Carts tayle, from the house of John Butcher in this Towne, to the house where Abraham Senior inhabitteth and from thence on the River side to the High Street, and from thence downe to the Markett house, And that thou Shalt have as many stripes laid on as to the Magistrates (who shall be present at thy execution) Shall be thought meet And from thence thou shall be taken and kept in Irons for the space of three Moneths from this day next ensueing, dureing which tyme thou shall be whipt at Three severall times more, in manner and forme as before is mentioned, that is to say on every third Seaventh day in each and every of the said three monenths, betweene the howers of Tenne and twelve of each said day; And that dureing thy said Three Moneths imprisonment thou thalt be made worke for thy bread; And shall pay the Court Charges and Fees: And after thy said three Moneths Imprisonment thou shalt for the space of one yeare and nyne Moneths then next ensueing, be brought (where thou canst be found within this Province) to each and every Quarterly Sessions at Burlington within the said tyme, And then and there be whipt in manner and forme as afore is mentioned.

[*order of Court*] ordered by the Court that Thomas Hardings Eare marks for Hoggs etc. may be altered according as hee hath ever marked his Hoggs, the former marke appeareing to be mistaken in the entring thereof, which is to be the Left Eare a Cropp and the Right whole.

[*Grand Juries Presentments*] They present the County for want of a Prison in Burlington for a County prison. Alsoe they present Burlington for not keeping London Bridge in repayre. Alsoe they present the Kings Highway Leading from Burlington towards Shrewsbury being out of repayre. Alsoe wee present Walter Reeves for marking his Swyne with another mans marke which is recorded before.

Henry Grubb plaintiff David Lillies Defendant Action of Debt: withdrawne.

Richard Basnett plaintiff William Cole defendant Action Debt: Continued.

Richard Basnett plaintiff Walter Pumphary defendant Attachment withdrawne.

William Hunt Plaintiff Walter Pumphary defendant Attachment withdrawne.

Thomas Gardner Plaintiff Walter Pumphary defendant Attachment Continued.

Joseph Pope Plaintiff Henry Beck defendant warrant Continued.

Henry Grubb plaintiff John Stanbanck defendant Attachment not executed.

Joane Huff plaintiff William Smith defendant Warrant withdrawne.

Edward Hunloke Plaintiff Walter Pumphary defendant Warrant: Continued.

John Hollinshead Plaintiff Walter Pumphary and Edward Hunloke Defendants Warrant not executed.

Edward Hunloke Plaintiff Walter Pumphary defendant warrant: Continued.

Isaac Horner Plaintiff Thomas Scholey defendant on Summons withdrawne.

William Crues Plaintiff John Throp Defendant a warrant withdrawne.

1687/8]   THE BURLINGTON COURT BOOK   81

Daniell Leeds Plaintiff   John Ithell defendant   Judgment acknowledged by Ithell and Entred for 4l. 18s. and Costs of Suite.
Edward Hunloke Plaintiff   Robert Salfert defendant   withdrawne.
William Stanley Attourney for Thomas Budd Plaintiff   Joshua Newbold Defendant   withdrawne.
William Stanley Attourney for Thomas Budd plaintiff   Robert Salfert defendant   withdrawne.
Abraham Senior Plaintiff   Robert Salfert defendant   warrant not executed.
Richard Basnett Plaintiff   David Lillies Defendant   withdrawne.
Henry Grubb Plaintiff   Samuell Abbett Defendant   withdrawne.
Joseph Pope Plaintiff   Godfrey Hancock senr. defendant   Summons Continued.
Joseph Pope Plaintiff   Godfrey Hancock junr. defendant   Summons Continued.
William Crues Plaintiff   Abraham Senior defendant   withdrawne.
James Marshall Plaintiff   Abraham Senior defendant   withdrawne.
Edward Hunloke Plaintiff   Walter Pumphary Defendant   Continued.
John Hollinshead Plaintiff   Thomas Williams defendant   withdrawne.
Constables for Burlington presented and Accepted   Christopher Weatherill, Thomas Rapier   Thomas Rapier Attested. Constables for West and East side of Northampton River   John Furnis and John Hyllyard   both attested.

[69 1688] [*Speciall Court*] Att a Speciall Court called and held the 31th of March 1688 upon the Accompt of Edward Hunloke Plaintiff against Walter Pumphary Defendant: Then Present   Elias Farr, James Marshall, Richard Basnett, William Myers   Justices.

Edward Hunloke Plaintiff   Walter Pumphary Defendant   Action Debt being for 500l. per bond   Defendant appeares not. The Jury   Jonathan Foxe, John Payne, Samuell Houghton, James Wills, Peter Daile, Benjamin Hoult, Abraham Senior, Benjamin Wheat, William Lovejoy, William Stanley, Mathew Allen, Seth Smith   Attested. The Bond for 500l. Read in Court, for performance of the Condition underwritten. Evidence   Richard Basnett, William Stanley, James Hill   Attested, prove the Bond, Alsoe the Award read and proved by Elias Farr and Thomas Revell. Alsoe John Fleckna, James Wills, Peter Daile, Samuell Houghton 4 of the Appraisers appointed by order from the Magistrates to value the worke in the building done at Lessa Poynt valued by them at 79l. Testify the same.

Mordeca Bowden then came into Court and charged Edward Hunloke for keeping of Falce bookes.

The Jury finde for the Plaintiff and bring in the 500l. by Bond appeareing forfeit.

Whereupon the Bench Considering the whole premisses: give Judgment upon the same Verdict for the Plaintiff for 74l. 2s. 2d. with Costs of Suite; And that Execution be issued forth thereupon on the Body or goods of the Defendant.

Edward Hunloke Plaintiff   Walter Pumphary Defendant   Action debt being for 60l. per Bond   Walter appeares not.

Evidence   Benjamin Hoult Attested, Proves the Bond, and sayth that hee sawe also Martin Hoult (his Father) put his hand as an Evidence thereto.

James Hill   Attested   Deposeth that when hee Attached the Goods of Walter Pumphary at suite of Edward Hunloke, William Huntley and William Fryday being alsoe then seized thereby, did then say they were the Servants of Walter Pumphary.

The Jury finde for the Plaintiff and bring in the 60l. by bond appeareing forfeit for non performance of the Condition thereof. Whereupon the Bench give Judgment for the Summe of 15l. being the principall Debt, with all dammages, charges and Costs of suite ariseing or comeing by reason thereof and alsoe That execution be issued forth for the Plaintiff thereupon on the body or Goods of the Defendant.

[*An Attestation of James Creeke in Court on the behalfe of Thomas Potts*]   James Creeke Attested, Deposeth that hee heard Walter Pumphary say that hee had in his Custody a bond or writing obligatory from Thomas Potts for a Considerable Summe; But that said Walter alsoe then said that it was all paid except a Trifle; And that if the same bond should be found after his decease it might be an occasion of Trouble to said Thomas Potts, to which Attestation the said James Creeke then subscribed his name.

[70 1688]   Att the Court held the 12th of the third Moneth 1688 and By adjournments continued to the 16th same Moneth.

Present there on the Bench   John Skene Deputy Governour   Robert Stacy, James Marshall, Edward Hunloke, Mahlon Stacy, Elias Farr, Richard Basnett, William Myers   Justices.

All Evidences Attested for the Grand Jury   The Grand Jury Returned Godfrey Hancock, Ananias Gaunt, John Day, John Wearne, Michaell Buffin, Robert Engle, Peter Harvey, Thomas Barton, John Haines, Thomas Butcher, William Wood, William Bustill, Thomas Harding   Attested.

Traverse Jury   Thomas Wright, William Evans, Daniell Leeds, George Parker, John Paine, John Tomlinson, Freedome Lippincott, John Wills, Ralph Trenoweth, Eleazer Fenton, Eliakim Higgins, John Langstaffe. Alsoe Thomas Stales, John Antram Attested with the rest in some cases instead of Eleazer Fenton and Eliakim Higgins.

Grand Jury finde the Bill against Caleb Carman senr., Jonathan West, Anthony Burgesse, Nathaniel Cripps, John Fleckna, Daniell England. Alsoe the Grand Jury upon Complaynt Present Caleb Carmen and sonnes, John

Peck etc. concerned, for takeing breaking up and disposeing of dubarkis Whales [24a] on this Shore contrary to Lawe.

Alsoe upon a Complaynt of Joseph Knight Against Edward Marshall and others presented.

Alsoe Walter Pumphary upon information to the Grand Jury from Arthur Cooke presented.

Alsoe Walter Pumphary upon information for melting and selling Plate etc. presented.

Alsoe Mordecai Bowden upon information for affronting the Authority and his open scandall of Edward Hunloke Merchant presented.

Alsoe presented the person or persons concerned for not finishing the Court house.

Alsoe presented yorkshire Bridge and the Bridge at Godfrey Hancocks for not being repayred.

Personall Actions

[withdrawne] John Hollinshead Plaintiff Walter Pumphary and Edward Hunloke Defendants Action of Debt agreed.

Joseph Hutcheson plaintiff Charles Sheepey Defendant action case, noe declaration Attachment the goods Attached to be delivered back and the action to be withdrawne.

John Tomlinson Plaintiff Charles Sheepey Defendant Tomlinson saith hee tooke noe Attachment out.

[Continued] Thomas Wright plaintiff Eleazer Fenton action of Trespasse, Thomas Wright requires the Defendants plea and soe continued by consent.

[withdrawne] Mordecai Howell plaintiff Daniell Howell Defendant action Debt agreed.

[withdrawne] William Coles plaintiff John Vanderlinden agreed.

[Continued] Edward Hunloke Plaintiff Mordecai Bowden Defendant Action continued, Bowden saith in Court that the Court will not suffer an Action for the King.

[withdrawne] Peter Fretwell plaintiff Francis Stephens defendant action case agreed.

[withdrawne] Richard Basnett plaintiff Thomas Milner Defendant action Debt agreed.

[withdrawne] Henry Grubb plaintiff Thomas Milner Defendant agreed.

[withdrawne] Joan Huffe widdowe Plaintiff Thomas Milner defendant agreed.

[24a] Sir Thomas Browne wrote of the "Sperma-ceti" whale: "Mariners called it a Jubartas, or rather Gibbartas. . . . The name Gibbarta we find also given unto one kind of Greenland Whales." See his *Works*, ed. C. Sayle (Edinburgh, 1927), ii, 86 (*Pseudodoxia Epidemica*, 6th ed., 1672).

[*Nonsuite*] Isaac Hargrave plaintiff   Walter Pumphary defendant noe declaration   the defendant requires a nonsuite; and its granted him.

[*withdrawne*]   Thomas Revell and Godfrey Hancock plaintiffs   Thomas Mann Defendant action trespasse, agreed.

Thomas Mann Plaintiff   Godfrey Hancock defendant   Warrant not served.

Walter Pumphary plaintiff   Gilbert Wheeler Defendant action of case entred, but declaration an Action of Trover; but however they come to tryall and the Plaintiff can make noe proofe therefore the plaintiff suffers a non-suite.

[*warrant and recording Courts order*]   Gilbert Wheeler according to his Bond appeares about his selling Rum, the Court demand the Fyne of 5l. formerly laid on him for selling Rum: Whereupon upon Mr. Wheelers request for mittigation the Court remitt it to 50s. provided Wheeler pay it in Silver money.

John Curtis plaintiff   John Heathcote Defendant   action case, Attachment   plaintiff declares, the Defendant appeares not, the Plaintiff proves his debt of 15l. 4s. 6d. that is to say Thomas Duglas deposeth that Defendant was borded with the Plaintiff for several Moneths but cannot certainly say how long; John Calowe deposeth hee knowes the Defendant was borded with the Plaintiff about soe long as is in the Accompt   John Curtis Attests to the truth of this Accompt given in: Judgment Awarded the Plaintiff by default. [25]Evidences Attested   Thomas Duglas, John Calowe   Plaintiff attested to the Accompt or booke.

[71 1688] [*Rests*]   David Lillies Plaintiff   Walter Pumphary Defendant warrant not Executed.

Mahlon Stacy plaintiff   Daniell Brenson Defendant action of Case   Defendant appears not, the Plaintiff proves the defendant had Summons And Proves his Debt, by his owne Attestation to his booke. Judgment awarded upon default. [26]Evidences   Thomas Revell   Mahlon Stacy   Attested.

The Persons found by Indictment called to the Barre.

[*John Dennis being the prosecutor*]   Caleb Carman, being Indicted Pleads not guilty, and referres himselfe to God and the Countrey, whereupon the Jury before are called, and all accepted, and Attested, the Jury finde him not guilty in Manner and form as hee stands Indicted; And hee thereupon afterwards was cleared by proclamation.

Jonathan West, at the Barre pleads not guilty to his Indictment, and referres himselfe to God and the Countrey. The Jury aforesaid called and all accepted, but John Tomlinson, and in his stead Thomas Stokes is called and Attested with the rest.

Evidence   Peter Jennings, John Budd junr.   Attested.

[25] The rest is in the margin.
[26] This is in the margin.

Peter Jennings Deposes hee sold to John Budd a peece of mettle at the request of Jonathan West.

John Budd deposes hee bought a peece of mettle of Peter Jennings and that when hee tryed it, it seemed to touch well, and to abide the hammer well.

Jonathan West being asked how he came by this mettle saith hee found it about a myle from Walter Pumpharys Plantation.

The Jury finde him not guilty. The Recognizance withdrawne.

Anthony Burgesse desires noe Traverse but referres himselfe to the Bench.

John Fleckna also referres himselfe to the Bench and desires noe Traverse.

Daniell England pleads not guilty, but requests his plea may be withdrawne and referres himself to the Bench and desires noe Traverse.

Nathaniell Cripps pleads not guilty, but after requests his plea may be withdrawne and desires noe Traverse but referres himselfe to the Bench.

[*Nathaniell Cripps*] The Benches sentence on Nathaniell Cripps, the Bench Fyne him in the Summe of Thirty Shillings to be paid for a particular use by the Deputy Governour appointed for the use of the Province into the hands of Thomas Gardner Treasurer: And to pay all Court charges to be paid within one weeke next.

[*John Fleckna*] The Benches sentence on John Fleckna, the Bench Fyne him in the Summe of Thirty Shillings to be paid for a particular use by the deputy Governor appointed for the use of this Province into the hands of Thomas Gardner Treasurer; And to pay all Court charges all to be paid within one weeke next.

[*Daniell England*] The sentence on Daniell England, The Bench fyne him in the Summe of Twenty Shillings to be paid to Thomas Gardner for the use aforesaid, And to pay all Court charges, all to be paid within one weeke next.

[*Anthony Burgesse*] The sentence on Anthony Burgesse, the Bench fyne him in the summe of Tenne Shillings to be paid to Thomas Gardner, for the use abovesaid, And to pay all Court charges, all to be paid within one weeke next. Remitted.

[*Walter pleads not guilty*] Walter Pumphary presented as before appeares at the Barre, And upon the presentment on Arthur Cookes information, Mary Skene appeareing not as Evidence against him, Walter is required, to give bond to appear next Court upon Indictment. Walter Pumphary presented as before upon information for melting and disposing of certaine Mettle etc. is there upon Indicted and appeares at the Barre and pleads not guilty, and referres himselfe for tryall to God and the Countrey, whereupon the Jury aforesaid called, and excepted onely Thomas Stokes instead of Eleazer Fenton, and John Antram instead of Eliakim Higgins are empannelled with the rest, And then the Jury Attested.

[*Evidence Henry Grubb, Edward Hunloke Attested*] Henry Grubb deposeth that as hee and another was takeing up the Floore of the house where Walter Pumphary (the last inhabitant dwelt) the Cup being Silver cup, was by them found under the Plankes of the floore, And when hee the said Henry brought it home, his wife seeing it said surely this is the Cup that was wanting in the sloope that was Cast on Shore.

[72 1688] Edward Hunloke Deposeth that Walter desired him to sell a peece of Plate for him at Yorke, which Mr. Hunloke received and weighed and tooke to Yorke and offered it to sale, which when the Goldsmith had tryed said it was not melted from Minerall as Walter had suggested but from silver plate and that if hee did not know Mr. Hunloke well hee should question him where hee had it; further Mr. Hunloke saith hee sold the plate or Bullen for 5s. per ounce and that it weighed 6 ounces and ¼.

[Evidence Richard Basnett Attested] Richard Basnett Deposeth that Anthony Tomkins (who had lost plate in the Sloop that was run ashore) gave him such an Account of the Cup which with others hee lost, That this Cup appeares to be the same Cup, And alsoe that the Inventory which Richard found in the drawer where the said Plate was taken from alsoe shewes this Cup to be the same that was taken out of the said Drawer.

The Jury finde the Prisoner guilty of putting a peece of melted Silver to Sale, and receiveing the returns thereof. And say that they beleeve from what they have heard and seene that the silver Cup brought before them in Court is the Silver Cup of the Widdowe Tomkins late wife of the aforesaid Anthony Tompkins deceased; Whereupon the Bench cause the Cup to be delivered in Court to Charles Pickering for the use of the Widdow Tompkins.

Mordecai Bowden presented by the Grand jury as before; appeares at the Barr, And saith hee knowes himselfe guilty with respect to the affaires of the Court charged against him, And that hee is ashamed of it and Sorry for it, And craves the favour of the Bench, as Alsoe for his slandering Mr. Hunloke, desires the Benchs and his favour therein.

The Bench order that Mordecai Bowden come now in open Court and acknowledge the premisses as followeth vizt, That hee hath abused the Government of this Province, And that the scandalous words formerly and alsoe before this Court by him spoken against Edward Hunloke Merchant, were spoken causlesly, to witt that the said Edward Hunloke keeps falce bookes and is a cheat, and that hee is very sorry for the same; And that the same confession shall be fairly written and subscribed by the said Mordecai and sett up and stand fourteene dayes to publick view on the Markett house of this Towne to the intent the same may be made the more publick; And that hee shall pay charges of Court.

[Joseph Knight] A Complaynt presented by Joseph Knight to the Grand jury the Grand jury present it: being against Edward Marshall etc. The Traverse Jury called and Empannelled and Attested.

[Evidence Richard Starre, John Machiver Attested]

Richard Starr deposeth that Edward Marshall owned hee owed Joseph Knight money for barrells and that Joseph demanded his money, and because Marshall could not pay him, Joseph said hee would have his barrells and sate him downe' upon them, whereupon Edward Marshall struggled with him and tooke the barrells away.

John Machiver sayth that Edward Marshall struggled with said Joseph Knight and tooke away their barrells.

The Jury goe togeather: The Plaintiff or Complaynant by Charles Pickering his Attourney desires the Jury may be withdrawne, which upon the Plaintiff Engageing to pay Costs is granted and the Jury withdrawne.

[*Walter Pumphays Sentence*] Walter Pumpharys sentence, hee being at the Barr: In regard Complaynts have been made and hath alsoe appeared before the Court that certaine plate hath beene Conveyed from severall Persons, And that notwithstanding the said Walter hath refused to make knowne to the Bench how hee came by the said melted peece of Silver, only pretending hee run it from minerall that is in the Countrey, which by Artists appeares cannot be done, the Court propose it to him that if hee will before some person; on the Bench doe the like, they shall beleeve that metle sold may be as hee sayth; but finding said Walters reply, to be only by evading words— The Bench fyne said Walter Pumphary Ten pounds and to be kept prisoner untill the same be paid: And to pay all Court charges.

Caleb Carman and sonnes, and John Peck etc. on presentment per Grand Jury called, Carmans and Peck etc. appeare and say they have sold noe Dubartus whales but what at first Thomas Mathewes gave them leave for. The Jury Empannelled.

[*Evidence John Throp, Richard Starr, Henry Johnson, Samuell Mathewes Attested.*] John Throp saith hee bought a Fish which was supposed a Dubartus whale and that there was made 11 Barrells oyle of it.

Richard Starr saith that hee was present when Throp bought the whale, And that the Carmans then owned the whale as their owne. And that Throp bought the whale as the said Carmans owne right.

[73 1688] Henry Johnson Attested saith that John Throp agreed with the Carmans onely for their labour upon the whale.

Samuell Mathewes saith that Ezekiel Eldridge (who had parte of the fish) said hee had sold his parte to Throp for 10s. and the rest had done the same, And that they sold the fish as theirs.

John Dennis Attested sayth hee knowes little of Throps buying the fish But hath heard said Carmans say that all drift whales that came ashore there, belonged to them by Thomas Mathews order.

Jury Attested: They goe togeather And find Caleb Carman and the rest concerned in the presentment not guilty according to the presentment.

[*Court order for Swyne in Burlington*] Ordered by the Court that all Swyne above 6 moneths old within the Island of Burlington which after the

Sixteenth day of the fourth Moneth next shall be found goeing abroad unringed be taken up and impounded by the overseers of the Highwayes in Burlington, or by their order, And be kept untill the owners thereof shall come and pay 5s. for each Swyne soe goeing unringed, or otherwise shall forfeit such unringed Swyne: To which intent and purpose it is alsoe hereby ordered that the overseers order a Common pound to be made in Burlington forthwith.

[*Order for finishing the Assembly house*]   Ordered that the Assembly house (presented by the Grand Jury) be finished before the 15th of the fourth Moneth next under the penalty of 50l. upon default thereof to be levyed upon Francis Collins the undertaker thereof.

[*Order for Repayreing Bridges*] Order that the Bridges at Burlington and at Godfrey Hancocks (by the Grand Jury presented) be repaired before 15th of the fourth Moneth next under the penalty of 10l. for default thereof.

Constables presented and Chosen; Daniell Leeds   about Birch Creeke. Thomas Folkes   about Chesterfield. John Wilford   about Nottingham. Samuell Mathews   about Cape May: Attested. Overseers for Highwayes within Burlington   James Wills, and Benjamin Hoult.

Att a speciall Court held the 3th of the 5th mo. 1688 on the Accompt of Richard Ford on the Complaynt of Peter Fretwill on Indictment. Then present on the Bench   Elias Farr, Richard Guy, Edward Hunloke, James Marshall, William Myers   Justices.

Grand Jury   Thomas Bowman, Joseph Pope, Samuell Houghton, James Wills, Samuell Furnis, James White, Richard Love, Thomas Gladwyn, James Creek, Isaac Smith, Abraham Senior, Robert Rigg, James Satterthwait   Attested.

Traverse Jury   Thomas Gardner, Charles Read, Benjamin Hoult, Thomas Potts, John Kinsey, Benjamin Wheat, Peter Woolcott, Peter Jenings, Henry Grubb, Joseph Adams, John Smith, John Fleckna   Attested.

Prisoner Arraigned pleads not guilty and committs the Tryall to God and the Countrey   the Prisoner Challenges none of the Jury.

[*Evidence   Peter Fretwell, John Greene, John Peck, Peter Jenings.*] Peter Fretwell Attested saith hee had certaine Clothes stollen the same day in the Indictment mentioned, and two Locks broken open in his dwelling house.

John Greene Attested saith that John Peck (Peter Fretwells boy) came crying to him at Joseph Popes afrighted towards night on the day before mentioned And was (as hee said) by a man that came creeping to Peter Fretwells house: And that the said boy then discribed the Prisoner by his Clothes and person agreeing with the same hee then had and now hath on.

John Peck Attested saith, this is the man (to witt the Prisoner) that came to the house and affrighted him, as is mentioned in the Indictment.

Peter Jenings Attested saith that the said boy described the Prisoner by his Clothes before hee came to see the Prisoner againe.

The Court adjourne for an hower.

The Court called And the Jury being called say they are agreed of their Verdict And that they finde the Prisoner guilty according to Evidence, of Creeping towards the house of Peter Fretwell and threatning his said boy with death if hee would not depart his Masters house (contrary to his said Masters charge who sett him to watch his house.

The Bench order the Prisoner to finde good security for his good behaviour towards all the Kings subjects and especially towards John Peck (the aforesaid boy) to pay all Court charges, or lye in Prison untill that be done.

Att the Court held for our Lord the King the 8th of the 6th mo. 1688. Then present on the Bench John Skene Governour Edward Hunloke, William Biddle, William Myers, Richard Guy, Daniell Wills, James Marshall, Mahlon Stacy Justices.

The Grand Jury Thomas Bowman, John Hollinshead, John Browne, Edmond Stuard, Freedome Lippincott, Peter Harvey, Thomas Butcher, Joseph Pope, John Budd, John Ogbourne, Abraham Senior, Thomas Stokes, Benjamin Hoult Attested.

The Traverse Jury John Shinn, Symon Charles, Thomas Wood, John Woolston, Samuell Andrews, Thomas Potts, John Day, Isaac Horner, Mathew Allen, George Smith, John Wilsford, Joshua Humphreys Attested.

John Tatham Esqr. Plaintiff Anna Salter defendant The declaration read. Evidences for the Plaintiff Anne Butcher, Edward Slade, Richard Pitman.

Anne Butcher Attested: Deposeth that the Defendant tooke goods of her the said Anne Butchers house without her consent.

Edward Slade Attested: Deposeth that the Defendant tooke away the debt booke late belonging to Gabriel Butcher her Husband deceased: And alsoe a Hyde of the Plaintiffs, Esqr. Tatham,

The Juryes Verdict The Jury finde for the Plaintiff and give him Twelve pence dammages and Costs of suite: And further the Jury explain their verdict (vizt, that the Defendant shall restore all the goods that were late Gabriel Butchers deceased to the said Plaintiff John Tatham Esqr., over and above the said Twelve pence dammages and Costs of suite: And Judgment is thereupon granted.

William Bustill and Uxor Plaintiffs Marmaduke Horsman Defendant Declaration Read.

Evidence for the Plaintiffs Nathaniell Duglas: Attested sayth nothing on the Behalfe of the Plaintiffs but what was acknowledged by the Defendant in effect.

The Juryes Verdict. The Jury finde for the Plaintiffs and give them 1 penny dammage with Costs of suit Judgment is thereupon Awarded.

[75 1688] James Hill Plaintiff John Tuely Defendant The Declaration Read and the Bond.

The Defendant himselfe appeares and acknowledges judgment for Nyne pounds with Costs of Suite: and judged [27] is entred.

Daniell England Plaintiff Jonathan Pyne Defendant Declaration Read The Defendant appeares not, the Court order judgment to be entred thereupon. The judgment above made null with the Consent of the Plaintiff Whereupon the Tryall goes on, and the Court proceed.

Evidence: Seth Hill Attested: Deposeth that the Defendant owned that hee had a heifer formerly John Storyes (in the declaration mentioned) but that hee had none of Daniell Englands, and that as belonging to Daniell England, hee would not deliver her.

The Juryes Verdict: The Jury finde for the Plaintiff and give him 5s. dammages with Costs of suite, And the Defendant to deliver the Cowe and Calfe at the Plantation late of John Story deceased within Six dayes after demand by the Plaintiff, or his order in good condition. judgment thereupon is entered.

Thomas Ollive and John Hollinshead Administrators of Joseph Blowers plaintiffs John Ogbourne Defendant The defendant (Ogbourne) confesses judgment upon the Declaration read: and judgment entred.

Thomas Ollive and John Hollinshead plaintiffs Attourneyes on behalfe of John Ogbourne versus Walter Pumphary Defendant The declaration Read and Letter Attourney from John Ogbourne alsoe read and owned per John Ogbourne The Bond of Walter Pumphrey read and proved.

The Juryes Verdict: The Jury finde for the Plaintiffs and give them the one hundred and Ten pounds due Per bond, with Costs of Suite: Judgment thereupon is entred.

Thomas Hutchinson Plaintiff Robert Hopper Defendant Action of Case declaration read.

Evidence for the Plaintiff Edward Butchers Attestation taken before Elias Farr, Edward Hunloke, James Marshall and Richard Basnett Justices, wherein the Deponent declares that hee did see delivered by the Plaintiff to the defendant Three thousand Pipe staves and Two thousand of heading at Treadhaven Creeke in great Chopt Anck River Mary Land in the Moneth of April 1685.

The Plaintiff alsoe Attested, Deposeth and Attests to the truth of an Accompt with the Defendant according to the declaration.

The Juryes Verdict: The Jury finde for the Plaintiff and give him 1s. dammages with Costs of Suite.

Thomas Hutchinson Plaintiff Robert Hopper Defendant Action Debt per bond The declaration read, The Bond read and allowed The Juryes verdict: The jury finde for the Plaintiff and give him 1s. dammages with

[27] *Sic.*

Costs of suite: To the end and intent the premises in Contest may returne and be sett in the right station.

Edward Hunloke Plaintiff   James Hill Defendant   The Action by order of Court Continued to next Court.

All Actions continued last Court are ordered to be continued to the next Court.

[76 1688] [*Presented*] Grand Juryes Presentments   [*John Crosby*] They present John Crosby for laying a pair Milstones at the Townes Landing at Burlington to the annoyance of the Province. [*Lawrence Morris*] Presented alsoe Lawrence Morris for setting a Haystack at the end of John Hollinsheads house in Burlington to the danger of the Towne. [*The Inhabitants of Nottingham*] Presented alsoe the Inhabitants of the Towne of Nottingham for not making a sufficient Bridge over the River Darwin. [*The Inhabitants near Daniell Bacons*] Presented alsoe the Inhabitants near Daniell Bacons for not makeing two bridges betweene said Daniels and Thomas Wrights over the runs lyeing in East Jersey Road: [*The Inhabitants of Burlington*] Presented alsoe the Inhabitants of the Towne of Burlington for not ringing their Swyne above three Moncths old:

[*The Fynes per order of Court*]   Their Fynes in case of Faylure   John Crosby if hee remove not his said milstones out of the River above highwater marke within fourteene dayes next to pay 3l. Fyne to be Levyed upon his goods and Chattells, with all dammages that shall arise after the forfeiture thereof: Thomas Butcher ordered to give him notice thereof.

Lawrence Morris, if hee remove not his Haystack within one weeke next to pay 5ol. Fyne, to be Levyed upon his goods and Chattells over and above all other dammages that may happen thereby. The Inhabitants of Nottingham togeather with all the Inhabitants on the Northeast side of Crosswicks Creek to make a sufficient bridge over the River Darrwin before the end of the Nyneth Moneth next, or otherwise to pay 2ol. Fyne to be Levyed upon their goods and Chattells: And to the end the same may be accomplished the Court appoint William Emley, Thomas Lambert, Robert Murfin and William Watson to be Assessours and the money soe assessed to be paid in to the hands of Mahlon Stacy and Thomas Hutchinson, who are alsoe hereby impowered to Levy the same (upon neglect of payment) by distresse and Sale of the goods and Chattells of the persons neglecting to pay the same.

Further ordered per Court that all persons keeping Swyne (vizt, Hoggs or Sowes in Burlington (sucking piggs onely excepted) shall either Ring them sufficiently within two weekes next, or keep them within their owne bounds or yards, under the penalty and forfeiture of 5s. for every such swyne as shall be soe taken up, by Joseph Pope or Bernard Devonish, or their order.

County of Burlington in West Jersey   Att the Court of Quarterly Sessions held at Burlington the first Tuesday in November being the 6th day of the same Moneth Anno 1688.

Present there   John Skene, Edward Hunloke, James Marshall, William Bidle, Richard Bassnett, William Meyers, William Emley, Daniell Wills Justices.

Grand Inquest   Thomas Wright, Thomas Scholey, Daniell England, Henry Ballenger, Edmund Steward, George Elkington, John Chapman, Robert Rigg, John Bunting, Thomas Gilberthorp, John Abott, Samuell Wright, Roger Parks   Attested.

All innkeepers, ordnary keepers and Alehouse keepers within this County called to shew their last Lycence and to take new ones from the Court.

Ordnary keepers Lycenced   Henry Grubb: Peter Jenings: Abraham Senior: Christopher Snoden. in Burlington and Hugh Staniland at Nottingham.

Joseph Hutcheson Recognizance Returned [*with Fyne of 30s.*] being by Justice Basnett bound to good behaviour for drinking quarrelling and fighting and other misdemeanours. Joseph Hutcheson appeares and referres and submitts himselfe to the Bench: The Bench Fyne thirty shillings and also to pay all Court charges: Adjourned to the 9th hower in the Morning. [   ][28] expense for the Province returned   it to him againe.

[**77 1688**] Presentments per Grand Jury   vizt, That a substantiall and good prison be built and finished in Burlington by this County before the Twenty Nyneth of September next upon penalty of Sixty pounds for default thereof. Alsoe, That a substantiall County Pinfold be built in Burlington betwixt this and the first of the first Moneth next under the Penalty of five pounds for default therein.

Alsoe, the Highway to East Jersey presented and ordered to be sufficiently repaired and that Bridges be made over the Creekes before 25th December next.

Alsoe, The Highway betweene Daniell Bacons house and Crosswicks Creek Presented.

Alsoe: The bridges over the Mill Creek and Pimsawking Creeke presented.

The Respective Division of Each Constablry or Township in the County returned by the Grand Inquest: And Approved per Court for present.

[*Nottingham*] Vizt, Nottingham Constablry to lye betweene Crosswicks Creek and Delaware River, and Northwards up the River soe farr as at present Inhabited.

[*Chesterfield*] Chesterfield Constablry to lye on the South side of Crosswicks Creek from the Indian Lyne to Thomas Farnsworths and soe by William Blacks Creek to Daniell Bacons and soe up his Creek to Thomas Scholeyes, and from thence to Widdow Sykes plantation to the Indian Lyne includeing in this Constablry all the said Plantations.

[*Mansfield*] The Constablry of Mansfield—to lye on the South side of

---
[28] Several words illegible in MS.

William Blacks Creek downe Dellaware River to the Towne bounds of Burlington and soe up Birch Creek to John Pancosts to Michaell Newbolds and soe to the North of the great Meadowe to Eliakim Higgin Plantation.

[*Springfield*] The Constablry of Springfield to lye on the Southside of Birch Creek to the Indian Lyne and to the Lyne formerly made betwixt the two Tenths and soe to the Towne Bounds.

[*Wellingborrow*] The Constablry of Wellingborrow, From Daniell Wills Plantation down Northampton River to Dellaware River, and soe up to the Towne bounds to George Elkingtons Plantation and soe to Daniell Wills Plantation, excludeing the same Plantation.

[*Northampton*] The Constablry of Northampton, from Daniell Wills Plantation, up Northampton River to the Indian Lyne and soe to the Lyne formerly drawne betwixt the two Tenths to the Towne bounds includeing Daniell Wills Plantation and George Elkingtons Plantation.

[*Chester*] The Constablry of Chester from Thomas Kendalls Plantation on the South side Northampton River, to Dellaware River, and soe to the most Southerly branch of Punsawking Creek from thence along the Road to Northampton River.

[*Eversham*] Constablry of Eversham, from the Kings Highway that Leads to Salem to the Indian Lyne, and soe along the Indian Lyne to the Easterly branch of Northampton River.

Constables chosen   John Browne Constable for Mansfield   appeared and Attested   Freedome Lippincott Constable for Wellingborrowe. George Smith Constable for Eversham.

Overseers for Highways Chosen   Joshua Wright overseer for Highways for Nottingham   John Bunting overseer for Chesterfield. Percifall Towle overseer for   John Crosby overseer for Springfield.

Next Sessions to be holden the first Tuesday in February next.

[78 1688] County of Burlington   Att the Court of Comon Pleas held 7th November 1688. John Skene Esqr. Judge thereof   Alsoe then on the Bench. Edward Hunloke, William Emley, Daniell Wills, Richard Basnett, James Marshall Justices on the Bench.

Jury Returned   John Hollinshead, Ananias Gaunt, John Crosby, John Roberts, John Payne, Daniel Bacon, William Hascor, Robert Pearson, Thomas Shinn, Robert Scholey, Abraham Senior, Hugh Staniland   Attested.

Thomas Wright Plaintiff   Eleazer Fenton Defendant [*my Fees 12s.*] Action Trespasse on case to the dammage of 3l. The defendant denyes the Trespasse   Evidences for the Plaintiff Robert Durham, Peter Fretwell and Edm[ond] Steward   Attested. Robert Durham saith that the Defendant confest hee tooke the Timber mentioned in the declaration from of the Land of the Plaintiff   Peter Fretwell saith the Logg or Timber was about two foot square and fifteene foot in Length.

Edm[ond] Steward saith the Plaintiff hath suffered great losse by falling of Timber in his ground, And that severall who have beene falling Timber and wood there said they was falling it for John Budd.

Jurys Verdict—They finde for the Plaintiff and give him 5s. dammage with Costs of suite: And Judgment thereupon Awarded.

Edward Hunloke Plaintiff   John Fleckna defendant [*my Fees 5s.*] Action Debt for 24l. The Defendant ownes the Bond for 24l. to be true. The Plaintiff ownes the receipt of 6l.   The Condition being for 12l. Soe Judgment Awarded for 6l. and Costs of Suite.

Edward Hunloke Plaintiff   William Smith defendant [*my Fees 5s.*] Action Debt   Defendant appears not the Plaintiff proves his Debt (being a booke Debt) by his makeing Oath to it: And ownes the receipt of 1l. 12s. 0od. soe rests 1l. 12s. 1d. which the Plaintiff craves Judgment for, with Costs of suite: Upon the Defendants not appearing: Judgment is granted for the said Remainder of debt with Costs of suite.

John Fleckna Plaintiff   Edward Smith Defendant [*my Fees 8s.*]   Action debt for 8l. 3s. 2d. The defendant ownes the debt and Confesses judgment And Judgment thereupon Awarded with Costs of Suite.

James Creek Plaintiff   Thomas Peachee Defendant [*my Fees 7s. and 2s. Exec[ution]*] Action debt for 2l. 11s. the Defendant appeares not and the Plaintiff makeing it appeare the Debt due, And acknowledges the recipt of 5s. Soe Judgment Awarded for 2l. 6s. the remainder thereof: (Two Evidences) with Costs of Suite.

Lawrence Morris Plaintiff   Richard Martin Defendant   Action debt Rests.

Execution taken out against Marmaduke Horsman at Suite of William Bustill and Wife the Sheriff makes returne the said Horsman is not to be found.

Execution against Walter Pumphary at Suite of Thomas Ollive and John Hollinshead (Administrators of Joseph Blowers Estate) The Sheriffs Returne is that hee hath Served the said Execution upon the Land and Plantation and houseing late in Walters possession and given possession thereof to the Plaintiff:

A Replevyn for William Myers against Godfrey Hancock senr. the Defendant since deceased.

Edward Hunloke Plaintiff   John Allen Defendant   Action of Debt Agreed and withdrawne.

Ordered by the Court etc. That all writts and processes to be brought in the Common Pleas shall issue under the hand and Seale of the Clerke of said Court: And that all Actions be entred in the Clerkes office before the warrant be served: And that the Declaration be Fyled in the office 14 dayes inclusively before each Court of Quarterly Sessions.

Next Court to be held immediately after the end of the next Quarter Sessions.

1688/9]   THE BURLINGTON COURT BOOK   95

[79 1688] Quarterly Sessions held at Burlington the First Tuesday in February being the 5th of the Moneth 1688. Present there   John Skene, Edward Hunloke, William Biddle, James Marshall, Daniell Wills, William Myers   Justices on the Bench.

Grand Jury Returned. John Tatham Esqr., Thomas Hutchinson, Thomas Folke, Joshua Eley, Peter Basse, William Budd, Percifall Towle, William Hunt, John Lambert, John Bainbridge, Isaac Marriott, Edward Rockhill, Robert Wilson, Thomas Scattergood   Attested.

Traverse Jury Returned   Thomas Gardner, Joseph Pope, Nathaniel West, Eliakim Higgins, John Woolman, Benjamin Hoult, Richard Finimore, William Foster, John Shinn junr., Henry Grubb, John Burling, Christopher Weatherill   Attested.

John Pancost for his not appearing on this Jury according to Summons fyned 20s. Samuell Taylor for absenting himself 5s.

The Sheriff hath noe Returnes on the Kings Acompt.

Coronor Makes two Returnes one of Godfrey Hancock junr. whom the Coronors Inquest judged to dye a naturall death: The other of one Ruth Birch who on her death bed accused Joshua Humphries her Master and his wife, of being the cause of her death. Joshua Humphries bound over to this Session appeares: And Daniell Wills prosecutes for the King: The Indictment drawne and given to the Grand Jury, and Joshua hath a Coppy thereof. Whereupon John Ingram and Mary Elkington Evidences for the King are called and Attested and sent to the Grand jury. The Grand jury bring in the Bill Ignoramus.

Constables called   Constables of Burlington Christopher Weatherill and Thomas Rapier, Nottingham   John Wilsford, Chesterfield   Thomas Folke, Chester   John Furnis, appeare and are dismist and new Constables for Burlington are James Satterthwait and Joseph Adams   Attested, Nottingham   Robert Pearson, Chesterfield   Robert Wilson, Chester   John Roberts.

Constables of   Mansfield   John Browne, Springfield   Daniel Leeds, Wellingborrowe   Freedom Lippincott, Northampton   John Hilliard, Eversham   George Smith,   appeare not.[29]

[*The order for Mary Pearson*]   Mary Pearson the servant woman of Christopher Snoden appearing to be a Vagabond and pretending to have a Husband who comes to her sometymes, but cannot make appeare Shee is marryed, and she and her pretended Husband being of evill report and behaviour, The Court order that the said Mary Pearson shall within foure days next finde sufficient security for her good behaviour and for her maintenance, or else within the said tyme depart the Province, or otherwise be whipt.

[*The order for Christopher Snoden*]   It appearing that severall misdeameanours and disorders have of late beene Committed by Christopher

[29] Except, apparently, Hilliard, who has "Attested" opposite his name in MS.

Snoden: The Court therefore order and hereby prohibitt him said Christopher Snoden from selling any strong Liquors untill next quarterly Sessions.

William Gill   Upon the Bond of John Hollinshead and James Wills his bondsmen Lycenced to keep ordnary etc.

[*Petition for the Highwayes over Northampton River*] Upon the Petition about the Highwayes from Burlington over Northampton River, Ordered by the Bench that the Highway over the said River, be from Robert Hudsons to John Wills and soe to be marked out from thence by the overseers who are to Summon and Attest 12 men of the Neighbourhood for a jury to lay out the same into the old way or the best and nearest way to Pannsaukin, and alsoe from Robert Hudsons to Burlington.

And John Wills appointed to keep the Ferry at Northampton River and to have a Lycence.

[80 1688]   Court of Common Pleas held 6th February 1688. Present: John Skene Judge, Edward Hunloke, William Myers, William Biddle Justices.

Jury Returned   Thomas Gardner, Joseph Pope, X Peter Fretwell, Nathaniell West, Eliakim Higgins, John Woolman, Benjamin Hoult, Richard Finimore, William Foster, John Shinn junr., Henry Grubb, John Burling, Christopher Weatherill   Attested.

John Ingram Plaintiff   Abraham Senior Defendant   withdrawne Dt.[30]

Daniell Wills senr. plaintiff   William Snead defendant   withdrawne Dt.

Abraham Senior plaintiff   John Renshaw defendant   withdrawne Dt.

William Righton Plaintiff   Samuell Harriott Defendant   Action Trover Continued.

Mathew Allen Plaintiff   Thomas Revell junr. Defendant   withdrawne Case.

William Myers Plaintiff   Edward Doughty defendant   withdrawne Dt.

Edward Hunloke Plaintiff   Mary Hancock widdow Defendant   withdrawne Dt.

Edward Hunloke plaintiff   James Hill Defendant   being a former Action Continued.

Alexander Steward Plaintiff   Mary Hancock widdow defendant   withdrawne Dt.

Edward Hunloke Plaintiff   Samuell Terrett Defendant   withdrawne Dt.

Richard Basnett Plaintiff   John Smith defendant   withdrawne Dt.

Richard Basnett Plaintiff   Robert Durham Defendant   withdrawne Dt.

Michael Thomas Plaintiff   Thomas Gardner Defendant   Continued.

Richard Basnett Plaintiff   John Renshawe Defendant   withdrawne Dt.

Andrew Smith Plaintiff   Samuell Oldale Defendant   withdrawne Dt.

John Ingram by a Petition Complaynes against Thomas French for parte

[30] Debt?

of his charge in his former Suit against French: Ordered that Thomas French be Summoned to appear next Court and to bring the receipts and payments hee hath in his hands.

Robert Styles and Priscilla his wife Plaintiffs   James Hill Defendant   Action Debt Declaration Read: Coppy of Thomas Howells Will read.

Evidence   John Hollinshead Attested: Deposeth that Daniell Howell told him this Deponent that hee the said Howell had paid the Plaintiffs what was due to them by Thomas Howells will except about 50s. But that the Plaintiff refused to accept the rest unless they might have all.

Juries Verdict: They finde for the Plaintiffs and that the plaintiffs be paid their Proportion according to the tenour of the Will, And they give the Plaintiffs 6d. dammages and Costs of suite. Judgment awarded.

John Hollinshead Plaintiff   James Hill Defendant   Action Debt per bond   The Defendant Acknowledges judgment upon the bond being per obligation 36l. and 18l. the Principall per Condition thereof, Judgment Awarded for the principall 18l. and Cost of Suite being 18s.

The Sheriffs returne of the Execution against Thomas Peachee at suit of James Creeke Executed and discharged.

Court dissolved untill the end of the next quarterly Sessions.

Att a private Sessions 16th February 1688.

Edward Hunloke, James Marshall, Richard Basnett and Daniell Wills Four of his Majesties Justices of the Peace at the request of Philip Richards of Philadelphia in the Province of Pennsylvania Mett togeather the 16th day of February 1688 at the House of Richard Basnett in Burlington and there held a private Sessions.

[*Philip Richards Complaynt.*] Philip Richards Complaynes that whereas hee Loaded severall goods on Board the Sloop Susanna (Peter Lawrison Master) as by Bill of Loading under the hand of the said Master dated 3th November 1688 ready to be produced in Court may appeare Shipt of at New Yorke and bound for Philadelphia abovesaid, which Sloop came on Shore to the Norward of Cape May, And that the said Sloop being come a shore as aforesaid, the Master and men left the Sloop and went a shore to seek for releife   in the interim Caleb Carman and Sonnes gott on board the said Sloop, and when the Master and his men came back to come on Board their Sloop, the said Carmans Vi et Armis, kept them of and would not suffer them to enter their said Sloop, unlesse they would yeild the said Carmans the halfe of the goods on board, which they pretended to have right to for saveing the goods therein (as they termed it) Whereupon the said Master and men (being overpowered by the said Carmans) was forced into a Complyance with them with reference to their owne particular goods, And in pursueance of which said forced Complyance the said Carmans have carryed away the said goods of the said Philip Richards mentioned in the Bill of Loading aforesaid, And have done Severall other matters and things in reference to the said goods in the said Sloop against the Peace of our Lord the King: Whereupon the said Philip Richards requests the said Magistrates to issue out processe against the said Caleb Carman and Sonnes and against all or any other person and persons that have beene concerned in the aforesaid unlawfull proceedings or reasonably suspected thereof To bring them up to Burlington in order to the binding them to make their personall appearance at the next court of quarterly Sessions to be held at Burlington aforesaid then and there to answer our Lord the King upon the Complaynt of the said Philip Richards.

Whereupon the Magistrates aforesaid order processe accordingly to be issued forth which is done. And Philip Richards bound for prosecution of his Complaynt next quarterly Sessions. Edward Hunloke, James Marshall, Richard Basnett, Daniell Wills   Justices.

[*1689 Sessions*]   Court of Quarterly Sessions held May 7th 1689. Present on the Bench   John Skene, Edward Hunloke, Daniell Wills, James Marshall, Richard Bassnett, William Emley   Justices.

Elias Farrs request to the Bench: ordered that hee bring in his Accompts and when they are adjusted hee may have his Quietus.

Grand jury   Joshua Wright, Thomas French, Samuell Oldale, Freedome Lippincott, John Hollinshead, Thomas Evans, Joshua Humphreys, John Langstaffe, William Ellis, Michael Buffin, John Pancost, Thomas Butcher, Henry Ballenger   Attested.

Traverse Jury   John Curtis, William Satterthwait, X Jonathan Eldridge, X Mathew Clayton, X Samuell Lovett, Abraham Hulins, John Harriot, Thomas Stokes, John Long, Thomas Shinn, X John Haynes, X John Tomlinson.

John Skene Esqr. Bill of Complaynt against Thomas Brock for a scandall   The Grand Jury bring in the Bill Ignoramus.

Christopher Snoden makes Complaynt against Thomas Peachee for 15l. 8d. per Bill out of his booke. Christopher Attests to the truth thereof, whereupon the Bench order Complaynant his said Debt with Costs of suite.

Edward Hunloke Gent. Complaynes against Edward Slade   Continued.

Daniel Leeds Constable formerly chosen, at this Session Attested. Ordered by the Bench that all Constables now in office shall stay in their places untill the yeare of the Major parte of the Constables now in being, shall be expired, that soe new Constables may all come in and goe out togeather.

Jury men not appeareing   Jonathan Eldridge, Mathew Clayton, Samuell Lovett, John Haynes   Fyned 10s. a peece and ordered that warrants be issued forth to the Constables or Sheriffe to Levy the same.

Constables not appearing   Burlington John Satterthwait, Nottingham Robert Pearson, Chesterfield Robert Wilson, Mansfield John Browne, Northampton John Hilliard, Chester John Roberts, Eversham George Smith

Fyned 10s. a peece and warrant alsoe order to be made to the Sheriffe to Levy the same.

[82 1689] Ordered That Six or more of the Neighbourhood may by agreement meet togeather and lay out their particular or private wayes betweene Plantation and Plantation and make report of such Highways by them laid out to the end if the same be approved of they may be established and Recorded.

Samuell Terrett an Evidence for Samuell Coles Attested Deposeth that his name subscribed as an Evidence to a Bill of John Cornish and James Sherwin to Samuell Coles is his owne hand writing and that hee is a witness and did see the said Cornish and Sherwin signe and deliver the same Legally.

Presentments by the Grand Jury

Wee present the Bridge upon the Mill Creek within the Liberty of the Towne of Wellingborrough upon the Kings Road and alsoe some bad Places betweene that and Burlington.

Wee present the Bridge by John Longs house upon Oneanickon Road to be repaired by the Towne of Burlington before the 20th day of this 3th Moneth 1689 upon the penalty of 40s.

The Grand Jury nominate the first of the third Moneth for the County of Burlington to meet to the Repayring of the Highwayes and alsoe the 10th of the 8th Moneth if need require yearly.

Court of Comon Pleas held May 8th 1689. There present John Skene Judge Edward Hunloke, Richard Bassnet, Daniell Wills, William Emley Justices.

Abraham Senior Plaintiff William Coles Defendant Action Debt The Defendant appears not The Bond being 36l. 10s. Debt with Interest proved by Edward Hunloke and Thomas Revell witnesses Attested: And the Debt of 2l. 16s. 4d. booke Debt since the bond, proved by Abraham Seniors Attestation thereto whereupon Judgment is awarded against the said Coles the Defendant for the said 36l. 10s. with Interest after 6l. per cent from the date of the bond and alsoe for the said debt of 2l. 16s. 4d. The interest for 2 yeares of 36l. 10s. is 2l. 3s. 9d. The execution therefore is for 41l. 10s. 1d.

William Crues Plaintiff Jonathan West Defendant Action Debt for 8l. 12s. Rests.

William Guest versus James Blake Action case Plaintiff appears not and at the Defendants request a non suit Granted.

James Blake versus James Read, Action for false Imprisonment the Plaintiff appears not and non suit Granted.

Edward Hunloke Plaintiff James Hill Defendant a former Action its Continued.

Abraham Senior Plaintiff   John Heesom Defendant   Action Debt withdrawne.

Thomas Revell Plaintiff   John Heesom defendant   Action Debt, withdrawne.

John Inian Plaintiff   William Wilobe alias Mathias Barksted Defendant   Action Debt the warrant not served.

Samuell Coles Plaintiff   John Cornish and James Sherwin Defendants   Action Debt   Continued.

Philip Richards Plaintiff   Edward Slade Defendant   Action Debt.   Continued.

Robert Stacy Plaintiff   Edward Slade Defendant   Action Debt. Rests.

Abraham Senior Plaintiff   Joseph Burgin Defendant   Action Debt withdrawne.

Abraham Senior Plaintiff   Samuell Scholey Defendant   Rests.

William Guest Plaintiff   James Satterthwait Defendant   Action Debt Rests.

[*August 6th 1689*] Court of Quarterly Sessions held August 6th 1689. Present there   John Skene, Edward Hunloke, James Marshall, Richard Bassnett   Justices.

Adjourned to the 5th 7ber or further order.

[83 1689] [*August 6th 1689*]   Court of Common Pleas held August 6th 1689.   Present There: John Skene Judge, Edward Hunloke, James Marshall, Richard Bassnett   Justices.

Samuell Cole Plaintiff   John Cornish Defendant   Continued.

Joan Huff plaintiff   John Heesom Defendant   Action Debt withdrawne.

Anthony Weston plaintiff   Edward Roberts Defendant   Action case withdrawne.

Edward Hunlocke plaintiff   James Blake Defendant   Action case withdrawne.

Abraham Senior plaintiff   George Goforth Defendant   Action debt Continued.

Edward Hunloke plaintiff   George Goforth Defendant   Action debt Continued.

William Fryley plaintiff   George Rowell Defendant   Continued.

Joseph Farrington plaintiff   Anthony Delayre defendant   Action Slander   Continued   the warrant not executed.

James Wills plaintiff   Samuell Burden defendant   Action Case   Withdrawne.

Philip Richards plaintiff   Edward Slade Defendant   Entred before and continued last Court   Continued this Court.

Benjamin Newberry, Daniell Leeds and Symon Charles Attourney for

Amos White Respectively enter Caveats against takeing out Letters of Administration of the Goods and Chattells of Robert Twyn Deceased.

Joseph Burgin Plaintiff   John Greene Defendant   Action case   Withdrawne.

This Court adjourned to the 5th 7ber next or further order.

September 5th 1689. Court of Sessions adjourned to this day called. Then present there: Edward Hunloke, James Marshall, William Myers, Richard Bassnett   Justices.

Edward Hunloke desired to have his Evidence concerning the discharge of 3l. laid on him for a Fyne for selling Rum. Whereupon James Hill and Bernard Devonish are Attested. And Doe respectively depose and say that they heard John Skene (when Deputy Governour) say, in open Court That Edward Hunlokes Fyne of 3l. aforesaid was satisfied.

Christopher Snoden upon the Complaynt of Richard Bassnett for keeping bad rule in his House appeares: James Blake Attested Sayth that hee came into the house of Christopher Snoden about 2 of the Clock in the night, and that hee sawe fower persons in the house drunk. The Court thereupon demand his Lycence, or by what authority hee keepes a publick house, To which hee answers hee hath paid 10s. for his Lycence, and if hee have it not hee is wronged.

The Court order upon this and other Complaints that Christopher Snoden shall sell noe more strong Liquor in Burlington: And that if it appeare before any one Justice of the Peace that hee shall notwithstanding sell any strong Liquor there, That then hee shall forfeit 40s. to be Levyed by warrant from any one Justice within this County.

[84 1689] Christopher Snoden for his abuse of the Bench required to finde Suretyes for his good behaviour; Hee replyes hee will Seeke for none because hee knowes hee can get none.

Peter Jenings Attested in Court Deposeth as followes, That hee knowes of his owne knowledge that Robert Wheeler and William Say or one of them have sold Rum to the Indians in Burlington about 2 Moneths agoe:

Court adjourned for 2 howers and then adjourned to the 1st of 8ber next.

May 12th 1690   Court appeare and called and all Actions and processe of this Court Continued, And the Court Adjourned to the 3th of June next.

Court adjourned to the 3th June 1690. John Skene, Edward Hunloke, William Biddle, James Marshall, Daniell Wills senr., Richard Bassnett, William Myers   Justices on the Bench.

Grand Jury Attested   Richard Guy, John Pancost, Eleazor Fenton, William Watson, Christopher Snoden, William Brightwen, Thomas Harding, William Wood, John Wearne, Abraham Senior, Thomas Dugglas, Daniell Leeds, John Shinn junr.

Traverse Jury Attested   Symon Charles, John Day, Eliakim Higgins, Peter Boss, William Budd, George Parker, Thomas Butcher, Christopher Weatherill, Benjamin Wheat, Samuell Ogbourne, Isaac Horner, John Warwin, Joshua Humphries.

Joseph Farrington Complaynes that Obadiah Hierton his servant will not performe his service to him said Farrington according to Contract. Master and Servant goe togeather and appeare again and declare they are agreed betweene themselves.

[*Hierton Fyned 20s.*]   But it appeareing before the Bench that Obadiah Hierton hath Contemned the Authority of this Province, for which offence hee referres himselfe to the Bench, The Bench thereupon order hee shall stand in the Pillory one Hower or pay 20s. said Hierton chuses to pay 20s. and Lawrence Morris promises payment thereof on behalfe of Hierton.

[*Indictment Elizabeth Chamnis*]   Peter Bosse Indictment on the behalfe of the King and Queene against Elizabeth Chamnis, The Indictment given to the Grand jury, and John Shinn and John Day Evidences Attested and sent to the Grand Jury; Grand Jury bring in the Bill ignoramus.

[*For a Tax for a County Gaol*]   Alsoe Grand Jury presented the necessity of a County Gaol and for stock[?] propose something of a Method for laying a Tax upon the County for that purpose and referre their proposall to the regulation of the Bench: [*Thomas Russell presented upon the information of William Wood and Thomas Dugglas*] And the[y] Present Thomas Russell upon the suspition of Fellony. The Bench thereupon order warrants to be issued forth to the Constables of each Townshipp to meet about the Tax and to chuse 2 persons in each Townshippe etc. and they to meet all at Burlington 23th June instant.

[*Alexander Steward Complaynt against John Skene for 50 Acres of Land.*]   Alexander Steward makes complaynt against John Skene his Master for his 50 Acres of Land by Contract: The said Alexander makes it appeare before the Bench hee hath honestly performed his service according to Contract: The Bench thereupon order that John Skene shall give him his Land.

John Skene offers an Appeal from this Session but the Bench take noe notice of it.

[85 1690]   Samuell Coles Plaintiff   John Cornish Defendant   Continued per Agreement of both parties.

[*Tryed*]   Edward Hunloke Plaintiff   George Goforth Defendant.

Jury Symon Charles and fellowes as before except John Daye Attested: Defendant appeares not: Declaration read: alsoe the Bond read, Abraham Senior an Evidence proves the Bond.

Jury Verdict   Jury finde for the Plaintiff and give him the Debt per the obligation due in Compensation of his Dammages and Costs of suite: And Judgment awarded: And Execution made out.

Thomas Ollive and John Hollinshead plaintiffs   Isaac Hargrave and Edward Hunloke Defendants   Continued by Consent of Both parties.

Edward Hunloke plaintiff   Isaac Hargrave Defendant   Action Debt Continued.

Eleazer Fenton plaintiff   John Budd Defendant   Continued.

James Satterthwait plaintiff   Obadiah Hierton defendant   withdrawne.

John Jenings plaintiff   Joshua Newbold Defendant   withdrawne.

Joshua Newbold Plaintiff   John Snape Defendant   withdrawne.

John Cornish plaintiff   Joshua Newbold Defendant   Continued.

Edward Hunloke plaintiff   John Hargrave Defendant   Continued.

Michaell Newbold plaintiff   Mathew Allen Defendant   withdrawne.

[See this Tryed further]   John Tatham Merchant on the behalfe of Doctor Daniell Cox Esqr.   John Dubrois Defendant   an Action upon the Case, The Action called, And the defendant desires a litle tyme to consider of the Plaintiffs Charge, which is granted by the Court and Complaynant.

Phillip Richards plaintiff   Edward Slade Defendant   withdrawne.

William Fryley Plaintiff   George Rowell Defendant   withdrawne.

Daniell Sutton Plaintiff   Elizabeth Chamnis Administratrix of John Chamnis Defendant   The declaration Read, and the Defendant ownes the Debt per Bill declared for in open Court, And acknowledges Judgment thereupon And, judgment accordingly is awarded. And Execution made out.

Edward Hunloke Plaintiff   William Fryley Defendant   William Fryley acknowledges judgment upon the Bond in open Court, And the Court Award judgment accordingly upon the bond for the discharge of the principall Debt in the Award and Dammages and Costs of suit.

William Fryley Plaintiff   John Heesom Defendant   Declaration and bond Read and the bond proved per 2 evidences (vizt) Christopher Snoden and John Fleckna, both Attested, The Court thereupon Award judgment upon the bond for payment 12l. 13s. the principall Debt with dammages and Costs of suite. And execution made out.

James Marshall plaintiff   Gilbert Wheeler Defendant   Defendant appeares not, declaration read, and alsoe the Bond and proved by 2 Evidences attested (vizt) Thomas Revell and James Hill, the Court thereupon Award judgment for 2l. 10s. silver money as [per] bond with Dammages and Costs of suite. See order of Court, in August   the Fyne and Costs to be 50s. in all.

Lawrence Morris Plaintiff   Abimelech Hudson Defendant   Declaration read, the Defendant ownes what is allready due to witt 3l. 10s. and 3 Bushells of wheat   Plaintiff and defendant deferr the Action a while.

[See this Tryed further]   Abraham Senior plaintiff   George Goforth Defendant   The Action deferred to the next day as see hereafter.

Edward Smith Administrator of William Smith plaintiff   George Goforth Defendant Edward Hunloke produces a power of Attourney from George Goforth and in regard the plaintiff hath not declared desires a nonsuite on the Plaintiffs behalfe which is called and granted Nonsuite.

Richard Russell Plaintiff George Goforth Defendant Edward Hunloke Attourney for Defendant as before craves a non suit against the Defendant not haveing declared in tyme, which is called and granted Non suite.

Court adjourned to 4th June.

[86 1690] June 4th [see this Entred and called as before] Abraham Senior against George Goforth called againe. The Jury Symon Charles and fellowes as last Attested. The Declaration Read: And the Bill read and proved by John Calowe an Evidence attested and Abraham ownes the receipt of 9l. 19s. 6d. upon the same Bill. Alsoe Abraham Attested to the truth of his booke Debt being 2l. 18s. 10d. The Jury finde for the Plaintiff and give him his debt remaining due per Bill and said booke Debt with 6d. damages and Costs of Suite: Judgment Awarded: And Execution made out.

John Joyner Plaintiff William Fryley Defendant withdrawne.

[Richard Guy and James Marshall order of Court] Richard Guy and James Marshall move the Court that in regard they have discharged their Trust (as farre as in them lies) touching their Administring upon the goods Chattells and estate of Robert Hopper, That they may have their Bonds in for discharge of the Persons who were security for them: And move that their owne particular Bonds may bee taken for yet remaynes to be done in the premises: The Court allowe and order the same to be done.

[Subpenas 2] John Dubrois Plaintiff Peter Perdriau and Elizabeth his wife, Elizabeth Montgault, Andrew Lawrance and Mary his wife, Daniell Lucas and Augustus Lucas Defendants. An Action of Slander and defamation, 2 subpenas one for plaintiff another for Defendant—Jury Symon Charles and fellows Attested. [Attested] Samson Gallais the Interpreter to the French people Attested.

[Attested] James Monjoy Attested, Saith hee heard Mrs. Rame and Mr. Perdriau saying to Andrew Lawrance, that if hee did not goe up to Burlington to doe what lay in his power to Undoe John Dubrois, shee the said Mrs. Rame said shee would never eat of said Andrew Lawrance bread more, And that shee said this because they had noe Lodging at Cape May. And further saith hee heard the said Perdriau say that Mr. Dubrois would run away. And that hee alsoe heard Perdriau say if hee would indeavour to undoe Mr. Dubrois that soe they might have an English overseer in his Roome. And further saith not.

[Attested] Isaiah Lebake Attested saith that hee heard Peter Perdriau and Andrew Lawrance say that John Dubrois had an intention to run away, these words were spoken as they came up from Cape May in a Boat, and further saith not.

[*Attested*] James Peyrard Attested, saith hee heard Andrew Lawrance say, that they were to indeavour to undoe Mr. Dubrois to tell falce things of him, these words were spoke in Burlington at the Bakehouse in December last. further saith not.

[*Attested*] Benjamin Godfrey, Attested, saith that Andrew Lawrance said to him (upon occasion of hee saying to said Lawrance that two such Testimonies as hee declared against Dubrois was enough to hang him) said Lawrance answered why then Mr. Dubrois wants onely the Rope: Further saith that Mrs. Rame said to Andrew Lawrance if hee would not goe up to Burlington to doe what hee could against Mr. Dubrois shee would never eat of his bread more, further saith not.

[*Attested*] John Gillent Attested saith, hee heard all the Defendants (except Augustus Lucas) say that Mr. Dubrois would run away, And that hee would sell and Convert the Goods of Doctor Coxe which hee had in his hand to his owne use. further saith not.

[*Attested*] Peter Reneare Attested saith hee heard Mr. Perdriau say to Mr. Dubrois that hee the said Dubrois intended to run away, but hee had prevented it: And that hee (this Deponent) supposeth the occasion of the Quarrell between said plaintiff and Defendants, was because Mr. Dubrois did not provide such a house for them as they expected: Further saith that Mr. Perdriau said hee had as much to doe to Command Mr. Dubrois, as Mr. Dubrois had to Command him: And that hee sawe Mr. Perdriau severall tymes come in threatening manner with his Fists Griped against Mr. Dubrois, And further saith not.

[*Attested*] John Cossen, Attested saith hee heard Mrs. Rame speake to her Sonne [87 1690] Andrew Lawrance to come up to Burlington, and that if hee would not come up shee would eate no more of his bread; further deposeth not.

[*Attested*] Nicholas Malherbe, Attested saith hee heard Peter Perdriau and Daniell Lucas senior say that Mr. Dubrois had a designe to take the Concerne of Doctor Cox into his owne hand, and goe away with it, And that after hee should gett the same into his hands, Escape who can, further deposeth not.

[*Attested*] Peter Lespine and Nicholas Martineo Evidences supenaed for the Defendants Attested. Peter Lespine saith hee heard Mr. Dubrois say that hee would gett what hee could out of Mr. Tathams hand and Then hee would laugh at him: Further saith that one day in the evening Mr. Lawrance told him in presence of Augustus Lucas that Mr. Dubrois would gett what hee could of Doctor Cox goods into his hands, and afterwards let every one shift for himselfe. And further saith that said Augustus Sonne told him that Mr. Dubrois said that if hee would stand by him the said Mr. Dubrois hee should goe shares with him in the profitts hee could make at Cape May, further saith that one day being at John Tests in Philadelphia Mr. Dubrois told him hee had a minde to send the Sloope to Boston and goe in her along Captain Eberad, And saith Peter Perdriau said to him (this Deponent) that Mr. Dubrois hath a minde to undoe us, but wee shall declare what wee knowe against him, further saith not.

[*Attested*] Nicholas Martineo, saith that Mr. Dubrois said hee would gett what hee could out of Esqr. Tathams hand, and then hee would laugh at him, And afterwards the said Mr. Dubrois said that when hee gott the Asse by the Tayle, hee knew how to Lead him, further saith not.

[*Attested*] David Lillies Attested, saith that the Whalemen by reason of the ill successe in the whalery, occasioned by reason of Mr. Dubrois comeing up the River with the Sloop, soe that they Lost the Whale: They thereupon said amongst themselves that Mr. Dubrois intended to make the best of the Doctors Concernes for himselfe: further saith not.

[*Verdict*] The Jury finde for the Plaintiff and give him 5l. Dammage and Costs and charges of suite. And judgment awarded thereupon.

Court adjourne to the 5th June.

June 5th 1690. [*See this entred as before*] John Tatham on the behalfe of Doctor Daniell Cox Plaintiff, John Dubrois Defendant, an Action upon the Case.

Jury Symon Charles and fellowes   Attested.

[*Entred plea*] The Declaration Read and opened: The defendant Pleads that John Tatham had noe power when the Action was Commenced to call the Defendant to Accompt   The Court Concurre togeather that hee had and hath a power to bring and prosecute this Action on the behalfe of Doctor Cox.

[*Doctor Cox Letter of Attourney read*] The Defendant requests to see Mr. Tathams Letter of Attourney from Doctor Cox which is produced and read: As to one parte of the Declaration, to witt, the Delapidations and defraud charged on the Defendant To be comitted to Patrick Robinson, Edward Hunloke, James Marshall and George Hutcheson to inspect and adjust the Accompts, And to make report to the next Court thereof: The abovesaid Commissioners are to meet at Burlington the 20th of this Moneth to proceed in the premisses.

Evidence for the Plaintiff

[*Attested*] George Taylor Attested Saith hee remembers that in January last (as hee supposeth) Mr. Dubrois came from Cape May to Newcastle with the Sloope, when the Whalery had occasion for her, And that the Whalemen had gott a Whale and kept her in hold 6 or 8 dayes but could not gett her in to shore for want of said Sloop, And before the Sloop [88 1690] came back from Newcastle the whale was Lost.

[*Attestation of Isaac Matchett*] Attestations of Isaac Matchett and others on the behalfe of the Defendant Showing upon what Accompt hee went up with the Sloop, which were taken before Mr. Salaway and Anthony Morris Justices in Philadelphia: Read in Court.

[*Attestations*] Attestation of Isaiah Ebrad on the Defendants behalfe taken before Justice Skene, shewing the reasons of Mr. Dubrois comeing up to Burlington, alsoe read in Court being for provisions.

[*Attested*] Benjamin Godfray Attested, saith that Mr. Dubrois sold some Beefe, but it was on the Accompt of the Whalery: Further saith that the chiefest reason of the other whalemen breaking Articles, was because of their want of supply with provisions, And because they was put to soe much trouble in going often for it; Further saith that if they had had salt they could have had meat; Mr. Tatham makes appear they had 26 Bushells of Salt downe to Cape May.

[*Attested*] Olliver Johnson Attested, saith that hee thinks the whalery men belowe on Doctor Cox Accompt had provision enough to serve the winter, and that hee stayed there amongst the whalemen untill 25th March, and that hee heard none of the whalemen Complayne for want of provisions, Mr. Taylor saith hee heard some Complayne for want of provisions, but the reason was because Mr. Dubrois would not give it them. George Taylor further saith that there is a vessel on the stocks at Cape May that was begun in James Budds tyme, But since James death nothing more is done to it, And that the reason was for want of Plank, And further saith that Mr. Dubrois spake to the whalemen to sawe Plank, at odde tymes, which they promised to doe, but did not.

[*Attested*] Peter Perdriau Attested saith that there was a Boat lost at Cape May belonging to Doctor Cox, which was lost by negligence, for want of help from the Shore.

[*Verdict*] The Jury finde for the defendant and give him his Costs of Suite, And Judgment Awarded for that parte of the Declaration which came before them with reference to neglect in the Defendant But the Judgment and order of Court for an Audit as to the Adjusting of Accompts remains accordingly to be done.

[*See this Tryed after:*] Peter Perdriau, Anthony Renavein, Peter Lespine, Nicholas Malherbe, Nicholas Martineo, Andrew Lawrance and Elizabeth Rame, (Servants of Doctor Daniell Cox) Plaintiffs Complayne against the said Doctor Cox their Master Defendant in an Action upon the Case. The Court order the Plaintiffs to prepare all their Contracts ready Translated out of French into English against Morning, and then to bring action on. Nicholas Malherbe, a single Action against Doctor Cox is alsoe ordered the same.

James Peyrard, Plaintiff Peter Perdriau Defendant an Action of assault and Battery—Plaintiff and Defendant agree to referre the cause to the Bench without a Jury, But the Lawe of this Province expressly requireing that assaults etc. shall be tryed by 12 men of the Neighbourhood: Jury called and Attested being Symon Charles and fellowes. Declaration read. Evidence.

[*Attested*] John Gillett Attested, saith that hee did not see the Defendant beat the Plaintiff but that hee did help the Plaintiff up hee being fallen downe, And that hee this Deponent was in the same Roome with Plaintiff and Defendant when the Quarrell was: Further saith hee heard the Quarrell betweene Plaintiff and Defendant and saith it was about a woman that was to goe downe passenger in the Sloope, and saith the Plaintiff asked the Defendant if hee should have parte of the money for the passenger, And the Defendant said that was nothing to him, hee would give Mr. Dubrois an Accompt of it: And Further saith hee heard stroaks but did not see any stroaks given.

[*Attested*] Daniell Lucas, Attested saith the Quarrell began as is aforesaid, and thereupon the Plaintiff reflected upon the Defendant by evill Language, and as the Plaintiff was at the Garden doore, hee tooke of his neckcloth and put it in his pockett, and went towards the Defendant as if hee had a minde to stryke him, whereupon the Defendant tooke up a padle in his owne defence and gave warning to the Plaintiff to stand of, saying if hee came upon him, hee (the Defendant) would stryke him, which the Defendant did: the deponent being asked if hee saw any blood, hee saith hee did.

[89 1690] [*Doctor Lanchads Bill read*] Alsoe a Bill made from the Plaintiff for the payment of 30s. for the cure to Doctor Lanchard Read in Court, with the receipt thereof.

[*The Doctors Certificate Read*] A Certificate from the said Doctor where the wound was (vizt, on the left side of the head, And that the wound was from 20th: 9ber to the 4th 10ber in cureing, And wherein alsoe the Doctor sette forthe that the Plaintiff Complayned of a paine in his Eye, which hee saith was occasioned by the stroak. [*Juryes Verdict*] The jury finde for the Plaintiff and give him 20s. dammages with Costs of suite.

[*A Complaynt against Henry Pope*] John Cowgill Attested saith hee heard Henry Pope at Christopher Snodens house Sweare (By God) three tymes, The Court Fyne him 8s. and Comit him to the Sheriffe till hee pay it. The Court upon his submission suspend the Fyne.

June 6th. [*See this entred before*] Peter Perdriau and the rest before mentioned against Doctor Daniell Cox called againe, Nicholas Malherbes particular Action agreed to come in Common with the rest only the Tooles that hee Attached hee desires may be appraised and sold to him towards payment of whats due to him: Alsoe the Complaynt of James Moÿe and the Petition of James Peyrard and John Gillett is to come in after upon the same Accompt with the rest.

Jury called Symon Charles and fellowes Attested. [*Interpretter Attested*] The Declaration Read Samson Gallais Attested truely to Interprett what shall be spoken out of French into English; And that the translating of the French Articles or Contracts with Doctor Cox into English is according to their principalls.

Peter Perdriaus Contract of Articles with Doctor Cox read: And also the rest.

[2 *Attestations*]   Peter Rainere and Benjamin Godfray Attested, say that Peter Perdriau came from Gravesend in prosecution of his Voyage december 6th 1688 Alsoe that Anthony Renavein, Nicholas Martineo and Andrew Lawrance came the same tyme from thence.

[*Attested*]   John Dubrois Attested, saith Peter Perdriau would not observe his orders, to goe into a certaine Creeke with the Sloop for her securrity, unless hee the said Mr. Dubrois would allowe one of the Servants of Doctor Cox to Pilate him in.

[*Attested*]   Daniell Lucas Attested saith that as to said Peter Perdriaus goeing into the said Creeke with the Sloop: Mr. Dubrois told Perdriau Captain Dixi should Pilate her in, but did not; whereupon Mr. Perdriau desired that hee might have another man to doe it, But Mr. Dubrois denyed it, whereupon Mr. Perdriau refused to goe into the said Creek and thereupon Mr. Dubrois putt him out from being Master of the Sloop. Peter Perdriau being further accused as being the occasion of the losse of the Red Boat.

[*Attested*]   John Gillet Attested saith hee knowes nothing of Peter Perdriaus being an occasion of the losse of the said Red boat. Mr. Tatham on the behalfe of Doctor Cox accuses the Complaynants in Generall for withdrawing from their Masters service, And that they said they will not worke.

[*Attested*]   James Peyrett Attested saith hee heard Peter Perdriau say hee would not serve Doctor Cox unlesse hee had his wages, And further saith that hee beleeves it was the said Mr. Perdriaus fault that the red boat was lost: But being asked the reason why hee beleeves soe, hee shewes none.

[*Attested*]   James Moÿer Attested saith hee knowes that since they were in their Masters service they have said noe body payes them, they had Commanders but noe payers But did never heare them say they would not worke.

[*Attested*] George Taylor Attested, saith that they are mentioned in Generall therefore hee can say litle; But as to some particulars hee hath heard Mr. Dubrois Command them to worke, and they answered if hee would not pay them they would not worke, And that [90 1690] others denyed to worke in Smiths worke, and said they wanted Implements to witt Sea Coale, And thereupon Mr. Dubrois gott other Smiths who did the worke with Charcoale: Further saith as to Anthony Renavien the Cooper hee heard him say hee could not worke being (as hee said) sick and that Mr. Godfray said to him sure if you can eat you can worke.

[*Mr. Dubrois deposition*]   Mr. Dubrois himselfe deposeth that hee cannot complayne against the Smiths; Hee said to them why cannot you worke with Charcoale as well as others: They said they could not Sauder with Charcoal, or Well great worke without Sea Coale.

[*Attested*] Olliver Johnson Attested being a Cooper, saith hee made 141 Barrells from 15 9ber to 25th March following, And the Doctors Coopers made being two but 145 Barrells from 15th January to 25th March following.

[*Attestation upon Anthony Renavien Accompt*] Upon the Accompt of Anthony Renavien who saith Doctor Cox promised him a sett of Tooles at the end of his service over and above his Contract. Peter Raniere saith hee heard the Doctor promise it. Mrs. Rame Covenant in right of her husband, As to which shee pleads for what was due to her husband to the tyme of his death, And that shee may have the Land and house built at Doctor Cox Cost according to the said Contract.

[*Verdict*] Juryes Verdict. The Jury find for the Plaintiffs (that is to say) for the plaintiff Peter Perdriau and give him his Debt per Covenants and Costs of suite. For plaintiff Nicholas Martineo and give him Debt per Covenants and Costs of suite. For the plaintiff Anthony Renavein and give him his Debt per Covenants and Costs of suite. For the plaintiff Anthony Lawrance and give him his Debt per Covenant and Costs of suite. For the plaintiff Nicholas Malherbe and give him his Debt per Covenant and Costs of suite. For the plaintiff Peter Lespine and give him his Debt per Covenants and Costs of suite. For the plaintiff Mrs. Rame and give her her debt per Covenants and Costs of suite that is to say what was due to her Husband to the tyme of his death and the land etc. as was Covenanted for dureing her life. And judgment awarded.

[*Elias Farr Accompt of Administratourship Adjusted and order of Court*] Elias Farre Administratour of the Goods Chattells and estate of Jane Garwood deceased haveing given in an Accompt before this Court of his said Administratourship, it appears there remaines upon Accompt in his hands to the Ballance the Summe of Three pounds one penny three farthings: which the Court order to remaine in his Custody untill the persons to whome the same belonge shall Legally make the same appeare.

Joshua Newbold Plaintiff William Wood Defendant action debt withdrawne.

Edward Hunloke plaintiff William Huntley Defendant Action of Accompt declaration read Jury Symon Charles and fellows Attested. James Hill produces a Letter of Attourney from the Defendant to appeare in defence of the Action: owned by plaintiff and Court.

[*An Evidence per an order*] The Defendant desires the Plaintiff to prove that Huntley was a servant James Hill confesseth that Huntley owned Himselfe a servant to Walter Pumphary when hee Attested him: The Plaintiff alsoe produced a Coppy of an order of Governour and Councell wherein they order to Seize Huntley as Pumphreys servant by Execution.

[Attested] Abraham Senior Attested saith hee knowes that Mary Bates had the Indentures both of William Fryley and William Huntley, and that shee said before Edward Hunlock should have them shee would give them their tyme, and saith Mary said shee had the Indentures from Pumphrey before Edward Hunlock seized them.

[Attested] William Fryley Attested saith hee knowes not whether Walter Pumphrey assigned them to Mary Bates before Edward Hunlokes Attachment was served or not.

[Verdict] Jury finde for the Plaintiff and give him 20l. dammages and Costs of suite, and Judgment awarded.

Edward Hunloke Plaintiff   John Heesom Defendant   withdrawne.
James Marshall Plaintiff   Joshua Newbold defendant   withdrawne.

[91 1690] [Petition] William Fryley a Petition in Court read Contayning a Complaynt against Edward Hunloke: The Court (in regard its a sodaine Surprisall to Edward Hunloke) appoint Fryley either to proceed next Court by this Petition, or by Legall way of Tryall, Fryley replyes hee will bring it by way of Action.

[Petition] Benjamin Godfray requests hee may have what wages hee deserves for his service to Doctor Cox, And that hee may bee dismist.

[Attested] Peter Reneire Attested on behalfe of said Godfray and alsoe Peter Perdriau, Attested   both say that Doctor Cox was willing to send him to Mr. Dubrois, and that hee should have such wages as his imploy deserved, And say that Doctor Cox did not intend said Godfray should come into this Countrey upon the termes of Servants who have onely the Custome of the Countrey. The said Benjamin Godfray haveing made it appeare, that there is noe Contract betweene Doctor Cox and him, And that hee came not over as a Countrey Servant but by Letter of recommendation from Doctor Cox, And that his service here for said Doctor seemes not at present soe necessary as was supposed, desires hee may have what hee hath deserved and be dismist of his service, which the Court thereupon order, onely that hee stay one Moneth in order to sett the affaires of the Doctor at the Cape in order, and what otherwise may be for the Doctors service in that tyme.

New Constables presented to be chosen and approved per Court. [Constables] Nottingham—John Roger Attested. Birch Creeke—Thomas Butcher Attested. Northampton—Joshua Humphries Attested. Willingborrow—Thomas Evans Attested before Daniell Wills. Cropwell—Thomas Wallis Attested. Burlington—Robert Riggs—Samuell Furnis Attested. Overseers for Highways. Mansfield—Michaell Newbold senr. Northampton—Anthony Elton. Willingford [31]—Thomas French. Burlington—Peter Fretwell and Samuell Harriott.

[31] A slip by the clerk. He corrected it above, crossing out "ford" and writing "borrow" above it.

[*order Court*]   ordered by the Court that new warrants be out against Nathaniell Cripps   John Fleckna and Daniell England for the respective Fynes on them formerly laid.

[*Order*]   This Court order that the Sheriffe take the Charge, and gather the Perquisitts appertayning to the Bench for each tryall, and alsoe to the Jury and Cryer, that is to say, 5s. to the Bench: 12s. the Jury and 6d. the Cryer for each Tryall, and in case a Declaration be delivered for Tryal and Plaintiff and Defendant agree not within two dayes before the Court, then the Sheriffe shall Collect gather or Levy 2s. 6d. for the Bench, 6s. the Jury and 6d. the Cryer for every such Action entred agreed after the said tyme: And alsoe the same halfe Fees for Bench Jury and Cryer shall be Collected by the Sherriffe for each Action wherein judgment shall be acknowledged in Court without a Jury.

This Court Dissolved   Next Court to be August 8th next.

Written out and Sealed a Comission according to the Courts order To Patrick Robinson Edward Hunloke James Marshall and George Hutcheson to inspect the Accompts of John Dubrois etc. and to make report thereof to next Court.

[92 1690] Att the Quarterly Court held August 6th 1690.   John Skene, Edward Hunloke, Daniell Wills, William Biddle, William Emley, Richard Bassnett, James Marshall, William Myers, Thomas Lambert, Justices present.   Grand Jury   John Shinn senr., Thomas Scattergood, John Calowe, Joseph Adams, Samuell Stacy, Michael Buffin, John Budd, Joshua Humphries, Daniell Leeds, Thomas French, Isaac Marriott, Anthony Elton, Samuell Taylor.   Traverse Jury   Thomas Gardner, Robert Murfin, William Black, Thomas Farnsworth, John Bunting, Mathew Watson, John Haynes, Peter Fretwell, John Day, John Abbott, Robert Wheeler, Daniell Sutton.

There are noe presentments or Indictment to the Grand Jury: Neither find they any thing presentable.

Samuel Coles Plaintiff   John Cornish Defendant   Agreed withdrawne.

Thomas Ollive and John Hollinshead plaintiffs   Edward Hunloke and Isaac Hargrave Defendants   Continued.

Edward Hunloke Plaintiff   Isaac Hargrave Defendant   Continued against John Hargrave Continued.

Eleazer Fenton plaintiff   John Budd Defendant   withdrawne.

[*Renew Execution*] William Fryley plaintiff   John Heeson Defendant   Execution satisfyed in parte.

James Marshall plaintiff   Gilbert Wheeler Defendant   discharged.

Lawrence Morris plaintiff   Abimelech Hudson defendant   withdrawne.

[*Renew warrant*] Nathaniell Cripps John Fleckna and Daniell England warrant not served.

Mary Hancock plaintiff   Walter Pumphrey defendant   Attachment noe goods found.

John Heeson plaintiff   James Blake Defendant   withdrawne.

Benjamin Wheat plaintiff   George Heathcote Defendant   Continued.

Francis Jonson upon Complaynt of Thomas Russell Comitted upon suspition of Murder; Russell run away and Jonson cleared by proclamation.

Thomas Wright plaintiff   John Calow Defendant   withdrawne.

[*make out Execution*]   John Calow plaintiff   William Lovejoy defendant   declaration read and Defendant acknowledges judgment for 50s. or Land and Judgment awarded for the said 50s. or the Land and Costs suite.

John Dubrois plaintiff   John Dewilde Defendant   withdrawne.

Peter Bosse plaintiff   Robert Hudson Defendant   Continued.

William Brightwen plaintiff   Gervas Bywater Defendant   Declaration read the Defendant appeares not. The Plaintiff Attests to the truth of his booke debt being 18s. 5d. being produced in Court, Judgment Awarded thereupon with Costs.

James Peyrard, James Mauger and John Gillott Plaintiffs Daniell Cox Defendant   Attachment noe goods founde.

Lewis Levalley plaintiff   Joseph Smallwood Defendant   agreed withdrawne.

Abimilech Hudson plaintiff   Richard Boyes Defendant   withdrawne.

Thomas Brock Plaintiff   Samuell Scholey Defendant   withdrawne.

Abram Senior plaintiff   Richard Boyer Defendant   withdrawne.

Abram Senior plaintiff   Samuell Scholey Defendant   withdrawne.

Daniell Wills Plaintiff   William Hill Defendant   Action Slander declaration read: Jury Attested   The Defendant confesses the words of the slander to be by him spoken: But Confesses hee spoke falce and desires forgivenesse: Jury find for Plaintiff and give him 12d. dammages and Costs suite. Judgment Awarded.

Richard Russell Plaintiff   George Goforth Defendant   Symon Charles appeares as Attourney for the Plaintiff   Letter of Attourney read and accepted in Court: the bond read and the acknowledgement thereof before Magistrates   The Jury find for the Plaintiff and give him his principall Debt upon the bond, that is to say 16l. 17s. 6d. and Six pence dammages and Costs suite, And judgment awarded.

Court Adjourned to 9th August being next day to 8 hr morning   Upon the Returne and report of the Audit appointed per last Court to inspect the Accompts of John Dubrois in answer to the charge given by John Tatham on the behalfe of Doctor Cox: It appearing by the returne of the same Audit that said Dubrois hath not Delapidated the Concernes of Doctor Cox wherewith hee was intrusted: The Court upon request of the Defendant Dubrois thereupon Award judgment for said Dubrois against the Plaintiff accordingly with Costs.

[93 1690] John Tatham Attourney on the behalfe of Doctor Daniell Cox Plaintiff, Peter Perdriau Anthony Renavein Peter Lespine Nicholas Malherbe Nicholas Martineau Andrew Lawrance and Elizabeth Rammey Defendants An Action upon the Case. Jury Attested Declaration Read: The Defendants Attourney on their behalfe demand a nonsuit in regard the charge in the declaration is in Generall termes and not specially exprest: The Court declare it as their opinion that the charge in the Declaration against the Defendants (according to Lawe) ought to have beene more particular: yet notwithstanding the Defendants declare they are willing to come to Tryall.

[*Evidence*] John Budd Attested saith hee knowes litle against the Defendants of his owne knowledge but saith that James Budd a litle before his death said that the service hee had in hand for Doctor Cox was soe hard by reason of the Defendants perversnesse they had broke his heart.

[*Evidence*] David Lillies Attested saith hee hath beene at worke with some of the Defendants, but as to their owne particulars hee can say litle, But saith James Budd said when hee was concerned with them at Cape May hee would bring Justice with him when hee went up to Burlington: And further saith that they wrought (to the best of his knowledge honestly) but when after they wanted victualls, they neglected.

[*Evidence*] Peter Reniere Attested saith that hee and the Defendants wanted provisions, And that their fare for two Monneths was onely Greene pease and some Butter. And that hee (this Deponent) was necessitated for want of provision to goe a fishing himselfe.

[*Evidence*] John Dubrois Attested, desires for his Testimony reference maybe had to what hee Attested last Court: And further saith there was a Generall Murmur amongst the French, and that they said pay us and wee shall worke: And that the reason of their soe murmuring, was because they was informed that John Tatham would pay noe further, therefore they desired to knowe who must be their paymaster: And further saith they had provisions, But that it was very sharp with them: And this Deponent being asked whether the Defendants came up from Cape May with his leave or not, hee deposeth some of them hee gave leave to. The Plaintiff and Defendants agree to withdrawe the Jury and Action: And that the Defendants and the other four persons who Complayned by Petition shall have their full wages to the 25th of March last paid them in goods at Cent. per Cent. and that Mr. Tatham on the behalfe of Doctor Cox shall discharge them the said Defendants and the other 4 aforesaid from their service that they may have liberty to goe where they please to worke.

[*Gilbert Wheeler part of his fyne of 50s. remitted*] The Court at the request of George Hutcheson remitt soe much of Gilbert Wheelers fyne as to make the Costs and Fine Amount onely to fifty shillings.

Thomas Farnsworth Constable for Chesterfield Attested. John Haynes

Constable for Eversham. Michaell Buffin nominated Constable for Mansfield. but desires to be excused because hee can neither write nor read. John Bainbridge overseer for Highways for Chesterfield instead of John Bunting.

Ordered per Court that Coppies of declarations be left with the Sheriffe for defendants 10 dayes before each Court.

Court order a warrant against Thomas Russell for 100l. being his bond forfeited in not appearing against Francis Johnson as Evidence for the King according to his Recognizance.

Persons nominated and appointed as a Jury for laying out Highwayes in the Lower parte of this County, And that they or the Major parte of them upon Accompt of death, absence or the like, shall have power to supply such vacancy amongst themselves by putting in others, vizt, John Skene, Thomas Ollive, Daniell Wills senr., Anthony Elton, Symon Charles, Francis Collins, Joshua Humphries, Daniell Leeds, John Day, John Shinn senr., Isaac Horner, Eleazar Fenton, John Woolman.

Court Dissolved   Next Court 3th 9th Moneth 1690.

[94 1690] Att the Quarterly Court held November 3th 1690   Edward Hunloke, Daniell Wills, William Biddle, Richard Bassnett, James Marshall, Thomas Lambert   Justices upon the Bench. Grand Jury Attested   Francis Davenport, William Righton, Samuell Harriott, John Woolston senr., John Day, John Payne, John Wills, Bernard Lane, John Woollman, John Butcher, Daniell Bacon, Christopher Weatherill, Thomas Wood. Traverse Jury John Wilsford, John Hollinshead, Roger Parkes, Percivall Towle, Peter Bosse, John Browne, Samuell Overton, Andrew Smith, Nathanill Dugglas, Thomas Kendall, Thomas Gardner, Thomas Scholey.

The Grand Jury have noe particular Bills from the Court But of their owne knowledge present John Wood of the County of Bucks in Pennsilvania according to the Contents in their presentment upon fyle. They alsoe present William Emley Thomas Wright and Joshua Wright for purchasing Lands of the Indians Contrary to the Lawe of the Province.

Actions

Thomas Ollive and John Hollinshead Plaintiffs   Isaac Hargrave and Edward Hunloke Defendants   The Plaintiffs upon the Action being brought in a wrong name require a non suite which is granted the Defendants   Nonsuite.

Edward Hunloke Plaintiff   Isaac Hargrave Defendant   Continued.

Edward Hunloke Plaintiff   John Hargrave Defendant   Continued.

Benjamin Wheat Plaintiff   George Heathcote Defendant   Continued.

[*declaration and Coppy 3s.*] Peter Bosse plaintiff   Robert Hudson Defendant   withdrawne.

Percivall Towle and John Pancost   John Woolston and John Browne Executors of Thomas Barton plaintiffs   Charles Robeson Defendant   defendant appeard not   Continued.

Edward Smith Plaintiff   John Gilbert defendant   upon the Defendants bondsmans request the Court Continued the Action upon promise to pay Interest.

Thomas Revell Plaintiff   Seth Hill defendant   withdrawne.

Peter Jenings Plaintiff   John Cornish Defendant   the Plaintiff Dead.

Samuell Stacy Plaintiff   Christopher Snoden John Fleckna and Joseph Smallwood Defendants   withdrawne.

Aaron Beswick and Abimelech Hudson plaintiffs   William Crues Defendant   Richard Basnett Attourney for Defendant requests a Continuance, the Court grant it.

Richard Basnett Plaintiff   John Hollinshead plaintiff   Gervas Bywater Defendant   declaration fyled   withdrawne.

[*John Tatham in person appeared and pleaded against the defendant Wood*]   John Tatham Esqr. Attorney for Daniell Cox Esqr. Plaintiff   John Wood Defendant   An action of Trespasse   Issue joyned the Defendant denies the Trespasse.

The Jury John Wilsford and fellowes Attested. Declaration opened [*the Plaintiffs Evidence   Attested*]   Thomas Lambert deposeth that John Wood the Defendant did acknowledge in his the Deponents heareing that hee the Defendant did take up certaine Lands above the Falls which Daniell Cox hath bought of Thomas Budd.

[*Attested*]   Richard Basnett Deposeth that hee heard the Defendant Wood say hee hath marked Trees in the Land (as above mentioned) and thereupon alsoe Cutt Hay, and alsoe that the Defendant Wood said hee would make the Tytle of Daniell Cox (the Plaintiffs) Land from Thomas Budd voyd.

[*Attested*]   Thomas Revell Deposeth that hee heard the Defendant Wood say that hee hath marked Trees and Cutt and stack Hay upon parte of that Land sold by Thomas Budd to the Plaintiff Daniell Cox above the Falls.

The Court adjourned untill 8th hower in the morning being 4th 9ber.

[*Verdict*] Court Called: The Jury gave in their Verdict in writing, as followeth (vizt) Wee of the Jury all agree in our verdict that John Wood defendant by his threatning speeches about the Land of Daniell Cox purchased of Thomas Budd disparaged and defamed publickly the Tytle of said Land Contrary to the Lawe of the Province to the damage of said Daniell Cox Plaintiff five pounds and Costs of Suite. The Bench thereupon grant judgment against the Defendant for the plaintiff for 5l. dammages and Costs Suite.

John Cornish Plaintiff   Edward Hunloke agent for John Langford Defendant   Jury Attested Declaration Read: Evidence for Plaintiff: Richard Basnett Attested saith the Defendant owned and promised to pay the Plaintiff either 11l. wanting 5s. or 11l. 5s. upon Accompt then made betweene plaintiff and Defendant for John Langford.

[95 1690] [*Verdict*] The Jury in the Action of Cornish bring in their Verdict and finde for the Plaintiff and give him his Debt Ten pounds fifteene shillings. And 2d. damage, and Costs of suite Judgment accordingly is awarded.

Court ordered that all Constables and overseers of Highwayes begin their yeare from the next Court, and that they then present new ones to be approved of and Attested then or else they soe fayling stay in another yeare.

Court at Burlington February 20 1690. Justices upon the Bench Daniell Wills, Edward Hunloke, Mahlon Stacy, William Emley, James Marshall, William Myers.

Grand Jury Present the County for want of a Prison and for want of keeping the County Court house in repaire.

Grand Jury John Curtis, Daniell Leeds, John Hollinshead, Robert Hudson, Edmond Steward, Thomas Raper, Percivall Towle, Thomas Folke junr., Seth Hill, Daniell Sutton, Samuell Andrews, Henry Grubb, John Day, Attested. Traverse Jury John Shinn senr., John Woolston senr., John Pancost, Thomas Gilberthorp, Samuell Bunting, Edward Rockill, William Matlock, John Antram, Josiah Appleton, George Smith, Stephen Day, John Crosby, Attested.

Edward Hunloke Plaintiff Isaac Hargrave defendant Rests.

Edward Hunloke Plaintiff John Hargrave defendant Rests.

Benjamin Wheate Plaintiff George Heathcote Defendant withdrawne.

Percivall Towle etc. Executors of Thomas Barton Plaintiffs Charles Robeson Defendant Declaration Read Articles Read and proved. Defendant appears not Judgment by default awarded for the 10l. in declaration etc.

Edward Smith Plaintiff John Gilbert Defendant withdrawne.

Aaron Beswick and Abimelech Hudson Plaintiffs William Crues Defendant: Hudson one of the Plaintiffs appears not—nonsuite.

John Wood presented last court indicted this Court but neither hee nor any to prosecute appeare soe suspended—suspended.

William Emley Thomas Wright and Joshua Wright Presented last Court and Indicted this Court, the persons Indicted appeare, but none prosecutes Grand Jury have noe Evidence and finde not the Bill: thereupon at the request of the Persons Indicted They are quitt by proclamation.

Samuell Oldale upon the Accusation of Anne Hartley Indicted, Anne Hartley Attested and sent to the Grand Jury: The Indictment found. Prisoner arraigned, and pleads not guilty and referrs himselfe for Tryall to God and the Country. The Traverse Jury abovenamed all accepted by the Prisoner And are Attested. Anne Hartley Attested, Deposeth that the Prisoner (her Father in Lawe) about Harvest last lay with her and had Carnall Copulation with her once, and afterwards about a moneth after hee once againe had carnall Copulation with her: Alsoe then read the Attestation of Mary Chamberlaine taken before Edward Hunloke James Marshall and Richard Basnett Justices That is to say that shee (the Deponent) being at the house of Oldale, hee offered to lye with her, And after that Anne Hartley told the Deponent that hee had Layne with her, And that the way hee Induced her to it was by telling her that hee had as many tymes as he pleased layne with her Sister Betty before shee dyed: This the Deponent saith shee heard being in the next roome. Traverse Jury finde him Guilty. And the Court February 23 agree upon and passe this sentence following, vizt, Samuell Oldale the Bench haveing Considered of the greatnesse and hainous nature of thy Crime of which at this Session thou hast beene found Guilty, Doe therefore Fyne thee in the Summe of 20l. to be paid for the use of the Publick, And also that thou shalt pay all Fees and charges of Court, all of which shall forthwith be Levyed upon thy Estate. And that thou shall this day betweene the howers of Eleven and two be whipt upon thy naked back at a Carts Tayle, And shall receive thirty stripes well laid on from the Assembly house to the Towne Landing in this Towne. Anne Hartleyes Sentence alsoe was passed as follows; Anne Hartley, The Bench haveing considered of the wickednesse of thy Fact of which thou hast declared thy selfe guilty, Doe therefore order that thou shalt this day betweene the howers of Eleven and Two be whipt at a Carts Tayle upon thy naked back from the Assembly house to the Towne Landing in this Towne and shall receive Twenty one stripes. Execution was accordingly performed. see the Courts order about Anne Hartleys Clothes towards the last proceedings of this Court.

[96 1690] Thomas Wright Indicted upon the Accusation of Daniell Wills for taking marking and selling of one Mare with her Colt being the proper Goods of said Daniell Wills:

Grand Jury finde the Bill: Thomas Wright called to the Barre, And Arraigned, And Pleads not Guilty, And referres himself for Tryall to God and the Countrey. The Jury called, The Prisoner excepts against Twenty one: The Jury called and accepted of by the Prisoner are Edward Rockhill, John Antram, John Crosby, Christopher Weatherill, Samuell Furnis, Mathew Allen, Thomas French, Thomas Butcher, Thomas Farnsworth, John Joyner, Thomas Gladwin, John Rogers and are Attested.

John Woolston senr. Attested Deposeth That to the best of his knowledge The Mare abovesaid is the same Mare that was left for Daniell Wills at Godfrey Hancocks, And that Thomas Wright told him (this Deponent) that his owne Mare had but one Walle Eye.

William Wood Attested, Deposeth That the mare that was left at Godfrey Hancocks for Daniell Wills was a Sorrilld Mare to the best of his remembrance.

John Calowe Attested deposeth That about May was 12 Moneths Thomas Wright Sold the Mare and Colt abovesaid to him (this Deponent) And that Thomas Wright when hee sold the Said Mare to him said Shee had but one Walle Eye.

Thomas Revell Labourer Attested Deposeth That hee hath seene the Mare abovesaid to day, And saith that shee hath the same marke that hee had heretofore marked a Mare which hee afterwards disposed of, which Mare had one Walle Eye and a peece.

Mary Hancock Attested, Deposeth That Shee hath heard John Scarbrough say that hee hath heard say that the Mare abovesaid was Thomas Wrights.

Thomas Potts Attested, Deposeth That hee heard say that a young Mare that was at Lessa Poynt with a Balld face was Thomas Wrights.

Richard More Attested, Deposeth That there was a Sorrill Mare with one walle Eye (and a yearling Colt) with a Balld face left at Lessa Point, And that Robert Durrham Said that the other Mare and Colt was Doctor Willses that was left there for him.

Thomas Wright being required to informe the Court what is Marke is Saith it is a hole in the neare Eare and a Slitt.

The Charge given to the Jury and they are ordered to seale up their verdict when agreed and present it to the Bench in the Morning: And then adjourned to 7th hower in the Morning.

February 21th   The Court Sett and the Jury appeare, And say they are agreed of their verdict, which by their Fore man they deliver Sealed to the Court, which is as followes: Wee of Jury are agreed of our verdict, And doe finde the Prisoner Thomas Wright guilty of takeing up marking and selling of the Mare with her Colt in the Indictment mentioned, which wee finde to be the proper goods of Daniell Wills.

February 23th   The Judgment or sentence of the Bench being as followes, Thomas Wright thou haveing beene found guilty of takeing up marking and selling of one Mare and Colt being the Proper goods of Daniell Wills, wee doe therefore order and appoint that thou make restitution according to the Lawe of this Province, whereupon Daniell Wills declares that upon Thomas Wrights paying Fees and charges of Court, hee acquitts him of the rest.

Joshua Newbold Plaintiff   Samuell Oldale defendant   Jury, John Shinn and fellows Attested, declaration Read: Plaintiff proves his Tytle to two thirds of the Mill Land and premisses by virtue of two deeds Recorded. It appeares the defendant hath noe present Legal tytle but an equitable right. It being required by the Court of the Defendant to show how hee comes to take and hold the possession of the premisses.

John Ogbourne Attested, deposeth that one evening (hee knows not when) hee heard the Plaintiff say to the Defendant that hee would have him goe on with the Mill and what necessary charges hee was at hee would pay his parte.

Thomas Terry Attested, Deposeth that what the defendant was out about the Mill, the Plaintiff said the Mill might pay it and that this was about 12 Moneths agoe.

William Monckhouse Attested, Deposeth the same in effect as above, and saith the words hee heard spoken as aforesaid was about January was 12 Moneths.

Edward Lancaster Attested, Deposeth that the Plaintiff hyred him to tend the Mill, and when accordingly hee went up to grinde at the Mill the defendant said hee would pull downe the damm: And that hee the said Miller went up againe by the Plaintiffs order to grind, And then the Defendant discharged him from meddleing with the said Mill, at his perill: The charge given to the Jury.

The Jury finde for the Plaintiff and give him 40s. damage and Costs of suite. Judgment Awarded accordingly, And that the Plaintiff be putt into possession of the Mill And Oldale by reason of his former threatning words to be yet continued bound to good behaviour. Joshua to keep true Accompts of the Mill.

[97 1690] John Dubrois Plaintiff John Tatham Esqr. Defendant withdrawne.

John Dubrois Plaintiff Daniell Cox Esqr. Defendant withdrawne Received 20s. per Bill from John Dubrois upon Mr. Tatham.

Charles Pickering on behalfe of himselfe and fellow executors of Anna Salter Plaintiff John Snoden Defendant Continued.

Charles Pickering Plaintiff John Tatham Esqr. Defendant withdrawne.

Anthony Elton and Elizabeth his wife Plaintiffs Mary Hancock Executor of Godfrey Hancock her late Sonne Defendant. Jury John Crosby, and fellows Attested Declaration Read, The Legacy proved vizt. 10l. thereof due per Coppy of the will which was Read and attested to be a true Coppy: The Defendant produces a Particular of Debts from the Father of the Testatour [31a] and from the Testatour alsoe, which the Attorney saith amounts to more than the Estate. But noe proofe made of the Truth thereof: The Jury find for the Defendant.

Henry Jacobson Falconbridge Plaintiff Thomas Bowman Defendant. John Shinn and fellowes (onely instead of William Matlock, Daniell Sutton) Attested Declaration Read

Eleazer Fenton produced a note from Peter Jegou and the Plaintiff which was Read in Court

Isaac Hargrave Attested saith, that Jegou desired the Defendant that this Deponent might goe out and take up a horse or horses that was in part-

[31a] "Testator" in MS.

nershipp betweene Jegou and the Plaintiff And that hee (this Deponent) did goe out and bring in a horse and Jegou marked him for himselfe and Delivered him to the Defendant to keep till further order. Jury Finde for the Plaintiff, and give him Costs of suite, Judgment Awarded.

Henry Jacobson Plaintiff   Thomas Wright Defendant   Action Trover withdrawne.

Joshua Newbold Plaintiff   Thomas Revell labourer defendant   warrant not served in tyme for this Court.

Henry Jacobson Plaintiff   Thomas Revell Defendant   Jury Attested Declaration Read, And proved   The Jury finde for the Plaintiff and give him the 17l. Declared for and 12d. dammage and Costs of suite. The Plaintiff ownes 7l. received.

Thomas Budd Plaintiff   Elizabeth Chamnis Administratrix of John Chamnis Defendant   Action Debt. Declaration Read, the Defendant appeares not, The Plaintiff Shewes and Reads the Bill for 20l. 10s. and the Court satisfyed with the truth thereof; Judgment thereupon Awarded upon default.

Charles Sheepey Plaintiff   William Righton Defendant   Jury (vizt) Joshua Wright, John Hollinshead, Samuell Furnis, Thomas Butcher, Thomas Farnsworth, John Joyner, Thomas Gladwin, Peter Fretwell, Henry Grubb, Samuell Ogbourne, Thomas Dugglas, Richard Love   Attested. Declaration Read, the declaration as to 2s. 6d. per day owned per defendant But the Defendant saith that hee is greatly dampnifyed for the Plaintiffs neglecting his worke.

Samuell Houghton Attested, saith that hee agreed with the Defendant to pay to the Plaintiff 2s. 6d. per day And that the Plaintiff was to stick to and followe the Defendants worke untill it was finished; But saith the Plaintiff neglected the Defendants worke, And that the defendant was thereby damnifyed, Jury find for the Plaintiff, and give him his Debt, and Costs of suite, Judgment Awarded.

William Biddle Plaintiff   Robert Butcher Defendant   Rests.

The returne of the warrants against Nathaniell Cripps discharged in Richard Basnetts hand. Warrant against Daniell England not discharged, can find noe effects. Warrant against John Fleckna, can find noe effects. Brightwens Execution against Bywater paid in part.

John Hollinshead Plaintiff   William Gill Defendant, Attachment Continued.

Abraham Senior Plaintiff   Joseph Smallwood Defendant   withdrawne.

Daniell Sutton and Lawrence Morris Plaintiffs   Abimilech Hudson Defendant   Attachment   Continued.

Ordered per Court that Anne Hartley be quitt from her Father in Lawes Jurisdiction, And that her said Father Samuell Oldale shall deliver to John Curtis and Thomas Dugglas (for the said Anne Hartley all such wearing

Clothes as doe or did apperteyne to her at the tyme of his and her Conviction or the value of such parte thereof as hee hath otherwise disposed of: And alsoe such other wearing Clothes which Elizabeth Hartley (sister of said Anne) had at her decease. onely the Court leave it to the discretion of said John Curtis and Thomas Dugglas to give some small Clothes thereof as they see meet to Mary the daughter of said Oldale.

[98 1690] [*John Cornish Acknowledgment*] John Cornish came into Court and acknowledged that hee hath Received of Edward Hunloke on the behalfe and by order of John Langford the Summe of 49l. 4s. 10d. ob: which order the said Cornish acknowledges that hee in an unadvised hast tore in peeces, And therefore that hee is willing and promises upon the demand of said Edward Hunloke to give him a receipt for the same.

[*For Townshipps laying out their owne highways etc.*] ordered That every Constablry or Townshipp shall and may amongst themselves nominate and appoint Twelve Freeholders or any number lesse not under the number of Six, who shall and may lay out Highwayes and other private wayes within their Townshipp: which wayes soe laid forth, they are to present before the next Sessions then following, where (if the same wayes shall appear to be Comodious, vizt, the same Highwayes or private wayes without being Complayned of as appearing too obnoxious to private persons concerned therein) the same shall be confirmed at the said Sessions.

[*order about bringing in the Tax*] Whereas the Grand Jury have at this Court againe presented the County for want of a Prison and alsoe for want of finishing the Assembly house or Court house; ordered therefore that the severall Townshipps bring in their Severall Taxes according to the former order of Sessions.

	New Constables for the severall Townshipps within the County Elected		overseers for Highwayes
[*Attested*]	For Nottingham.	Thomas Gilberthorpe	John Lamber
[*Attested*]	For Chesterfield.	Edward Rockhill	Samuell Bunting
[*Attested*]	For Mansfield.	William Ellis	John Woolston senr.
[*Attested*]	For Birch Creek.	Samuel Ogbourne	Eleazer Fenton
	For Northampton	Thomas Stoakes	John Woolman
	For Willingborrow	Abraham Hulings	Thomas French
	For Cropwell Alias Chester	William Clarke	John Rudderowe
	For Vale of Eversham	Robert Engle	William Hewlings
[*Attested*]	For Burlington	James White	Percivall Towle
		Bernard Lane	William Righton

March 21th 1690/1. Att a private Court then held at the House of Richard Bassnett in Burlington for the County thereof in West Jersey.

1690/1]   THE BURLINGTON COURT BOOK   123

There present Edward Hunloke, James Marshall, Richard Bassnett Justices.

The Sheriffe then made his returne of the warrant of Execution against the Estate of Samuell Oldale for his Fyne of Twenty pounds and Costs and Charges of Court wherein judgment past against him last Court held February 20th last: Upon the said Oldales refusall of payment of the said Fyne and Costs and Charges. Vizt, The Sheriffe hath Seized the Third part of his Mill and of the Land belonging thereto with the Utensills and Appurtenances And hath sold the same by publick proclamation and burning of an Inch of Candle or Auxion the 18th instant to Edward Hunloke for Twenty Eight pounds: Whereupon John Heesom haveing bargained heretofore with the said Samuell Oldale for the said Third parte of said Mill Land and premises, and haveing onely given a Bond to said Oldale for the makeing a Tytle of the same premises; by the appointment and free consent of said Oldale (who alsoe gave and delivered in the said Bond) made and Executed the Deed of Conveyance of said Third parte of Mill Land and premises to the said Edward Hunloke.

[99 1691] Court at Burlington May 8th 1691. Justices present Edward Hunloke, Daniell Wills, James Marshall, Richard Bassnett. Grand Jury Thomas Gardner, Thomas Hooton, Thomas Evans, Joshua Humphries, Samuell Kimball, Michaell Buffin, Thomas Briant, John Gardner, Henry Ballenger, Abraham Senior, Thomas French, John Roberts, Thomas Gladwin Attested. Traverse Jury Symon Charles, John Woolston senr., John Wills, John Day, John Haynes, Thomas Butcher, John Paine, Daniel Sutton, Anthony Elton, John Hollinshead, Elias Burley, Samuell Harriot Attested.

[*Henry Beck and Alice Rawood presented*] The Grand Jury present Henry Beck and Alice Rawood the daughter in Lawe of William Black for Comitting Fornication. Henry Beck appeared on the behalfe of himselfe and said Alice (shee being not able to come) And acknowledged the aforeside Cryme: And on the behalfe of himselfe and said Alice submitted to the Judgment of the Bench.

[*Order of Court*] The Court haveing thereupon Considered of the aforesaid Cryme, order as followes (vizt) That the said Henry Beck give security for the Indemnifying the Court of Burlington, And for mainteynance of the Bastard Child; And that the said Alice Rawood after shee shall be delivered and well, shall be whipt, or pay 5l.

[*Thomas Peachee and Mary presented*] Alsoe they present Thomas Peachee and Mary (his now wife) for Committing Fornication before marriage To appear next Court.

[*William Emley and Mary, presented*] Alsoe they present William Emley and Mary (his now wife) for Comitting Fornication before Marriage To appear next Court.

[*John Hollinshead presented*]   Alsoe they present John Hollinshead for damming up the Highway betweene Ponsaukin and Burlington.

Edward Hunloke Plaintiff   Isaac Hargrave defendant   Rests.

Edward Hunloke Plaintiff   John Hargrave defendant   Rests.

Percivall Towle etc. Plaintiffs   Charles Robinson defendant   Execution to be renewed.

Joshua Newbold Plaintiff   Samuell Oldale Defendant   Execution but the goods not sold.

Thomas Budd Plaintiff   Elizabeth Chamnis Defendant   Execution [*Land seized and sit* [?] *to Sale but it being before mortgaged to Thomas Bud Court order Sheriffe to give plaintiff possession.*]

Charles Sheepey plaintiff   William Righton Defendant   Execution.

John Hollinshead Plaintiff   William Gill Defendant   Continued.

Freedom Lippincott Plaintiff versus Thomas French Defendant   Continued per Order of Court.

Christopher Snoden Plaintiff versus John Hollinshead Defendant   the Plaintiff Nonsuited.

Christopher Snoden Plaintiff versus John Cornish Defendant   withdrawne.

John Gardner Plaintiff versus William Righton defendant   Continued.

Thomas Brock Plaintiff versus John Heesom Defendant   Continued.

Thomas Brock Plaintiff versus Ralph Syddall defendant   withdrawne.

Christopher Snoden Plaintiff   John Heesom defendant Jury Attested, declaration read, and Bill obligation for 9l. 14s. 7d. Debt. The defendant declares hee beleeves the Bill was Executed by him, but saith hee was drunk when hee did it. Henry Pope Attested saith hee sawe John Heesom the Defendant seale etc, the Bill, and that to the best of his knowledge hee was sober: And as to the 34s. 11d. in the declaration mentioned due per booke, the Plaintiff produced his booke but it makes nothing out, John Fleckna Attested saith that the Defendant and hee the deponent, and others came to the Plaintiffs house and brought Rum with them at their owne charge, And that they drunke the same at the Plaintiffs And the said Plaintiff putt the same Rum to their charge, at the same rate as sold in an ordnary: The Letter of Attourney alsoe Read from the Defendant to the Plaintiff [**100 1691**] wherein it appeares the defendant impowered the Plaintiff to Act for him as in the Plaintiffs declaration mentioned. [*Verdict*] The Jury are agreed of their Verdict, and find for the Plaintiff, vizt, as to the Bill under hand and Seale they find 7l. 14s. 7d. remaining due, As to the 34s. 11d. the booke debt they find nothing thereof due, And as to the Charges paines etc. mentioned in the declaration as Attourney for the defendant they find 4l. 18s. 0d. with 6d. dammages and Costs of suite. Judgment thereupon Awarded.

Thomas Ollive Plaintiff versus Edward Smith defendant   Jury Attested Action of the Case for 25s. 10d. per booke The Plaintiff produced the booke in Court and the Accompt therein (as appeares by adjusting thereof) appeares to bee a just debt. [*Verdict*] The Jury are agreed of their Verdict, and find for the Plaintiff and give him his debt declared for with 2d. dammages and Costs of suite. Judgment thereupon Awarded.

James Hill the Surviveing Executor of Francis Beswick deceased Plaintiff versus William Crues Defendant The defendant Crues appeares not personally: But John White as his Attourney appeares: And saith hee will not be concerned in paying any thing if the defendant should be Cast,[32] but onely will appeare to defend the Case. The defendants bond forfeited.

[*Charles Sheepey perjured and Pilloryed*] Charles Sheepey appeares in Court and upon his Attestation informes against Abraham Seniors Selling Rum as followes, hee deposeth that hee hath seene Mary the wife of Abraham Senior give Rum to an Indian or Indians Twice at one tyme and tooke wampam for it, and saith it was about half a yeare ago, And that hee did not discover it untill about a Moneth last past, when hee (this deponent) was sett in the Stocks upon Mary Seniors Accompt; And further saith John Fleckna and Henry Pope was by when shee delivered the said Rum and that they sawe it, John Fleckna and Henry Pope being thereupon Attested say they never sawe Abraham Senior or his wife give or sell any Rum to any Indian or Indians (except onely to one Indian called Indoweys William Biddles man, when hee came downe from William Biddles an Errand: Whereupon Sheepey againe answered and said that was not the Indian hee speakes of, and further then said that Fleckna and Pope was not by when Shee Sold the Rum to the Indian. Whereupon it plainly appearing that the said Sheepey hath given a false Evidence, the Court order that hee be sett in the Pillory forthwith one hower, And hee noe more to be admitted in Evidence.

[*Court Order*] The Court order that Christopher Snoden sell noe more Rum or strong Liquors without Lycence at his owne perill.

Christopher Snoden Plaintiff Abraham Senior Defendant Action Case: Jury being Symon Charles, John Woolston senr., John Wills, John Haynes, John Payne, Daniel Sutton, John Hollinshead, Elias Burley, Samuell Harriott, John Day, Thomas Butcher, Anthony Elton Attested. Declaration Read. The defendant ownes that hee agreed to pay 10l. to the Plaintiff when Charles Sheepey should earne it, that is to say, 40s. first to the Plaintiff, and next 40s. to himselfe, as in the declaration, And saith hee hath accordingly paid it. [*Verdict*] The Jury are agreed of their Verdict, And find for the Plaintiff, and give him 6d. Dammage with Costs of suite and Court charges. Judgment awarded.

[*Court order for Ordnaryes*] Ordered that all Ordnary keepers come in to take their Lycence, or otherwise as the Justices shall see meet where-

---
[32] *I. e.*, convicted.

upon Henry Grubb, Abraham Senior, Richard Bassnett, Thomas Kendall upon their giveing bond to be Lycenced.

[*Order of Court about Priscilla Hudson*] whereas Priscilla late wife of Francis Beswick deceased hath late Marryed one Abimelech Hudson who hath spent and Consumed a great parte of what was the said Priscilla's and hath left her, And shee being in want, Its ordered therefore that James Hill (the Surviveing Executor of Francis Beswick) shall and may take sell and dispose of such parte or parts of the goods and Chattells and Cattle as apperteyned to her share as her thirds, as shall be needfull for her mainteynance.

Court Dissolved   next Court August 8th next.

[101 1691] June 15th 1691. Anne Bradgate servant to Peter Bosse being brought before Edward Hunloke James Marshall and Richard Bassnett Justices Confest Shee Stole from John Stephens about 13 ounces of Cotton. And upon her Examination further Confesses shee hath stollen from her Master and Mistress Bosse as follows (vizt) That shee Cutt of 3 Aprons of Course Cloth and that shee put 2 of them with a parcell of wooll (which shee stole) in the old house, and the other shee let hang in her Masters house. And further saith that Saunder Stewards wife desired her to take up 3l. of Soap from William Gills wife on her Mistress Accompt and told her shee would help her to money for it, and that then shee might pay for it. Further saith that shee hath severall times stollen pins from her Mistress, And that shee stole 6 pence in wampam from her Mistress and further that shee alsoe stole 2 nyne penny bitts from her: Shee is againe Committed to prison untill June 19th next.

[*Spetiall Court*] Held at Richard Bassnetts in Burlington June 19th: 1691. Att a spetiall Court held before Daniell Wills Edward Hunloke James Marshall and Richard Bassnett   Justices at the House of Richard Bassnett in Burlington.

Thomas Ollive and John Hollinshead Plaintiffs versus Edward Hunloke and Isaac Hargrave defendants   upon Bond. The defendants acknowledge the Bond due and are willing to answer and Respond the Condition thereof, deducting what hath beene paid thereof which is five pounds. Execution to be made out for the same and Costs. Bench order Judgment and Execution against Isaac Hargrave and Edward Hunloke to be for 75l. according to Condition of the Bond and soe much more (as dammages and Costs suit) as will clear the Plaintiff of both Actions.

Edward Hunloke Plaintiff   John Hargrave and Isaac Hargrave defendants   upon Bond. [*Evidences*] Thomas Kendall an Evidence Attested saith hee did see the Bonds above said Sealed and delivered by the abovenamed John and Isaac Hargrave to Edward Hunloke, as alsoe the other from Isaac Hargrave and Edward Hunloke to Thomas Ollive and John Hollinshead. Henry Grubb alsoe Attested deposeth the same, Isaac Hargrave acknowledges the Bond and Judgment thereupon. Execution to be made out for the same and Costs. And for the other of Edward Hunloke against Hargraves; Execution to be 75l. and soe much more as will indempnifye said Edward.

June 19th 1691. John Stephens then appeares and discharges Anne Bradgate as to what Shee stole from him as above Whereupon none else appearing to prosecute Shee is per order of Court discharged by proclamation paying her Fees and Court charges: Whereupon Peter Bosse her Master refuseing to pay the Fees and Court charges for her, The Sheriffe per order of Court for discharge of Fees and Court charges Sells her to Anthony Elton for one yeare then next ensueing hee paying 20s. for the discharge of Fees etc. and Anthony Finding her sufficient meat drinke washing and Lodging.

Anne Bradgate the prisoner above, being brought into Court, Complaynes that James Blake came into the House where shee was Prisoner and asked her if shee was a Prisoner there, and further asked her if shee lay there, shee said yes, Hee then asked her if she had a Soft bed to doe a job upon: And alsoe that said Blake said hee would come to her againe and bring her something, And that hee after gave her some bread and meate and told her hee would come againe and bring her a Pott of Beere; And further saith hee did come againe, and not finding her went up the staires into the Chamber, but shee not being there (haveing hid her selfe for feare of him) hee came downe againe and went away. James Blake appeares, And denyes that hee said any such words to the said Anne as above, or that hee went into the house where shee was prisoner. Elizabeth Bassnett saith shee sawe James Blake goe into the Prison house (where the said Anne Bradgate used to be kept) last night, but did not see him come out againe. Elizabeth Decoo saith shee sawe James Blake goe into the said Prison twice and stay in some tyme last night. Susanna Decooe saith shee sawe James Blake goe into the said Prison house twice and that shee heard him goe up the staires there last night. Sarah Whitten saith shee sawe James Blake goe into the Prison house twice and that shee heard him goe up staires there last night. James Blake submitts to the Bench, whereupon they order him to find sureties for his good behaviour for one yeare and a day and to pay the Constables, and all other Fees and charges occasioned by his misdemeanour and to pay over and above Ten shillings.

Upon the Verdict against Abraham Senior at suite of Christopher Snoden (being for the Plaintiff with 6d. dammages and Costs suite, the Magistrates find the true meaning thereof to be that the Accompt being cleared, that what Sheepey hath earned over and above necessary charges, Snoden have the first 40s. and Senior the next 40s. untill Snodens 10l. should be paid: It appeares before them there is 10l. 17s. cleared whereof 6l. is due to Snoden and 4l. to Senior, soe the next 40s. is due to Senior there being 17s. of it in his hand and 14s. in James Marshalls hand if James find it paid in the yeare and soe forwarde: And the 3l. 7s. due from John Crosby is to be divided according to the agreement above when it becomes due.

Court dissolved.

[102 1691] County Burlington. Court of Sessions held August 8th 1691. Edward Hunloke, William Biddle, Daniell Wills, Mahlon Stacy, Richard Bassnett Justices on the Bench. Grand Jury returned Thomas Gardner, George Hutcheson, Samuell Furnis, Joseph Adams, Christopher Weatherill, Thomas Gladwin, Thomas Butcher, William Fryley, William Righton, Abraham Senior, Henry Grubb, James Wills, Richard Love Attested. Traverse Jury returned onely appeared Samuell Andrews, Thomas Scattergood, Isaac Horner, John Butcher, Henry Ballenger, William Hewlings.

[*Sheriffs Returne of Execution against John and Isaac Hargrave at suite of Edward Hunloke.*] James Hill Sheriffe makes returne of the Execution against John and Isaac Hargrave; That hee hath Seized their house and Plantation within the County of Burlington: which was appraised June 22th 1691 by James Wills Samuell Stacy and Samuell Furnis to the Summe of Sixty one pounds Five shillings: And was then accepted by Edward Hunloke (the Plaintiff) at same vallue as parte of satisfaction of the same Execution.

[*Sheriffs returne of Execution against Isaac Hargrave and Edward Hunloke at suit of Thomas Ollive and John Hollinshead.*] James Hill Sheriffe makes returne of the Execution against Isaac Hargrave and Edward Hunloke at Suit of T. O. and J. H., That hee hath Seized the House and Plantation of Edward Hunloke which was by him accepted as above in parte of Satisfaction for the Execution above, which was againe appraised June 22th 1691 by James Wills Samuell Stacy and Samuell Furnis to the Summe of Sixty one pounds five shillings: And that hee hath alsoe Seized other goods of said Edward Hunloke, all which being appraised (with the house and Plantation) amount to more then the vallue and Summe mentioned in the same Execution and charges; All which hee hath published the Sale of: but are yet remaining in his Custody unsold.

John Hollinshead Plaintiff   William Gill defendant   Continued.

John Gardner Plaintiff   William Righton defendant   withdrawne.

Thomas Brock Plaintiff   John Heesom defendant   rests.

Andrew Robeson and wife Plaintiffs   Mary Lawrie Executor of Gawen Lawrie Defendant   Action debt per bond   warrant not served.

Joseph Burgin plaintiff   Joshua Newbold defendant   warrant not served agreed.

Joseph Smallwood plaintiff   Obiadiah Hierton Defendant   withdrawne.

Daniell Leeds Plaintiff   Mahlon Stacy defendant   rests.

John Cornish Plaintiff   James Sherwin defendant   declaration fyled Continued.

William Righton Plaintiff   Charles Sheepey Defendant   Continued.

Freedome Lippincott plaintiff   Thomas French Defendant   rests.

Returne of Grand Jury   Upon the Indictment of William Emley and Mary his wife find Billa vera. Upon the Indictment of Thomas Peachee and Mary his wife: find Billa vera.

They alsoe present Eleazer Fenton and Elizabeth his wife for Comitting Fornication before marriage.

They alsoe find it necessary that the former tax for building of a County prison to the value of 6ol. to defray the charge thereof and other necessary things about the Court house goe forward. They alsoe find it necessary that the Highway from Yorkshire bridge to the Highstreet in Burlington be laid forth: which per order of Court they lay out the same day as followes: From a stake sett up in the Highway by Mahlon Stacyes house toward Nathaniell Cripps house North west and by west, the former parts of the said street being before laid forth to Mahlons stake aforesaid The breadth of said street to be equivolent with the street. Alsoe they present the Township of Springfield for want of repayres of Mattacopenny Bridge. Alsoe they present the Towne of Burlington for want of repayres of John Longs Bridge.

Thomas Peachee etc. and William Emley etc. called. Thomas Peachee appeares and upon the Indictment ownes that hee gott Mary (now his wife) with child before Marriage and submitts to the Judgment of the Bench The Bench order him to pay 5l. or his wife to be whipt   upon his further submission the Bench remitt their sentence upon his good behaviour hee paying Court Fees.

William Emley and Mary his wife appeare not. Mahlon Stacy and John Wilsford Attested deposed that the Marriage of William Emley and Mary his wife was on 8ber 1690 to the best of their remembrance, or however within 2 or 3 dayes under or over, And that about 20 weeks then next following she (his said wife) was delivered of a Sonne. Whereupon further processe made out for their appearance next Court.

Court dissolved   next Court 3th 9th Mo. 1691.

[103 1691]   Att the Court of Sessions held November 3th 1691. Edward Hunloke, William Emley, Mahlon Stacy, William Biddle, Richard Bassnett Justices present. Grand Jury Thomas Gardner senr., Daniell Bacon, George Smith, Josiah Appleton, Walter Reeves, Peter Fretwell, John Hollinshead, John Joyner, Daniell Leeds, John Roberts, Thomas Dugglas, William Hunt, John Gardner Attested. Traverse Jury Symon Charles, John Payne, William Budd, George Elkington, Nathaniel Dugglas, John Ogbourne, Edmond Stuard, John Calowe, Nathaniel West, John Hillyard, John Tomlinson, Samuell Houghton.

John Hollinshead plaintiff   William Gill Defendant   Rests.
Thomas Brock plaintiff   John Heesom defendant   Rests.
Daniell Leeds Plaintiff   Mahlon Stacy defendant   withdrawne.
William Righton plaintiff   Charles Sheepey defendant   rests.
William Emley and Mary his wife upon Indictment   William appeares: but not proceeded in.
Eleazer Fenton and Elizabeth his wife upon Indictment Eleazer appeares: but not proceeded in.
John Cornish Plaintiff   James Sherwin Defendant   the Defendant appeares not to defend. Plaintiff declares for 11l. per Bill and alsoe per another Bill for 2l. 0s. 11d. both Bills read: James Hill Attested proves both Bills: The Plaintiff ownes the receipt of 7l. indorsed upon one of the Bills and about 5 or 6 hundred of Bords: The Court award Judgment for 6l. 0s. 11d. with Costs of Suite.
Grand Jury present the overseer of Nottingham for not clearing the Highway upon Complaynt. Alsoe they present Daniell England, Nicolas Martino, John Powne, John Cassoone, Christopher Snoden, Thomas Williams, Robert Cole, James Barroe for breach of an order made at a Towne meeting of Burlington the 11th 6th Mo. last.
[*declaration and Coppy etc.*]   George Hutcheson Plaintiff   Alexander Steward defendant   withdrawne.
[*declaration and Coppy*]   Samuell Oldale Plaintiff   Richard Moore defendant   withdrawne.
Thomas Peachee versus Abraham Senior and wife, noe Record of a declaration.
Henry Grubb plaintiff   William Fisher Defendant   withdrawne.
A warrant drawne against Edward Hunloke at suite of Thomas Ollive and John Hollinshead in an Action of Case from the Sessions: But William Emley refused to Signe and Seale the Same, And there are but two Justices besides him on the Bench.
Court dissolved.
Court of Sessions held February 20th 1691. Edward Hunloke, Daniell Wills, William Emley, William Biddle, James Marshall, Richard Basnett Justices present. Grand Jury Returned   John Daye, John Warren, Lawrence Morris, James Satterthwait, Ananias Gaunt, Robert Wheeler, Thomas Potts, John Burley, John Browne, Thomas Kendall, Nathaniell West, John Woolman, Thomas Rapier   and Attested. Traverse Jury returned. William Wood, Benjamin Wheat, Isaac Marriott, John Bainbridge, Elias Keich, Nathaniell Dugglas, Mathew Watson, James Croft, Joshua Humphries, John Budd, Samuell Houghton, Nathaniel Ricketts.
There are noe Bills for the Grand Jury.
The Grand Jury present the County for neglect of Repairing the Court house.

[104 1691]

New Constables returned and Chosen		New overseers for Highways returned and Chosen
Nottingham—	John Abbott	John Lambert remaines haveing presented none
Chesterfield—	William Black	Samuell Bunting remaines haveing presented none
Mansfield—	John Curtis	John Woolston remaines haveing presented none
Birch Creek—	John Tonkan	Ananias Gaunt and John Butcher
Northampton—	Walter Reeves	John Woolman remaines haveing presented none
Willingborrow—	John Scott	Thomas Harding
Croppwell—	William Clark remaines,	John Rudderow remaines for want of another
Eversham—	Robert Engle remains,	William Hewlings remaines for want of another.
Burlington—	Robert Wheeler and Daniell Sutton Attested	John Budd and Samuell Furnis

John Hollinshead Plaintiff William Gill Defendant Continued.

[*Trespasse*] John Hollinshead Plaintiff William Fryley Robert Rigg, Richard Davis, John Cornish and John Pears Defendants withdrawne paid.

[*Case*] Thomas Wright Plaintiff John Greene Defendant withdrawne.

Mathew Allen Plaintiff Bernard Devonish defendant Continued.

[*Case*] Bonaventer Dominion versus Joshua Newbold plaintiff dead.

Mordeca Howell versus Thomas Smith Defendant warrant not served.

John Budd Plaintiff William Biddle Defendant withdrawne.

Robert Wheeler Plaintiff John Greene Defendant withdrawne.

[*Case*] Richard Basnett and wife Executrix of William Frampton Plaintiffs William Lawrence senr. defendant withdrawne.

[*Case*] Robert Coles Plaintiff John Baker defendant withdrawne.

[*Case*] Hector Dicks Plaintiff William Righton defendant Continued.

[*Case*] Hector Dicks Plaintiff William Righton defendant Continued.

Thomas Peachee and uxor against Abraham Senior and uxor withdrawne.

Nathaniell Cripps Heire to John Cripps Plaintiff versus Charles Pickering Defendant one of Executors of Anna Salter deceased on behalfe of him selfe and fellow Executors Action of debt on bond. noe warrant taken or served but they are to come to tryall by Consent. the Plaintiff hath fyled a declaration and sent Charles a Coppy. But Charles appeares not.

[Case] John Calow Plaintiff. Thomas Wright Defendant Tryed, Jury called and Thomas Wright the defendant excepted against William Wood And therefore Thomas French was added to the Jury aforesaid instead of William Wood. And then the Jury Attested, And the declaration Read, The Defendant ownes hee sold the Mare and Colt mentioned in the declaration and that they were againe taken from the Plaintiff. Attested for plaintiff William Wood saith that upon the Mare and Colts being taken away from John Calow, Thomas Wright was willing the Mare and Colt should be viewed, that it might appeare what they were worth. And that hee this deponent viewed the Mare etc. but put noe valew upon them, because Thomas Wright said hee would give John as good a Mare and Colt againe, And that the said John was Contented therewith. Verdict The Jury finde for the Plaintiff and give Him his five pound for the mare and Colt and Forty five Shillings dammages, with Costs of suite. Judgment thereupon Awarded and the Costs to be silver money or Equivolent to it.

[Slander]   John Calowe Plaintiff Thomas Wright Defendant Action of defamation The Jury before Attested, the Declaration Read [Attested] Henry Glassum saith that hee heard Thomas Wright say, that John Calowe is a Rouge And that hee is a forsworne Rouge, And that hee could prove him a forsworne Rouge. [Attested] Thomas Peters saith that Thomas Wright said hee would prove John Calowe a forsworne Rouge. for hee Attested that Thomas Wright said the Mare had but one wall eye. [Attested] Thomas Potts, saith Thomas Wright said hee would prove John Calow a forsworne Rouge. [Attested] Joshua Wright, saith that hee was with Daniell Wills, and Daniell asked Thomas Wright what Wall Eyes the Mare had and Thomas said I know not: and Further that hee the said Joshua after the Court asked Calowe about said Mare, why hee witnessed soe in Court; And hee answered, Thomas Wright hath Sued mee. [Attested] Daniell Wills, Saith that at some publick time John Calow and hee the Deponent mett, and Calow desired Daniell to speake with Thomas Wright; And accordingly Daniell mett with Thomas Wright, And asked him about the Mare and said Thomas said my Mare hath but one wall eye, and that this deponent said then I will looke noe more after her, for shee is not myne. [Attested] John Joyner saith that at last Fall Generall meeting Thomas Wright came in and Daniell Wills and John Calow and discoursed of a Mare, and Daniell thought the Mare to be his: and Thomas said my mare hath but one wall Eye. [105 1691] The Tryall before Comitted to the Jury, And the Court order that they Seale up their Verdict when agreed and bring it in to the Court, And then the Court adjourne to the 23th instant at 9th hower in the morning.

February 23th 1691. The Court mett and calld.

[*Court Order*]   Ordered by the Court That all Plaintiffs who shall take out any processe against any Defendant or Defendants from the Court, shall pay for their proceedings as they goe on therewith.

[*Verdict:*] The Jury called and appeare and give in their Verdict Sealed; They find for the Plaintiff and give him two pence dammage and Costs of suite. The Court Award and order judgment to be entred according to the Verdict, for full Costs of Suite with 2d. Dammage, And Costs to be Current silver money or Equivolent.

William Righton Plaintiff   Charles Sheepey Defendant   Jury Attested, William Wood againe taken in to the Jury and Thomas French dismist. The Declaration Read. The Defendant requires the Plaintiff to prove his declaration.

[*Attested*]   Samuell Houghton being already Attested as a Jury man, Saith that the Defendant Charles, was as much engaged to the Plaintiff in carrying on the building as hee (this deponent) who was the Master Bricklayer. And further saith that there was agreement betweene Plaintiff and defendant for carrying on the building, but cannot say that it was agreed betweene them that, the Defendant should abide by it untill it was finished.

[*Attested*]   Thomas Revell Deposeth that William Righton came to seeke out the Defendant Charles to come to his worke, and that said Charles would not come but went to Snodens and gott drunk.

[*Attested*]   William Righton junr. deposeth that hee knowes that his Father (the Plaintiff) Hyred the Defendant Sheepey with Samuell Houghton to build his House, and that said Sheepey was to have Two Shillings per day, And further saith that upon the Plaintiffs paying the said Defendant Twenty Shillings of wages, hee (the Defendant) promised hee would not leave the worke untill it was finished.

[*Verdict*]   The Jury find for the Plaintiff And give him forty one Shillings Dammages and Costs of suite   Judgment awarded for Costs of suite Currant silver money, or Equivolent. and 2d. dammages.

[*Case*]   Abraham Senior Plaintiff   William Whitty Defendant   Upon attachment Plaintiff appeares: Defendant called, but appeares not. Jury Called and Attested: Declaration Read.

[*Evidence*]   The Plaintiff produces his Bill under the Defendants hand, with two witnesses in Court for four pounds. And Attests there is nothing thereof discharged. And alsoe produces his booke in Court for the Debt of forty one Shillings and Three pence, the particulers whereof being read and Cast up in Court, The Plaintiff alsoe Attests to the truth of his booke and that nothing thereof is paid: And soe its Comitted to the Jury.

[*Verdict*] The Jury find for the Plaintiff and give him his Debt of six pounds one Shilling and three pence, and Twelve pence dammages and Costs of suite. Judgment Awarded for said Debt and dammages And that for Costs of suite it be Currant silver money or Equivolent.

[*Court Order*] Whereas upon the returne of several Surveys of Land at this Court a Caveat is entred against Recording the returne of Mahlon Stacyes Survey of Land, And that Caveats are still upon the Returne of the Surveys of Christopher Weatherills and the Land late belonging to his wife in right of Joseph Pope her former Husband which was formerly brought in: Ordered therefore at this Court, that if any person or persons have any thing to object against the Recording of any of the said particuler Surveys aforesaid, they are required to make publick their objections in 6 Moneths next onely Edward Hunloke (as Attourney for Doctor Cox) desired to be excused in his Assent to this order.

[**106 1691**] Thomas Ollive and John Hollinshead Plaintiffs Edward Hunloke Defendant Edward Hunloke (the Defendant comes from the Bench and desires Daniell Wills to come from the Bench (as haveing undertaken the Vindication of the Plaintiffs Cause by his owne words) whereupon Daniell comes of the Bench.

William Emley, William Biddle, Richard Basnett, James Marshall, on the Bench.

Declaration Read at the Defendants request. The Defendant pleads the former judgment and Execution against him etc. by the Plaintiffs for the same debt declared for in Barr to this Action.

The Plaintiffs, by and with their Attourney John White sett forth as in their Declaration that the Defendant did on the 21st January 1690 oblidge himselfe etc. and did assume upon himselfe to pay and satisfye to the Plaintiffs according to the obligation given them by Isaac Hargrave and this defendant for 150l. without any trouble or suite in Lawe If they the said Plaintiffs would then give further day for payment of certaine Bills of Exchange, The which tyme they gave even to the 20th May then next ensueing. The which assumption the Defendant haveing not performed they desire the Action may proceed to Tryall by a Jury.

The Defendant in answer thereunto says hee acknowledges That hee being (as security) become bound with Isaac Hargrave in an obligation of 150l. to the Plaintiffs with Condition for true payment of Bills of Exchange etc. And being about the tyme set forth in their (the Plaintiffs) declaration, upon the poynt of being Arrested upon the said Bond (apprehending the great dammage hee might sustaine in his Creditt abroad thereby) did under his hand assume to pay the same as they alledge, and does acknowledge likewise they did stay till the 20th of May as aforesaid,

But further saith that after the said 20th of May (not minding or regarding the Defendants said assumption) The said Plaintiffs sue the said Isaac Hargrave and the now Defendant to a Speciall Court, where appearing They produce the said Hargraves and the Defendants obligation, and by their acknowledgment of the Bond due, obtained Judgment and Execution as aforesaid, And further pleads that the said assumption ought not to appeare against the Defendant the Bond being satisfyed: and therefore being noe cause of Action, Pleads a Barr.

The Plaintiffs etc. further sett forth that the Debt is not paid And that the former Judgment and Execution not legally answered and served upon the Goods and Chattells of the said Defendant according to the tenour of the Writt of Execution Delivered the Sheriff. And therefore crave the Action may proceed to Tryall, And desire the Writt of Execution might be produced in Court.

The Sheriffe brought in the originall Writt of Execution which was Read

The Records of the former Judgment and proceedings of Court, as alsoe the Sheriffs Returne of the Execution Read.

The defendant thereupon alleadges that the Sheriffe haveing an overplus in his possession due to the Defendant, the whole Debt damages and Costs being Legally and fully satisfyed, according to the Sheriffs Returne upon Record, Craves a Barr.

Some Cases in Lawe touching the premisses out of severall Law books, asserted on both sides and Read.

The Issue, left to the Bench, whether for a Barr, or to proceed to Tryall: Uppon hearing of both sides, The Bench order as Follows (vizt)

The Bench haveing Considered the premisses are satisfyed, that the Barr pleaded aforesaid lies against the Plaintiffs Action, And thereupon order the said Action voyd.

And further that whereas upon the Plaintiffs Complaynt the Judgment before obtained against the said Defendants is not discharged, And that the premisses taken in Execution are overprized, and therefore cannot bee sufficient to discharge the said Judgment, The Court order that the premisses taken in Execution and apprized remaine in the Sheriffs Custody, And that hee continue a Publication of the sale thereof; And if within Six Moneths next noe person or persons will give the Vallue they are apprized to, That then four or more of the Magistrates of this County shall appoint Twelve Honest judicious men of the Neighbourhood to reprize the premisses allready taken in Execution, and if then the same premisses fall short of makeing satisfaction, That then Execution shall and may be renewed against the Defendant for seizing of more of the goods and Chattells of the Defendants soe as may make up full payment and satisfaction of the said Judgment and execution, unlesse the Defendants upon demand doe and shall pay and discharge such remaining parte of the said Judgment as the premisses aforesaid when soe reprized will not discharge.

Court dissolved   next Court being May 8th 1692.

[107 1692]   Att the Court of Session Held May 8th 1692. Called May 9th the 8th day being First day. Edward Hunloke, William Biddle, James Marshall, Richard Bassnett Justices on the Bench.

Grand Jury John Wilsford, John Wearne, John Calowe, Joshua Newbold, John Gardner, Thomas Peachee, James Wills, William Hunt, Daniell Leeds, Isaac Horner, Roger Parke, Daniell Bacon, Henry Grubb Attested.

Traverse Jury Francis Davenport, William Hickson, Thomas Folke junr., Robert Murfin, Samuell Overton, Abraham Senior, Samuell Houghton, John Budd, John Bainbridge, William Budd, Mathew Champion, John Crosby.

Upon an Indictment of John Shawe against him fyled, Henry Johnson prosecutor. Katherine Johnson, Abigaell Johnson, Nicholas Martineau Attested for the Grand Jury   appear to the Grand Jury.

Upon an Indictment fyled against Jonathan West and Mary his wife, John Pound, prosecutor. There are noe Evidences.

Ephraim Allen Committed to the Sheriffe per Richard Bassnett upon Hue and Crye comeing from East Jersey. Thomas Webley called to prosecute, appears not   Whereupon at the request of said Allen hee is cleared by Proclamation paying his Fees.

The Grand Jury find the Indictment against John Shawe. In the Indictment of Jonathan West and Mary his wife they bring it in Ignoramus.

They present Peter Groome and the reputed wife of Thomas Wright, for that they Lead a debauched and Lacivious life one with the other against the Peace of our Soveraigne Lord and Lady the King and Queene and alsoe against the wholesome Lawes and Constitutions of this Province.

They Present the Justices of this County for not takeing timely care for Erecting a Prison.

They Present the County of Burlington for not repairing the Highwayes already laid out, and for not takeing due care for makeing and laying out lawfull Highwayes where they are wanting. vizt To the Falls.

The Indictment against John Shawe being found by the Grand Jury as above. Whereupon the Prisoner is called for and sett to the Barr, And Arraigned. Upon his Arraignment hee Pleads not Guilty. And referres himselfe for Tryall to God and the Countrey.

The Jury called, The Court advise the Prisoner that hee may take notice of his Exceptions   their names as followes Francis Davenport, Symon Charles, Samuell Andrews, William Hickson, Thomas Folke junr., Robert Murfin, Samuell Overton, Abraham Senior, Charles Read, William Budd, Mathew Champion, John Crosby.

The prisoner haveing his liberty to make his Exceptions declares he knowes nothing against any of them but that they are honest men. The Court adjourned to the 7th hower in the Morning being 10th May Instant.

The Prisoner in the meane tyme before the Jury are Attested desires a Coppy of the Jury, which is granted before the Court rise.

May 10th The Court being sett, The Prisoner is called for, and sett to the Barr. The Jury above being called over, the Prisoner excepts against them all one by one.

Whereupon, Another Jury is called, Namely John Tatham, John Budd, John Bainbridge, Thomas Bowman, John Petty, John Abbott, Samuell Houghton, Benjamin Wheat, John Peers, William Fryley, Nathaniell Cripps, John Scott. Indictment Read againe and Prisoner pleads not guilty. The Prisoner Accepts of them Whereupon they are Impannelled and Attested.

Katherine Johnson Sworne, And upon oath deposeth, That Shaw (the Prisoner came to the house of Henry Johnson, and said to this deponent hee would give her 1s. for a Shoot with his Gun at the Fowles, which this Deponent refused, And that then said Shaw proffered her 2s. and after 3s. for a Shoot: And that shee then said if you will give mee 3s. you shall shoot at the Cock: and that then said Shaw snapt with his gun at the Cock and the Gun went not of, And this Deponent then said your Gun is not charged, you doe but fright us, And said Shaw then said, you shall see that; And that then this Deponent frightened the Cock away, and said you shall not shoot at them if you would give mee 3s. apeece, whereupon said Shaw [108 1692] Clapt the Gun to his Shoulder and kneeld upon one Knee and fyred the Gun, And that hee was then within the field hard by the Doore, And that hee Shott by the sides of both the houses, which were houses Inhabitted, And saith there was Benjamin Johnson (in the Indictment mentioned) a Boy who was in one of the houses was slaine by the said Shott of said Gun: And deposeth the Boy was Shott in the left eye, in the right Jaw Bone and the right side of the Temples of his head of which wounds in about Six dayes after hee dyed: The Court asked the Deponent which way the Cock at which Shaw was about to Shoot stood? To which she deposeth, that at first the Cock when shee gave leave to shoot at him, was distant from the house and out of danger; But when said Shaw snapt with his Gun and it went not of, then this Deponent threw at the Cock and frighted him away, and that after that Shaw fyred: Further deposeth that shee was by the said Shaw when hee Shott, And that when said Shaw Shott, Shee did not see said Boy; but that immediately after she saw her Sister lift up the Boy and Cry out, John Shaw thou hast kiled my Brother, And that said Shaw afterwards said there was a Slugg in the Gun: And further saith not.

Abigaell Johnson Sworne, Deposeth, that shee was in the house when said John Shaw came to the house of Henry Johnson, And that then the Boy (that was afterwards slaine) was with her in the house that was downe staires and that hee went up stairs, And that shee then heard the Gun goe of, and that the said Boy (her brother) then fell downe into her Armes, And that shee looked forth presently and Sawe the Gun in John Shaws hand, And that shee said to him, what hast thou done? thou hast killed my brother. And the Court asking her whether Shaw knew the Boy was in the house, She saith hee did know it: And further saith the boy had one wound in at the left Eye, another at the right jaw bone, and another in the right side of the Temples of his head, Of which wounds in about Six dayes after hee dyed, And that shee saw high Swan Shott taken out of the wood which was hard by where the boy was shott. And further saith not;

Sarah Marsh Sworne, Deposeth that shee heard of the boye's being wounded in about an hower after he was shott, And that she was sent for by John Shaw, and the boye's Sister to dresse and take care of the boy, and that shee tooke what care of the boy shee could; And that shee does not know but that the boy did dye of the wounds hee received as aforesaid. And saith that the boy had a feaver upon him before hee dyed, but beleeves the wounds was the occasion of it. And further saith not.

Nicholas Martineau Sworne, deposeth, that when hee heard of the boy his being wounded, he (this Deponent) went to see the boy next morning; And that hee saw the boy drest, which when hee saw hee beleeved it would kill the boy, for hee saw the wounds, one whereof was in at the left Eye, which he beleeves would have been the death of any man (if shott soe) The other Shott was in at the jaw bone, and that they in dressing tooke out severall teeth, And that they did not perceive anyway where the Shott came out againe, And another Shott was in at the Temples and came out about two Inches of, in the head; and that said Shaw signifyed hee was Troubled for the boy, And that said Shaw owned hee did Shoot of a Gun when the boy was wounded: And further saith not:

The Returne of the Neighbours (in the nature of an Inquest Read: The Evidence of Shamgar Hands taken before Samuell Mathews Constable Read.

The Kings Attourney Generall Pleads in behalfe of their Majesties against the Prisoner at the Barr. And demands Justice from the Bench against the Prisoner according to Forme of Law.

The Court demand of the Prisoner if hee have anything to say for himselfe, before the Jury goe togeather, The Prisoner desires hee may have Counsell, being ignorant in the Lawe.

To which the Court reply if hee want to know any particuler in Lawe touching the premisses, hee shall be informed; but if it be in matter of Fact, Counsell against the King cannot be allowed him.

Whereupon the Jury goe together, and after some Considerable tyme returne And being called over etc. And asked if they be agreed of their Verdict, they answer yea, And by John Tatham Esqr. (their foreman) deliver their Verdict in writing sealed up, vizt, That they find the Prisoner (John Shaw) Guilty of Homicidium per infortunium, or Homicide by misadventure: being asked what goods and Chattells the prisoner was possest of etc. they answer none that they know of: The Sheriffe charged to secure the Prisoner.

The Prisoner being called for and sett to the Barr, The Court aske him if hee have anything to say before sentence be pronounced upon him. To which hee hath nothing to say.

The Court adjourne to the 9th hower in the Morning being the 11th May instant.

May 11th. After the Court being sett, And the Prisoner brought and sett to the Barr: The Court require the Clerke to Read his sentence being as follows. vizt, John Shaw thou shalt forfeit all thy goods and Chattells debts and duties whatsoever.

The Court adjourne for 2 howers.

[109 1692] [*Henry Johnson Constable sworne.*] Henry Johnson Chosen Constable for the Precincts of Cape May for one yeare next, or till further order: And Sworne.

Henry Johnson and Nicholas Martineau being nominated and appointed by the Justices to make an Estimate and Appraisement of the Estate of John Shaw aforesaid Whereupon after they had beene sometime togeather to Consider thereupon Doe Appraise the same to the Summe of Thirty pounds.

Civil Actions

John Hollinshead Plaintiff   William Gill Defendant   Continued.

Mathew Allen Plaintiff   Bernard Devonish defendant   Continued.

Jonathan West and Mary his wife Plaintiffs   John Pound Defendant Action slander.

Thomas Peachee Plaintiff   John Jones Defendant   Warrant not served.

Judith Morrell Executrix of Gilbert Morrell Plaintiff   Dennis Rotchford Defendant   Action debt   Continued.

Dennis Rotchford Plaintiff   Judith Morrell Executrix of Gilbert Morrell Defendant   Continued.

John Tatham Esqr. Plaintiff   John Gibbs and Ephraim Allen Defendants   withdrawne.

Robert Coles Administrator of John Baker etc. Plaintiff   Anthony Woodward Defendant   Continued.

Thomas Coddrington Plaintiff   Robert Cole defendant   Action Trover Continued.

Sheriffs returne of the Execution against Thomas Wright at suit of John Calowe Is That the Plaintiff is Satisfyed.

Hector Dicks Plaintiff William Righton Defendant Action Case. Plaintiffs Declaration for 38s. 6d. Read The Defendant Pleads non Assumpsit.

Jury—Francis Davenport and Fellows (except instead of Symon Charles Samuell Andrews and Charles Read) are put in Samuell Houghton John Budd and John Bainbridge. The Plaintiffs bill of particulers Read amounting to forty three shillings six pence. The Plaintiff is Attested, And Deposeth that the particulers in his Bill produced and Read are just and true and are due from the Defendant (save onely hee (the said Plaintiff) acknowledges the receipt of 5s. thereof, And the remainder makes up 38s. 6d. declared for. [alsoe and [33] *Attestation of Samuell Harriotts proveing some parte of the Bill Read.*]

The other tryall of the same Plaintiff against the same Defendant coming on the Jury stay and take oaths together.

Hector Dicks Plaintiff William Righton Defendant Action of the Case, The Jury above, Attested Plaintiffs Declaration Read, setting forth the Defendants breach of a bargaine made between Plaintiff and defendant.

The Defendant Pleads hee hath broken noe such Covenants as the Plaintiff setts forth in his Declaration.

The Plaintiff produced a writeing Concerning the bargaine betweene Plaintiff and Defendant which was Read.

[Attested] Samuell Furnis upon his Attestation proves the writing, which was the heads of the Contract betweene Plaintiff and Defendant.

[Attested] Charles Read upon his Attestation Deposeth, that the Plaintiff came to him to draw up Covenants betweene him and the Defendant, And that the Plaintiff and Defendant came after togeather to draw up the Covenants, and said Deponent said hee should have the heads of their agreement, which being produced, the Defendant differed with the Plaintiff and disliked the Covenants, and the Plaintiff stuck by them. Samuell Furnis further saith William Righton (the Defendant) came to him, and said to him said Furnis thou was a foole in writing this Agreement, why did thou not burne them?

[Attested] Sabella Righton upon her Attestation that the Plaintiff asked the Defendant (her father) if hee would buy hides, And hee (the said Defendant) bid him goe to worke and hee would doe what was right.

[Attested] Peter Fretwell upon his Attestation, Deposeth that William Righton came to him to assist him in the Tanyard, And that when hee (this deponent) came there, hee found much Leather and skins which in 24 howers would have spoyled, which was for want of Bark provided.

Samuell Furnis upon his Attestation further deposeth, that the Plaintiff would have had a workman sent for (in regard of the said Plaintiffs sick-

[33] *Sic.*

nesse) And that said Plaintiff said hee would pay him his wages: But that the Defendant was not willing to have one sent for.

The Premisses given up to the Jury aforesaid, who are to agree of their verdicts; And in regard the Court adjourned to next morning, they are required to keep togeather, and to Seale up their verdicts (when agreed) before they part. [110 1692] [*Plaintiff and Defendant appeare*] May 11th 92. Court called and sett, The Jury called and Appeare, And being demanded whether they find for Plaintiff or Defendant they say (by their Foreman) for the Plaintiff in both Actions, And deliver up their Verdicts Sealed, to the Court, which are opened and Read, being as follows, First Action wee find for the Plaintiff and give him his Debt of Thirty Eight Shillings Six pence, and Costs of Suite, Judgment Awarded thereupon. in the Second Action wee find for the Plaintiff, and give him Twelve pounds dammage and reasonable Costs of Suite, Judgment thereupon Awarded.

The Defendant required an Appeale from the Juries Verdicts to the Assembly The Court say though they find noe Law for it in the book of Assemblies Acts, yet if hee will assigne reasonable and lawfull grounds for his Appealing to the Assembly, And pay the Costs, It shall be granted, which hee did not doe.

Joshua Newbold and Samuell Oldale referre themselves to the Bench to put an end to their difference in all Accompts relateing to the Mill.

Court dissolved Next Court to be August 8th 1692.

Att a Private Session at Richard Bassnetts at Burlington held the 25th June 1692 at the request of Robert Styles senr.

Justices present Edward Hunloke, Daniell Wills, James Marshall.

Grand Jury Thomas Wright, Andrew Smith, Joseph Adams, Elias Burley, Isaac Marriott, Thomas Gladwin, Nathaniell Dugglas, James Satterthwait, Henry Bursham, Lawrance Morris, Abraham Senior, Nathaniell Cripps, William Fryley. Robert Styles senr. John Rudderow and William Pitchforward Indicted for Riottously entering upon the Land of Robert Styles junr. and Cutting downe his Corne there, upon the Complaynt of said Robert Styles junr. The said Styles junr. and Mordeca Howell on the 21th June instant were Attested before Edward Hunloke that the said Styles senr. etc. did on the 20th June instant forcibly etc. enter on the Land as aforesaid and after warning given by said Styles junr. Cutt downe the Corne of said Styles and said they would carry it away etc. which Attestation was delivered to the Grand jury, And Peter Long was alsoe Attested and sent to the said Jury: The Grand Jury gott amongst themselves Robert Styles senr. (being one of the Prisoners) And afterwards bring in the Bill Ignoramus.

The Prisoners at their request are cleared by proclamation. The Court dissolved.

Att the Court of Session held August 8th 1692.

Justices present   Edward Hunloke, Daniell Wills, William Biddle, James Marshall, Richard Bassnett. Richard Bassnett as Attourney Generall comes of the Bench.

Grand Jury Impanelled and Attested. Thomas Bowman, Samuell Andrews, John Joyner, Samuell Ogbourne, John Shinn junr., George Elkington, Samuell Harriott, Thomas Folke junr., John Calowe, John Warren, Andrew Smith, James Croft, John Snoden. Peter Bosse and William Budd Summoned for Grand Jury and appeared not fyned 10s. a peece. Traverse Jury   Mathew Allen, Thomas Dugglas, John Gardner, William Fryley, John Petty, Samuell Furnis, Charles Read, Thomas Gladwin, William Hickson, John Hollinshead, Christopher Weatherill, Henry Grubb. James Wills being present in Court and called to serve on this Jury, for his peremtory refuseing to serve fyned 10s.

The Bill against Harry the Negro man Servant of Isaac Marriott given to the Grand Jury for Buggering a Cow.

Mary Myers senr., Mary Myers Junr. Attested and sent to the Grand Jury.

The Grand Jury Find the Bill   The Prisoner upon the Indictment Pleads not Guilty. And Isaac Marriott his Master and the Prisoner (his Servant) referre the Tryall to God and the Countrey   The Traverse Jury above called, and accepted by the Master and Attested.

Evidence   Mary Myers senr., Mary Myers junr. Attested. Mary Myers deposeth that about the tyme mentioned in the Indictment the Prisoner was gott upon a Cow, And that her Children saw the same, And called her to see, And there shee then saw him ride upon the Cow And that hee was in Action as Buggering the Cow and that shee stood still, And that after the Cow had the usuall Motions of Cows when they had taken the Bull, And that when hee came of to goe away, the Cow turned and looked after him, And that hee after stooped and tooke up Grasse or leaves and as Shee supposes wiped his Members: And that the cow was Lawrence Morris Cow.

Mary the Daughter, deposeth that Shee saw the Negro doe the same that her Mother hath deposed as above. [111 1692]   Juryes Verdict as to the Negro:

Wee have Considered Evidence and Circumstances and alsoe viewed the Place which might give him opportunity   Doe beleeve and Judge him Guilty of the Fact.

The Prisoner brought, And being demanded if hee have anything to say why Sentence should not passe upon him, Answers not: but is silent.

Sentence   The Bench haveing Considered of the Sentence according to the Law, Command the Clerke to read the same to the Prisoner, which hee accordingly read, As follows Thou Harry! shalt be kept in Safe

Custody untill the Sixth day commonly called Fryday the nyneteenth day of this instant August, And that (betwixt the howers of Tenne and Twelve in the Forenoone of the same day thou shalt be hanged by the neck till thy body bee dead, dead, dead, And God have Mercy on thy Soule: And that the Cowe with which thou Committed the Buggery shalt the same day be slaine. Many of the Freeholders and Inhabitants of this County preferre a Petition to the Bench for Spareing the Negroes life, And to inflict other punishment upon him, The Bench say they will Consider on it.

Actions

Mathew Allen Plaintiff   Bernard Devonish defendant   withdrawne.

Robert Cole Plaintiff   Anthony Woodward Defendant   withdrawne.

Thomas Codderington Plaintiff   Robert Cole Defendant   the Plaintiff Called to prosecute appeares not   the defendant craves a nonsuite and its granted.

Judith Morrell Executrix etc. Plaintiff   Dennis Rotchford defendant   Plaintiff declares the Bond produced and Read   the Defendant appeares not to defend. At the Plaintiffs request Judgment awarded by default, upon the bond for what remaines due and unpaid, with Costs Suite.

Dennis Rotchford Plaintiff   Judith Morrel Executrix etc. defendant   Plaintiff appeares not to prosecute the Defendant craves a non suite; its granted.

Peter Resneire Plaintiff   Daniell Cox Esqr Defendant   Edward Hunloke as Attourney for Defendant appeares and desires the Action may be Continued   the Action Continued by Consent.

Daniell Sutton one of the Trustees for Priscilla Hudson Plaintiff   Isaac Decow Defendant   Defendant appeares not to make Defence. Declaration Read   Imanuell Smith Attested proves the Bill   Judgment Award upon default or nihil dicit.

James Marshall Plaintiff   Joshua Newbold Defendant   withdrawne.

Thomas Wright Plaintiff   Richard Moore Defendant   neither Plaintiff nor Defendant appeare.

Thomas Wright Plaintiff   John Greene Defendant   neither Plaintiff nor defendant appeare.

Edward Hunloke etc. Plaintiff   Robert Styles Defendant   Continued.

Nathaniell Cripps Sonne and Heire of John Cripps Plaintiff   Charles Pickering one of Executors of Anna Salter Defendant   Plaintiff and Defendant referre the matter in Controversie to the Bench. Court withdrawnes.

Court order   ordered by the Court that a Jury of Twelve men of the Neighbourhood (Inhabitants within the Townshippe of Wellingborrow) be Summoned to meet togeather and to lay out Convenient Highwayes, which are wanting within the said Townshipp of Wellingborrow: Which wayes when layd out, are to Present to the next Session for the approbation thereof: To be Summoned by the Constable of said Townshipp.

Charles Pickering requests on the behalfe of the late wife of Isaac Bowde to inspect into the Accompts of the late Administratour [34] of the Goods and Chattells late of Adlord Bowde (the late Father of Isaac) deceased which the Court Grant.

[112 1692] [*Northampton Towne Bounds Recorded at request of Daniell Wills on the behalfe of the inhabitants of Northampton.*] The Bounds of the Townshippe of Northampton are as follows Beginning at the House on Northside of Daniell Wills Lyne, And soe up by Northampton River westerly side And soe turning with that Branch of the Crick Southerly by Henry Burrs. And from thence to the head of that branch, And from thence to William Budds, and soe along by Isaac Horners and Widdow Skenes and soe by Samuell Jennings and right along by the Towne bounds untill it come to the Northerly Lyne of the Land of Daniell Wills and soe up to his house againe, which Lyne of his Land Devides betweene Willingborrow and Northampton.

The Highway for William Biddle and others From Widdow Hancocks To turne into the way formerly called John Cripps way, And from the said Way by a Lyne of Marked Trees laid out for the Mill way to James Crofts Plantation, Then downe to the Bridge And thence through Samuell Stacyes Land to William Biddles.

The way for severall persons beyond John Curtis: And for others to their Meadow on the way from Widdow Hancocks to Turne out of the old East Jersey way neare Widdow Hancock and soe straight on the way last marked out to Thomas Revells, and soe to Widdow Towles Plantation And soe straight on the Beaten Cart Road, And soe leaveing the Beaten Cart way below John Curtis Hill, and soe Crosse his Land belowe his house, and soe Crosse his Land to John Calows Land and soe Crosse the Land late belonging to William Ellis, then Crosse Nathaniell Dugglas Land, then Crosse Thomas Dugglas Land to a Crick or Runne bounding on a Plantation belonging to William Biddle, As the beaten way now lies.

And for those who have Meadow at Mount Pleasant to Turne to that part of the Meadow lyeing beyond John Curtis house on the way abovesaid Crosse John Curtis Land to the same Meadow: And for the other part of the Meadow on the Southwest side John Curtis house; To keep on the beaten wayne way aforesaid and soe on the Southwest side of John Curtis Graveyard to the same Meadow: And John Woolstons way to his part of Meadow there, to Turne out of the aforesaid wayne way into that Cart Road by him allready made to his Meadow: Alsoe Michaell Buffin to have

[34] "Administrator" in MS.

his way to his part of Meadow there, on the said Cart Road of John Woolston, And through John Brownes Land to his Meadow.
Court Dissolved.

Quarterly Sessions November 3th 1692. [*Adjourned to 10th instant*] Edward Hunloke, Andrew Robeson, William Biddle, Mahlon Stacy, Justices Present. The Court adjourned to 10th instant. [*Called November 10th and Adjourned to the 21th instant.*] Court called November 10th and adjourned to the 21th instant. [*November 21th 1692 Court called*] November 21th 1692, the Deputy Governours Comission Read. November 21th 1692 Court called and opened being then present on the Bench Edward Hunloke Esqr. Deputy Governour. John Tatham Esqr., William Biddle Gent., Thomas Lambert Gent., Thomas Gardner Gent., William Righton Gent. Justices. The Justices Comission Read. Grand Jury Thomas French, William Hunt, Joshua Humphries, Anthony Elton, John Snape, William Budd, William Foster, Edward Rockhill, Samuell Bunting, John Bunting, Robert Hutcheson, Robert Hudson, Richard Fennimore Attested. Traverse Jury Henry Grubb, John Payne, John Hollinshead, Thomas Harding, William Hascor, Henry Ballenger, Abraham Senior, Peter Fretwell, John Gardner, John Hilliard, John Joyner, Nathaniell Duggles.

Grand Jury present the Towneshipp of Mansfield for want of repayring the Bridge at Nathaniell Ricketts.

Charles Pickering and fellow Executors Plaintiffs John Snoden Defendant an Action of Slander and defamation The Jury Attested Declaration Read. Evidences 1 A Deed of Lease and release for a Sixth parte of a propriety Sold by Richard Mew to William Snoden and John Hooton; Read. 2 Alsoe the Assignment from William Snoden to Thomas Fairman in Trust for Anna Salter read. 3 Alsoe the assignment from Thomas Fairman of his Trust in the Premisses aforesaid to Anna Salter read. 4 Alsoe the Deed from Anna Salter John Hooton etc. Deed of Lease and Release to John Cripps (father of Nathaniell Cripps) read. 5 Isaac Horner Attested, Deposeth that hee was about buying the Land in Question of Nathaniell Cripps, And that after wards hee met with John Snoden (the Defendant) And that hee the said John Snoden said John Cripps had not a Tytle to the Land (in Question) And that there upon hee the said John Horner would not further proceed in purchaseing the said Land. 6 James Hill, Attested deposeth that John Snoden said that as to the Land in question although hee himselfe would not doe any thing in relation to the Land in question, yet his Heires in tyme to come might make claime to it. [*Juryes Verdict*] The Jury finde for the Plaintiffs and give them four pounds damages with Costs of Suite and Judgment is thereupon Awarded.

[**113 1692**] High Sheriffs Attestation [*James Hill Sheriffe Attested*] I James Hill High Sheriffe for the County of Burlington doe Solemnly promise in the presence of God that I will true Allegiance Bear to our Soveraign Lord and Lady the King and Queen and to their Lawfull Heires and Successours, And that I will truely diligently and effectually Serve and Execute all warrants writts Executions and other precepts to me directed from the Governour and Deputy Governour of this Province and either of them, And from the Justices or any of them within my Bayliwick, And that I will doe execute and perform all other matters and things relateing to my said office to the uttermost of my Power and ability according to Law: James Hill.

Mahlon Stacy Francis Davenport Daniell Wills, Justices absent, not Attested. Thomas Lambert, William Biddle, Thomas Gardner, William Righton and Daniell Leeds Justices all tooke their Attestation In the presence of God that they will true allegiance beare to our Soveraigne Lord and Lady King William and Queene Mary and their Lawfull Successours.[35]

Coronours[36] Attestation. I Daniell Wills Coroner for the County of Burlington Doe Solemnly promise in the presence of God, That I will true allegiance beare to our Soveraigne Lord and Lady the King and Queene and to their Lawfull Heires and Successors: And that I will well and truly doe execute and performe my said Duty and office of Coroner[37] within the County aforesaid according to Law.

[order of Court]   ordered by the Court that the present Constable and Constables of every respective Towneshipp within this County shall be Collectour[38] and Collectours for the present Tax or Poll within his and their Constablry and shall pay in the same to the Treasurers.

[Order of Court]   Whereas upon the Accompt now given in by Daniell Wills for the Prison it appeares that the former Tax laid upon this County for building the prison will come farr short of paying what is allready done and what remaines yet to be done; ordered therefore that there be the one Moyetie or halfe of the Tax formerly laid upon this County, to be laid in like manner as the former Tax as an Additional Supply for the carrying on and finishing the same prison, And that warrants accordingly be issued forth for paying of the whole at or before the Twenty fifth of December next.

adjourned to the 8th hower in the morning being 22th 9ber instant. Court opened. The Jury aforesaid to witt Henry Grubb and fellows called: Abraham Senior and Nathaniell Duggles appeare not and are fyned three Shillings a peece: And Anthony Elton and Richard Fennimore are put in their stead.

Peter Resniere Plaintiff   John Powne Defendant   withdrawne.

---

[35] "Successors" in MS.
[36] "Coronors" in MS.
[37] "Coronr" in MS.
[38] "Collector" in MS.

Edward Hunloke Esqr. Plaintiff James Hill Defendant Continued.

Edward Hunloke etc. Plaintiffs Robert Styles Defendant Defendant appears not Judgment awarded by default upon the bond for Charges.

Nathaniell Cripps Plaintiff Robert Stacy and fellow executors of Anna Salter Defendants Jury Attested vizt Henry Grubb and fellows (except Abraham Senior and Nathaniell Duggles) And in their stead are Anthony Elton and Richard Fennimore). The defendants Plead theres noe cause of Action.

Evidences 1 The Deeds read for Evidence to prove the first part of the Declaration. 2 Thomas Revell Attested, deposeth that Anna Salter gave order to him to put John Hooton and John Snoden with her selfe in the Deed to John Cripps. 3 James Hill Attested deposeth that Charles Pickering (one of the defendants promised to make John Snoden Signe and Seale the Deed aforesaid. 4 Samuell Jenings Evidence read in Court shewing why hee refused to Grant Nathanial Cripps a warrant for takeing up the Land in question. 5 Isaac Horner Attested Deposeth that the reason why hee refused to buy the Land in question was because John Snoden told him Cripps had not a good tytle to it. [114 1692] 6 The Plaintiffs Bill of Particulers of his dammage Read. 7 The Deed of Lease and Release from John Hooton to Anna Salter for half of a Sixth parte of a propriety Read. 8 Richard Bassnett Attested Deposeth that Charles Pickering told Nathaniell Cripps that hee should have what Security and tytle to the Land in question could be given: Alsoe that Nathaniell Cripps required dammage of Charles which as hee (this deponent) thinks is about 3 or 4 yeares agoe. 9 Samuell Furnis Attested deposeth that Robert Stacy told this Deponent that it was their appointment that Charles Pickering should make Nathaniel Cripps a Tytle, And that it was Charles fault it was not done. [Juries Verdict] The Jury finde for the Plaintiff and give him Sixteene pounds dammages and Costs of suite. Judgment is thereupon Awarded. The Plaintiffs desire an Appeale to the next Generall Assembly: The Court grant this Appeale, upon paying Cost of this suite, And giveing bond and Security to prosecute the same with effect and abideing etc. the determination of the same Assembly and pay all Costs of the same appeale.

Edward Hunloke Esqr. Plaintiff Abraham Senior Defendant upon bond for 40l. Silver money for non payment of 21l. like money the Defendant acknowledges judgment thereupon.

John Hollinshead appears in Court and desires to have the Record of Court proceedings in February 20th 1691 wherein Thomas Ollive and John Hollinshead were Plaintiffs and Edward Hunloke Defendant Read which was done. John Hollinshead desires to have some further processe against Edward Hunloke with relation to the last proceedings. The Court haveing heard and Considered the proceedings of the former Court are not satisfyed how a new processe may be granted against the Defendant in the same Action that has judiciously past the Court and proceeded to Execution and returne thereof made in Court by the Sheriffe, And therefore judge that the goods and Chattels taken in Execution ought to satisfye the Debt according to apprizement.

Adjourned to 8th hower in the Morning 23th 9ber instant.

November 23th 1692. Court opened; The warrant of Execution by Edward Hunloke against William Fryley. The Sheriffs returne thereof, That the House and Lott of Fryley in Burlington is seized for satisfaction of the Execution Ordered thereupon that the premisses taken in Execution be sett to sale and sold for satisfaction and discharge of the same Execution.

The two warrants of Execution by Hector Dicks against William Righton: The Sheriffs returne thereof That the Judgments obtained by Hector Dicks against said William Righton in both Actions are discharged.

Made out 3 warrants (vizt) against Lawrence Morris against Peter Bosse William Budd and James Wills and against Abraham Senior and Nathaniel Duggles. And the two former warrants vizt Morris and Bosse Budd and Wills delivered to the Sheriffe.

James Wills Chosen Packer for this County. and Attested: as followes I: J. W. doe Solemnly promise in the presence of God, that I will Exercise the office of a Packer justly and uprightly according to my best knowledge, That I will not authorize or put my marke upon any Barrel of meat, but such as shall Containe Thirty one Gallons and an halfe at Least, And the meat both as to the saveing and quality thereof to be merchantable and in good Condition.

The Court demanded the Sheriffe to bring his Prisoner Harry the Negro man Servant of Isaac Marriott before them, The Sheriffe returnes a non est inventus; The Court require the Sheriffe to lay out for him and secure him.

[Court order] Ordered by the Court that the Person and Persons Inhabitants and resyants within the Townshipp of Burlington who have not full filled their Six dayes worke at the Bridges and Highwayes within the said Townshippe for the yeare last past, shall pay for each and every day they have soe neglected the same worke, Two Shillings And drawne and by order of Court signed a warrant to the Constables for that purpose.

Court dissolved. next Court to be February 20th 92.

[115 1692/3] Att the Court of Session February 20th 1692/3. Edward Hunloke Deputy Governour. John Tatham, William Biddle, Daniell Wills, Francis Davenport, Mahlon Stacy, Thomas Lambert, Thomas Gardner, William Righton, Daniell Leeds Esqrs. Justices upon the Bench. Court Called. Grand Jury returned John Day, Mathew Grange, Samuell Taylor, Henry Beck, Robert Chapman, Andrew Smith, Richard Harrison, Jonas Keene, Elias Toy, William Biddle junr., Nathaniel West, John Browne,

George Elkington   Attested. Traverse Jury returned   John Shin senr., Isaac Horner, Peter Harvey, Thomas Eves, Joseph Birch, Thomas Haynes, Thomas Scattergood, John Rudderowe, Joshua Humphries, Daniell Wills junr., Samuell Ogbourne, John Antram.

[*The presentment of Grand Jury*]   The grand Jury agreed of their verdict   By them Agreed that every Towneship within this County of Burlington, Shall have a Towne meeting to raise a tax to defray their Constables Charge at or before the first of the First Moneth: And that at the same meeting, every Townshippe shall agree to raise money to pay for killing wolves.

[*Kings road through Mansfield*] The Highway for East Jersey, Through the Townshippe of Mansfield, read and approved and ordered to be Recorded, being as followes. Beginning at the Bridge from Widdow Hancocks, and forward, and to turne out of the old East Jersey road neare Widdow Hancocks, and to go the Right hand road last marked out, to Thomas Revells: from thence to Widdow Towles Plantation, and soe downe to the Bridge neare Widdow Towles, And then on the way that Leads from said Bridge towards Samuell Andrews, untill it meets with a Lyne of Marked Trees straight to the Creek now called Chesterfield Creek, where there's a good Conveniency for a bridge; and is to be made and maintained equally betwixt the Inhabitants of Chesterfield and Mansfield, neare to Edward Rockhills.

[*Kings Road through Wellingborrow*]   The Highway through the Townshippe of Wellingborrow, read and approved, and ordered to be recorded, being as follows. To begin from the Mill Creek bridge in Salem Road, and soe as straight as may be to Widdow Peachees Plantation; And also a Publick highway from Abraham Hewlings Plantation straight through the Township towards Burlington; which said highway was agreed upon and subscribed the 28th 9th Mo. 1692 by John Payne, Thomas Harding, Robert Hudson, Thomas Eves, Freedom Lippincott, Daniell Wills, Abraham Hewlings, Richard Finnimore, John Scott and Samuell Kemble. Alsoe Thomas Ollive in his life tyme, and Daniell Wills (one of the Executors of Thomas Ollive, promised that for a Bridle way, the Inhabitants of Wellingborrow and all other passengers shall have free passage over the Mill Damme late of said Thomas Ollive, but not for a drift way. This alsoe read and ordered to be recorded.

[*Another agreement of the Inhabitants of Wellingborrough.*] Alsoe the agreement following then read and ordered to be recorded   Whereas the Inhabitants of the Towne of Wellingborrough being mett togeather at the house of Thomas Ollive in the County of Burlington, have agreed that every Loaden Cart that shall passe over the Mill damme shall pay Three pence a tyme, and every Empty Cart passing and not returning Loaden shall pay two pence a tyme, and every horned beast of one yeare old and upwards shall pay one penny a head for every tyme goeing or comeing over the said damme, And whosoever shall deny payment as aforesaid shall forfeit his owne priviledge: witnesse our hands this first day of the Seaventh moneth 1692. Thomas French, Thomas Ollive, Thomas Harding, Robert Hudson, John Paine Richard Finimore, Abraham Hewlings, John Scott, Thomas Eves.

New Constables for the yeare Ensueing Nottingham Thomas Tindall, Chesterfield Daniell Bacon, Mansfield James Croft, Birch Creek alias Springfield John Tonkan, Northampton Walter Reeves instead of him Isaac Horner, Wellingborrough Thomas French, Cropwell alias Chester Elias Toy, Eversham John Haynes, Robert Engle Attested May 8th 96, Burlington Peter Fretwell and Nathaniel Duggles.

[116 1692/3] New Overseers for the yeare Ensueing Nottingham Thomas Gilberthorpe and Joshua Eley, Chesterfield Thomas Folke junr., Mansfield John Curtis, Springfield Ananias Gaunt and John Butcher, Northampton John Woolman, Wellingborrough Richard Finimore, Chester John Rudderowe, Eversham waved untill the next Assembly be over: William Hewlings, Burlington Peter Bosse and Henry Grubb.

Edward Hunloke Administrator of John Cutcher Plaintiff Thomas Bowman Defendant Action of debt for 160l. Current of New Yorke per bond The Defendant desires the Action may be deferred untill next Court The Court by the Plaintiffs agreement require the Defendant to give security to answer etc. the Action next Court: which the Defendant not doeing the Action proceeds. The Jury aforesaid Empannelled and Attested. Declaration Read: The Plaintiffs Letters of Administration of the said John Cutchers Estate in this Province, produced and read: Alsoe the Bond read, with the proofe of the Notary Public of New England Subscription: And William Coles Attestation to the defendants Executing said Bond, taken before Elias Farr then Justice alsoe read. Thomas Bowman produces a Bill of certaine Barrells of flower delivered to John Cutcher in his life tyme pretending satisfaction of the bond: But it appeares the flower was by him given to said Cutcher 14 Moneths before the Bond, as per date of the Bill and the Bond (upon fyle appeare). The Jury find for the Plaintiff the Bond as due, with Costs of Suite Judgment thereupon Awarded the principall and Interest amounting to more then the obligation. Execution was made out for 96l. 3s. debt, for 6il. 15s. 6d. Interest and for 2l. 1s. 6d. Costs is 160l. 0s. 0d.

Edward Hunloke Plaintiff Thomas Bowman Defendant Action upon the Case Jury above Attested The Declaration Read: Alsoe the deed of Mortgage from the Defendant to the Plaintiff read: and owned by the Defendant. The Plaintiff Attestes that hee hath disbursed upon the premisses to the value of 500l. As his Bill produced appeares. The Jury are agreed in their verdict and find for the Plaintiff vizt, that the Defendant shall either pay the Improvements and the money on the Mortgage, or make the Plaintiff a Tytle (Consonant to the Covenant in the Mortgage for makeing such Legall assurance as the Plaintiff shall require) of the one hundred Acres etc. mentioned in the Mortgage and Costs of Suite: Judgment thereupon Awarded.

Richard Finimore Plaintiff   Thomas French Defendant   Action of Trespasse: Jury aforesaid Attested   Declaration Read: [*Evidence*] Abraham Hewlings Attested Deposeth that hee knowes the Land in Question, And that the Defendant hath made a Ditch upon the Plaintiffs Land (according to the Survey made to the Plaintiff) since the Plaintiff had the Land Surveyed to him. [*Evidence*] Daniell Leeds. the Attestation tendred, But Daniell refuses to take the Attestation of declaring the whole truth unlesse hee may be borne harmlesse: whereupon his Attestation is waved. [*Evidence*] John Antram (being Attested on the Jury) Deposeth that one hundred Acres was Surveyed to the Plaintiff before any other had taken it up (And five Acres of Meadow (being the Land in Question) the said Deponent saith was then Surveyed to the Plaintiff before any other had taken it up. The Jury find for the Plaintiff and give him fifty Shillings dammage with Costs of suite. Judgment thereupon Awarded.

[*Returne of Executione against Fryley satisfyed.*] Upon the Returne of the Executione at suite of Edward Hunloke against William Fryley. Edward Hunloke (the Plaintiff) declares the same Satisfyed.

Isaac Marriott and Daniell Sutton Plaintiffs   a Negro called Will Defendant   Action Debt   the Negro hath made his escape from the Sheriffe.

Edward Hunloke Plaintiff   James Hill Defendant   Continued.

Thomas Revell Plaintiff   John Cornish Defendant   Action case   Continued.

Richard Hartshorne and Thomas Hilbourne upon their request for Admistration of John Hootons Estate. See the Proceedings of Court and order or issue thereof in the booke of Registry for Admistrators   See alsoe the determination of Court in the businesse of Christopher Weatherill: about Accompts etc. and Thomas Gardner as Trustee for Nathaniell Pope in the same Registry for Administrations.

[**117** 1692/3] [*Court Order the Severall Townshipps proportions Trebled Nottingham 20—60, Chesterfield 19—57, Mansfield 18—54, Springfield 18—54, Southampton 20—60, Wellingborrow 9—27, Eversham 9—27, Chester 14½—43-6, Burlington*] Ordered that warrants be directed to Each Constable about the Poll Tax, To warne in all the Inhabitants to some Convenient place in the Township and make a Duplicate of every Inhabitant, and those hee and shee is Concerned to pay for at or before 7th March next: And that the Constable gather in 2s. 6d. for every head 16 yeare old and upwards and pay in the same to the Treasurers on this side or before 30th March next And in case any person or persons refuse or neglect payment thereof to Levy the same by distresse and sale of the offenders goods: And that at the Towne meeting they nominate in each Townshippe assessours [39] to lay an equall Tax, upon Lands and Cattle for paying for killing wolves and discharge of Constables charge etc. to be put into the hands of such as shall be chosen in each Townshipp for that purpose: That to that end 3l. be raised in the Township of Nottingham and Proportionably the rest.

[*Court order for Cryer*] ordered by the Court that the Cryer from hence forward shall have for every Tryall 1s. and for every non appearance of a Jury man 9d.

[*Order of Court*] Whereas it appeares that Nicholas Tregidgon (the Servant of Seth Hill) hath at severall tymes runaway from his said Master And hath put his said Master to great charge in goeing and sending after him and bringing him back to his Master For the makeing satisfaction therefore to his said master for his losse of tyme and expences, The Court doe order and appoint the said Nicholas Tregidgon shall serve his said master Seth Hill or Assignes for two yeares next ensueing this twenty firsth of February 1692/3.

Court dissolved.

Att the Court of Quarterly Sessions att Burlington May 8th 1693. Edward Hunloke, John Tatham, William Biddle, Daniell Wills, Thomas Gardner, Daniell Leeds Esqrs. Justices present. Grand Jury Robert Wilson, Eleazer Fenton, Robert Murfin, Thomas Wood, John Abbott, John Sharp, Michael Newbold, John Snape, John Tomlinson, Joshua Newbold, Thomas Wilkinson, Robert Engle, George Willhouse Attested.

The Grand jury upon the Bill to them preferred against Gennett Monro Find the Bill. Att the request of the Attourney Generall the further hearing of the aforesaid Prisoner is deferred untill further order.

The Grand Jury present the halfe of the Bridge and the Peece of Low Land which the way lies through by Widdow Hancocks as being not passable: And alsoe the Lane by Widdow Farrs and the Bridge in the said Lane: All which belong to the Township of Springfield. Springfield Township fyned 40s. (but if they amend the Premises in three weeks next then the Fyne to be remitted, otherwise to be paid.

The Constables of each Townshippe called to appeare. Whereof Daniell Bacon Constable of Chesterfield, John Tonkan Constable of Springfield, Elias Toy Constable of Cropwell appeared not and are fyned 10s. a peece.

Upon a Complaynt of Mary Turner against William Turner her Husband, who was Comitted to the Sheriffe, and Lett at Liberty upon Bayle, John Cornish being his Bayle, The said William Turner not appearing: John Cornish is ordered to bring in said Turner, or pay the 100l. Bond or lye in Prison in his roome.

---

[39] "Assessors" in MS.

John Tatham Esqr. Plaintiff   Thomas Hatchley and Martha his wife Defendants   Action Case   Withdrawne.

Abraham Senior Plaintiff   John Hickman Defendant   Attachment Action Debt   withdrawne.

John Hollinshead Plaintiff   John Rush Defendant   Action Debt   warrant not served.

William Deane Plaintiff   John Rush Defendant   Action Debt withdrawne.

[118 1693]   John Cornish Plaintiff   James Sherwin defendant   Action Trespasse Continued.

Walter Reeves Plaintiff   John Payne Defendant   Action Trespasse Tryed. Jury Called: vizt, John Curtis, Mathew Watson, William Bustill, Samuell Bunting, William Evans, John Ogbourne, Henry Ballenger, Michael Buffin, Thomas Harding, Robert Pearson, Thomas Tindall, Lawrence Morris   Attested. The Plaintiffs Declaration Read: The Plaintiff not proving his Tytle where the Trespasse is by the Declaration sett forth to be made, but it appearing that the Defendant had the First Survey thereof. The Jury find for the Defendant.

[*Execution taken out for 15s.*] William Fryley and wife Plaintiffs   John Port Defendant   Action Slander. The Defendant craves a non suit in regard the Plaintiffs appear not. The non suit calld and Judgment awarded for the Defendant for Costs.

John Hollinshead Plaintiff   John Rush Defendant   Action debt Attachment   Withdrawne.

Evidences for Walter Reeves Henry Morley and Thomas Cleverley, Attested: See their Depositions below thus marked ☞

Alsoe Walter Reeves Plaintiff   Joshua Humphries Defendant   an Action of Trespasse. The Plaintiff not goeing on with his Action against the Defendant Suffers a non Suite. which is granted and called upon the Defendants request And judgment for the defendants Cost awarded.

The Sheriffs returne of Executione in the Action of Mr. Edward Hunloke as Administrator of John Cutcher against Thomas Bowman is as follows   Vizt, That the Sheriffe hath Seized Severall of the Goods of said Thomas Bowman and hath had them appraised: which falling short of satisfying the Execution, hee hath alsoe Seized one hundred Acres of Land next adjoyning to the one hundred Acres at Wingerworth Poynt in said Mr. Edward Hunlokes Tenure, which was appraised to the Summe of Twenty pounds: All which in the whole amount to the Summe of
which is in parte of Satisfaction of the same Execution.

The Sheriffs returne of Execution in the Action of Mr. Edward Hunloke against Thomas Bowman for non performance of Covenants in the Mortgage by him made to Mr. Hunloke: is as follows. Vizt, That the Sheriffe hath Seized goods Sufficient for discharge of the same Execution. Mr. Edward Hunloke in Court Attested That the Bill of Charge by him given in to Thomas Bowman amounting in the whole to Five hundred Twenty Eight pounds Fifteene Shillings is a true Accompt. Mr. Thomas Bowman in Court promised to Seale and Execute the Deed for the Confirming and Releasing the one Hundred Acres and premisses by him formerly Mortgaged unto Mr. Edward Hunloke, This night being the 8th May 1693: which afterwards hee performed before John Tatham Esqr. William Biddle, Thomas Gardner and Thomas Revell Justices who alsoe as Evidences signed thereto.

☞ In the Action above of Walter Reeves against John Payne. Henry Morley Evidence on the behalfe of Walter Reeves Attested, deposeth that Walter Reeves came to Joshua Humphries and said he had an Attachment in James Hills hand to Attach the stack of Hay upon a peece of Marrish upon the further Branch of Rancokus Creek, the Hay belonging to John Payne and Joshua Humphries: But the said Walter said that for Joshua Humphries sake hee would wave the Attachment and lose the Charge thereof: And Joshua said if Walter would let it alone that tyme hee would stack noe more there, because it lay unconvenient for the Creek. Thomas Cleverley Attested deposeth That hee knowes litle, but onely that the Land in Controversie was Surveyed to Walter Reeves.

John Bainbridge requests that the Survey of some Particuler Lotts of which hee hath given Daniell Leeds an Accompt, may be suspended for one Moneth next, that in the meane while hee may make his right thereto appeare. which the Court grant.

The Court upon the Promise of the persons following to give Recognizance according to Law grant Lycences to them namely Richard Bassnett, Henry Grubb, Thomas Kendall, Abraham Senior, And order Thomas Revell accordingly to make out their Lycences and take their Recognizances according to Law:

Court Adjourned untill further order.

[119 1693] Att the Court of Quarterly Sessions held August 8th 1693. Edward Hunloke Esqr. Deputy Governour. William Biddle, Daniell Leeds, Francis Davenport, James Marshall, Thomas Lambert Esqrs. Justices on the Bench. Grand Jury Isaac Marriott, Thomas Kendall, Daniell Sutton, James White, Henry Bircham, Robert Wheeler, Thomas Gladwin, William Fryley, John Petty, Seth Hill, Abraham Senior, Richard Finimore, Samuell Ogbourne Attested. Traverse Jury Peter Resniere, Thomas Potts, James Satterthwait, Jonathan West, Lawrence Morris, Henry Grubb, Samuell Houghton, Samuell Furnis, James Wills, Bernard Lane, Nicholas Martineau, Richard Love Attested in the Case of Nathaniel Cripps versus Charles Pickering etc.

[*Daniell Smith paid Fyne*] Daniell Smith and Thomas Peachee Summoned and called but appeare not Daniell Smith Fyned 10s.

Grand Jury present John Budd and Samuell Furnis late overseers for Highways within Burlington, for detaining the Townes money and not giveing an Accompt thereof to the Towne meeting.

Robert Hutcheson and his wife Complayned of by Mathew Smith and Elizabeth his wife for selling Rum to the Indians before Edward Hunloke Esqr. Deputy Governour upon their oath against said Hutchesons wife were by said Deputy Governour bound to prosecute them this Court: And George Hutcheson gave his Engagement for said R. Hutchesons appearance: Robert Hutcheson and his wife called but appeare not. Mathew Smith and wife Attested and sent to the Grand Jury: The Grand Jury thereupon present Robert Hutcheson and wife Robert Hutcheson and wife called againe but appeare not. The said Mathew Smith upon their Attestation prove before the Court that said R. Hutchesons wife have sold Rum to the Indians since the last Act made against it whereupon the Court Fyne Robert Hutcheson 5l. according to the Act of Assembly: The Informers Remitt the halfe of what belongs to them: And the Bench Remitt the halfe of the other parte of the Fyne: the whole remitted is 50s. And the remainder being 50s. George Hutcheson for want of Robert Hutchesons appearance to pay the same 50s.

[*Fyne*] Elias Toy Constable of Cropwell Robert Engle Constable of Eversham for their non appearance Fyned 10s. a peece excused by reason of sicknesse.

[*Sheriffs returne of Executione against Thomas French*] The Sheriffe in the Executione against Thomas French at suite of Richard Finimore, That hee hath upon Executione Seized Goods from said French and hath them in possession.

John Cornish Plaintiff James Sherwin defendant Continued againe.

John Peares Plaintiff George Heathcote Defendant Action Case Continued.

Thomas Clarke Plaintiff John Peares Defendant Action Case Continued.

John Crafford Plaintiff Benjamin Devell Defendant Action debt warrant not served.

John Crafford Plaintiff Benjamin Devell Defendant Action debt warrant not served.

Abraham Senior Plaintiff Richard Francis Defendant Action Case withdrawne.

Abraham Senior Plaintiff Henry Pope defendant Action Case withdrawne.

Lawrence Morris and Nathaniel Cripps Plaintiffs John Crafford defendant Action debt withdrawne.

William Fryley Plaintiff John Peares defendant Action Case withdrawne.

John Port Plaintiff Benjamin Wheat defendant Action Case referred.

Richard Bassnett Plaintiff William Gill Defendant Action debt: Defendant called and appears not: Declaration Read, the Bill for 5l. 11s. principall debt read: James Hill proved the Bill upon Attestation The Court grant judgment upon the Bill for 5l. 11s. and Costs of Suite.

Nathaniel Cripps Plaintiff Charles Pickering etc. Defendants Jury Attested: Declaration Read: Jury find upon their owne knowledge for the Plaintiff and give him 4l. with Cost of Suite and 30s. dammage.

Thomas Revell on the behalfe of the Comittee in England Plaintiff John Powson Defendant Action Case. Defendant called, and appears not and it goes by default: The Declaration read, the Contract read and proved, the Court give judgment for 40s. dammage and Costs of suite.

[Court order] Ordered by the Court that the Justices of this County who appear not at each quarterly Court (unlesse sickness, or their being forth of the Province prevent) shall pay for each Court they appear not Three Shillings.

[120 1693] Att a Private Session held October 18th: 1693 Upon the Accompt of William Wardell. There Present Edward Hunloke Esqr. Deputy Governour. John Tatham, John Worlidge, Francis Davenport, Daniell Wills, Daniell Leeds Esqrs. Justices.

William Wardell (who was 16th October instant Comitted) being under indisposition of Body, requested to make his humble Submission and to Committ himselfe to the hearing and determination of a Private Session, which is this 18th October 1693 called at the House of Thomas Kendall in Burlington. Att the request of the abovenamed Wardell, to make his Submission to the Justices: The Court called William Wardell called And Confesses hee hath had Carnally to doe with Phillis, the Negro Woman, servant to Thomas Lambert: And Committs himselfe to the Mercy of the Bench. The said Wardell (the Prisoner) by others in his behalfe requests hee may have his Punishment laid upon his Estate. The Judgment of the Bench That the said Wardell shall be whipt at a Carts Tayle to morrow betwixt the howers of 10 and 12. from the Markett house to the River and shall receive Thirty Nyne Stripes well laid on: And pay all the Charges that hath been expended by Thomas Lambert in prosecuting him, And alsoe pay all Court Charges: or instead of the Thirty Nyne Lashes to pay the Summe of Five Pounds, And pay the Summe of Forty shillings over and above to Thomas Lambert for his losse of time in his Negro womans service: William Wardell called, And his Sentence above, Read: And the said Wardell chuses to pay five pounds instead of the Lashes, and to pay the other Costs and other Charges: Which Amounts in the whole to Nine Pounds, one shilling and Six pence.

November 3th 1693 Court of Quarterly Sessions then holden. Then present upon the Bench   Thomas Revell, William Biddle, Daniell Wills, Francis Davenport, Daniell Leeds, William Righton   Justices. Grand Jury Returned   John Roberts, William Hewlings, Henry Ballenger, William Matlock, Timothy Hancock, William Evans, James Bingham, William Clarke, Josiah Appleton, William Hasker, John Mason, Thomas Gladwin, Richard Boyes   Attested.

The Lawes signed by the Governour last Assembly Published.

Constables Called: Elias Toy Constable of Cropwell appeares not. Excused.

[*Grand Juryes Returne*]   Wee the Jury of Inquest for this County doe give it as our Verdict that there be a Tax laid Containing one third part as much as the Provinciall Tax Amounts to in this County: and to be laid in the same manner: And also that the owners of Negroes shall pay one penny per pound for their Negroes according to their worth or value: And that the said Tax be paid to George Hutcheson, whom wee appoint Treasurer for this County, who shall have power and hereby order to pay each Assembly man what appears to be his due, And the overplus (if any be) shall be made use of for finishing the Court house.

[*Court Order*] Order per Court that Warrants be Issued forth to the Constables of this County Consonant to the Act for the Tax, And alsoe for the Tax now laid upon the County according to the Grand Inquests presentment.

[*Court Order*] Order per Court that James Hill Sheriffe sue the Bonds given by Dennis Rotchfords bondsmen at suite of Judith Morrell etc.

Traverse Jury called   John Hollinshead, John Day, Samuell Furnice, Samuell Houghton, Samuell Ogbourne, John Wearne, Laurence Morris, Thomas Bryan, Henry Grubb, Christopher Weatherill, John Gardner, James Wills   Attested.

Daniell Wills junr. Plaintiff   Eliakim Higgins defendant   Action Case withdrawne.

Mahlon Stacy Plaintiff   Francis Tunneclift Defendant   Action Case withdrawne.

Samuell Furnice Plaintiff   William Fryley Defendant   Action case withdrawne.

James Marshall Plaintiff   William Fryley Defendant   Action case withdrawne.

Richard Bassnett Plaintiff   James Sherwin defendant   Action case withdrawne.

Richard Bassnett Plaintiff   John Heesom Defendant   Action case withdrawne.

Richard Bassnett Plaintiff   John Peares Defendant   Action case withdrawne.

[121 1693]   Walter Reeves Plaintiff   William Biddle Defendant   by

Consent of Plaintiff and Defendant   Jury before Attested. William Biddle comes of the Bench.

The Declaration Read: The Plaintiffs Deed Read: The Plaintiffs deed is not Recorded: Noe Returne of the Survey of Land which the Plaintiff Complaynes for as his right by the Deed is upon Record.

[*Attested*] Anthony Elton Attested upon the Plaintiffs Accompt But can say nothing for the Plaintiff.

[*Attested*] Daniell Wills came of the Bench and is Attested: And deposeth that the Plaintiff was advised not to Survey the Land in question for that it was laid forth before.

[*Verdict*] Jury are agreed of their Verdict and find for the Defendant. The Court give Judgment against the Plaintiff for Costs of suite.

John Peares Plaintiff   George Heathcote defendant   The Action last Court Continued   The Plaintiff requests hee may proceed   The defendant three times called to defend his Action   but appeares not. The Court endeavoured to perswade the Plaintiff to forbeare this Court: But the Plaintiff will not yeild thereto. Whereupon the Declaration is read   and is in Law Confessed by not appearing.

Articles betweene Plaintiff and Defendant read: [*Attested*] Thomas Clark and [*Attested*] Alexander Bennett   Evidences Attested. Thomas Clark deposeth that hee hath done severall peices of work for the Defendant by the Plaintiffs order, for which the Plaintiff hath paid him. Alsoe Alexander Bennett Deposeth that hee hath done severall peices of worke for the defendant by the Plaintiffs order, for which the Plaintiff hath paid him: And further deposes, that George Heathcote (the Defendant) did tell him (this deponent) in comeing from Philadelphia, that hee would pay the said Plaintiff, what was due to him for his work that hee had done for him the said Defendant. [*Attested*] The Plaintiff produces his Bill of the particulers of the worke by him etc. done for the defendant   And Attests that its a true bill and that the worke hath accordingly been done and performed which Bill Amounts to 12l. 07s. 00d. And acknowledges the receipt of 7l. 8s. 0d. The Plaintiff alsoe proves himselfe dampnifyed by the Defendants turning him of from the work Contrary to the Articles of Agreement in the Summe of 40s. Whereupon the Court Award Judgment in behalfe of the Plaintiff against the said Defendant for the Summe of 4l. 19s. 00d. Debt   for the Summe of 2l. 00s. 00d. Dammages   And for Costs of Suite being 1l. 10s. 09d. And Execution Accordingly made out to the Sheriffe.

Court dissolved.

[*Daniel Wills senr. by John Cook Chosen his Guardian*] January 6th 1693. Then came John Cooke, the sonne of John Cooke late of the County of Burlington in West New Jersey And made his free Choyse of Daniel Wills senr. to be his Guardian, Before James Marshall, Francis Davenport and Thomas Revell Justices, at the house of Henry Grubb in Burlington, And the said Daniel Wills was then Admitted Guardian as aforesaid by the said Justices. And said Daniel Wills then Accepted thereof.

[*Edward Andrews also chose Edward Rockhill for his Guardian*] January 6th 1693. Then came Edward Andrews the Sonne of Samuell Andrews late of the County of Burlington in West New Jersey And made his Free Choice of Edward Rockhill of the County aforesaid to be his Guardian, Before James Marshall Francis Davenport William Biddle Daniell Wills and Thomas Revell Justices at the House of Henry Grubb in Burlington And the said Edward Rockhill was then admitted Guardian as aforesaid by the said Justices, And the said Edward Rockhill then Accepted thereof.

[122 1693/4] Court of Quarterly Sessions at Burlington February 20th 1693. Edward Hunloke, John Tatham, James Marshall, Nathaniel Westland, Francis Davenport, William Biddle, Daniel Wills, Thomas Gardner, Mahlon Stacy, William Righton Esqrs. Justices present. Grand Jury John Wilsford, Robert Murfin, Robert Wilson, Robert Pearson, Samuell Overton, John Woolston junr., John Ogbourne, John Abbott, William Hickson, John Bunting, John Payne, Samuell Bunting, Richard Haynes Attested. Traverse Jury Samuell Harriott, William Wood, George Elkington, John Haynes, Benjamin Moore, Thomas Scholey, John Warren, Robert Hudson, John Gardner, Thomas Dugglas, John Calow, Mathew Champion.

[*Fynes*] James Sherwin and William Budd for their neglect in appearing being Summoned for Jurors fyned 10s. a peece.

New Constables presented and Chosen.

Nottingham ....William Watson: hee hath hyred Robert Pearson and the Court accepts him Attested.
Chesterfield ....William Wood—Attested
Mansfield ....Nathaniel Records—Attested
Birch Creek ....John Ogbourne senr. Attested
Northampton ....William Budd
Wellingborrough ....Thomas Eves—Attested
Cropwell alias Chester ....James Sherwin—Attested
Eversham ....Jonathan Eldridge—Attested
Burlington ....Henry Bircham and Abraham Senior— Attested

New Overseers for the Highwayes.
Nottingham ....John Wilsford and Robert Pearson
Chesterfield ....Samuell Taylor
Mansfield ....John Horner
Birch Creek ....William Atkinson and John Antram
Northampton ....John Wills

Wellingborrough . . . . Abraham Hulings
Cropwell . . . . John Rudderow   Continued
Eversham . . . . William Huling is still Continued
Burlington . . . . Peter Fretwell and James Wills

    John Tonkan brought his Complaynt against Susanna Reeves for Scandalizeing him which is offered to the Grand Jury Whereupon Joseph Stockton and John Stockton are sworne and Isaac Marriott Attested Evidences and sent to the grand Jury.

    And the Court Adjourne for 2 howers.

    Grand Jury returne, And they Find the Bill or Complaynt of John Tonkan against Susanna Reeves. Whereupon Susanna Reeves is called for and appeares, And being asked whether shee will Traverse or Submitt to the Bench, Shee saith shee submitts to the Bench. Joseph Stockton and John Stockton being againe both Sworne to give their Evidence to the Bench, Depose that the same Night the said Susanna Reeves layes the Scandall upon John Tonkan, that hee lay with her at John Gardners barne, they came out of Burlington in Company with John Tonkan, and the said Susanna Reeves parted from them at Yorkshire Bridge, And the said Deponents and said John Tonkan Rode togeather untill they came to Mattacopenny Bridge and then John Tonkan Rode before them to his owne house to make a Fyre against the said Stocktons should come, And that they the said Deponents stept in to Samuell Ogbournes house and warmed themselves a while and then Rode on to John Tonkans House where they found him, and hee had made up a good fyre. Isaac Marriott Attested, Deposeth that whereas the said Susanna Reeves and her father reported that the said Tonkan and said Susanna Reeves (the same day before that night in which shee reports the Scandall abovesaid) was drinking togeather at said Isaac Marriotts house, the said Deponent Deposes that hee saw noe such thing. Benjamin Moore Attested, Deposeth, that the said Susanna Reeves said to him, That it was not her that slandered said Tonkan, but it was her Mothers wicked lyes. [*Judgment and Sentence of the Bench*] Susanna Reeves haveing submitted her selfe to the Bench as above, The Bench order, That the said Susanna Reeves for her Scandalizing the said John Tonkan, Shall tomorrow betweene the howers of 12 and 2 be whipt betweene the Court house and the River not exceeding Forty Lashes well laid on. And Shall also pay Court Charges And order her to be secured in Prison until the tyme of her whipping, and after until the Court Charges be paid or secured to be paid.

    Adjourned to 8 in the Morning.

    February 21th. Jane the wife of Samuell Ogbourne was sent for to Court And Deposed that the two Stocktons abovesaid came into her house, And as they since told her that it was the same night that the Slander abovesaid was raised upon. But said John Tonkan came not in with them and that the said 2 Stocktons stayed and warmed themselves a while and rode away.

ordered per Court that a warrant be drawne and given for Execution of the Sentence abovesaid which was done: And the said Susanna was accordingly whipt.

[123 1693/4] [*This Cause was heard the 20th day*] Thomas French Plaintiff Richard Finimore defendant Action Trespass: Plaintiff and Defendant called and appear. Jury Attested. The defendant Pleads hee hath made noe such Trespass, As the Plaintiff setts forth.

[*Evidence*] Thomas French junr., Attested deposeth that the Defendant did cutt grasse upon the Meadow of the said Plaintiff which hee bought of John Woolston.

[*Evidence*] Charles French Attested deposeth that the Defendant with one hee brought with him did last Hay tyme Mow grasse upon the Meadow of said Plaintiff which hee bought of John Woolston. A Tarry of a Deed from John Woolston to the Plaintiff read, Also the Deed it selfe from said Woolston to the Plaintiff Read, Also a deed of Defendants read.

[*Evidence*] Daniell Leeds Attested Deposeth that in the first weeke of February 1682/3 hee Surveyed the 5 Acres of Land in Question to the Defendant by virtue of a warrant And that afterwards hee did Survey the said Meadow to Thomas French for feare said Thomas should sue him as hee did before, which hee then threatned if hee refused.

[*Evidence*] John Antram Attested, Deposeth that hee helped Daniell Leeds to Survey the 5 Acres in Question, which was before Thomas French Surveyed it.

[*Evidence*] Daniell Wills senr. Attested deposeth that the Land in question had beene Thomas Frenches, if hee would have taken to it, but hee took up other Land in Liew of it, and let the Land in Question lye voyd for any others that would take it.

[*Evidence*] John Woolston senr. Attested that the Land in Question was parte of the Land hee sold to Thomas French, which Land was parte of the land to him the Deponent then belonging by Lott.

[*Evidence*] Isaac Marriott Attested Deposeth that the 5 Acres of Meadow which Benjamin Scott threw up and which Daniell Leeds afterwards Surveyed for Richard Finimore was not Meadow but Myre.

[*Evidence*] Abraham Hulings Attested Deposeth that hee beleeves that the Propriety Lyne formerly Run Cutts of this Land in question from the Land late of John Woolston. And further that the said Defendant Surveyed the 5 Acres Meadow in question before the Plaintiff brought the Surveyor to Survey the whole.

[*Evidence*] William Hulings Attested, but what hee had to offer was not thought materiall or needfull. Court adjourne to Thomas Kendalls.

[*Verdict*] Jury goe togeather and after a Considerable time returne, being agreed of their Verdict. And by Samuell Harriott (their foreman) say they find for the Defendant, and soe they say all. Plaintiff desires an

Appeale, The Court tell him, hee performing the Conditions of an Appeale hee may have it, The Court give the Plaintiff tyme untill tomorrow to Consider of it; And the next day being asked if hee desire an Appeale, hee is not willing to have it: Judgment awarded and entred.

[*Court order*] Ordered per Court that there be an Equall Divident of that part of the Reall and personall Estate late Samuell Andrews which is bequeathed betweene the late wife of said Samuell and Edward his late Sonne According to the will of said Testatour, and that the Moyetie or Share belonging to said Edward (as appeares by said Will) be delivered to Edward Rockhill (the joynt Executor with said Mary Andrews and Guardian of said Edward) to be by said Guardian improved for the use of said Edward his Heires Executors Administrators and assignes.

[*2 Caveats*] Mathew Allen enters A Caveat against Recording Isaac Conoroes 500 Acres Land alsoe a Caveat against the Recording of Jacob Conoroes 500 Acres Land And Daniell Leeds ordered to bring them both in next Court And Mathew Allen then to appear and give notice to the other two.

James Marshall plaintiff William Fryley defendant Attachment withdrawne.

Clement Shinn Plaintiff Charles Woolverton defendant withdrawne.

Charles Woolverton plaintiff John Greene Defendant withdrawne.

Hugh Hutchins Plaintiff William Huntley Defendant Action Debt Attachment Noe effects.

Henry Pope Plaintiff Francis Austin Defendant withdrawne received 1s.

Abraham Senior Plaintiff Edward Slade Defendant Continued.

Abraham Hooper Plaintiff John Rush Defendant Continued received 1s.

Sheriffs returne of Executione against Walter Reeves not Served.

Abraham Senior Plaintiff Henry Pope Defendant withdrawne.

[*Presentment*] Grand Jury present Peter Groome and the reputed wife of Thomas Wright for their Scandalous liveing togeather.

John Peares Plaintiff James Hill Sheriffe Defendant Plaintiff and defendant Appear and both referre the Cause to the Bench. Bench order that the Sheriffe shall pay Peares for his last judgment and Execution, And also the Charge of this processe. The Court give James Hill a Moneths respite to pay the same.

John Shinn Administrator of Bonaventer Dominicy Complaynes versus William Righton both appeare John Gardner Attested to the truth of an affidavit (Saveing one or two small things therein hee could not be positive in. Samuell Harriott Attested Deposeth that hee heard Bonaventer etc. a litle before his decease say his Master Righton was indebted to him. Both

Complaynant and defendant referre the Matter to the Bench. (See further).

[124 1693/4] [*Presentment*] Mary Fryley presented by the Grand Jury for selling Liquor without Lycence and keeping bad order. [*Court order*] Mary Fryley sent for before the Court, where for her Misdemeanour in presumeing to keep any sourt of ordnary without Lycence Shee is Fyned 5l. And order that Shee forbeare keeping Liquors or house of publick Entertainment for the future without Lycence. But the Bench remitt the said fyne of 5l. because of her Condition.

[*Ordered Court*] Ordered that Susanna Reeves shall Serve John Antram for one yeare to Commence from this day 21st February 1693/4 in Consideration That the said John Antram hath payd downe the Charges of Court on her behalf being 44s. And also in Consideration that John Pay to said Susanna 16s. more; Provided Shee serve him the said one whole yeare, which said Susanna promises to doe.

Upon the further Consideration of the Complaynt of John Shinn against William Righton, William Righton is required to give a distinct Accompt of what is betweene him and the Estate late of Bonaventer aforesaid, in order that John Shinn may bee Cleare of his Accompts and Charge of same Estate as Administrator thereof and have his Quietus. William Righton replyes hee will give noe further Accompt then hee hath done: whereupon the Court order to take their owne Course therein: Afterwards being informed by two Witnesses whereby there seems to be litle or nothing due from William Righton to said Bonaventer a litle before his death, The Bench wave further proceeding therein untill some or one of the Magistrates take an opportunity to goe to William Rightons and Attest his wife in the premises.

[*Presentment*] Thomas Peachee etc. being presented by the Grand Jury hee and Mary his wife appear. Thomas Peachee being required the reason why hee hath put away his wife and live severally from each other, Answers that the reason thereof is because Shee abuses and Scandalizes him and therefor in regard they could not live in any Peace or Comfort togeather, they made an agreement to live apart each from other: Whereupon the Court aske them both if they are not willing to come to a Reconciliation and live togeather as husband and wife ought to doe, And admonish them soe to doe; Mary Peachee thereupon saith shee is heartily willing and desireous thereto. Thomas Peachee saith hee is also willing they should be reconcyled togeather Provided Shee will acknowledge shee hath Scandalized him wrongfully: Shee replies Shee is ready and willing to acknowledge Shee hath done evilly in giveing forth bad reports of him because hee is her Husband and therefore shee ought not soe to doe, But saith shee will not owne that shee hath told lies of him to her knowledge: But after some good admonitions from the Bench, They both promise they will forgett and never mention what unkind speeches or Actions have formerly past betweene them or Concerning each other; and thereupon are willing each of their papers which they made and signed one to another for their parting shall be Cancelled and burnt which is accordingly done; And they are againe reconciled togeather, and Hee said Thomas promisses shee behaveing her selfe with tendernesse and love to him, hee will remaine as a Loveing and a Carefull Husband to her and endeavour to make the best provision for her and the Child that hee can.

[*Court order*] Ordered per Court that Nottingham and Chesterfield Townshipps Shall meet togeather and lay out that way that may sute the Inhabitants of Nottingham Townshippe and thereabouts and also that parte of East Jersey through their Townshipps, And afterwards Mansfield Townshippe shall Carry on the same way through their Townshippe as they judge may best sute, And shall make report thereof to the next Court of Session.

Court Dissolved.

Court of Quarterly Sessions: May 8th 1694.

Edward Hunloke, John Tatham, James Marshall, Nathanael Westland, William Biddle, Thomas Gardner, Daniell Leeds   Esqrs. Justices present. Grand Jury   Samuell Harriott, James Wills, Daniell England, Henry Burr, Thomas Shinn, Samuell Furnis, Thomas Gladwin, Thomas Potts, James Sherwin, Thomas Raper, Bernard Lane, Daniell Smith, Lawrence Morris Attested. Grand Jury give in their Bills of presentment. Traverse Jury   John Shinn senr., Daniell Wills junr., Thomas Kendall, John Petty, Peter Fretwell, Benjamin Wheat, Samuell Ogbourne, Eleazer Fenton, Thomas Williams, Nicholas Martino, Thomas Eves, Thomas Bibb.

[125 1694] [*Grand Juries Bill and order thereupon*]   Wee of the Grand Jury are agreed That a Convenient Post Road be made from Crosswicks to Widdowe Hancocks and soe to Yorkshire Bridge, And from Burlington to Hulands poynt, best and nearest for the Accomodation and good of the County and to be done at Counties Charge. The Court order the same to be done accordingly.

The Grand Jury also Present as Nusances the wood Stones and Rubbish Lyeing in the Streets of Burlington.

Peter Groome and Anne the reputed wife of Thomas Wright upon the Grand Juries presentment last Sessions appeare this Session in Court. Their Indictment Read, Peter Groome Pleads not guilty and referres himselfe for tryall to God and the Country, Anne Wright also pleads not guilty and referres her self for tryall to God and Country.

Peter Groome for his Standing before the Court with his Hatt on with other Contemptuous behaviour in Contempt of the Court Fyned 5l. and to be Secured untill it be paid. Peter the next day appeares and desires Favour for his unseemly behaviour as above, acknowledging hee had gott over much strong drink, whereupon the Court remitt his Fyne of 5l. for the offence above and Fyne him 50s. for his appearing before the Court drunk; which hee paid. And said Peter and also said Anne both bound to appear next Session, upon the same Indictment.

[*The Caveat entred against Jacob Conoroes Land taken of*] Mathew Allen declares that the Caveat by Him Entred last Court against recording the Survey of Jacob Conoroes 500 Acres may be taken of and it is ordered to be taken of.

Samuell Stacy etc. Plaintiff   James Croft Defendant   Action of Case Plaintiff and Defendant appeare: Jury called, and Declaration read and Defendant pleads   Jury above Attested: Declaration opened. The Articles betweene Henry Stacy and James Croft read and owned by the Defendant. Also a Bill under the hand of the Defendant for 50s. Sterling read Also another for 2l. 15s. 2d. for utensills. Also the Defendant acknowledges the 5l. received of William Biddle. Also a Letter from Mrs. Stacy sent to James Croft read. Also Elias Farr the Attourney for Henry Stacy and for Henry's Executors his release to the defendant Read. Thomas Croft and Thomas Garwood both Attested and prove the release sealed and Executed by Elias Farr to the Defendant. Lawrence Morris Attested, Deposeth that hee heard Henry Stacy say hee had Leant 50s. to James Croft.

[*Verdict*] The Jury called and Appear: And say they are agreed of their verdict, And that they find for the Defendant and Soe they say all: The Plaintiff requests an Appeale, which under the provisoes Limitted in the Laws for Appeales is granted.

[*Caveat entred*] A Caveat entred against the Survey of Lawrence Morris (being parte of Jonathan Fox his Survey) entred per Francis Davenport on behalfe of Jonathan Fox.

Michaell Newbold Plaintiff versus Peter Greene Defendant   Action Case.

[*Received 2s. 6d.   Declaration and Copy 4s. Fyling 1s. Subpoena 1s. Cont[inuance?] 1s.*]   John Fleckna and James Johnson plaintiffs per Mathew Miller their Attourney versus John Rush Defendant   Attach[ment]   Action Case Continued.

[*Received 2s. 6d.*] John Fleckna and James Johnson plaintiffs per Mathew Miller their Attourney versus John Rush defendant   Attachment not served.

Mathew Allen's Caveat entred last Court now to be heard per order last Court: Mathew Allen declares the 500 Acres for Jacob Conoroe hee takes of: see that it may be recorded   see this entred above.[40]

Abraham Senior Plaintiff   Edward Slade Defendant   Continued.
Abraham Hooper Plaintiff   John Rush Defendant   Continued.

[40] This paragraph crossed out in MS.

Court Dissolved.

May 9th 1694. The Provinciall Court or Court of Appeales in Law Then called.

Samuel Stacy appeares to prosecute his Appeale against James Croft: The Court adjourne to the 15th Instant: And the Appeallant and Appealee agree: The Appeallants appeale is withdrawne.

[126 1694] County of Burlington in the Province. West New Jersey May 12th 1694. Court of Oyer and Terminer called before The Honourable Andrew Hamilton Esqr. Governour of the Province Judge thereof, And Severall of the Justices of this County being on the Bench.

Upon the Tryall of Jannett Monro. Grand Jury returned and Impannelled Nathaniel Dugglas, James Satterthwait, John Wearne, John Rogers, Thomas Tindall, Marmaduke Horsman, Bartholomew Minderman, Nathaniel Cripps, George Elkington, John Hilliard, Daniell Marshall, John Rush, Restore Leppincott Attested.

Jury of Life and death Richard Stockton, Peter Resniere, John Langstaffe, Richard Ridgway, John Joyner, Joshua Eley, Anthony Elton, Christopher Weatherill, Mathew Allen, Michael Newbold, Joshua Newbold, Thomas Dugglas, Attested. The Charge given The presentment upon the Coroner's Inquest, given to the Grand Jury with the returne of the same Inquest also: The Grand Jury returne and bring in the Bill, Billa vera.

The Sheriffe required to bring the Prisoner to the Barre The Prisoner Arraigned: And upon her Arraignment pleads not Guilty: And referrs her selfe to God and the Countrey. The Jury of life and death called being above named: And the Prisoner required as they are called to make her Challenges or Exceptions against any of them, if shee please; Shee saith they are strangers to her, but shee freely accepts them whereupon they are Attested.

The Kings Evidences against the Prisoner called for.

Dugglas Ireton (the wife of Obadiah Ireton) Attested, Deposeth, that a Child was found in a Tubb of water by an Indian near John Bainbridge house: And that shee being informed thereof came and found it there: And further Deposeth that the Child had a kind of blackish spott in its neck: and further saith not.

Sarah Bainbridge (the Prisoner Mistress) Attested; Deposes that shee was never sure that said Jannett (the Prisoner) was with Child but onely had suspition thereof: And therefore shee asked her the question, And shee said Jannett Denyed shee was with Child, but said shee was dropsicall; And further that shee (this Deponent) knowes nothing of the Child ever being alive; further saith not.

John Bainbridge (the Prisoners Master) Attested; Deposeth that hee Saw the Child, and that hee saw it at first in the Well, And that hee looked on the Child and the Child bended a litle in the neck, And that there appeared a litle blewish Circle on the Childs neck; But that hee did not apprehend it to be any thing of the Cause of the Childs death: And that hee put the Child in the ground and acquainted the Constable forthwith further saith not.

John Joyner (One of the Jury) saith hee tooke the Child up after it was by John Bainbridge Covered, And that hee washed the Child, And there was a black spott upon the neck of the Child, But that hee could not perceive anything of a wound or that it was the Cause of its death. And further saith not.

Daniell Wills (Coroner and Chyrurgeion) Attested, Deposeth that hee saw the Child after it was taken out of the Earth and washed, And that it had a small blackish Ring upon its neck; But that hee thinks it might be onely a Setleing of blood and further saith not.

Francis Davenport Attested, deposeth that hee being one of the Coroners Jury, Saw the Child, And that hee and others of the Jury saw a black spott or Ring on the Childs neck; And it was the opinion of him and others that the same spott or ring was a Signe of violence done to the Child.

John Bainbridge further saith that hee did not know the Prisoner to be with Child, but did Suspect it, And therefore that hee gave his wife Charge to be carefull of said Prisoner.

Proclamation made for all the rest of the Kings Evidence to drawn neare and give their Evidence for the King. Kings Attourney Generall Pleads that the Prisoner by vertue of an Act of Parliament is Guilty unlesse shee can make it appeare the Child was dead borne: To this the Judge and other of the Justices say that Law was made Ad Terrorem.

Prisoner Pleads the Child was still borne in the night in bed, but that shee can give noe Evidence thereof, there being none with her.

The Governour gives the Charge to the Jury, that if they finde what has beene Evidenced is proofe Sufficient of the Prisoner's murdering or killing the Child, they are to find her Guilty, otherwise not guilty.

Adjourned untill five at night: Court opened, Jury appear and called over, the Prisoner sett to the Barre, The Jury by Richard Stockton (their Foreman) say they are agreed of their Verdict: And that they find Jannett Monro (the Prisoner) not Guilty. and soe they say all.

The prisoner is ordered to be passed over for such tyme to some person or persons for soe long time as may discharge the Charges of Court which is 3l. 16s. 00d. And Satisfye her Master John Bainbridge for remainder of her time.

And Shee is cleared by proclamation.

Court dissolved.

[**127** 1694] Court of Quarterly Sessions and Pleas held August 8th 1694.

Edward Hunloke, James Marshall, William Biddle, Daniell Wills, Francis Davenport, Daniel Leeds, John Curtis, Peter Frettwell Justices on the Bench.

Grand Jury   William Righton, John Wills, John Roberts, Michael Buffin, John Tomkin, Peter Harvey, John Meredith, Ananiah Gaunt, George Smith, William Hewling, William Hunt, Samuell Tayler, Robert Chapman Attested.

Traverse Jury   William Wood, Edmond Steward, Isaac Horner, George Parker, Thomas Wallis, John Hollinshead, John Shinn junr., John Abbott, Robert Pearson, William Biddle junr., Nathaniel Cripps, John Petty.

[*Order of Court about the Constables for every Townshippe*]   Ordered by the Court that for the Ease of the Constables of Each Townshipp, That the Constables of Nottingham and Northampton Townshipps appear next Court: and next the Constables of Chesterfield and Wellingborrow, Next the Constables of Mansfield and Chester, next the Constables of Springfield and Eversham, And that at every Session one of the Constables of the Towne of Burlington appeare to serve the severall Courts: And that is [40a] order shall be followed Successively.

[*Order of Court about Groome and Wright*]   In the Indictment against Peter Groome and Anne the reputed wife of Thomas Wright, both called, but said Anne appeares not: Thomas Wright by Peter Groome (who appeares) desires (in regard hee is sick and that his wife cannot be spared from him) that the Court will deferre the matter untill next Court. The Court in kindnesse to said Thomas Wright deferre the proceedings untill next Court of Session.

[*The Grand Juryes returne is on fyle*]   Upon the Grand Juries returne for the repayreing amending and perfecting the Court house decently and that the Charge thereof be defrayed forth of the last County Tax. The Court thereupon send for George Hutcheson the receiver of the County Tax: and hee saith hee hath not money received of said Tax to defray the same.

[*Presentment per Grand Jury*]   The Grand Jury also Present that there is a High road wanting to goe through the Towne Bounds of Burlington to answer the Road that leads to Rancokus Point. [*Courts order thereupon.*] The Court thereupon order that the Inhabitants of Burlington lay out and returne to the next Session a Highway Convenient to answer that or meet the way that Leads to the Poynt of Northampton River.

[*John Poynsett cleared*]   John Poynsett upon the Complaint of Alexander Skene, being by Recognizance bound to this Court: Appeares   The Complaynant appeares not, with any processe against him: and said Poynsett is cleared by Proclamation And the Recognizance withdrawne.

[*The business relating to Edward Andrews and Edward Rockhill*]   Edward Andrews the sonne of Samuell Andrews deceased, came into Court and desired to Nominate and Chuse another Guardian instead of Edward Rockhill his present Guardian: Whereupon the said Edward Andrews Giveing satisfactory reasons to the Court for his soe doing, And also at his Mothers

[40a] *Sic.*

request, the Court Grant it: And hee nominates Mordecay Andrews his brother for his Guardian: The Court admitt said Mordecay his Guardian, Provided hee give sufficient bond to discharge his said Guardianshippe faithfully and to indempnifye the aforesaid Edward Rockhill the former Guardian: which the said Mordecay hath done: [*And Edward Rockhills dismission*] Edward Rockhill as joynt Executor with Mary Andrews, And as Guardian to the aforesaid Edward Andrews, Then gave in an Accompt of his receipts and disbursements Concerning the same Estate, which is adjusted and accepted; And hee desires to be dismist of his Executorshippe and as Guardian aforesaid To which the Court give their Assent: The Ballance of said Accompt which being adjusted before the Court and in presence of Mary Andrews the other Executrix it appeares that the said Edward Rockhill as joynt Executor aforesaid, And as Guardian to said Edward is indebted to the Estate in the Summe of Fifty and three shillings and four pence halfe penny and noe more: But said Edward Charges nothing in his Accompt for his paines and expenses therein: The Court therefore upon Consideration thereof thinke fitt to allow him five pounds: Soe it appeares there rests due to said Edward Rockhill from the Estate Forty Six Shillings Seaven pence halfe penny.

[*An Agreement of Doctour*[41] *Peachee and Mary his Wife*] Agreed by Doctour Peachee and Mary his wife before the Court at Burlington the 9th August 1694, that in Consideration the said Mary with her Sonne will depart this Province for England, either by the way of Mary Land, or some other Port within three weeks next, And soe not be further chargeable to the said Doctor Thomas Peachee: Hee the said Thomas Peachee hereby promises to pay to or for the use of the said Mary Peachee, Three pounds, or if shee desires it five pounds this day; And at or before her departure from hence (to the intent and purpose aforesaid) the Summe of Fifteene pounds more, being in the whole twenty pounds: to which the said Mary Peachee also hereby agrees, And in testimony hereof [**128 1694**] The said Thomas Peachee and Mary Peachee have hereunto sett their hands the day and year abovesaid. This done in Court before us Edward Hunloke: Daniel Leeds, James Marshall, Daniel Wills, Thomas Revell Justices.   Thomas Peachee   Mary Peachee.

Court of Pleas.

John Fleckna and James Johnson Plaintiffs by Mathew Miller their Attorney versus John Rush defendant   Action case entred last for last Court Plaintiffs nor defendants appear: Continued.

Jacob Spicer Plaintiff versus William Biddle junr. Defendant   Action Trespass on Attachment on a negro. The declaration not agreeing with the warrant The Court order the Plaintiff to pay Costs of suite.

Thomas Kendall and James Wills Plaintiffs versus Henry Pope Defendant   Action Debt   neither Plaintiff nor defendant appeare   Action Continued.

[41] "Doctor" in MS.

Richard Bassnett Attourney for Philip Richards Plaintiff versus John Rush Defendant   Action Withdrawne.

Isaac Marriott Plaintiff versus John Heeson Defendant   Action Debt Withdrawne.

Thomas Gladwin Plaintiff versus Francis Rawle Administrator of Samuell Borden Deceased defendant   Action Case   withdrawne.

Abraham Senior Plaintiff versus Charles Sheepey Defendant   Action Debt   withdrawne.

Lewis Levally Plaintiff versus Nathaniell Dugglas Defendant   Action upon the Case   warrant not executed.

Mathew Allen Plaintiff versus John Rush Defendant   Action Debt withdrawne.

Stephen Day Plaintiff versus Thomas Williams Defendant   Action Trespasse   withdrawne.

Mathew Miller Plaintiff versus John Rush Defendant   Action defamation   neither Plaintiff nor defendant Appeare   Continued.

John Tatham Esqr. and Daniell Leeds Plaintiffs versus Mary Myers Defendant, action upon the Case   The Jury called over: being as before   and attested: the declaration Read. Plaintiffs open the Case. The Defendant desires to see the Warrant for the Plaintiffs Survey: Which is produced and Read: Then the Defendants Tytle to the Land in question, per deed Read Also the Defendants Survey produced and Read.

[*Evidence*]   John Antram called by the Defendant for Evidence Attested   And Deposeth that the Land now in Widdow Myers tenure when Surveyed per William Emley; They begun as soone as they came at fast Land over London Bridge and soe went on upon fast Land to the Tannhouse Run, And soe back againe the Courses to the Bridge aforesaid   And that hee (this Deponent when the Lynes were soe run, asked the Surveyor, what must become of the Swamp Land; And hee answered, It must run in with the rest.

Act of Assembly, Concerning Resurveyes etc. Read: Also William Myers Tytle to one Eighth and one Sixty fourth parte of a Propriety Read. The Charge to the Jury given And they goe togeather.

[*Juryes Verdict*]   The Jury returne to the Court: And are called over. And answer distinctly: And declare they are agreed of their Verdict   and say they are agreed of their Verdict   And say they find for the Defendant And soe they say all.

Mr. Tatham (one of the Plaintiffs) in behalf of himself and Daniell Leeds (the other Plaintiff) requires an Appeale to the next Provinciall Court of appeales in Law: The Court respite their Answer untill the Morrow Morning following Att which tyme the Court called againe: And the Plaintiffs require noe Appeal. thereupon judgment awarded.

Court Dissolved.

[129 1694] Court of Quarterly Sessions and Court of Common Pleas holden November 3d 1694. A Quorum then appeares on the Bench. The Courts called but finding the Court was not likely to finish and being the last day of the weeke, The Courts adjourned to the 8th November instant.

November 8th 1694, The Court Session called John Tatham, Nathaniell Westland, William Biddle, Francis Davenport, Thomas Gardner, John Curtis, Peter Fretwell Esqrs. Justices on the Bench.

Peter Groome and Anne the reputed wife of Thomas Wright (who was ordered to appear at this Session called 3 tymes and appeare not, their Bayle bonds forfeited, and ordered to be put in suite.

The Grand Jury returned Thomas Gilborthorp, John Browne, Thomas Williams, Nathaniell West, John Bunting, Thomas Folke junr., Joshua Newbold, Mathew Watson, Benjamin Field, Jacob Perkins, Peter Harvey, William Foster, Samuell Furnis. Thomas Gilberthorp refuses to appeare by reason of his privilege as an Assembly man. Nathaniell West, Benjamin Field, Thomas Folke junr., Peter Harvey, Joshua Newbold, Samuell Furnis, all sick. The Grand Jury not full the Session therefore adjourne for 2 howers.

Post Meridiem The Court of Session Called, The Grand Jury not full by reason of sicknesse The court therefore adjourne untill further order.

[*Court of Common Pleas*] Court of Pleas called Jury for the Court of Pleas called Benjamin Wheat, Thomas Harding, Thomas Scattergood senr., Thomas Scholey, John Warren, Joshua Humphries, John Butcher, Henry Ballenger, John Woolman, James Bingham, Henry Beck, Marmaduke Horsman.

James Hill Plaintiff as Sheriffe Phillip Richards Defendant Action of Debt on bond declaration and Copy delivered the Action Continued upon the promise of Mr. David Lloyd that the Debt and charges should be paid etc.

Henry Low Plaintiff versus Isaac Conoroe Defendant Action upon ye Case The Defendant called and appeares not The action called again after dinner, but the said defendant still appeares not but lets it goe by default. The Court require the declaration to be read, which is read, and the plaintiff to prove his debt brings John Adams who is Attested, and deposes that the defendant bought the Horse as is sett forth in the declaration for 5ol. to be paid as is alsoe declared.

The Bench grant judgment for 5ol. with Costs of suit.

John Calowe Plaintiff versus John Tuelie Defendant Action Trover etc. The Jury to witt Benjamin Wheate and fellows Attested. Declaration read; Defendant Pleads not guilty in manner and forme.

[*Evidence*] John Joyner Attested, Deposeth that to the best of his knowledge the Horse in question is the Plaintiffs proper goods, And saith that the Defendant said to him (this Deponent) that his (the Defendants) Brother John had markt his Horse; but thought that this in question was not the same

Horse; And further Deposeth that hee held the Horse of the Plaintiffs while another person (to witt Thomas Dugglas markt him.

[*Evidence*] Thomas Dugglas, Attested saith that John Calow sold a Mare and Colt to John Joyner, and that at the spring John Joyner markt the Colt and turned him forth, And saith that the Horse in question hath the same naturall and Artificiall markes which the said Colt had, And that the Horse in question hath used the same walk that the said mare and Colt used and that to the best of his knowledge, as he beleeves the Horse in question is the Plaintiffs.

[**130 1694**] [*Evidence*] Michael Newbold, Attested, Deposeth that hee was Imployed by the Plaintiff to Cutt his Colt, And that the Horse was not to be found And that the Defendant said hee had gott his Horse Gelt, And that the Horse in question is ungelt.

[*Evidence*] Edmond Stuard, Attested, Deposeth that hee beleeves the Horse in Question is the Defendants hee having severall times seene him with the Mare, And that the Defendants Colt (as the person that was to Geld him said) was not Gelt But had a Scratch and a peece of a stone Cutt of.

[*Evidence*] John Hancock Attested, Deposeth that the Defendants wife had such a Colt as is in question, And that hee did marke the Colt for her (the Defendants wife) And that its the same marke with the Colt in question.

[*Evidence*] of Mordecay Anderson and Mary his wife Being their affidavit taken before Thomas Revell Justice, was presented in Court and read.

The Jury have their Charge given and are ordered to seale up their Verdict when agreed, and to deliver it to the Court when the Court shall sitt tomorrow in the morning. And soe goe togeather. And the Court adjourne untill to morrow morning at the 8th hower.

November 9th 1694 The Court sett. The Jury are called and all appear, They by their foreman deliver up their verdict sealed, Wherein they find for the Plaintiff with Cost of suite (vizt) That the Plaintiff have his Horse and Costs of suite, and soe they say all. Judgment awarded thereupon.

The Governour comes to the Bench.

Jeremiah Basse Attourney for Daniell Cox Esqr. Plaintiff versus Mahlon Stacy and George Hutcheson etc. and Administrators of Thomas Hutcheson etc. Defendants Action Continued.

Lewis Levalley Plaintiff versus Nathanaell Dugglas Defendant Action of Trespasse upon the Case Plaintiff and defendant Appear. The Plaintiffs Declaration Read the Defendant putts in his plea Speciall, The Plaintiff offers a demurre thereupon. The Bench order the Court to withdraw that they may Consider of it and give their opinion therein. The Bench give their opinion, That in regard of the infancy of the Province, advantage may not be taken against the formality of a Plea.

The Defendant pleads in Generall, that what hee did was in his owne defence.

The Jury called; being the same Jury as before; Benjamin Wheate, the Defendant makes his Exception against. And Christopher Weatherill is added to the Jury, and Benjamin put by. And then called and Attested.

[*Evidence*] Anne Prickett Attested, Deposeth, That the Plaintiff called the Defendant a Rouge and a Cheating Rouge, And the defendant said call mee not Rouge for I will not beare it; and that shee saw the Plaintiff thereupon pull of his Neckcloth and lay it by, And then struck the Defendant a box on the Eare, and that hee the said Plaintiff Struck the Defendant a second blow, And that then the Defendant took the Plaintiff by the Collar and threw him downe.

[*Evidence*] Josiah Prickett Attested, Deposeth, that hee came into the House and saw that the Defendant had throwne downe the Plaintiff, and that Hee (the Deponent) tooke the Defendant of, And that then the Plaintiff made at the said Defendant againe to strike him and the said Defendant said, pray to not hold mee to be murdered, and thereupon hee (the Deponent) let him goe.

[*Evidence*] John Petty Attested, Deposeth that after the quarrell, hee saw the Plaintiff, and that hee seemed to aile litle, onely hee had like a little Scarre on his Eye.

[*Evidence*] Thomas Dugglas, Attested, Deposeth that after the Quarrell, he saw Levally (the Plaintiff) and that hee had a plaister on his Eye, And that Eleazer Fenton said, the Plaintiffs Shin was the worst hurt hee had.

[*Evidence*] Thomas Bibb, Attested, Deposeth, That the defendant 2 or 3 dayes after the quarrell went with him (the Deponent) to see the Plaintiff, And that the Plaintiff then said hee was not drunk when the Quarrell happened: And further saith that to his knowledge the Plaintiff is a quarrelsome person, which was in Court apparent.

[*Evidence*] John Joyner Attested, Deposeth that hee (hearing The Plaintiff was not well) went to see him and asked him (amongst other things) if hee was drunk when the quarrell was, and hee answered noe, And that the Plaintiff then said hee struck the Defendant first, and said hee thought to have boxed him (the Defendant) sufficiently: but found his hand too heavy for him; but further said hee hoped it would be good for him, for it should be a warning to him for strykeing persons any more.

[*Evidence*] John Poynsetts Attestation in Writing being taken before authority is produced and Read in Court.

[*Evidence*] Richard Francis Attested, Deposeth, That the Plaintiff some time before the Quarrell came into a house where hee (this Deponent) was, and struck him on the face.

[*Evidence*] Doctor Thomas Peachee, Attested, Deposeth, that the Plaintiffs head and face was extreamly swelled, before hee sent for him to him And that the Plaintiff suffered much afterwards, which was as hee beleeves the effect of the blowes in the quarrell, but cannot ascertaine it. The Charge given to the Jury, And they goe togeather And after some time returne to the Court, And being all called over and they make answer they are agreed, say by their Foreman, they finde for the Defendant   Judgment is awarded for the defendant for his Costs.

[131 1694] John Tatham Esqr. Plaintiff   John Budd Defendant   Action of defamation etc. The Defendant Pleads that an Action of Scandalli Magnat in this Action Lies not.

The Plaintiff Demurrs to this Plea.

The Bench see good the Court shall proceed upon the Declaration as an Action of Defamation.

The Defendant Pleads the Generall Issue, not guilty in manner and form.

The Jury (To witt Thomas Harding and fellowes in the last action onely Christopher Weatherill dismist and Thomas Bibb put in, in his stead) Are Attested. The Declaration Read.

[*Evidence*] Jeremiah Bass, Attested, Deposeth that hee heard the Defendant Budd say to the Plaintiff Tatham, Thou hast shortned, or I beleeve thou hast Shortned the dayes of my Brother, and the said Plaintiff then asked what Brother, the said Defendant replyed my Brother James, and hee further said hee Would push it as farre as it would goe; And that the Defendants wife said shee beleeved that her Brother James was poysoned; but did not beleeve that John Tatham had poysoned him. And that the said defendant Budd then replyed; it was John Tatham that had poysoned him. This the Deponent said hee (immediately after the speakeing of the words   (for his memories sake perceiveing hee was likely to be called to give Evidence thereof) writt downe, And presently Fetcht the writing it selfe, and read it, which agreed with the words laid in the declaration and the time and place.

[*Evidence*] Captain John Jewell Attested, Deposeth that hee (with many others being in the House of Henry Grubb, on or about the time in the Declaration laid) did heare the defendant Budd say to the Plaintiff Tatham; Thou hast shortned my Brothers dayes, And the said Plaintiff then asking what Brother, hee, (the Defendant) answered my Brother James.

[*Evidence*] Mary West Attested, saith little to any purpose (which by reason of the presse of people could not be taken).

[*Evidence*] Jonathan West Attested, deposeth that James Budd after hee was dead Swelled and looked black, and wrought in his Belly and att his mouth, and that after hee was put into the Coffin he swelled much. And that hee with others thought he burst in the coffin.

[*Evidence*] Certaine Depositions of Mr. John Inians taken before one of the Magistrates in East Jersey Concerning one Hollwells words before his death, produced and Read.

[*Evidence*] Depositions of Mrs. Mary Inians also taken before the same Magistrate, Concerning the said Hollwells words, also produced and Read.

[*Evidence*] The deposition of one Mary Ashley taken before Justice Wilcocks in the Province of Pennsylvania, produced and Read.

[*Evidence*] William Budd, Attested, Deposeth that hee met his Brother James walking in Burlington, And that hee told this Deponent hee was under great trouble, for that hee had a Letter in his pockett wherein his death was designed.

[*Evidence*] Peter Bosse, Attested, desired for his Memories sake hee might read or give in his Depositions in writing which hee attested to the truth of and put his hand, which was Read.

[*Evidence*] Nicholas Martineau, Attested, Deposeth, that James Budd said his heart was almost broke, and said that John Tatham would not pay him money necessary for his businesse hee had undertaken.

[*Evidence*] Elizabeth Bosse Attested, Deposeth, that according to her judgment, James Budd dyed not the Comon death of all men. And further that shee beleeves James Budd dyed of Poyson.

[*Evidence*] Priscilla Love, Attested; but saith litle to the purpose (which (by reason of the presse of the People then made) could not be taken. The Jury have their Charge given, and by reason its night are ordered to seale up their Verdict when Agreed, and to deliver it to the Court when sitting. And soe goe togeather.

And the Court adjourne to the 8th hower next morning.

November 10th 1694, The Court appeare and is called, The Jury called and appeare, And by Thomas Bibb (whom they appointed their foreman deliver in their Verdict Sealed, wherein they find for the Plaintiff and give him Twenty pounds dammage with Costs of suite and soe they say all. The Court grant Judgment thereupon.

John Beach per order of Court Entred Cryer of the Court etc.

Stephen Jones Plaintiff versus John Jones defendant   Action Case, noe appearance of Plaintiff or defendant   the Action Continued.

Abraham Senior Plaintiff   John Ratliffe Defendant   withdrawne.

William Righton Plaintiff   John Heesom defendant   Continued.

John Rudderow Plaintiff   John Jones Defendant   Continued.

Jeremiah Basse Attourney for John Reeve versus William Righton Defendant   Entred by Consent to come to tryall next Court, declaration drawne, and Copy sent and fyling the same. but the Plaintiff orders it to be put by.

Court Dissolved.

[**132** 1694] [*Nathaniel Pope*] January 19th 1694. Nathaniel Pope Sonne of Joseph Pope late of Burlington deceased Chose Francis Davenport and Edward Rockhill Guardians for him, before Nathaniel Westland Thomas Revell and Peter Fretwell Justices, and Admitted and gave Bond for performance of their Trust.

Court of Session and Court of Pleas held February the 20th 1694. Present on the Bench   The Honorable the Governour Hamilton. Edward Hunloke, John Tatham, Jeremiah Basse, Nathaniel Westland, William Biddle, Daniel Wills, Francis Davenport, Mahlon Stacy, John Curtis, Daniel Leeds, Peter Fretwell Esqrs.

Grand Jury Impannelled   Isaac Marriott, John Scott, Bartholomew Minderman, Anthony Elton, Freedom Lippincott, Henry Grubb, Robert Engle, John Wilsford, Thomas Folke junr., John Day, John Browne, William Matlock, William Biddle junr.   Attested.

Traverse Jury   Walter Humphries, Richard Love, Thomas Raper, Restore Lippincott, William Black, Thomas Wallis, Michael Newbold, Nathaniel Duggles, William Hunt, John Hancock, Thomas Williams, Robert Wheeler.

Nathaniel Records Constable of Mansfield returnes severall persons who have not paid their Tax, for the Townshipp. [*Court Order*] The Court order a warrant to distreyne particularly upon the Delinquents.

New Constables: Nottingham: William Hixson Attested. Chesterfield: Thomas Folke junr. Attested. [*Continued*] Mansfield   William Beel junr. Attested. Birch Creek   William Bustill Attested. [*Continued*] Northampton [*William Budd the last years Constable never attested nor appears*]. [*Continued*] Wellingborrough   Richard Finimore. [*Continued*] Cropwell or Chester   Mathew Allen Attested. [*Continued*] Eversham   Josiah Appleton. [*Continued*] Burlington   Josiah Prickett and Jonathan West Attested.

Overseers for Highwayes Nottingham   John Abbott and John Bryerley. Chesterfield   Andrew Smith. [*Continued rest*] Mansfield   James Croft. Birch Creeke   Continued as before. Northampton   John Wills. Wellingborrow   Freedome Lippincott. Cropwell   George Glave. Eversham   James Bingham. Burlington   Christopher Weatherill   Thomas Raper.

Jacob Perkins bound by Recognizance to this Session called and appeares; The Grand Jury find the Bill: The Prisoner declares he will Traverse. 21st February   Jacob Perkins his Indictment read, and hee Arraigned, And Pleads not guilty: And referres himself for tryall to God and the Countrey. [*Revell Attorney General*] [42] The Traverse Jury before mentioned Attested The King's Attourney for this Session appointed is Thomas Revell   Attourney calls for the King's Evidences against the Prisoner: Thomas Bibb the Sheriffe Attested deposeth that on the 25th December last by vertue of a warrant hee Arrested John Powson in the Indictment mentioned at the house of Mathew Allen and was bringing him to Burlington and that said Pawson endeavoured to make his escape by runing over the Creek, and that hee the said Sheriffe Rid about, and Came where hee found Pawsons footing and followed the same to Jacob Perkins where hee heard Powsons voyce in the house, And that hee thereupon threw open the Doore and went into the said Jacob Perkins house and Siezed the said Powson his prisoner: And that hee

---
[42] Along the margin in a different hand.

the said Sheriffe then said, Mr. Perkins: this is my Prisoner, I charge you to assist mee: And that said Jacob Perkins refused: saying, assist thee who art thou, The Sheriffe replyed I am their Majesties Officer, and said Jacob said thou the Sheriffe, thou a turd: And Heaved his fist at the said Sheriffe: And in the meane time the Prisoner Run away over the River on the Ice. Jury Goe togeather: And after some time returne: And give in their Verdict against the Prisoner at the Barre; for the King that the Prisoner is guilty: The Bench Fyne him 5ol. And Court Charges: But Suspend the Fyne upon his good behaviour.

Peter Groome and Anne Wright request they may come to tryall, that their Bondsmen may be cleared: The Court grant it. The Traverse Jury called and Attested (they makeing noe exceptions against any of them) The Indictment Read. The King's Attourney Calls for the King's Evidences: Thomas Duggles Attested Deposeth that the said Groome and Anne Wright did for some time Cohabit togeather. But saith that Thomas Wright her husband beat her and turned her out of doores which her Husband confesses in Court. Michael Newbold Attested deposeth the same with Thomas Duggles. Henry Beck Attested Deposeth that hee saw Anne Wright have a swelld face, And that shee said Thomas (meaning her Husband) had beat her, And that Thomas Wright replyed shee caught him by the Throat: And hee this deponent asked said Thomas what the matter was of their falling out, And Thomas replyed that shee was minded to live with Rogues. Thomas Chapman, Attested, Deposeth that hee knowes the said Groome and Anne Wright Lived disorderly togeather for some time, as above appeares, but knowes nothing of any particular Act. The Charge given to the Jury and they goe togeather. And find for the King: The Bench Fyne Groome and Anne Wright 5l. a peece and Court Charges: And order them both to be bound to good behaviour for 12 mo. and a day. The Court Suspend the Fyne of 5l. upon Wright's wife untill next Court Because of her Husband's purse etc.

[*Court Order*] Ordered that the County Tax wherein the Negroes are Taxed shall for this tyme be paid but that it be noe president. And that hence forward they shall not be Taxed in a Poll and as Chattells both.

[**133** 1694/5] [*Presentment*] Grand Jury present John Bryerley and his wife Mary for haveing a Child within 21 weekes next after marriage.

[*Presentment*] They also present Andrew Davisse and Mary his pretended wife for haveing a Child and goeing togeather contrary to the Law of the Province.

Also The Grand Jury doe give it as their Judgment That a Rode be laid out the best and nyest way to the Point calld Hewlings Point from Burlington.

[*Thomas Revells Bill*] The Bill of Thomas Revell for severall businesse done for the County amounting to Six pounds Thirteene Shillings Six pence allowed by the Bench.

Court of Pleas opened.

John Hugg junr. Plaintiff John Silver Defendant Action Trespasse Continued because Plaintiff or defendant appeare not.

John Tatham Esqr. Plaintiff Henry Beck Defendant Action Case Withdrawne.

Jeremiah Basse Gent. Plaintiff John Pawson Defendant Action Case, warrant served but Powson made his Escape.

Thomas French Plaintiff Daniell Leeds Richard Finimore and Abraham Hewlings: Defendants Action Trespasse Plaintiff and Defendants appeare, Declaration Read: The Defendants plead not guilty of a Trespasse in manner and forme. in regard the Land upon which the Plaintiff declares the Trespasse to be done is not the Plaintiffs Land. [2 *Deeds for Evidence*] The Jury before named, called over and Attested: Plaintiffs Deed from John Woolston: And Thomas Ollives deed to John Woolston read. [*1 Instrument for Evidence*] Also an Instrument for an Exchange of Land with William Biddle read.

[*John Woolston senr.*] John Woolston senr. Attested Deposeth that hee sold to the Plaintiff 200 Acres of Land next to William Peachees Land but knowes not what or how much Meadow belonged thereto.

[*William Hewlings*] William Hewlings Attested, Deposeth that hee hath taken Speciall notice of the Land in question, And saith that according to the Lynes which hee and others found left by Hancock the Surveyor as the Common report went, by those Lynes the Land in question is not within Thomas Ollives Propriety.

[*Abraham Hewlings*] Abraham Hewlings Attested, Deposeth that the Land in Question is within William Peachees Line and not within Thomas Ollives propriety The whole matter opened to the Jury and they goe togeather: And upon their returne say they are agreed of their Verdict. And that they find for the Defendants. The Bench at the defendants request grant Judgment for Costs: Plaintiff desires an Appeale which the Court under the Provisoes in the Law in that behalf agree to. (Vizt, to pay the Costs of this Tryall and give bond and security to prosecute his Appeale with Effect; neither of which are done (while the Court sitts.

George Porter Plaintiff William Biddle Gent. Executor of William Ellis Defendant Action of the Case William Biddle comes of the Bench. Plaintiff and Defendant appeare, The Declaration Read, the Plaintiff declares theres noe such Bill as the Plaintiff setts forth.

[*Evidences*] [*Nathaniel Records*] Nathaniel Records Attested, Deposeth that hee did see a writing before William Ellis came into the Countrey which had a Seale to it and the name William Ellis Subscribed which hee beleeves (haveing seene the hand writing of said Ellis) to be his owne hand, wherein William Ellis was to pay to the Plaintiff Sixteene pounds English money.

[*Mordecay Andrews*] Mordecay Andrews Attested, Deposeth, that hee heard William Ellis say, hee did owe George Porter (the Plaintiff) money, but that hee could not pay him without selling Land, And that hee would sell noe Land for it, for that George Porters Bill was Burnt, and hee had nothing to show for it, But said hee would pay him when hee was old, and it would doe him most good then, for if hee had it hee would make it away, but doth not remember that hee heard Ellis say how much hee owed him.

[*John Browne*] Attested Deposeth that William Ellis was formerly sick at his this Deponents house and made his will, And that said Ellis then gave this Deponent an Accompt of his Debts but said nothing of any Debt due to the Plaintiff.

[*John Curtis*] being A magistrate on the Bench Deposeth that a few days before said Ellis dyed hee this Deponent writt said Ellis Will and that said Ellis then said the greatest debt hee owed was to William Biddle which as appeared was but about 20s. The whole matter opened to the Jury And they goe togeather: And upon their returne being called over, say they are agreed of their Verdict, And that they find for the Plaintiff and give him Sixteene pounds English money and Costs of suite; The Plaintiff craves Judgment thereupon. And Judgment is accordingly awarded.

Court dissolved.

Speciall Court   February 23d 1694.

Att a Speciall Court Called the 23d of February 1694 at the house of Henry Grubb in Burlington: at the request of Jeremiah Basse Attourney for Doctor Coxe Plaintiff and George Hutcheson and Mahlon Stacy Administrators of Thomas Hutchinson etc. Defendants. Jeremiah Basse Gent. (Attourney for Daniell Coxe of the Cittie of London in the Kingdome of England Esqr.) Plaintiff haveing brought an Action of Debt against George Hutcheson and Mahlon Stacy and also them as Administrators of the Estate of Thomas Hutchinson late of the County of Burlington aforesaid Deceased Defendants in an Action of debt for 900l. of Lawfull money of England per bond. Which Action at the Court held at Burlington the 3d November 1694 being Continued by order of Court: Att the request of said Plaintiff and defendants this Speciall Court was called there being present Edward Hunloke: John Tatham: Thomas Revell: Daniell Wills and Peter Fretwell Justices on the Bench. Court called and opened: Plaintiff and Defendants appeare: Declaration Read.

An Authentick Coppy of the bond read: The Defendants owne the Bond: But say they have paid 186l. 19s. 2d. thereof, which the Plaintiff ownes, as haveing seen and stated the Accompt with the Defendants: The Defendants thereupon (saving to themselves what they may farther make appeare paid thereof) Confesse judgment   And the Court Order judgment accordingly to be entred.

It is in Court acknowledged by Plaintiff and Defendants that theres onely one Hundred and forty pounds remaines due upon this Bond and judgment.

Court Dissolved.

[134 1695] Court of Session and Court of Pleas held at Burlington May 8th 1695. Justices on the Bench   Edward Hunloke, William Biddle, Daniell Leeds   Justices   Nathaniel Westland. Grand Jury Returned   Francis Collins, John Wills, Thomas French, John Haynes, Mathew Allen, Mathew Champion, John Paine senr., John Crosby, John Cheshire, Peter Rensiere, Samuell Furnis, John Longstaffe, James Croft   Attested.

William Budd Constable of Northampton for not appearing to be attested and for not Executing said office   Fyned 10s.

Richard Finimore Chosen new Constable refuses to be attested.

John Tomlinson appeares not on the Traverse Jury.

Josiah Appleton Chosen New Constable appeares not: Fyned.

Henry Grubb prosecutor for the King; Indicts Andrew Walbridge, being bound by Recognizance to this Session: hee appeares. Evidences for the King: Thomas Elton and Thomas Cleverly   are Attested and sent to the Grand Jury   Grand Jury bring in the Bill Ignoramus. Andrew Walbridge cleared by proclamation.

John Bryerley and Mary his wife upon presentment last Session: processe made out to the Constable to Seize them and take them before next Justice in order to be bound over to answer this Court, the Constable saith Mahlon Stacy promised they should appeare; But they are called and appeare not.

Andrew Davisse and Mary his pretended wife presented last Court, processe made out against them, but they are both out of the province.

Traverse Jury in the Action of Edward Hunloke versus John Pidcock   Mathew Watson, William Evans, Thomas Tindall, Michael Buffin, John Sharp, Abraham Hewlings, Thomas Duggles, John Petty, Joseph English, John Antram, Isaac Horner, George Elkington   Attested.

Edward Hunloke Merchant Plaintiff   John Pidcock Defendant   Action of Debt on Bond   Plaintiff and Defendant appeare. declaration Read   The Defendant pleads a former Mortgage in Barre. The Court agree that the Defendants Plea is noe Barre; John Brock Attested Deposeth that a peece of Parchment (but the Defendant then replyed it was paper) was brought to Court and Edward Hunloke desired Pidcock (the Defendant) to acknowledge it in Court, and that Pidcock would make noe answer but went his way out of Court and did not acknowledge it: And Edward Hunloke desired the Clerk of the Court to Record the same. Thomas Williams Attested proves the Bond declared upon. The Jury goe togeather and bring in their Verdict for the Plaintiff.

And the Jury desire the Bench to take care that upon discharge of the Verdict the Defendant may have full discharge from the Plaintiff from all

Claymes dues etc. whatsoever. That the Plaintiff be debarred from any Clayme by virtue of any pretended Mortgage or otherwise the Court order Judgment accordingly.

The Plaintiff in Court declares that hee is willing if the Defendant will pay downe his principall money with the Just Interest upon the same and Costs hee will accept thereof in satisfaction of the Judgment and discharge the Defendant.

The Defendant desires an Appeal to Equity, The Court reply that upon his giveing Bond etc. and discharge of what the Law requires in that behalf hee may have it.

Daniell Wills Attourney for Plaintiff Samuell Stacy   Henry Grubb Defendant   Action Trespasse, they proceed by Consent. The defendant requires a nonsuite which the Court (seeing Cause for) grant.

John Hugg Plaintiff   John Silver Defendant   Continued.

Court Dissolved.

Court of Session and Court of Pleas held at Burlington August 8th 1695. Justices on the Bench   Edward Hunloke, John Tatham, Nathaniel Westland, Francis Davenport, Mahlon Stacy, William Biddle, John Curtis, Daniell Wills, Peter Fretwell, John Adams, Samuell Harriott, John Hollinshead. Grand Jury Returned   William Emly, William Righton, Henry Burr, George Smith, Robert Hudson, Nathaniel West, Nathaniel Cripps, John Wearne, Seth Hill, Samuell Taylor, Thomas Kendall, Daniell Wills junr., Lawrance Morris, Attested. They say they have nothing presentable.

Executions returned   Calow versus Tueley Satisfyed. French versus Leeds etc. Satisfyed. Reeves versus Biddle Satisfyed. Lowe versus Conoroe Satisfyed. Levalley versus Duggles   Levalleys Goods and person not to be found in the Province.

William Budd for not appearing as Constable for many Courts and not returning a new Constable fyned 10s.

Jacob Perkins, Charles Byles, Barnett Lane, Jurors not appearing fyned 10s. per man.

[135 1695] John Heath Plaintiff versus Joseph Crosse defendant   Action upon the Case. Jury   Joseph Adams, Thomas Eves, John Shinn junr., Richard French, George Parker, John Woolston junr., John Abbott, James Wills, Mathew Forsyth, Peter Resniere, Nicholas Martineau, Freedom Lippincott Attested. Declaration Read   Seth Hill Attested: Deposeth that hee received a Barrell of Tobacco (declared for) of the Plaintiff which hee delivered for the use of the Defendant. The Plaintiff Attested: Deposeth that the defendant gave him order to send up the Tobacco in Question according to the Plaintiffs Accompt in writing given in to Court. The Jury goe togeather. Upon their returne (being called over) say they are agreed of their Verdict, And that they find for the Defendant with Costs of suite. The Court Grant Judgment thereupon.

The Plaintiff desires an Appeale in Law, which is granted under the provisoe of the Law for Appeales. Plaintiff and Defendant after the Tryall agree to referre the Case, which is agreed and plaintiff and defendant satisfyed and discharged.

Severall Surveyes brought in and published and approved.

[*Highway for Eversham Approved*] The Highway hereinafter mentioned, being laid out by 12 of the Inhabitants of Eversham brought to the Session and approved of (Vizt) Beginning at John Heines his Landing and from thence over a brook neare Benjamin Moores, and from thence to a Brook near Robert Engles and from thence to a brook neare John Boartons and from thence to the Kings Road neare the Widdow Eltons Plantation, And another Road begining at the Kings Road upon the South side of Mulberry Creek and from thence neare to Richard Appletons house, And from thence neare to James Binghams Plantation, And from thence over Mulberry Creek at Jonathan Eldridge his Land and from thence neare to John Sharps, And from thence to John Heines his Landing.

Court Dissolved.

[136 1695] Court of Session and Court of Pleas held at Burlington November 4th 1695. The Honorable Governour Hamilton then on the Bench Also Edward Hunloke, John Tatham, Francis Davenport, Mahlon Stacy, Daniell Wills, John Adams, Samuell Harriott, John Hollinshead   Justices.

Grand Jury George Deacon, Christopher Weatherill, William Hewlings, Samuell Bunting, John Butcher, Thomas Scattergood senr., Robert Pearson, William Quicksall, Richard Ridgway, John Woolman, Thomas Harding, John Warren, William Clarke   Attested.

William Lovejoy and Anne Penston bound over to this Session.

A Bill of Indictment against William Lovejoy and Anne Penston the Wife of Stephen Penston, now the pretended wife of said William Lovejoy: presented to the Grand Jury.

Thomas Sharp, Thomas Penston, Edward Burrows Evidences for the King being (at the request of John Petty Complaynant for the King) Subpoened appeare not the said Thomas Sharp for his pregmaticall answer by a Letter and not appearing fyned five pounds, and said Penston and Burrows fyned Twenty Shillings a peece. Andrew Smith and John Rudderow Appear not and are fyned 10s. a peece and William Atkinson Fyned 10s. for refuseing to take Attest on the Traverse Jury.

Edmond Steward attested for the King against Lovejoy Attested, and sent to the Grand Jury.

The Grand Jury find the Bill against William Lovejoy and said Anne Penston: But in regard the King's Evidences appeare not, the further Tryall is deferred untill next Session: And the Recognizance still stands.

Grand Jury Also bring in their Verdict That one hundred pounds be raised within this County, towards the Building of a Bridge at the Point neare

Mr. Tathams: Provided that the repairations thereof (when built) lye not upon the County to mainteyne: And further that the said one hundred pound be imployed to the use aforesaid within twelve Moneths next after the said one hundred pound shall be paid in: ordered by the Bench with the advice of the Grand Jury that the Tax shall be raised after the Method of the last provinciall Tax.

Court of Pleas opened November 5th.

The Jury for Tryalls or Petty Jury   William Wood, Thomas Scholey, Edmond Steward, James Bingham, Joshua Humphris, Thomas Stokes, John Ogbourne senr., Henry Beck, William Foster, John Tomlinson, John Lee, John Meredith.

The Complaynt of Thomas Meach on the behalfe of the King etc. against William Righton Master of the William and Mary called: And the Complaynt read. Complaynant and Defendant appeare: The Defendant requests the Court to see into, and to give their Judgment with relation to the Complaynants power of Seizure at the Port of Burlington, by vertue of his Commission.

The Court give their opinion, that the Complaynants power of Seizure, is limitted by his Comission to the Province of Mary Land and Pennsilvania and therefore appeares not to reach the Port of Burlington:

The Court thereupon (at the request of the Defendant) order the Vessell to be sett at Liberty from the Complaynants Seizure.

Edward Hunloke Esq. (Collectour [43] within this Province for his Majestie) desires the vessell William and Mary may be seized which is accordingly Seized: And the said Edward Hunloke and Defendants agree to try her this afternoone. But the Defendants enter into Bond to produce their Clearance of the Vessell from England: and shee is cleared from this Seizure.

Nathaniell Cripps Plaintiff   Benjamin Clarke Defendant in an Action of Defamation in the Tytle of the Plaintiffs Land to the dammage of 100l. The Defendant appears not but by his Attourney.

The Court order the same appearance to be entred and taken: The defendant pleads there's a variance betweene the Plaintiffs declaration and the writt, therefore the Defendant craves judgment of the Court that the writt may abate   A reference being proposed, the Plaintiff and Defendant agree, And withdraw the Action.

Court of Session.

John Bryerley being presented for haveing Carnally to doe with his wife before Marriage, at a former Court desires the Thing may not be called in Court: hee acknowledges his Crime and submitts to the Governours pleasure as to the Fyne and promisses to pay the Court charges.

The returne of the Jury from Chesterfield Township in obedience to a warrant to Lay out the Kings Road through said Township: which High way they returne, But the Governour desired it might be waved this Court.

[43] "Collector" in MS.

Henry Grubb Plaintiff   Thomas Philips Defendant   Attachment Action Case   Action called, the Defendant appeares not, Declaration Read. Judgment awarded by Default and the goods, being a Cow called forfeit.

Isaac Decow Plaintiff   Isaac Hargrave defendant   Attachment Action Case   Action called, the Defendant appeares not: Declaration Read: Judgment awarded by Default and the goods called forfeit.

Samuell Jennings Plaintiff   Samuell Vaus junr. defendant   Action Case withdrawne.

Abraham Senior Plaintiff   Samuell Vaus junr. defendant   Action Case withdrawne.

Abraham Senior Plaintiff   Samuell Vaus junr. defendant   Action Case withdrawne.

[137 1695]   Att a Speciall Court at Burlington December 5th 1695 Held at the House of Henry Grubb on the Accompt and request of Stephen Solly being in the Common Goale at Suite of John Tatham Esqr. Justices then upon the Bench   Thomas Revell, Francis Davenport, John Curtis, Peter Fretwell, Samuell Harriott. The Jury   Thomas Kendall, Joseph Adams, Bartholomew Minderman, Peter Resniere, Samuell Furnis, James Wills, Nathaniel Cripps, Thomas Raper, Robert Wheeler, Bernard Lane, Lawrence Morris, Daniell England   Attested.

Court Called. John Tatham Plaintiff   Stephen Solly Defendant   Action of the Case   Plaintiff and Defendant appeare. The Declaration Read. The Defendant ownes the bargaine declared upon and the receipt of part of the premisses charged in the Plaintiffs Bill   The Jury goe togeather: And returne agreed of a Verdict: Vizt, They find for the Plaintiff, with Twenty Shillings dammage and Costs of suite, and Tenne pounds Eight pence which they find the Defendant Debtor in Accompt by the Bill, And that the Plaintiff shall receive what goods shall be returned at the price charged as part of said 10l. oos. o8d. Judgment is awarded accordingly. Then Bench, Sheriffe, Clerk, and Jury give all their perquisits of the tryall to the Defendant. Court dissolved.

Court of Session and Court of Common Pleas held at Burlington February 20th 1695/6. Edward Hunloke, John Tatham, Nathaniell Westland, Mahlon Stacey, John Hollinshead, John Adams, Francis Davenport, Peter Fretwell   Esqrs. Justices on the Bench.

Grand Jury   Daniell Leeds, Thomas French, Walter Humphris, Anthony Elton, Bartholomew Minderman, Richard Love, Nathaniell Pettit, Robert Engle, Thomas Williams, Thomas Raper, Frederick Keene, Thomas Lambert, Thomas Curtis   Attested.

The Constables of each Townshippe called. Burlington Constables appeare not. Nottingham: vizt William Hixson: John Lambert keeps ordnary know if hee have Lycence. Chesterfield Thomas Folke junr. omnia Bene. Mansfield William Biddle junr. omnia Bene. Springfield William Bustill saith hee is informed of John Ogbourne and John Tomlinson and Samuell Vaus about killing Hoggs. Evidence against Ogbourne is John Tonkan and against Tomlinson and Vaus is William Wood and John Warren.

New Constables for the yeare Ensueing   Overseers
[Attested]   Nottingham: Samuel Overton   Gervas Pharoe
[Attested]   Chesterfield: Mathew Watson   Roger Parks
[Attested]   Mansfield   Thomas Duggles   Michael Buffin
[Attested]   Springfield   Mathew Champion   John Longstaffe
                                                                            and Isaac Decow
[Attested]   Northampton   George Parker   John Wills
[Attested]   Wellingborrow   Jacob Perkins   John Scott
[Attested]   Chester alias Cropwell   William Matlock   George Glave
                                                                            Samuel Baker
                                                                            keeps ordnary
                                                                            know if Lycenced.
[Attested]   Eversham   William Hollinshead   William Evans
[Attested]   Burlington   Peter Resniere and Seth Hill

The Townshipps have raysed noe money according to the warrants sent out by order of last Session for the building the Bridge at the Poynt in Burlington.

William Lovejoy and Anne Penstone Continued bound to this Court called and appeare: and say they will Traverse the Indictment   The Court Finding the Indictment in relation to Lovejoy etc. Insufficient Quash the Indictment.

Traverse Jury   Henry Grubb, [*Appeared not and fyned 10s.*] William Black, Henry Bircham, William Hunt, Gervas Pharoe, Robert Wheeler, Richard Ellison, John Browne, Thomas Wallis, Michael Newbold, Thomas Renshall, Thomas Atkinson, John Haynes.

John Bryerley Attested deposeth that hee heard Richard Ridgway say that his sonnes under pretence of Killing Wild Hoggs; they (with others) had killed severall marked Hoggs, and that the said Richard said hee had paid a deale of money for agreement.

Samuell Nicholls Plaintiff   Peter Monseur Defendant   Action Trespasse   Jury called and Attested, declaration Read. Daniell Leeds Attested Deposeth that the Meadow upon the front of the Upland and now in Question belongs to Captain Hance. Jury find for the Defendant, And judgment Awarded thereupon.

[138 1696]   John Tatham Plaintiff   Abimelech Hudson   defendant Action Trespasse Continued.

Bernard Lane Plaintiff   Walter Reeves Defendant   Continued.

Thomas Peachee Plaintiff   Thomas Potts Defendant   Action of Case Continued.

Edward Hunloke Plaintiff   Stephen Solley Defendant   Debt   Stephen

Solley acknowledged judgment upon the bond and Judgment Awarded and entred.

Upon Complaynt of Daniell Sutton against William Sanford his Apprentice, for runing away and stealing and Cheating: said Daniell being willing to part with his said Apprentice And the Apprentice also willing to leave him and to goe to John Petty, the Court order the said Daniell Sutton to passe over his Apprentice to said John Petty or to any other person, And the said Apprentice to serve such Master Seaven yeares from this 20th February 1695/6 And order that said Sanford shall be severely Whipt at a Carts tayle (onely the execution to be remitted untill his first misbehaviour) and the Charge of Whipping to be at his Masters Charge, and his Master to be allowed a Moneths service more for it.

Sarah, the Negro Woman of the Widdow Gardner brought for stealing and defaceing the Indian Belt presented by the Sachem to the Governour shee Confesses the Fact, and Submitts: The further processe left untill the Governours pleasure be knowne therein.

The Business about Packing etc. in relation to Joseph White left to further Consideration.

Court Dissolved.   Adjourned.[44]

Court of Session and Court of Pleas held at Burlington May 8th 1696. Edward Hunloke, John Tatham, Nathaniell Westland, John Hollinshead Esqrs. Justices on the Bench. Grand Jury. Francis Collins, Isaac Marriott, Mathew Allen, John Paine, George Elkington, John Longstaffe, Henry Burr, John Bunting, Joshua Eley, John Cheshire, Samuell Furnis, John Sharp, Edmond Steward   Attested. Traverse Jury   John Wills, Thomas Tindall, Michael Buffin, Joseph English, John Antram, Isaac Horner, Abraham Hewlings, Abraham Bickley, Henry Ballenger, William Black, John Meredith, Henry Bircham.

The Jury upon the returne of their warrant for altering the Highway in Thomas Wrights Plantation, being not throughly agreed; ordered that they make a Review and bring in their Report.

Court of Session adjourned: Court of Pleas opened.

Samuell Pereys Plaintiff   James Verier defendant   Action Case   Plaintiff and Defendant appeare: The Declaration Read, The defendant Pleads that the Bill or assumpsit is naked and without Consideration. The Court are of opinion theres noe ground of Action upon this Assumption it being naked and without Consideration: Whereupon at the Defendants request a Non Suite is granted and judgment Awarded.

Bartholomew Minderman Plaintiff   Thomas Bibb and Thomas Duggles Executors of John Joyner Defendants   Action Case   Plaintiff and Defendants appeare, Declaration Read. The Jury Attested; The debt declared

[44] This word is in a different hand.

for being not proved, the Jury goe togeather: And bring in their Verdict for the Defendants   The Defendants crave judgment which is granted   Judgment Entred.

Thomas Wright Plaintiff   John Tatham Defendant   Plaintiff and defendant appeare, declaration Read, There being a defect in the declaration (to witt one of the parties Complayned of left out of declaration) the Defendant requires a nonsuite, which is granted.

[*2 Caveats against Surveys*] Upon the Reading of severall Surveys in Court, a Caveat is entred against recording 60 Acres in Cedar Swamp in Comon betweene John Haines and Thomas Wilkins: And also against recording 50 Acres of Cedar Swamp to Richard Haines.

Jacob Lamb bound by Recognizance to this Court of Session; William Wood (his Bayle) appeares for him, and desires if there be noe processe against him, the said Lamb, hee may be cleared by proclamation, whereupon proclamation being legally made and noe Complaint appearing, the said Lamb is cleard, paying his Fees. The Recognizance withdrawne.

[*An Agreement betweene the Townes of Eversham and Chester*] 29th of the 12th Mo. 1695/6. Att a meeting of the two Townshipps of Eversham and Chester at the House of James Adams it is agreed by us whose names are under written, the Division of the Townes shall be as follows; That the Lyne betwixt John Hollinshead and John Wills shall be the bounds, and the Widdow Eltons land to be in Eversham, and William Hollinshead and John Adams and James Adams and Thomas Rodman   Mathias Bellows, Samuell Burroughs and John Copperthwait all to be in Chester with this Condition that the said Towne of Chester doe forever hereafter discharge the said Towne of Eversham from doeing any duty toward either makeing or repairing, or being at any charge whatsoever belonging to the two Bridges called by the name of Mulberry Bridge and Cropwell bridge, And the said William Hollinshead, John Adams and James Adams doe agree and by their signing hereof doe confirme the Towne Road already laid out from John Haines to Mulberry bridge and promise, not to stop nor alter the same without the Consent of Township of Eversham, In witnesse whereof wee hereunto Set our hands the day and yeare abovewritten. John Adams, Mathew Allen, Thomas French, William Evans, Henry Ballenger, John Hollinshead, George Gleave, Thomas Wilkins, Francis Austin, James Sherwin, Robert Engle, John Borton, Jonathan Elridge, John Sharp, James Adams, William Matlock, Stephen Day, John Wills, William Hollinshead, Thomas Wallis, Thomas Horton.

Both Courts dissolved.

[**139 1696**] [44a]   Court of Sessions and Court of Pleas held at Burlington August 8th 1696   on the Bench   The Honourable Governour Andrew

[44a] Different handwriting.

Hamilton alsoe Mahlon Stacy, Francis Davenport, William Biddle, Daniell Wills, John Hollinshead, John Adams, Peter Fretwell Esqrs. Justices on the Bench.

The Lawes made last Assembly published. The Justices Comission Read.

Grand Jury William Elmley, William Righton, Robert Hudson Thomas Kendall, William Biddle junr., Thomas Williams, Thomas Foulke junr., Daniell Sutton, Jon. Hamell, Richard Fennimore, James Croft, James Sherwin, John Shinn junr., William Foster Attested.

The Bill of presentment Against Thomas Wright sent to the Grand Jury.

Edward Hunloke, Thomas Revell, Samuell Furnis Esqrs. Attested and sent to the Grand Jury as Evidences on the behalf of our sovereign Lord the King against Thomas Wright.

Traverse Jury Called William Wood, James Wills, John Abbott, George Parker, John Woolston junr., Joshua Newbould, Stephen Day, Eleazer Fenton, William Haskew, George Smith, Lawrence Morris, Richard Ellison ordered to Attend the Court.

Post Meridie The Grand Jury returne the Bill of presentment Against Thomas Wright Ignoramus And the Bill against Josiah Prickett Ignoramus.

The Court of Common Pleas opened.

Thomas Wright Plaintiff Peter Groome defendant Action upon the Case: Plaintiff and Defendant appear, the Jury before named Called and Attested: the Declaration Read. the defendants pleas is; he did nott Assume in Manner and form. George Parker Attested, deposeth that he was with John Milbourn A smith and that he the said Milbourn said he had workt up severall Iron tooles that were Thomas Wrights for Peter Groomes use:

Peter Groome Plaintiff Thomas Wright defendant Action upon the Case: Plaintiff and defendant appear: The Jury Attested the declaration Read: the defendants Plea is; he did nott assume in manner and form: The Jury (for Expedition sake) goe out with both Tryalls.

The Grand Jury being Informed by the Bench of the Necessity of raising a Tax for the defraying of the just debts of the County: Etc. make the return following (Vizt) August the 8th 1696 County of Burlington Being informed by the Honorable Governour, And Justices now sitting in the Court of Quarter Sessions of the necessity of raising a Tax: for defraying the just Debts of the County etc. Wee the Grand Jury for the Body of this County (according to the power and Trust in us Invested, by virtue of an Act of Assembly thereby Enabling us, to raise Moneys for defraying the said Debts etc.) doe accordingly order, that by and with the Consent of the Governour and Justices, A County Tax shall be raised which shall Amount to one full third part of the Provinciall Tax payable by the said County The same Method in Assessing, Collecting And paying in at the same time (viz) the 2nd day of February next Ensueing etc. to be exactly observed ordered that Peter Fretwell shall be Treasurer for the said Tax. This Motion Approved on by the Bench.

[140 1696] The Bench with the Grand Jury order that the Kings Road between Chesterfield Bridge and Crofts Bridge be Recorded according to the return of the Grand Jury then present (viz) beginning at Chesterfield Bridge, shall run from Thomas Foulkes Cartway newly made, to John Moores field And from thence to the New bridge, thence the New Road to James Crofts Bridge.

Traverse Jury Come in and bring in their Verdict; in the Action for Thomas Wright Plaintiff and Peter Groome defendant, they find for the Plaintiff the Summ of Sixteen pounds Eighteen Shillings and four pence Debt: with Costs of suite And their Verdict for Peter Groome Plaintiff and Thomas Wright defendant is they find for the Plaintiff the summ of Seaven pounds Eleaven shillings and Seaven pence with Costs of suite; Judgement given on both Actions and Entred.

Reneir Vanhist Plaintiff John Leeds defendant Action upon the Case Leeds now Estate Capiendum.

Mr. Edward Hunloke Plaintiff John Jooston defendant Action upon the Case withdrawne.

Isaac Marriott Plaintiff Richard Dell defendant Action upon the Case withdrawn.

Elizabeth Basnett Plaintiff William Dean defendant Action upon the Case withdrawn.

Samuell Kimball Plaintiff William Dean defendant Action Case withdrawn.

Samuell Kimball Attorney to Benjamin Kimball Plaintiff William Dean defendant Action of debt withdrawn.

William Carter Plaintiff John Hawkins defendant Action Case withdrawn.

Court order that Warrants be Issued out to the Respective Constables in Each Township of this County of Burlington in order to require them to warn in the Inhabitants of their particular Townships to bring in an Account of their lands and stocks taxable by the late Act of Assembly and to chuse their Assessours and Collectours for the Provinciall Tax and for the County Tax ordered to be raised by this present Court.

Court order that Josiah Prickett and his baile stand till next Court.

[*The Kings Highway through Nottingham township approved on*] (viz) The Highway hereinafter mentioned, being laid out by 12 men of the Neighbourhood of the Township of Nottingham and brought to the Sessions and approved on, A Right line to begin at a Certain Hickery tree near Croswicks Bridge and runs thence to a little Runn, that Arises in Thomas Gilberthorps Meadow, where William Watsons Way crosses over the said Runn, And thence to a stake in the middle of a Certaine parcell of land of Thomas Gilberthorps on the further side And then Anthony Woodward to Choose his best Convenience to the said Roade.

Court Dissolved.

Court of Quarter Sessions held at Burlington November the 3d 1696. Francis Davenport, William Biddle, Daniell Wills, John Hollinshead, Peter Frettwell Justices on the Bench.

The Grand Jury Daniell Leeds, Thomas Rapier, John Bunting, Thomas Harding, John Woolman, Edmond Steward, Benjamin Feild, William Bustate[?], Joshua Humphreys, William Hulings, John Tomlinson, James Bingham, John Tonkins.

The Grand Jury Attested the Bill of presentment Against John Ogbourne junr. sent to the Grand Jury. John Hollinshead junr., Anthony Elton, Nathaniel Cripps Evidences in the behalf of our Soveraigne Lord the King against John Ogbourne Attested and sent to the Grand Jury.

[141 1696] Post Meridies. The Bill of presentment Against Thomas Wright sent to the Grand Jury. John Tatham Esqr., Mr. Thomas Revell Evidences on the behalf our Soveraigne Lord the King Against Thomas Wright Attested and sent to the Grand Jury.

The Court Appointe Thomas Bibb Kings Attorney for the present Court.

Traverse Jury Called Christopher Weatherill, Ralph Hunt, Robert Pearson, John Waring, Thomas Schooley, Mathew Champion, William Quicksall, Thomas Stokes, Thomas Scattergood Junr., Henry Becke, John Rudroe, Michael Newbould. William Clarke not appearing in the Traverse Jury the Court fyne him ten shillings.

The Burgesse of the Towne of Burlington Exhibited to the Court the Recognisances of Elizabeth Basnett, Henry Grubb, Thomas Kendall, George Willis And Robert Hudson for the keeping of Ordinaryes which were then Approved on by the Court and ordered to be Kept on fyle by the Clark.

The Grand Jury return in the Bill Against John Ogbourne junr. that they doe not find the within Named John Ogbourne Guilty of this presentment. And on the Bill presented Against Thomas Wright they returne That they Cannot find this Bill in Manner and forme abovesaid.

The Grand Jury present Mattacopany Bridge being out of Repaire.

John Ogbourne junr. Cleared by Proclamation, of being Suspected to have broke the Lord's day.

The Court order that Samuell Harwoods former Survey of thirty five Acres of Land Adjoyning to his plantation be Recorded.

The Court dissolved.

December the 28th 1696. [*Benjamin Wheate by Theophila Cripps Chosen Guardian*] Then appeared Theophila Cripps the daughter of John

Cripps late of Burlington in the Province of West New Jersey And made her free Choise of Benjamin Wheate to be her Guardian, before Mahlon Stacy Peter Fretwell and John Hollinshead Justices, at the house of Henry Grubbs in Burlington and the said Benjamin Wheate was then admitted Guardian as aforesaid, by the said Justices. And the Benjamin Wheate Accepted thereof. And gave bond for the trust to him Committed.

The Court of Quarter Sessions and Court of Common Pleas held at Burlington February the 20th 1696/7. The Honorable Governor Andrew Hamilton   Mahlon Stacy, Francis Davenport, William Biddle, Daniell Wills, John Hollinshead, Peter Fretwell, John Adams   Justices on the Bench. The Grand Jury   Mathew Alleine, Anthony Elton, William Hixon, Richard Love, Thomas Curtis, Richard French, Jervas Pharo, James Adams, Thomas Wallis, Henry Ballinger, Daniell Smith, Matthew Watson, Matthew Graunge. Joshua Eely Attested and sent to the Grand Jury.

[142 1696/7] New Constables Chosen   [*Samuell Overton*] [*Attested*] Nottingham   Anthony Woodward, Chosen but Samuell Overton serves in for him. [*Attested*] Chesterfield   Marmaduke Horseman, serves for John Warren. [*Attested*] Mansfield   Joseph English. [*Attested*] Springfield   William Hunt. [*Attested*] Northampton   William Parker. [*Attested*] Wellingborrough John Hudson. [*Attested*] Chester Alias Cropwell   Stephen Day. [*Attested*] Evesham   Thomas Wilkins. [*Attested*] Burlington   Thomas Potts but John Beech serves for him and is Attested   and Samuell Terrett. [*Attested*] Maidenhead   Ralph Hunt.

The Inhabitants above Assinpink ordered by the Court to be a Township of themselves by the name of Maidenhead.

Traverse Jury   William Hunt, Theophilus Phillips, Thomas Moss, Thomas Atkinson, John Boorton, Robert Chapman, Thomas Wilkins, Thomas Potts, Joseph White, John Hancocke, John Butcher, John Hollinshead Junr.

Abraham Heulings Plaintiff   Thomas French defendant   The Plaintiff and defendant Appeares but Thomas French the defendant sayes he is Incapacitated to Joyne Issue with the Plaintiff at this Court whereupon the Court Admitt of a Continuation of theire Action and order that the defendant shall Answer the said Abraham the Plaintiff peremptorily at the next Court in the Suite before Commenced or Else Judgment to pass against him the said defendant by default.

Josiah Prickett bound by Recognisance to this Court to Answer the Complainte of Elizabeth Sweatnam, but nothing Appearing against him he is quitt by Proclamation.

Robert Turner Plaintiff   Mounce Cocke defendant in a plea of debt Continued at the request of the Plaintiff   withdrawn.

Nathan Alleine of East Jersey Plaintiff   Peter Groome Defendant in a plea of debt   ye said defendant non est Inventus.

John Bownde of East Jersey Plaintiff   Javes Cottrell defendant   Action upon the Case   withdrawne.

John Ogbourne Junr. Plaintiff   Josiah Prickett defendant   Action upon the Case   withdrawne.

Samuel Jennings Plaintiff   Richard Dell defendant   upon the Case withdrawne.

William Woode Plaintiff   Thomas Greene and Thomas Atkins defendants   upon Trover and Conversion   withdrawne.

Robert Wheeler Plaintiff   Samuell Perrett defendant   upon the Case the defendant not summoned and the Sheriffe to pay the Charge by order of Court.

The Court order that the hundred pounds given by the Grand Jury at the Court held 9ber the 3d 1695 for the Building a Bridge over Assiscunke Creeke shall be paid by Warrants Issued out for the payment of the Same by the first day of May Next which shall be Assessed Collected and paid after the Manner of the Provinciall Tax unto Peter Fretwell who is Appointed Treasurer for the same.

The Court order that five men (viz) Francis Davenport John Hollinshead John Adams Peter Resneire and William Wood view that part of the Creeke Called Assiscuncke Creeke Alias Birch Creeke (between Peter Fretwells house and the point neer Mr. Tathams House) and sett out and Affix a place that may be most Commodious and less Chargeable for the Erecting a Bridge over the Creeke aforesaid And make report of theire proceedings therein to the Clarke of the County of Burlington at or before the 25th day of March next, And the vote of the Major part shall Conclude the whole, And that the five persons aforesaid shall meet at the Towne of Burlington at the House of Henry Grubbs on the first of March next, And then they shall Assigne theire owne times of meeting afterwards According as they shall see meete.

Court dissolved.

[143 1697]   Court of Quarter Sessions held at Burlington May the 8th 1697. Mahlon Stacy, William Biddle, Daniell Wills, Peter Fretwell, John Adams, John Hollinshead   Justices on the Bench. Grand Jury   Thomas Gilberthorp, John Bryarly, John Pane Senr., John Antram, Turolas Suillavan, Elias Toy, Peter Resneire, George Elkinton, Henry Burr, William Mattlock, Thomas Tindall, Matthew Forsyth, Robert Pearson   Attested.

Mr. Thomas Revell Attested and sent to the Grand Jury.

The Grand Jury present Nathaniell Pettit Moses Pettit and Mordecai Andrews for selling Strong Liquors without a Licence and for Keeping disorder in theire houses for which Crimes the Bench fine them twenty shillings per man.

The Grand Jury present Ralph Hunt for selling strong liquors without a License for which Crime the Bench fine him twenty shillings And Mr.

Thomas Revell promised on the behalf of the said Ralph Hunt to pay the said twenty Shillings to the Honorable Governour Hamilton, And the said Ralph Hunt being present desires of the Bench a license for a victualling house which the Bench grant he the said Hunt giving bond for his good behaviour in that Imploy According to law, The Bench order that the Clerke take his Recognisance and signe his license on the behalf of the Court.

The Grand Jury present Samuell Furnis for not recording or refusing to record his deed therefore the Bench according to the law in that Case fine him the said Furniss twenty shillings, And as by the law one half thereof belongs to the Recorder he remitts his share being ten Shillings. The Burgess of the towne of Burlington Exhibited to the Court the Recognisances of Elizabeth Basnett, Henry Grubb, Thomas Kendall And George Willis for the Keeping of Victualling houses which were Approved on by the Bench and the Clerk was ordered to Keep them on fyle.

The Court of Pleas held the eighth of May 1697. Traverse Jury John Wills, Joshua Eley, John Hucheson, Frederick King, John Sharp, John Meredith, John Haines, Francis Austin, William Evans, John Cheshire, William Hunt, Richard Haines. William Budd not Appearing on the Traverse Jury fyned by the Bench ten Shillings.

John Tatham Esqr. Plaintiff   Thomas Green defendant   withdrawn.

Samuell Peres Plaintiff   James Verier defendant   withdrawn.

Abraham Heulings Plaintiff   Thomas French Senr. defendant   Action of Slander and defamation   the Plaintiff and defendant Appear. the declaration Reade, the defendants Plea is not guilty. the Jury Attested.

[*Evidences*] John Woolston Senr. Attested deposeth he Knowes little or nothing in the said Matter. John Pane Senr. Attested, deposeth that he cannot remember he heard the Express words in the declaration mentioned as Scandalous but however words to that Effect.

[144 1697] [*more Evidences*] Thomas Harding Attested deposeth that he heard Thomas French the defendant speake words to the same effect as in the declaration are mentioned that the said Abraham Hulings had took a false Attestation in that Tryall between the said Thomas as plaintiff and Fennimore etc. defendants.

Daniell Leeds Attested deposeth he being on a grand Jury the 20th day of February 1695/6 with the said defendant etc. And then the said defendant said unto the said Jury if they would not present Abraham Hulings for perjury he would not Consent to them In others matters, And further the said deponent saith that at the request of some of the Plaintiffs neighbours he went and viewd a line of partition between Thomas Olives propriety and William Peachees propriety And he found that the Meadow which was in Controversie between the said French the defendant and Richard Fennimore was on William Peachees side of the Line.

Thomas Eeves Attested, deposeth that he heard Thomas French the defendant say that the said Abraham the Plaintiff had bore false wittness Against him the said French and that he was at running a line with about fifty Markt trees which doubtless was the Partition line between the said Thomas Olive and William Peachee and that the Meadow formerly in Controversie was on Peachees side of the Line.

John Hollinshead Junr. Attested, deposeth that at the Court held the twentieth day of February last he heard Hulings the said Plaintiff say that he was Accused by the defendant French of perjury And the said Hulings desired the Court would permitt them to proceed whereunto the said French replyed it was time enough for he Could prove itt.

Thomas Wilkinson Attested, deposeth that the line before Mentioned was itt he always tooke to be the partition line between Thomas Olive and William Peachee and Knew noe other and the meadow before mentioned was on Peachees side of the line. two letters produced by the Plaintiff wherein the defendant Accuses him the said Plaintiff of bearing false wittnes Against the said Defendant. The Jury goe out.

Edward Shippen and Uxor Plaintiffs   Elizabeth Basnett Senr. defendants   an Action upon the Case by Consent. the declaration read the Plaintiff therein declares for Seaven hundred And twelve pounds three Shillings and three pence half peny. The Defendant Acknowledges the whole debt declared for, the Plaintiff Craves Judgment   The Bench give Judgment therein.

The Jury returne they find for the Plaintiff Abraham Heulings with five pounds dammages and Costs of Suite   Judgment thereon Awarded.

Susannah Elton Plaintiff   John Hollinshead Junr. defendant   in an Action upon the Case   the declaration read and the defendants Plea is not Guilty. The Jury Attested. [*Evidences*] Thomas Hooton Attested, deposeth that by the said Plaintiffs order he was Killing severall of the Plaintiffs Hoggs and the said defendant Came to him at the same time and said to him the deponent, what you are killing them, yes replyed the deponent but not all, then said the defendant how many doe you want the deponent replyed two asanded [45] one and Another, to the which the defendant replyed I have Killed two whats that to any body. Turolas Suillavan Attested, deposeth according to the tenour of the aforesaid Hootons deposition. Anthony Fryer Attested, deposeth according to the tenour of the said Hootons deposition. Mary Leeds Attested, deposeth that the two Hoggs John Hollinshead Kild were hers the said deponents And that she had raised them up. [145 1697] George Gleave Attested, deposeth the widdow Baker hired him the deponent and John Hollinshead Junr. the defendant to Kill two Hoggs which they did, The Jury goe out.

[*Mr. Thomas Revell Mr. Thomas Gardner Guardians to John Gosling*] John Gosling son of John Gosling late of the towne of Burlington in the

---

[45] *Sic.*

Province of West New Jersey deceased Appeared before the Bench And made his free Choice of Mr. Thomas Revell and Mr. Thomas Gardner to be his Guardians, who were Admitted to be Guardians by the Bench to the said John Gosling and have given bond for theire faithfull discharging the trust in them reposed as Guardians.

The Jury returne. They find for the Plaintiff Elton with four pounds dammages and Costs of Suite. Judgment Awarded thereon.

Court Order. That Justice Fretwell shall view the warrants late writt by the Clerke for the raising a hundred pounds for the building a Bridge over Assiscunke Creeke And if the said Justice Frettwell shall find them according to the Method prescribed by the Court held the twentieth day of February last past that then he being Treasurer for this County shall pay the Clerke for the same one pound and five Shillings And this order shall be his receipt for the same paid as Aforesaid.

Court dissolved.

Att a Speciall Court of Pleas held the Eleaventh day of June 1697. The Lawes made Last Assembly published and the Justices Commission Read. Mahlon Stacy, Daniell Wills, Peter Frettwell, John Hollinshead, Justices on the Bench.

Edward Hunloke Esqr. Plaintiff John Hamell Defendant in a Plea that he doe hold to him a Certaine Covenant between them made.

Traverse Jury Called Francis Collins, Thomas Kendall, Edmund Steward, Peter Resnier, Eleazer Fenton, Nathaniell Cripps, George Elkinton, John Wills, Joseph Adams, Daniell Smith, Thomas Bryan, Thomas Renshaw. The declaration read. The defendant promises to Joyn Issue in the Afternoon. Post Meridie. The Plaintiff promises to Answer to a Cross Action brought by the defendant And to Joyn Issue thereto. The Bench Continue the Action Commenced by Edward Hunloke Esqr. against John Hamell till the Court of Common Pleas to be holden the eighth day of Augut next And the Bench Continue the Cross Action brought by the defendant John Hamell Against Edward Hunloke Esqr. till the Court of Common Pleas to be held the eighth day of August next.

Court dissolved.

[146 1697] Court of Quarter Sessions held the 9th day of August 1697. Mahlon Stacy, Francis Davenport, William Biddle, Daniell Wills, Peter Frettwell, John Hollinshead, John Adams Justices on the bench. The Grand Jury Isaac Marriott, Richard Love, Abraham Bickley, James Croft Senr., Nathaniell Douglass, John Bourton, Christopher Weatherill, George Smith, Edmund Steward, Thomas Williams, Josiah Appleton, John Hutcheson, Thomas French Junr. Anthony Elton and Thomas Renshaw fyned ten Shillings per man for not Appearing on the Grand Jury.

[*Court Order*] Nathaniell Pettitt and Moses Pettitt paying the officers fees are suspended the payment of theire fines untill the Court held the third day of November next they in the mean time having liberty to Apply themselves to the Governour for the remitting theire fines.

The Bench fine Thomas Foulk Senr. twenty Shillings for Selling of Strong liquors and victualls without a license.

the Court Adjourne for two houers. Post Meridie   The Court Sitt and Adjourne the Court of Sessions for two houers.

The Court of Pleas opened. Traverse Jury   Thomas Wood, Richard Stockton, Robert Pearson, Job Bunting, Eleazer Fenton, Jonathan Eldridge, William Heulings, James Bingham, John Hancocke, Michael Newbould, Thomas Wallis, Thomas Tindall   They Appeare.

Edward Hunloke plaintiff   John Hamell defendant   they appeare, the declaration Read, the defendant John Hammell requests that a Cross Action of his may goe on with the plaintiffs Action. The Bench Consider of it And Agree by the Major parte on the Negative. The defendant putting in no plea the Bench Award Judgment upon a Nihill dicit. The defendant Craves an Appeale which the Bench Admitts of with these provisoes that the defendant John Hamell and William Wood give A sufficient bond to the plaintiff Edward Hunloke to prosecute the Appeale at the next Court of Appeales under the penalty of five hundred pounds they the said Hamell and Wood being bound Joyntly and severally And pay Cost of Suite, which is done (viz the provisoes fulfilled.

[147 1697]   James Adams Plaintiff   Thomas Hooten and Anthony Fryer defendants   the declaration read   the defendants plead not guilty the Jury aforesaid Attested. William Hollinshead Attested deposeth that he Knew two of the piggs in Controversie to be the Plaintiffs.

[*Evidences*] Elizabeth Adams Attested deposeth that she heard her son the plaintiff Ask Anthony Fryer one of the defendants who had Markt his Swine to which Fryer replyed he had helped Thomas Hooten to Marke two of them which two she thought was two of three in Controversie.

George Gleave Senr. Attested deposeth that he saw one shoate or Hogg Markt with Thomas Hootens Mark which he supposed was one of those in Controversie. George Gleave Junr. Attested deposeth but little Materiall or Nothing.

James Sherwin Attested deposeth that in November last was a yeare he gott Thomas Hooten the Plaintiff to help him to Kill some Hoggs And the said deponent then having some Shoates which went Away from the said deponent and Hooten, the said Hooten the plaintiff Asked him the deponent what he would doe with them that were gone the said deponent replyed he would give them to him the said Hooten.

John French Attested deposeth that he was talking with James Adams the plaintiff in the spring of the year last past about some Shoates and the said plaintiff said to the deponent he had Some Shoates of about a year old

And the deponent replyed and said Matthew Allein had some of that Age.

Thomas French Junr. Attested. Thomas Wilkinson Attested deposeth that James Adams and William Hollinshead having Killed two young Sowes and John Bourton Claiming them James Adams the Plaintiff replyed in these words (viz) I look on it my Privilege to Kill them, And I have some running in the woods, And Thomas the deponent being by and Thomas Hooten and John Bourton, he the said Adams the Plaintiff said to them that they might take the same privilege Against him. John Bourton Attested deposeth according to the tenure of the aforesaid Evidence.

Abraham Heulings Attested. The Jury goe togeather. The Jury returne and bring in theire Verdict and find for the defendants, Judgement Awarded.

August the 10th Court of pleas opened.

John Horner Plaintiff John Bainbridge defendant they appear the declaration read, there being a deficiency in the declaration the defendant Craves a Non Suite which the Bench grants.

[148 1697] Edward Hunloke Esqr. Plaintiff Robert Wheeler defendant withdrawn.

Robert Wheeler Plaintiff John Tatham Esqr. defendant withdrawn.

John Joosten and John Hammell Plaintiffs Edward Hunloke defendant the declaration read, the defendant pleads he had not the Copy of the declaration within the time limitted by the law in that Case which the Bench Consider on it and give theire Judgment that it was an Errour on the plaintiffs part that they had not got the declaration ready ten dayes before the Court and further say they cannot proceed to tryall this Court. Whereupon the defendant Craves a Non Suite which the Bench grants. The Plaintiffs John Joosten and John Hammell request of the Bench a Speciall Court for a further Tryall of their Covenants with Edward Hunloke which the Court grants And order it to be held the twenty seaventh day of this Instant August at Burlington.

[Court order John Scott and George Douglass] John Scott of Wellingborough in the County of Burlington Exhibited to the Court a Scotch boy named George Douglass which he the said Scott bought of James Trent as by a Certaine Bill of Sale given by the said Trent to him the said Scott dated the twenty first day of July last past may more fully Appeare, And the said Scott having noe Indentures with his said Boy, He requests of the Court to Assertaine and fix a Certaine term of yeares for the said George Douglass serving him the said Scott According as the law in that Case directs, which said Boy is ordered by the Bench to Serve nine Yeares from this ninth day of August 1697 to him the said John Scott his heires Executors Administrators or Assignes.

[Court order Abraham Heulings Daniell Camrone] Abraham Heulings of Wellingborough aforesaid Exhibited to the Court a Scotch boy named Daniell Camrone bought by him the said Heulings of James Trent as by a

Certaine bill of Sale given by the said Trent to the said Heulings dated the twenty first day of July 1697 may more fully Appeare, And the said Heulings having noe Indentures with his said Boy he requests of the Court to Assertaine and fix a Certaine term of yeares for the said Daniell Camrone serving him the said Heulings According as the Law in that Case made directs, which said Boy is ordered by the Bench to Serve nine yeares from this ninth day of August 1697 to him the said Heulings his Heires Executors Administrators or Assignes.

[*Court order John Lambert George Slaiter*] Whereas John Lambert of Nottingham in the County of Burlington exhibited to the Court a Scotch boy named George Slaiter bought by him the said Lambeth of James Trent as by a Certaine Bill of Sale given by the said Trent to the said Lambeth bearing date the twenty first day of July 1697 may more fully Appeare; And the said Lambeth having noe Indentures with the said Boy he requests the Bench to Assertaine And fix a Certaine term of years for the said Slaiters serving him the said Lambeth According as the law in that Case directs which said Boy is ordered by the Bench to serve Nine yeares from this Ninth day of August 1697 to him the said Lambeth his heires Executors Administrators or Assignes.

Court Dissolved.

[149 1697] at a Speciall Court of Pleas held the 27th day of August 1697. Francis Davenport, William Biddle, Peter Frettwell, John Hollinshead Justices on the Bench. The Jury William Elmley, Francis Collins, Thomas Eeves, John Haines, Christopher Weatherhill, William Hulings, William Evans, Jonathan Eldridge, John Sharp, John Bryarley, Henry Burr, Joseph Cross.

John Joosten and John Hammell Plaintiffs Edward Hunloke Esqr. defendant the plaintiffs and defendants Appeare (viz) William Wood Appeares for John Joosten.

Court order that they Come to tryall Notwithstanding some debate about the granting of the present Speciall Court.

The defendant requires a sight of the deed given by the defendant to the Plaintiff which upon the Defendants Assumpsitt to the Bench to redeliver the said Deed Againe; is delivered to him the said defendant to peruse till after dinner. Post Meridie the defendant delivers the deed Againe And proceed no further to tryall.

The Court dissolved.

Att the Courts of Quarter Sessions and Common Pleas held the third and fourth dayes of November Anno Domini 1697. Mahlon Stacy, Francis Davenport, William Biddle, Daniel Wills, Peter Frettwell, John Hollinshead, John Adams Justices on the Bench. Court of Quarter Sessions opened. The Grand Jury Restore Lippincoate, William Fisher, John Pane Senr., Robert Wheeler, Thomas Douglass, Thomas Scattergood Junr., William Bustale,

Joseph White, Thomas Stokes, William Foster, John Tonkins, Samuell Taylor, John Bourton   The Grand Jury Attested receive their information and goe togeather.

John Horner Complaynant against John Bainbridge on the behalf our our Soveraigne Lord the King for the said Bainbridges breach of the Peace. John Horner Called and Appeares not.

Henry Pope Attested and sent to the Grand Jury.

Seth Hill Attested and sent to the Grand Jury.

The Court of Quarter Sessions Adjourned till two a Clocke in the Afternoon.

The Court of Common Pleas opened. The Traverse Jury   John Longstaff, Matthew Watson, Edward Rockhill, Samuell Bunting, Isaac Decoo, Alexander Stuart, John Abbott, Nathaniell Cripps, Samuell Kimball, Matthew Champion, John Ogbourne Junr., Abraham Houlings.

Christopher Snoden Plaintiff   Charles Shippey defendant   the defendant Appeares not   it is referred longer by the Bench.

[150 1697]   Hugh Hutchin Plaintiff   Thomas Cleverly defendant   the plaintiff Called and Appeares nott the Action Continued.

The Court adjourned till two a Clock in the afternoon.

Post Meridiem the Court sitts.

Christopher Snoden plaintiff   Charles Shippey defendant   The Plaintiff and defendant Called and Appeare, The declaration reade. The defendant pleads Satisfaction. the Jury Attested. Abraham Senior Attested, deposeth that Charles Shippey hath paid two or three peices of eight to him the deponent on the Account of Christopher Snoden since the said Christopher went into England And that by the said Christophers order, And that the said deponent Kept the said Shippey in his house Sick for three or four months, some time after the said Snoden went to England.

The deposition of Thomas Cleverlie read in Court.

The Jury receive theire Charge and goe togeather.

Benjamin Wheate the King's Attorney putt in an Information on the behalf of our Soveraigne Lord the King Against Daniell Englands vessell for that the said vessell had Imported and had on Board Sugar which did not truley and without fraude belong to the People of England, Ireland, Dominion of Wales or Towne of Berwicke upon Tweed as proprietors or right Owners thereof.

The Court of Quarter Sessions opened.

Joseph White is Absent from the Grand Jury and Continues absent during the time of the Court.

The Grand Jury return to the Court and Exhibit Severall presentments which are on file in the Clarks office.

The Traverse Jury returne and bringe in theire verdict And find for the defendant Shippey. Judgement Awarded.

The Plaintiff Christopher Snoden Craves an Appeale, the Bench grant it he the said plaintiff fullfilling the terms And Conditions of an Appeale According as the Law for Appeals prescribes which he hath done.

John Horner plaintiff John Bainbridge defendant Action of Trespass on the Case, the plaintiff Called, Appeares not, the Action Continued.

The Court Adjourns to Henry Grubbs House forthwith.

The Court Adjournes till Seaven a Clock in the Morning.

The fourth day of the Instant November. The Court Sitt, the Quarter Sessions opened And John Bainbridge is required by the Court to find further security for the peace the which he refuses therefore is Committed to the Sheriffs Custody, till he doe.

[151 1697] The Court of Common Pleas opened, and Adjourned for one hour. The Court Sitt, It being under the Benchs Consideration whether Edward Hunloke were a quallifyed Officer to make lawfull Seizures of Vessells It past by the Bench in the Affirmative.

The Jury Attested to try the Issue of that Cause depending Between our Soveraigne Lord the King the Honourable Governour Andrew Hamilton And Edward Hunloke Against Daniell England According to the Information before Mentioned.

Moses Grasberry Attested, deposeth that Daniell England had been on Board a ship that the deponent brought into this River before he the deponent gave any order to the said Daniell and that he the said Daniell had taken a part of the Rigging from the Ship without the deponents Knowledge And after some time the deponent by virtue of Governour Markhams Commission to him gave Daniell England liberty to worke in the vessell and save what Sugar he Could, provided he would give this deponent such a share thereof as other persons (viz) Samuell Rowland etc. were to give him, but further the deponent saith that the said England never Came to give him any share of the Sugar he had saved as aforesaid.

The Jury receive theire Charge and goe out togeather, the Jury returne and say they are Agreed of theire Verdict, And find for the Defendant England, Judgement Awarded.

Peter Indian by name upon his voluntary will and Consent and with the Approbation of this Court bound himself a servant to Mordecai Howell of the County of Gloucester in this Province of West New Jersey for the term of eight yeares from the third day of November Anno Domini 1697.

Martin Scott of the Towneship of Nottingham in the County of Burlington Exhibited to the Court a Scotch boy named James Haddgard which he the said Martin Scott bought of James Trent, as by a certaine Bill of Sale given by the said Trent to him the said Scott dated the twenty first day of July Anno one thousand six hundred ninety and seaven may more fully appeare, And the said Scott having noe Indentures with the said boy, he desires of the Court to Assertaine and fix a Certaine term of yeares for the said James

Haddgard's serving him the said Scott According as the Law in that Case directs, which said Boy is ordered by the Bench to serve Nine yeares from the Ninth day of August last past to him the said Martin Scott his heires Executors Administrators or Assignes.

Thomas Lambert of the Towneship of Nottingham abovesaid did by Martin Scott Exhibit to the Court a Scotch boy named John Young which he the said Thomas Lambert bought of James Trent as by a Certaine Bill of Sale given by the said Trent to him the said Thomas Lambert [152 1697] dated the twenty first day of July Anno one thousand Six hundred ninety and seaven may more fully Appeare. And the said Thomas Lambert having noe Indenture with the said Boy, he desires of the Court to Ascertaine and fix a Certaine term of yeares for the said John Youngs serving him the said Lambert, According as the Law in that Case directs, Which said Boy is by the Bench ordered to Serve nine yeares the ninth day of August last past to him the said Thomas Lambert his heires Executors Administrators or Assignes.

Court order that some worke done and boardes used in the Court house shall be paid by the County Treasurer out of the County Treasury. Also Court order that the County Treasurer buy and pay for a table now in the Court house out of the County Treasury.

Nathaniell West the sonne of Nathaniell West late of the County of Burlington deceased desired of the Court that Thomas Bibb and Clement Dungan may be his Guardians which the Court Admitts of they the Said Thomas and Clement giveing Security (to perform their Guardianship truely) to some two of the Magistrates of this County.

Court Dissolved.

Court of Quarterly Sessions held at Burlington February the 21st and 22nd dayes of 1697/8. Mahlon Stacy, Francis Davenport, William Biddle, John Adams Justices on the Bench. Grand Jury Walter Humphreys, John Woolman, Mathew Alleine, Nathaniell Ricketts, Richard French, Michael Buffin, Daniell Smith, Thomas Haines, James Adams, John Rogers, John Snape, George Parker, Thomas Curtis Attested. The Traverse Jury John Test, John Antram, Henry Beck, Isaac Horner, Thomas Hooten, Joshua Newbould, Thomas Harding, Joshua Wright, John Butcher, Marmaduke Horsman, Thomas Dugglass, Thomas Scholey.

John Banbridge being bound to the peace and to his Appearance at this Court is Acquitted from the said bond.

New Constables chosen [*Attested*] Maidenhead John Bryarley. [*Attested*] Nottingham William Quicksall. [*Attested*] Chesterfield Henry Beck. [*Attested*] Mansfield James Antram is returned by Joseph English but Appeares not. James Antram afterwards Appeares [*Attested*] Springfield John Snape. Northampton William Parker he returns none therefore is Continued. [*Attested*] Wellingborough Abraham Heulings. [*Attested*] Chester Alias Cropwell Frederick King. [*Attested*] Evesham

Richard Haines. [*Attested*] Burlington Thomas Scattergood and James Satterthwaite but James serves for Abraham Bickley.

[*Court order for granting licenses*] The Bench order that from hence forward no Justice or Justices shall give any license to any person within this County (Burlington Towne Excepted) in any Private Manner or any other wayes then in the Quarter Sessions held at Burlington, that is to say for selling of Strong liquors.

Court Adjourned for two houres.

[**153 1697**] Post Meridie The Court of Pleas opened, the Quarter Sessions Adjourned for one hour longer.

James Read plaintiff John Rudroe defendant Thomas Gardiner by a letter of Attorney read and Approved in Court Appeares for James Reade. The Plaintiff and defendant Called and Appeare the declaration read wherein the plaintiff declares for fifty pounds upon bond, the defendant pleads satisfaction. The Jury Attested heare the Cause receive theire Charge and goe out togeather, they are out a while and returne, and say they are Agreed of theire Verdict and find for the Plaintiff James Reade four pounds and seaven shillings with Costs of Suite. Judgement Awarded. The Plaintiff by Thomas Gardiner Craves Execution for the four pounds and seaven Shillings the defendant (having paid and promised to pay the Cost of Suite) which was granted to be Issued out when the said plaintiff requires it.

John Scott plaintiff Jacob Perkins Junr. defendant withdrawne.
William Wood plaintiff Thomas Greene defendant withdrawne.
Mary Ewer plaintiff John Test Defendant withdrawne.
Bridgett Guy plaintiff Thomàs Williams defendant Continued.
The Court of Pleas dissolved.

the Court of Quarter Sessions opened Againe. the Grand Jury returne and bring in some presentments nott materiall to be recorded.

[*Court order*] The Justices with the Concurrence of the Grand Jury order that a Tax be laid on this County after the Manner of last County Tax.

the Sessions Adjourned till next morning. the 22nd day the Court opened.

[*The Treasurer gives up his Accounts*] Peter Fretwell Treasurer for the County of Burlington Exhibited to this Court his Accounts in what he hath received of the Countyes money in the last County Tax and likewise his disbursements in paying the County debts, And his Accounts were by the Court Approved on, And upon the Adjusting of the same the ballance was eighteen Shillings due to the County and in the said Treasurers hands now for the Countys use, And the said Peter Fretwell shall nott be liable to any further Stating of his Accounts for the said Tax only the eighteen Shillings Aforesaid.

Court Order That the Constables of Maidenhead shall Summons in twelve Sufficient Men of the same Towneship such as the Constable shall see meet and Expedient for the laying out a Kings Highway through the said Towneship to begin at the partition line of the two provinces West and East Jersey thence along to Assinpinck Creeke, the said Constable making returne of the said twelve Mens or the Major partes proceedings in the Same, to the Next Court of Quarter Sessions to be holden at Burlington.

Court order that any three Justices out of Sessions may signe the Warrants that are to be Issued out for the County Taxes raising.

Court of Sessions dissolved.

[154 1698] Court of Quarter Sessions held the ninth day of May 1698 at Burlington. Francis Davenport, William Biddle, Peter Frettwell, John Hollinshead, John Adams Justices on the Bench. post Meridiem Mahlon Stacy Justice Comes on the bench. the Grand Jury Anthony Elton, Roger Parks, William Hickson, William Pancoaste, Thomas Foulke Junr., Timothy Hancocke, Benjamin Field, Gervas Pharo, John Hudson, Benjamin Moore Junr., Joseph Croft, Henry Ballenger, John Woolston Junr. Attested.

Thomas Billingham an evidence for John Powell on the behalf of the King Against Anne Reeves Attested and sent to the grand jury.

John Hollinshead Burgess of the Towne of Burlington Exhibited to the Court four Recognisances from ordinary Keepers, (viz) from Henry Grubb Thomas Kendall George Williss and Elizabeth Basnett and theire Suretyes And were by the Court Approved on and ordered to be Kept on file by the Clerke.

The Constable of the Towneship of Northampton saith he hath Executed the Warrants for the provinciall and county Taxes and Joshua Humphreys was Chosen Collector for the said Taxes.

Abraham Bickley Collector of the Provinciall and County Taxes in the Towne of Burlington being sent for and is by the Court Examined what he hath in Collecting the said Taxes he Acknowledges he had nott yett Collected them but promised the Court that he would Speedily and pay inn the same to the treasurer, and desires the Court would remitt his former Transgression, And the Court say theyle Consider on it.

The Court of Common Pleas opened. The court Adjourns till two a Clocke in the afternoon. Post Meridem the Court of Quarter Sessions opened. Traverse Jury Thomas Eeves, John Browne, William Hunt, Thomas Renshall, William Satterthwaite, John Haines, Richard Bickam, Thomas French Junr., Mordecai Andrews, Joseph Smith, Obadiah Hierton Robert Chapman.

Anne Reeves the Wife of John Reeves bound by Recognisance to this Sessions. A Bill Against the said Anne sent to the Grand Jury they returne the same Billa vera.

The Prisoner Arraigned and upon her Arraignment pleads nott guilty, And refers her self to God and the Countrey for tryall.

The Jury Called, the Prisoner required to view them as they are Called and make her Exceptions Against them, if she please; She makes no Exceptions of any, the Jury Attested. the Indictment Reade.

Thomas Billingham an Evidence for the King Attested and deposeth that on the day mentioned in the Indictment he the said deponent was in the field and the said Anne Coming home haled him, but the deponent not Coming Immediately She the said Anne went and putt up her horse, And when she Came backe the deponent mett her, at the doore And went into the house with her, and after a little time the said Anne desired the deponent to goe and give the horse some Meate, which the deponent did, and afterwards Came into the house againe, and the said Anne Askd him whether there was any Rumme in the house the deponent replyed there was, Then the said Anne Askt the deponent to milk the Cow and she would make some Milk punch, and Accordingly the deponent did, and when the deponent came in the said Anne Askt him for the Broome he replyed twas in the Chamber she bid me fetch it, so he went to goe up Staires and hee see the doore only fast with a bolt went up two or three Stepps, and the said Anne Seeing him goe up readily Askt [155 1698] the deponent whether they left the doore soe, the deponent replyed he thought it was as John Powell left he thought, then the said Anne replyed said Ile warrant the Indians have been here and broke open the doore, (which was before She came to the doore) And afterwards she Cryed I,le warrant John Powells Money is gone, and she and the deponent went into the Chamber and she bid him looke into the Chest and see whether the Money was there, and shee bid him pull out the drawers in the Chest and see for itt, but when the deponent and Anne Saw noe Money, she said againe that I,le warrant John Powells money is gone, And further the deponent saith he believes the doore of the Chamber was broke open, and further saith nott.

The Jury receive the Charge and goe out togeather, the Jury returne, the said Anne the Prisoner Sett to the Barr, the Jury being Askt whether they were Agreed of theire verdict they replyed yes, and by theire Foreman Thomas Eeves say they find the said Anne Reeves not guilty.

Sarah Bainbridge the wife of John Bainbridge being bound to Appeare at this Sessions she Accordingly Appeares, And the King's Attorney pleaded the King's wittnesses were nott ready, the Court Continue her upon fresh baile till the next Session and have put her into the Sheriffes Custody till she give Security for the Same.

John Bryarley Constable of Maidenhead bein Asked by the Court what he hath done in the Execution of the Warrants for the late provinciall and County Taxes, he replyed he warned in the Inhabitants of the said Towne upon a Certaine day and the Major parte of them mett, but they did nott proceed Any further in order to Choose Collectors or to Any other Matter relating the said Taxes According as they were required by the Tenour of the said Warrants, whereupon the Bench fine the Inhabitants of the said

Towneship the summe of one hundred pounds for theire default therein, but mitigated and restricted to the Summe of ten pounds upon Condition only theire respective Taxes both provinciall and County be paid in a months Time from the present day.

John Snape Constable of Springfield being Askt what he did in the Execution of the Warrants for the provinciall and County Taxes last putt out, to which he replyed, he did summons in all the Inhabitants of the said Towne to a certaine place According to the tenour of the warrants, And further saith that a Certaine part of the Inhabitants Complyed with the warrants (whose names are returned by the Constable and would have Chosen Assessors and a Collector for the levying and Collecting the said Taxes but they being lesser parte of the said Inhabitants were overvoted by the Major parte, and soe could nott Proceed According to the method prescribed in the warrant yet they say they have their Money ready, and will pay the same to the Treasurer And whereas the Major parte aforesaid (whose Names are likewise returned by the Constable) did refuse and Neglect to proceed According to the Method prescribed in the said warrants and have nott paid theire respective Taxes, whereupon the Bench fine them fifty pounds but Mitigated and restricted to the Summe of ten pounds upon this Condition only that they pay theire respective Taxes in a Months time from this present Court.

Court order   Peter Fretwell Treasurer of the County of Burlington to pay the Grand Jury thirteen Shillings for this present Service.

John Bryarley returns a Court order granted last Session held at Burlington for the laying out a Kings high way from the partition line of East and West Jersey to Assinpinke Creeke (viz) Beginning on the said line at Yorke old Roade at the Corner of Joseph Worths land, thence to the eight Mile Runne, thence through Jonathan Daviss his land Improved and Inclosed, thence over the Six mile Runne through Theophilus Phillips land, thence over severall Mens lands and over Thomas Smiths land to the five mile Runne thence over Mahlon Stacyes land to Assinpink Creek near the Mill of Mahlon Stacy.

Our Soveraigne Lord the King William the third over England etc. and the Honourable Andrew Hamilton Governour and Edward Hunloke Esqr. Plaintiffs   William Righton Junr. defendant   Action of debt   the Sheriff saith non est Inventus.

Peter Resnier plaintiff   John Curso defendant   Action upon the Case withdrawne.

Nathaniell Westland Merchant Plaintiff   James Wills defendant   Action upon the Case   withdrawne.

Court dissolved.

[156 1698]   [46] Court of Sessions and court of Pleas held at Burlington, August the 8th 1698. Justices on the Bench   John Tatham, Thomas Revell,

[46] Different handwriting.

Nathaniell Westland, George Deacon, William Emley, Thomas Bibb, Anthony Elton, Joshua Ely, Michaell Newbold, John Test. Grand Jury Roger Park, John Hutcheson, Moses Petit, Robert Pierson, William Hixson, Henry Beck, Richard Fennimore, John Rudderow, Bernard Lane, Robert Wheeler, Abraham Brown Junior, John Bainbridge, Obadiah Hierton. Traverse Jury John Hammell, Ralph Hunt, Samuell Vaus Senior, Richard Ellison, Joshua Newbold, Benjamin Jones, John Hilliard, James Sherwin, William Foster, John Hancock, Daniell Sutton, Edmund Steward.

The court opened. A Return made by John Hollinsheade Speciall coroner pro hac vicetantum made to the Court of the verdict of a Jury by him Impannell'd June the 21th 1698 for the viewing of the body of Joshua Buddin Son of William Buddin Who was Drowned accidentally and their doings were approved of by the Court.

The court adjourns for two hours. The Court opened post meridiem. The grand Jury being call'd over and some Sworn and the rest Attested went out, and Soon after Return and presented a petition that Peter Fretwell the late treasurer might be called to an account for the Money which he received of the county Wherewith the bench concurs and appoint Nathaniell Westland Thomas Revell John Tatham George Deacon Thomas Bibb and Daniell Leeds to audit the Account. The grand Jury go out againe having recommended to them by the Bench to enquire and inspect if they can find of any that have profaned the Sabbath day By fetching up wild horses thereon and two persons (viz) Richard Ridgway and Ralph Hunt being Attested to declare their knowledge in that affair were Sent to the grand jury, and Emanuell Smith is presented to the jury upon Suspition of having clipt the coine currant Within this Province. The grand Jury come againe into Court and return that they cannot find the bill against Emanuell Smith for want of Evidence And that they cannot find of any that had lately prophaned the Sabbath day by fetching up of Wild horses thereon of which as is aforesaid they were charged by the bench to enquire.

Jacob Ong appeared in court to answer to a complaint against him for riding on gallop in the fair time Betwixt the Market house and the water Side and affront offered to the Constable wherewith he was charged But no person appearing to prosecute against him he was cleared by the court.

Court of Pleas opened.

Edward Hunloke Plaintiff versus John Tatham Defendant in an action upon the case; The said Plaintiff and defendant called Both appear, the Defendant pleaded that the Declaration was not filed ten days before the court, whereupon he craved a non Suit, which the court granted and Judgment for the costs of Suit and awarded execution for the Same.

Peter Resnier Plaintiff versus Daniel England Defendant in an action upon the case. Said Plaintiff and Defendant called both appear in court the Declaration Read. The defendant pleaded that whereas he being a free holder was arrested therefore the arrest was not legall, which plea the court over ruled [[No]te *the reason why the court would not admit the Defendant plea was, because he was about departing the province at the time of the arrest [   ]ing give any [public]k notice thereof [befor]ehand]* [47] and ordered that the defendant pay the cost of Court [157 1698] and that the Said Defendant Shall give Sufficient Security to make the Plaintiff as good a title to the land mentioned in the Declaration as he can by the Next courts direction.

John Bainbridge appeared at this court in the behalfe of his wife pursuant to a bond given by her and Sureties for her appearance at this court. But no person appearing to prosecute against her She was Cleared by Proclamation.

Joseph Scattergood Plaintiff against John Pears Defendant in an action of Debt, The Plaintiff and Defendant called the Plaintiff appeared, the defendant appeared not, the Declaration Read. The debt proved by a bill produced from under the defendants hand and Isaac De Cow being attested declared that he heard the Defendant confesse and acknowledge the Said bill Whereupon the Court did award Judgment against the Defendant by default for the debt and costs of Suit and execution for the Same.

Bernard Lane Plaintiff versus John Pears defendant in an action upon the case, The Plaintiff and Defendant called   the Plaintiff appears the Defendant appears not   the declaration Read the Plaintiff being attested proved the Debt as in the declaration Specified. Whereupon the court gave Judgment for the Same and costs of Suit against the Plaintiff by default, and ordered execution.

Robert Wheeler Plaintiff versus Thomas Atkins Defendant   an arrest Withdrawne.

Elizabeth Kilcop Plaintiff versus Zechariah Pricket Defendant   an arrest withdrawn.

Cornelius Van Standt Plaintiff versus John Peterson defendant   an arrest withdrawn.

John Ogborn Junior Plaintiff versus Hugh Hutchins Defendant   Summons Withdrawn.

William Brown Complaint against Henry Beck Defendant the complainant as a Servant having proved his wages   1l. 7s. 6d. to be to him due from the Said Henry Beck his Master the Court thereupon order the Said Henry Beck his Master to pay the Said complainant his Servant the Said Wages of 1l. 7s. 6d. Together with the Charge of this said Complaint.

Henry Beck was convicted to have been guilty of Severall misdemeanours both by his menaces to James Antram Constable who was commanded to Serve the Justices Warrant or precept and also By Scurrilous reflecting expressions to Michaell Newbold Justice Before whom he was brought by force after Denial upon threats to give obedience unto the Said Justice's Warrant

[47] In margin.

or precept and the said Henry having been therefore required by the Said Justices to find Security for his good behaviour and did refuse to find Security accordingly Wherefore the said Justices did by Mittimus Send the Said Henry Beck to prison till he Should give Security for his good behaviour.

The court of Quarter Sessions held by adjournment August the 9th 1698. John Tatham, Thomas Revell, Nathaniell Westland, George Deacon, Daniell Leeds, John Test, Thomas Bibb, Anthony Elton   Justices on the Bench.

after much Debate and hearing the allegations of two persons viz John Langstaff and Alexander Steward before the court concerning a way in dispute betwixt them, the court ordered that within 14 days next coming the Way in dispute Shall be laid out by these persons (viz) Hananiah Gaunt Benjamin Jones Samuell Vaus Thomas Dugglas William Bustill Joseph English and Thomas Curtis Without any favour or affection to any person or parties and as it will best accomodate the countrey and families that are to passe that way and least hurt and damnify any mans Plantation and Improvement, and that Michaell Newbold Justice Shall tender to the said Persons an oath or attestation that they will lay out the Said Road accordingly, and that the Way pitcht and fixt upon by the plurallity of votes of the Said persons Shall be a finall decision concerning the Same.

Emanuell Smith entered into Recognizance with two manucaptors (viz) Edmund Steward and John Ogborn for said Emanuells personal appearance at next court.

[**158 1698**] Ordered by the Court that the fines laid upon the Township of Springfield and Maidenhead by the court held at Burlington May the 9th 1698 be Remitted upon their payment of the Provinciall tax when Legally done.

Court Dissolved.

Court of Sessions and court of Pleas held at Burlington November the 3d 1698. The Grandjury   William Fisher, Jonathan Davies, Johannes Lawrenson, Nathaniell Petit, Samuell Overton, Thomas Overton, John Stockton, Thomas Wilson, Thomas Green, Jacob Perkins Senior, Samuell Taylor, John Cluff, Thomas Potts Junior. Justices on the Bench   John Tatham, Thomas Revell, Nathaniel Westland, John Jewell, George Deacon, Thomas Bibb, John Test, Michaell Newbold, Daniell Leeds   Esquires. The Court open'd. The Grand Jury some swore and the rest attested received their charge and go out.

Henry Beck appear'd at this Court pursuant to his bond given for his appearance at this court and Submitted and acknowledged his error and was thereupon Discharged by the court.

Emanuell Smith pursuant to his Recognizance appear'd at this Court.

The Traverse Jury were called   John Tuley, John Ogborn Senior, John Scholey, George Parker, John Woolston, Daniell Wills, Joseph Scattergood,

William Bustin, John Tonkan, Michaell Buffin, John Powell, Jonathan Curtis.

The Persons Subpena'd to give Evidence for our Soveraigne Lord the King against Emanuell Smith were called, (Viz) John Hollinshead John Buntin and Richard French. John Hollinshead appear'd not. John Buntin and Richard French appeared and being attested Were Sent to the Grand Jury. The Grand Jury Return ignoramus upon the Bill preferr'd against Emanuell Smith Because they had no evidence of the clippings being found In the Said Emanuell Smiths Chest.

The court adjourn'd for two hours to Sit again post meridiem in the court house which being accordingly Sit adjourned forthwith to Thomas Kendall's house. the court opened at Thomas Kendalls house.

Edmund Steward Plaintiff versus John Long Defendant in an action upon the case withdrawn.

The grand jury return into court and present Richard French for that Whereas there was a Road laid out by a lawfull Jury from the widow Hancocks house to the meadow known by the Name of William Biddles meadow through the Township of Mansfield, he the Said Richard French to the nusance of the kings Subjects fenc'd the Road and laid great trees therein to Impede his Said Majesties Subjects from a free passage therein. They likewise present Christopher Weatherill for Scandalizing John Tatham by Saying that he is a Papist, They also present Lawrence Morris for that he with two Negro's on the Lords Day being the 25th of September last came up the River with a float of Loggs or timber, and further present Thomas Vaus, for Selling Rum to the Indians whereby great disturbance did accrew to his Neighbours and particularly to Thomas Wilkinson.

Benjamin Kemble and Edward Kemble Plaintiffs and Samuel Kemble defendant being called the Said Benjamin and Samuell appear, the declaration being for a debt upon bond was read, the Defendant desires to have the action continued, the court order that if Plaintiff and defendant will plead each his own cause they Shall proceed to trial otherwise that the action Shall be continued till next court They consent to plead each for himself and proceed, the Defendant did plead Satisfaction of the Said bond the Traverse Jury being Attested to try the Said cause go forth and Soon Return and give their Verdict for the plaintiff whereupon the Court awarded Judgment for the Said bond. The court adjourned till nine of the clock the next day.

[159 1698] Justices on the bench John Tatham, Thomas Revell, Nathaniell Westland, John Jewell, George Deacon, Michael Newbold, Thomas Bibb Esquires.

The court find John Abbot Thomas Folke Junior and Samuell Buntine each in the Sum of Ten Shillings for not appearing at this court to Serve upon the grand jury according to Summons. The court also find Jonathan

Eldridge Richard Boyes and Jonathan West for not appearing at this court to serve upon the Traverse Jury.

Captain John Jewell produced an account in court of four pounds due to him by Ballance from John Joyner which account the court allow'd of the said John Jewell being Sworn to the truth of his said account and that he was Nowaies reimbursed or Satisfied of the Sayd ballance and the court ordered That the executors of the Said John Joyner Should pay the Said ballance out of the Estate of the Sayd John Joyner.

Edward Hunloke mov'd the court to have his cause tried with John Tatham, and John Tatham consented to come to triall upon condition that Edward Hunloke would pay half the charges of his Suit against the Said John Tatham at the last court which the said Edward Hunloke promised to do.

William Menor Plaintiff and Jacob Perkins defendant in an action upon the case being called appear the declaration read the defendant pleads Satisfaction the traverse Jury attested to try the cause, Leonard Van de Grift, being Sworn deposed that he Saw the defendant deliver unto the Said Plaintiff four barrells of cyder in Satisfaction for the four pounds due to him the Said Plaintiff as wages from the defendant and also that he had heard the Plaintiff acknowledge that the Defendant had fully paid and Satisfied him therewith Nicholas Van der Grift being Sworn Deposed to the same purpose, Abraham Hewling being attested deposed that Isaac Perkins told him he had expresse order from his father the Said defendant to Francis Jarvis that he should not pay any money upon the account of the cyder to the Sayd Menor, The Sayd Isaac Perkins being Sworn deposed that his father the Said defendant gave him order to tell the Sayd Francis Jarvis that he Should Stop only Seaven Shillings from the Said Menor out of the price of the Cyder. There was produced in Court an attestation of Francis Jarvis taken before Anthony Morris Justice in Philadelphia, which attestation is on file, and is of the tenour following (viz) Philadelphia November the 2d 1698, Francis Jarvis of this place declareth that in or about the month of October 1697 was then at Jacob Perkins house in West Jersey the Said Jacob Perkins delivered to Francis Jarvis about four Barrells of cyder to Sell for the Sayd Jacob Perkins at twenty Shillings per Barrell and to pay the money to William Maynard The cyder not yet being Sold but Remains in the custody of the abovesaid Francis Jarvis, the Said Francis Jarvis being forbid by the said Perkinses Son to pay any money to the abovesaid William Maynard etc. Francis Jarvis.

The court adjourn'd for two hours and met and opened post meridiem. Thomas Bibb, appointed to be County treasurer. Justices on the Bench John Tatham, Thomas Revell, Nathaniell Westland, John Jewell, George Deacon, Thomas Bibb, Michaell Newbold, Daniell Leeds.

Whereas William Fisher paid Thirteen Shillings unto the grandjury the court ordered that the Same Should be discounted unto him in his tax.

The court order that whereas the Grandjury have presented Richard French for Stopping and Incumbring the road aforesaid through Mansfield that a publication Shall be Set up warning the Said Richard French to Remove the said Incumbrance out of the Said Road before the 29th Instant otherwise that he shall pay the Sum of five pounds as a fine.

[160 1698] The Traverse Jury Return into court and give their verdict that they find for the Plaintiff William Menor, Whereupon the court granted Judgment accordingly, and the Defendant crav'd an appeal which would not be granted because it was under the value.

John Tatham and Edward Hunloke appear in court and Implead each other, and at Length agree to refer the matter in controversy between them.

John Neve Plaintiff versus Samuell Oldale Defendant An action upon the case withdrawn.

Samuell Oldale Plaintiff versus Peter Fretwell and Samuell Furnis executors of James Hill Defendants in an action upon the case Withdrawn.

William Brown Plaintiff versus Nathaniell Allen Defendant in an action of trover and conversion withdrawn.

Thomas Pots Junior Plaintiff versus Randolph Simmons Defendant in an action of debt withdrawn.

Daniell England Plaintiff versus John Dewsbury's house and lot in Burlington and against the heirs of the Said Dewsbury an action upon the case.

[It is of a Road in dispute between John Langstaffe and Alexander Steward Whereof mention is made in the Last courts proceedings, the return of the sayd Jury is on file.] A Return made by a Jury to the court of a way by them laid out or confirmed pursuant to an order of court to them Directed for that purpose and the court approved of their proceedings.

Whereas the grandjury presented Thomas Vaus for Selling rum to the Indians the court ordered that the fine prescribed by the law upon such offenders Shall be forthwith Levied of the Said Thomas Vaus. Whereas the grandjury presented Christopher Weatherill for Scandalizing John Tatham and Whereas the Said Christopher Weatherill appear'd in court and Submitted he was discharged. and whereas the grandjury presented Lawrence Morris aforesaid for bringing loggs up the River on the Lords day and that he the Said Lawrence Appeared in court and excused his Said offence, by Shewing that what he did was in a case of necessity, the court dischargd him.

Peter Resiner appeard in court and mov'd that Daniell England might be ordered to make him a Sufficient title to the house and lot upon the Island of Burlington Sold him by the Said Daniell pursuant to an order of last court Daniell England by his attourney John Tatham appear'd in court but his power not appearing to be full enough and he not having the writings relating to the premisses the court could do nothing in the matter.

The court adjourn'd till the tenth instant.

The court of Quarter Sessions held November the 10th 1698. Justices on the Bench   Thomas Revell, Nathaniell Westland, John Jewell, Michael Newbold.

The under Sheriff made Return of the execution made by him against Jacob Perkins in the Suit of William Menor and that the Same is Satisfyed.

A Warrant was Sent for Thomas Vaus and Serv'd upon him by the undersheriff, whereupon Thomas Douglas promised on the behalf of the Said Vaus that he the Said Vaus should appear or Send Effects to Satisfy the Sayd fine But neither was performed only Samuell Vaus and Thomas Dowglas appeard on the behalf of the Sayd Thomas Vaus and being demanded by what power they appeared could Shew none, But told the court the Sayd Thomas vaus would traverse which the Court would not admit of by reason that the Said Thomas Vaus did not personally appear to give Security for his appearance at the next court and his good behaviour in the Mean while.

Then the court adjourn'd till the 20th of February or New Summons.

[161 1698]   Court of Sessions and Pleas held at Burlington February the 20th 1698. The court opened. Justices on the Bench   John Tatham, Thomas Revell, John Jewell, George Deacon, Thomas Bibb, Anthony Elton, Daniell Leeds, William Emley, William Hewling. The Grandjury   Thomas Potts Senr., Thomas Kendall, Richard Fennimore, John Arnold, William Ogborn, John Brierley, John Shin Junr., Henry Beck, Robert Powell, Ralph Hunt, Charles Miller, John Hutcheson, John Moore. The Traverse Jury   Joseph Adams, Joseph White, Edmund Steward, Eleazar Fenton, Thomas Dowglas, Mordecai Andrews, Marmaduke Horsman, James Croft, Hugh Hutchin, Nathaniell Petit, Richard Harrison, Samuell Terret.

Constables being called, John Brierley constable of Maidenhead appeard and Return'd John Clerk Who had been chosen by the Said Town) for his Successor whom the Court accepted of and forasmuch as the Said Clark was not present ordered him to be brought before William Emley Justice to be Sworn to Serve for the said Town in the office of a constable for the ensuing Year. Ralph Hunt overseer of the highways within the Said Township   appeard and return'd Thomas Smith who had been chosen by the Said Town for his Successor in the office of overseer of the high wayes for the ensuing Year and was accepted of.

Joshua Elyes complaint was then prosecuted.

Richard Dell Plaintiff versus Thomas Wells defendant   in an action of the case   withdrawn.

William Quicksall constable of Nottingham being called appeard and Return'd Isaac Watson for his Successor for the ensuing Year whereupon Isaac Watson was called but did not appear whereupon he was fin'd in the Sum of twenty Shillings. James Antrum Constable of Mansfield being called appear'd and being askt Whether he had anything to present presented Richard Francis and Edward Andrews, for that each of them carried a gun

1698/9]   THE BURLINGTON COURT BOOK   213

on the Lords Day, and being askt Who he Return'd for his Successor Return'd Mordecai Andrews. John Snape constable of Springfield being call'd appear'd and being askt what he had to present return'd   Langstaff for his Successor and return'd a warrant to him directed to Summon certain Delinquents in the Said Warrant mentioned, to appear at this Session for their refusing to pay their tax, which warrant upon Examination he was found not to have executed according to the tenour thereof, and was therefore continued In his office untill he should make full execution of the Same   Henry Beck constable of Chesterfield being called appear'd and Return'd Marmaduke Horsman for his Successor for the ensuing Year, Marmaduke Horsman appear'd, William Parker constable of Northampton being call'd appear'd and was continued in his office for the Ensuing Year. Abraham Hewling constable of Wellingborough being call'd appear'd and made Return of a Warrant to him directed to bring in Isaac Perkins to appear at this sessions, and the said Isaac Perkins appear'd and Submitted and was fin'd in the Sum of Twenty shillings all which excepting five shillings was Remitted unto him In consideration of his povertie, the said Abraham Hewling made a complaint against Jacob Perkins for saying that he was perjured in his office in that he did not execute a warrant to him directed according to the tenour thereof to Effect but they accorded the matter Betwixt themselves in the presence of the Court. Abraham Hewling Return'd John Mills for his Successor but he not appearing it was ordered that the Sayd Abraham should bring the Said Mills before Some Justice within this County to be attested to Serve in the office of constable for the ensuing year, The constable of Chester alias Cropwell being called appear'd not and was continued in the office. There was a return made of a road laid out from the Kings new Road through William Fishers Land Edward Boultons land James Crafts land Edmund Wells land, over the Creek for the conveniency of the Neighbourhood, and was approved of, the constable of Eversham being call'd appear'd and Return'd Richard Boise for his Successor. Thomas Scattergood and James Satterthwait the constables of Burlington being called appear'd and Return'd Isaac De Cow and Thomas Clerk for their Successors for the ensuing Year.

The Court adjourned for two hours.

William Atkinson presented a petition to the Court that he might have a confirmation of a certain Road leading from his house to the Kings road.

William Emley Speciall coroner pro hac vice tantum made Return to the Court of a verdict given by a Jury by him Impannelled to view the Body of Matthew Clayton who had been accidentally drowned in Delaware River which said Jury was Impannelled the Last day of October 1698 and it was approved by the court.

[162 1698]   Thomas Bibb Burgesse of the Town of Burlington delivered into Court a Recognizance by him taken of Martha Wearing Inholdresse Which is on file.

William Hewlings was attested by John Tatham Justice, to bear true alleageance to our Soveraigne Lord King William and to be true to the Governour and government of this Province, and truely and faithfully to Serve In the office of a Justice of peace within this county of Burlington.

The Court adjourn'd for two hours, and then opened again post meridiem, the Justices on the Bench being John Tatham, Thomas Revell, George Deacon, John Jewell, Daniell Leeds, Thomas Bibb. The Grandjury being called the persons abovenamed appeard and Some being Sworn and the rest attested they went forth. The traverse Jury being call'd the abovesaid persons appear'd.

an order was granted to John Snape constable of Springfield to lay out a road from William Atkinson house to the Kings road leading to Burlington.

Jacob Perkins Plaintiff and William Menard defendant in an action upon the case being called did appear. The Declaration read the court ordered them to Withdraw Whilst they confer about the matter, and being call'd In again the court told them they would take time till the morrow to consider of their cause.

Thomas Black being attested in court to give his Evidence to the Grandjury was Sent unto the Same.

Thomas Craft Plaintiff and William Brown Defendant in an action of debt being called both appear'd, And upon the Plaintiffs allegation that his Evidence was not ready the action was continued.

Edward Hunloke Plaintiff and George Glave Defendant in an action upon the case being called Edward Hunloke appear'd and desired the action might be continued which was accordingly done.

Peter Resnier Plaintiff and Daniell England Defendant in an action upon the case Peter Resnier appear'd and John Tatham Esquire appear'd as an atturney for the defendant, And the Declaration being read the Matter was defer'd till the next day.

Daniell England Plaintiff against John Dewsbury's Estate being Called John Tatham Esquire atturney for Daniell England appear'd and Desir'd a continuance which Was granted,

John Ogborn Plaintiff John Hollinshead defendant, being called the Plaintiff appear'd the defendant appeard not.

Joshua Horner was attested for the grandjury.

Thomas Bibb Plaintiff against Thomas Dowglas and Emanuell Smith an action of Debt, withdrawn.

John Jewell Plaintiff and Thomas Gardiner defendant being called they both appear'd, and the court thought fit to continue the matter till the next day.

William Brown Plaintiff and Thomas Craft defendant being called they both appear'd, and the action Was continued till the next court.

The grandjury return'd into Court and presented William Biddle for not prosecuting the law against Edward Andrews, whom the said Biddle did charge with the stealing of two Swine from him the Said William Biddle, the Grandjury did move to have the former County treasurer brought to an account.

The Court of Pleas held by adjournment the 21st day of February 1698. Justices on the Bench   John Tatham, Thomas Revell, John Jewell, George Deacon, William Emley, Daniell Leeds, Thomas Bibb, Anthony Elton, William Hewlings.

The court opened and immediately adjourned till the 14th of March next.

An order was granted to Abraham Hewlings constable of Wellingborough to Lay out a road from Richard Fennimore's house to his land on the Southeast of Jacob Perkins his Land and so onward to John Tests Mill.

John Snape having return'd a Warrant to him directed for to bring in to this Sessions certain persons in the said warrant named for refusing or neglecting to pay their tax, unexecuted, had the Same renewed.

The court of Sessions and Pleas held by adjournment at Burlington March the 14th 1698. The court opened. Justices on the Bench   John Tatham, Thomas Revell, Nathaniell Westland, George Deacon, Daniell Leeds, John Test, Joshua Ely, Joshua Newbold. The Grandjury being called the Court adjourn'd for two hours to Sit again at Thomas Kendalls house. The Court opened, and the Grandjury being called answered to their names being the Same as appear'd at the former Setting.

[163 1698]   A Return was made to the court by Michaell Newbold of a way laid out through Richard French his land, by persons chosen by him the said Newbold and French and was approved by the court and ordered to be recorded Which is as followeth, from a white oak and a Stump markt near the house Standing in the Road laid out and So along towards Michaells house as it is now markt by us to the meadow Side, and from thence as Michael Sees cause as farr as the Said Richards land goes, as the said Richard Willingly consented to and offered of himself.

Thomas Wallis exhibited a boy named Rees Price to this court whom he had bought of Richard Owen, as by assignment Endors'd upon a certain Indenture bearing date, the 16th of June 1698, did appear, and desir'd that the Court would Confirm the Said Boy unto him according to the tenour of the Said Indenture and Indorsment, and to Limit the Time for which he Should Serve him and the Sayd boy then declaring that he was Willing to Serve the Said Wallis, The court then ordered that he should Serve him until he Should attain unto the age of twenty and one years Which will be in June 1704.

A Return was then made by John Test of a way laid out from his Mill, to Richard Fennimores land on the Southeast Side of Jacob Perkins his land, and so onward to the said Fennimores house.

Jacob Cooperwhait was Return'd Constable for Chester alias Cropwell.

William Fisher Plaintiff versus Sarah Farr Defendant in an action of Debt.

Abraham Brown Plaintiff versus Richard French defendant in an action of trover and conversion withdrawn.

Robert Wheeler Plaintiff versus Henry Jacob Defendant in an action of the case withdrawn.

Robert Wheeler Plaintiff versus John Hutcheson defendant in an action of the case withdrawn.

Thomas Potts Junr. Plaintiff versus Anthony Ashmore defendant in an action of debt withdrawn.

Jonathan Curtis Plaintiff versus John Butcher defendant in an action of Defamation of title in land withdrawne.

Joseph Wood Plaintiff versus Robert Cole Defendant in an action of debt withdrawn.

John Robards Plaintiff versus Edmond Steward defendant in an action of the case withdrawn.

John Cooperthwait was return'd constable for Chester at this court, Jacob Bromeley and Anthony Dawson, both by Subpanaes appear'd at this court.

Court Held March the 15th 1698. The Court opened. The Governour present John Tatham, Thomas Revell, George Deacon, Nathaniell Westland, Anthony Elton, Daniell Leeds, Joshua Ely, William Emley Justices on the Bench. The Traverse Jury called.

Daniell England Plaintiff against John Dewsburies Estate called Daniell England by his atturney John Tatham Esquire appear'd to prosecute, his power of atturney was read, and the declaration was likewise read, and no person appearing on the behalf of the Said Dewsbury, legally to make any defence, the court Granted a Judgment against the Said Estate.

Peter Resnier Plaintiff against Daniell England then appeard in court and Desired time till the afternoon to prepare himself which the Court granted.

John Jewell and Joshua Barkstead Plaintiff against Thomas Gardiner Defendant being called the Plaintiffs appear'd the Defendant being call'd three times appear'd not but Sent a paper to the Court which was overruled and rejected, and the court gave Judgment by Default against the defendant, and ordered that a writ of enquiry Should be issued out to enquire of damages returnable the next court.

[*take in here what is placed in the next page between the parallel lines.*] [48]

Richard Dell and Elizabeth his wife Plaintiffs and Elizabeth Basnet Defendant being called the Plaintiff and Defendant appear'd the defendant crav'd a continuance, the Court ordered the defendant to bring in her ac-

[48] See p. 218.

counts within twenty daies next coming and in the mean time continued the action.

Jacob Perkins Plaintiff and William Menard defendant being called appear'd, and it was put to the vote Whether the action should be tried, and it was carried by the majority of votes of the bench in the Negative Whereupon the action was dismist.

[164 1698] William Brown appeard and desird to have his action against Thomas Craft trid which would not be admitted In regard that it had been continued till next court.

John Ogborn Plaintiff and John Hollinshead defendant being call'd the Plaintiff appear'd, the defendant appeard not and the action was continued.

A Return was made of a way laid out by a Jury pursuant to an order of the former Sitting of this Court from William Atkinson's house to the King's road leading to Burlington and the court approv'd of it and ordered it to be Recorded and is as followeth, Beginning at two markt trees by the creek Side in John Butchers land Right opposite Against William Atkinsons house going in a Strait line to the other markt trees containing two Rod wide going into the Kings Road, Wee (viz) the Jury do allow him a Road with gates.

John Snape Constable made Return of a warrant to him directed to Summon in certain delinquents for their Refusall to pay their tax which warrant he had executed as he reported, whereupon the Court ordered that Such as refused to pay should be distrain'd.

James Satterthwait appear'd at this Sessions who had been bound to appear to answer for searching Daniell Suttons house without a legall warrant, and John Hollinshead being then and there present asserted that himself is Burgesse and as Such might give power to Search, and James Satterthwait was then askt if he would Submit to the Bench or have his case presented to the Grandjury, Whereupon he desired a little time to consider of it which being granted he soon return'd again and answered that he did not understand the matter they might do what they would, and being examined concerning What he was charg'd withall, he ownd that he Went along with the Said John Hollinshead to the said Daniell Suttons house to Search for Some goods and that in the Said house he did make Search among Some of the said Daniell goods, So the said James Satterthwait being convict of Searching the said Daniell Suttons house without a legall Warrant was fin'd in the Sum of five pounds, John Hollinshead was convict of not prosecuting and giving evidence against Emanuell Smith Whom he had committed, and was therefore fined in the Sum of ten pounds, he was likewise convict of Commanding and going along with the said James Satterthwait to Search the said Daniell Suttons house without a legall warrant in contempt of Authority, and was therefore fined in the Sum of ten pounds and the said John Hollinshead and James Satterthwait were committed to custody till they Should pay their Said respective fines and give Security for their good behaviour.

ordered by the Court that Moses Langstaff shall be brought in by John Snape to Daniell Leeds Justice to be Attested to Serve in the office of a Constable for the ensuing Year.

Mons Cocks and his wife were presented to the Grandjury for taking fifty Shillings and Sixpence from an Indian, and Jacob Bromely, and Anthony Dawson being both Sworn to give their evidence in the case were Sent to the Grandjury, and the Grandjury return'd ignoramus upon the Bill.

Mons Cock was convict at this court of Selling Strong liquors without licence and was thefore ordered to pay thirty Shillings as a fine, and he was also convict of Selling Strong liquors to the Indians, and was therefore ordered to pay the fine by the law prescribed in Such case (viz) five pounds.

John Hollinshead James Satterthwaite and Mons Cock were committed for not performing what was laid upon and required of them Respectively as aforesaid.

Whereupon the Court adjourn'd till eight a clock on the morrow morning.

Peter Resnier appeard, in court in the afternoon to prosecute his Suit upon bond against Daniell England Whereupon it was debated in court Whether the said bond were forfeited or no, and Whether it ought to Come upon triall, the Court after Some deliberation gave their Judgment it ought to come upon tryall from which Judgment Daniell England Crav'd an appeal which upon the usuall conditions was granted by the Justices upon the Bench (viz) Thomas Revell Nathaniell Westland Daniell Leeds Joshua Ely William Hewlings William Emley [*add this to the foregoing page*].

Christopher Snoden Plaintiff Thomas Gardiner Defendant being called the Plaintiff appear'd the defendant being Called three times appear'd not, whereupon Judgment Went against him by default Which was for ten pounds damages with costs of Suit.

The court ordered Thomas Bibb to pay the Grandjury for three daie's attendance at this Court.

Nathaniell Petit and Mary his wife having been in the Sight and presence of Joshua Ely Justice convicted of keeping bad order in their ordinary, as keeping persons drunk and breaking the Sabbath and other Misdemeanors is presented to this Court Whereupon the Court order his licence shall be taken from him the said Petit.

[165 1698] There was an order of Court for William Sanford to Serve his Master John Petty for the time limited and reasons Mentioned in the Same order which is on file.

The Sheriffe return'd that the execution was Satisfied which was awarded against Samuell Kemble upon a Judgment granted the Last Court to Benjamin and Edward Kemble executors of the last Will and testament of Hanna Scott late deceased upon a bond put in Suit against the Said Samuell Kemble by them the Said executors.

ordered that Whereas there is a difference Between the Inhabitants of Maidenhead about two Roads Leading from their said Town to Sanpink a precept shall be directed to the Constable of the Said Town requiring him to Summon the said Inhabitants to come together at Such time and to Such place as shall unto him Seem convenient and there put it to the vote whether of the said roads shall Stand and that that Road which Shall be pitch upon and approv'd of by the majority of votes shall be the Establisht road.

The Court adjourned till eight a clock in the morning next day.

The Court of Session opened the 16th day of March 1698 The Governour being present John Tatham, Thomas Revell, Nathaniell Westland, George Deacon, William Emley, Daniell Leeds, Joshua Ely Justices on the Bench.

Peter Fretwell was then brought into court by the high Sheriff by virtue of a precept unto him directed and the sheriff returnd the said precept which being read the said Peter Fretwell was askt whether he would So far Submit to authority as to give up his accounts of the County tax to the persons appointed to audit accounts With him, he desired Some time to consider he withdrew for a little While and after return'd into Court and denied to give any answer, whereupon he was by mittimus Sent to prison for not rendring his accounts as aforesaid and not acknowledging the government and giving Security for his good behaviour.

The Sheriff returnd a non est inventus upon the warrant to him directed to bring in Thomas Gardiner into this Court.

It was then adjudged by the court that whereas John Garwood paid his tax unto John Shin Senior and he received the Same Since the collectors were chosen that it was a contempt of authority in them both, Wherefore they were fined in twenty Shillings apiece.

New Constables for the ensuing Year Maidenhead John Brierley. Nottingham William Quicksall. [attested] Chesterfield Marmaduke Horsman. [attested] Mansfield Mordecai Andrews. Springfield Moses Langstaff. Northampton William Parker. [attested] Wellingborough John Mills. Chester, alias Cropwell John Cooperthwait. [attested] Eversham Richard Boise. [attested] Burlington Isaac De Cow and Thomas Clark.

The Court adjournd till the next day being the 17th of March was then opened, Justices being on the Bench Thomas Revell, George Deacon, Nathaniell Westland, Daniell Leeds.

The court dissolv'd.

[166 1699] Court of Quarter sessions and Pleas holden at Burlington on May the 8th 1699. Justices on the Bench Thomas Revell, Nathaniell Westland, George Deacon, John Jewell, Daniell Leeds. The Grandjury William Fisher, John Bainbridge, Thomas Potts Junr., Robert Pierson, Thomas Tindall, William Foster, Abraham Brown Senr., Thomas Smith, Thomas Runnion, Enoch Anderson, Recompence Kerby, James Sherine, Benjamin

Jones Being called appeard and were some Sworn and the rest attested receive their charge.

James Satterthwait, pursuant to a bond by him given appeared at this court and no person appearing to prosecute against him he was dismist.

Traverse Jury Edmond Wells, William Bustin, Abraham Hewlings, Charles Wolverton, John Hilliard, Abraham Brown Junr., Obadiah Hierton, Henry Beck, John Brierly, Emanuell Smith, Joseph Scattergood, Joseph Pancoast. The traverse Jury being called appear'd and answered to their names.

And then the Court adjourn'd for two hours.

Court of Pleas opened post meridiem. Justices on the Bench Thomas Revell, Nathaniell Westland, Daniell Leeds, Michaell Newbold.

Peter Resnier Plaintiff Daniell England Defendant being called, appear'd. The defendant insists to have the benefit of an appeal which he alledged to have been granted the Last court, But the Court not consenting The defendant complies to go to triall at common law, the Jury called appeard and were attested to try the cause the Declaration read the bond read the plea given in and read the condition of the bond read The traverse Jury go out and Return into court again, the Plaintiff and Defendant call'd come in, the Jury being askt who they find for they by their foreman declare they find for the Plaintiff, the Defendant Craves an appeal from the verdict as vitious.

The grandjury came into Court and return'd two presentments which were read in court the one of a way Between Mill Creek and York Shire bridge, and the other of Samuell Jenings for saying that our Governours commission is unlawfull and they that made it do not dare to Stand by it.

Thomas Revell, Nathaniell Westland, Daniell Leeds, Anthony Elton, Michael Newbold Justices on the Bench.

Richard Dell appeared to prosecute against Elizabeth Basnett Elizabeth Basnet appear'd and being required to give in her accounts did alledge her present Incapacity and promised to give her accounts the twelfth instant.

Thomas Bibb as Burgesse of the Town of Burlington did exhibit to the Court four recognizances by him taken, (to wit) of Henry Grubb, George Willis Elizabeth Basnett and Martha Wearing Inholders The said Thomas Bibb as treasurer made his Complaint to the Court that John Hutcheson Collector of part of the provinciall and county tax doth neglect to pay in the Same Whereupon it is ordered that a Warrant shall be issued out for to Levy the same.

[167 1699] Justices on the Bench. Thomas Revell, Nathaniell Westland, John Jewell, Anthony Elton, Michaell Newbold, George Deacon.

John Ogborn Plaintiff John Hollinshead defendant being called the Plaintiff appear'd the Defendant being Called three times appeard not, the Declaration Read and Judgment was given by Default against the Defendant the Judgment being for Eleven pounds fourteen Shillings and four pence with Costs of Suit amounting to three pounds and ten Shillings.

William Pancoast being then attested Declared that before Jane Pancoast was married to Thomas Crosse he was present when there were five cows that belonged to Anne and Abigail Curtis Whereof the Said Deponent bought two, and the other three She the Sayd Jane Pancoast Was minded to take to halfs. Jonathan Curtis being attested deposed that the said three cows in the Custody of the Said Jane Pancoast were the proper goods of the said Anne and Abigail Curtis at the time of the Intermariage of the said Jane and Thomas Crosse Two of Which Said Cows being red the executors of the said Thomas Crosse did Sell unto William Atkison, the third died before She came to the hands of the sayd Executors.

Thomas Revell, John Jewell, George Deacon, Nathaniell Westland, Daniell Leeds, Anthony Elton, Justices on the Bench.

The Court at Daniell Englands request confirmed the Judgment to him granted at the Last court against John Dewsbury's Estate.

Thomas Brock Plaintiff versus John Foulk alias Owen Defendant in an action of debt Withdrawn.

John Test Plaintiff versus Charles French Defendant in an action of the Case Withdrawn.

John Jewell, George Deacon, Michaell Newbold, Anthony Elton, Daniell Leeds.[49]

Jacob De Cow Plaintiff versus Mordecay Andrews Defendant in an action of the case Withdrawn.

Abraham Redwood Plaintiff versus Joseph Heron Defendant an action of the case withdrawn.

Joseph Pigeon Plaintiff versus Bewley Marshall Defendant an action of the case withdrawn.

Daniel Leeds Plaintiff versus Jonas Moon Jasper Moon and William Pancoast Defendants in an action of debt withdrawn.

The honourable Jeremiah Basse Esqr. Governour and Thomas Revell Gent. Agents for the honourable the West Jersey Society Plaintiffs Complain'd against Nathaniell Westland Gent. Late agent for the Said Society Defendant in an action upon the Case with relation to the accounts of the Sayd Defendants for considerable quantities of goods and merchandize of the Said Society to him the Said defendant Delivered: Whereupon the Court did appoint four men to audit accounts with the Said Defendant (Videlicet) George Deacon and Daniell Leeds on the behalf of the Plaintiffs And Joseph Row and John Meredith on the behalf of the defendant, and to fix the Ballance between the Sayd Society and the Said Defendant, Then the Court adjourned till Seaven of the Clock in the morning next day.

[49] *Sic.* Probably the court adjourned and met again, with these justices present.

The Court of Sessions and pleas held at Burlington May the 9th 1699. Justices on the Bench   Thomas Revell, Nathaniel Westland, Daniel Leeds. the Court opened.

Upon the verdict given Yesterday by the Jury for the Plaintiff Peter Resnier the court gave Judgment for Sixty eight pounds in full Discharge of the bond, the Defendant Daniell England Crav'd an appeal which was granted he the said Daniell England paying the costs of Suit and giving Sufficient Security to prosecute his appeal to effect As the Law in that Case doth require which Conditions he the Sayd Daniell England performed by paying the Costs and giving bond to prosecute.

Whereupon the court adjourned till the 19th instant.

[168 1699]   The Court of Pleas held by adjournment the 19th of May 1699. Justices on the Bench   Thomas Revell, Nathaniell Westland, Daniell Leeds. the Court opened and adjourn'd till the morrow morning 8 aclock.

The Court of Sessions and pleas holden at Burlington August the 8th 1699. The Governour present. Justices on the Bench   John Tatham, Thomas Revell, John Jewell, Nathaniell Westland, George Deacon, Daniell Leeds. The Court opened.

Thomas Bibb Burgess of the Town of Burlington Delivered into Court John Neves bond Henry Greens Recognizance Thomas Renshaws recognizance and Daniell Mecartees Recognizance, for their Severall appearances at this Court, all which being called (together with Thomas Roberts Who was also bound to appear at this Sessions) did Appeare and Were continued till next Sessions Excepting only the said Thomas Renshaw who upon Paying of his fees was Dismist.

William Cole Plaintiff versus John Test Defendant   an action of the case   withdrawn.

Isaac Conorroe Plaintiff versus John Jenings Defendant   in an action of debt   withdrawn.

Jacob De Cow Plaintiff versus Mordecai Andrews defendant   an action of the case   withdrawn.

Henry Green Plaintiff versus William Richards Defendant   an action of Slander   withdrawn.

Edward Hunloke did appear and make Report to this Court that for rent due to him from James Layton his late tenant he had made Distreis of the goods found in the said Laytons house, and did desire the Court to grant him licence to dispose of the said goods for the satisfying of the said rent Which the Court granted he the Said Edward Hunloke promising to Swear before Some Magistrate to the Truth of his account.

The Jury's being called, and Severall not appearing, So that full Juries could not be made, the court Could not proceed in businesse, and therefore the Court Dissolved.

The Court of Quarter Sessions and Pleas held at Burlington November the 3rd 1699. The Governour present. Justices on the Bench Thomas Revell, Nathaniell Westland, John Jewell, George Deacon, Daniell Leeds, Joshua Ely, Michaell Newbold, Anthony Elton, John Test. The court opened. The grand Jury Mathew Allen, James Craft Senr., Andrew Heath, Robert Pierson, Thomas Tindall, Johannes Lawrenson, Samuell Hunt, James Price, William Bustin, Thomas Wood, John Hammell, John Moor, Thomas Dugglas all which being called answered to their names. [169 1699] The Traverse Jury Thomas Wright, John Ogborn Junr., Eleazer Fenton, Ralph Hunt, Thomas Smith, Abraham Brown Junr., Jasper Smith, Nicholas Martineau, John Hilliard, Richard Harrison, Edmond Wells, Jacob De Cow being called appeared.

    The Grandjury being attested received their charge and Went out, and then Daniell Mecarty Henry Green Abraham Carlile Alexander Stuart and John Neve were called to appear according to their Severall Recognizances or bonds John Neve appeard and Thomas Bibb Burgess, Who had taken bond of John Neve for his appearance, gave an account to the Court Why the Said John Neve was bound over, (viz) Because the Said Neve having cohabited in this Town of Burlington with Mary Friley did after carry her away with him out of the Province and Returned again into the Sayd Province without her, Whereupon the Court finding that the Said Mary is Safely return'd into this town and no evidence appearing against the Sayd Neve for any crime the Court Thought fit to withdraw the Said Neves bond he paying his fees.

    Matthew Champion being attested to give evidence for the King in Daniell Mecartees Matter Was Sent to the Grandjury.

    Abraham Carlile appeared and the examinations taken of him and Hanna Biddle were Sent to the Grandjury.

    The Recognizance taken of Thomas Kendall as Inholder was Return into the Court by the Burgess of the Town of Burlington.

    Humphrey Hughes appear'd, and being presented by the grandjury for that he was suspected to have Carried away or Secured certain privateers, Submitted to the Bench, and was adjudged to pay a fine of ten pieces of eight, and to pay the Sheriffs and Clerks fees.

    Thomas Bibb also recommended to the Court a Negro, called Will whom he had committed, as one that might give Some light in Daniell Mecartees Businesse.

    The Court adjourn'd for two hours. The Court opened post meridiem. Justices on the Bench Thomas Revell, Nathaniell Westland, John Jewell, George Deacon, Joshua Ely.

    Josiah Pricket Plaintiff versus Jonathan Fearman defendant an action of debt withdrawn.

    Alexander Stuart appeard according to his bond, and also Mary Grant appeared to prosecute against him, a paper evidence against the Said Stuart was sent to the Grandjury. The Sayd Stuart having commenced a civil action against the Sayd Mary Grant, their Severall actions were continued till next court.

Thomas York and Mary His wife Plaintiffs against Martha Wearing and Robert Dummer defendants being Called appeared, and alledging the absence of their evidence crav'd a continuance Which was Granted.

Martha Wearing Plaintiff against Jeremiah Reading Defendant being called appear'd, Jeremiah Reading appear'd not, his bondsmen Thomas Potts Senr. and James Craft Junr. being called Thomas Potts Senr. appear'd and being admitted by the court to personate the sayd Jeremiah Reading The Declaration was read and by reason of some uncertainties or unsufficiencies therein was Quasht and the Sayd Martha Wearing thereupon non Suited.

The Grandjury Return'd into court and exhibit Several presentments, (viz) one against Joshua Ely Justice another against John Neve and Mary Friley, another against Robert Dummer and Martha Wearing and another against Alexander Stuarts wife and another against Daniell Mecartee, and another against Abraham Carlile and Hanna Biddle, and another of the Road Betwixt John Hancocks and York Shire bridge Which are on file, they likewise exhibit a presentment against John Tatham, and another against Humphrey Hughes.

[170 1699] Richard Dell Plaintiff and Elizabeth Basnet Defendant appear in court, and their matter is deferred till the next day.

The Court of Quarter Sessions and Pleas held at Burlington the fourth of November 1699. The Court opened, Justices on the Bench, Thomas Revell Nathaniell Westland George Deacon Joshua Ely.

James Wills his Negro Will was brought into Court and examined concerning goods which He was suspected to have received of or delivered unto Daniell Mecartee, Sayd he Sold the Sayd Mecartee a Shirt Which he Stole from the Widdow Basnets house.

Daniell Mecartee being brought into Court and askt how hee came by one Shirt which the same was found in his house, Denied that ever he Saw or knew anything of the said Shirt untill the Same was found In his house.

The Court having considered the evidence given against the Said Daniell Macartee and Negro Will and Thereupon finding them guilty of the fellonious Stealing of certain goods Belonging unto Severall persons of the Town of Burlington, The Court gave Judgment that the Sayd Daniell Mecartee on the same Day being the fourth of November 1699, Between the hours of one and two of the clock in the afternoon Shall be Whipt at a cart tail from the Court house down to the Water Side and thence back again to the Courthouse With thirty nine Stripes Well laid on, and also that if the said Daniell Mecartee Should be found within this Province after the Seaventh day of the sayd Month of November, that then he the Said Daniell Mecartee Should be taken up again and Whipt as aforesaid.

Likewise the Court ordered that the Said Negro Will Should, at the time and in the Space aforesaid, be Whipt at a Cartstail with thirtynine Stripes well Layd on.

Thomas Revell Plaintiff and Mons Cocks Defendant in an action of Debt upon bond being called the Plaintiff appear'd the defendant appear'd not, the declaration read, the bond read and prov'd and a Judgment thereupon granted for five pounds with costs of Suit.

Richard Dell Plaintiff and Elizabeth Basnet Defendant, appeared in Court, and after Some debate the Declaration read, Whereunto the defendant pleads Plenius Administravit, and the accounts read Severall other papers as receits articles and a bond read, and after Some debate the Defendant engaged on the behalf of William Framptons children that his Eldest daughter Elizabeth Shall before the next Court acknowledge her Self Satisfyed with the hundred pounds mentioned in the Sayd articles and by vertue thereof unto her belonging, And also that Security Shall be given before the next court That Thomas and Sarah Residue of the sayd William Framptons children, When They come to age Shall accept of their Respective hundred pounds to them by vertue of the Sayd articles due and belonging, and So the cause was continued till next court.

A Return of a Road through Maidenhead made to the Court and approved of by the Same, as followeth   May the 4th 1699, In order to the amendment, wee of the Jury Begining at the partition Line So runing as Markt trees shall direct to the eight mile run to a White oak in the Land of Johannes Lawrence Soe Runing as Markt trees Shall direct to a White oak tree Standing before Ralph Hunts door by the run So running as Markt trees Shall direct to Bridge over the Six mile run in Robert Lannings Land So running as markt trees Shall direct through the Land of William Acres and through the Land of Jasper Smith and through the land of Thomas Smith to the Five mile run to a hiceree tree So running through the Land of Samuell Matthews and So through the Land of Samuell Stacy as Markt trees Shall direct to Shabakunck bridge, So as markt trees Shall direct through the Land of Mahlon Stacy to the mill of Mahlon Stacy, Sign'd by, Ralph Thomas Smith Samuell Hunt Theophilus Phillips Joshua Anderson John Lanning Joseph Smith Hezekiah Bonham.

The Court adjourn'd for two hours.

The Court opened Post meridiem. Justices on the Bench   Thomas Revell, Nathaniell Westland, John Jewell, George Deacon, John Test, Michaell Newbold.

[171 1699]   Thomas Roberts being called appeared, and Joseph Steward being called appear'd not nor any other to prosecute against the said Thomas Roberts, therefore the Said Thomas Roberts was dismised paying his fees.

Henry Green being called, appear'd But no person appearing to prosecute against him he was Dismissed paying his fees.

John Neve and Mary Fryley came into Court and were ordered to part and not to cohabit togeather any longer under the penalty of Ten pounds.

Robert Dummer and Martha Wearing came into Court and were ordered to Marry or part Within one Month after this time under the penalty of Ten pounds. Martha Wearing being convict of having Spoken abusively and contemptibly of Thomas Revell Justice Was by the bench fin'd in five pieces of eight Which in consideration of her poverty Was remitted unto her.

Abraham Carlile came into Court and being convicted of having comitted fornication With Hannah Biddle Was fin'd in the Sum of five pounds Which being tendered unto the Governour by the sayd Abraham the Said Governour was pleased mostly to give and Restore again unto the Said Abraham in consideration of his poverty.

Whereupon the Court adjourn'd.

The Court of appeales held at Burlington the 5th of october 1699. Justices on the Bench   Thomas Revell, Nathaniell Westland, Joshua Ely.

The Court opened, and no business presenting the Court adjourn'd till the 12th instant.

The Court of Appeales held by adjournment at Burlington the 12th of October 1699.

Justices on the Bench   John Jewell, George Deacon, Anthony Elton, John Test. The Court opened.

Daniell England Apellant against Peter Resnier Appellee being called Appeared not, Peter Resnier Appellee Appear'd and crav'd to have an issue put to the matter depending betwixt him and Daniell England, the court Takes time to consider of it and adjourn for an hour and an half.

The Court opened post meridiem, Justices on the Bench   John Jewell, George Deacon, Anthony Elton, John Test.

Daniell England appellant called three times appear'd not. Peter Resnier appellee appear'd and crav'd a confirmation of the Judgment given at common law at his Suit against the sayd Daniell England, Whereupon the Court after mature deliberation and consideration of the former Courts proceedings in that matter Gave it as their Judgment that the Judgment of the Court at common law for Sixty eight pounds payable by the Sayd Daniell England to the Sayd Peter Resnier is and Shall be confirmed, and that the Sayd Appellant Shall pay the Costs of Court amounting to one pound and Sixpence Whereupon the Court Adjourn'd.

[172 1699]   [50] [*Court of Sessions and Pleas February 20th 1699*]   Court of Sessions February 20th 21th 22th 1699. Justices on the Bench   Mahlon Stacy, Francis Davenport, Peter Frettwell, William Biddle, John Adams, John Wills, Joshua Newbould, Ralph Hunt   Esqrs. Thomas Gardiner Kings attorney   Joseph Cross Sheriffe.

Grand Jury   foreman Hannaniah Gant, Thomas Raper, Matthew Fore-

[50] Different handwriting.

sith, Thomas Bryan, Joseph White, William Bustill, Joseph Smith, John Tonkin, John Butcher, Richard French, John Ogborn Senr., James Craft, Thomas Wilson, Richard Ridgway, William Black   Attested   charge given.

[*Petition*]   Petition of some of the Inhabitants above the Falls for a New Townshipp to be called Hopewell as also for a New Road and Boundaries of the said Town read—and upon file. Order'd That there be a Town there called Hopewell and that the Boundaries thereof be as follows (vizt) To begin at Mahlon Stacyes Mill And so along by York: road, untill it comes to Shabbucunck, and up the same untill it meet with the line of Partition that divides the Societies 30000 acres Purchase from the 15000 and then along the line of the said Societies 30000 acres Purchase to Delaware River.

[*Petition*]   Petition of some of the Inhabitants of Springfield and Northampton Townshipps concerning the altering of a Road (read) and upon file. Order'd   Concerning the said Petition, That Peter Frettwell and Joshua Newbould two of the Justices appoint six indefferent men out of each Townshipp to lay forth Said Road and make report thereof next Court for their Approbation.

Upon a Motion by Edmund Steward concerning altering the Road by Thomas Wrights Plantation in Burlington Town bounds to avoid bad way. Order'd   That Peter Frettwell and Joshua Newbould Justices give a Warrant to the Constables or Constable of the Town of Burlington to Summons twelve men as a Jury to view and lay out a Roadway between Yorkshire bridge and William Fishers Plantation to prevent the hollow way by said Wrights Plantation.

Order   That the Inhabitants of the Out plantations adjoyning to Springfield Townshipp do at present belong to said Townshipp only Thomas Willson to belong to Chesterfield Townshipp till further Order.

Restore Lippincut brought an Irish boy into Court (he having newly bought him to serve him till the age of One and Twenty Years) and craved that the Court would give an Estimate of his age, the boys name being Daniel MacCay. Order'd   By the Court, That the said boy named Daniel MacCay be adjudged at Eleven Years of and so to serve ten Year, as by the his Contract.

James Shinn brought also an Irish boy named John Anderson on same Accompt and the Court Order'd   That the said John Anderson be adjudged, ten years and to serve Eleven years pursuant to his Contract.

Joshua Tomkins aged 14 years or thereabouts an Orphan, John Hollinshead his late Guardian being deceased craved of the Court that Peter Frettwell might be admitted his Guardian—The Court Order'd   That upon Peter Frettwells giving Security according to Law is admitted said Tomkins Guardian and the Letter of Guardianshipp be given him as such.

Benjamin Wheat Guardian to and for Theophila Cripps she being of age and in Court acknowledging she had received just Accompts and all the

Estate which he received of hers to her full Satisfaction and said Wheat craving his Quietus   Order'd   That said Wheat's Bond be delivered up and he released of his said Guardianshipp.

Peter Frettwell Treasurer making Complaint that several of the Collectors for several of the Townshipps in Burlington County have not paid in their Collections either in the Provincial or County Taxes   Ordered   That a Warrant be sent to those several Collectors that have not yet brought in their Accompts nor paid in their respective Collections (which Warrant is to be sign'd by the Justices) that they bring in their respective taxes and the Duplicates according to Law, to said Frettwell County and Provincial Treasurer by the next Quarter Sessions.

Order'd   By the Court That the Court Record book be forthwith new bound by Matthew Wattson, and be paid at the County charge.

Constables and Overseers chosen for this year by the Several Townshipps in this County and by them return'd to and allow'd off by the Court as follows (vizt) for

	Constables	Overseers
Maidenhead	Theophilus Philips Attested	Hezekiah Bonum
Nottingham	Caleb Wheatly Attested	Thomas Tindall
Chesterfield	John Arnold or Duke Horsman for him Attested	Thomas Scholey and John Moor
Mansfield	Edward Andrews Attested	John Hancock and Richard French
Springfield	Moses Langstaff	John Shinn Senr. and Jarvis Pharo
Northampton	John Woolstone Attested	Thomas Stookes and William Budd
Wellingborough	John Pain Senr. Attested	Thomas Harding
Chester alias Cropwell	John Cooperthwaite Attested	Joseph Heritage
Eversham	John Boarton Attested	Benjamin Moor
Burlington	Samuel Gibson Attested William Bustill Attested	Lawrence Morris and Joseph Smith
Hopewell	Stephen Willson Attested	Andrew Heath

The Grand Jury came into Court and delivered three Presentments as follows viz   The grand jury present   Abraham Brown Senr. for entertaintaining another mans Wife contrary to her husbands mind   Sundry persons Selling Strong drink without a Licence vizt James Crofts Widdow Hancock and John Jackson etc. Benjamin Kembal and William Fennymore for playing at Unlawfull Games.

The Grandjury brought in a paper intimating that they had accounted with Peter Frettwell County Treasurer, and there remains in his hands Four pounds, two Shillings and one penny as Ballance (at present received).

Ordered   That James Crafts Widdow Hancock and John Jackson be fined twenty Shillings a piece for Selling Strong drink without a Licence.

Order   James Crofts craving a Licence to keep an Ordinary which upon his giveing Security according to Law is admitted.

Ordered   That Robert Dummer and George Parker (they craving a Licence) have liberty to keep an Ordinary in Burlington giving Bond and Security according to Law.

William Fennymore brought into Court upon the Grandjuries Presentment   Order'd   That he find Security for the good behaviour or go to prison   Samuell Gibson appear'd as his Security and the Court accept of the Bonds.

Elizabeth Basnett Widdow being bound by Recognizance to the King in Twenty pounds and Isaac Marriott and Benjamin Wheat in Tenn pounds a piece for the well behaving of said Basnett in keeping an Ordinary and performing the Condition of Said Recognizance the Court unanimously agree and adjudge the said Recognizance to be forfeited by the said Basnett permitting and countenancing in her house an Illegal and clandestine marriage between one Robert Hickman under Custody of the Sheriff as a Suspected Pirate (and that to the knowledge of said Basnett) and Mrs. Dorothy Tatham Eldest daughter of John Tatham Esqr. and after said Marriage in provideing conniveing and suffering them to go to Bedd together in her house to the great damage grief and affliction of the parents of said Mrs. Dorothy, the Reproach of the Province, and Scandal to the Christian proffession and Civil Society and Neighbourhood. [173 1699]   Order'd   By the Court that the said Recognizance being forfeited, the forty pounds therein mentioned be Levied on the goods and Chattells of the Said Widdow Basnett Isaac Marriott and Benjamin Wheat according to Law, her Licence be taken from her and She permitted to Sell no other drink than what she has in her house and a Months time and no more granted her to sell said drink.

Nathaniel Cripps and Bernard Lane made Complaint against some of the Inhabitants of the Town of Burlington about the high wayes which Complaint is referr'd till next Court.

The Court of Pleas held at Burlington February 20th and 21th dayes.

Justices Present on the Bench   Mahlon Stacy, Peter Frettwell, William Biddle, Joshua Newbould and John Adams Esqrs.

[*February 21th*] Action   Thomas Wetherill Plaintiff   James Wills Defendant   The Declaration read. The defendant by David Lloyd his Attorney offered some things in barr to the action but was overruled by the Court and order'd to go to Tryall. The Jury Attested in this Tryall   John Meredith, Samuel Taylor, Thomas Foulk junr., John Bunting, Jacob Decow, Thomas Potts junr., Joseph Pancoast, Thomas Garrett, Eliezar Fenton, John Ogborn junr., John Tantam, John Moor. The Declaration again read And the Contract or Covenant between the Plaintiff and Defendant read.

[*Evidence*] Thomas Scattergood Attested saith he owns that Thomas Weatherell the Plaintiff was sometimes Mowing and Some times digging of a Cellar when his (said Plaintiffs) Master (the Defendant) was at work in his Shopp, but knows nothing of his said Masters refusing or not learning him his Trade, but says he had heard the Plaintiff say several times that he believed his Master would not teach him his Trade and on that Accompt had him before John Hollinshead Justice.

[*Evidence*] Peter Frettwell Justice says he knowes that James Wills was brought before the Justices, and Said James promised an Amendment and that if there were any Deficiency there was time to amend it.

[*Evidence*] Charles Levallee Attested, declares that he saw the Plaintiff hooping and Setting or locking on of hoops on a New Cedar Buckitt and at another time asking him the Plaintiff what he had been doing, he replyed he had been shaving hoops all day for Buckitts. The Jury find for the Plaintiff Twenty pounds damage and Costs of Suit.

[*Tryall February 21st*] John Robards Plaintiff appears John Tatham Defendant by his Attorney Thomas Clark appears The Declaration read. The Defendants Plea is he does not owe the money declared for to the Plaintiff.

The Jury Attested in this Tryall is the same as above only Daniel Wills instead of John Meredith. The Declaration again read.

The Plaintiff produceth his Accompt and is sworn to it.

[*Evidence*] Thomas Curtis Sworn saith that about Fourteen months ago the Defendant John Tatham, carried his Son John down to Philadelphia and there meeting together in Company with Israel Taylor, was saying that his Sons Arm was broken and was not well Sett, and would have had them (the Deponent and said Taylor) to have broken the said Childs Arm again and to have Sett it anew that it might be Strait it being somewhat crooked before, but they refused it, But sometime after the Child happening to break his Arm again, this Deponent then Sett it and cured it.

[*Evidence*] Thomas Clark sworn sayes that last Wednesday or this day Week he was at Coll.[53a] Markhams, and he heard said Markham say that the things or Medicines that the Plaintiff (as by his Accompt or bill delivered to the Defendant and shewed to said Markham) used about the Fracture of the Childs Arm was not proper to be used. These Evidences of the Defendants was brought in Order to prove the little Skill the Plaintiff had in Chyrurgery.

[*Evidence*] Abraham Bickley Attested said that when his wife was very ill he addressed himself to the Doctor (the Plaintiff) And when Griffith Owen and John Rodman two Phisitians was told by this deponent what the Plaintiff had administred they both approved thereof.

[*Evidence*] Thomas Gardiner Attested says as to a Bone Setter he can

[53a] "Coll¹" in MS.

say little concerning the Plaintiff having had no occasion, but as to a Physitian he can say much in his behalf.

[*Evidence*] Edward Hunloke Attested says that as to a Physitian he has experienced him (the Plaintiff) to be (to the best of this Deponents knowledge) a person well worthy and deserving his Esteem And further saith, that before said John Tathams Arm was broke the Second time it was (as this Deponent believes) in a very likely way to be well (if it were not then cured) he said Child being at play among the boyes.

[*Evidence*] Samuel Furnis his Paper Evidence read and upon file.

[*Evidence*] Nathaniel Dugles attested sayes that haveing his Shoulder out of Joint and ill of it asking the Plaintiff whether it was right Sett, The Plaintiff said he believed it was and gave him a Strengthening Plaister which did him Good.

[*Evidence*] John Hilliard Attested Say's that this last Fall his Child fell off a horse and broke her Arm, and brought to the Plaintiff and he sett it well and Strait and cured it.

The Jury find for the Plaintiff, for Three pounds two Shillings debt and Costs of Suit, And upon the Plaintiff Moving for Judgment on said Verdict: Judgment was awarded accordingly.

John Pain and Uxor Plaintiffs   George Deacon and Daniel Leeds Defendants   withdrawn and half fees paid.

Alexander Steward Plaintiff   Mary Grant Defendant   continued.

The Court dissolv'd.

[**174 1700**] [*Court of Sessions and Pleas held May 8 1700*] Court of Quarter Sessions May 8th 1700. Justices on the Bench   William Biddle, John Wills, Joshua Newbould, Peter Frettwell, John Adams, Thomas Lambert   Esqrs. Thomas Gardiner Kings Attorney   Joseph Cross Sheriff   Edward Hunloke Clerk.

Grand jury   William Wood Foreman, Harmannus King, John Cheshire, John Hutcheson, Joshua Wright, John Lambert, John Abbot, Thomas Curtis, Thomas Scattergood, George Parker, Joseph Steward, Abraham Brown, Benjamin Field   Attested.

Richard Allison Attested Constable for the Townshipp of Mansfield instead of Edward Andrews.

William Pain John Poynsett attested to give their Evidence to the Grand Jury and also Charles Levally and Martha Dummer Attested on same Accompt.

[*Order about the highway by Wrights Plantation*] According to an Order from the Court of Quarter Sessions held at Burlington the 20th day of February 1699 for the Laying out of an high way from Yorkshire bridge to William Fishers Plantation for the preventing of the hollow place a little on this side of Thomas Wrights Plantation, We whose names are here subscribed being the Jury appointed for the laying out of the same, have done it according to the best of our Judgments The said Road begins at the riseing of Sand Hill and so thence as marked to the Run in Springfield Road thence along said Road neer about ¼ of a mile and thence as marked to Henry Scotts field, thence through said Field to the Creek commonly called Mill Creek in said Scotts Land as may appear by Stakes and markt Trees. Wittnesse our hands this 13th day of First Month Anno Domini $1\frac{699}{700}$ Thomas Scattergood, George ⊃ Willis his mark Isaac Decow Joseph Smith Isaac Marriott, Henry P Burcham his mark, Robert Wheeler John Ogborn Junr. Bernard Lane, James Wills George Parker, Jonathan W West his mark.

Return of the alteration of the Road of Springfield and Northampton Townshipps,—Read, and order'd to be recorded—as follows [*By road by John Langstaffs*] March 26th 1700. These may Certifie the Court That We whose names are here Subscribed, by virtue of a Warrant to us directed by Peter Frettwell and Joshua Newbould Justices of the Peace have to the best of our Understanding Survey'd and Laid out the best and most commodious and convenient By-road for accomodateing, the back Inhabitants to the least prejudice of the Neighbourhood, Beginning at the Towns bounds by John Langstaff and so along the Old path untill a come to the Line between John Langstaff and Alexander Stewards and so along the same Line, and from thence Straight to the path by William Ogbourn and so along the Path till a come to the Said Ogborns corner tree by the Creek so over the Creek into the old Path, so along the same path by Samuel Barkers house leading into the Kings road,—Thomas Stokes, George Elkington John H Hilliard his mark Thomas T Ridgway his mark, Samuel Coate, John ⊢ Scholey his mark John ID Dixson his mark William Dean John Crosby.

Court adjourn'd for two houres.

[*Presentment John Lawdell*] The Grand Jury came into Court and upon Indictment against John Lawdell (which is upon File in the Provincial Clerks Office) they found the Bill.

[*Presentment*] The 8 day of 3 month 1700 Whereas Complaint has been made that Mattacopeny bridge is not passable, We of the Grand jury do find cause to present it Signed by me William Wood Foreman.

The 8th 3 mo. 1700 We the Grand jury for the Body of this County have considered the occasion that this County has of Money but the methods of raiseing of it We are not satisfied with Therefore considering the Assembly is so near Sitting We think fitt to leave it to their Consideration to take such Methods as they shall think fit, and in order thereto We have drawn up a few Lines by way of Petition to offer to their Consideration Signed by me William Wood foreman.

Court adjourn'd till to Morrow Morning.
May 9th Court opened.

[*Petition*] A Petition exhibited by Nathaniell Cripps and Bernard Lane, Suspended till next Court.

John Ogborn craved of the Court to have an Execution upon a Judgment formerly obtained against John Hollinshead Senior. Ordered and advised by the Court that said Ogborn would once more offer a referrence to William and John Hollinshead Executors of their said Father John between this and next Court.

[*Pleas*] The Court of Pleas May 8th 1700. The same Justices on the Bench as Sate in the Court of Quarter Sessions as above.

[*Action*] Alexander Steward Plaintiff appears Mary Grant Defendant appears The Declaration read and the plea (both on File) read and put the issue to a Jury. The Traverse Jury Peter White, Samuel Taylor, Robert Chapman, John Watson, William Spencer, William Parker, Daniel Smith, Bernard Lane, Robert Wheeler, Henry Beck, Andrew Heath, Isaac Gibbs Attested. The Declaration again read.

[*Evidence*] Daniel Leeds being called to his Attestation refused that, and was willing and desired to have the Oath administered to him according to the Law of England which was done accordingly by order of Joshua Newbould to this purpose viz As soon as Mary Grant the Defendant, came to the said Plaintiffs house the Constable John Snape came to him (said Plaintiff) and told him the Neighbours were not Satisfied about the womans being there, which might prove a Charge to the Town (She being with Child) Upon which the Plaintiff went to this Deponent Daniel Leeds (he being then a Justice) and told him that Mary Grant (the Defendant) was an Industrious Woman, and was Spinning for his Wife and Should be no charge to the Town, while at his house.

[*Evidence*] William Budd Attested sayes, his Wife being at the Defendants Labour and there being nothing at all to drink, She sent home to fetch something to drink and comfort the Woman. The Plaintiff and Defendants Accompt read.

[*Verdict*] The Jury find for the Plaintiff One Shilling damage and Costs of Sute and the Court give judgment accordingly.

[*Action*] William Dean Plaintiff appears John Cluft defendant appears The Defendant acknowledges Judgment for Four pounds Sixteen Shillings and Costs Upon request of the Defendant The Court Order a respite of Execution till first of June.

[*Action*] Henry Jacobs Plaintiff appears John Cook Defendant appears The Action calld, the Declaration read, The Declaration by the Court is quasht by reason the words in the said Declaration are not Actionable, and advise both Plaintiff and Defendant to try their Title by Consent before next Court.

[*Action*] Martin Harding Plaintiff Appears Joshua Ely and Daniel Price Defendants Joshua Ely appears The Declaration read The Court give a Barr to the Action because Martin Harding sues When Mark Harding was pretended to be beaten. The Plaintiff nonsuited.

The Court adjourn, till next Court in August.

[*175 1700* August Court] [*Court of Sessions and Pleas August 8th 1700.*] Court of Sessions. August 8, 9, and 10 dayes. Thomas Gardiner Kings Attorney Christopher Wetherill Sheriffe. Justices present on the Bench Mahlon Stacy, Francis Davenport, William Biddle, John Adams, Richard Ridgway, Joshua Ely, Joshua Newbould, Robert Wheeler.

Grand jury Thomas Eves, John Day, Thomas Gilberthorp, Ralph Hunt, John Warren, John Haines, Francis Austin, Restore Lippincut, Anthony Elton, Thomas French, Jarvis Farrow, George Smith, Benjamin Field, Matthew Champion, Joshua Humphries Attested and their Charge given them.

The Recorder informing the Court, That the book of the Records of the Deeds of the Land in this County is unbound and comeing to pieces and they viewing the same [*Order'd*] That Matthew Watson forthwith bind the same, and shall be paid for it out of the next County Tax.

[*Ordered*] Also by the Court that two books be bought (and paid for by the County Treasurer Forthwith) one for the recording of Wills and Letters of Administration etc.—The other for the Grand jury for to keep their Minutes.

The Grand jury came into Court and delivered several papers, vizt. [*Treasurer Accompted with the Grand jury*] Burlington the 8th of 6th Month 1700. This day the Treasurer brought in his Accompts to the Grand jury, and they are approved on and We find that he has paid £1 3s. 11d. more than he has in his hands of the Countyes money Signed in behalf of the Grand-jury Thomas Eves Foreman.

Another Paper concerning sundry persons not paying in their last County tax to the Collector, and that the Collectors of some Townshipps have not paid what they received to the Treasurer. They desire the Court to take some Care therein, the County being dissatisfied about it.

[*Presentments*] Two Presentments, viz, in one William Wardhill of Hopewell is presented as a person Guilty of committing Fornication with her that is his now wife before Marriage, and the other John Robards of Burlington is presented on the same Accompt.

Court Adjourned till to morrow Morning.

August 9th Court open'd. The Grandjury being informed by the Bench of the necessity of raiseing a County Tax for the defraying of the County debts do bring in a Paper as follows (vizt)

[*County Tax*] Burlington County the 9th of August 1700 We of the Grandjury for the body of this County have considered and examined the

Estate of this County and find that the County is greatly in debt We likewise find upon Examination, that there is several that hath not paid their last County Tax to the great dissatisfaction of several in the said County Therefore We do agree that the old Arrears shall be paid at or before the twenty third day of November next Likewise We do agree that there shall be a Tax raised in the said County in manner following that is to say. Upon every Acre of Land cleered fenced and improved, one half penny per Acre, and upon every hundred Acres of Land unimproved 4d. per hundred And upon every Neat beast of one year old and upwards 4d. per head and upon every horse or Mare of one year old and upward 8d. per head; And for every Sheep three farthings per head, And for every hogg or swine that is sold liveing or dead 4d. per head, and for every Negro of 15 years of age and Upwards, the Master or Owners thereof shall pay 2s. 6d. per head And all persons resideing in Townes or Elsewhere whose Estates are not so visible, as those that consist of Land and Stock, shall pay 2d. for every pound their Estates shall be appraized worth, And all persons who are Freemen and not indented Servants of 20 years of age and upwards within this County who shall not appear Taxable by estate or Stock to the value of three Shillings Shall notwithstanding pay the Summe of 3s. to this said tax, This said Tax shall be paid into the hands of Thomas Gardiner whom We have chosen Treasurer for the same at or before the 23th day of November next ensueing the date hereof, The Collectors for gathering the said Tax and paying to said Treasurers hands shall have their usual price 1s. per pound, And the Treasurer for receiveing and paying the same, to the Countyes use shall have 6d. per l. Signed in behalf of the Grand jury per Thomas Eves foreman. Two of the Grandjury viz Anthony Elton and Ralph Hunt Declare in open Court their dissent to said Tax. The Bench concurr with the Grand jury in the above Tax.

[*Presentment*] The Grand jury present John Neve for liveing with and keeping Company with Mary Fryley Wife of William Fryley contrary to Law.

Order'd That the presentments brought in by the Grand jury be put in Prosecution next Court.

Ordered that Michael Newbould Robert Pierson and Isaac Gibbs be and are fined 10s. a piece for their nonappearance upon the Petty Jury and that a Writt be Issued out to levy distress. The Court adjourn to to morrow morning 8 a clock.

August 10th Order'd That at the request of Ralph Hunt, he have and is Licensed to keep an Ordinary giveing bond etc. which was done.

[*Sessions Ended*] The Court of Sessions dissolved.

[*Court of Pleas*] Court of Pleas August the 8 and 9 dayes.

Justices present on the Bench the same as in the Court of Sessions (excepting Francis Davenport). Petty Jury call'd and appear'd Isaac Horner, James Price, John Murfin, John Stockdon, William Hunt, Jonathan Eldridge, James Crofts Senr., Samuel Kemble, Nathaniell Pain, John Ogborn Senr., Henry Beck, Daniel Smith.

[*Steward against Roberts*] Joseph Steward Plaintiff call'd and appeared. Thomas Roberts Defendant call'd three times and doth not appear. It was by the Court enquired of the Sheriff whether he delivered the defendant a Summons, The Sheriff said he found no body at home but put the Summons in at the Keyhole of the door of his house, and was inform'd afterwards that his (the Defendants) wife said that she or her Children would burn it, Which by the Court was adjudg'd that the Summons was well serv'd. The Declaration read (and on file) The Plaintiff craving for Judgment by default.

[*Judgment*] Ordered by the Bench that Judgment for default be and is awarded for the Plaintiff And that a Writt of Enquiry be made and issued out for a Jury to Enquire of the damages by the Plaintiff Sustain'd, and that the said Writt be returnable the next Court.

[*Abraham Brown against West*] Abraham Brown Senr. Plaintiff William West Defendant both call'd and appear'd The Declaration read (and on file) The Defendant by Thomas Revell his Attorney in barr to the said Action sayes The Cow declared for was seized by the Sheriff of the County of Monmouth in East Jersey—Attachment of the Sheriff of Monmouth County in East Jersey read. The Sheriffs Attestation read, The opinion of the Court is They have nothing to do with this Cause in this Court, the Cow sued for here, being under Attachment in another Province and therefore the

[*Judgment*] of the Court is, that being no Cause of Action the Action is thrown out.

[*Braithwait against York*] Manning Braithwait Plaintiff called and Thomas Revell by Warrant of Attorney appear'd for him. Thomas York Defendant call'd and appeared. And they agreed.

[176 1700 August Court, and adjournment to September 19th 1700]

Daniel England by Thomas Clark his Attorney, came and inform'd the Court, That he had a Scire facias concerning the Estate of John Dewsbury, and craved that accordingly the person or persons concern'd might appear and show cause why Execution should not be had against said Estate, which said Scire facias was under the Governours hand. The Clerk informs the Court that he had lately received a Letter from the Governour, and which he shewed them, wherein the Governour sayes that there was so many things contain'd in the said Writt of Scire Facias that he was a Stranger to, and was so little a time before the Court that he could not have that advice that he could depend upon and therefore thought it not safe to proceed in it that Court, and order'd the Clerk to advise the Justices, and Daniel

England thereof before the Court, which was done. Court adjourn'd till to morrow post Meridiem.

[*Adjourn'd*] August 9th. Open'd   Judgment of the Court That it be Suspended, till the 19th of September next: And the Court demanding the Paper or Writt of Scire facias Signed by the Governour and by said Thomas Clark read in Court, The said Clark refused to deliver it till the Court possitively ordered him to deliver it, and then he delivered it to his Client, and he to the Clerk of the Court to remain upon file.

The Court adjourn'd till the 19th of September next.

[*Court of Pleas by Adjournment September 19th 1700*] Court of Pleas held by adjournment September 19th 1700. Justices on the Bench   Mahlon Stacy, Francis Davenport, William Biddle, John Adams. Thomas Gardiner Kings Attorney   Christopher Wetherill Sheriffe.

[*Verdict of the Jury of Enquiry in the Cause of Steward Plaintiff   Roberts Defendant*] The Jury ordered by the last Court to Enquire what damages Joseph Steward Plaintiff sustained by Thomas Roberts Defendant did give their Verdict Seal'd to the Sheriff who produced the same in Court which is in these words following (vizt) The 7th of the 7th month 1700. We of the Jury of Enquiry do all agree in our Verdict, And upon Serious and diligent Enquiry do award the Said Steward for damages Thirty pounds —Signed by Benjamin Wheat   John Bunting   John Tantum, John Abbot Henry Barr, Thomas Folkes, William Foster   James Shinn, Samuell Taylor, Thomas Bryan   John Tonkin, Isaac Horner.

[*Judgment*] The Court award Judgment according to the Verdict and upon the Plaintiffs motion Order Execution to be forthwith granted.

[*Action*] Robert Stacy   Richard Whitfield, Thomas Fairman and John Hart Executors of Anna Salter Widdow deceased Plaintiffs   Jone Dewberry Executor of her husband John Dewsberry deceased Defendant   The Plaintiffs call'd. Daniel England produces a Letter of Attorney under their hands and Seals to appear for them. The Defendant call'd appears not, The Sheriff call'd to make return of the Writt of Summons which he delivers in his return was in these words, viz The Defendant is not to be found in my Baylywick   Christopher Wetherill Sheriff.

[*Petition*] Peter Resnier exhibited a Petition to the Court which was read intimateing that though he might not be imediately concern'd in this present Action, Yet it being about a Title of Land which Daniel England had formerly sold him, and for prevention of Fraud and Law Suits craves that his Attorney might speak to the action brought against the Defendant, and to unfold the undue practices therein used.

[*Answer*] The Court are of the Opinion that no Person being impowered by the Defendant to appear for her, cannot be admitted, only Thomas Clark, Resniers Attorney desireing leave to speak a few words, and prayed that Daniel Englands Letter of Attorney might be proved in Court, The Evidence to the same being call'd and appearing in Court, Mahlon Stacy one of the Justices on the Bench saying he knew Robert Stacy's hand, and looking upon the Letter of Attorney Affirm'd that his name thereto Sett was his Writing, and the Court approved thereof. The declaration Read. The Court was informed that the Summons being upon an Action of Trespass upon the Case and the Plaintiffs declareing in an Action of Covenant the Action ought to abate. David Lloyd Attorney for Daniel England moves that, that being a Mistake it might be altered and amended according to the Declaration—which the Court order'd accordingly. The Letters Testamentary read. A Deed of Sale of Goods read. The Deed of Mortgage from John Dewsberry and Jone his wife to Anna Salter read. The Plaintiffs crave judgment against the Defendant by default.*

[*Order*] The Court order that the Jury Summon'd and then attending the Court, be Attested (on this Occasion) to Enquire what damages the Plaintiffs Sustained by the Defendants or her late husband takeing away the Goods Sold to Anna Salter—and the Jury being Attested (vizt) Abraham Bickley, John Hammell, John Brown, Thomas Stoakes, John Hudson, Benjamin Moor, Nathaniell Cripps, Henry Scott, Joseph Smith, Anthony Fryer, Richard Smith, Martin Scott were attested accordingly. Verdict of the Jury in these words We The Jury of Enquiry on the Action between the Executors of Anna Salter Plaintiff and Jone Dewberry Defendant do find damage for the Plaintiffs Fourty four pounds and costs of Suit. And Judgment being moved for, by the Plaintiffs Attorney

[*Judgment*] The Court give and award Judgment according to Verdict and that the Plaintiffs may have Execution [*Received Execution and Return in the November Court next.*] upon the Estate of John Dewsberry For the same. *The Evidence of Ann Potts taken before Justice Mott of Philadelphia was given to the Jury as also Benjamin Wheat and Ruth Bibb attested in Court to give the Jury of Enquiry what Evidence they could about Jone Dewsberry's takeing away the Plaintiffs Goods etc.

Edward Hunloke Plaintiff against the Estate of Ebinezar and John Langford, The Plaintiff call'd appears The Attachment (by the Government) granted against the said Estate was read, and the Sheriffs Return of the same, read. Declaration read (as follows) viz **Province of West New Jersey, County of Burlington** per Edward Hunloke of the same County Merchant **P**laintiff against the Estate of Ebinezar Langford, and John Langford late of the said County of Burlington Merchants **deceased** in an Action of the case. A dwelling house and One thousand Acres of Land and Appurtenances commonly called or known by the name of Langford Plantation lying on Northampton River in the County aforesaid and late belonging to the said Ebinezar and John Langford was attached to answer the Suit and Complaint of the said Edward Hunloke the Plaintiff in a Plea,

That Whereas the Said Ebinezar and John Langford from and since the Tenth day of November, in the year of our Lord One thousand Six hundred Eighty and Six, And in the second year of the Reigne of James the Second King of England etc. The Said Ebinezar and John Langford have had and received from the Plaintiff in money, merchandize and other effects to the value of Two Hundred Sixty Seven pounds fifteen Shillings and nine pence as by the Plaintiffs Accompt ready to be produced in Court more fully may appear Which they the said Ebinezar and John Langford did promise and assume upon themselves to pay and Satisfie the said Plaintiff for, Together with the Intrest thereof, Yet Nevertheless The said Ebinezar and John Langford nor either of them nor any other person for or on their or either of their behalfs, The said Sume of Two hundred Sixty Seven pounds Fifteen Shillings and nine pence with the Interest thereof to the Plaintiff hath not paid and rendered but the same to render have neglected Whereupon the Said Plaintiff brings his Suit and Craves Judgment etc.

[177 1700 September Court by Adjournment—And November Court] The Plaintiffs Accompt of Debit and Credit produced in Court, and Article by Article read and by the Plaintiff Proved, and also the Assumptions of the said Ebinezar and John Langford under their hands produced and proved.

[*Judgment*] The Court after mature deliberation, consideration and Examination of the several Articles of the Said Plaintiffs Accompt and approving the same as also the Assumptions above mentioned. The Court award Judgment against the said Ebinezar and John Langfords Lands and Tenements (there being no other Effects of theirs in the Said Province) as by the high Sheriff was attached in this Suit for payment of Two hundred Sixty Seven pounds Fifteen Shillings and nine pence debt, and twenty Seven Shillings and three pence Costs of this Suit. And the Magistrates in Court Signe an Execution against the said Estate which is as follows vizt

[*Coppy of the Execution see for the Return hereof in the next Court of Pleas (Seal) (Seal) (Seal)*] County of Burlington in the Province of West New Jersey— To the Sheriff of the said County or his Deputy Greeting Whereas Edward Hunloke of Burlington in the County aforesaid Merchant by a Writt of Attachment served on the Land and Plantation late belonging to Ebinezar and John Langford Merchants deceased Lyeing on Northampton River in the said County at the Court of Pleas held at Burlington by Adjournment the 19th day of September instant, prosecuted his Action against the Estate of the said Ebinezar and John Langford for the Summe of Two hundred Sixty and Seven pounds Fifteen Shillings and nine Pence current money of the Said Province which said Sume haveing appeared in Court and by Law to be due to the said Plaintiff by his Accompt produced and proved Whereupon the Said Edward Hunloke obtain'd at the Court aforesaid Judgment for the Said Summe of Two hundred Sixty Seven pounds Fifteen Shillings and nine pence debt and Cost of Suit. These are therefore in his Majesties name to Will and require you forthwith in Execution the Goods Chattells Lands and Tenements which now or late did belong to and are the proper Estate of the Said Ebinezar and John Langford or either of them where you can find the same within your Jurisdiction, to take and Seize, and the same to appraise Sell grant and convey according to the Law of the said Province for the discharge and satisfying of the said Edward Hunloke the Plaintiff his said debt of Two hundred Sixty Seven pounds Fifteen Shillings and Nine pence current money of said Province debt and twenty Seven Shillings and three pence costs of Suit Returning the overplus (if any be) to the Executors or Administrators of the said Ebinezar and John Langford when demanded And make return of this Execution and of your doings herein at the next Court of Pleas to be held at Burlington aforesaid for the Jurisdiction thereof   Hereof faile not as you will answer the contrary And for your so doing this Shall be to you a Sufficient Warrant Given under our hands and Seals this 20th day of September Anno Domini 1700 being R R^s Gulielmi Terti Angliae etc. Duodecimo.

Mahlon Stacy, William Biddle, John Adams   Justices.

Action   Elizabeth Tatham Executrix to John Tatham Esqr. deceased Plaintiff   Jeremiah Basse Esqr. Defendant   both Plaintiff and Defendant being called 3 times and none appearing   The Court Ordered the said Action to be thrown out.

Action   Jonathan Jennings Plaintiff   Richard Cantrill Defendant both Plaintiff and Defendant call'd three times but neither appear'd. Court order that in both the above Actions, The Plaintiffs viz Elizabeth Tatham and Jonathan Jenings pay halfe fees.

Court of Sessions and Pleas November 4th and 5th 1700. Court of Sessions opened. November 4th (the 3d day the time for the Court appointed being of a Sunday) Anno Domini 1700. Present. The Honourable Coll. Andrew Hamilton Governour. Justices   Mahlon Stacy, Francis Davenport, William Biddle, John Adams, Samuel Furnis Burgess, John Wills came the 5th day. Thomas Gardiner Kings Attorney   Christopher Wetherill Sheriff. Grand-Jury   John Shin Senior, Robert Wilson, Samuell Bunting, Thomas Coleman, Robert Pierson, Thomas Raper, John Scott, John Snape, William Black, John Sharp, William Evans, George Beard, Joseph Parker, Daniel Wills   Attested and their Charge given them by the Governour.

John Hancock on behalf of his Mother the Widdow Hancock desires she may be Licenced to keep a Victualling house or Ordinary. Which the Court grants, She observeing the Methods the Law requires.

William Cooper on behalfe of Hanna Wolston Widdow brought into Court a Boy called Robert Gannington to be bound to her for Seven years from the time of his Arrival   The boy declaring his willingness, The Court order him to be bound for the said time.

[*Burdens Presentment*] A Bill or Indictment being delivered to the Grand jury from the Kings Attorney against Benjamin Burden, the Grand jury come into Court, and deliver said Bill, with these words written thereon, We the Grand jury do find this a truebill—John Shin foreman.

The Court adjourn'd till Afternoon. and then again Opened.

Benjamin Burden Sett to the Barr—The Bill or Indictment read in these words (vizt) [*Indictment*] We the Jurors for our Sovereign Lord the King, and for the body of this County, do present That whereas Benjamin Borden of Freehold in the Province of East Jersey, The Eleventh or twelfth day of October 1700 at this Town of Burlington, of Set purpose and deliberately and with malicious intent, did Sett forth amongst other things, this false Seditious and Scandalous matter to defamation of our Governour Coll. Andrew Hamilton (that he the said Governour was run away) with an evil intent to disturb the Peace of this Province, and contrary to divers Statutes made and provided and to the evil Example of all others in the like cause offending etc.

To which Indictment the Prisoner pleaded Not Guilty—The Court demanding of him, Whether he would referr himself to the Bench or put himself upon his Tryall by Jury—The Prisoner answered he would put himself upon Tryal by the Country.

The Petty Jury Attested were—Matthew Watson, John Lambert, John Cheshire, Thomas Ridgway, John Shin junr., John Hilliard, George Elkington, Samuell Lippincutt, John Powel, Thomas Bishop, Thomas Smith, Matthew Foresith. [*a Paper Evidence*] The Deposition of George Willis   George Willis being Solemnly Attested saith That Benjamin Borden comeing into his house the last night or Evening, And some Enquiry being made of what News from East Jersey (he comeing from thence) the said Benjamin Burden replyed and reported, That the Governour was ran away, and further saith not, Attested the 12th day of October 1700 before me—Samuell Furnis Burgess.

[178 1700 **November Court**] [*Evidence*] George Willis in open Court being Attested saith, that Benjamin Burden comeing into his house (Said Burden Comeing then from East Jersey, was asked what news from thence, he answered that the disturbances there were not yet quieted And further the said Burden said—Suppose the Governour is run away, and further saith not.

[*The Prisoners Plea*] The Court demanding of the Prisoner what he had to say for himself The Prisoner denyes that ever he spoke any such like words. The Court adjourn'd to Henry Grubbs—and there opened the Court of Pleas   The Court of Sessions adjourn'd to to morrow morning 8 a Clock.

November 5th, The Court of Sessions opened.

[*the verdict*] The Jury bring in their Verdict in these words (vizt) We the Jury are all agreed that the Prisoner (according to the Evidence) is guilty of saying (Suppose the Governour is run away). The Court asking the Prisoner, whether he had anything to offer in Arrest of Judgment or otherwise and haveing nothing material to move to the Court

[*Judgment*] Judgment of the Court is, The he (the Prisoner) be and is fined One hundred pounds and Costs of Suit, remanding into the Sheriffs Custody till paid etc.

Peter Fretwell brought into Court a Letter of Guardianshipp Impowering to call all Persons to an Accompt etc. That have any of the Estate of Joshua Tomkins Orphan. The Letter of Administration to John Hollinshead on the Estate of Elizabeth Tomkins alias Hambley (mother of the said Joshua) read. A Letter of Guardianshipp granted by Governour Markham in Pennsilvania to John Hollinshead for the said Joshua read. The Inventory of the said Elizabeth Hambley deceased produced by John Hollinshead Junior, read, as also the Vandue Paper or Accompt of her Goods as Sold at the vandue read, which amount to £26 12s. 1d. more than the Goods were appraysed at by the said Inventory. John Hollinshead Accompt of Disbursements about the said Estate and upon said Orphan read, Amount to £70 3s. 10d. there being some Articles in Said Accompt of Disbursements that the Magistrates could not find reasonable to allow, Upon the whole the Magistrates allow said Hollinshead Accompt to be £64 3s. 10d. And to deduct out of that, the said £26 2s. 1d. to the Orphan, which was made of the Goods more then appraysed at in the Inventory And so the Accompt is to be Stated, And Whereas Peter Frettwell desired that the Interest of the Orphans money might be demanded and had of William and John Hollinshead Executors to their father, the aforesaid John Hollinshead deceased The Court Stand to the above Accompt as Stated, Then said Frettwell demanded the money, They craved time, the money being out of their hands, which upon giveing Bond for the Money and the Interest from this time to come, is by the Court allowed of only Peter Frettwell is to have five pounds part thereof in a Week or two William and John Hollinshead paid for the charge of the Court in this Affair Six Shillings, which Said Frettwell is to allow to them in part of the money by them to be paid.

[*Packers*] Ordered By the Court That Joseph White and Thomas Wetherill Coopers be Packers for this County of Burlington till next Assembly or further Order, which they accepting off were Attested in open Court accordingly.

John Wills appeared in open Court and declared he was well Satisfied with the draught of his Fathers Will brought in by Thomas Gardiner being not fully Executed he (James Wills the father) being taken Senceless before it was Executed, And also said John Wills declared that he would stand and abide by the same, And was also willing that Thomas Gardiner and

Peter Frettwell should execute (as Executors or Administrators) the said Instrument it being as his fathers Testatio Mentis.

Nicholas Brown being brought into Court by the Sheriff upon Suspition that he gave his Assistance and was Confederate in the Escape of his Prisoner Benjamin Borden, who escaped from the Sheriff and run away upon said Browns horse.

[*Brown's Recognizance*]   The Court order Said Brown be bound over to the next Court and find Security in mean time for his good Behaviour Whereupon Nicholas Brown Recognizes himself to be indebted to our Sovereign Lord the King in the Summe of Four hundred pounds And John Hollinshead and Nathaniel Cripps Recognize themselves to be indebted Joyntly and Severally in Two hundred pounds, To be Levied on their Goods and Chattells Lands and Tenements Conditionally That the said Nicholas Brown shall be and appear personally at the next Court of Quarter Session to be held at Burlington the 20th day of February next And in the mean time to be of Good behaviour to all his Majesties Liege People, And that he shall abide the order and determination of the said Court. This was acknowledged by the said Nicholas Brown John Hollinshead and Nathaniel Cripps before the Magistrates in open Court.

This Court adjourn'd till the 12th of this Instant for granting out Warrants to the Several Townshipps about the Provincial County Taxes.

[*Court of Pleas*] Court of Pleas opened November 4th 1700. Justices on the Bench   Mahlon Stacy, William Biddle, John Adams, John Wills came on the 5th day.

Isaac Decow Plaintiff call'd and appeared. The Declaration read and bill under the Defendants hand read and prov'd. Samuel Leonard Defendant call'd 3 times appeared not, But sent to the Clerk a Paper which he would have put in as his Plea, which was read and shown to the Court in these words as follows

[*Leonards Plea*]   Samuell Leonard Isaac Decow contra   And the said Leonard in his own Person comes and defends the force and Injury and prays Oyer of the Writeing Obligatory and a day assigned to plead for that he saith he cannot plead untill he hath seen the bond, And of this, he prayes the Judgment of the Court. The Court after Consideration of the said Plea, (the defendant not appearing as he set forth therein) disallow of the Plea, And the Plaintiff craving Judgment on default and haveing proved his bill as abovesaid do give Judgment and Order the Plaintiff Seven pounds due by his Said bill and costs of Suit. The Plaintiff moving for Execution on said Judgment The Court order it to be forthwith drawn and executed.

Benjamin and Edward Kemble Plaintiffs   Samuell Kemble Defendant in an Action of Debt upon two Bonds   Plaintiffs and Defendant call'd and all appear. The Declaration read, the Bond of Seventy Pounds read, The Defendant acknowledges Judgment. The Plaintiffs declareing they were willing to remitt the Penalty and be content with the Principal being Thirty five pounds and the Interest thereof with Costs of Suit—Whereupon

[*Judgment*] The Court grant Judgment for the same Accordingly—And the other bond of Thirteen pounds being also read—The Defendant Acknowledges Judgment—And the Plaintiffs being likewise willing to do as in the other bond The Court grant Judgment upon this bond for Six pounds ten Shillings with Interest and Costs of Suit. The Plaintiff craving for Execution—The Court order Execution to be issued out and Levied forthwith.

Edward Kemble Plaintiff Samuel Kemble Defendant in an Action of Debt upon Bond. The Plaintiff and Defendant call'd both appear. The Declaration read, The Obligation read which is for Fourscore pounds. The Defendant acknowledges Judgment thereupon. The Plaintiff declareing notwithstanding his Obligation he is willing to accept of the Principal being Forty pounds with the Interest and Costs of Suit [*Judgment*] The Court award Judgment for the Plaintiff for Forty pounds with Interest and costs. And upon the Plaintiff moveing for Execution the Court order it accordingly.

[179 1700 **November Court of Pleas. February Court**] [*Action*] Samuel Jenings Plaintiff Griffith Morgan Defendant in an Action of Detinue for keeping a Bond from the Plaintiff in the Defendants Custody. The Declaration read. The Defendants Plea viz he sayes he never had the Bond in his Custody to his knowledge but is willing that he and his wife should Legally discharge him Said Plaintiff.

[*Judgment*] The Court award that the Plaintiff is discharged of that Bond (haveing proved the payment thereof in Court) And that the Defendant deliver it up to the Plaintiff, or give and execute a Legal discharge therefrom under the hand and Seal of him (the said Defendant) and his wife within a Months time—and the Defendants to pay the cost of this Suit.

[*Action*] Joseph Pidgeon Plaintiff Mons Cock Defendant in an Action of Debt upon Bond The Plaintiff call'd and appear'd. The defendant call'd 3 times but did not appear—but his wife appear'd. The Declaration read, The Obligation being for Twenty pounds read. The Plaintiff desireing no more than the Principal being Ten pounds with the Interest and Costs, and being craved upon default.

[*Judgment*] The Court award Judgment by default, for the Summe, Interest and Costs as above, the Bond was delivered the Plaintiff by order of Court.

[*Action*] Edward Smout Plaintiff Call'd appeares by Mr. Thomas Revell his Attorney John Cropp Defendant call'd 3 times does not appear. The Plaintiff desires the Court to ask the Sheriff, for the Return of his Warrant of Attachment delivered to him by Mr. Revell. The Sheriff makes return, That he could not find (nor was shown) any effects of the Said Cropp the Defendant in his Baylywick.

[*Action*] Christopher Snoden Plaintiff Charles Sheepey Defendant call'd and both appear'd. The Declaration read The Defendants Attorney craving a former Declaration it being not to be found—Therefore the Action is continued till next Court.

[*John Ogborn*] John Ogborn craves an Execution against John Hollinshead Estate, upon a Judgment formerly obtained. [*Order*] The Court wave doing anything in said request of Said Ogborn, because the Methods that the Law prescribed he said Ogborn hath not performed in respect to said former Judgment.

[*The Return of the Sheriffs Execution about Langfords Land, etc.*] Christopher Wetherill Sheriff made Return of the Execution Edward Hunloke obtained against the Estate of Ebinezar and John Langford in Manner Following (vizt)—October 1st 1700 I have Levyed the within Execution upon the house and Five hundred Acres of Land late belonging to John Langford, on Rancocus Creek alias Northampton River, And other five hundred acres of Land adjoyning to the aforesaid Plantation which did lately belong to the within mentioned Ebinezar Langford per me— Christopher Wetherill Sheriffe—And further Endorsed—We whose names are underwritten, by order of the Sheriffe have appraised the above mentioned house, and Said One thousand Acres of Land at Two hundred Forty and Seven pounds Wittnesse our hands—John ⊢ Mus his mark George ⋀ Gleave his mark John Hollinshead—All which Writeings viz the Execution Return and Appraysement being viewed considered and approved off in Court The Sheriff by advice and Order of the Court, (they haveing also viewed and approved of the Deed) did seal and Execute in Court a deed of Said Land and Plantation, for the consideration of Two hundred Forty Seven pounds part of Said Hunlokes debt, And the Justices sett their hands thereto as Wittnesses.

[*The Execution and Return thereof, about the Executors of Anna Salter Estate of Dewsburys*] County of Burlington to wit to the Sheriff of the Said County or his Deputy Greeting—Whereas Robert Stacy Thomas Fairman, Richard Whitfield and John Hart Executors of the Testament of Anna Salter Widdow deceased brought and prosecuted their Action against Joan Dewsbury Executrix of John Dewsbury deceased at the Court of Pleas held at Burlington by adjournment the 19th of September instant, and obtained a Verdict by a Jury of Enquiry for Forty four pounds and Costs of Suit, and Judgment thereupon awarded accordingly—These are therefore in his Majesties name to will and require you forthwith in Execution, the Goods Chattells Lands and Estate of which now or late belonged to the said John Dewsberry deceased where you can find the same within your

Jurisdiction to take and Seize And the same to appraise and sell, for the discharge and Satisfieing of the Said Plaintiffs the Said Summe of Forty four pounds damages and Two pounds ten Shillings and Six pence costs of Suit returning the over plus (if any be) to the said Joan Dewsbury the Defendant And make return of this precept, and of your doings herein at the next Court of Pleas to be holden at Burlington aforesaid Hereof fail not as you will answer the contrary And for so doing this shall be your Warrant Given under our hands and Seals this 20th day of September Anno Domini 1700 Annoque RR Gulielmi Terty Anglia etc. Duodecimo.—Mahlon Stacy William Biddle John Adams Justices.

[*Sheriffs Return*]   September 24th 1700 Then I have served the within Execution upon the house and three Acres of Land belonging formerly to John Dewsbury in the Island of Burlington, Per me Christopher Wetherill Sheriff.

[*The Appraisors Return*] West New Jersey—Burlington the 24th September 1700. Whereas Daniel England as Attorney to the Executors of Anna Salter deceased obtain'd a judgment against the Estate of John Dewsbury deceased for Forty four pounds debt, and damages, with Two pounds ten Shillings and Six pence costs the 19th Instant And for the Appraiseing of said Estate We whose names are underwritten being appointed Appraysers by said Court of the said Estate We haveing been on the premisses and have carefully viewed the same doth Appraise the said Houseing with the three Acres of Land thereunto belonging all being and lyeing neer the West End of the Island of Burlington, to the Summe of Forty pounds current money of this Province In Wittnesse whereof We hath hereunto Sett our hands the day and year first above written—Isaac Marriott, Henry Grubb, Samuell Furnis James Wills.

[*Court of Sessions and Pleas February 20th 1700/1*] Court of Sessions opened February 20th 1700. Present   The Honourable Coll. Andrew Hamilton Governour   Justices Mahlon Stacy, Francis Davenport, William Biddle, John Adams, John Wills, Samuell Furnis Burgesse. Thomas Gardiner Kings Attorney   Christopher Wetherill Sheriffe. Grand-jury   Francis Collins, Edward Rockhill, John Hutchinson, John Brown, William Evans, Thomas Eves, John Day, John Scott, Joshua Humphreys, Seth Hill, John Woolman, Joshua Wright, Thomas Wilkinson, Matthew Champion   Attested And the Charge given them by the Governour after the several Constables were examined (viz)

The Governour and Court called the several Constables of the Severall Towns to enquire of them what they had done in pursuance of their Severall Warrants directed to them to Convene the Inhabitants of their Several Townshipps about chuseing their Assessors and Collectors about rayseing the Provincial and County Tax. To which the several Constables answered as follows [**180 1700 February Court of Sessions**] Theophilus Philips Constable of Maiden answered to the above Question that he summoned the Inhabitants who all appeared but two or three but chose no Assessors or Collectors. Stephen Willson Constable of Hopewell made answer that he Summoned the Inhabitants who mett at the place appointed but refused to chuse Assessors or Collectors, excepting Joshua Ely John Hutchinson Thomas Hough and himself (said Constable) who were willing to chuse. Caleb Wheatly Constable of Nottingham made answer that the Inhabitants in said Townshipp mett and chose William Emley and Samuel Overton Collectors. Duke Horseman Constable of Chesterfield answered that the Inhabitants in said Town mett and chose Assessors and Collectors Benjamin Field and Thomas Foulke junr. Richard Ellison Constable of Mansfield answered that the Town mett but they chose no Assessors or Collectors, the reason he gives is that the General party in the Town would chuse none. Springfield Constable call'd, but there was nothing done there, because there was no proper Constable in the Towne. John Woolston Constable of Northampton call'd did not appear, but Justice John Wills informs the Court that at their meeting (he being of that Town) they chose Assessors vizt the said John Wills and Anthony Elton and Collectors Joshua Humphreys and Daniel Wills. John Pain Constable of Wellingborough made answer that he called the Meeting they Mett but chose no Assessors or Collectors but he said Constable was willing to choose and pay And so were Thomas Eves John Scott, John Hudson Thomas Harding and Richard Bickham. John Cooperthwait Constable of Chester, made answer he call'd a Town Meeting they Mett but chose no Assessors or Collectors. John Boarton Constable of Eversham answered, he Summoned the Inhabitants they mett but then chose none but at another Meeting Soon after they chose William Hewlings Collector. Samuel Gibson and William Bustill Constables of Burlington replyed They call'd the Town Meeting who Mett and chose Assessors and Collectors.

Then the Governour gave the Grand jury their Charge and the Court adjourn'd till 2 a Clock P. M.

2 a Clock P. M. the Court Opened.

[*New Constables*] New Constables chosen for the several Townshipps as follows vizt Maidenhead Theophilus Philips serves again Att[ested]. Hopewell Jonathan Davis attested afterwards. Nottingham Caleb Wheatley serves again Attested. Chesterfield. Samuel Taylor Attested. Mansfield Joseph Pancoast Attested. Springfield Peter White afterwards Attested. Burlington Daniel Smith and Joseph White Attested. Northampton Daniel Wills Attested. Wellingborough Charles French Attested. Chester Mons Cock, not appearing, John Cooperthwait by order of Court stands till the other be Attested. Eversham Josiah Appleton not appearing, the old one Stands till the other be Attested.

The Grand Jury come into Court and Present

[*Presentments*] Anne Stevens for being privately delivered of a Manchild, which was dead—to be tryed at the Provincial Court.

Dorothy Roberts for bearing a Bastard Child.

[*Petition*] Henry Beck craves of the Court for their Order to lay out a Way from his Mill to the River. Ordered That Francis Davenport appoint the men to lay out the Way, and to make Return the next Court.

[*Recognizance*] Memorandum George Green of the County of Burlington in the Province of West Jersey doth Recognize himself in the Sume of Fifty pounds current money of said Province unto our Lord the King, and William Spencer of Same County doth also Recognize himselfe in the Summe of Fifty pounds of like current money to our said Lord the King To be levied upon their Goods and Chattells Lands and Tenements Upon Condition that the said Green do appear at the Quarter Sessions held the 8th day of May next at the Town of Burlington to answer the Complaint that shall be alledged against him And in the mean time to be of good Behaviour towards all his Majesties Liege People (especially to Hannah his Wife). It being read to them, they both acknowledged it in open Court.

[*Apprentice bound*] Thomas Fenton bound himself by Indenture for Six Years and a quarter of a Year to Thomas Raper in open Court, and the said Indentures wittnessed by the Justices, and the Court approved the same.

[*Apprentice bound*] Thomas Shinglefield, bound himself by Indenture (with the Approbation of the Court) to William Petty junr. for Seven Years from the fourth day of November Last and Wittnessed by the Justices.

[*Petition*] The Petition of Obadiah Hierton against John Ogborn, read the Court consider of it and [*Judgment*] Award Judgment for Nine Shillings and costs.

The Court adjourn till to morrow Morning 9 a Clock.

February 21th day The Court opened. [*Presentment*] The Grand jury Presented Nicholas Browne for assisting Benjamin Burden (being then a Prisoner in the Sheriffs Custody) to make his Escape.

[*Petition*] John Brown and Jacob Decow Petition the Court for a Private Road to the Mill, Whereupon the Court order [*Order*] That William Biddle appoint twelve men to view and lay out the most convenient Road to the Mill, and make report thereof at next Court for Approbation.

[*Recognizance*] Thomas Cleverley of the County of Burlington Yeoman doth Recognize himself to be held and firmly bound unto our Lord the King in the Summe of Forty pounds current money of this Province And Jonathan West doth also Recognize himself in the Summe of Forty pounds of like current money unto our said Lord the King To be levied upon their Goods and Chattells Lands and Tenements Upon Condition that the said Thomas Cleverley be and appear at the Provincial Court to be held the

Eleventh day of April next, Then and there to answer to what Shall be alledged against him. The Recognizance being read they both own'd it in open Court.

[*Nicholas Browns cause*] Nicholas Brown was called, appears according to his Recognizance taken last Court, And the Grand jury haveing this Court presented him, as above, The Court demanded of him Whether he would Submitt to the Court, or Traverse it—He referres him Self to the Bench and craves their favour.

The Court adjourn till to Morrow Morning.

February 22th day—Court opened. Nicholas Brown call'd appear'd— The Court haveing considered his Offence, They Award [*His Judgment*] That he the said Nicholas Shall pay the Cost and Charges of Benjamin Burdens Suit, And his own Cost last Court and this and then to be discharged.—Which the Said Brown did thankfully and imediately comply with.

Daniel Blewit and Henry Grubb being bound by Recognizance that the said Blewit should appear at this Court to answer such Complaint as should appear against him—The said Blewit and Grubb were call'd who both appeared—The Court Order That the said Recognizance be continued till next Court (if they are so willing) the which they did own and acknowledg to do in the open Court.

[181 **1700 February Court of Sessions.**—**Court of Pleas**] Thomas Clark the Lawyer requested a Warrant from the Court to bring Captain Samuell Leonard before them for breach of the Peace—which was granted—And Captain Leonard appearing, The said Clark charged him with striking hime —said Leonard bids him prove it. John Hollinshead Attested saith that Samuel Leonard and Thomas Clark being at the Widdow Basnetts about some differences between them calling one another abusive names as Sorry Rascal, and old fool, the said Leonard struck the said Clark. William Hollinshead Attested saith, he was at said Basnetts but not at the begining of the words they had and what words past before he could not say, but as the said Leonard stood by the fire he looking upon said Clark uttered these words to him You are a Rascal and so Struck him.

The said Leonard confessed in his Passion he might strike said Clark, and leaves it to the Court.

The Court award said Leonard to pay the Costs being Nine Shillings which was paid accordingly.

The Court of Sessions adjourn'd to the 3d of March next.

Court of Pleas opened February 20th 1700. Justices Present   Mahlon Stacy, William Biddle, John Wills, John Adams, Richard Ridgway.

[*Action*] George Curtis Plaintiff   Henry Wells and Edmund Wells defendants   Withdrawn in Court.

The Court adjourn till to Morrow Morning.

February 21th The Court opened. [*Action*] Samuel Jenings Plaintiff Edward Andrews Defendant called and both appear'd. The declaration Bond and Articles read. The Defendants Attorney craves a Barr, for that there was no Consideration mentioned in the declaration. The Court overrule that Plea, Then the Defendant put in his Plea, That he doth not owe the money in manner and form as sett forth in the Declaration And put it upon that Issue. The Jury called as followed (vizt) William Wood, William Biddle junr., William Hunt, John Butcher, John Moore, Thomas Scattergood, Hermannus King, James Adams, William Spencer, Thomas Garwood, David Curtis, John Pain all Attested. After the declaration Bond and Articles read Neither Plaintiff nor Defendant had anything to object or offer but leaveing it with the Jury. After the Jury had been out some time—The Jury found for the Plaintiff.

[*Judgment*] The Court give Judgment That the Plaintiff shall have One hundred pounds with Costs of Suit.

[*Action*] Christopher Snoden Plaintiff Charles Shippey Defendant both call'd and appear'd. The Declaration read. The Defendant puts in his Plea That he had performed the Covenant. The abovementioned Jury Attested.

William Righton his Affidavit read.

[*Wittnesse*] John Smith Attested sayes That this Winter Charles Shippey told him, that he acknowledged he owed the Plaintiff, Christopher Snoden Seven pounds ten Shillings. Two paper Orders under Sheepeys hand, One upon Daniel Garner for Fifty Shillings, the other upon Robert Chapman for Forty five Shillings.

[*Wittness*] William Emley attested sayes He was the said Plaintiffs Attorney and had Effects in his hand for him, but he said Defendant would never come to him, nor would not Serve him, neither could he find the Defendant except at an Ale house in Burlington. A paper from Francis Horner read.

[*Evidence*] Nathaniel Cripps Attested sayes that Abraham Senior brought Charles Shippey into his house in a Languishing Condition for Six or Seven Months time as soon or presently after the Plaintiff went to England.

[*Verdict*] The Jury find for the Plaintiff Sustaining the Damage of Fifteen pounds with Costs of Suit, The Plaintiff craves Judgment.

[*Judgment*] The Court give Judgment according to Verdict.

[*John Ogborns Petition*] John Ogborn came into Court and demanded an Execution upon a Judgment by him formerly obtained against John Hollinshead since deceased. [*John Hollinsheads Answer*] Upon which demand John Hollinshead Executor to his said Father John Hollinshead by his Attorney, inform'd the Court That his father being Burgess or chief Magistrate of the Town of Burlington had committed said Ogborn to Prison for breach of a Law Afterwards said Ogborn Sued the said Hollinshead upon that Accompt and said Hollinshead not appearing at that Court to answer said Action, Judgment was given against him by default at a Court of Pleas held at Burlington May 8th 1699. Now it is humbly offered to this Court, That said Ogborn does demand this his Execution illegally, As first he makes this demand without a Scire Facias etc. 2dly John Hollinshead committing said Ogborn to Prison being done while he was in the Execution of his Office and as Burgess, The Executors are not answerable now for it, it being only a Personal Trespass and when he died the Action died with him. The Court demanding of said Ogborn what he had to offer against said Allegations, He answered he would say no more at that Court.

[*Order*] The Court are of Opinion not to grant an Execution, And Order said Ogborn to make no more Such demands on that Accompt.

[*Action*] Anthony Woodward Plaintiff Samuel Taylor defendant continued.

[182 **1700, 1701 Court of Sessions by adjournment March 3d. Court of Sessions and Pleas, May 1701**] [*Sessions*] Court of Sessions held by Adjournment March 3d 1700. Present Francis Davenport, William Biddle, John Adams, John Wills, Justices.

Ordered That the Privy Seal be at present made use of in all Warrants and business concerning the County Courts of Session instead of the Justices Seals, till there can be a County Seal provided. The Warrants to the Several Constables of the several Townshipps about raiseing the Provincial and County taxes were Signed by the Justices in open Court. The Governour comeing into Court, Sent for Robert Wheeler Justice, to join with the other Justices in Signeing the above mentioned Warrants which he waveing and refuseing The Governour with advice of the Court discharged him from acting any more as Justice.

[*Court of Sessions and Pleas May 8th 1701. adjourn'd to 26th May instant*] Court of Sessions opened May the 8th 1701. Justices Edward Hunloke, Peter Frettwell, John Wills, present. Thomas Gardiner appointed Clerk for the present Court. The Court adjourns till the 26th instant May. Att the same time and place and by the same Justices the **Court of Pleas** was called and the same time and place adjourned.[50b]

[*Sessions by Adjournment*] Court of Sessions held by Adjournment May 26th 1701. Present Francis Davenport, Thomas Gardiner, John Wills, John Adams, Richard Ridgway Justices. Christopher Wetherill Sheriff Thomas Gardiner Kings Attorney Edward Hunloke Clerk.

Grand Jury Matthew Watson, Joshua Humphryes, Thomas Hooten,

[50b] This paragraph in different handwriting.

Nathaniel Paine, Thomas Harding, Thomas Bishopp, Edward Gaskill, Joseph Heritage, Timothy Hancock, Matthew Champion, John Antrum, Jacob Lamb, Alexander Stewart, William Matlock all Attested. The Charge given them by Francis Davenport.

Daniel Sutton bound by Recognizance to appear at this Court was calld and nothing appearing further against him was cleer'd and discharg'd paying his Fees.

[*John Slow*] John Slow Prisoner was by the Sheriff sett to the barr, the Justices Mittimus was for his said Slows Stealing a shirt and selling it. The Prisoner confesses himself Guilty and referrs himself to the Bench. The Justices Order

[*Ordered*] That the Prisoner John Slow alias Stanton pay four fold for the Shirt which was affirm'd worth ten shillings And therefore

[*Judgment*] Judgment is awarded that he pay Forty Shillings and costs and charges of the Court, and that he continue a prisoner till paid.

Henry Low bound by Recognizance to the Peace and for his Personal Appearance at this Court was call'd 3 times but did not appear. George Gleave junr. desires this Court to Suspend this business till next Court which is granted.

George Green bound by Recognizance in open Court last Sessions being called appeared and none comeing to prosecute him in this Court Ordered by the Court that he be dismist paying his Fees which he did.

Thomas Cleverly being bound by Recognizance to this Court from the last Court of Sessions was called and appeared, and it be proved that he appeared at the Provincial Court and there being discharged was also dismist here.

[*Anne Stevens*] Anne Stevens being by order of the Provincial Judges and Justices to be sold publickly at a Vandue for dischargeing the debt and costs of her Tryall and paying the overpluss to her former Master Thomas Cleverly, And at her instance and request Hugh Huddy at the time buying her by bidding most—She in this open Court declared that altho by the order of the said Provincial Court She was to be disposed of but for the remaining time of her Indentures which was not full three Years to come yet notwithstanding according to her promise [to?] the said Huddy she of her own free will in open Court declared that she was willing and would be oblidged to serve said Huddy or his Assigns for the full term of three years from the time of her going to him.

[*Presentments*] The Grand jury in Court by bill present Richard Caving, Henry Roe, Mordecay Andrews John Clough William Dean Jonathan Curtis, Thomas Renshaw, Moses Langstaff, for that they did forcibly on the 18th day of March Last past break open the Prison door of this County. Again the say—We do also present John Woolstone William Fisher, John Ogborn junr. and Richard Ellison for that they four men was their Mouths and Leaders to this Tamultuous Action Signed by the Foreman Matthew Watson, the 26th May 1701.

Joseph Cross Thomas Bryan John Warren Thomas Scoley John Crosby Thomas French and Samuel Coles being returned upon the Jury and not appearing or sending any Excuse The Court for their Contempt of Authority fine them in tenn Shillings a piece.

The Court broke up by Proclamation.

[*pleas by Adjournment*] Court of Pleas held by Adjournment opened the 26th day of May 1701. Justices Present Francis Davenport, Thomas Gardiner, John Adams, Richard Ridgway, John Wills.

[*Action*] Anthony Woodward Plaintiff Samuel Taylor Defendant both call'd 3 times neither appeared The Court at the desire of Anthony Woodward by Henry Gleave continue the Action till next Court.

The Court adjourn till the next Court in course.

[**183 1701 August Court of Sessions**] [*Court of Sessions and Pleas August 1701.*] Court of Sessions open'd August 8th 1701. Present Francis Davenport, William Biddle, John Adams, Robert Wheeler Burgess, Thomas Gardiner, Samuel Furnis, Richard Ridgeway Justices.

Grand Jury John Day, Joseph Cross, Caleb Shreeve, John Boarton, John Hammell, Joseph Scattergood, James Bingham, John Hollinshead, James Crafts Senr., Michael Buffin, Samuel Gibson, Richard French, Richard Smith, Joseph Smith Attested, and Charge given them.

Richard Boyes upon Complaint of John Boarton was by Justice John Wills bound to his good behaviour till, (and to appear at) this Court, who being called, appear'd, and Nothing being alledged against him, he was dismist by the Court paying his Fees.

[*Mill Road for Brown and Thomas Curtis allowed of and ordered to be recorded by the Court.*] The 4th of the 1st Month 1700/1 Then laid out a Mill road for John Brown and Thomas Curtis as followeth (viz) from their owne Land through Richard Gibbs Land the most convenient way for them both to Michael Buffins Creek, thence through Michael Buffins Land to John Underhills Land, so through Hugh Hutchins along by his house into his Lane, from thence to Edward Andrews and so along the most convenient way to the Mill,—by us whose names are underwritten—Abraham Brown junr. Edward Boulton, Caleb Shreeve, Benjamin Scattergood Robert Powell Francis Parks, Jacob Decow, James Anteram Richard French Joseph Pancoats, David Curtis, Nathaniel Records.

[*Presentments*] The Grand jury bring in two Presentments as follows in these words viz—We do present John Neve and Mary Fryley for liveing together as man and wife, her husband William Fryley according to the best of our knowledge being Yet alive. 2dly We so present the Bridge and the Causeway on this side Hancocks belonging to the Inhabitants of Springfield.

Robert Edwards being upon Complaint of Lemuel Oldale bound by

Recogniz.nce to the Peace and to appear at this Court but the said Lemuel haveing nothing further against him, he said Edwards was by the Court dismist paying his Fees.

[*Evidence about Seth Hills being Suspected for clipping etc.*] Thomas South, being Attested in Court and before the Grand Jury (then in Court) Saith that Elizabeth Hill daughter of Seth Hill about November last being in the Chamber makeing the Bed, asked the Deponent to come up to her, and in looking in her Fathers Closett among some odd things, found in a Coffee dish some Clippings to the value of about ten or twelve Shillings, he put them down again and knows no further of them but says that the said Elizabeth said She knows nothing of them Clippings unless her father might receive them from Emmanuel Smith. Elizabeth Hill being attested saith That Thomas South (the above Evidence) was never in her Chamber or Fathers Closett as he attested nor did she ever see any Clippings in her Fathers house. [*is Cleer'd*] An Indictment was then given to the Grand jury chargeing the said Seth Hill for clipping of money—but soon after they return and bring in Ignoramus, and he is discharged paying his Fees.

[*Thomas Peachees Guardians discharged*] Richard Fennimore on behalf of himself and Abrahem Hewlings as Guardians to Thomas Peachee, the said Peachee being of Age and in Court and haveing nothing to offer against their being discharged according to their desire

[*Order*] The Court order them to be discharged and their Bonds given up paying the usual fees—The Court adjourn till to Morrow Morn.

August 9th. [*Seth Hill prosecuted by John Neve for offering abuse to his wife*] Seth Hill upon Complaint made by John Neve before Robert Wheeler Burgess being bound by Recognizance to appear at this Court to answer said Complaint being call'd appear'd.

[*Evidence*] Mary Fryley alias Neve being solemnly Attested in open Court declared as follows. That Seth Hill upon the 24th day of May Anno 1700 and at several other times before he was mareyed to his second wife (and while he was a Widdower) he came to the Deponents house, and requested her to lett him lye with her useing some Arguments to prevail with her and saying he would not hurt her etc. he would have her put her hand into his breeches, and to that purpose took hold of her hand and when he could not put her hand into his breeches he pul'd out his private Members and put them into her hand and in a delusive manner prayed her to be kind. Another time he came to this Deponents house, sent for Rum and milkt the Cow himself to make Milk punch but made it so strong they could not drink it, at which time Elizabeth Pears was with the Deponent the Deponent went towards the Water side but had not been long out of the house, before said Peers call'd to this Deponent saying She would not serve her so to go out of the house, and as this Deponent came into the house She found the said Hill had thrown her upon a Chest and ruffled her clothes above her knees. One other time at this Deponents house this Deponent saith he said Hill would have tempted her to debauchery and would flatteringly say to her he had nothing against her, but that she kept company with John Neve and at same time would have debauch't her praying her to be kind to a Man, alledgeing he would not hurt her but urgeing and praying her to let him try one inch saying Mary do, pray Mary do let me try but one inch.

[*Evidence of Elizabeth Pears taken before Justice Stanbury*] The Declaration of Elizabeth Pears, upon a certain time in Burlington, I being at the house of John Neve—Seth Hill when it was night came to the house abovesaid and brought Milk and sent his daughter with Rum, and came himselfe and made Milk-punch, Then and there did he endeavour to debauch me the abovesaid Pears by all the Allurements he could use, and not only that but would a forct me, had I not call'd for help, he took me by force and threw me upon a Chest, in the said house had forct me had I not call'd out.

Elizabeth Peers was legally attested to the Truth of the above written the 13th 4 mo. 1701. before Nathan Stanbury Justice.

[*Evidence*] John Pears attested saith he comeing home from Henry Becks where he was at work, he asked his wife where she lay such a night when it thunder'd and lightned so much she said She was at Mary Neves, and that Seth Hill made milk Punch and would have abused her and Mary Neve and would have forc't her. Seth Hill being asked by the Court what he had to offer or say against the above Evidence he said it was all false, for he was never in said Neves house but when he said Neves was at home or askt to come in, And further saith he does not remember that ever he was in Company with them Women alone, nor ever offer'd an Abuse to them or either of them.

John Neve and Mary Fryley being presented by the Grand jury as above—The Court order said Neve to find Security to answer the same.

[*John Neve Recognizance Joseph White*] John Neve and Joseph White do Recognize themselves joyntly and severally to be indebted unto our Sovereigne Lord the King in the Summe of One hundred pounds to be levied upon their Goods and Chattells Lands and Tenements on Condition the said John Neve and Mary Fryley do appear at the next Quarter Sessions held here for said County to answer said Presentment found by the Grand jury. John Neve and Joseph White both appearing acknowledge the above Recognizance.

[**184 1701 Court of Sessions and Pleas August.**] [*Mingo Seth Hills Negro bound to this Court appears is Cleer'd*] John Neve haveing attested before a Magistrate that he went in fear of his life by some threatening words given forth by a Negro man named Mingo (servant to Seth Hill) Whereupon the said Negro being committed till Security was given for his Appearance at the

Quarterly Sessions was then called and appeared. The Court demanding of said Neve whether he was yet under any fear or terror of the said Negro said Neve answered he was under no great fear now nor would not insist upon keeping him longer a Prisoner or be under Bail, Whereupon the Court order upon his Master Seth Hills paying the Costs and Charges the said Negro to be dismist.

[*John Neve bound by Recognizance is cleer'd*] Seth Hill Attesting the Peace against John Neve before a Magistrate, the said Magistrate bound said Neve by Recognizance to appear at this Court, who accordingly appears. The Court demanding of said Hill whether he was yet under any fear or terrour of the said Neve the said Hill answered he was not now afraid, Whereupon the Court order'd the said Neve to be dismist and cleer'd paying his fees etc.

[*John Neve complains against Mingo for abuseing and Scandalizeing him*] Mingo (Seth Hills Negro) was call'd in Court upon Complaint of John Neve, For that the said Mingo reported and said that on the 13th day of July last about 9 at night the said John Neve offered and by force did lye with his said Mingo's Wife (a Negro Woman) and that the said Negro Woman cryed out. The Court asks Mingo what proof he could make of this he answered That his Wife told him so and that was all he knew.

[*Evidence*] Jonas Moon Attested saith That the same night being the 13th July he was with John Neve till 11 a clock and was talking with him all the while and that there was no such thing while he was there—And further saith that Mingo said he saw said Neve a topp of his Wife. Peter Knowles, (being under Age was not Attested but) said he lay in the house all night and that there was no such thing as he knew off.

[*Judgment*] The Court Considering the Premisses give Judgment as follows That for the Malicious Scandalous and false report made by said Mingo against the said Neve That he said Mingo, on Monday next in the Town of Burlington be publickly whipt on the bare back receiveing thirty Stripes Severely laid on, and committed to Prison till all charges be paid (viz) as well upon Neves Attesting the Peace against him as the Charges of this Scandal.

Order'd that the Clerk give the Sheriff a Warrant for Executing said Judgment.

[*Seth Hills Recognizance*] Seth Hill and Henry Grubb in open Court Recognize themselves to be bound to our Sovereigne Lord the King in the Summe of Forty pounds a piece To be Levied upon their Goods and Chattells Lands and Tenements On condition that Seth Hill appear at next Court of Sessions to answer to such Matters as shall be objected against him concerning Mary Neve. Seth Hill and Henry Grubb both appearing acknowledge the same.

[*William Pettys Complaint against George Wickham*] William Petty junr. makeing Complaint in Court against George Wickam, shewing That altho he said Petty paid for his said Wickams passage from England into this Province and other necessary charges, The said Wickam abuses his said Master and will not serve him by entring into Indentures or otherwise according to the Custome of the Countrey—And Whereas the Law of this Province obliges all above the age of 21 years that are transported hither from England shall Serve for the term of 4 years (to commence from their Arrival in this Province) to such Person or his Assignes that shall pay for their Said Passage

[Order] The Court therefore Order That the said George Wickam Serve the said William Petty junr. or his Assignes for the term of 4 years to commence from the 29th September last past according to the Law and Custome of this Province.

Court of Pleas opened August 8th 1701. Justices present Francis Davenport, William Biddle, John Adams, Samuell Furnis and Richard Ridgway.

[Action] Joseph Rowe Plaintiff call'd Mr. Thomas Revell by Warrant of Attorney appears for him. John Towle Defendant call'd appears. Mr. Revell by his Obligation became bound for Mr. Rows personal Appearance at this Court to prosecute his said Action to effect. Mr. Row appear'd not.

The Declaration read—The Defendant demurres because he is sued upon an Assumpsit and a Quantum Meruit, there being no consideration in the declaration mentioned. The defendant put in his Plea in writing to this effect, That he did Not assume in manner as the Plaintiff declares, and further saith he paid the Plaintiff 3l. 16s. 8d. in full discharge and Satisfaction of his trouble etc. The Plaintiff replyed and sayes it was not in full Satisfaction. The Jury call'd Benjamin Wheat, Abraham Bickley, Matthew Champion, William Biddle junr., John Stockton, John Petty, Benjamin Moor, Zachary Prickett, William Bustill, Thomas Clark, Thomas Wetherill, Thomas Hooton and Attested.

The Declaration read. The Plaintiff brings in a Paper Affidavit sign'd and taken by Michael Booth and Edey his Wife before John Moll Justice in Philadelphia, which was read. A Letter produced by the defendant from John Towle and Elizabeth Towle in England to Francis Davenport and others which was also read. After the several Allegations on both sides the Jury go out and bring in their

[Verdict] Verdict in Writeing (vizt) We the traverse Jury find for John Towle the Defendant with Costs of Suit—Benjamin Wheat Foreman.

[Action] Thomas Middleton Plaintiff called, appears Richard Allison Defendant call'd 3 times appear'd not. The declaration read, the Bond read, and proved by Samuell Furnis and Thomas Gardiner Wittnesses to the Bond. The Plaintiff Craves Judgment by default,

[*Judgment and Execution granted*] which the Court grant but change the Bond to the conditional Summe of £24 – – Interest and costs of Suit, and upon request Execution was Order by the Court.

[*Action*] Richard Boyes Plaintiff appears Abimelech Hudson Defendant call'd 3 times appears not. The Declaration read. the Bill under the Defendants hand read and proved. [*Judgment*] The Court give Judgment for £4 10s. and Costs.

Henry Beck and Joseph Scattergood Plaintiffs call'd appears William Gabitas call'd 3 times appears not. The declaration read. The Bond read, The Plaintiffs crave Judgment by default.

[**185 1701 November. Court of Sessions and Pleas**] [*Order of Court*] The Court order, That a Writt of Enquiry be issued out, to enquire what damages the Plaintiffs have Sustained and Judgment to be awarded thereupon.

[*Action*] Samuel Furnis Plaintiff call'd appears. Robert Powell and Mary his Wife defendants, call'd appear by their Attorney Thomas Clark, the Declaration read, The Defendants [*Plaintiff Nonsuited*] crave a Nonsuit which is by the Court granted.

Court of Sessions and Pleas November 3 1701. Court of Sessions opened November 3d 1701. Present Francis Davenport, William Biddle, Samuel Furnis, John Adams, John Wills Justices. Isaac Marriott Sheriff Thomas Gardiner Kings Attorney.

Grand-Jury Benjamin Field, Christopher Wetherill, William Wood, John Bunting, Edward Rockhill, Martin Scott, John Shinn junr., John Garwood, Samuel Bunting, William Boarton, William Stevenson, Thomas Bryan, Henry Burr Attested And Charge given them by Francis Davenport.

adjourn'd till 2 a Clock.

John Neve and Mary Fryley called in Court to answer the Recognizance given for their appearance at this Court. John Neve appears, and produceth a Certificate and Affidavit of Joseph Crosse and William Page under Edward Shippens hand as Justice, that said Mary Fryley or Neve was very Sick and so could not be at the Court.

[*Order*] The Court upon said Neve's request continue the cause till next Court he said Neve and his Security in open Court declareing they were willing to Stand bound by Recognizance as in the preceeding Court till the next Court in February.

[*Order*] The Court order that the several Assessors and Collectors appointed by Act of Assembly for the several Townshipps in this County be call'd to give Accompt what they have done in relation to the Tax. Hopewell—Andrew Heath and William Spencer Assessors and Nathaniel Petit Collector call'd appear not. Maidenhead—William Hixson and John Brierly Assessors and John Bainbridge Collector call'd appear not. Nottingham—

William Emley and Thomas Tindall Assessors and Samuel Overton Collector call'd appear not. Chesterfield—Benjamin Field one of the Assessors and Collectors call'd appears. The Court ask't him what done concerning the Tax, he sayes he has been about and demanded the Tax, and has made Return of those that refused. Mansfield—Thomas Curtis and James Crofts Senr. Assessors call'd appear'd not but Richard French the Collector being call'd appeard, and sayes he was willing to do his duty But the Assessors not acting, he could do nothing. Springfield—Thomas Duglis and William Hunt Assessors, and John Snape Collector call'd appear not. Northampton—William Budd and Anthony Elton Assessors call'd appear not. Thomas Bryan call'd appears. Burlington—The Assessors call'd appear, and Say they have Assessed the Townshipp. The Collectors call'd, at present do not appear. Wellingborough—Thomas Eves and John Ward call'd, Thomas Eves appears and says he has acted by himself but Ward would not Act, John Hudson collector appears. Chester—Abraham Hewlings Assessor Call'd—Justice Adams informs the Court that he has done his duty, John Hollinshead and Thomas French Collectors call'd The Court are inform'd they have been doing their duty. Evesham—Henry Ballenger and William Evans Assessors and William Hewlings Collector call'd appear'd not.

The Court adjourns till 8 in the Morning.

November 4th. Seth Hill and Henry Grubb do again in open Court declare they are willing to stand bound by Recognizance as in the preceeding Court till the next Court in February.

Jacob Perkins was call'd (being bound by Recognizance) and appeard, the Recognizance and Mittimus read, and is discharged pay the usual Fees.

Court of Pleas opened November 4th 1701. Present Francis Davenport, William Biddle, Samuel Furnis, John Adams Justices.

The Petty Jury that Attended the Court was as follows, vizt Thomas Lambert, Matthew Watson, William Hollinshead, Abraham Hewlings, John Abbott, Joseph Steward, Edward Bolton, Thomas Potts, Henry Beck, Obadiah Hierton, William Hackney, Thomas Gilberthorp.

[Action] Seth Hill Plaintiff John Neve Defendant call'd appears— Declaration read The Defendant put in his Plea That the Action cannot lye, 1st he sayes in his Declaration he was legally discharged, but an Ignoramus is not a full Legal Discharge for that it may again come before another Grand jury.

[Order] The Court order the Writt to abate, and the said Hill should pay Costs of Suit.

[Action] George Curtis Plaintiff Henry Wells Defendant call'd appear—The Declaration read—The Defendant puts in his Plea in Writing —The Plea is over-ruled and for want of an issueable Plea—Judgment is awarded by default. The Defendant afterwards came into Court and confest Judgment for 7l. and Interest according to Declaration upon Condition that Execution be Suspended for 2 months time—which the Court allow of.

[*Action*] Nicholas Brown and Elizabeth his wife Executors to Thomas Cook her former husband Plaintiffs—call'd—appear. Thomas Webley Defendant call'd 3 times appeard not. The Declaration read. The bill under the Defendants hand read, and by an Affidavit of John West one of the Wittnesses taken before Jedidiah Allen Justice in Shrewsbury produced and read in Court, proved. The Plaintiffs crave Judgment The Court order Judgment to be entred by default.

[*Action*] John Parker Plaintiff John Ward Defendant call'd appear— The Defendant comes into Court Confesses Judgment for Eighty pounds according to the Condition of the Bond with Interest and Costs of Suit, and the Plaintiff remitts the Penalty.

[**186 1701 November Court of Pleas and Adjournment February Courts**] [*Return of Samuell Jenings Writt of Execution*] Christopher Wetherill the former Sheriff made a Return of an Execution obtain'd by Samuell Jenings against the Estate of Edward Andrews—the Return is in these words, endorsed (vizt) This Execution was laid on the Plantation of Edward Andrews the 29th day of May 1701 by me Christopher Wetherill Sheriffe—Henry Grubb and Samuell Gibson present—The said late Sheriff affirmed in Court that at the time of serving said Execution there was some Persons there that said The said Plantation he then levied his Execution upon was not belonging then to Edward Andrews but that he had sold it— And Samuell Jenings saith he hath this day seen a deed under said Andrews hand wherein he had convey'd away the said Plantation.

[*Court order upon it*] Upon the above Return and no other Effects or Estate real or personal to be found of said Andrews—The Said Samuell Jenings craves a further Execution to be granted against the body of said Andrews—Which the Court order accordingly.

The Court adjourn till the 25th day of this month.

Court of Pleas held by Adjournment the 25th day of November 1701. Opened. Present William Biddle, John Wills, Thomas Gardiner, Samuel Furnis Justices.

[*Action*] John Bunting Plaintiff John Gilbert Defendant call'd appear. The Defendant acknowledges the Bond and the Court give Judgment for Sixteen pounds.

Seth Hill for abusive words and Actions to and in the Court and to some perticular Magistrates then sitting was required by the Court to find Security for the behaviour and to answer for said Abuse at next Court of Sessions. which upon his refusing was committed to prison.

Court of Sessions and Pleas February 20th and 21th 1701/2. Court of Sessions opened February 20 1701/2. Present Mahlon Stacy, William Biddle, John Adams, John Wills, Thomas Gardiner, Samuel Furnis, Richard Ridgway   Justices. Isaac Marriott Sheriffe   Thomas Gardiner Kings Attorney.

Grand Jury Benjamin Field, Thomas Raper, Abraham Bickley, Thomas Eves, John Warren, Nicholas Martineau, John Smith, Benjamin Jones, John Snape, George Willis, William Ogborn, Isaac Gibbs, John Hudson, William Biddle junr. Attested, and the Charge given by Mahlon Stacy and Thomas Gardiner.

Constables the ensueing Year, for Hopewell   Elnathan Davis Attested. Maidenhead   Theophilus Philips Constable last Year, being calld not appearing, And the Court being informed the Town had chose him for the Year ensueing the Court confirm'd their choice and ordered him to stand by his former Attestation. Nottingham   John Lambert chose Thomas Tindall of his owne voluntary Will Attested in his Stead. Chesterfield   Charles Millward   Attested. Mansfield   William Foster   Attested. Springfield   John Stockdon Attested. Burlington   Joseph Smith and John Wetherill Attested. Northampton   Henry Burr   Attested. Wellingborough   Thomas Peche Attested. Chester   John Rudderow appears not Ordered that Justice Adams Attest him. Eversham   Josiah Appleton Constable for the late year call'd appears not. Thomas Hooton chose by the Town appears and Attested.

A Warrant granted by the Court to fetch Josiah Appleton late Constable of Eversham before them to answer to such things as shall be objected against him Signed Per order of Court—Edward Hunloke Clerk.

The Grand jury come into Court and inform, that they understand that several presentments of former Grandjuries have not been duly prosecuted, perticularizing one thing (which they believe may be on Record) about Thomas Williams getting his wifes daughter with Child, And altho he is fled from Justice, Yet the Woman is yet in the place and ought to answer for it.

[*Presentments*] The Grand Jury in open Court present Dorothy Roberts for haveing a Bastard Child.

[*Presentment*] The Grand Jury Present Rebecca Bennett now wife of John Scholey the daughter in Law of the above mentioned Thomas Williams for Committing Fornication with her Father in Law (if she be not formerly presented and so appear upon Record.

[*Andrew Heath Presented pleads Guilty*]   The Grand Jury present Andrew Heath for committing Adultery with his daughter in Law Francis Venables. The said Andrew Heath being call'd to the Barr, and the Presentment being read to him, and asked whether Guilty or not Guilty—He pleads Guilty and craves the Favour of the Bench. The Court order the Sheriff to take him into Custody.

[**187 1701/2 February 1701 Courts**] [*the 21th February   Heaths Sen-*

tence] Andrew Heath Prisoner was call'd to the Barr being Yesterday convicted by his own Confession.

The King's Attorney orders the Law of the Province against Adultery to be read and thereupon crave Judgment against the prisoner accordingly.

The Court therefore grant Judgment and give Sentence That the said Andrew Heath pay Ten pounds and Costs, and be remanded to Prison till paid, And find Security for the Behaviour.

[*Josiah Appletons Tryall*] Josiah Appleton who was sent for by Warrant From the Court and by vertue thereof brought into Court, appears Complaint was made against him for that he haveing brought a Person named Robert Willcocks before Justice Gardiner for Felony, but forbearing now at Court to prosecute him according to promise, and Stiffleing the King's Evidence.

[*Evidence*] Thomas Wetherill attested saith James Bingham on behalfe of Josiah Appleton desired a Warrant from Justice Gardiner for him said Appleton to bring a Felon before him, But Justice Gardiner [50a] to said Bingham that said Appleton should make Complaint in person: which he doing a Warrant was granted and the Felon brought before said Justice, The Felon upon Examination confest the Fact, and to the best of this deponents remembrance he said Appleton promised to prosecute the prisoner Upon which said Justice granted a Mittimus to Send the said Roger Willcocks to prison.

[*Evidence*] Daniel Smith Constable Attested saith. That Josiah Appleton bringing (by vertue of a Warrant from Justice Gardiner to him said Smith directed) a Felon before said Gardiner, But he heard nothing of a Bond discourst off to Prosecute the said Felon.

[*Evidence*] Justice Thomas Gardiner declares to the Court That he discoursed with said Appleton about his giveing Bond to prosecute the said Willcocks the Felon at next Court But being willing to save charges took his word to prosecute And Further informs the Court that said Appleton both as Complaint and as the Kings Officer (being a Constable) he ought to prosecute for the King. But the said Appleton (for reasons to himself best known) letting fall the prosecution and not appearing against the prisoner according to his duty, the said Gardiner (as Attorney for the King) informs the Court that this Acting of Said Appleton was a Stiffling the Kings Evidence a Prevention of Justice and Contempt for the Laws and thereupon moved for Justice against him and thereupon the Court give Judgment

[*Sentence*] That the said Josiah Appleton for his said Offence be fined and shall pay Twenty Shillings with Costs and Charges.

[*Presentment of Roger Willcocks his Tryall and*] The Grand Jury present Roger Willcocks for Felloniously carrying away one great Coat, from the house of Josiah Appleton the 20th day of December 1701. The said

[50a] [said].

Appleton thereupon being Arraign'd at the Barr, Guilty or not Guilty, the said Appleton the Prisoner pleaded Guilty. The 21th day of February being sett to the Barr and upon his Conviction the day before of Stealing a Coat by his owne Confession, The King's Attorney moved the Law might be read against Felons which was done and further moves for Judgment according to said Law Thereupon the Court give Judgment

[*Sentence*] That the said Roger Willcocks the Prisoner pay four fold (vizt) the Coat being valued at 15s. he pay Three Pounds with Costs etc. and be committed to prison till paid.

[*Presentment of Nathaniell Pettit*] The Grand Jury present Nathaniell Pettit for Selling of Rum without Licence, and keeping People drunck from day to day in his house contrary to Law. he being call'd appear'd not.

[*Presentment of Seth Hill: his Tryall and*] The Grand Jury present Seth Hill For his Abuse and Contempt of Authority on the 25th day of November 1701 being Sett to the Barr, and asked whether Guilty or not Guilty, he pleads Guilty and craves the favour of the Court. The 21th February The prisoner Seth Hill Sett to the Barr, The said Hill being presented by the Grandjury for abuse and Contempt of Authority and being Convicted by his Confession The Court takeing the heynousnesse of his Crime into Consideration it being for his notorious abusing the Magistrates on the Bench in Open Court For Assaulting the high Sheriffe and other most Enormous Crimes give Judgment and Sentence against him as follows (vizt)

[*Sentence*] That he pay Forty pounds fine with cost of Suit etc. To find Security for his Behaviour, and committed to prison till said Sentence be fullfilled.

[*William Fisher Attests the Peace against John Henry*] William Fisher upon his Solemn Attestation declares that he goes in fear of his life from John Henry. John Henry answers; That his Attestation ought not to be taken for that he (meaning said Fisher) is a Theef and a Murdrer and was burnt in the hand.

[*Evidence*] John Poinsett Attested saith, That he working and being at William Fishers, he has heard John Henry say several times that he would burn his house (meaning said Fishers).

[*Evidence*] Eleazer Fenton Attested saith That in Fishers house (John Henry being there) there was some discourse about his said Fentons being in Dobsons house (the wife of John Henry) at New York, The Woman being reputed to keep a common Bawdy house And Said Fenton discoursing to Said Henry, telling him what he heard, The Said John Henry thereupon, threatned the Said Fenton, and said he would lye in wait and kill him —And the Said Fenton begg'd his pardon, for what he said to him, Yet he continued his Malice and threatening. Whereupon the Court Order

[*Court Order*] The said John Henry to find Security for the Peace and his good Behaviour till the next Court of Sessions or to go to Prison and if a Prisoner, Fisher to allow him three pence a day, And the Said Fisher to pay the Costs and Charges hereof which he said Fisher promised to do.

[*Recognizance Andrew Heath*] Andrew Heath in open Court Recognizes himself to be bound to the King in the Summe of Fifty pounds to be levied upon his goods and Chattells, Lands and Tenements On Condition that he be of good abearing and keep his Majesties Peace to his Said Majestie and all his Liege People for a Twelve Month and a day.

[*Recognizances of Neve and Hill Continued*] John Neve his Recognizance and Security given last Court for his and Mary Fryleys appearing at this Court, As also Seth Hill his Recognizance the last Court for his appearing at this, are both continued till next Court, because the River not being open nor fast is very hazardous so that Neve could not come to this Court.

[*Warrant for N. Pettitt 2s. 6d.*] By Order of Court the Clark made a Warrant to cause Nathaniell Petitt to be brought before Justice Mahlon Stacy to answer to his presentment of this Court at next Court of Sessions, given under the Clerks hand and County Seal.

[*A Quietus granted to the Executors of Thomas Gladwin deceased*] The Court haveing appointed Justice John Wills to inspect the Accompts of Samuel Furnis Robert Wheeler and Joseph Adams as Executors to Thomas Gladwin deceased in order for their Quietus the Justice Wills haveing inspected and duley Examined their Accompts Reports That he finds their Accompts just and true, and that they have fully administred upon the same Estate, And also haveing given publick Notice of their Intentions of Sueing out their Quietus according to Law and Nothing appearing to the contrary.

The Court therefore grant them their Quietus as haveing fully Administred.

[**188 1701/2 February Court of Pleas**] [*Court of Pleas February 20 and 21th*] Court of Pleas opened February 20th 1701/2. Present William Biddle, John Adams, Samuel Furnis, Thomas Gardiner, Richard Ridgway Justices. Isaac Marriott Sheriffe Edward Hunloke Clerk.

Action John Joyner Plaintiff call'd appears Thomas Duglis Sole Surviveing Executor of John Joyner (the Plaintiffs father) deceased Defendant call'd appears. The Declaration read. The Defendant is willing to pay the remaining of the Legacy of Twenty pounds left him (the Plaintiff) by his father which the Plaintiff is willing to accept, And as the Defendant charges, The Plaintiff acknowledges to have received of the Executors in money and Sundry Goods, to the value of Fourteen pounds one Shilling and six pence. For the remainder Five pounds Eighteen Shillings and Six pence The Court give Judgment That the Defendant pay the same to the Plaintiff with Costs etc.

1701/2]   THE BURLINGTON COURT BOOK   265

Action   Henry Wells Plaintiff   Robert Powell Defendant both appear. The Declaration read. the Defendant confesses he owes the money But prayes Releife against the Obligation. The Condition being but for Twenty pounds. The Court gives Judgment for the said Twenty pounds to be paid to the Plaintiff with Costs, Interest etc.

Action   Edward Hunloke Plaintiff against the Estate of Thomas Bibb late of Burlington deceased. The Declaration read the Bond read,—after several Debates by Nathaniel Westland, and hearing of all sides,—The Court gives Judgment as follows (viz) That Edward Hunloke have his just debt of Eight pounds twelve shillings and six pence and Costs of Suit etc. which amount to Thirty eight Shillings and six pence more.

Action   Edward Hunloke Plaintiff call'd appear'd. Thomas Clark Defendant call'd three times not appearing. The Plaintiff moveing for Judgment by default. The Court order Judgment accordingly to be Entred by default. And the Court further Order the Jury then Summoned and Attending, should be attested to make Enquiry of the damages, with Costs etc. The Jury of Enquiry find for the Plaintiff Fifty Shillings damages and Costs of Suit which upon both Juries and Bench etc. come to Three pounds and two pence more as per bill of Costs etc.   allowed.

[51] [*September 1702   An order of Court for Recording some minnitts as Follows*]   Burlington the 29th of September 1702. Att a Court held the day and yeare and Place aforesaide, Wee upon the Information and request of our present Clarke Hugh Huddy haveing received and perused the minnuts which our late Clerke Edward Hunloke had taken in short for the Courts of May last past and Said Hunloke Dyeing before he had reduced the Same Into the Records, and findeing the same to be just Except where wee have crost it out, doe order Said Huddy to Transcribe them and put them into the Bookis of the Records of the Same. William Biddle Thomas Gardiner Francis Davenport John Wills Justices.

[*Court of Sessions May 8th 1702*]   May Court of Sessions opened the 8th day 1702. Present Francis Davenport, John Addams, John Wills, Richard Ridgway, Mahlon Stacy, Samuell Furnis   Justices. Isaac Marriott Sheriffe   Edward Hunloke Clerk.

Grand Jury   William Wood, Joshua Humphy, Hormanus King, Richard French, Richard Smith, William Satterthwait, John Woolman, John Antram, Anthony Elton, Robert Pierson, George Elkinton, Thomas Middleton, John Tautam.

Petty Jury   William Petty senr., Thomas Eves, Thomas Bryan, Daniel Wills, John Bryerly, Thomas Folks junr., Richard Fennymore, Emanuell Smith, Samuell Taylor, Thomas Wilkins, Richard Haines, Isaac Decow.

Evidence   Elizabeth White and Elizabeth Brown attested in Court and Were sent to the Jury.

[51] Different handwriting.

Evidence Euphane Dunbarr, being attested saith that young George Gleave upon the Thurday next before Last November being the Twenty eight day of October lay with her and Got her with Child (being demanded where) it was in his fathers howse in the night below Stairs. George Gleaves Bond or Recognizence for appearance at this Court Read.

[189 1702 May Court of Sessions] [*Recognizances of George Gleave and his sonn*] George Gleave Junr. and George Gleave Senr. doe Recogniz Themselves Jointly and Severally unto our Lord the King in the Summe of Fifty pounds a piece To be levied upon there Goods and Chattells and Tennements upon Condition that the said George Gleave Junr. appeare at the next Court of Quarter Sessions to answer the Complaint of Euphane Dunbarr, and in the mean time to be of Goode abearing to all his Majesties Liege people. Acknowledged by them in open Court. The Court adjourned till 2 a Clock.

The Court opened.

[*Evidence*] Joseph English and William Cordery attested and sent to the Grand about Whites business.

John Henery Prisoner upon account of William Fisher called appears. A Deposition of Henry Green before Justice Ridgway.

[*Presentment John Neave and Mary*] John Neave and Mary presented formerly for cohabiting togeather as man and wife the Saide Fryley being yett alive.

[*A Licence from the Governor of Maryland*] A Licence from Governor Blackston of Maryland to Marry said Neve and Mary Fryley and a Certificate from Mr. Sharp Minister, of there being marryed the The Court order the said licence and Certificate to be recorded.

[*Evidence*] Nicholas Braddocks affidavit before Nathan Stanbury read.

[*Evidence*] Alexander Armstrongs affidavit taken before Justice Gardiner read.

[*John Neave and Marys Clearance*] The Court considering that none appears to prosecute Give Judgment for theire Clearance.

[*Order of Court to bring Rebecca Bennet before Justice Ridgway*] Rebecca Bennett now wife of John Scoley presented last Court call'd 3 times does not appear. The Court order Richard Ridgway Justice to grant his Warrant to bring her before him to binde her in a Recognizenc to appear at Next Court or commit her.

[*Rencocus Ferry presented*] The Jury present the Causey on the South Side Rancocus Ferry. The Court wave it till Hollinshead and Lippincuts agree whose it is, and how they are Oblidged to mend it.

[*Samuell Coates Recognizance with George Beard*] Samuell Coates and George Beard in open Court acknowledge themselves Indebted to our Soveraigne Lord the King in the Summe of Forty pounds to be Levied upon there or either Goods and Chattles Lands and tenements on condition that the said Samuell Coates be of Good abearing and keep his Majesties Peace as well towards all his Majesties Liedge people as perticularly towards Elizabeth White and Elizabeth Brown till the Next Court of Sessions acknowledged by them in Court.

[*Evidence*] Elizabeth White and Elizabeth Brown attested say they are afraid that Samuell Coates will abuse them or Ravish them and are afraid of there lives and Crave of the Justices to binde him to the good behaviour and the Peace   The Court order Said Coates to find Security accordingly.

[*John Boarton Bound by Recognizanc*] John Boarton acknowledged himself to be bound unto the Honourable Coll. Andrew Hamilton in the Summe of Tenne Pounds. To be Levied on his Goods and Chattles Lands and Tenements upon Condition that he pay the fine due by the Law inflicted upon Dorothy Roberts. He acknowledges the Same in open Court. he has paid the Cost.

[*An order of Court for John Henrys discharge*] John Henry a prisoner upon William Fishers account since last Court and nothing now appearing against Said Henry—The Court order to be discharged paying his fees and alsoc order the said William Fisher to deliver to said Henry all his said Henrys Goods and Effects in his said Fishers Custody or procurement according to his said Fishers promise to the saide Court.

[*Nathaniell Pettet fined*] The Court Fine Nathaniell Pettit for selling Rum and without Licence and by Proofe Keeping a very disorderly howse. The Summe of Tenn Pounds and cost and Charges of Suite and Comitted to prison till performed.

[*Seth Hill accquited by Proclamation*] Seth Hill by Proclamation is accquitted of his Charge or Crime of Clipping of mony Formerly in the Court of Sessions charged or Inform'd against him. Seth Hill by Proclamation is accquitted of all Crimes wherein he stands bound by Recognizance to answer to all Matters or things conserning Mary Neve.

[*John Neave and Mary Fryley Cleard of their Recognizance on paying the Charges*] John Neve and Mary Fryley appear according to there Recognizance and nothing appearing against them are Cleerd. John Neve and Thomas Clark promises and Oblige themselves in open Court to pay Neves Cost and Charges of this business to the Clerk when the Bill is Drawn up.

John Neve and Mary Fryley by proclamation is Cleerd of there Recognizance for there appearance.

[**190 1702 May Court of Pleas**] [*Court of Pleas May 8th and 9th*] Court of Pleas Opened May the 8th 1702. Present   Mahlon Stacy, Francis Davenport, Thomas Gardiner, John Wills, John Addams, Samuell Furnis, Richard Ridgway   Justices.

Action   John Hollinshead Plaintiff   George Gleave and Isabella his wife Defendants   All appear the Declaration read   The Defendants Plead not guilty in manner and forme. The Jury before call'd and attested.

[*Evidences*] Evidences Samuell Danford, John Midleton, Francis Spencer, Charles Spencer, Thomas Eves, Sarah Cleverly Thomas Cleverly Sarah Connore all attested.

[*Ditto*] John Middleton saith That the first time Vizt about the 15th of January Isabella Gleve told this Deponent that he the said deponent had a bad master, meaning John Hollinshead he being hired by his Said Master John Hollinshead, and telling him in the presence of Saide Hollinshead Negro, that he had Whipt, abused his said Hollinsheads Negro formerly and had killed him. [*Ditto*] Francis Spencer Saith that about the 21st of November Isabella Gleve told her that John Hollinshead had beaten or abused his Negro till he dyed.

[*Ditto*] Samuell Danford in June was Twelve month he was at Plow with John Hollinshead and that George Gleave and Isabella his wife told him that Said John Hollinshead had killd his Negro.

[*Ditto*] Charles Spencer. Saith That he heard the Negro that attempted to hang himself his Master asked him how he came to doe Such a thinge the Said Negro said That it was by Some Words Spoke to him by Gleaves wife that he had abused and beaten one Negro much and killd another.

[*Ditto*] Thomas Eves says that he was present and Says to the same effect as the last.

[*Ditto*] Sarah Cleverly John Hollinshead was agreeing with her about a boy and went with the boy as farr as Gleaves Intending to put him to him said Hollinshead, after some discoorse Isabella Gleave told her that If the Child was hers shee would kill'd the Child or bury him that she might know the end of him. This was said about three years agoe.

[*Ditto*] Thomas Cleverly saith he lived at John Hollinshead and all the time he lived there which was in the life time of the Negro that was Said to be killed, and he never Saw Said Hollinshead abuse his Negro or Servants.

[*Ditto*] Sarah Conneroe saith she lived at John Hollinshead about half year dureing most in the time of the said Negro lived and she never or knew of any abuse or hardship used to the Negro.

[*Ditto*] William Powell attested Saith that the twenty Fift day of Aprill he came to Hollinsheads howse to goe over the Ferry he Sayes that he saw the Negro as he was goeing to the howse but the Girle Missing and calling the Negro the Deponent told he Saw at the Barn where she goeing to call the Negro she runs back and Says he was hanging himself upon which this deponent says he found him hang'd with his tongue out of his mouth and after cutt down was quarter of an hower before he came to himselfe. John Weatherell and Robert Stephens attested.

[*Ditto*] John Weatherall Saith he was at George Gleaves to gett barke, being at Georges and John Hollinshead Servant asked whether there (viz John Hollinshead) Negro Jack was there but it was answered he was not after that John Hollinsheads wife asked for him and Gleaves wife Said he

1702] THE BURLINGTON COURT BOOK 269

was there upon which Said Hollinsheads wife forbad them to keep any of there Servants or encourage them to Come to there howse And the Negro upon his goeing away said he would See the end of it.

[*Ditto*] Robert Stephens saith much to the Same effect. Adjour'd till tomorrow morning.

[*Judgment*] The Jury find for the Plaintiff twelve shillings Damadge and Costs of Suite, Judgment being moved for the Court give Judgment accordingly.

Action Edward Hunloke Plaintiff John Ogborn Defendant The Plaintiff call'd appears The Defendant Call'd appears not, the Declaration read the Debt proved by the Plaintiff the Court order and give Judgment for the Plaintiff for eleven pounds Fifteen shillings and Costs.

Action Henry Beck and Joseph Scattergood Plaintiffs John Pears Defendant Call'd, neither appear'd pay halfe Fees and continued.

John Petty Plaintiff Isack Horner Defendant Cald neither appeard pay half Fees and continued.

Action William Beaks Grimston Bowde Thomas Bavin the Plaintiff call'd 3 times not appearing The Court with Patience waiteing a longe time for some body that Might to appear for the Plaintiff but none apeareing the Court gives nonsuit against the Plaintiff and order the Prisoner to be discharged.

[*William Beaks Jonathan Daviss Defendant*] Action William Bekes Plaintiff Jonathan Daviss Defendant The Plaintiff called 3 times appears not the Defendant craves a Nonsuite which (after much patience of the Court) the Court give a Non Suite.

This is a true Coppy of the minuits left by Mr. Edward Hunloke and Recorded by me Hugh Huddy.

[191 1702 August Court of Sessions] [*Court of Sessions August 8th 1702 Being the first year of the Reigne of Queen Anne*] Court of Sessions opened the 8th day of August 1702. Present Francis Davenport, William Biddle, John Wills, John Addams, Samuell Furnis, Richard Ridgway Justices. Henry Grubb Sub-Sheriffe Thomas Gardiner kings Attorney Hugh Huddy Clerk.

The Justices cummission of the Peace for the County of Burlington from the Honourable Coll. Andrew Hamilton Governor Read. The said Governors Commission to Thomas Rapier Sheriffe Read A Deputation from Said Rapier to Henry Grubb as Subsheriffe Read and accepted by the Court. The Said Governors Commission to Hugh Huddy Clerke Read.

Constables Called Joseph Smith, John Ruddero appears Thomas Tindall, John Wetherell appears.

Grand Jury Eliakim Warden att[ested], Dan Sutton, James Verey, John Wells Junr., Robert Edwards, John Chesshire, Nathan Allen, William Hackney, Richard Smith, Michael Buffen, Thomas Scattergood, William

Gabitas, Edmond Wells, Samuell Gibson, Attested and Charge Given by Francis Davenport.

Traverse Jury   Benjamin Wheat, Thomas Smith, Daniell Smith, Christopher Wetherell, Thomas Curtis, William Bustin, Obadiah Ireton, Mathew Watson, William Matloke, Henry Beck, Anthony Fryer, Jonathan Lovett.

Court adjour'd till 2 of the Clock.

Mett againe The same Justice Present and adjour'd till the 29th of 7ber 1702.

Court of Pleas opened at the same time. and Place and adjourn'd as aforesaide.

[*Court of Sessions and Pleas 7ber the 29th 1702*]   Court of Sessions opened September 29th 1702. Present   Francis Davenport, William Biddle, Thomas Gardiner, Justices. Henry Grubb Sub sheriffe   Hugh Huddy Clerk.

The Grand Jury aforesaid Called.

The Court adjourn'd till 2 of the afternoon. Mett againe the same justices and John Wells Justice.

And for as much as neither Grand nor Pettit Jury appeared full by reason of Sickness the Court dismist all till a new Summons.

Court of Pleas opened at the same time and place. Before   William Biddle, Francis Davenport, Thomas Gardiner, John Wells   Justices present. Called   And a full Jury not appearing adjourn'd or rather dismissed till November Court which comes of Course the 3rd day of November Next.

[**192 1702 November Court of Sessions**]   Court of Sessions opened the 3rd day of November 1702.

At A Generall Quarter Sessions of the Peace held for the County of Burlington at Burlington the 3d of November in the first year of the Reigne of our Sovereigne Lady Anne by the Grace of God of England Scotland France and Ireland Queen Defender of the Faith etc. Annoque Domini 1702

Before   William Biddle, Thomas Gardiner, Samuell Furnis, Richard Ridgway   Justices. Henry Grubb Subsheriffe   Hugh Huddy Clerk.

Grand Jury William Emley, Samuell Bunteing, John Warne, Robert Person, John Ogborn Senr., William Evans, John Copperthwaite, John Hamill, Thomas Haynes, Thomas Bryan, Nathaniell Cripps, John Hollingshead, Andrew Smith, Johanis Larransen   Attested and Charge given by William Biddle.

Constables Called   Charles Millard apears, John Stocden   ap[ears], Joseph Smith ap[ears], John Wetherell ap[ears], Thomas Peache ap[ears].

Traverse Jury called over   Edward Rockell, John Bembridge, John Murfen, John Bunting, William Biddle Junr., Mathew Champion, Charles French, Richard Fennimore, Nicholas Martineau, Thomas Eves, Daniell Wells, Thomas Wallis.

Court adjourn'd till 2 of the Clock.

Mett againe the same justices and Mahlon Stacy. Euphan Dunbar attested in open Court and Sent to the Grand Jury. John Wetherell attested in open Court and sent to the Grand Jury.

Adjourn'd till tomorrow 8 of the Clock.

November the 4th Then met and present Mahlon Stacy William Biddle Thomas Gardiner. After Court opened Sarah Gilbert attested and sent to the Grand Jury. Mary Wheate attested and sent to the Grand Jury.

Adjourn'd till 2 of the Clock. Then mett and present as before And Richard Ridgway Justice present.

[*Rebecca Bennet now Scowly Sentence*] Rebecca wife of John Scowly late called Rebecca Bennett was presented by the Grand Jury for committing fornication with one Thomas Williams to which presentment her husband John Scowly in her behalfe Submitted therefore the Court considders and adjudges that the said Rebecca or her said Husband pay the Summe of five pounds to the use of the Governor or receive the Corporall punishment according to Law.

[*Eupham Dunbar Sentence*] The Grand Jury allso present Eupham Dunbar for haveing a Basterd Child as alsoe for Committing fornication with one George Gleaves to which Indictment Shee pleaded Guilty Therefore the Court considder and addjudges that Shee pay the Summe of five pounds to the use of the Governor or receive the Corporall punishment according to Law.

[*Presentment*] The Grand Jury also Present John Stockton Constable of Springfield for Neglect of his office.

[*Presentment*] Thomas Duglis overseer of the High Ways for the Township of Springfield presents James Shinn William Budd William Fuller William Blouk Benjamin Cambell Mordecay Anderson for refuseing to doe there Servis at the Highways.

[*George Gleave Junr. presented and his Recognizance with John Hollinshead*] The Grand Jury alsoe present George Gleave Junr. for fornication as above who appears and Traverses his presentment till next Court, and produces John Hollingshead of this County yeo man who together with the said George Gleve Jointly and Seaverally Recognices themselves to be bound to our Sovereigne Lady the Queen in the Summe of fourty pounds a piece to be Levied upon there Lands and tenements Goods and Chattells etc. Sub Condition That George Gleve appear next Court and prosecute his Said presentment with effect.

[193 **1702 November Court of Sessions**] [*Presentment Highways*] Richard Ridgway Justice presents a return of Thomas Duglas and Samuell Frettwell, that John French William Brown and Samuell Coate for Neglecting there Service and duty at the highway.

[*William Richards and John Tonken Recognizance*] William Richards held and firmly bound unto our Sovereigne Lady the Queen in the Summe of fourty pounds Silver monys, and John Tonken in the Summe of Twenty pounds upon Condition that William Richards appears next Court to answer what Shall be objected against him and in meane time to be of good behaviour.

[*Mary Kendrick presented for Fellony*] The Grand Jury also present Mary Kendrick for Feloniously takeing out of the howse of Sarah Gilbert of Burlington a Summe of Silver money about four pounds Who appearing Pleded Guilty Therefore the Court considers and adjudes that the Saide Mary Kendrick pay to the said Gilbert twelve pounds and to remayne in Custody till complyance Therewith and paying her fees. Mary Bown accquitted by Proclamation.

Robert Person did not prosecute Richard Rumsey according to his Recognizence of fourty pounds. Adjourn'd the Court to Henry Grubbs for halfe hower Justices present as before, mett againe.

[*An order of Court for Selling William Dickinsons Maire*] Whereas William Dickinson late of the County of Burlington was taken and Committed to the Goale of Said County for makeing and Coyning Falce monys which at the same time he was possessed of a Black mare which said Dickinson sometime after broke the Kings Prison and left many Charges unpaid for the defraying of Which this Court orders the Sherriff to sell the said Mare and return said monys next Court to Satisfy Said Debts.

The Court adjourn'd till it comes in Course.

[52] [*Court of Pleas November 3rd 1702*] Pleas Holden and Tryed at Burlington. the third day of November in the first yeare of the Reigne of Anna Queen of England etc.

Before Mahlon Stacy William Biddle Thomas Gardiner and Richard Ridgway Justices.

William Fisher came and Exhibited into the Court then and there a certaine Bill against John Henery of a Plea of Trespass on the Case which said Hill followeth in these words Vizt Burlington to wit Said John Henery of the County of Burlington was attached to answer William Fisher of the Same County Yeoman of a Plea of Trespass on the Case And Whereupon the Said William by Thomas Clark his attorney complaines for that Whereas the Said William is a good true and faithfull Leige Subject of Sovereigne Lady the Queen and as a just and Honest person without any Kinds of Fellony Murder Theft cheating dishonesty or any base and wicked crime or Suspicion of the Same Wholy free Clear and unsuspected hath always from the tyme of his Nativity until this present time lived remained and Continued And of good name fame Credit and Estimation amongst all her majesties Leige Subjects to whome he was Known hitherto hath allways been Esteemed reputed and accounted and hath Conserv'd himselfe and all his Effects Safe and untainted and in nowise Subject to the Reigour of the Law

[52] Different handwriting.

for Such like offences made and provided. By reason whereof the said William hath deservedly had and obtained the Love favour and good will of his Neighbours and other his Majesties good Subjects. Nevertheless the Said John being not ignorunt of the premisses but envying the State and Condition of the Said William and maliciously intending not Only the good name Creditt and reputation of the Said William to ruine and utterly destroy and to bring the Said William into hate and evill oppinion of his neighbours and other her Majesties Liege people but allso designing him the Said William into infamy trouble and danger of his life to bring on the twentieth day of February in the 14th year of the Reigne of William the third late of England etc. King Anno Domini 1701/2 at Burlington in the County of Burlington aforesaid haveing Speech and Communication with divers Leidg Subjects of our Sovereigne Lady the Queen then and there being present of and Concerning him the Said William in their presents and hearing did then and there openly and publickly with a Loud and audible voice falsely and maliciously affirm pronounce and declare and publish of the Said William the said false feigned Scandalous Malicious and approbious words following (Vizt) That he (meaning the said William the plaintiff) is a Theife and a Murderer and was (meaning againe the Said William the Plaintiff) burnt in the hand: Whereas in truth the Said William no fellony or murder did ever Comit or perpetrate (or ever did receive the ignominy of being burnt in the hand) by pretext of the Speaking publishing and declaring of which Said falce Malicious and Scandalous words the Said William [**194 November Court of Pleas 1702**] is not Onely Extreamly hurt and damnified in his good name credit and Reputation aforesaid on which his means of livelyhood very much depends but also he the said William is mightily hindred in his Lawfull business For and by reason of the aforesaid false Malicious and Scandalous words his Neighbours and other her Majesties Leige People (which before Speaking and publishing of the Said false Malicious and Scandalous words which with him the Said William use to deal and Converse) decline and refuse to have further Conversation with him and also by reason thereof He the said William is in danger of being brought under the punishment which the Law directs and provides for Felony murder and such Like Enormous Crimes Whereupon the said William Saith he is worse and hath damage to the Valew of five hundred pounds Current money and there of brings his Suits etc.

And the Said John in his own proper person Came and defended the Force and Injury when Etc. And Saith that the aforesaid William his action against him ought not to have or maintaine because that before the Comencing of the action and before the tyme in which twas Supposed the said words were Spoken the Said William was burnt in the hand for felony in the Fort of New York So that it was Lawfull for him to Say the Said Words And this he averred and prayd Judgment if the said William ought to have his Said action against him. And the Said William Saith that he for any thing by the Said John above Alledged from haveing his action ought not to be barred because he Saith that the Said John did Speake the said words Specified in the Declaration the day and year aforesaid in manner and forme as the Said William above against him has Complained of in his own wrong and with out any Such cause as by the Said John alledged with out that; that the Said William was burnt in the hand as the Said John has alledged and this he desires may be inquired of by the Country And the Said John in like manner Therefore twas Comanded the Sherriffe that he Cause to Come 12 good and Lawfull of the Neighberhood by whome etc. who returnes Edward Rockell etc. who being duly attested Say that they finde for the Plaintiff and that he was damnified by the Speaking of the Said False and Scandelous words by the said Defendant in the Summe of 200l. besides Costs of Suite Therefore tis Considered that the said William Shall recover against the said John the damage aforesaid by the Jury aforesaid in form aforesaid attested as also the Summe of 1l. 19s. 4d. for there Cost and Charges of the Said William in this action Expended which in the whole amounts to the Summe of 201l. 19s. 4d. and the Said John in mercy etc.

Be it also Remembered that the Same day year and Place Came William Beakes and Exhibited into Court a Certaine Bill against John Hutchinson of a Plea of Debt which bill followeth in these words Burlington to wit Said John Hutchinson of the County of Burlington yeoman was Summoned to answer William Beaks of a Plea that he render unto him the Summe of fourteen pounds Current Silver Money which to him he Oweth and from him unjustly detaineth etc. And Whereupon the Said William by Thomas Clark his atturney Complaines for that Whereas the said John the Twentieth day of October in the thirteenth year of the Reigne of William the third late of England etc. King Anno Domini One thousand Seven hundred and one at Burlington in the County of Burlington by his certaine writing Obligatory under his hand and Seal having date the day and year aforesaid became houlden and firmly bound unto the Said William in the said Summe of fourteen pounds Current Silver money to be paid to the Said William when he the Said John Should be thereunto required nevertheless the said John altho often required (viz) the tenth day of February in the thirteenth year aforesaid at Burlington aforesaid and often afterwards the Said Summe of fourteen Pounds [195 **November Court of Pleas 1702**] nor any part thereof to the Said William hath not paid nor Contended but the Same to pay hitherto hath and Still doth utterly refuse and deny to the damage of the Said William twenty pounds and thereof brings his Suit etc. And bring here into Court the writing aforesaid with debt aforesaid in forme aforesaid doth testifie whose date is the day and year aforesaid etc. Thomas Clark Que 28th July 1702 and the said John by Samuell Terrett his Attorney Comes and defends the force and injury when etc. And nothing in Bar of the said action of the Said William doth say by which the Said William against the Said John remains Undefended thereof therefore tis Considered that the said William recover against the Said John the Summe of 8l. 11s. 6d. for his debt aforesaid being the Summe mentioned in the Condition of the Said Obligation with Lawfull Intrest, As also the Summe of 2l. 8s. 2d. for his Cost and Charges in that Suit Expended which by his Own assent was adjudged by the Court and the Said John in mercy etc.

Be it also Remembred that the Same day year and Place came Isaac Marriott and then and there Exhibited into Court a Certaine Bill against Richard Cauin of a Plea of Trespass on the Case which Said Bill followeth in these words, Burlington to wit Richard Cauin late of the County of Burlington was attached by his goods and Chattles to answer Isaac Marriott of Burlington merchant of a Plea of Trespass on the Case And Whereupon the Said Isaac by Thomas Clark his atturney Complaines For that whereas the said Richard the Last day of December in the year of the Reigne of our late Sovereigne Lord William the third King of England etc. the thirteenth Anno Domini 1701 at Burlington in the County of Burlington aforesaid was Lawfully indebted to the Said Isaac in the Sum of Five pounds Eight Shillings and Eight pence current money of West New Jersey for Sundry goods and Merchandises by the Said Isaac at the Special Instants and Request of the Said Richard to the Said Richard before that tyme Sold and delivered And being So there of indebted He the Said Richard afterwards to witt the Same day year and place aforesaid In Consideration thereof did upon him selfe assume and to the Said Isaac then and there faithfully promist that He the said Richard the Said Summe of five pounds Eight Shillings and Eight pence to the said Isaac when he Should be afterwards thereunto required would well and truly Content and Satisfie and pay. And altho the Said Richard hath paid to the Said Isaac the Summe of Fourteen Shillings in part of the Said Summe of five pounds Eight Shillings and Eight pence Never thelesse as to four pounds fourteen Shillings and Eight pence Residue of the Said Five pounds Eight Shillings and Eight pence the Said Richard tho often afterwards required (viz) the first day of January in the thirteenth year aforesaid at Burlington aforesaid to the Said Isaac hath not paid nor in any wise Satisfied but the same to pay hath and Still doth utterly refuse and deny to the damage of the Said Isaac ten pounds current money and there of he brings his Suit etc. Thomas Clark Quer 16th July 1702 And also the Defendant was Solemnly caled three tymes appeared not but make default and the Plaintiff prays Judgment for his damages by occasion of the premises which against the said Richard he ought to recover which after deliberation was granted by default but because tis unknown to the Court what damages the said Isaac by occasion of the Premisses has Sustained Tis Comanded the Sherriffe that by the Attestation of good and Lawfull men of the County aforesaid he dilgently inquire what damges the said Isaac has Sustained by Occasion of the premisses aforesaid as also for his Cost and Charges in this Suit Expended And the Inquisition which the Said Sheriffe Shall thereupon take he make to appear before the Justices of the Said Court to be held at Burlington aforesaid the twentieth day of February next under his Seale and the Seales of the Said Jurors etc.

Be it also Remembred that the Same day year and place Came William Gabitas and Exhibited into Court a certain Bill against Joseph Scattergood of a Plea of Debt which Said Bill followeth in these words (Vizt) See the declaration on the file. And altho the Said Joseph was Sollemnly Called 3 tymes did not appear but made default therefore it is Considered that the Said William ought to recover against the said Joseph the debt aforesaid upon which the Said William Craves Judgment onely for 18l. 10s. and Interest with Cost of Suit and remits the rest of the Said debt upon which the Court by the Consent of the Plaintiff [**196 November Court of Pleas 1702**] adjudges that he recover the Summe of 19l. 05s. 00d, as also the Summe of one pound Eighteen Shillings for his Costs and Charges in that behalfe Expended And the said Joseph in Mercy etc.

Hugh Wright Plaintiff versus Thomas Embly Defendant, Being called Hugh Wright appears in his own proper person and was attested that several of his Evidence could not be procured to attend at this instant and praied the action might be Continued and it was Continued accordingly.

The Court Adjurned till two of the Clock. Then mett and present as before with Richard Ridgway Justice.

Be it also Remembered that the Same day year and Place Came Samuell Jennings and then and there Exhibited into Court a Certaine Bill against John Smith which Said Bill followeth in these words (Vizt) Burlington to wit Samuel Jenings of Burlington in the Said County Merchant Plaintiff Complaines against John Smith of the Said County Blacksmith Defendant of a Plea That Whereas the said Defendant on the First day of December 1686 at Burlington aforesaid did borrow and receive of the said Plaintiff Certaine Smiths Toole and Materials hereafter mentioned to witt One pair of Bellows and irontue and one anvill One vice one pickhorne One great hammer Two hand hammers a nailing hammer Ladle hammer and a rivetting hammer Six pair tongs To ax Mondrils a toole for nailes for Cart Wheell nine Chissils and punches to bolsters one Butteris five files Two halfe round one round and two Flatts and a Wireble Steady [53] to be delivered to the Said Plaintiff when he the said Defendant should be thereunto required and altho the said Defendant afterwards to witt one Fourteenth day of September last past at Burlington aforesaid and at Severall other days

---

[53] *Sic.* The Smithsonian Institution writes that this doubtless refers to "a *variable steady* which is a steady that can be varied as to height. The steady is a tool that stands on the floor to support the end of a long piece of metal while the other end is being worked on." See also note 57 below.

and tymes was required to redeliver the Said tooles and Materials to the Plaintiff Neverthelesse the said Defendant hath not redelivered them but the Same to redeliver hath denyd and Still doth deny and Converts the said and Materials to his own use To the Plaintiff Damages of Twenty pounds And there of he brings Suit etc. And altho the Defendant was Sollemnly called 3 times he did not appear but made default And the Plaintiff prays Judgment for his Damages by occasion of the premisses which against the Said John he ought to recover which after deliberation was granted by default but becase tis unknown to the Court what damages the said Samuell by occasion of the premisses has Sustained Tis Commanded the Sherriffe that by the attestation of good and lawfull men of the County aforesaid he diligently Enquire what damages the Said Samuell has Sustained by occasion of the premisses aforesaid as also for his Cost and Charges in this Suit Expended And the Inquisition which the Said Sheriffe shall there upon take he make to appair before the Justices of the Said Court to be held at Burlington aforesaid the 20th day of February next under his Seale and the Seales of the Said Juriors etc.

Thomas Andrews Plaintiff versus Isaac Web Defendant Plaintiff appears by Thomas Clerke his Attorney But Defendant not appearing therefore the action is ordered to Continue untill next Court.

Be it also Remembered that the same day year and place Came John Jones by Thomas Clark his atturney and then and there Exhibited into Court a Certaine Bill against Mouns Cox of a Plea of Debt which Said Bill followeth in these words (Vizt) Burlington to wit Mouns Cox of the County of Burlington Otherwise called Mouns Kocks of the County of Burlington Yeoman Was Summoned to answer John Jones of Philadelphia merchant of a Plea that he render unto him the Summe of Four Pounds Eighteen Shillings and Eight pence current money of Pensilvania which to him he oweth and from him unjustly detaineth etc. And Whereupon the said John Jones by Thomas Clerke his atturney Saith For that whereas the Said Mouns Kocks the twenty Sixth day of June in the first yeare of the Reigne of our Sovereigne Lady Anne of England etc. Queen Annoque Domini 1702 at Burlington in the County of Burlington aforesaid by his Certaine writing or bill Obligatory which the Said John Sealed with the Seale of the Said Mouns produced here in Court whose date is the day and year aforesaid did acknowledge him Selfe to owe and be Indebted to the said John in the Said Sum of four pounds Eighteen Shillings and Eight pence Pensilvania money to be paid to the Said John his heirs Executors administrators Assignes or Lawfull atturney at or before the twenty fifth day of July Next [197 November Court of Pleas 1702] Ensuing after the date of the Said Bill to which payment well and truly to be made the Said Mouns Obliged himselfe His heirs Executors and administrators in the said Summe of four pounds Eighteen Shillings and Eight pence Pensilvania money firmly by the said Bill or writing And the Said John in fact Saith that the said Mouns hath not paid to him the said John the Said Summe of four pounds Eighteen Shillings and Eight pence at or before the Said twenty fifth day of July which to him at or before the Said day he ought to have paid according to the Forme and effect of the Said Bill by which action accrueth to the Said John to required and have from the Said Mouns the Said Four pounds Eighteen Shillings and Eight pence Nevertheless the Said Mouns altho often requested the Said Summe of Four Pounds Eighteen Shillings and Eight pence to the Said John as yet hath not rendred but the Same to him to render hitherto hath denyed and Still doth utterly refuse and deny Whereupon the Said John Saith He is damnified to the value of Eight pounds Current Money And thereupon brings Suit etc. Thomas Clarke Quer 20 8bris 1702 and the said Mouns appears by his wife who defends the force and injury when etc. and nothing in Barr to the action of the Said John doth Say by which the Said John remaines against the said Mouns undefended thereof therefore tis Considred that the said John recover against the Said Mouns his Debt aforesaid togeather with 1l. 15s. 8d. for his Cost and Charges in the Suit Expended which by the said Court is adjudged and the said Mouns in Mercy etc.

Be it also Remembered that the same day year and place came Mathew Champion and then and there Exhibited a Certaine Bill against Nicholas Martino of a Plea of Debt which Said Bill followeth in these words Burlington to wit Nicholas Martineau of Burlington Otherwise called Nicholas Martineau of Willingborough in the County of Burlington Carpenter was Summoned to answer Mathew Champion of Springfeild yeoman of a Plea that he render unto him the Summe of thirteen pounds which to him he oweth and from him unjustly detaines etc. And Whereupon the Said Mathew by Thomas Clark his atturney Saith For that whereas the Said Nicholas Martineau the first day of October in the Year of our Lord god one thousand Seven hundred and one at Burlington in the County of Burling within the Jurisdiction of this Court granted himselfe to be held and firmly bound to the Said Mathew in the Said Summe of thirteen pounds Current money of the Province of West New Jersey to be paid to the Said Mathew when he Should be thereunto required Neverthelesse the Said Nicholas altho often Required the Said thirteen pounds nor any part thereof to the Said Mathew hath not rendred nor paid but the Same to pay hath hitherto and Still doth utterly refuse and deny Whereupon the Said Mathew Saith he is worse and hath damage to the valew of twenty pounds money aforesaid and thereon brings his Suite etc. and brings into Court the writing aforesaid which the debt aforesaid in forme aforesaid doth testifie whose date is the day and year aforesaid etc. Thomas Clarke and the Said Nicholas Cometh and defendeth the Force and injury when etc. And nothing in barr of the Said action of the said Mathew doth say by which the said Mathew remaines against the said Nicholas undefended there of Therefore tis Considered that the said Mathew recover against the Said Nicholas the Summe of 6l. 10s. 0 for his Debt aforesaid being the Summe Mentioned in Condition of the Said writing Obligatory with Lawfull interest as also the Summe of fifteen Shillings for his Cost and Charges in this Suite by the Said Mathew Expended which by his own assent was adjudged by the Court And said Nicholas in mercy etc.

Be it also Remembered that the same day year and place Came Isaac Marriott and then and there Exhibited a Certaine Bill against John Garwood of a Plea of trespass on the Case which said Bill followeth in these words Burlington to wit John Garwood of the County of Burlington was Sumoned to answer Isaac Marriott of Burlington aforesaid merchant of a Plea of Trespasse on the Case And Whereupon the Said Isaac by Thomas Clark his Attorney Complaines For that whereas the Said John the twenty Second day of April [198 **November Court of Pleas 1702**] in the year of our Lord One thousand, Seven hundred and two at Burlington in the County of Burlington with in the Jurisdiction of this Court did togeather accompt with the said Isaac of divers Summes of Money to the Said Isaac by the Said John for divers goods and Merchantdizes by the Said John From the said Isaac before that tyme had and received and by the said Isaac to the Said John before Sold and delivered) before that tyme due and owing and being in arrears unpaid And upon which accompt the Said John was found in arrears towards the Said Isaac in the Summe of Five pounds Six Shillings and five pence Current money of the Province of West New Jersey upon which the said John In Consideration thereof did upon himselfe assume and to the Said Isaac did then and there faithfully promiss that he the Said John the said five pounds Six Shillings and five pence to the said Isaac when thereunto required would well and truly Content Satisfie and pay Neverthelesse the Said John his promiss and assumtion aforesaid not regarding but intending to deceive and defraud the Said Isaac in that behalfe the Said five pounds Six Shillings and five pence nor any part thereof to the said Isaac hath not Satisfied nor paid Altho often there unto by the Said Isaac afterwards required (Vizt) the Sixteenth day of October in the year aforesaid at Burlington aforesaid but the Same to pay did utterly refuse and deny and Still doth refuse Whereupon the said Isaac, Saith he is damnified to the Valew of ten pounds Current money and thereof brings his Suite etc. Thomas Clarke Quer 20th 8bris 1702 and altho the Said John was Sollemnly Caled 3 times did not Come but made default upon which the Said Isaac proving the accompt made up with the Said John upon his Solemn Attestation and that he never had received any part or parts of the Said Summe mentioned in the said declaration Therefore it is Considered that the said Isaac recover against the Said John the Summe of 5l. 6s. 5d. for his Debt as also the Summe of 1l. 16s. 2d. for his Costs and Charges in the Suit by the Said Isaac Expended and Said John in Mercy etc.

Be it also Remembered that the same day year and place Came Hugh Huddy and Margaret Hunloke also by Thomas Clerk their Atturney and then and there Exhibited a Certaine Bill against Thomas Midgley of a Plea of debt which Said Bill followeth in these words (Vizt) Burlington to wit Thomas Midgley late of Burlington Sadler was attached by his Goods and Chattles to answer Hugh Huddy and Margarett Hunloke Executors of the last will and Testament of Edward Hunloke late of Burlington aforesaid merchant deceased of a Plea that the render unto them the Summe of Ten pounds money of this Province of West New Jersey which from them he unjustly detaines etc. And Whereupon the Said Hugh and Margarett by Thomas Clerke their atturney Say for that whereas the aforesaid Edward in his Life tyme (vizt) the first day of November in the Eleaventh year of the Reigne of William the third late of England etc. King Annoque Domini 1699 at Burlington aforesaid did demisse to the aforesaid Thomas Midgley one Message or dwelling house with a garden and other appurtenances there unto belonging Situate lyeing and being in the town of Burlington aforesaid to have to hold to the said Thomas and his Assignes from the said first day of November untill the full end and terme of one whole year from thence next following fully to be Compleat and Ended and from year to year So long as boath parties were So Content rendring therefore yearly to the said Edward or his assignes four pounds Current money of West New Jersey to be paid in own and Equall percent in two Severall payments that is to say two pounds one moyety thereof at or upon the Second day of May and the Other moiety thereof at or upon the Second day of November in every year yearly So Long as the Said Thomas Should hould the Same by virtue of which Demisse the aforesaid Thomas in to the Messuge and garden aforesaid with the appurtenances did enter upon and was thereof Possessed and the said Messuage Gardien and appurtenances for the Space of two years and halfe did occupy and posses and the said ten pounds due for the two years and halfe rent Ending the Second day of May in the yeare one thousand Seven hundred and two to the Said Edward in his life tyme did not pay By which action accrewed to the Said Edward to have and receive of the Said Thomas the Said ten pounds Nevertheless the Said Thomas altho often required the Said ten pounds to the said Edward in his life time or to the [199 **February Quarter Sessions 1702**] the said Hugh and Margarett Since the death of the Said Edward hath not rendred but the Same to render did deny and Still doth deny to render to the Said Hugh and Margarett but unjustly detaineth Whereupon they Say that the[y] are worse and have damage to the valew of fifteen pounds and thereon bring their Suite etc. and produce here in Court the Letter of administration by which it appears that they are Executors of Said Edward and ought to have admission etc. Thomas Clarke Quer And the Said Thomas by Vesulah Midgley his atturney Comes and defends the force and injury when etc. nothing in Barr of the said action doth Say by which Said Hugh and Margarett remaine undefended against the said Thomas thereof Therefore tis Concidered that the said Hugh and Margarett recover against the said Thomas the Summe of 7l. 14s. od. which is all that appear to the Court to be due from the Said Thomas to the said Plaintiffs for the Rent aforesaid as also the Sum of one pound fifteen shillings and 10d. for their Costs and Charges in this Suit Expended by the Said Hugh and Margarett which by their own assent was adjudged by the Court and Said Thomas Midgeley in mercy etc.

[54] February Court of Sessions opened.

At a Court of Generall Quarter Sessions of the Peace Holden at Burlington for the County thereof Twentieth day of February in the first year of the Reigne of our Sovereigne Lady Anne of England etc. Queen Annoque Domini 1702 Before William Biddle, Francis Davenport, John Wills, John Addams, Samuell Furnis Justices of the Peace for the Said County.

The Sheriffe of the County of Burlington Returned the names of the persons which he had Summoned for a grand Inquest to Serve for this Sessions who being called appear and Are as followeth William Wood, John Woolman, Abraham Hewling, James Bingham, Isaac Watson, Jarvis Farrow, Richard French, Thomas Ridgway, Annania Gant, Job Stocton, Daniell Smith, Henery Marlow, Joseph English All appeared Who being attested According to Law and the Charge Given to them by Francis Davenport Withdrew by themselves.

The Severall Constables being Called Appear and Make their Returnes of New Constables who also appearing were Attested to their office for the year Ensuing and are as followeth For Hopewell William Spencer. Nottingham Thomas Tindal. Chesterfield John More. Springfield Samuell Coates. Burlington Thomas Middleton and Thomas Wetherill. Northampton Thomas Bryan. Chester Robert Stiles. Willingborough Henery Wells.

[200 February Quarter Sessions 1702] The Sheriff also returned the Panell of the Traverse Jury who being Called Over appeared as followeth Thomas Gilberthorpe, John Abbott, Richard Eare, Thomas Wilkins, Thomas Eves Junr., William Hollingshead, Abraham Broune Junr., Caleb Sheriffe, Joshua Humphery, John Hudson, Samuell Levincole, James Addams all appeared.

Court adjournes till two of Clocke in the after Noon Post Meridiam two of Clock Court mett againe and Opened before William Biddle, Francis Davenport, John Wills, John Addams, Richard Ridgway Justices.

George Gleve called upon his Recognicence and Imeadiatly Answering

[54] Different handwriting.

the Court order that the Recognicence be Continued till next may Court.

William Richard called appears upon his Recognicence and upon the Queens Attorneys Motion orders said Richards Recognizance to be Continued till next may Court.

Charles Garrett tent in twenty Pounds Silver Money, Thomas Kendall tent in twenty Pounds Like Money to our Lady the Queen Sub: Conditiond that Garrett be of good behaviour and appear at next May Court.

Whereas Last November Court Mary Kendrick was Convicted by her Own Confession for feloniously Stealing Four Pounds Money of this Province or thereabouts from Sarah Gilbert It was then adjudged by the Court that the Said Mary pay to the Said Sarah the Sum of twelve pounds Money aforesaid According to an Act of Assembly of this Province for four fould Restitution or Retalliation And Whereas the Said Mary has not Wherewithall to Satisfie the Same It is ordered by this Court That for the Satisfaction of the Said Summe shee be Sold by the Sheriffe of this County to Serve so Many years as may pay her said Judgment and Fees of Court.

John Moore desires Licence to Keepe a Victualling House or Ordinary which the Court grants he Observing the Method the Law requires.

A petition of the Inhabitants of the townshipp of Nottingham was read in these words   Nottingham the 19th 12th Mon. 1702 To the Honerable the Queens Justices present Sitting—Whereas there has been for more than twenty Years past a Highway Leading from the Falls towards Burlington over Croswick Creeke through the Plantation now of Samuell Overton which Much Shortens the Journey as well for the Conveniancy of Travelors as also for the Inhabitants of the townshipp of Nottingham and Whereupon the Inhabitants at their last towns Meeting Were Unanimusly Concenting and did there all Concent and agree (Excepting the Said Samuell Overton) that the same should be so Continued and remaine as a free Bridle stye and Way for travelers etc. And therefore humbly prays the Concurrance of the Court in Confirmation of the Same   Signed in Behalfe of the Towne per William Emley Clerk. Whereupon the Court Orders that it Shall Continue a Bridle way.

The Grand Enquest bring in a presentment as on the file.

[201 February Court of Pleas 1702]   Pleas Holden and Tryed at Burlington for the County thereof the twentieth day of February in the First year of the Reigne of Anna Queen of England etc.

Before   William Biddle, Francis Davenport, John Wills, John Addams, Richard Ridgway   Justices.

Be it Remembred that Samuel Jennings Came and Exhibited into the Court then and there a Certaine Bill against Jonas Moone in a Plea of Debt Which Said Bill followes in these words Burlington to wit Samuell Jennings of Bridlington in the County of Bridlington In the Province of West New Jersey merchant Complaines against Jonas Moon of the Said

County Yeoman in a Plea of Debt for that Whereas the Said Plaintiff Sold and delivered to the Said Defendant Certaine Wares Goods and Merchandizes to the Valew of three pounds and ten shillings of Lawfull Money of the Said Province and the said Defendant being So Indebted the Said three pounds and tenn Shillings to the Said Plaintiff hath not yett paid altho the said Defendant by the said Plaintiff within the Jurisdiction of this Court hath Severall times been thereunto required two the Said Plaintiffs Damage the Summe of   And thereupon brings his Suit etc. And the Said Jonas appeared in his proper person and defends the force and Injury When etc. and Saith that he Cannot gainsay the Action of the Said Samuell aforesaid Nor but that he doth owe to the said Samuell the Summe of two pounds Sixteen Shillings and four pence as the Said Samuell declares against him wherefore tis Considered that the Said Samuell Recover against the said Jonas the Said Debt of two pounds Sixteen Shillings and four pence as also the Sum of Eighteen Shillings as well for his Damages which he Sustained by reason of the detention of the Debt aforesaid as also for his Cost about the Suit in that behalfe Expended appointed by the Court and by his assent adjudged which damages in the Whole do amount to the Summe of 3l. 14s. 04d. and the Said Jonas in Mercy etc.

Be it also remembred that the same day and year and place Came Hugh Huddy and Margarett Hunloke Executors of the Last Will and Testament of Edward Hunloke deceased by Thomas Clerke their Attorney and Exhibited into Court then and there a Certaine Bill against Jonas Moone of a Plea of Trespasse on the Case which said Bill followes in these Words Burlington to wit Jonas Moone Late of Burlington Labourer Was Attached to answer Hugh Huddy and Margarett Hunloke Executors of the Last Will and Testament of Edward Hunloke deceased of a Plea of Trespasse on the Case And Whereupon the Said Hugh and Margaret by Thomas Clerke their Attorney Complaines for that Whereas the Said Jonas in the Life tyme of the said Edward (Vizt) the Nineteenth day of June in the twelfth year of the Reigne of William the Third of England etc. King at Burlington aforesaid was Lawfully Indebted to the aforesaid Edward in the Summe of three pounds Sixteen shillings and Eight pence Current Money of West New Jersey for Sundry Goods and Merchandizes by the said Edward in his Life tyme to the Said Jonas before that tyme sold and delivered And by the Said Jonas from the Said Edward had and Received and being So thereof Indebted he the Said Jonas in Consideration thereof did afterwards (Viz) the Same day year and place upon himself assume and to the Said Edward in his Life tyme then and there faithfuly promisse that he the Said Jonas the said three pounds sixteen shillings and Eight pence to the Said Edward when he should be thereunto afterwards Required would well and truly Content Satisfie and pay Neverthelesse the Said Jonas his promisse and assumption aforesaid not regarding but intending the Said Edward in his Life tyme and the said Hugh and Margerett after the death of the Said Edward in that behalfe to deceive and defraud the Said three pounds Sixteen Shillings and Eight pence Nor any part thereof unto the Said Edward in his Life tyme or to the Said Hugh and Margarett or Either of them Since the death of the said Edward hath not paid nor them nor Either of them therefore hath any Wise Contented Altho thereunto the Said Jonas by the Said Edward in his Life tyme often and by the Said Hugh and Margarett After the death of the Said Edward Afterward (Viz) the tenth day of december in the first year of the Reigne of our Sovereigne Lady Ann of England etc. Queen at Burlington aforesaid was Required but the [**202 February Court of Pleas 1702**] Same to him to pay did refuse and the same to the said Hugh and Margarett to pay as yett doth refuse and deny to the Manifest Hindrance of the Execution of the Last Will and Testament aforesaid and to the damage of the said Hugh and Margarett Six pounds Current Money and thereof they bring their Suit etc. And bring into Court the Letters Testamentary of the Said Edward by which it Manifestly appears to this Court that the Said Hugh and Margarett are Executors of the Last Will and Testament aforesaid and thereof have Administration etc. And the said Jonas appeared in his proper person and Defends the force and Injury when etc. And Saith he Cannot gainesay the Action of the Said Hugh and Margarett aforesaid not but that he doth owe to them the said Summe of three pounds Sixteen Shillings and Eight pence in Manner and forme as the said Plaintiffs above against him have thereupon declared therefore tis Considered that the Said Hugh and Margarett recover against the said Jonas the debt aforesaid as also the Sum of 1l. 13s. 4d. as well for their damages which they have Sustained by reason of the detention of the Said Debt aforesaid as also for their Cost and Charges by them about the said Suit in that behalf Expended Alowed by the Said Court and by his assent adjudged which damages in the Whole amounts to the Sum of 5l. 10s. 00d. and the Said Jonas in Mercy etc.

 Be it also remembred that the same day and year and place Came then and there Hugh Wright and Exhibited into a Court a Certaine Bill against Joshua Ely of a Plea of Debt which Said Bill followeth in these words Burlington to wit Joshua Ely of the County of Burlington Otherwise called Joshua Ely of Hopewel in the County of Burlington in the Province of West New Jersey Batchelor was Summoned to answer Hugh Wright of Philadelphia Merchant of a Plea that he render unto him the Summe of Eighteen Pounds Current Silver money of West New Jersey aforesaid which to him he Oweth and from him unjustly detaineth etc. And Whereupon the said Hugh by Thomas Clerke his Attorney saith for that Whereas the Said Joshua the Second day of October in the first year of the Reigne of our Sovereigne Lady Anne Over England etc. Queen at Burlington aforesaid by his Certaine Obligatory under his hand and Seal did grant himself

[1702/3] THE BURLINGTON COURT BOOK 285

to be held and firmly bound unto the said Hugh in the Said Sum of Eighteen pounds money aforesaid to be paid to the said Hugh When he should be thereunto required Neverthelesse the said Joshua altho often required the said Sum of Eighteen pounds to the said Hugh as yett hath not rendred nor paid but the same to him to render hitherto hath and still doth utterly refuse and deny Whereupon the Said Hugh Saith that he is worse and hath damage to the Valew of twenty pounds Money aforesaid and thereof brings his Suit and bring hereinto Court the Writing aforesaid with the Debt aforesaid in forme aforesaid doth testifie whose date is the day and year aforesaid etc. And the said Joshua Appearing in his Own proper persons prays Oyer of the Condition of the Said Obligation which being read to him in these words The Condition of the Obligation is such that if the above bounden Joshua Ely and John Hutcheson or Either of them the Heirs Executors or Administrators of them or Either of them Shall and Will Well and truly Satisfie Content and pay or Cause to be Well and truly Satisfied Contented and paid unto the abovenamed Hugh Wright his heirs Executors Administrators or assignes the full and Just Sum of Nine pounds like Currant Silver Money of West New Jersey aforesaid at or on this Side the Five and twentieth day of the Tenth Month called December Which Shall Be in this present year of our Lord One thousand Seven hundred and two At one Entire payment without any Manner of Cover Fraud or Further delay that then this present Obligation to be Void and of None Effect or Else the Same to remaine and Abide in ful power and Virtue Joshua Ely with (seale) John Hutcheson with a (seale) Sealed and delivered in the present of John E Ely Joyce Hutcheson And the (his mark) said Joshua defended the force and Injury when etc. And Saith that he cannot gainsay the Action of the said Hugh aforesaid nor but that doth Owe unto him the said Eighteen pounds in Manner and forme aforesaid as the said Hugh above against him thereupon hath Declared Whereupon the Said Hugh remitts the Penalty of the Obligation and Craves Judgment for the Sum Mentioned in the Condition of Said Obligation with his Interest and Cost of Suit therefore tis Considered that the Said Hugh Recover against the Said Joshua the Summe of Nine pounds Mentioned in the Condition of the Said Obligation as also the summe of 1l. 9s. 8d. as well for his Interest or damages Sustained by reason of the detention of the said debt as also for his Costs and Charges by him about the suit in that behalfe Expended and allowed by the said Court by his consent and adjudged with damages in the whole amount to the summe of 10l. 9s. 8d. and the said Joshua in Mercy etc.

[203 **February Court of Pleas 1702**] Be it also Remembred that the Same day year and place the Sheriffe of the County of Burlington aforesaid returned a Certaine Writt of Enquiry of Damages to him directed in these Words Burlington to wit Anne by the Grace of God of England etc. Queen To the Sheriffe of the County of Burlington Greeting Whereas Isaac Marriot of Burlington Merchant Lately before Our Justices of the Court of Comon Pleas held at Burlington for the County thereof Exhibited his Complaint against Richard Cauin Late of the County of Burlington for that Whereas the Said Richard the Last day of December in the year of the Reigne of our Late Sovereigne Lord William the third King of England etc. The thirteenth Anno Domini 1701 At Burlington in the County of Burlington aforesaid Was Lawfully Indebted to the Said Isaac in the Summe of five pounds Eight Shillings and Eight pence Current money of West New Jersey for Sundry goods and Merchandizes by the said Isaac Att the Special Instance and Request of the Said Richard to the Said Richard before that tyme Sold And delivered and being So thereof indebted He the said Richard afterwards to Witt the Same day year and place aforesaid in Consideration thereof did upon himself Assume and to the said Isaac then and there faithfully promisse that he the Said Richard the Said Summe of five pounds Eight Shillings and Eight pence to the Said Isaac when he Should be Afterwards thereunto required Would well and truly Content Satisfie and pay And Altho the Said Richard hath paid to the said Isaac the Summe of fourteen Shillings in part of the Said Sum of five pounds Eight Shillings and Eight pence Neverthelesse as to four pounds fourteen Shillings and Eight pence Residue of the Said five pounds Eight Shillings and Eight pence the Said Richard tho often afterwards Required (vizt) the first day of January in the thirteenth year aforesaid at Burlington aforesaid to the Said Isaac hath Not paid nor in any wise Satisfied but the Same to pay hath And Still doth utterly refuse and deny to the damage of the Said Isaac tenn pounds Current Money and thereof he brings his Suit And the aforesaid Richard Caluin [55] altho in the Said Court before the Said Justices Was Solemnly Called did Not Come but Made default and the Proceedings in the Said Court is in Such Manner that the aforesaid Isaac his damages by Occasion of the premisses of the Said Richard Ought to Recover but because it is Not Known What Damages the aforesaid Isaac hath Sustained by Occasion of the premisses Wee Comand thee that by the Solemn Attestation of honest and Lawfull men of this Bailywick thou diligently Enquire what Damage the Said Isaac hath Sustained as well by Occasion of the premisses as for his Costs and Charges by him About his Suit in that behalf Expended and what Inquisition thou Shalt make therein thou shalt Make Manifest before the Justices at Burlington the twentyeth day of February Next Ensuing under thy Seale And the Seales of them by Whose Attestation thou Shalt make the Inquisition and have thou there their names and this Writt. Wittnesse Thomas Gardiner at Burlington the 27th day of

[55] Calvin?

November in the Second year of the Reigne of our Sovereigne Lady Anne of England etc. Queen Anno 1703 Thomas Gardner upon which the Said Sheriffe made the return in these Words Burlington 12th December 1702 the Execution of this Writt appears by A Schedule hereunto Annexed Henery Grubb. Which Schedule follows in these words Burlington the 12th day of the 10th month 1702 Wee of the Jury of inquery Summonsed to appear At the House of Henery Grubb have agreed and find for the plaintiff Isaac Meritt One Shilling with Cost of Suit As Wittnesse Our hand the day and year abovesaid Henery Grubb Sub Sheriffe John Brown Thomas Brian John Antrim Samuell Gibson John Snape Edward Boulton Benjamin Wheate Francis Collings William Petty John Hamill William Bustill George Elkinton. Therefore it is Considered that the said Isaac recover of the said Richard the damages aforesaid by the Inquisition aforesaid in forme aforesaid found as also the Sum of one pound sixteen shillings for his Costs and Charges to the Said Isaac by the said Court adjudged which said Damages in the Whole to the Sum of 6l. 10s. 8d. and Said Richard in Mercy etc.

Be it also remembred that the Same day year and place the Sheriffe of the County of Burlington aforesaid Returned a Certaine Writt of Enquiry of Damages to him directed in these Words Burlington to wit Anne by the grace of god of England etc. Queen To the Sheriffe of the said County of Burlington Greeting Whereas Samuell Jenings of Burlington Merchant Lately before Our Justices of the Court of Comon Pleas held at Burlington for the County thereof Exhibited his Complaint against John Smith Late of the County of Burlington for that Whereas the said John One the first day of December 1686 at Burlington aforesaid Did borrow and receive of the said Plaintiff Certaine Smiths Tools and Materialls hereafter Mentioned to Witt One pair of Bellows and Iron tue and one Annvill One Vice One Pickhorne One great hammer Two hand hammers A Nailing hammer One Ladle hammer and a rivetting hammer six pair of Tongs Two ax mondrills a Tool for Nails for Cart Wheels [205 [56] February Court of Pleas 1702] Nine Chissels etc. Punches two bolsters One Butteris five files to half Two half round One round and two flatts Wanble Steady [57] to be redelivered to the Said Plaintiffe when the Said Defendant Should be there to required and altho the Said Defendant afterwards to Witt On the fourteenth day of September Last past at Burlington aforesaid and at Severall Other days and tymes Was Required to redeliver the Said Tools and Materialls to the Plaintiff Neverthelesse the Said Defendant hath Not redelivered them but the Same to redeliver hath denyed and Still doth deny and Convert the Said Tools and Materials to his Own use to the Plaintiffs Damage of Twenty pounds and thereof he brings his Suit etc. And the afore-

[56] Pages 205 and 204 are transposed in the MS.
[57] *Sic.* See note 53 above.

said John Smith altho in the Said Court before the Said Justices was Sollemnly Called did Not but Made default And the proceedings in the Said Court is in Such Manner that the Aforesaid Samuell his Damages by Occasion of the premisses of the Said Richard Ought to recover but because it is Not Known What Damages the said Samuell hath Sustained by Occasion of the premisses We Comand thee that by the Solemn Attestation of honest and Lawfull men of thy Bailywick thou diligently Enquire What Damages the Said Samuell hath Sustained as Well by Occasion of the premisses as for the Costs and Charges by him About his Suit in that behalfe Expended and what Inquisition thou Shalt make therein thou shalt make Manifest before the Justices at Burlington the 20th day of February Next Ensuing under this Seale and the Seales of them by Whose Attestation thou shalt make Inquisition and have thou there their names and this Writt Wittnesse Thomas Gardiner At Burlington the 27th day of November in the first year etc. of the Reigne of our Sovereigne Lady Anne of England etc. Queen Anno Domini 1702 Thomas Gardner upon Which the Said Sheriffe made the returne in these words Burlington 12th of December 1702 The Execution of this Writt appears by a Schedule hereunto Annexed Henery Grubb Sub Sheriffe Which Schedule follows in these Words Burlington the 12th of the 10th Month 1702 Wee of the Jury of Inquery Summonsed to appear at the House of Henery Grubb have agreed of Our Verdict and find for the Plaintiff Samuell Jenings five pounds with Cost of Suit as Wittnesse Our hands this day and year above said John Brown Thomas Brian John Antram John Snape Samuell Gibson Edward Boulton Benjamin Wheat Francis Collings William Petty John Hamill George Elkinton William Bustill therefore it is Considered that the said Samuell recover against the Said John the Damages aforesaid by the Inquest aforesaid in forme aforesaid found as also the Summe of 1l. 17s. od. for his Cost and Charges to the Said Samuell by the Said Court adjudged which Said Damages in the Whole to the Summe of Six pounds seventeen shillings and Said John in Mercy etc.

Be it also remembred That the Same day year and place the Sheriffe of the County of Burlington Aforesaid Returned a Certaine Writt of fieri facias to him directed in these Words Burlington to wit Annæ by the grace of god of England etc. Queen Defender of the faith etc. To the Sheriffe of the County of Burlington or his Lawfull Deputy Greeting Wee Comand you that of the goods and Chattles of Thomas Midgley Late of the Town and County of Burlington aforesaid Sadler in your Bailywick you Cause to be Levied as well a Certaine Debt of Seven Pounds Fourteen Shillings Current Moneys of this Province of West New Jersey which Hugh Huddy and Margaret Hunloke Executors of Edward Hunloke Deceased in Our Court of Comon Pleas held before Our Justices thereof at Burlington aforesaid Recovered against him the Said Thomas Midgley as also One pound Six

1702/3]   THE BURLINGTON COURT BOOK   289

Shillings and four pence moneys aforesaid which to the Said Hugh and Margaret in the Same Court was Adjudged for their Cost of Suit in That behalfe Expended And that you have the said Summe of Moneys before our Justices at the Next Court of Comon Pleas to be held at Burlington aforesaid the Twentieth day of February next Ensuing the date hereof to render to the Said Hugh and Margarett for the Debt aforesaid and Cost aforesaid Whereof the Said Thomas Was Convict and that you have then and There this Writt Wittnesse Thomas Gardner At Burlington aforesaid this fifth day of November in the first year of Our Reigne Annoque Domini 1702 Thomas Gardner upon which the Sheriffe made the Returne in these words Burlington December 17th 1702 Levied part of this Writt and paid to plaintiffs by Order and Consent of the Defendant Henery Grubb Sheriffe.

Be it also Remembred that the Same day year and Place the Sheriffe of the County of Burlington aforesaid returned a Certaine Writt of fieri facias to him directed in these Words Burlington Annae by the grace of god of England Scottland France and Ireland Queen Defender of the faithe Faith etc. To the Sheriffe of the County of Burlington Greeting Whereas Joseph Pidgon of Philadelphia Merchant Lately in Our Court of Pleas Held at Burlington aforesaid (Vizt) the third day of November in the twelfth year of the Reigne of William the third Late of England etc. King before Mahlon Stacy William Biddle and John Addams then Justices of the Said Court of Pleas [204 **February Court of Pleas 1702**] Burlington aforesaid by the Consideration of the said Court of Pleas did recover against Mouns Cocks of the County of Burlington aforesaid yeoman as Well a Certaine Debt of Tenn pounds Current Money of the Province of West New Jersey as also four pounds fourteen Shillings and Ten pence which to the Said Joseph in the Said Court was Adjudged for the intrest and damages which he Sustained by reason of the detaining of the Said Debt Whereof the Said Mouns is Convict as by the record and process thereof in the Said Court before the said Justices at Burlington aforesaid Sitting Manefestly appears NevertheLesse Execution of the Said Judgment as yett remaines to be done as by the Insumation [58] of the said Joseph wee have received And because wee desire that those things which in the said Court are Justly Ordered and that the Debt and Executiond [58] thereof be demanded Wee Comand you that by good and Lawfull men of your bailywick You make Known to the Said Mouns That he be before Our Justices at Burlington aforesaid the twentieth day of this Instant february to Shew Case if Any or What he has to Say Why the said Joseph Executiond [58] for the Debt intrest and damage aforesaid Should not have according to the forme of the Said Recovery if to the Said Mouns it seems Expedient And have there the names of them by Whome you Make this Known to him as also this Writt Wittnesse Thomas Gardner att Burl-

[58] *Sic.*

ington aforesaid the Nineth day of February in the first year of Our Reigne
Anno Domini 1702/3 Thomas Gardner Elias Toy, William W̅ Macklac,
                  his
                  mark

upon which the Sheriffe made this Returne Burlington 10th February 1702/3 Then Made Known the Writt Within Mentioned by Elias Toy and William Macklack good and Lawfull men of my Bailywick Thomas Rapier Sheriffe Which being read the Said Mouns Was Solemnly Called three tymes to answer if he had any thing to Say why Execution According to the Said Recovery thereto Should Not be granted but the Said Mouns appeared not but made default therefore it was Considered and adjudged that Execution Shall be Awarded etc.

 Be it also remembered that the same day year and Place the Sheriffe of the County of Burlington aforesaid returned A Certaine Writt of fieri facias to him directed in these Words Burlington to wit Annæ by the grace of god of England etc. Queen Defender of the faith etc. To the Sheriffe of the County of Burling or his Deputy Greeting Wee Comand you that of the goods and Chattles of John Henerick in your bailywick you cause to be Levied the Summe of Two hundred and one Pounds Nineteen Shillings and four pence which to William Fisher Was Adjudged in Our Court of Comon Pleas held at Burlington aforesaid before Our Justices thereof as well for his Dammages Which he had by Occasion of Certaine falce Malicious and Scandolous Words Spoken by the Said John of and to the Said William at Burlington aforesaid as also for his Costs and Charges about the Suit in that behalfe Expended Whereof the Said John is Convict as appears by the record of the Said Court and that you have the Said Summes of Money at Burlington aforesaid the Twentieth day of February Next Ensuing the date hereof before our Said Justices to render to the Said William for his Damages and Cost aforesaid And that you have there this Writt Wittnesse this Nineteen day of November in the first year of Our Reigne Annoque Domini 1702 Thomas Gardner Burlington 17th December 1702 Levied part of this Writt which is ready Henery Grubb Sheriffe Which being Considered the Court adjudged the goods Levied by Said Writt to be sold or Else to deliver to the Said William.

 Be it also remembered that the same day year and Place the Sheriffe of the County of Burlington aforesaid returned a Certaine Writt of fieri facias to him directed in these Words Burlington to wit Annae by the grace of god of England etc. Queen Defender of the faith To the Sheriffe of the County of Burlington or his Lawful Deputy Greeting We Comand You that of the goods and Chattles of John Hutcheson of the Township of Hopewell in the County of Burlington aforesaid yeoman in Our Bailywick you Cause to be Levied as well A Certaine Debt of Eight pounds Eleven Shillings and Six pence current Money of this Province of West New Jersey which William Beaks of the County of Bucks in the Province of Pencilvania in Our Court of Comon Pleas held before our Justices thereof at Burlington [206 1702] aforesaid recovered against the said John Hutchinson as also Two pounds Eight Shillings and Two pence money aforesaid which to the said William in the Same Court Was Adjudged for his Cost of Suit in that behalfe Expended And that you have the Said Summes of Money before Our Justices of the Next Court of Comon Pleas to be held at Burlington aforesaid the Twentieth day of February Next Ensuing the date hereof to render to the said William for his Debt aforesaid and Costs aforesaid whereof the Said John Was Convict and that you have then and there this Writt Wittnesse Our hand and County Seale at Burlington aforesaid this fifth day of November in the first year of Our Annoque Domini 1702 Mahlon Stacy Thomas Gardner upon which the Sheriffe made a Returne in these words Burlington 17th December 1702 Levied the Summe within Mentioned and have it all ready payd it to Plaintiff by Consent of Defendant Henery Grubb Sheriffe.

Burlington to wit Att a Court of Quarter Sessions of the Peace held Att Burlington for the County of Burlington this Eighth of May 1703 and in the Second year of the Reigne of Our Sovereigne Lady Ann of England etc. Queen Before Francis Davenport, Thomas Gardiner, John Addams, Samuell Furnis Justices.

The Court being called and opened in Usual Manner the Justices having received Information of the Death of Coll: Andrew Hamilton Our Governour, thought proper to advise till the Eighth of August Next Ensuing and in the Mean time (to respitt all Recognizances) And then in Solemn Manner adjourned the Court till Said Eighth of August or further order.

Burlington Att a Court of Pleas held at Burlington for the County of Burlington this Eighth of May 1703 and in the Second year of the Reigne of Our Sovereigne Lady Ann of England etc. Queen Before Francis Davenport, Thomas Gardner, John Addams, Samuell Furnis Justices.

The Court being Called and Opened in usuall Manner the Justices haveing received Information of the Death of Coll. Andrew Hamilton Our Governour thought proper to advise till the Eighth of august Next Ensuing and the Meane time to Continue all prosses and Actions and then in Solemne Manner adjourned the Court till Said Eighth of August or further Order.

[207 1704] [59] Burlington January 11th 1704 at a Private Sessions held at George Willis our present Clerk Hugh Huddy desired to receive Orders Concerning Severall Minutes of Court and other things done in Captaine Jewells time at Severall Courts they not being Entred on the booke of Records Wee the Justices Present Order Said Huddy to Keep the Said Minutes etc. Carefully on file or in bundle and to enter all proceedings Since

[59] Handwriting different.

on the Old or former Booke of Court Records As Wittnesse our hands Thomas Revell, J. Bass, Robert Wheeler.

December Court of Sessions opened. At a Court of Generall Quarter Sessions of the Peace holden at Burlington for the County thereof the 12th day of December in the third year of the Reigne of our Sovereigne Lady Anne of England etc. Queen Annoque Domini 1704/5 before Thomas Revell president, Nathaniell Westland, William Budd, Joshua Newbold, Michaell Newbold   Justices.

The Sheriff of the County of Burlington returned the Names of the Persons which he had Sumoned for a Grand Enquest to Serve for this Sessions who being Called appear and are as followeth—Vizt. foreman Jonathan Davis, Alexander Locker, Jasper Smith, Phillip Philips, Benjamin Hardin, and Byall Davis, William Green, Samuell Hunt, Henery Cook, Nathaniell Pettit   Sworne   William Hollingshead, Joseph Pankis, William Hauster, Joseph Decow, William Hackney, Christopher Wetherill, John Wills, John Hollingshead   Attested   Who being Sworne and Attested According to Law and the Charge Given them by Alexander Griffith Esqr. With drew by Themselves.

The Court Adjourned for two hours.

Then Mett and opned the Same Justices present and William Hewlings. The Severall Constables being Called appears and Makes their Returnes of New Constables who also appearing were Sworne and Attested to their offices for the year Ensuing and are as follows—Maydenhead   Powell Hoofe. Hopewell   Byall Davis. Nottingham   Richard Willgoose for Issac Watson. Chesterfield   John Moore. Mansfield   Nathaniell Richards   Richard French. Springfeild   William Mackintosh for Alix: Steward. Northampton   Thomas Bishop. Welingborough   John Hudson [60]   Moses Rapp Sworn. Eversham   Benjamin Muse [60]   Symon Woodrof Sworn. Chester   Thomas French. Burlington   William Fenimore and Obediah Ireton.

On Motion of Mr. John More The bench thought fitt to Continue the tryall of Robert Edwards till Next Court Under the Same bayle.

William Wood being Called appeared and requested a Coppy of his Inditement the bench orders it he paying for it and to Come to tryall or Submit next Court of Sessions in Coors.

The Court Adjourns to George Willis forthwith   The Same Justices present. [208 1704] the Grand Jury Called and appeared delivered in a presentment against Thomas Munyon for unlawfully Marking of Hoggs Contrary to Law Signed by Jonathan Davis foreman   the Court Adjourned untill the first Tuseday in March Next.

Pleas holden and tryed at Burlington for the County thereof the thirteenth day of December in the third year of the Reigne of Our Sovereigne Lady Anne Queen of England etc. Anno Domini 1704/5   Before Thomas

[60] This name crossed out in MS.

Revell Judge, Nathaniell Westland, William Budd, Joshua Newbold, Robert Wheeler, and William Hewlings   Justices.

Thomas Hickman Plaintiff versus Robert Hickman Defendant   Called boath appeared by their Attorneys Michael Jobson for Said Thomas the Plaintiff and Alexander Griffith Esqr. for Robert the Defendant   The Matter being debated the Justices on the Bench on Mature Consideration Gives Judgment for one hundred and fifty pounds this Country Money with Costs of Suit   April 25th 1705 by a letter under hand of the Plaintiff the Judgment was Sattisfye per Defendants.

The Court adjourns for two howers Mett againe and opened   Justices the Same.

William Biddle junr., and Joseph Parker being Sumoned in the grand Jury Called three times and Not appearing are fined by the bench ten Shillings each.

Ordered that Joseph Kirkbride paper Concerning the Reverend Mr. John Tolbott that Coppyes thereof be posted on three of the Most publique places in the Town (Vizt) one at the gate of the Quakers burieing ground one at the Markett place and the Other at George Willisses.

Then the Court Adjourned till the first Tuseday in March Next imediately after the Court of Sessions Shall end terminate.

March Court of Sessions Opned 1705. At A Generall Quarter Sessions of the Peace holden at Burlington for the County thereof the Sixth day of March in the third year of the Reigne of our Sovereigne Lady Anne etc. Queen Annoque Domini 1705 before Thomas Revell Chairman, Jeremiah Bass, Nathaniell Westland, William Budd, Daniell Leeds, Robert Wheeler, William Hulings   Justices. The Sheriff of the County of Burlington returned the names of the Persons which he had Summoned for a Grand Inquest to Serve for this Sessions who being Called appeared and are as followeth (Vizt) Nathaniell Cripps foreman, Hugh Sharp, James Shinn, Thomas Ridgway, Thomas Haines, William Parker, John Powill, Samuell Lepincoat, Joseph Parker, William Hunt, Peter Wood, John Snape, Richard Ares, James Burcham, Robert Lucas, Richard Fenimore, Daniell Smith, Isaac Gibbs, Who being Attested According to Law and the Charge given to them by Thomas Revell Esqr. with drue by them Selves.

[209 1705]   Constables called and Answered to their Names.

Ordred by the bench that all presentments or Inditements found Last Court Shall be Tryed this Court to prevent Delays.

The Travers Jury Called and butt tenn returned which Answered to their names And were ordred to give their Attendance the afternoon then by Proclamation the Court was Adjourned to the hours of 2 in the Afternoon.

Then Mett the Court opened the Traverse Jury Called Sworn and Attested Excepting Samuell Frettwell and John Garriot who were Comitted for refuseing to take of their hatts or Suffring any Other to take them of

While Solemnly Attested. Jacob Perkins foreman, John Bullock, Nicholas Martinew, William Dean, William Ogbourn Sworn Anthony Frayer, John Antrum, William Parkes, Joseph Scattergood attested Recompence Kerby, Edward Boulton, Richar Ridgway Junr. Attested.

Robert Edwards Called upon his Recognizence Appears his Indictment Read Evidences for the Queen Daniell Sutton Sworne Declared he Saw Robert Edwards to take Daniell Gardiner by the hair of his head and threw him down to the Ground and hurt him.

[*Evidences*] George Kendall Sworne declares the Same with Daniell Sutton. Daniell Gardner Sworne declared that Said Edwards took him by the heir of his head and did throw him down to the Ground and did hurt his throat with his hand And did put his Knee on him And brused him.

[*Evidences*] Susannah Kendall Sworn declared there was a well which was between Said Kendall and Edwards and the Said Gardiner was drawing of Water and Shee the Said Kendall Saw him the Said Edwards to take the Said Gardiner by the hair of the head and did throw down to the Ground and hurt the Said Gardiner Very Much. The Charge given the Jury and Sent out Obedia Ireton Constable Sworen to Attend them.

Where as there has been a diferance between the Townshipp of Midenhead and hopewell Concerning a Devident or Division of the Two Townshipps It was Ordred that Six of one of the Townshipps and Six of the Other Shall Meet and agree about a Division and make their report which they of hopewell haveing refused to Chuse their men it is Now ordred by the Court that the Two Townshipps Shall Stand as before till further orders (Vizt) All Maidenhead.

[*Evidences*] Ralph Cougill and Thomas Billingsham was Attested and Sent to the Grand Inquest concerning John Rumsey and William Cales wife and Marcy Pumphry.

[*Indian Kings Complaint*] Indian King Charles Complaines to the Bench Against the Wife of Mons Coxks for Cheating him of four Pounds it being Money Shee had of him in the Street at Philadelphia the bench Satisfied the Indian that he Shall be heard before my Lord.

William Budd Complained to the bench that his Apprentice Stephen Hodgkins running from his Said Master Budd and took away his Indenture and Made them Away, it is ordred by the Said bench that the Said Apprentice Shall Serve his Said Master three years from the Sixth of November Next.

Court Adjourned to George Willses.
There Mett and Opened Justices the Same.

[210 1705] The travers Jury returnes Robert Edwards in Guilty of an Assault of the Body of Daniell Gardner the bench in Mature Consideration Orders payment of three pounds and Costs of Suit down in Court and in open Court Robert Edwards and Walter Pumphry Recognized themselves in The Sum of Forty pounds for payment of the fine with Costs of Suit at or before the tenth day of May next the Grand Jury Called over Answered to their Names Nathaniell Cripps foreman and gave in their presentments.

Henry Tuckness Appeared to his Inditement and desires till Next Court to Plead but Since Submitts to the Court on Mature Consideration is fined Twenty Shillings with Costs of Suit.

Mons Cocks Called appeared to his Inditement and desires till Next Court to Plead. Memorandum the Bench are Satisfied Mr. Bass has taken Recognizence for Mons Cocks his Appearance Next Sessions and Also Recognizonce for his good behaviour.

Mary Cole and her husband William Cole appeared and desires to Stand tryall this Court Since Retracts Standing to tryall and Submitts to the Court defferred till tomorrow and is discharged by paying his fine Two Shillings and Sixpence with Costs of Suit.

William Bayley Called appeard to his Inditement and Submitts to the Court on Mature Consideration is fined forty Shillings and Costs of Suit.

Inditement of Seth Hill returned   Ignoramus.

Inditement of Peter Cock returned   Ignoramus.

Nicholas Martenew is presented by the Grand Jury for Scandolusly by Liveing with Elizabeth Rumsey the wife of John Rumsey. Nicholas Martinew upon his presentment appeared and desired to Consider till next Morning then Appeared Again and promised in Court to refraine the Company of Elizabeth Rumsey.

The Grand Jury present Alice Chissell of the town of Springfield for bearing of a basterd Child.

The also present Mary Allen for bearing of a basterd Child.

The Grand Jury Are dismissed with Thanks for their good Services and ordred them thirty Shilling at Henry Grubbs.

Joseph Parker who was fined Last Court for not appearing upon Evidence Now produced of his ilness is dismist per order of Court.

Adjourned to the Court house Eight in the Morning. Then Mett Same Justices and Joshua Newbold and Michael Newbold.

Elias Toy and Fredrick Toy Acknowlidg them Selves indebted to Our Sovereigne Lady etc. Queen her heirs and Successors in the Summe of forty pounds each Lawfull Moneys of this Province to be Levied on their Goods And Chattles Lands and Tenements   Sub Condition

That if the Said Alias Toy and Fredrick his Sonne Shall make their personall appearance at the Next Court of Quarter Sessions to be holden for this County the first tuseday in June Next And Shall prosecute Mons Cocks upon an Inditement found against them this Court then this Recognizence to be Void and of None Effect or Else to be in full force and Virtue.

The Attorney Generall Moved in the behalfe of the Town of Burlington Concerning John Henry that he Might be Maintained by William Fisher Esqr. it being a former agreement Made by Said Fisher with Said Henry and that the Town May No further Lyable at the Charge. [211 1705] Ordred by Said Court that the Said William Fisher at his Own proper Cost and Charge Shall remove Said John Henry from this Town of Burlington to Soapas being the place from whence he Came or Otherwise to be Taxed to the Poor rate according to the Words of the Statutes in that Case made and provided.

Thomas Munyan presented by the Grand Jury the former Court for unlawfully Marking of hoggs being now Called appeared and Confessed he did Mark one that was not his own In the Opinion of the bench it is Not inditable being Satisfied he had No designe of Stealing the hogg by reason he informed Severall of his Neighbours of it some of them declared.

Christopher Snoden Complaines in Court against the Executors of Edward Hunloke deceased for detaineing thirty one Shillings and Eleven pence being Moneys in his hand for Accompt of James Layton over pluss of Goods taken by Snoden the Sheriff and delivered into the hands of Said Hunloke.

Nicholas Martinue Called and Sworn declared that he heard Mr. Hunloke declare in his Sick bedd that he had goods in his hands did Amount to the Value of thirty one Shillings More then Are due Which was delivered him by the hand of Said Snoden Sheriff taken by him by distress from James Layton a Tennant of Said Hunlokes and Said Hunlokes reason was because he had Some of the goods unsold.

The Bench haveing further Seen an Appraisement of the Goods Seized by warrant directed to the Sheriff Snowden under the hands of Appraisors Amounting to £8 18s. 6d. and the Charge £1 6s. 7d. and Mr. Hunloks Debt appearing to be £6 os. od. in the hole is £7 6s. 7d. so remaines due £1 11s. 11d. which Sum it is the Opinion of the bench Unanimusly Shall be delivered to the Said Snowden then Sheriff.

Court of Sessions Adjourned Till first tuseday in June Next According to the Ordinance.

March Court of Pleas Opened 1704. Thomas Revell Judg Jeremiah Bass, Daniell Leeds, Nathaniell Westland, William Budd, Robert Wheeler, Joshua Newbold, Justices.

Adjourned for half an hour. Mett againe Justices the Same present Except Jeremiah Bass.

Daniell Sutton Plaintiff John Wills Defendant Called boath appeared Daniell Sutton in his proper Person appeared And John Wills per Thomas Clark his Attorney. The Defendant Demurrs Generally and the Plaintiff agrees to the Demurrer and after a Long discoors by Daniell Suttons Attorney Alexander Griffith Esqr. and Thomas Clark Esqr. the bench Maturely Considering what boath had pleaded gave their Opinion that the words are Actionable and give Judgment upon the Demurrer for the Plaintiff And that a Writt of Enquiry Issue out for Damages.

Court Adjourned for 2 hours. Court Opened At George Willisses Justices the Same.

four papers of Acknowledgment of William Wood Signed by his own hand in Court Concerning Daniel Leeds Esqr. in these Words following Whereas it is Evidenced that I William Wood did Say Daniell Leeds is an Atheist Now these May Certifie that if I did Say any Such Words I Speak them unadvisedly and do declare I am hartily Sory for it for in My Concience I do not beleave it nor intend any Such thing   As Wittness my hand this Seventh day of March Anno Domini 1704 William Wood [212 1704] are by Order of Court to be posted at the Most publique places in the town of Burlington One at Church Porch one at Court house one at George Willisses the other Mr. Leeds desposes of as he sees fitt.

Cour Adjourned till first tuesday in June According to the Ordinance.

Pro New Jersey Comit Bur. to wit At a Court of Quarter Sessions begunn the fifth day June 1705. Present   Thomas Revell Esqr. President, Daniell Leeds, Nathaniell Westland, Robert Wheeler, William Budd, Joshua Newbold, Michael Newbold, Roger Parkes, William Hewlings Esqrs. her Majestys Justices of the Peace.

The Grand Jury Called over and Sworn and Attested and are as follows Vizt Richard Ridgway senr., Thomas Scoley, William Evans, John Shinn Junr., Mathew Champion, Edward Gaskins, John Butcher, John Woolman, Samuell Gipson, Jacob Lamb, Daniell Wells, John Goslen, Richard Haines, Zachariah Prickett, Benjamin Scattergood, John Browne, Nathaniell Paine, Caleb Shrieve, John Garrot, Thomas Garrot, Samuell Cole, John Smith, Charles French, Joseph Welch, Michael Buffen, John Petty.

The Sheriff Came into Court and made his protest against the County prison for Want of Sufficient Repaire and Referred to the Consideration of the Court and the Grand Jury being then present which protest he Desired Might be Entred which was ordered Accordingly.

The Constables Called answer to their names.

Mouns Cocks being called appeared his Indictment Read pleaded Not Guilty and put himselfe upon the Country and the Queens Attorney Doth the Same.

Mary Allen Called upon her Presentment did Not Appear the Court Allow her till Afternoon.

Alice Chissell Called but not Appearing Ordered that the Usuall process Issue out against her to Appear next Court.

The Traverse Jury Called and Appeared and are as follows Vizt Thomas Valles, Robert Stiles, Thomas Holton, Thomas Wilkins, Abraham

Hewlings, Henry Ballenger, William Hollinshead, William Hackney, Preserve Brown, Robert Chapman, William Atkinson, John Ogbourn.

[**213 1705**] The Court Adjourned till 3 clock in the Afternoon. Mett againe According to Adjournment Present Justices as aforesaid.

The Travers Jury Called over Attested and Sworen.

Mouns Cocks Called and Appeared. Elias Toy Called and Sworne Declares that his Sonn Frederick did hear Mons Cocks Son Say he Would Shoot his hors and that on the fifteenth day of February 1704 and the Sixteenth Day one of his horses was Shott Dead and another Wounded and that by traceing of the blood found it to be done in Mouns Cocks Ground.

Mr. Rudderow Sworen Declares that he Saw a hors Dead and did goe to Mouns Cocks house and Inquired of him About his horse who Answered he Knew Nothing of Such a horse goeing from Mons Cocks house Mett with Charles Steelman and Tould he found a hors dead Who upon the Same Said it was his brother Law Elias Toys hors then boath of them with Some Others Did goe to the Ground Aforesaid and Traced the blood and Track of the horse afore in the Snow.

Fredrick Toy Called and Not appeared.

Mons Cocks Leaves it to the Jury. The President gave Direction and Sent the Jury out. Nathaniell Richards Constable to attend the Jury.

William Fisher Esqr. High Sheriff Tendered in Court unto Mouns Cocks forty Eight Shillings and Seaven Pence being over pluss of good that Ware Taken in Execution from said Mons Cocks and Sold at a Vandew Mons Cocks Refused the Tender of Said Money.

Lewis Levally and William Fenimore Sworen and Sent to the Grand Jury in the buisness of Wetherill and Yorks Daughter.

Mary Allen Called three times and Not Appearing the Court Orders Obediah Ierton Constable to goe and bringer into Court She Could not be found the Court Orders the usuall Process to Issue out.

Robert Edwards Called three times not Appeared.

Walter Pumphry Called three times not Appeared.

The Court ordred that there Recognizence be put in Suit.

The Court Adjournes for halfe an hour. Meet againe According to Adjournment Justices the Same.

Dom. Reg. vs. Mouns Cocks   The Traverse Jury Called and Answered to their names and give in their Verdict that the Defendant is Guilty According to the Inditement.

The Queens Attorney Craves Judgment.

The Court give Judgment that the Said Defendant Mouns Cocks is fined Ten pounds and to be Discharged paying the fine and All Costs and Charges.

The Grand Jury Present Mary Levally for Takeing a falce Oath. The present Edward Fisher for Refuseing to Assist the Constable in Keeping the

Queens Peace. [**214 1705**] The Grand Jury Agree that the Presentments Delivered in by them Shall be putt into forme altering No Matter of Substance.

Edward Fisher Appears and Craves time to Consider the Court Grant it.

Ordered by the Court that John Wetherills Recognizence be Discharged by paying his Fees.

Obediah Ierton and Griffith Morgon entered into Recognizence for Mouns Cocks Appearance at this Court Said Mouns Cocks Appearing it is ordered by the Court the Said Recognizance be Discharged by paying the Fees.

Adjourned till 8 in the Morning. Then Mett present Thomas Revell President Joshua Newbold William Hewlings Roger Park William Budd Justices. The Court Opened.

The Court Order John Brown to be fined 15s. for Refuseing to have his hat taken of at the time of takeing the Attest to the Dishonour of Allmighty God.

The Court Order John Petty to be find 10s. for not Appearing and Answering to his name being Sumoned to be of the Grand Jury.

Edward Fisher Appears and Craves till next Court to travers the Court grants it.

Adjourned till first Tuesday September next.

Court of Pleas Opened This 6th of June 1705. Present Thomas Revell President. Joshua Newbold William Hewlings Roger Park William Budd Justices. The Jury Called over and Answered to their names.

Alexander Griffith Plaintiff versus John Bullock Defendant boath appeared and After Sum Debate agreed to put it to Arbitration in face of Court the being to Chuse two men Which Two men not agreeing they Should Chuse a Third Man to end it which is to be done Timely Enough before the Court Breaks up this entred per order of Court.

Court Adjourned till two a Clock the After noon. Mett Againe Present Thomas Revell President. Daniell Leeds Nathaniell Westland Joshua Newbold William Hewlings and Robert Wheeler Justices.

William Fisher Esqr. Plaintiff Called and appeared versus Samuell Richardson and Thomas Gardiner Defendants Called Thomas Gardiner appears Samuell Richardson Called Not to be found within the Bayliwick as by the Returne of the Coroner. [**215 1705**] The Writt Read and the Bond produced Wherein Thomas Gardiner was Security for the Appearance of Samuell Richardson at the Court of Comon Pleas holden in Burlington the fourteenth day of Xbr 1703 Which Bond the Said Thomas Gardiner Acknowledges to be his Act the Condition of Which bond Was Read The Declaration Read Whereupon Alexander Griffith Esqr. Moved for Thomas Gardiner to put in his Plea it is the Judgment of the Court that the Said Thomas Gardiner ought to put in a Plea or a Demurrer Whereupon the Said Thomas Gardiner Replyed that being Joyntly bound with Samuell Richardson and being arrested and Samuell Richardson Not to be found the Said Thomas Gardiner Cannot enter a Plea till Such time as Samuell Richardson is found or out Lawd and then the Said Gardiner is Ready to Enter his Plea or Joine Issue to Said Action. And the Said Alexander Griffith Esqr. Saith that the Said Gardiner ought to put in a Plea or take Advantage of the Matter before Mentioned by way of Abatement or Demurrer for Want of either of Which he humbly Moves the Court for Judgment It is the Opinion of the Court Nemine Contra Dicenti that Judgment be given and Entred against Said Gardiner for Refuseing to Plead or Enter a Demurrer Whereupon Judgment was granted and Execution thereuppon.

Adjourned to George Willises for halfe houre. Met againe Present Thomas Revell President   William Budd, Robert Wheeler, and Joshua Newbold. Court Opened. Court Adjourned to the first Tuesday in September Next.

The 13th of June 1705. Then Surveyed and Laid out a Comon high Way beginning at Thomas Bishops Land into the fork of Northampton River and goes thence as the Path Now lyeth to Thomas Haineses thence Along the Said Path to a black oak Marked by Robert Dimsdells Thence through the feild as it is Marked to a Run of Water then over Said Run as it is Now Marked to the great bridg over the North branch of Said River thence as it is Marked to a black Oak by Nathaniell Cripps fence thence upon a Streight Line to a Dead Hickery Standing in the feild then Along the Road as it was formerly to Burlington the Said Road to be four Rodd in Breadth Laid out and Confirmed by us the Day and Year Abovesaid Joshua Newbold Thomas Rapier John Wills   Commissioners.

[216 1705] [60a]   At a Private Sessions held at George Willises the 20th Day of June 1705. Present Thomas Revell President   Daniell Leeds, Nathaniell Westland, Robert Wheeler   Esqrs. Justices of the peace.

Whereas William Fenimore Constable Removeing out of Town and Obediah Ierton Constable Removeing out of Town humbly Offered to And Request of this honorable Bench that two Others might be Chosen in their places The bench on Mature Consideration grant it and Make Choice of Lewis Levally and John Doson who being present were Sworen According to the forme.

Province of Nova Cesaria   Comit Burlington to wit At a Court of Quarter Sessions begunn the fourth Day of September 1705. Present Thomas Revell president   Daniell Leeds, Jeremiah Bass, Nathaniell Westland, Robert Wheeler, Michael Newbold, Roger Parks   Justices.

The Sheriff Called. Returnes the Venire with the List of the Juries. The Grand Jury Called over and Sworen and Attested and are as follows

[60a] Different handwriting.

Vizt—John Bainbridge, Ralph Hunt, Jonathan Stout, Edmond Wells, James Adams, William Macklack, Joseph Herritage, Thomas Duglis, Abraham Hewlings, Samuell Taylor, Thomas Tindall, Jonathan Davis, Junr., Allexander Locker, Richard Bort, Henery Meshall, Ezekiah Bonham, Joshua Andrison, John Heart Senr., William Marrell, Permains King, John Cerkett, James Burchim.

The Charg given the Grand Jury and Sent out William Markintash Constable to Attend them.

Edward Roberts Called on his Recognizance. Mr. Secretary Answers to the Bench The Bench Orders the Discharge of his Recognizence Nothing Appearing Against Him.

Constables Called over and Answered to their Names Except Simon Woodrooff Who is Fyned ten Shilling for his non Appearance and Thomas Bishop Fyned twelve Shillings for goeing home without Leave of the Bench.

Thomas Duglis and Richard Burt Summoned on the Grand Jury and not Appearing are fyned ten Shillings Each.

Mary Rogers Attested in behalfe of the Queen and Sent to the Grand Jury.

[217 1705] William Richards was bound to the good behaviour by Recognizence Called and Appeared. Nothing Appearing Against him is Discharged paying his Fees.

Mary Allen Called three times and Not Appeared. Mr. Attorney Generall Moved that A Capias goe Against her She Not Appearing upon the Summons.

The Court Adjourned till two of the Clock in the Afternoon. Mett againe According to Adjournment The Court Opened. Presant Thomas Revell President. Daniell Leeds, William Budd, Robert Wheeler, Roger Parks Justices.

Alce Chissell Called three times Not Appeared. Mr. Attorney Generall moveing that process Issue out Against her the Bench Orders it.

Edward Fisher Called Appears the presentment read he pleads Not Guilty and puts himselfe upon the Country.

The Jury Called Sworn and Attested and Sent out on the Same to Attend them The Sheriff for Affronting the Judg and Justices very Contemptious and Approbrous Words Was Ordered to be Committed to the Goal by the two Constables John Doson Richard French till it be further Considered on.

Obediah Ierton Sworn Deposeth That by Order of my Lord he was to Keep the peace at A Bunfyre then Made But at the Same time by one John Kendall was Abused upon which the Constable Desired Severall to Assist him but were put by and further Desired Edward Fisher to Assist him who Denied him with Scandelous words bidding him to Kiss his Brich and Diswaded Others from Assisting him the Said Obediah the Constable.

Ordered by the Motion of Mr. Attorney Generall that all Alehouse Keepers within the Town and County of Burlington Doe Come and Enter their Lycences with the Clerk of this Court in Due time.

John Manners Complaines Against John Abbott for giveing forth Severall Slanderous Words etc.

Caleb Wheatly Attested Declares John Abbott Told him the Said Wheatly when at his house and Walkt with him Some Distance of his house and fell into A Discours About his Servant Maid Ann Hartly and Told me that John Manners Smelt Mairish and Something Concerning A foall fearing Least he had Done Something towards this foall I Cried out oh Sadd Wee had more Words and from more to Less I Know Not what he Said but Slyney[?] he Asked me If I had any Tame Creatures and bid me have a Care of my Creatures and my Daughter in Law further Saith Not.

Sarah Wheatly Attested Declares that Discoursing with John Abbotts wife there was in the house A Very Civill Man who did Chase A Mare About the feild but She Knew not for What nor the mans Name as the Said Abbots husband Informed her further Saith not.

Joseph Myers Attested Declares that he was at John Abbotts house and he asked if John Manners Designed to goe to Law with him the Said Abbott I told he Did he Asked what it was About I told him that it was About Caleb Wheatly then he said Wheatly had Remarked and Informed About it and it was out of Very Malice that he told him or Else he would not have done it and that he was greeved and Confessed before Thomas Lambert further Saith Not. Robert Pearson Attested Declares Ann Abott and John Manners met at his house and had Discours Concerning Abbott and Manners and Shee Said he was not fitt to live nor Dye nor fitt for men nor Womens Company. [**218 1705**] John Manners Attested Affirmes the Same with Robert Pearson and further that he said Manners Should be Ashamed to Meet any Person on the Road and Lett any Body see my face and Gett a helmett on my head and gett into A hole or Cave.

[*Joseph Myers Said*] More John Abbotts Wife Said that John Manners was a Very Wicked man and She did beleive that there was Nothing Impossible with God but She Did beleive it was as possible for the Devill to Come to A Reformation or be a Good man as him.

John Abbot Attested and Sent to the grand Jury to declare the Best of his Knowlidg in the behalfe of the Queen. Ann Watson Attested and Sent to the grand Jury in behalfe of the Queen.

Ann Abbott Attested and Sent to the grand Jury.

George Kendall Called Appears Nothing Appearing Against him is Discharged paying his Fees.

The Court adjourned to George Willis forthwith. Then mett Justices the Same. Court opened.

Its Agreed by the Court Nemine Contra Decente That William Fisher Esqr. Sheriff of this County of Burlington be Amerced five pounds to our Sovereigne Lady the Queen for his Aprobious Words and Contemptious behaviour to Said Court and that he pay the Moneys Down or Enter into Recognizance for payment or Otherwise to Remaine in Custody.

The Sheriff Sent for the Order read The Sheriff Refuses to pay the fyne he is ordered to be Keept in Custody of the Same Constables John Doson and Richard French.

The Travers Jury Called over Appeared Some Sworend Some Attested and are as follows Vizt and Sent out John Hammell, Nicholas Martinew, Jacob Perkins, John Wetherill, Robert Lannings, Charles Millward, Edmand Stuard, John Arney, Joseph Scattergood, Thomas Peachee, Henery Bell, John Wilkins, William Richards.

The Travers Jury returned in Court in the Buisness the Queen versus Edward Fisher and Answered to their names and Agreed John Hamil to Speak for them who Delivered in This Virdict We find the Defendant not Guilty.

The Bench Ordered Edward Fisher to be Cleared by paying his Fees Otherwise to remaine in the Custody of the Corroner Till they are paid. paid.

The Court Ordered Obediah Ierton to be taken into Custody of the corroner for Contempt of the Court and Refuseing to Serve the Office of A Constable.

Adjourned till nine Clock to Morrow Morning at the Court house. Then Mett Court opened presant Thomas Revell president, Daniell Leeds, Robert Wheeler, Joshua Newbold, Nathaniell Westland, William Budd, Roger Parks Justices.

The Grand Jury Comes into Court and were Called Over by their names Each answering Thereunto and gave in their presentments.

[219 1705] Burlington September the fourth 1705.

Wee of the Grand Jury Doe present Thomas Foulks of Chesterfield in this County for Begetting a Basterd Child With Mary Horner late of Mansfield.

We also present George Kendall of Burlington for Breach of Peace.

Wee also present Nathaniell Pettit Junr. Bartholmew Thatcher William Wardell and John Richardson all of Hopewell for Breach of Peace on the first of this Instant at or Near the house of Henery Bell in hopewell Aforesaid.

Wee also present Andrew Heath of Hopewell for Takeing into his Custody Docking Gelding And Marking with his own Mark a Young hors Aged About Two Years Sold by Thomas Coleman to John Clark but not then Delivered Signed per order per me John Bainbridg foreman.

Wee also present John Abbett for Defameing of John Manners and also that the said John Abbett did Contradict his own Evidence Signed per order per me John Bainbridg foreman.

Wee of the Grand Jury for the Body of this County Doe present Thomas Revell by the Name of Thomas Revell of the Town and County and Town of Burlington Gent. and John Ward of Wellingborough in the County Aforesaid for Concealing a Person Charged with fellony Namely George Glave Junr. and Also bidding the Said Gleave make the best of his way one of the Two Desireing John Wetherill to Shew the Said Gleave when he might goe over the flatts from the Island of Burlington to the Intent he might Not be taken   Signed per order per John Bainbridg.

I John Doson Constable of the Town of Burlington Doe present Thomas Clerk Lawer for Swearing by his Maker in Vaine as Wittness my hand   mark   John |D Doson.

Burlington the 4th of September 1705. Wee of the Grand Jury for the Body of this County with the Concurrance of the bench Doe Levy A County Tax for the finishing of the prison and Court house Vizt One Shilling and Sixpence for every hundred pounds that the Estate of Every Inhabitant within this County Shall be Vallued at and every Inhabitant Vizt householders and Sojurners whose Estate Shall not Amount to the Value of one hundred pounds to pay to the Tax ten pence to be paid in money or wheat at a price Equivolent at that Mill that is Most Convenient for Each Township the Collectors to be Allowed twelve pence per pound   Signed per order by me John Bainbridg foreman.

Thomas Foulk Junr., Nathaniell Pettit, Bartholemew Thatcher, Andrew Heath, William Wardell, John Richardson   All Called None Appeared. John Abbott Called Appeared and Pleads Not Guilty Desires to Travers Till Next Court. George Kendall Called Appeared and Submitts and is fyned Sixpence that being paid and Costs of Suit he is to be Discharged.

Ordered by the Court with the Consent of the Jury that the presentments be Drawn into form and Process goe out Against the Offenders.

John Abbott Acknowledges himself Indebted to our Sovereigne Lady the Queen in the Sum of fourty pounds and John Lambert in the Sum of twenty pounds to be Levied Upon their Goods and Chattles Lands and Tenements. Sub Condition that Said Abbott Personally Appears at the Next Court of Quarter Sessions to Answer to Such things as Shall be Aledged Against him.

[220 1705]   The Grand Jury Sent out William Markintosh Constable Ordered to Attend them. William Fisher Esqr. Sworen and Sent to the Grand Jury in behalfe of the Queen. Edward Fisher Sworen and Sent to the Grand Jury. John Wetherill Attested and Sent to the Grand Jury.

William Hackney Acknowledgeth himselfe Indebted unto our Sovereigne Lady the Queen in the Sum of fourty pounds Peter Fretwell in the Sum of Twenty pounds to be Levied upon their goods and Chattles Lands and Tenements. Sub Condition that William Hackney personally Appears next Court of Sessions and in the meantime to be of the peace and Good behaviour etc.

Caleb Wheatly Sarah Wheatly Joseph Myers Robert Person John Manners doth Acknowlidg themselves held and firmly bound unto our Sovereigne Lady the Queen in the Sum of twenty pounds Each. Sub Condition that they and ever of them be and personally Appear at our next Court of Quarter Sessions to Prosecute the Presentments Against John Abbott and not to depart the Court without Lycence.

Court Adjourned for two howers. Mett againe Justices the Same. The Grand Jury Appeared and gived in their presentments and Agreed of Drawing them into forme and Are Dismist.

Emanuell Smith Acknowledgeth himselfe held and firmly bound unto our Sovereigne Lady the Queen in the Sum of twenty Pounds and George Willis in the Sum of Ten Pounds. Sub Condition that Emanuell Smith Doe personally Appear at the Next Quarter Sessions to Aswer to Such things As Shall be Aledged Against him and in the mean time to be of the peace and Good behaviour Taken before Thomas Revell Alexander Griffith Justices of the peace.

The Court Adjourned till next Tearm.

Court of Common Pleas Opened in form   Present   Thomas Revell Esqr. Judg, Daniell Leeds, Robert Wheeler, Joshua Newbold, Nathaniell Westland, William Budd, Roger Parks   Esqrs. Justices of the peace.

John Jones Plaintiff Appears per Alexander Griffith Esqr. his Attorney. James Price Defendant Appears per Thomas Clark his Attorney. Ordered by the bench that Whereas the Plaintiff not Appearing in Person is required to give in Security to Prosecute next Court this Action Against James Price and that he give Notice fourteen days before into the Ofice.

Edward Pateman Plaintiff Called Appears by Alexander Griffith Esqr. his Attorney. William Hackney Defendant Appears by Thomas Clerk his Attorney who Pleads Non Assumsitt and by Consent to Come to tryall next Court.

Grace Townsend Plaintiff Called and Not Appeared. William Watts Defendant Appears Continued.

The Court Adjourned to George Willis till five a Clock. [221 1705] Then mett Justices the Same. Court Opened.

The Bench Orders on a Motion made by John Ward Corroner that Satisfaction may be Entered upon A Judgment Granted Against Thomas Gardner Defendant upon Payment of Cost of Suit.

The Court Adjourns till it Comes in Cours.

Province of Nova Cesaria Burlington to wit At A Court of Quarter

Sessions Begun the Eleventh Day of December Anno Domini 1705. Presant Thomas Revell Esqr. President, Daniell Leeds, Nathaniell Westland, Robert Wheeler, Michaell Newbold, William Budd Justices. There being no Sheriff The Corroner Called and Returns the Venire with a list of the Grand Jury. The Grand Jury Called Over Answered to their names Some Sworen Some Attested And are as follows (Vizt) William Bustill Foreman, John Hammell, Thomas Tindall, Ralph Hunt, John Rogers Sworn. Jonathan Davis, Henry Scott, William Atkinson, Benjamin Wright Sworn. Joseph Scattergood, Thomas Scooley, Robert Chapman, John Day, John Copperthwait, Samuell Gibson, John King, Ambrose Field Attested.

The Charge given The Grand Jury by Thomas Revell Esqr. President.

The Bench Orders Benjamin Hardin to be Called he being Called Appears.

Nathaniell Wade Called to Prosecute Benjamin Hardin and Rebecka his Wife he being Called three times and Not Appearing Ordered that his Recognizence be forfeited. The Bench further Orders that Benjamin Hardin and Rebecka his wife no person Nor anything Appearing Against them that they be Cleared by Proclamation first paying the Court Charges Memorandum paid them.

Jacob Hewlings and Ann his Wife Called both Appears. Jacob Perkins, John Ward Appears upon their Recognizence. Jacob Perkins, Moses Napp Appears upon their Recognizence. Jacob Lamb, Thomas Bishop Appears upon their Recognizence. Henry Wells, Richard Ellison Appears upon their Recognizence.

[222 1705] Sworen and Attested in the matter of Jacob Hewlings and Ann his Wife as follows Vizt John Engle Attested Affirms his Deposition formerly given to the Justices. Thomas Hooton Attested. James Addams Attested. Jacob Perkens Junr. Sworen. Rachell Sharp Sick Appears not but the Evidence Shee had given formerly was read to the Jury in Court. The Grand Jury Sent out Powell Hooffe Constable to Attend them. Elias Toy Sworen. William Evans and Elizabeth his wife Attested Henry Ballenger Attested Jonathan Eldridg Attested Rice price Attested Francis Lee Sworen Joseph Herritage Attested John Chambers Sworen Sarah Roberts Attested All sent to the grand Jury Richard French Constable Ordered to Attend them.

The Court Adjourned till 2 in the Afternoon. Then mett Justices Present Thomas Revell President. Daniell Leeds, Nathaniell Westland, Robert Wheeler, William Budd Esqrs. Justices. Hester the wife of James Addams Called Appears Attested. Sarah the wife of Joseph Copperthwaite Attested and Sent to the grand Jury upon a Bill of Indictment Preferred to the Grand Jury in the Case of Ann the Wife of Jacob Hewlings.

The Constables Called over Answers to their names and presents New Constables for Each Township Which are as follows Vizt For Maidenhead

Jasper Smith, Hopewell Zebulon Heston and (John Parks) Excused Richard Wildgoos, Nottingham William Emley, Chesterfield Benjamin Wright, Manfield Hugh Hutchins, Springfield William Ogbourn, Northampton Joseph Parker, Wellingborough Charles Spencer, Eversham John Inskipp, Chester Isaac Coneroe, Burlington Thomas Middleton and William Bagley Sworen and Attested.

John Abbott Called three Times Appeared and Requested for two howers Consideration the Bench Grants it.

The Bishop Presents Alce Chissell for bearing of a Bastard Child.

[223 1705] Thomas Foucks Junr. Called three times not Appeared Ordered A Capias goe out against him. John Manners Attested Declared That he Sumoned Thomas Foucks by Venire to Appear at this Court the Wife of Thomas Foucks Informed him that Thomas her husband was gone up Among the Indians.

Also Nathaniell Pettit William Wardell and John Richardson. Ordered that A Capias Goe Out Against these that have not Appeared on their Venire.

John Abbott Called and Appeared with Thomas Clark Esqr. his Attorney. The Queens Attorney produces an Indictment Drawn in form which was read. John Abbott Requests Till the morning to Consider the bench grants it.

Andrew Heath Appears The Queens Attorney Desires he may Plead to his Presentment Heath Pleads not Guilty and puts himselfe upon the Country The Attorney Likewise.

The Grand Jury came into Court and Delivered up the papers relateing to The Queen Versus Ann Hewlings with the presentment Signed Ignoramus The Bench Orders Shee be Cleared by proclamation paying her fees Paid them.

John Woolston and John Jennings Called Appears and are Sworen in behalfe of the Queen Versus Jacob Lamb.

Court Adjourned till Tomorrow 10 of the Clock. Then mett Thomas Revell president Daniel Leeds, Nathaniell Westland, Robert Wheeler, William Budd Justices.

Queen versus Perkins Moses Napp Sworen and Sent to the grand Inquest.

Thomas Peachee Called Appears Sworn and Sent to the Jury John Doson Constable to Attend him.

William Talbot of Pencilvania his Deposition Sent to the grand Inquest.

William Talbot of the Ferry and his wife and Thomas Peachee and Isaac Perkins Sworen and Sent to the grand Inquest Against Hackney.

John Abbott Called Appears.

Thomas Coleman John Clark John Bainbridg Called Appears.

The Court Adjourned till 2. Then mett Justices present the Same as before. Court Opened.

William Talbott and his wife Called Appears Attested and Sent out to the grand Jury in behalfe of the Queen and Also Moses Nap and Jacob Perkins they being first Sworen John Doson Constable to Attend them.

[224 1705] The Travers Jury Called over Answered to their names and are as follows Vizt Thomas Duglass foreman, James Wild, Daniell Sutton, Obediah Ierton Sworn. John Claiton, Thomas Eves, William Foster, John Chesheir, Isaac Watson, Jonathan Eldridg, Timothy Hancock, John Hudson Attested.

Queen versus Heath Wittnesses following.

John Clerk Called Appears being Sworen Declares that he bought A Mare and Colt of Thomas Coleman which is two Years of Age and Upward Unmarked Ungelt and not Dockt Andrew Heath Sent word to Said Clark that he Should Come and See if this was the Colt he bought of Coleman then he came finding heath not At home told his wife it was the Same Colt further Saith not.

John Bainbridg Called Appears and is Sworen Declares that Andrew Heath Did Say that he marked Said Colt and branded him to and that was only the Strings of the Stones because no body Else Would Mark him further Saith that John Clark Did Tell Andrew Heath that Said Heath had Marked Said Colt with Said Heaths Mark which Said Heath Did own in Court.

Thomas Coleman Called Appears and Sworen Declares that he heard that there was A Colt at Andrew Heaths then he went there to Heaths and found that it was the Coult he had Sold to John Clerk and that the Said Colt was Markd Gelt and Dockt.

The Travers Jury Sent out John Doson Constable to Attend them The Bench Orders Andrew Heath not to Depart the Court without Lycence.

Mary Allen Called three times Appears not Ordered pluries Capias goe against her.

Alice Chissell Called three times Appears not Ordered Capias Goe out Against her.

Emanuell Smith Called Appears Nothing Appearing Against him he is Discharged of his Recognizence by Proclamation by paying his fees.

Richard Ellison Called Appears Sworen and Sent to the Grand Inquest.

Queen versus Henry Wells Called Appears.

The Travers Jury Returned in Court and dilivered the Verdict following—Wee of the travers Jury are All Agreed and Doe find Andrew Heath Guilty of Marking a Colt through a Mistake of John Clark by Thomas Dugliss foreman. The Bench on Mature Consideration finds him three Dollers with Costs of Suit And that he Shall Stand Comitted till he pay the Amercement with Fees in the Custody of the Corroner.

Queen versus John Abbott John Abbot called Appears John Manner Cald Appears The Travers Jury Sworn and Attested. The Bench Orders there goeing to tryall upon A Persentment Delivered in Last Court.

The Grand Jury returned two bills into Court Against Jacob Perkins billa Vera As on file will Appear. Mr. Perkins Desires to travers and Pleads not Guilty in the Presentment of Ward And that of Naps the Same and to Come to Tryall next Court. The Queens Attorney Joynes Issue. The[y] Also Returns into Court the Bills Against William Hackney Ignoramus.

[225 1705] Queen versus Abbott Caleb Wheatley Attested and Delivers his Deposition in Writing As on file his wif and Joseph Myers Also Attested. Declares the Same as at Last Court. Robert Pearson Sworn Deposeth once upon a time John Manners and Ann Abbott being at his house fell into Discours the Said Ann Abbott Said the Said Manners was Neither fitt to live nor Dye nor fitt for men nor Womans Company further Saith not. Obediah Hierton Sworen Declares that A Day or two After the Last Court Ann Hartly Came to the prison Window where he the Said Hierton Wass and Enquired if it were John Manners in Prison he Answred no and Asked where Shee had been for that her Master John Abbott had been to Seek for her and Shee the Said Ann Hartly told the Said Hierton that her Master and their folks would have her to Say Something Against John Manners but Shee had Nothing to Say Against Said Manners.

The Travers Jury Sent out John Doson Constable to Attend them.

Jacob Lamb Cleared by Proclamation Paying the Fees of Court Paid them.

Jacob Perkins Acknowledgeth himselfe held and firmly bound unto our Sovereigne Lady the Queen in the Summe of fourty pounds And John Tomkin in the Summe of twenty pounds to be Levied upon their goods and Chattles Lands and Tenements. Sub Condition That Jacob Perkins Appears next Court of Quarter Sessions then and there to Abide the Order and Determination of Said Court and Not to Depart the Court without Lycence.

The Court Adjourns to George Willises for half an hower. Then Mett and Opened Justices the Same As before. The Travers Jury Came into Court were Called over and Answered to their names and Delivered in the Virdict following Vizt Wee of the Travers Jury are All Agreed and Doe find John Abbott Guilty of Speaking Defaming Words Against the Said John Manners his Creditt and Reputation per Thomas Dugliss foreman. The Bench on Mature Consideration finds John Abbott three Pounds York money with Costs of Suit and that he stand Comitted in the Custody of the Corroner till fyne and Fees are paid.

Thomas Clark Esqr. Calld on his Presentment Appears not Ordered that a Venire goe out Against him.

Queen versus Thomas Revell Esqr. and John Ward Thomas Revell Esqr. Called and John Ward Gent. Called on their presentment Drawn into form its on the fyle read They Desire Sight of the Warrant before they will plead Entred per order Nathaniell Westland and Robert Wheeler Justices.

The Court Adjourns Till the first Tuesday in March.

[226 1705] Court of Comon Pleas Opened. Present Thomas Revell Judg Nathanell Westland Robert Wheeler Justices. Court Adjourned till tomorrow morning at the Court house by Nine of the Clock. Then Mett Court Opened. Present Thomas Revell Judg Daniell Leeds Nathaniell Westland Justices.

Edward Patemen Called versus William Hackney Called neither Appears Order the Continuance.

Mary Hancock Called versus Walter Pumphray Appears by her Attorney produces the bond and Declaration upon which the Bench Awards Judgment by Default Defendant Called Not Appears.

Ralph Cowgill versus Walter Pumphary Neither Appears in person but both Requested the Corroner and Clerk to Acquaint the bench they Desire a Continuance the bench Order it.

Alexander Griffith Esqr. Called Appears versus John Kible Gent. Called Appears not Continued.

The Court Adjourns to George Willis for halfe hower. Then Mett Justices the Same. The Court Opened and Adjourned to the first Tuesday in March Next.

Prov: Nova Cesa: Comt Bur: to wit At a Court of Quarter Sessions begun the fith day of March 1705 Present Thomas Revell Esqr. President, Jeremiah Bass Daniell Leeds Nathaniell Westland Robert Wheeler Joshua Newbold Michaell Newbold Roger Parks Esqrs. Justices of the Peace. Commissions Read Comission for Clerk Read. The Justices delivered in their Recognizences. The Corroner Returns the Venire with A pannell of the Grand Jury thereunto Anexed. The Constables Called Answered to their names Except William Emly Constable of   Who Not Appeared. The Grand Jury Called over Answered to their names Some Sworen Some Attested as per the pannell and Are as follows Vizt William Hixon, Andrew Heath, Alexander Lockert, John Sto[c?]ton, John Tuely, John Moore, William Scooley, Jonathan Roberts, William Spencer, John Hart, Abraham Brown, William Earle, Samuell Couts, David Jones, Jonathan Woolman, William Biddle, Isaac Gibbs, Isaac Horner, Michaell Buffin, Edward Rockhill, John Lambert, Henry Burr, Benjamin Wheat, Nathaniell Fretwell. [227 1705] The Charge Given by Thomas Revell Esqr. President.

Thomas Folks Attested and Sent to the Grand Jury.
William Ogbourn Constable Sworen and Sent with him.
The Petty Jury Ordered to Attend the Afternoon.
The Court Adjourned for two howers.
Then Mett Justices the Same Court Opened.
The Petty Jury Called and Answered to their names Some Sworen and Some Attested as per the pannell   Edmond Stuard, Emanuell Smith, Obediah Hierton, William Dane, Alexander Bennett, John Park, Enoch Andrews, John Tuely, John Wills, Robert Lucas, George Elkinton fined 10s., William Hollingshead. Talis men   Thomas Tindall, Seth Hill, William Budd Junr. Excused, William Atkinson.

Dom. Reg. versus Eldad Davis. The Grand Jury Came into Court and Answered to their names. William Meriall Sworn and Sent with the Grand Jury. Evidences for Our Lady the Queen Thomas Smith and Andrew his brother they being present. The Grand Jury Came into Court and delivered in the bill Against Eldad Davis billa Vera and Delivered in Another Bill Against Richard Ridgway Ignoramus. The Grand Jury are Dismissed with thanks for their Service.

Adjourned to George Willises for one houre. Then mett Justices the Same Court Opened.

Ordered Mr. Andrew Heath and Mr. Nicholas brown have Lycences for the Keeping A Common Victualling house etc.

Ordered the Delinquents on the Grand Jury fined Ten Shillings Each.

Adjourned till tomorrow Ten of the Clock. The Sixth of March 1705 then mett at the Court House   Justices on the bench the Same. Court Opened in forme.

Dom. Reg. versus William Hackney   Called Appears is Cleared by Proclamation paying his fees.

Dom. Reg. versus Jacob Perkins   Called Appears and Acknowledgeth himselfe Guilty and Submitts to the bench is fined Three pounds and Stands Comitted till he pays fine and fees and to find Security for his behaviour Twelve Months.

Dom. Reg. versus Jacob Perkins   Called Appears and Acknowledgeth himselfe Guilty and Submitts to the bench is fined Three pounds and Stands Comitted till he pays fine and Fees and to find Security for his behaviour Twelve Months.

Dom. Reg. versus Mary Allen   for bearing A Bastard Child Continued till further Consideration.

Dom. Reg. versus Alice Chissell   for bearing A Bastard Child Writt returned not to be found.

Dom. Reg. versus Thomas Foulks   Called Appears and Submitts to the Bench fined Fifty Shillings and Costs of Suit   Received Costs of Suit.

[228 1705]   Dom. Reg. versus Thomas Revell Esqr. and John Ward

Called they Demand a Warrant   The Queens Attorney Moves that Mr. Revell puts in his plea in order to Come to Tryall   The Court will Consider on it.

Dom. Reg. versus John Dorson   Called three Times and his baile Daniell Sutton Neither Appears   John Dorson.

Dom. Reg. versus Nathaniell Pettit, Bat. Thatcher, William Wardell, John Richardson   Called Appears Submits to the bench. The bench Orders Twelve Shillings fine and costs of Suit and Stand Comitted till its paid.

John Wetherill Called and Appeare Cleared by Proclamation.

Dom. Reg. versus Dorson.

Dom. Reg. versus Thomas Clark Esqr. Called and not Appears.

The Court Adjournes to the First Tuesday in June.

Court of Pleas Opened   Presant   Thomas Revell Esqr. Judg   Justices the Same. Proclamation made for Sylence. The Judges Comissions Read   The Coroners Commission Read.

John Manners versus John Abbot   both Called and Appeared Deferred till the Afternoon. Then Appeared per their Attorneys   The Plaintiff by Alexander Griffith Esqr. and John Moore Esqr. his Attorneys. and the Defendant by Thomas Clark Esqr. and refused to plead Wherefore Judgment is given per Default. Ordered that a Writt of Enquiry Issue out.

Edward Pateman versus Hackney   Continued three Courts   The Plaintiff Called Appears not   the Defendant Called Appears and Craves A Non Suit The bench Grants it.

Ordered by the bench that any person not being an Inhabitant in this County bringing any Action as Plaintiff Shall first Give Security to Prosecute the Said Action and pay the Condemnation if Cost this before any Writt Shall Issue out of the Office.

Alexander Griffith Esqr. versus John Kible   Continued three Courts before this. The Plaintiff Called Appears the Defendant Called not Appears Judgment Granted per Default.

Adjourned till two of Clock. Then Mett Justices the Same.

John Ogbourn versus Samuell Gooldy and Elizabeth his Wife   Caled both Appears Deferred till the Afternoon. The Defendants Craves Oyer of the Deed—Granted and to put in their Plea Twenty days before next Court. The Plaintiff Move for Speciall bayle to be given in. The Bench Ordered that he Should Stand and Abide the order and Determination of the Next Court or Surrender his body.

[229 1705]   Whereas William Alcot being bound To Thomas Emley for Nine Years and three Months to Learne the Trade of a Carpenter and the Said William Alcot being Assigned to William Budd Junr. who is no Carpenter to Serve the Said Tearm of Years Therefore the Court orders that he the Said William Budd When the Said William Alcot has Served

Seven Years and three Months of the Tearme Abovesaid Shall have his Choice Either for his Aprenticeship to Expire then or to Serve the Whole Tearm and have the Trade of A Cooper or receive Ten pounds Now Current money without A Trade. Ordered in Court to be Entred.

The Court Adjourns till Next in Course.

[*June Court 1706*] Att a Court of Quarter Sessions begun this fourth day of June Anno Domini 1706. Court Opened presant Thomas Revell Esqr. President, Daniell Leeds, Robert Wheeler, Michaell Newbold, William Budd, John Bainbridg, Nathaniell Westland Esqrs. Justices of the Peace. The Grand Jury Called over Answered to their names all Attested and are as follows Vizt A List of the Persons Sumoned to Serve on the Grand Jury William Haines, John Hollingshead, John Bacon, Richard French, John Shinn Junr., Isaac Horner, William Biddle Junr., Samuell Taylor, Nathaniell Crips, William Hollingshead, William Hunt, Josiah Suderick, John Paine, John Surkett, Josias Gaskins, John Day, George Elkinton, Samuell Lippincott, John Woolman, Thomas Stoakes, William Gabitas, Joshua Humphry.

Robert Edwards Called upon his Recognizence.

John Smith Called upon his Recognizence.

John Sadler Called upon his recognizence Appears.

Noah Lawrance Sworen and Sent to the Grand Jury in behalfe of our Lady The Queen.

The Grand Jury Sent out Zebulon Heston Constable Ordered to Attend them.

Court Adjourned till three of the Clock post Miridiem. Then mett and opened Justices on the bench the Same.

Jane Gilbert of Hopewell Sworen and Sent to the grand Jury.

Overseers of the high ways Chosen for the Townships following as follows Vizt for Maidenhead: Joshua Anderson and John Hart Senr. Hopewell: Jonathan Davis Junr. and Abraham Temple. Nottingham: Thomas Gilberthorp and Isaac Watson. Chesterfield: Samuell Taylor John Blackfield.[61] Mansfield: William Foster and Jacob Decow. Springfield John Ogbourn Senr. and Charles Wolverton. Northampton Joshua Humphries and William Budd Senr. Eversham Jonathan Eldridg William Hasker. Wellingborough John Hudson. [*230 1706*] for Chester William Hackney. Burlington John Wills and Thomas Wetherill.

Dom. Reg. versus Alce Chissell and Mary Allen Alce Chissell Called three times appears not Gone of Continued. Mary Allen Called on her recognizence Appears not Continued.

Ordered by the bench at the Complaint of Magdalen Harden Against Abraham Temple for non Satisfieing Said Complainant for Ploweing and

---

[61] "Field" is partially crossed out. Perhaps the name is only "Black."

harrowing A Certain Quantity of Acres of Ground that Said Temple pay her the Said Magdalen Harden the Summe of Three pounds Current Silver money of the Province of New Jersey.

John Dorson Called upon his Recognizence Non Appears   Continued. Eldad Davis Called non Appears has not been warned.

The Court Adjourns to George Willises for halfe an hower Then mett Court Opened Justices on the Bench the Same. The Grand Jury Returned in Court Called over and Answered to their names and Gave in this Presentment following Wee of the grand Jury for the body of this County of Burlington Doe present Jonathan Curtis of the Township of Hopewell for that he the Said Jonathan did on or About the Twentyeth day of Second Month Last past overtake on the Rhoad Some Distance from Any house Jane the Wife of Samuell Gilbert of the Same Township and place aforesaid and did Violently pull her down from her mare and Indeviour to force her to Uncleaness. Signed in the behalfe of the Grand Jury per Joshua Humphries foreman. Burlington 4 4th mo. 1706. Said Curtis Submitts. The Grand Jury are Dismissed with thanks for their good Service.

At the Motion of Mr. Michaell Newbold Ordered that Ann Newbold be with her Unkle till next Sessions and that Jacob Decow and Michaell Newbold be Sent for before Mr. Revell Mr. Bass and Mr. Wheeler and that there be report made of it at the Next Court of Sessions.

James Allen Sworen Deposeth that William Cols and his wife had Differance and he heard said Coles wife Say to her husband bidding him Carrie home John Hamills bacon or the mans bacon the Said Deponent Could not Tell which.

Jasper Smith Constable of Maidenhead Called Appears not fined Tenn Shillings.

Joseph Parker Constable of Northampton Called Appears not fyn'd Tenn Shillings and that Said Parker be fyned 30s. more for Contempt in Refuseing to Receive the Warrant for Destraineing the Quaker fines for twenty Shillings per Annum pursuant to the Militia Act.

Mr. Noah Lawrance Acknowledgeth himselfe Indebted unto our Sovereigne Lady the Queen in the Summe of thirty pounds and Mr. Samuell Furnis in the Summe of twenty pounds to be Levied upon their Goods and Chattles Lands and Tenements etc. Sub Condition that if Said Noah Lawrance Appear before his honor Coll. Richard Ingoldesby Lieutenant Governor of New Jersey New York etc. when thereunto required in the mean time to be of the peace and Good behaviour.

Dom. Reg. versus Jonathan Curtis Said Curtis Submits. Ordered by the Court that Jonathan Curtis be fyned three Pounds to our Sovereigne Lady the Queen with Costs of Suit and remaine in Custody till fine and Fees are paid and to Enter into recognizence for his Good behaviour for one year.

[231 1706] Ordered that John Smith and Robert Edwards be Discharged per Proclamation by paying their Fees. (paid them). Robert Edwards by reason No Recog[nizence] Appear against him.

The Court Adjourns till it Comes in Cours.

[*Pleas opened*] Court of Common Pleas Opened Present Thomas Revell Esqr. Judg Justices the Same as before.

John Ogbourn Plaintiff versus Samuell Goldy and Elizabeth his wif Executors of Eleazer Fenton boath Called Mr. Clark Appears for the Plaintiff The Defendant Called not Appears.

Adjourned till Tomorrow Eight of the Clock.

Quinto June Mett againe According to Adjournment Justices on the Bench the Same Except John Bainbridg.

John Manners versus John Abbott Ordered by the Bench that Judgment on the Writt of Enquiry pass Against the Defendant John Abbot for 32l. 10s. with Costs of Suit etc.

Jonathan Curtis Acknowledgeth himselfe Indebted unto our Sovereigne Lady the Queen in the Summe of fifty pounds and Jonathan Stout in the Sum of twenty five pounds to be Levied upon their goods and Chattles Lands and Tenements etc. Sub Condition that Said Curtis be of the peace and good behaviour Towards all her Majestys Leige People for the Space of Twelve months and one day. Jonathan Curtis Acknowledgeth himselfe Indebted to our Sovereigne Lady the Queen in the Summe of Ten pounds and Jonathan Stout in the Summe of Tenn pounds to be Levied upon their goods and Chattles Lands and Tenements etc. Sub Condition that Said Curtis Pay three Pounds fine to our Sovereign Lady the Queen with Costs of Suit etc. Att or before the next Court of Sessions.

Memorandum the Justices Received of the Corroner their Fees for Two Courts the Sum of three Pounds Eight Shillings (that is to say) for December and March Last past and they gave the Corroner A Receipt for the Same.

The Court Mett and Opened Judg and Justices the Same.

Richard Francis Plaintiff versus Walter Pumphray Hugh Huddy versus Walter Pumphary Joseph Welch versus Walter Pumphary The Goods that were Taken from Walter Pumphray upon Attachment its the Opinion of the Court that the Said Goods remaine in Custody of the Corroner till further orders for the Security of the Complainants.

The Court Adjourns till next in Cours.

Whereas I John Abott have Spoken Severall unadvised words Against John Manners these are therefore to Satisfie all persons that I am Very Sorry that I have Spoke any Such words for to take away his Reputation as Wittness my hand the 5th of June Anno 1706 Signed per John Abbot.

[232 1706] [62]At a Court of Quarter Sessions begunn this third Day of September 1706. Presant Thomas Revell, Robert Wheeler, John Rud-

[62] Different handwriting.

roe, Daniell Leeds, Michaell Newbold, John Bainbridg, Nathaniell Westland, William Budd, Joshua Newbold Esqrs. Justices of the Peace. The Court Opened Proclamation Made.

The Grand Jury Called over Sworn and Attested.

Proclamation for Sylence made and the Charge given to the grand Jury and Sent out a Constable Ordered to Attend them.

Memorandum the high ways of the Town of Burlington being presented by his honor Richard Ingoldesby Esqr. Lieutenant Governor of the Provinces of New Jersey New Yorke etc. Ordered that if the High Street be not repaired within Two Months that process Issue out against the Overseers Also the Rhoad Along the River Delaware.

Benjamin Wright Constable of Chesterfield Called not appeared there is notice Taken of him for his Omition in not returning the Warrant for take Accompt of the Peoples names etc.

William Ogbourn Constable of Springfield Called not Appeared Excused being Sick. Joseph Parker Constable of Northampton not Appeared Excused.

Memorandum Thomas Kimsey Junr. Acknowlidged himselfe Indebted to our Sovereign Lady the Queen in the Sum of twenty Pounds and Thomas Kimsey Senr. in the Summe of Twenty Pounds to be Levied on their goods and Chattles Lands and Tenements etc. Sub Condition that Said Thomas Kimsey Junr. doe appear at our next Court of Quarter Sessions to Answer Such things As Shall be Aleidged against him and in the mean time to be of the good behaviour.

The Court Adjourned for Two howers. Then Mett Presant Thomas Revell, Robert Wheeler, John Rudroe, John Bainbridg, William Budd Esqrs. Justices.

Proclamation Made. The Court Opened in forme.

Dom. Reg. versus Eldad Davis Called three times not Appearing— Ordered that further process Issue out Against him.

James Allen and John Hamill being Sworen and Sent to the grand Jury in behalfe of our Sovereign Lady the Queen Against William Cale.

Dom. Reg. Versus Mary Allen Called three times and not Appears Ordered her Recognizance be prosecuted.

Dom. Reg. versus Alce Chissell.

Dom. Reg. versus John Dorson.

Dom. Reg. versus Thomas Revell Esqr. and John Ward Gent. Continued.

[233 1706] A List of the Persons Sumoned to Serve on the Grand Jury John Hains, John Brown, William Parker, Joseph Devonish, Henry Burr, William Forster, James Burcham, Isaac Horner, Edward Gaskings, William Earle, Judea Allen, Isaac Gibbs, Richard Fenimore, Ananias Gant, Benjamin Moore, William Evans, Edward Rockhill, John Abbott, Thomas

Ridgway, Jonathan Eldridg, Henry Ballenger, Thomas Wilkins, John Brooks, John Engle.

The Travers Jury Called over answered to their names and are as follows Vizt

A Callender of the names of the Persons Sumoned to Serve on the Traverse Jury as follows Vizt Thomas Hooton, Timothy Hancock, Francis Osten, William Asker, John Lambert, John Borton, William Borton, Thomas Eves, John Middleton Excused, William Bustill, John Gosling, Joseph Scattergood, Richard Apleton, Reece Price, Thomas Wakefield no Freeholder, Joseph Scattergood, William Bustill.

Memorandum Jasper Smith Constable of Maidenhead being fyned Ten Shillings for not Appearing Last Court of Sessions he now producing Severall Good reasons for not then Appearing Ordered by the bench that the fine Aforesaid be remitted.

Zebulon Haston Constable of Hopewell brought a bill of Charges against Abraham Temple it's Allowed by the Bench. Ordered by the bench that Abraham Temple pay unto Zebulon Haston Constable of Hopewell the Sum of Two Pounds and Two pence remainder of Fees due to him.

Hugh Huddy Esqr. Sworn and Sent to the grand Jury.

The Grand Jury Came into Court Called over and answered to their names and gave in the presentment Following. The 4th day of the 7th mo. 1706.

Wee of the Grand Jury at this day doe present the high Way from Springfield to Burlington Betwixt the place Called Redd hill and Longs bridg Near unto the Division of the Towns we of the Grand Jury doe present that high way. Signed by the foreman of this Jury John Hains.

Proclamation made The Court Adjourned to George Willises for halfe an hower. Then mett Presant Thomas Revell, Daniell Leeds, Robert Wheeler, John Bainbridg, John Rudroe Esqrs. Justices.

[234 1706] Proclamation made Court Opened in forme.

Ordered that Andrew Heath be discharged of his Recognizence by paying his Fees Proclamation.

Ordered that John Brown be fyned Ten Shillings for not Appearing being Summoned to Serve on the Grand Jury Unless he gives Satisfactory reason to the Court for not Appearing. The abovesaid fyne is paid.

Benjamin Wright Constable of Chesterfield Called not Appearing Ordered that Said Benjamin Wright be fyned Ten Shillings Unless he gives Satisfactory reason to the Court for not Appearing.

Upon the Complaint of John Hamill for our Sovereign Lady the Queen against William Cale [Cole?] found by the Grand Jury Ignoramus.

William Bayley Called upon his Recognizence Apeared Ordered that he be discharged of his Recognizence paying his Fees.

The Court Adjourns Till it comes in Course.

Court of Common Pleas Opened Presant Thomas Revell and Daniell Leeds Esqrs. Judges Robert Wheeler, John Bainbridg, John Rudroe Esqrs. Justices.

The Court Adjourns till Tomorrow Morning Eight of the Clock. Then Mett According to Adjournment Presant Thomas Revell and Daniell Leeds Esqrs. Judges Jeremiah Bass, Robert Wheeler, William Budd Esqrs. Justices.

Proclamation made and the Court Opened in forme.

John Ogbourn Plaintiff versus Samuell and Elizabeth Goldy Defendants both Called Neither Appears it rests.

Alexander Griffith Esqr. Versus Samuell Harriot Called both Appears. Ordered that Mr. Samuell Harriot give in Speciall Bayle to the Action or be in the Custody of the Sheriff till it be given in.

Peter Parqenett versus Samuell Brown withdrawn.

William Smith versus Rebecca Stacy withdrawn.

Rebecca Stacy versus William Smith withdrawn.

[235 1706] Nehemia Allen and Benjamin Wright versus Samuell Brown withdrawn.

Thomas Price versus Samuell Brown Withdrawn.

James Allen versus Ralph Boon withdrawn.

Richard Boys versus John Mason and Mary his wife Withdrawn.

Nathan Allen versus Henry Wells Withdrawn.

Thomas Revell Esqr. versus Nathan Allen Executor of the Last will and Testament of Benjamin Field Deceased Withdrawn.

John Wetherill versus John Martin Withdrawn.

Hugh Huddy versus Andrew Heath Withdrawn.

Alexander Griffith versus Richard Boys Withdrawn.

The Court Adjourned Till the Second Tuesday in December next.

[*December Court of Sessions 1706*] Att a Court of Sessions begunn the Tenth of December 1706. Presant Daniell Leeds, Nathaniell Westland, Robert Wheeler, William Budd, John Rudroe Esqrs. Justices of the Peace.

Proclamation made The Court Opened in Forme. Proclamation for Sylence made The Comission of Hugh Huddy Esqr. to be high Sherriff of the County of Burlington Read. The Comission of Charles Huddy To be Clerk of the County of Burlington read. Proclamation for Sylence made. The Grand Jury Called over answered to their names and were Sworen and Attested and are as follows Vizt [236 1706] A Callender of the names of the Persons Summoned to Serve on the grand Jury Abraham Hewlings, William Hunt, Hugh Sharp, John Tantum, John Sheen, Abraham Brown Junr., Mathew Champion, John Black, John Ogbourn, John Ogbourn Junr., Henry Cook, William Forster, George Willis, Emanuell Smith, Daniell Sutton, Joseph White, Henry Scott, Nicholas Martinew, William Fenimore, Daniell Smith, Nathan Allen.

[1706]   THE BURLINGTON COURT BOOK   319

The Charge Given to the Grand Jury and Sent out.
The Constables Called over all Appeared.

Dom. Reg. versus Alce Right   Memorandum   Joseph Parker Acknowledgeth himselfe Indebted unto our Sovereign Lady the Queen in the Summe of Fifty Pounds to be Levied on his goods and Chattles Lands and Tenements etc. Sub Condition that said Alce Right Appears at the next Court of Sessions to be held for our County of Burlington at Burlington on the fourth Tuesday in March next.

Dom. Reg. versus Hanath Underhill   for bearing a Bastard Child. Hanath Underhill called upon her Recognizence and did not Appear   John Arrison Surity for Hanath Underhill Called To bring in the body of Said Hanath Underhill who did not. Ordered That The Recognizence be prosecuted.

Proclamation made the Court Adjourns to Two howers to meet at George Willises.

The Court Mett According to Adjournment. Presant   Daniell Leeds, Nathaniell Westland, Robert Wheeler, Michaell Newport,[63] William Budd, John Rudroe   Esqrs. Justices. Proclamation made. The Court opened in Forme.

New Constables Chosen as follows Vizt   For Maidenhead: Robert Lanning. Hopewell: Enoch Andrasson. Nottingham: William Watson. Chesterfield: John Murkett. Mansfield: Thomas Potts. Springfield: John Dixon. Northampton: Jacob Lamb. Wellingborough: Thomas Eves Senr. Eversham: John Inshipp. Chester: Joseph Herritage. Burlington: Henry Scott and John Smith.

[237 1706]   Thomas Kimsey Junr. Called upon his recognizence Not Appeared. Thomas Kimsey Senr. Security for Said Thomas Kimsey Junr. Called to bring in his body who did not. Memorandum   Thomas Kimsey Senior Acknowledgeth himselfe Indebted unto our Sovereign Lady the Queen in the Summe of Forty pounds current Silver Money of the Province of New Jersey to be Levied on his goods and Chattles Lands and Tenements etc. Sub Condition that Thomas Kimsey Junr. doe appear at our next Court of Sessions to be holden for our County of Burlington on the first Tuesday in March next to answer Such things as Shall be Aledged against him.

The Grand Jury came into Court and gave in the presentment Following   Burlington the Tenth day of December 1706   Wee of the Grand Jury for the body of this County doe present Alce Wright of the Township of Northampton for haveing a basterd Child the Eighth of this Instant   Satisfied Mr. William Budd and Joseph Parker. Signed by our foreman Abraham Hewlings.

Proclamation made the Court Adjourned Till Tomorrow morning Nine of the Clock.

[63] Error for Newbold.

December the 11th 1706   The Court mett According to Adjournment. Presant   Daniell Leeds, Nathaniell Westland, Robert Wheeler, Michaell Newbold, John Rudroe   Esqrs. Justices of the peace.

Proclamation made   The Court Opened in Forme.

Dom. Reg. versus Alice Chissell   Called not Appear.

Dom. Reg. versus Mary Allen   Called not appear   per order of the Lieutenant Governor Cossion [63a] of process be Entred in this Cause paying fees.

Dom. Reg. versus Thomas Revell Esqr. and John Ward   Continued per order of Court.

Dom. Reg. versus John Dorson·   Discharged of his recognizence per order of Court by paying his Fees.

Dom. Reg. versus William Cole   Called on his recognizence Appeared. Ordered that he be discharged of his recognizence by paying his Fees.

The Court Adjourns Till the 4th Tuesday in March Next.

[238 1706]   At A Court of Common Pleas held this Eleventh day of December 1706. Presant   Daniell Leeds Esqr. Judg, Nathaniell Westland, Robert Wheeler, Michaell Newbold, John Rudroe   Esqrs. Justices of the Peace.

Proclamation made. The Court Opened in Forme.

Alexander Griffith Esqr. Called appear   versus Samuell Harriott Called not appear   ordered that it be Deferred till the Afternoon.

Thomas Revell Esqr. versus Francis Collings   Ordered that it be continued till next Court.

The Court Adjourned for Two howers.

The Court Mett According to Adjournment. Presant   Daniell Leeds Esqr. Judg   Nathaniell Westland, Robert Wheeler, Michaell Newbold, William Budd, John Rudroe   Esqrs. Justices.

Proclamation made   The Court Opened in forme.

Alexander Griffith Esqr. versus Samuell Harriott   ordered That it be continued Till next Court.

The Court Adjourns Till it comes in Course.

[*March Court 1707*] At a Court of Sessions begunn the 25th day of March Anno Domini 1707. Presant   Thomas Revell, Daniell Leeds, Nathaniell Westland, Robert Wheeler, Joshua Newbold, John Rudroe   Esqrs. Justices of the Peace. Proclamation made   The Court opened in forme. The Grand Jury Called over answered to their names Sworen and attested and are as follows Vizt   A Calender of the names of the Persons Summoned to Serve on the Grand Jury on the 4th Tuesday in March 1707. Andrew Heath, John Antrum, Michael Boven, James Shinn, Restore Lipincot, Joshua Humphrys, Joseph Smith, John Bacon, John Wetherill, John Stokes, James Antrum, Thomas Bishop, Thomas Garwood, William Gab-

---

[63a] Cessation. See a similar order, p. 329 below.

itas, Charles French, John Black, John Farnsworth, Joseph Devonish, Thomas Duglass, Thomas French.

[239 1707] The Constables of the Severall Townships Called over All Appeared Except Enoch Anderson Constable of hopewell Who is Excused by the Court and Thomas Potts Constable of Mansfield who is also Excused and William Watson Constable of Notingham who is fyned by the Court Ten Shillings for not appearing—10s.

Ordered That the Town of Nottingham be fyned for not Chuseing of fitt man for Constable.

John Adams Attested and Sent to the Grand Jury in the behalfe of our Sovereign Lady the Queen versus Thomas Munion Also Judeth Lippincot Attested and Sent.

Proclamation made   The Court Adjourns Till Three Clock post Meridiem   The Court mett According to Adjournment   Presant   Presant Thomas Revell, Daniell Leeds, Nathaniell Westland, Robert Wheeler, William Budd, John Rudroe   Esqrs. Justices of the Peace.

Proclamation made   The Court opened in forme.

Benjamin Hixon Sworen and Sent to the Grand Jury on the behalfe of our Sovereign Lady the Queen versus Andrew Heath.

Dom. Regine versus Eldad Davis   Eldad Davis Came into Court pleads Guilty and Submits to the Court.

Memorandum   That Whereas by a Late Town Meeting at Burlington Assumeing in themselves A power of Removeing Thomas Wetherill and John Wills overseer of the high Ways of the Town aforesaid an[d] Appointing Others in their roome its the Opinion and order of the Bench Nemine Contra dicent That the Said John Wills and Thomas Wetherill Still Continue overseers of the Township aforesaid and that they Enter upon repaireing of the high Ways within a fortnights time. And That the Court disaproves of Chuseing any Others in their Stead.

Memorandum   its ordered by the bench Nemine Contra Disenter That Each person that has a Lott that Fronts the high Street in Burlington they Shall repair it to the Middle of the Street Against their Oposite Neighbour and that it be done within Six Months at the farthest (That is to say) from Mr. Jannings house that Thomas Kendall Lately Dwelt in Soe down to the Town wharfe.

Dom. Reg. versus Alce Wright   Called appears and Confess her Selfe Guilty of bearing a basterd Child and Submitts to the Court   Alce Wright Sworen and upon her Oath declares that Shee knew not the name of the person that begott the Child but declares that Shee should know him if Shee Saw him againe.

Ordered by the bench Nemine Contra Disenter that the Overseers of the high Ways of Each Township within the County of Burlington aforesaid that were Chosen Last June Court the remain overseers untill the fourth Tuesday in March 1708 and till Other Overseers are Chosen and Sworen or Attested in their offices.

The Court Adjourns To George Willises forthwith. The Court Mett According to Adjournment Presant Justices on the Bench The Same.

Griffen Morgen Sworn and Sent to the Grand Jury Against Mouns Cox wyfe.

Thomas Houghton Samuell Lippincot Sary Hancock Mary Price and Rice Price Attested and Sent to the Grand Jury in the behalfe of our Sovereign Lady the Queen versus Thomas Munion.

The Court Adjourns Till Tomorrow morning Nine of the Clock.

[240 1707] [25th March 1707] The Court Met According to Adjournment presant Daniell Leeds, Robert Wheeler, William Budd Esqrs. her Majesties Justices of the Peace.

Proclamation made The Court Opened in forme.

Proclamation made the Court Adjourns to George Willises forthwith. Ther mett and opened in form Justices on the Bench as follows Thomas Revell, Daniell Leeds, Nathaniell Westland, Robert Wheeler, William Budd, John Rudroe Esqrs. Justices of the peace.

Dom. Reg. versus Eldad Davis Eldad Davis Came into Court in his own proper Person and pleads Guilty and Submitts to the Court The Court on Mature Consideration fynes him one Shilling and Eight pence and order that he be Discharged by paying fynes and fees of Court etc. (payd fyne and fees).

Ordered that unless the bridg or Causeway Lyeing in the Road Leading from Burlington to Springfield being in the Township of Burlington be repaired at and before the Last day of June next that the Overseers be fyned Three pounds.

Daniell Dean Sworen and Sent to the Grand Jury in the behalfe of our Sovereigne Lady the Queen versus Andrew Heath.

Memorandum George Lowther Esqr. personally appeared in Sessions and Acknowledged himselfe Indebted unto our Sovereign Lady the Queen in the Summe of Tenn pounds to be Levied upon his goods Chattles Lands and Tenements etc. Sub Condition That his Tenants The Pottash family now on his Plantation in the Township of Chester Nor Neither of them Shall become burthensome or Chargable to The Said Township etc.

[*Eversham New overseer*] John Brook Sworen Overseer of Eversham for one Whole year.

The Grand Jury Came into Court and gave in Presentments following

Dom. Reg. versus Thomas Kimsey found by the grand Jury Ignoramus and Nothing appearing against him he is Discharged per proclamation paying his fees.

Dom. Reg. versus Alce Wright for bearing a basterd Child. Called Appeared pleads Guilty: The Court gave her Choyce to pay the fyne of five pounds and fees of Court or Suffer Corporable punishment According as the Law directs in Such Cases She Chewses to pay the fyne and fees etc. (and payd them to the overseer) of the Poor. Ordered by The Court That Shee be fyned five pounds to be paid as the Laws directs in Such Cases with fees of Court etc. and that Shee be Comitted unto the Common Goal till fyne and fees are paid etc.

Dom. Reg. versus Grinla Cox   Indictment brought in by the Court [64] Ignoramus   Called on her recognizence appears   Ordered That Shee be in Custody of the Constable till Shee pay the Court fees etc.

Dom. Reg. versus Moses Pettit   Indictment brought in by the grand Jury Ignoramus   Ordered That he be Discharged by paying his fees.

Dom. Reg. versus Enoch Anderson   Indictment brought in by the Grand Jury Ignoramus   Ordered That he be discharged paying his fees.

Dom. Reg. versus Andrew Heath   information brought per Grand Jury Ignoramus. Ordered That he be discharged paying his fees.

[241 1707] [union] [65] presentment for Scandolizeing Judeth Lippincote found per the Grand Jury Billa Veras as follows Vizt   Burlington to wit The Jurors for our Sovereign Lady the Queen and the body of the County of Burlington being Sworen and Attested to Enquire upon their Oaths and Attestations doe present That Thomas Munion of the Township of Chester and County aforesaid Yeoman on the first day of March or thereabouts in the fifth year of the Reign of our Sovereign Lady Anne by the Grace of God of England Scotland France and Ireland etc. Queen Defender of the faith etc. at the Township of Eversham and County aforesaid openly and publickly Wickedly in the Presence of Severall of her Majesties Leige Subjects these falce and Scandelous and Wicked Words following of one Judeth Lippincote of the Township of Eversham and County aforesaid Spinster did publish declare and utter (Vizt) I have Seen Judeth Lippincotes Privett parts   meaning Judeth aforesaid   And felt them as often as you   Speaking to Thomas Hooton then being Maried Eight years   Have felt your wifes and I can Lye with her when I Please   by Occasion of Which falce and Wicked Words and publication thereof the Said Judeth abused and Scandelized in Contempt of her Majesties Laws and against the peace of our Said Sovereign Lady the Queen her Crown and Dignity—found per the Grand Jury Billa Vera and Signed per Joshua Humphries foreman.

The Grand Jury are Dismissed with thanks for their Service.

Thomas Munion Called appears and Pleads not Guilty and desire to traverse till next Court.

Dom. Reg. versus Benjamin Nixon   Wee of the grand Grand Jury doe present Benjamin Nixon for Speaking these Scandelous words Against Two

[64] *Sic.*
[65] Mutilated.

of our Magistrates the Queens Justices of the Peace vizt Thomas Revell and Daniell Leeds he the Said Nixon Saying (in the Case of Andrew Heath and Davis and Dean) that They the Said Thomas Revell and Daniell Leeds had put down words which he the Said Nixon did not Speake Signed by our foreman Joshua Humphries.

Memorandum Thomas Munion Personally appears and Acknowlidgeth himself Indebted unto our Sovereign Lady the Queen in the Summe of Twenty pounds Current Silver Money of the Province of New Jersey and Thomas Kendall in the Summe of Ten pounds and Thomas French in the Summe of Tenn pounds to be Levied on their goods and Chattles Lands and Tenements etc. Sub Condition That the Said Thomas Munion Personally appears at our next Court of Sessions and prosecute his Travers to afect and to be of the good behaviour etc.

Richard Ridgway Junr. is fyned Tenn Shillings not appearing being Sumoned on the Grand Jury

The Court Adjourns Till it Comes in Cours.

The Court of Comon Pleas opened Present on the Bench Thomas Revell Daniell Leeds Esqrs. Judges Nathaniell Westland Esqr. Justice of the Peace. The Petty Jury Called over and Are as follows

A Calender of The names of the persons Sumoned to Serve on the Petty Jury The 4th Tuesday in March 1706/7. Charles Wolverton, Nathaniell Pope, Daniell Smith, Samuell Lovett, John Carlyn, Henry Burcham, Samuell Furnis, Isaac Decow, Christopher Wetherill, Thomas Kendall, John Wills, Thomas Scattergood, Emanuell Smith, Thomas Wetherill, Bernard Lane. [242 1707] Proclamation made The Court Adjourned Till Tomorrow Morning Nine of the Clock. March 27th The Court mett According to Adjournment Presant Thomas Revell Daniell Leeds Esqrs. Judges Nathaniell Westland Esqr. Justice. Proclamation made the Court opened in forme.

Shershaw Cary Plaintiff versus Nathan Allen Defendant Called Plaintiff Appears Mr. Cary per George Lowther Esqr. his Attorney and Mr. Allen per Alexander Griffith Esqr. his Attorney. The Jury To trye the Issue Sworen Attested and Sent out. Charles Volverton Not appearing is fyned five Shilling being Sumoned on the Jury of Travers Paid his fine (paid said fyne) Charles Mathews Sworen and declared to the Jury. John Antrum Attested and declared to the Jury.

Alexander Griffith Plaintiff versus Samuell Harriot Defendant Harriot Appears by George Lowther his Attorney and pleads not Guilty. Ordered That a Venire goe out to Trye next Court.

Cary versus Allen The Travers Jury Came into Court Called over and Answered To their names being ready to give in their Virdict Mr. Cary Called Three times withdrew himselfe appears not Adjudged by the Court that the Plaintiff be Nonsuited.

Martha Dummer versus Robert Skeen   ordered That Speciall bayle be given in to the Action per the Defendant.

Martha Dummer versus Robert Skeen   ordered That Speciall bayle be given in per the Defendant and that he remain in Custody of the Sheriff till it be given in in both Actions.

Proclamation made The Court Adjourns Till it Comes in Course.

[*7ber Court of Sessions 1707*] At A Court of Sessions begun the 23th Day of September Anno Domini 1707. Presant   Thomas Revell, Jeremiah Basse, Robert Wheeler, Daniell Leeds, John Rudroe, William Bustill Esqrs. Justices of the Peace.

Proclamation made the Court opened in forme.

[*William Watson fyned 40s.*]   Proclamation made The Sheriffe Corroner and Constables called all appeared Except William Watson Constable of Nottingham who is fyned per the Court Forty Shillings.

The Grand Jury Called over Sworen and attested and are as follows A Calender of the names of the Persons Summoned to Serve on the Grand Inquest (Vizt)   Robert Stiles, Thomas Tindall, Elias Toy, Jacob Hewlings, Charles Stillman, John Walker, Mouns Skeen, William Ogbourn, William Atkinson, John Hancock, Robert Pearson, John Woolman, Thomas Crafts, John Tooly, Moses Pettit, John Brooks, John Hart, John More.

Proclamation made. The Court Adjourned till Two of the Clock Post Meridiem.

[243 1707] The Court met according to Adjournment   Presant Thomas Revell, Jeremiah Bass, Robert Wheeler, Daniell Leeds, John Rudroe, William Bustill   Esqrs. Justices of the Peace.

Proclamation made The Court opened in forme.

The Grand Jury returned and answered to their names and gave in a Presentment against William Cale which is as follows

[*Dom. Reg. versus William Cale presentment*] The Jurors for our Sovereign Lady the Queen and the Body of the County of Burlington to Enquire being Sworen upon their Oaths doe present that William Cale Late of the Town and County of Burlington Laberour on the first day of June in the Sixth year of the Reign of our Sovereign Lady Anne of England etc. Queen Defender of the faith etc. and Continually after untill the Twenty Seacond of September in the Same year a Common house of Drinking Carding and unlawfull gameing for the Proper gain of the Said William at the Town and County aforesaid hath Keept and hath then and there received harboured and Supported Diverse Vagabond and Other Idle and Suspected persons of Evill conversation as well as Diverse Servants and Negroes of the Inhabitants of the Town aforesaid at unseasonable times and that the Said William on the first day of September in the year aforesaid in his house aforesaid the aforesaid unlawfull game of carding at Two of the Clock in the Morning of the Same day and Likewise with unlawfull and imoderate Drinking did at the Town and County aforesaid did keep and himselfe Excersise Suffer allow and maintain to the Common nusance and Disturbance of the Inhabitants against the Peace and against the forme of the Statute etc. Billa Vera Robert Stiles foreman.

Dom. Regine versus Richard Pearse Called on his recognizence appears nothing appearing against him he is Discharged per proclamation per order of Court and the officers in Consideration of his Poverty forgave him the fees.

Dom. Reg. versus Thomas Munion being presented at our Last Court for Scandaliseing Judeth Lippincot Called appears pleads Guilty and Submitts to the bench.

Dom. Reg. versus Benjamin Hixon Presented Last Court Called on his presentment not appears. ordered a Capias goe out against him.

The Court Adjourns for one hower. The Court mett according to adjournment Presant Daniell Leeds, Jeremiah Bass, Robert Wheeler, John Rudroe, William Budd Esqrs. Justices of the Peace.

Proclamation made the Court opened in forme.

The Grand Jury returned and gave in a Presentment against Thomas Howton which is in the words following (Vizt) The Jurors for our Sovereign Lady the Queen and the body of the County of Burlington to Enquire being Sworen upon their Oaths Doe present that Thomas Howton of the Township of Eversham in the County of Burlington Yeoman on the Tenth day of March or thereabouts in the fifth year of the Reigne of our Sovereign Lady Anne by the grace of God of England Scotland france and Ireland etc. Queen Defender of the faith etc. at the Township of Hopewell and County aforesaid these falce Scandelous and Malitious words following of Thomas Revell Esqr. one of her Majesties Councill for the Province of New Jersey and one of her Majestys Justices of the Peace for the County aforesaid in the Execution of his office then being publickly malitiously and falsly did Speake proclaim and utter (Vizt) [244 1707] (he did not care to goe before Thomas Revell) Thomas Revell aforesaid meaning (because he would wright Nothing as a body did give in. for body may Say what he will he will write as he pleases for I Know him Since he would have Served Thomas Wallis and I Such a Trick when we went to give in the Words that Joseph Cooper Should Say he writt clear another thing then what wee Said and when I found fault with it he Tould me I might wright my Selfe if he Could not please me. In contempt of her Majesty and her Government against the peace of our Said Lady the Queen her Crown and Dignity etc. Vera bill Robert Stiles foreman.

Dom. Reg. versus Thomas Hooton Called on his presentment appears Ordered That he pleads Dureing the Sitting of this Court.

Dom. Reg. versus Thomas Munion Called appears Submitts Ordered that he be fyned to our Sovereign Lady the Queen in the Summe of

Six Shillings and that he be discharged paying fyne and fees of Court.

Proclamation made the Court adjourned till Tomorrow morning Eight of the Clock.

7ber 24th The Court meet according to Adjournment Presant Thomas Revell, Daniell Leeds, Jeremiah Bass, Michael Newbold, John Bainbridg, William Budd, John Rudroe, William Hewlings, William Bustill Esqrs. Justices of the Peace.

Proclamation made The Court opened in forme.

[*Dom. Reg. versus John Reevs*] The Grand Jury returned gave in a presentment against John Reeves Ignoramus.

Dom. Reg. versus Thomas Hooton Called on his presentment Appears and pleads not Guilty and desires to traverse Till next Court. Ordered That he Come to Tryall next Court and that he be continued on his former recognizence and that a Venire be awarded etc.

Dom. Reg. versus William Cale Called on his presentment appears and pleads not Guilty. Ordered That he Come to Tryall by consent. The Jury Sworn and Sent out Henry Scot Constable Sworen to Attend them.

The Township of Wellingborrow versus the Township of Chester Concerning the Charge of a poor man etc. Ordered by the bench nemine Contra Dicente that the Said Townships be of an Equall charge of Expences at his Sickness funerall and Court Charges etc.

Dom. Reg. versus Thomas Wetheril bound per recognizence to his behaviour and appearance at this court being called on his Recognizence appears. Ordered That he be Discharged of his recognizence by paying his fees.

Dom. Reg. versus Thomas Hooton Called on his recognizence appears Ordered that he be discharged of his recognizence by paying his fees.

Dom. Reg. versus Thomas Billingsham bound per recognizence to his good behaviour and appearance at this Court etc. Called on his recognizence appears. Ordered That he be Discharged of his recognizence by paying his fees etc.

Memorandum of the names of the persons that has not mended before their Lotts to the Middle of the Street according to an order made at our Last Court of Sessions are as follows Vizt William Gabitas Two Lotts: Daniell Smith one Lott: Thomas Gardiner Two Lotts: Samuell Jennings one Lott Samuell Furnis for Henry Margorem one Lott. Ordered That the persons aforesaid be fyned Tenn Shillings each for each Lott for the Contempt of our Said Last Court order and that unless the[y] Repair it According to Said Last court Order within three months that they be fyned Twenty Shillings More each that Makes Default.

[245 1707] [*Dom. Reg. versus John Clarke presentment*] The Grand Jury returned into Court Called over and gave in a presentment against John Clarke in the Words following Vizt

The Jurors for our Sovereign Lady the Queen and the body of the County of Burlington to Enquire being Sworen upon their Oaths doe present That John Clarke of the Township of Hopewell in the County of Burlington aforesaid Gentleman on the Twentyeth day of September in the Sixth year of the Reign of our Sovereign Lady Anne of England Scotland France and Ireland etc. Queen Defender of the faith etc. at the Township of Hopewell and County aforesaid one Elizabeth Scusdouck late of Bristol in the Province of Pencilvania Spinster being apprehended by Enoch Anderson Constable of Hopewell by Virtue of a Warrant of Hue and Cry for stealing goods from the Possession of Ann Richardson did aid Assist hide and Convay away in Contempt of her Majesties Laws and against the peace of our Said Sovereign Lady the Queen her Crown and Dignity etc. Signed Bill of Vera   Robert Stiles foreman.

Dom. Reg. versus John Clarke   Called on his presentment not appears Ordered That a Venire doe goe out to Sumons him to appear next Court.

Dom. Reg. versus John Poinsett   bound per recognizence to his good behaviour and appearance at this Court was called appears and Nothing appearing Against him Ordered That he be discharged of his recognizence per paying his fees.

Dom. Reg. versus Peter Morrow   being bound to his good behaviour and appearance at this Court was Called appears and nothing appearing against him Ordered That he be Discharged of his Recognizence paying his fees.

Dom. Reg. versus Thomas Renshale   being bound to his good behaviour and appearance at this Court was Called appears and nothing appearing against him Ordered That he be Discharged of his recognizence paying his fees.

The Grand Jury is Discharged with thanks for their good Service etc.

Dom. Reg. versus John Reeves   Ordered That John Reeves doe give in Security for his good behaviour.

Dom. Reg. versus William Cale   The Traverse Jury returned Called over and Answered to thier names being asked whether Said Cale was Guilty or not The foreman made answer that he was guilty and Soe they Said all.

[*John Prickett bound prentice to Zachariah Prickett*]   Ordered by the Court Nemine Contra Dicente That John Prickett doe from this day Serve his unkle Zachariah Prickett (untill he shall Attaine to the age of Twenty years) in any Service his Said Uncle Shall imploy him about Dureing which Time his unkle Shall provide him with Sufficient meat Drink Washing and Lodging and Shall give him one breeding mare with the increase till he attains Said age of Twenty years and at the Expiration of Said Terme he Shall pay Said John Prickett the Summe of Twenty pounds (Nevertheless and Notwithstanding this order) If Josias Prickett the father of the Said John Shall Take away his Said Sonn before the Expiration of the aforesaid

Terme of his Attaining to Twenty years that then this order to be of none Effect or Else this to be in force.

Dom. Reg. versus William Cale Ordered by the Court nemine Contra dicente that William Cale be fined to our Sovereign Lady the Queen in the Summe of Tenn Pounds and that he Stand Comitted untill fine and fees are paid. William Cale Called not appears his Securitys called to bring in the body of Said Cale who did not. Ordered That unless Said Cale appears dureing the Sitting of the Court that his recognizence be prosecuted.

Dom. Reg. versus Negroe Peter Ordered he be Discharged Paying fees.

[246 1707] Dom. Reg. versus John Reeves Called not appears his Securitys called to bring in his body who did not. Ordered That unless Said Reeves doe appear dureing the Sitting of this Court that his recognizence be prosecuted.

Upon The Complaint of Samuell Oldal concerning his makeing of a bridg over Assinpinck Creek and being not paid for it Ordered by the Court Nemine Contra Dicente that Theophile Phillips John Bainbridg John Clarke and Capt. Ralph Hunt be appointed to assess upon such persons as are Lyable to pay for the building of a Certain Bridg over Assinpinck Creek equally upon Such persons in the Township of Maidenhead and Hopewell (who have not Subscribed etc.) in three months time and on Default of payment of Such Assessment to Straine etc. and that they meet to assess it within Six weeks.

Dom. Reg. versus John Reeves Called appears Ordered That unless John Reeves find Security for his entring into Recognizence to Answer the new breach of the Peace which was the forfeiture of his old recognizence that he Stand Comitted to the Sheriffs Custody.

Proclamation made The Court Adjourns until the fourth Tuesday in March.

[*Pleas opened.*] Court of Common Pleas opened Presant Thomas Revell, Daniell Leeds Esqrs. Judges Jeremiah Bass, Michaell Newbold, John Bainbridg, William Budd, John Rudroe, William Hewlings, William Bustill Esqrs. Justices of the Peace.

Proclamation made the Court adjourned till Tomorrow eight of the Clock. The Court mett according to adjournment Presant Judges and Justices the Same as before except Mr. Michaell Newbold.

Proclamation made the court opened in forme and adjourned to George Willises to meet forthwith.

Dom. Reg. versus John [H]arrison Ordered That Sessation of Process be entred by order of his honor the Lieutenant Governour paying his fees.

Elizabeth Elton versus John Fisher and John Markett action upon the Case Withdrawn.

Daniell Leeds Esqr. versus Daniell Hall and Charles French   action of Debt   Withdrawn.

William Clayton versus Edward Jannings   action upon the Case   Withdrawn.

John Myers versus Samuell Oldal   action   Withdrawn.

John Wills versus Walter Pumphray   action the Case   Withdrawn.

John Rawson versus Edward Jannings   action   Withdrawn.

William Mott versus Samuell Gibson   action   Withdrawn.

Proclamation made the Court adjourns till it comes in Course.   God Save the Queen.

[247 1707]   At A Court of Sessions held for the County of Burlington at Burlington on Tuesday the 23th day of March 1708.   Presant   Thomas Revell Esqr. President   Daniell Leeds, Michael Newbold, Michael [66] Newbold, William Bustill   Esqrs. Justices of the Peace.

Proclamation made The Court opened in forme.

The Grand Jury called over answered to their names and are as follows   A Calender of the names of the Persons Sumoned to Serve on the Grand Jury Vizt   John Woolston, William Hackney, Mathew Watson, William Petty Junr., Samuell Kimball, Thomas Douglas, John Stockton, John Tompkin, Mathew Champion, Samuell Goldy, John Day, Thomas Curtis, Thomas Garwood, John Warren, Benjamin Scattergood, John Ogbourn Senr., John Ogbourn Junr.

Proclamation for Sylence made Then Said Jurors Sworen Attested and the Charge given them and Sent out   Thomas Potts Constable to attend them.

Dom. Reg. versus John Clarke   Called on his presentment Appears and protests himselfe not Guilty and Lays himselfe upon the Mercy of the Court. The Court will advise.

The Court adjourned till 2 of the Clock Post Miridiem. The Court mett according to Adjournment   Presant   Thomas Revell, Daniell Leeds, Joshua [67] Newbold, Jeremiah Bass, Michaell Newbold, William Bustill Esqrs. Justices of the Peace.

Proclamation made the Court opened in forme.

Dom. Reg. versus Thomas Howtin   Called on his presentment appears and Submits. Ordered that he be fyned two Shillings and Sixpence—0.2.6. and that he be discharged by paying fyne and fees.

The names of the Constables Chosen for the Ensueing year as follows— for Maidenhead   Henry Mashon. Hopewell   Alexander Lockert. Nottingham   Robert Pearson [68] William Beaks. Chesterfield   Charles Miller [68] John Bullock. Mansfield   Henry Cook. Springfield   Thomas Wilson.

[66] Error for Joshua. See below.
[67] "Michaell" erased and "Joshua" written in.
[68] This name crossed out.

[1707/8] THE BURLINGTON COURT BOOK 331

Northampton   Walter Reeves   Sworen. Wellingburrow   Jacob Perkins Sworen. Eversham   Henry Morley. Chester   Samuell Burgis Sworen. Burlington   James Wild and James Thompson Sworen.

The Court adjourns to George Willises forthwith to meet. The Court mett according to adjournment   Presant as before.

Ordered by the Court that John Arrison doe pay unto Thomas Curtis thirty Shillings for Charges of the keeping of Hannah Underhill and that he pay the Constable fees if destrayn be made for Said Summe and the Clerks fees for Said Court order and Coppy Signed per order of the Court per the Clerke of the Court.

[248 1707]   The names of the overseers of the high ways and the Overseers of the Poor Chosen for the Ensueing year are

Overseers of the highways   Overseers of the Poor
Maidenhead
Hopewell   William Green and Jonathan Hunt
Nottingham   William Quicksall and
  Mahlon Stacy
Chesterfield
Mansfield   Robert Edwards and
  Caleb Shreef
Springfield   John Day and Thomas   Samuell Goldy and Thomas Wilson
  Staples
Northampton
Wellingborrow
Eversham
Chester
Burlington   Isaac Decow and Rich- Nathaniell Pope and Samuell Lovett
  ard Wright

The Court adjourned to meet at George Willise's forthwith. The Court mett according to adjournment   Presant as before. Proclamation made and the Court opened in forme.

Dom. Reg. versus John Clarke   John Clarke Called appears. Ordered that Said John Clarke be fyned three bitts to our Sovereign Lady the Queen and that he be discharged of his presentment by paying said fine and fees of Court.

Proclamation made   The Court adjourned untill Tomorrow morning Nine of the Clock.

Wednesday the 24th day of March 1707/8   The Court mett according to Adjournment   Presant   Thomas Revell, Daniell Leeds, Joshua Newbold, William Bustill   Esqrs. her Majesties Justices of the Peace. Proclamation made the Court opened in forme.

The Grand Jury came into Court and gave in a presentment against Moses Knap Vizt   Wee of the Grand Jury present Moses Knap for a breach of the peace Signed by our foreman John Woolston. The Grand Jury went out againe.

Dom. Reg. versus Moses Knap   Called on his presentment   Appears pleads Guilty and Submitts to the Bench.

Dom. Reg. versus Thomas Craft   being bound to his good behaviour and his appearance at this Court Cald appears. Ordered That he be discharged by proclamation by paying his fees.

The Court adjourned till two of the Clock Post Miridiem. Post Miridiem The Court mett According to adjournment. Presant Justices as before. Proclamation made the Court opened in forme.

Mr. Attorney Generall Moved in behalfe of the Sheriff that protest against the insufficiency of the Prison be entered. Ordered by the bench that it be entered Accordingly.

[249 1707]   Dom. Reg. versus Moses Knap   Called appeares and is fyned by the Court three bitts Ordered That he be discharged of his presentment paying fyne and fees.

The Grand Jury came into Court Answered to their names and give in the presentments following

[Com. Burlington to wit Dom. Reg. versus William Bewker] The Jurors for our Sovereign Lady the Queen and the body of the County of Burlington to Enquire being Sworen and Attested upon their Oaths and Attestations doe present that William Bewker of the Township of Springfield and County of Burlington aforesaid Yeoman on the Eighteenth day of December in the Sixth year of the Reigne of our Sovereign Lady Ann Queen of England etc. at the Township of Springfield and County aforesaid upon the body of Mary Smallwell the Wife of John Smallwell fornication did comitt against the peace of our Said Lady the Queen and against the forme of the Act in that case made and provided etc. (Signed on the backside)   Bill of Vera John Woolston foreman.

Com. Burlington   The Jurors for our Sovereigne Lady the Queen and the body of the County of Burlington to Enquire being Sworen and Attested upon their Oaths and Attestations doe present that Mary Smalwell The Wife of John Smallwell of the Township of Chesterfield and County of Burlington aforesaid Yeoman on the Eighteenth day of December in the Sixth year of the Reign of our Sovereign Lady Ann Queen of England etc. at the Township of Springfield and County aforesaid with William Bewker of the Township of Springfield and County aforesaid Adultry did Comitt against the peace of our Said Sovereign Lady the Queen and against the forme of the Act in that case made and provided etc. (Signed on the backside) Bill of vera John Woolston foreman.

Dom. Reg versus Mary Smalwell   Called appears pleads Guilty and Submitts to the bench   Ordered That by her own Choice Shee receive So many Lashes on her bare back According as the Act in that case made provides and that Shee remain in Custody till Said Law is answered and the Court Charges Answered.

Dom. Reg. versus William Bewker Called on his presentment Submitts and throws himself at the mercy of the Court. Ordered That Said Bewker be fyned the Summe of five pounds and that he be discharged of his presentment paying fyne and fees and that he remain in Custody of the Sheriff till fyne and fees are paid and untill he Give in Security for his good behaviour for one year Especially Toward Michaell Newbold Esqr. one of her Majesties Justices of the peace for this County.

The Court Adjourns until the fourth Tuesday in 7ber next.

Court of Common Pleas opened Presant Thomas Revell, Daniell Leeds Esqrs. Judges Justices the Same as before.

The Dockett Called over as follows

John Ward versus Walter Pumphary action Debt Withdrawn.

John Budd versus John Staples action on the Case Writt returned Non est Inventus.

Ann Mills Junr. versus Thomas Craft action Slander Withdrawn.

Alexander Griffith Esqr. versus Isaac Wood Action Slander Withdrawn.

John Burris versus Peter Hall Debt and dammages 4l. 16s. Withdrawn.

Mary Williams Executrix to Robert[?] Williams versus John Dorson action Debt 6l. 10s. Withdrawn.

[250 1707] Andrew Heath versus Charles Smith action upon the Case Dammages 12l. Withdrawn.

Alexander Griffith versus George Willis Case Dam. rec. Retraxit in propia persona.

Hugh Huddy versus William Fuller Debt Withdrawn.

William Rogers versus Charles Smith Case ad Dam. 14l. Withdrawn.

Alexander Griffith Esqr. versus James Paul.

The Court Adjourns until it Comes in Course.

At The Court of Sessions held for the County of Burlington at Burlington on Tuesday the 28th of September 1708. Presant Thomas Revell, Daniell Leeds, J. Bass Esqrs. Justices Robert Wheeler, William Bustill Esqrs. Justices.

Proclamation made and the Court opened in Forme Proclamation for Sylence made. And the Comission of the Peace to the Justices was Read.

Proclamation made and the Sheriffe was called to make returns of the precept to him directed and delivered returnable this day that the Justices might proceed thereon who appeared and made returns Accordingly The Constables of the Severall Townships in this County were Called and All Appeared Except William Beeks Constable of Nottingham.

The Grand Jury were Called over appeared and are as followeth A

Callender of the names of ther persons Sumoned to Serve on the Grand Jury Vizt Nicholas Martinaux, William Gabitas, Nicholas Brown, Jacob Decow, John Warren, Isaac Horner, Richard Ayers, Jonathan Wright, William Forster, William Hunt, Joseph Inducto, Isaac Decow, Emanuell Smith, Thomas Wetherill, John Bacon, John Lambert, Richard Wright. The Grand Jury was Sworen and Attested and the Charge Given to them and Sent out with a Constable to Attend them.

Benjamin Furnis and John Hollinshead was attested and Sent to the Grand Jury on the behalfe of our Sovereign Lady the Queen and a Constable to attend them.

Dom. Reg. versus Law[rence] Howton Being bound by recognizence to the behaviour and Appearance at this Court Called appears Ordered that his appearance be Entered and that he be Continued on his Recognizence untill the Last day of the Court.

Proclamation made and the Court Adjourned till Two of the Clock in the afternoon. The Court mett According to Adjournment Presant Justices as before and Theophilus Phillips and Enoch Anderson Esqrs. Justices. Proclamation made and the Court opened in forme.

Dom. Reg. versus Nicholas Brown and James Duff Called appears upon their Recognizence. Ordered That they find Sufficient Security to Answer etc. next Court Continued on their former Recognizence till next Terme.

[251 1708] Dom. Reg. versus Richard Blackham Called appears on his Recognizence. Ordered That he Attend Dureing the Sitting of this Court.

Dom. Reg. versus Mouns Cox Called appears on his Recognizence. Ordered That he Attend Dureing the Sitting of this Court. Ordered That Mouns Coxe be Comitted into the Sheriffs Custody till he find Security for his Attendance (his former Surity not being Willing to Continue bound) Dureing the Sitting of this Court.

Dom. Reg. versus Law[rence] Howton Ordered that unless any body appear against him Dureing the Sitting of this Court that he be Discharged of his Recognizence paying his fees.

The Grand Jury Returned in Court called over all Answered to their names and brought in three Indictments Ignoramus Dom. Reg. versus Richard Blackham on Indictment for breach of the Peace Brought in per the Grand Jury Ignoramus. Dom. Reg. versus William Hackney on Indictment for not doeing his Duty as an overseer of the highways etc. Brought in per the Grand Jury Ignoramus. Dom. Reg. versus Mouns Coxe on Indictment for marking hoggs etc. Brought in per the Grand Jury Ignoramus.

Dom. Reg. versus Law[rence] Howton Called on his recognizance and nothing appearing against him   Ordered That he be discharged by Proclamation paying his fees.

Dom. Reg. versus Mouns Cox   Ordered That he Stand Comitted untill he give Security for his appearance at the next Court and for his good behaviour in the mean time.

The Grand Jury delivered into Court and presented to the Court the following writing   Vizt   Burlington 28th of September 1708. Wee of the Grand Jury for the Body of the County of Burlington with the Consent of the honorable Bench haveing Laid before us the Necessity of repaireing the Courthouse doe appoint a County Tax to be Levied on the Severall Townships in this County as followeth to be paid in Silver money or good Merchantable Wheat at price Current to be brought into the Treasurer William Bustill for the Said County at or before the first day of the Eleventh month next Ensueing the Date hereof. Wee Doe also Appoint with the Consent of the bench William Bustill and William Gabitas to Call in the Residue of the Moneys belonging to Said County out of the hands of Samuell Furnis and Nathaniell Westland and Lett out the worke of the aforesaid Courthouse   Signed per our foreman Nicholas Martinaux.

The Townships in the County of Burlington Amwell   £00:12:00. Hopewell   £03:10:00.   Maidenhead   £03:00:00.   Nottingham   £03:00:00. Chesterfield   £05:00:00.   Mansfield   £03:14:00.   Springfield   £04:00:00. Burlington   £06:00:00.   Northampton   £02:10:00.   Wellingborrow £01:10:00.   Eversham   £03:00:00.   Chester   £02:00:00.   [Total] £37:16:00.

Signed per our foreman Nicholas Martinaux.

The Grand Jury Discharged with thanks for their Good Service.

[252 1708]   Jonathan Davis Came into Court and Desired to be Qualified to be a Babtest Preacher According to the Act of Tolleration. Curias Advursare [69] Vult.

Proclamation made   The Court Adjourned till the fourth Tuesday in March next.

At The Court of Comon Pleas held this day   Presant   Thomas Revell Daniell Leeds Esqrs. Judges. Justices the Same as before. Proclamation made and the Court opened in forme. Proclamation made and the Court Adjourned Till Tomorrow Nine of the Clock 7ber 29th   The Court met according to Adjournment   Presant   Judges and Justices the Same as before. Proclamation made and the Court opened in forme. The Docquett Called over as follows

Martha Dummer versus Edward Fisher   withdrawn.
Martha Dummer versus Symon Nightingall   Withdrawn.
John Smith versus Robert Edwards   Withdrawn.

[69] *Sic.*

John Borton versus Robert Small   Withdrawn.

Armstrong Smith versus James Robinson   Withdrawn.

Samuell Beaks versus Henry Woodhealth   Debt ad Dam. 6l. The Plaintiff Called Mr. Attorney Generall appeares for him   The Defendant Called appeared in person and confessed Judgment   Ordered That Said Henry Woodhealth Stand Comitted unto the Sheriffs Custody on Execution till the Debt and fees are answered.

John Poinsett versus Phillip Howell   action upon the Case   Dam. 10l. Withdrawn.

Proclamation made and Court adjournes to meet again imediately after our next Court of Sessions which beginns on the fourth Tuesday in March next. God Save the Queen   Cha. Huddy Clerk.

At A Court of Private Sessions held at Burlington for the County thereof the 29th of September 1708   Presant   Thomas Revell, Daniell Leeds, Robert Wheeler, William Budd, John Rudroe, William Bustill Esqrs. Justices of the Peace. Jonathan Davis came into Court in order to be Quallified according to the Act of Tolleration as a baptist preacher and Accordingly took the Oaths and Subscribed the Articles and was Quallified according to Said Act And it is Ordered (at his request) that the now Dwelling house of Said Davis be the Place recorded for the meeting house for him and his Congregation for their publick worship: Gave him a Certificate of the Same per order of the Court Signed by the Clerk.

[253 1708][70]   At   A Court of Quarter Sessions held for the County of Burlington at Burlington on Tuesday the Twenty Second day of March 1709. Presant   Thomas Revell, William Budd, William Bustill, Michaell Newbold, John Rudroe, William Budd   Esqrs. Justices.

Proclamation made and the Court opened in forme.

The Grand Jury called over and answered to their names and are as follows   foreman John Wills, Joshua Humphris, Henry Ballenger, John Murfin, John Tantum, Powell Hoof, John Touly, Samuell Goldy, William Matlack, James Adams, William Budd Junr., Samuell Hunt, Isaac Watson, Joshua Anderson.

The Grand Jury Sworen and attested and the Charge given to them by Thomas Revell Esqr. and Sent out Jacob Perkins to attend them. The Severall Constables of this county Called over. Ordered that the Constable of Maidenhead (to wit) Henry Mashon be continued in his offices for the following year. Said Order is reversed and Said Constable is fyned fifteen Shillings.

A List of the Constables appointed to Serve for the following year for Amwell   George Green   John Arburton.[71]   Maidenhead   Timothy Baker. Hopewell   Thomas Smith.   Nottingham   Samuell Radford.   Chesterfield

---

[70] Handwriting of another person.
[71] This name added in a different hand.

1708/9]   THE BURLINGTON COURT BOOK   337

Thomas Craft. Springfield   Samuell Fretwell. Northampton   John Powell. Wellingborough   Jacob Perkins Jnr. Eversham   Francis Osten. Chester   John Hollingshead [72]   Anthony Fryer. Burlington   Robert Stevens and Robert Hosier.

Dom. Reg. versus Law[rence] Howton   Appears and desires his Appearance to be Entered. Ordered it be Entered Accordingly.

Proclamation made and the Court Adjourned till two of the Clock post Meridiem   The Court Mett According to Adjournment   Proclamation made and the Court Opened in form. Present as Before Except Mr. Revell and Mr. Newbold.

Dom. Reg. versus Brown and Duff   Ordered they be discharged per proclamation paying their fees. Proclamation made and no body Appearing Against them they are Accordingly Discharg'd.

[254 1708]   Dom. Reg. versus Mouns Cox   he is Discharg'd   paying his fees and Satisfieing the Widdow of Charles Steelman deceased.

Dom. Reg. versus William Baker   in recognizence   he is discharged paying his fees.

The Constable of Maidenhead made return The Town would not raise the money for repairing of the Court house as Taxed Last Court.

The Constable of Hopewell made due return of the Warrant to him directed for the Calling of A Town Meeting and Elected Two Collectors which made no returns of any money which was taxed Said Township Court to repair the Court house.

Proclamation made and the Court Adjourned Till The Second Tuesday in June next.

Court of Comon pleas Open'd. Present as before Except Mr. Revell and Mr. Newbold. The Doggett Call'd over. Overseers for the highways Chosen as follows Vizt   for Mansfield   Edward Belton and Edward Barton   Hopewell   John Ely and William Green   Springfield   Jobe Hogdon and William Ogbourn   and for the Other Townships ordered that the overseers Chosen Last year do remain.

Proclamation made and the Court Adjourn'd Till it Comes in Cours. God Save the Queen.   Cha. Huddy Clerk.

[73] At a Court of Generall Quarter Sessions held att Burlington for the County of Burlington on the Second Tuesday of June 1709. Present Thomas Revell, Daniel Leeds, Michael Newbold, Robert Wheeler, William Bustill, Enoch Andrews   Esqrs. Justices. Proclamation made the Court open'd in forme. The Grand Jury call'd over and answered to their names and are as follows   Foreman William Wood, Caleb Shreve, Armanus King, Thomas Scoley, Edward Kemp, John Gosling, Robert Hunt, Joseph Pancust, Samuell Lipincott, Andrew Heath, John Dane, Thomas Eves Junr.,

[72] This name crossed out.
[73] Different handwriting.

John Sharp, Jonathan Eldridge, John Moore, Nathaniell Folwell, James Tomson, John Wetherill, Richard Ridgeway, Thomas Staples, John Haine, Thomas Wilkin, Henry Cook.

Ordered by the Court that Peter Leister and Joseph Stout Collectors for Hopewell do bring in their Accounts within fourteen Days and the Same for John Bryerly of Maidenhead or otherwise fin'd Twenty Shillings.

[255 1709] John Hollinghead is to appear next Court to answer his refusall of taking the office of Constable according to an Order in Court which Mr. Sheriff had promis'd to Acquaint—

The Collector of Northampton.

The Collector of Eversham.

Michael Miles Appearing and being Charged with Assault and battery he desired the Court that he might Confess his fault and Submitted himself to the Court. Michael Miles own'd himself Indebted to the Queen in 40l. to be Levied etc. on Condition to be of good behavior to the next Court of Quarter Sessions and to appear then and there etc. Michael Miles Fin'd two peices of Eight.

This fourteenth day of June 1709 Appeared in Custody of the Sheriff before Judges Revell Esqr. Mr. Robert Wheeler William Bustill Daniell Leads Michaell Newbolt John Rudrow Esqr. a Negro man by name Caser belonging to Samuel Davis Yeoman of Hopewell: Complaint was made to the Said Justices by Jonathan Johnson of Maidenhead that the Said Negro Stold from him one shirt to the Value of 30l.[74] the Said Negro being Charged with the Said Complaint before the said Justices and the Said Negro being askt by the Court what he had to Say for himself Denied the fact in behalf of the Queen Justice Andrews he declared that the Said Negro upon a writt Appareing before him had Confessed the fact and own'd it to be true and also the Said Johnson upon Oath being Sworn did Depose in behalf of the Queen that he had Lost the Shirt and that he never Saw it Since and that it was of the Same Cloth that he had upon his back whereupon it was Ordered by the Court that the Said Negro shall receive forty Lashes upon his bare back and be likewise burnt with a hott Iron on the most Vizable part of the left Cheek Near the Nose with the Letters T C: and also make restitution to the party Injured and pay Such Charges as the Court Shall Direct of etc.

The Court Adjourn'd till it Comes in Course. God Save the Queen.

At a Court of Quarter Sessions held for the County of Burlington at Burlington on Tuesday this thirteenth day of September 1709. Present Daniell Coxe, Hugh Huddy, Thomas Revell, William Bustill, Jeremiah Bass, Daniell Leeds, William Budd, Enoch Andrews, Michael Newbolt Esqrs. Justices.

Proclamation made the Court open'd in Forme. The Sheriff Accord-

[74] *Sic.*

ing to Order return'd the Jury which are as followeth   Grand Jury: Andrew Heath, Dene [Done?] John Moore, Nathaniell Falwell, James Thompson, Henry Cook, John Dawson, John Thomkins, George Willis, Daniell Sutton, Richard Ellison, John Alburtus, John Ogborn Senr., John Ely, Benjamin Hardin. Sent William Alburtas Constable to Attend the Grand Jury.

[256 1709]   John Hollingshead did not appear According to an Order of the Last Court. Michael Miles appeard and is Discharg'd paying his fees; Abraham Temple call'd and Appear'd order'd to Appeare to Morrow morning. Henry Peeps[?] calld and Appear'd ordered to appear to Morrow Morning. Edward Kemp Call'd before the Court for his Contempt and ordered to remaine in Custody of the Constable till to morrow Morning. The Court Adjourn'd till to Morrow morning att Nine a Clock.

Edward Kemp being return'd by the Sheriff of this County to Serve on the grand Jury appear'd when call'd and being requir'd to take the oath of a Grandjuryman and Serve as Such refused soe to do tho he own'd it was not Contrary to his profession to Serve or take an Oath were upon the Court proceeded to fine him and fined him in the Summe of 4l. for his Contempt and refusall aforesaid. Ordered that he be taken and Stand Committed untill he paid it its further Ordered that he find two Sureties for his good behaviour in the Summe of   and his appearance next Court or in Default thereof he be and remaine in the Custody of the Sheriff.

Ordered by the Court that Samuell Fretwell and Samuell Godling do referr their Buisiness to two Arbitrators and if they cannot agree to Chuse and Umpeer and so to Determine the matter.

The Grand Jury came into Court and being Call'd over according to forme they present the Court with a paper the tenor of which followeth in these words. September the 14th 1709. Whereas by an Act of General Assembly of this Province Entituled an Act for the Destroying wholfs Panthers Crows black birds etc. the Justices of the peace on Concurrence with the grand Jury in Each Respective County in this province are impowered and required to raise Such Summ or Summs of money as are appointed by the Said Act as also to appoint and Nominate Assessors and Collectors in Each respective County we the Justices of the Peace for the County of Burlington in Concurrence with the grand Jury to be doe appoint the following Summes of money to be Levied in the respective Townships for the Said Service Vizt:

	l	s	d
For the Township of Eversham	04	00	00
For the Township of Chester	02	10	00
For the Township of Wellingborrow	01	00	00
For the Township of Burlington	05	00	00
For the Township of Northampton	04	10	00
For the Township of Springfield	04	00	00

For the Township of Mansfield	04	00	00
For the Township of Chesterfield	05	00	00
For the Township of Notingham	03	00	00
For the Township of Hopewell	03	00	00
For the Township of Maidenhead	02	10	00
For the Township of Armwell	01	00	00
	£39	10	00

Whereas we the grand Jury with the Concurrence of the bench appoint Assessors and Collectors in Each Respective Township as follows Vizt for the Assessing and Collecting we do appoint for Eversham Township William Huyllings and John Inship Assessors John Haines Collector: For the Township of Chester John Rudrow and Hugh Sharp Assessors and Jacob Huylings Collector For the Township of Wellingborrow Abraham Huylings Senr. and Richard Fenimore Assessors and Captain John Ward Collector For the Township of Burlington Emanuell Smith and Nicholas Martinux Assessors and Richard Wright Collector for Northampton Township John Woolston and William Budd Senr. Assessors and William Budd Junr. Collector for Springfield Township Thomas Douglas and John Hogdon Assessors and John Ogborn Junr. Collector For Mansfield Township Thomas Potts and James Crafts Junr. Assessors and William Biddle Junr. Collector For Chesterfield Township Nicholas Brown and John Thorne Assessors and Jonathan Wright Collector Notingham Township Thomas Tindall and William Emly Assessors and Robert Pearson Collector For Hopewell Township William Green and Jonathan Davis Assessors and Daniel Howell Collector For Maidenhead Township Ralph Hunt and Robert Layning Assessors and James Price Collector For Amwell Township John Reading Senr. and John Wilkinson Assessors and Samuell Green Collector We of the grand Jury doe likewise Nominate and Appoint Robert Wheeler to be Treasurer for this County Tax with the Concurrence of the bench We do likewise order and Appoint that this Tax Shall be Assessed and Collected and to be paid to the Treasurer in Currant Money of this province betwixt and the first day of January next Ensueing by me foreman Andrew Heath.

[**257 1709**] On the Humble Petition of Edward Kemp Acknowledging his great fault the Court reduced his fine to twenty shillings on payment of which with his fees he is to be Discharged.

Ordered by the Court that the Measure of Beer and Ale Cask be According to the Statute of England and that the Weight of Bread be pursuant unto the Standard of Weight by the order of the Same as is now adjusted.

September the 14th 1709.

Whereas William Bustill and William Gabitas hath Appear'd before us the grand Jury for the County of Burlington against Samuell Furnis Esqr.

for the not payment of the Ballance of the former Accompts as for former Grand Jury made up with him We of the grand Jury doe agree to Leave it to the Honourable bench. Signed by the foreman: Andrew Heath.

The Court of Quarter Sessions Adjourn'd till it Comes in Course.

Court of Pleas open'd the 14th September. Present as before.

Adjourn'd till to Morrow att tenn a Clock.

The Court mett According to Adjournment   Present as before. Proclamation being made the Court open'd in forme. The Sheriffs return of the grand Jury the greater Number whereof refus'd to Swear being Quakers Whereupon the bench order'd the Sheriff to make up his Pannell of others that are not Quakers.

Abraham Temple being bound by Recognizence to appear this Sessions for his Misbehaviour towards Enoch Andrews one of the Justices of this County has Appear'd on his humble Submission and request is Discharg'd paying his fees.

Henry Poops being bound over by Recognizence to appear here at this Sessions to answer for a pretended Fornication Committed by him on Mary Henton has appear'd and the grand Jury having return'd two bills of Indictment about the matter ignoramus the Court Order'd him to be Discharg'd by proclamation paying his fees Alexander Griffith Esqr. Attorney Generall Dissented thereunto: Discharg'd as aforesaid paying his fees.

Thomas Revell and Daniell Leeds Esqrs. two Justices etc. having given Judgment against Richard Allison on the Complaint of Nathaniel Westland for the Summe off Twenty two Shillings from which Judgment the Said Allison appeal'd to this Court and the Court on hearing the proofs and Allegations of both parties revers'd and the Said Judgment and order'd that the Said Allison be restor'd to all things he lost thereby and have the Usuall and Lawfull Costs.

[*Atty*] [75] A Commission from George Ingoldesby to Thomas Clark Gent. to practice as an Attorney and Councill at Law was read and allowed.

Ward Against Holbrooke That a Declaration be Accepted of this Court by the Consent of the plaintiffs Attorney and that he plead a fortnight before next Court and Come to tryall next Court by Consent if not Judgment.

Maclamere Against Gust   Ca[?] Bond assign'd.

[*Regula Generalis*] [76] Its ordered by the Court that all persons whatsoever that Shall Commence an Action against any person or persons whatsoever that Such person or persons soe Commencing his or their Action Shall file his or their Declaration fifteen days before the return of Such Writt or Else a non pros. to be Enterd, Except in Such Cases where any Plaintiff sues out a Writt in less time then fifteen days before the Court then Such

---

[75] Written along the margin in a different hand.
[76] Written along the margin in a different hand.

Plaintiff is to file his Declaration in fifteen Days before the Terme Ensueing the return of the Plaintiffs Writt or Else Non pros. to be Enter'd in the Clerks Office all non Residents to Give Security to pay all Cost if they are Nonsuite on the return of the Writt or non pros. to be Enter'd.

The Court Adjourn'd till it Comes in Course.

[258 1709] At the Court of Quarter Sessions begun the Second Tuesday in December 1709. Present: Coll. Coxe, Coll. Huddy, Mr. Revell, Mr. Sonmans, Mr. Leeds, Mr. Bustill, Mr. Budd Esqrs. Justices.

Court call'd over: the Jury call'd all appear'd and Sworn (Except John Burlace) and sent out John Arrison appear'd and refused to take the formal Oath and having no Certificate from the Quakers.

Dom. Reg. Against George Willocks.

Dom. Reg. Against John Barton.

The Court adjourns till three a Clock Post Meridiem. The Court mett According to Adjournment: Present Coll. Coxe, Coll. Hudey, Mr. Revell, Mr. Leeds, Mr. Andrews Justices.

Judith Allen Sworn and Sent etc.

Mr. Hillocks appears on his Recognizence and desires his Appearance might be Enterd Ordered that his Appearance be Entered.

John Borton appears on his Recognizence ordered he attend during the Courts Sitting.

The Court Adjourns till to morrow Morning at 9 of the Clock. Mett According to Adjournment. Present Coll. Coxe, Coll. Hudey, Mr. Revell, Mr. Andrews Esqrs. Justices.

Mr. Willocks call'd upon his Recognizence appears at the motion of Mr. Attorney Generall Order'd that Mr. Willocks be Dischargd of his Recognizence and that he Enter into a new Recognizence for his Appearance and to answer at the next Court of Oyer and Terminer to be held at Burlington Tuesday next in him in the Summe of £100 with two Suretyes in the Sum of £50 each for the peace and that in the mean time he be in Custody till Such Suretys be given in.

The grand Jury return'd call'd over appears; Thomas Wilkings Thomas Borton John Wills and Joshua Humphris, all sent to the Grand Jury to Inform them Concerning the boundrys of two Towns (Vizt) County of Burlington the 21st of November 1709 Then laid out a Road (for the benefitt of the Inhabitants of the Township of Eversham and Others) the Same road being the breadth of two rods Beginning at Salem road in the fork of Pansaquen in the township of Chester (and answers the road formerly laid out to the South branch of Ponsaquen Creek to Samuell Borroughs) thence as it is now mark'd through John Cowperthwaits Land etc. to Richard Apletons fence corner as it now stands and along the Same thence as it is now mark'd to the bridge by Jonathan Elderidges thence as it now Lyeth through Jonathan Eldridges Land thence as it is now Mark'd to William Evans field and Over a Corner of the Same to a tree Mark'd on the other side thence a Long the Road as it is now mark'd to Thomas Lippincotts Land thence along [259 1709] as it now mark'd to a Small Hickrey By Richard Haines fence corner thence through the field on a Straight line to a Mark'd tree at the other Corner thence as it is now mark'd to a Little Gully thence as it is now mark'd to the corner of Zachariah Prickets field thence as it is now mark'd to a Spanish Oak by the west branch of Rancocus Creek and over the Same thence as it is now Mark'd to Richard Airess Mill: Also one other road laid out the Same day to a Landing on the South branch of the aforesaid Creek beginning at the Gully aforesaid and so along the old path as it is now mark'd to Zachariah Prickets fence and Along by the Same thence as it is now mark'd to the Landing at the place call'd the fording place the aforesaid Roads being mark'd with two Nocches in the trees the said roads being as aforesaid two Rod roads. The Said roads was laid out by us the day and year above Said. Joshua Humphris   John Wills Commissioners.

The Court Adjourned till 3 a Clock Post Miridiem. Mett According to Adjournment   Present as before. Court Open'd.

Dom. Reg. against John Borton   On Indictment Ignoramus. Ordered that he be discharged of his Recognizence paying his fees.

The Court Adjourn'd for one hour, at George Willis. Meet According to Adjournment   Present as before. The Grand Jury came into Court and gave in and Account of further Division betwixt the Township of Northampton and Eversham. Order'd by the Court that it be Enter'd which is as followeth Vizt   County of Burlington the 14th of December 1709: Whereas it hath been represented to us who are of the Grand Inquest for the body of the Said County that there is a Necessity of a farther Division to be made betwixt the Township of Northampton and Eversham: We therefore do agree that the Said Division do begin where the former record leaves of and thence to the forking of the Said South Branch and then beginning Just at the Said fork and thence going to a Certain Bridge over a Creek call'd Mill Creek or Thomas Evans's Run near the Indian Town Call'd Coerxing[?] and along the same to the head thereof. Signed by Jacob Heulings Foreman.

They also brought in an Account of Charges of the Township of Northampton in help Building a Bridge which is in the Town of Eversham. Ordered that Each Township Chuse each of them two men and that be at the next Court of quarter Sessions to be try'd in that matter.

Court of Common Pleas open'd and Adjourn'd till tomorrow Morning Mett according to Adjournment   Present as before.

John Rowland against John Holbrook   Mr. Attorney Generall appears for the Plaintiff and Moves that the Deffendant put in his Plea at or before the first of February next or Judgment Granted   Mr. Bass appears for the Deffendant moves that the Plaintiff being not an Inhabitant of the Province that he give in Security to pay Cost if Cost Granted   Mr. Attorney Generall Moves in Said Case that the Deffendant give in Special Bayle in to Said Action in a fortnights time Granted.

[**260 1709**] John Ward against John Holbrook   Mr. Attorney Generall moved in the behalf of the Plaintiff that Judgment be Enter'd according to the rule of Last Court Granted.

Court Adjourn'd till 3 Post Meridiem. Court Mett according to Adjournment   Present as before. Motion made by Mr. Attorney General as follows   On the Motion of Mr. Attorney General that the former rule made in this Court for the fileing Declarations fourteen days before the return of the Writt was in many cases very Inconvenient. Ordered that the Said Rule be sett aside and the Plaintiff in Every Action doe by some one of the Attorneys of that Court file their Declaration the first day of the Court next after the taking out of the Said Writt or a Non pros to be Enter'd.

Henry Scott against Samuell Smith   Mr. Attorney Generall appears for the Deffendant. Ordered it be Continued till next Court.

[*Regula Generalis*] [77]   Ordered that the Attorneys for the Plaintiff shall be Accountable for the fees to all the Officers of the Court for their Clyents for which they are Implyed by.

The Court Adjourns till it Comes in Course.[78]

[77] Along margin, in a different hand.

[78] Rest of this page blank. Remainder of record is in reverse paging, and contains several pages of road records, 1707–1709, and an old index to some of the matter in the court record.

INDEX

INDEX

Key to Abbreviations

A	Anglican *	op	overseer of poor
a	attorney	p	plaintiff
c	constable	pj	petty juror
cp	complainant, accuser	Q	Quaker *
cr	coroner	Q?	probably Quaker
d	defendant	Q??	perhaps Quaker
g	governor or deputy	r	recognizance, held for court
gj	grand juror	s	sheriff or deputy
i	indicted, presented	sv	servant
j	judge, justice	t	tavern
ka	king's or prosecuting attorney	tl	tavern license
oh	overseer of highways	w	witness

Abbott, Ann, Q, w, 302.
Abbott, Jane, w, 15.
Abbott, Jno., Q, 237; c, 131; d, 312; gj, 92-316; i, 302; oh, 176; pj, 112-281.
Abbott, Sam., d, 48-81; i, 15.
Account. *See* Actions.
Acres, Wm., 225.
Actions: account, 110, 127, 239; assault, battery, 14, 20, 46, 234; jury trial required, 107; assumpsit, *quantum meruit*, 257; attachment, 2, 14, 44, 75, 80, 83, 84, 113, 121, 133, 162, 165, 184, 236, 239, 315, forfeiture of goods, 75, vs. an estate, 238; battery, 20, 46; bond, 126, 134, 147, 218, 246; case, 12, 14, 15, 16, 20, 24, 35, 41, 42, 44, 45, 48, 51, 59, 60, 61, 71, 74, 83, 84, 90, 99, 100, 101, 103, 106, 107, 114, 125, 130, 132, 140, 150, 151, 153, 155, 156, 157, 165, 169, 170, 175, 178, 181, 185, 186, 188, 189, 192, 194, 205, 206, 207, 209, 210, 211, 214, 216, 221, 222, 329, 330, 333, 336; debt, 13, 14, 19, 24, 23, 35, 39, 42, 43, 44, 45, 47, 48, 50, 51, 59, 60, 63, 69, 70, 80, 81, 82, 83, 90, 94, 97, 98, 99, 100, 103, 110, 113, 121, 128, 132, 139, 150, 151, 153, 155, 156, 162, 169, 170, 179, 180, 185, 189, 191, 205, 207, 209, 211, 214, 216, 221, 222, 223, 225, 243, 277, 278, 280, 282, 284, 330, 333, upon bond, 244; defamation, 13, 116, 132, 170, 183, 193, 211, 216, 304, 309, 324, 326, of title in land, 216; false imprisonment, 99; forcible entry, 20; *in personam*, die with person, 251; libel and slander, 273; malpractice, 108; slander, 60, 61, 62, 64, 86, 100, 113, 132, 139, 153, 222, 302, 333, and defamation, 104, 145, 193; thievery, 126, 127; trespass, 8, 9, 12, 49, 58, 61, 62, 67, 68, 74, 83, 93, 116, 151, 153, 161, 169, 170, 172, 178, 181, 185, 200, 272, 275, 279, 283; trespass on the case, 3, 9, 66, 238; trover, 48, 61, 84, 121, 139, 171; trover and conversion, 2-3, 33, 192, 211, 216, 276.

Adams, Hester, Q, w, 306.
Adams, Jas., Q, 187; gj, 191, 201, 301, 336; pj, 250, 281; w, 306; *v. Hooten and Fryer*, 196.
Adams, Jno., Q, 187, 192; j, 181-291; w, 171, 321.
Adams, Jos., Q, A 1702, 264; c, 95; gj, 112-141; pj, 64-88, 181-212.
Administration of estates, 34, 162, 242, 243; excrs. and admrs.—parties pltf., 23, 103, 115, 117, 120, 125, 139, 143, 147, 150, 162, 237, 240, 260, 280, 283; excrs. and admrs.—parties deft., 120, 121, 132, 142, 172, 178, 179, 186, 211, 237, 238, 264, 265, 315; approving accounts, 264; caveat against, 101; discharged as admr., 104, 110;

---

* Identifications of Anglicans are mostly from G. M. Hills, *History of the Church in Burlington* (Trenton, 1876), especially pp. 214 ff. Those of Quakers are based chiefly upon the Burlington and other monthly meeting minutes in custody of the Philadelphia Friends Yearly Meeting, 302 Arch Street, and an early Chesterfield minute book in the Historical Society of Pennsylvania, Philadelphia; also upon various printed works, particularly W. W. Hinshaw, *Encyclopedia of American Quaker Genealogy*, ii (Ann Arbor, 1938), and A. M. Gummere, "Friends in Burlington," in *Pennsylvania Magazine of History*, vii (see especially pp. 266, 370).

INDEX

Administration of estates (*Continued*)
execution vs. an estate, 238, 239; foreign letters of administration, 150; moneys in executors' hands seized, 160; request for, 151; registry for, 151; *plenius administravit*, 225; sale of goods for deceased children, 126.
Admiralty, 97.
Adye, Capt. Jno., d, 14.
Alberson, Wm., Q, 28; gj, 51.
Alburtus, Jno., gj, 339.
Alburtus, Wm., c, 339.
Alcot, Wm., 312.
Aldridge [Alrichs], Peter, w, 68.
Aletasters, 19.
Allen, Eph., Q, 136; d, 139.
Allen, Jas., w, 314, 316; *v. Boon*, 318.
Allen, Jed., Q?, 260.
Allen, Jno., 45; d, 24-94; i, 58; sv, 24; w, 68; *v. Gray*, 48; *et ux. v. Pumphary*, 58.
Allen, Judea, Q, gj, 316.
Allen, Judith, w, 342.
Allen, Mary, sv, d, 24; p, 58.
Allen, Math., Q, non-Q 1701, 1, 70, 162, 165, 176, 187; c, 176; d, 20-25; gj, 180-223; pj, 23, 73-166; w, 50; *v. Bartlemews*, 3, 4; *v. Cole*, 10, 20; *v. Davison*, 48; *v. Devonish*, 131; *v. Revell*, 96; *v. Rush*, 170.
Allen, Mary, i, 295-316.
Allen, Nathan, Q, d, 318, 324; gj, 269, 318; *v. Groome*, 191; *v. Wells*, 318.
Allen, Nath., Q??, d, 10, 211.
Allen, Neh., d, 10; *and Wright v. Brown*, 318.
Allen, Thos., d, 10, 13, 16; w, 15.
Allison, Rich., Q?, c, 231; d, 257; *v. Westland*, 341.
Anderson [Andrews?], Enoch, c, 319-328; gj, 219; i, 323; pj, 311.
Anderson, Jno., 25, 28, 46; d, 34.
Anderson, Jno., sv, 227.
Anderson, Josh., 225; gj, 301, 336; oh, 313.
Anderson, Mary, w, 172.
Anderson, Mordecai, i, 271; w, 172.
Anderson, Sam., gj, 43.
Andrews, Edw., Q, 159, 161, 168, 253; c, 228, 231; d, 250; i, 212, 215.
Andrews [Anderson?], Enoch, j, 334-342.
Andrews, Mary, Q, 162, 169.
Andrews, Mordecai, Q??, 169; c, 213, 219; d, 221; i, 192, 252; pj, 203, 212; w, 179.
Andrews, Sam., Q, 31, 61, 149-168; gj, 74-142; pj, 60-136.
Andrews, Thos., Q??, *v. Web*, 277.
Andros, Sir Edm., xxi-xxv, xxviii-xxxiv.
[Anglican] Church, 297; in West Jersey politics, xxxix.
Animals, punishment of, 143.
Antram, Jas., Q, 253; c, 201, 212; gj, 265, 320.
Antram, Jno., Q, 1, 31, 163, 287; d, 34; gj, 192,
252, 320; oh, 159; pj, 73-201, 294, 324; w, 151, 161, 170; *v. Potts*, 34.
Appeal, from Burlington court, xliii f.; from decision of two justices, 341; ignored, 102; to assembly, 141, 147, refused, 62; to England, refused, 25; to equity, 181; to provincial court, 162, 165, 170, 182, 196, 200, 218, 220, 222, 248; refused, 211.
Appeals, Courts of, xliv, xlvi, xlviii; 166, 226, 248.
Appearance, by wife, 244; refusal, 56; no, 94, 225, 226.
Appleton, Jno., Q??, gj, 74.
Appleton, Josiah, c, 176, 180, 247, 261; gj, 129-195; i, 262; pj, 117.
Appleton, Rich., 182, 342; pj, 317.
Appraisers, 41, 63, 81, 128, 135, 139, 148, 245, 296.
Apprentices. *See* Masters and servants.
Arbitration, xlvii, 3, 29, 39, 44, 46, 70, 299, 339.
Arburton, Jno., c, 336.
Armstrong, Alex., w, 266.
Arney, Jno., Q??, pj, 303.
Arnold, Jno., c, 228; gj, 212.
Arnold, Rich., Q, 1, 28; cp. 29; d, 16.
Arrison. *See* Harrison.
Ashley, Mary, w, 175.
Ashmore, Anth., d, 216.
Ashton, Jno., Q, 30; d, 54.
Assault. *See* Actions, Crimes.
Assessors chosen, 30; appointed, 339.
Assinpink (St. Pink) Creek, 6, 7, 203, 205, 219, 329. *See also* Birch.
Assiscunck, *alias* Birch Creek, 30, 192, 195.
Assumpsit. *See* Actions.
Atheism, charge of, 297.
Atkins, Thos., d, 192, 207.
Atkinson, Thos., Q, 214; pj, 185, 191.
Atkinson, Wm., Q 1686, sworn 1705, 213, 216, 221; gj, 56, 306, 325; oh, 159; pj, 182, 298, 311.
Attachment. *See* Actions.
Attestation, 53, 82, 108, 132, 151, 153, 158, 160, 161, 166, 170, 206, 223, 236, 261, 263, 266, 271, 294, 302, 306; "false," 58, 193; of various officers, 5-7, 64, 66, 146, 148, 214; put in minutes, 61; read in court, 54, 210, 255; refused, 151, 233. *See* Oaths, Witness.
Attorney, 9, 20, 44, 50, 67, 87, 100, 116, 120, 134, 154, 214, 229, 230, 236-238, 244-246, 249, 250, 267, 272, 274, 275, 277-281, 283, 284, 293, 296, 307, 310, 315; becomes bound to appear for defendant, 257; commission as, 341; letter of, 104, 106, 216, 236; prosecuting, xlii; refusal of, 138, 237; request for, 138; rule re, 344; will not pay if defendant is cast, 125.
Auditors, 113, 221.
Austin, Fran., Q, 187; c, 337; d, 162; gj, 234; pj, 193, 317.

INDEX

Austwick, Onesiphorus, cp, 48.
Ayers, Rich., Q, 343; gj, 293, 334; pj, 281.

Bacon, Dan., Q, 31, 91; c, 150, 152; gj, 115-136; his creek, 92; pj, 54-93.
Bacon, Jno., Q, gj, 313-334.
Bagley, Wm., c, 307.
Bail, forfeiture, 152, 171.
Bainbridge, Jno., Q 1678, sworn 1705, xxxix, 204, 207, 258, 307, 329; d, 197, 199; gj, 95, 206, 219, 301; j, 313-327; oh, 115; pj, 130, 136, 270; w, 62, 166, 308.
Bainbridge, Sarah, Q, r, 204, 207; w, 166.
Bakehouse, 105.
Baker, Jno., 139; d, 131.
Baker, Sam., Q?, 185.
Baker, Tim., c, 336.
Baker, widow, 194
Baker, Wm., r, 337.
Ballinger, Henry, Q, 187, 259; gj, 92-203, 317, 336; pj, 128-186, 298; sv, 14; w, 306.
Baptist preacher, 335, 336.
Barker, Sam., xxvii, 232; v. Tuely, 24.
Barkstead. See Wilobe.
Barkstead, Josh., p, 216.
Barnes, Wm., 31.
Barrels, 87.
Barroe, Jas., i, 130.
Bartlemew, Geo., 1; d, 3, 8; v. Loyd, 16; v. Willis, 14.
Bartlemew, Mary, d, 3, 8.
Barton, Edw., Q, oh, 337.
Barton, Thos., Q, 32; gj, 32-82; pj, 8-69.
Basnett, Eliz., Q, 224; d, 194, 216; tl, 190, 220, 229; w, 127; v. Dean, 189.
Basnett, Rich., Q, xi, xxxv, 23, 26, 29, 39, 63; a, 116, 170; cp, 74, 101; cr, 71; d, 49, 59; j, 69-142; ka, 142; oh, 49; pj, 14-67; t, 97-141; tl, 19, 126, 154; w, 74-147; and Hollinshead v. Bywater, 116; v. Chamnis, 71; v. Cole, 80; v. Durham, 96; v. Gill, 156; v. Heesom, 157; et ux. v. Lawrence, 131; v. Lillies, 81; v. Lotter, 20; v. Milner, 83; v. Newman, 24; v. Peares, 157; v. Pumphary, 80; v. Renshawe, 96; v. Rush, 170; v. Sherwin, 157; v. Smith, 96; v. Thrumball, 20.
Basse, Jeremiah, A, xxxviii; a, 172-179, 221, 343; d, 240; g, xxxiv, lii, 216-223; j, 176, 292-338; secretary, 301; w, 174; v. Hutcheson and Stacy, 179; v. Powson, 178; v. Righton, 175; v. Stacy, et al., 172; and Revell v. Westland, 221.
Basse, Peter. See Bosse.
Bates, Wm., Q, 28, 111; gj, 44.
Bavin, Thos., d, 269.
Bayley, Wm., A, i, 295; r, 317.
Beach, Jno., 175; c, 191.
Beach, Rich., cp, 8.
Beaks, Sam., v. Woodhealth, 336.

Beaks, Wm., Q, c, 330, 333; v. Bowde and Bavin, 269; v. Daviss, 269; v. Hutchinson, 274, 291.
Beard, Geo., 266; gj, 240.
Beard, Wm., Q, 1, 31; c, 62; gj, 54; pj, 9-49; w, 22.
Beck, Henry, Q, xxxvi, 207, 248; c, 201, 213; d, 80, 178, 207; gj, 148, 206, 212; i, 123; pj, 171-270; w, 177; and Scattergood v. Gabitas, 258; and Scattergood v. Pears, 269.
Bell [Beck?], Henry, 303; pj, 303.
Bellows, Mathias, 187.
Bennett, Alex., pj, 311; w, 158.
Bennett, Edm., cp, 34.
Bennett, Rebecca. See Scholey.
Berkeley, Lord Jno., xv.
Berry, Rich., 53.
Beswick, Aaron. See Boswick.
Beswick, Fran., Q, 1, 31, 125, 126.
Beswick, Priscilla. See Hudson.
Bewker, Wm., i, 332.
Bibb, Ruth, w, 238.
Bibb, Thos., xli, lii, 190-223, 265; d, 186; ka, 180; j, 206-212; pj, 164, 174; s, 176; w, 173, 176; v. Dowglas and Smith, 214.
Bickam, Rich., Q, 247; pj, 203.
Bickley, Abr., Q, 203, 238; c, 202; gj, 195, 261; pj, 186, 257; w, 230.
Biddle, Hanna, i, 223-226.
Biddle, Wm., Q, xi, xii, xxvii, xl, 29, 31, 39, 125, 144, 165, 178, 209; d, 46, 131, 157, 178; gj, 310; i, 214; j, 12-281; v. Butcher, 121.
Biddle, Wm., jr., Q, xxxviii, 340; c, 176, 184; d, 169; gj, 148-188, 261-313; pj, 168, 250-270.
Biles, Wm., Q, 2; v. Young, 24.
Bill of exchange, 50, 120, 134.
Billingham, Thos., Q?, r, 327; w, 203, 204, 294.
Binge, Sam., 71.
Bingham, Jas., A, 182, 262; gj, 157, 190, 253, 281; oh, 176; pj, 171-195.
Birch Creek, 49, 93 (alias Springfield), 150. See also, Assinpink.
Birch, Jos., pj, 149.
Birch, Ruth, sv, 95.
Bishop, The, cp, 307.
Bishop, Thos., Q., 300; c, 292, 301; d, 48; gj, 252, 320; pj 241.
Black, Jno., Q, gj, 318, 321; oh, 313.
Black, Thos., Q, w, 214.
Black, Wm., Q, 1, 31, 123; c, 131; gj, 51, 226, 240; his creek, 92; i, 271; pj, 9, 112, 176-186.
Blackham, Rich., Q?, i, 334.
Blacksmith, 188, 276; work, 109; tools, 276, 287.
Blackston, Gov., of Maryland, 266.
Blake, Jas., d, 99, 100, 113; r, 127; w, 101; v. Read, 99.
Blewit, Dan., r, 249.
Blowers, Jos., 30, 90, 44; d, 48; pj, 42.
Boards, planks, 10, 107.
Bom, Cor., cp, 39, 40.

Bond, 8, 29, 179, 180, 207, 218, 243, 244, 260, 262; discharged, 208; for appeal, 147; for appearance, 220, 223; forfeited for non appearance, 115, 157; to prosecute, 272, 295; to support bastard, 123. *See also,* Actions, Recognizance.
Bondsman, admitted to "personate" defendant, 224; to produce prisoner or lie in prison, 152; unwilling to continue, 333.
Bonham, Hez., 225; gj, 301; oh, 228.
Books, bound, 228, 234; bought, 234.
Boon, Ralph, d, 318.
Booth, Edey, 257.
Booth, Mich., 257.
Borden, Benj., xxxvi; i, 241-243.
Borden, Sam., Q, 31, 170; d, 100.
Borrowes, Jno., Q??, w, 52.
Borton, Eliz., Q, d, 13.
Borton, Jno., Q, 1, 30, 182, 187; c, 228, 247; cp, 253; gj, 32, 195, 199, 253; i, 343; oh, 49; pj, 1-56, 191, 317; r, 267, 342; w, 197; *v. Small,* 336.
Borton, Thos., Q?, w, 342.
Borton, Wm., Q, gj, 258; pj, 317.
Bosse, Eliz., w, 175.
Bosse, Peter, Q, lii, 126, 127, 148; cp, 102; gj, 69-142; oh, 150; pj, 48-115; w, 175; *v. Hudson,* 113.
Boston, 106.
Boswick, Aaron, Q, *and Hudson v. Crues,* 116.
Boulton, Edw., Q, 213, 253, 287; oh, 337; pj, 259, 294.
Bowde, Adlord, 144.
Bowde, Isaac, 144.
Bowde, Grimston, d, 269.
Bowden, Mordecai, 30; cp, 81; gj, 54; i, 83; *v. Pickering,* 44.
Bowman, Henry, d, 13, 49.
Bowman, Thos., Q, 26-67; d, 53, 120, 150; gj, 40-142; pj, 137.
Bown, Mary, 272.
Bownde, Jno., *v. Cottrell,* 192.
Boyden, Jas., Q, w, 69.
Boyes, Rich., c, 213, 219; d, 113, 318; gj, 157; pj, 210; r, 253; *v. Hudson,* 258; *v. Mason et ux.,* 318.
Bradbury, Jno., cp, 35.
Braddock, Nich., w, 266.
Bradgate, Anne, cp, i, sv, 126-127.
Bradway, Edw., Q, xxii-xxv, 5.
Braithwait, Manning, *v. York,* 236.
Bramma, Benj., 28.
Branding, 338.
Branford, —, 65.
Brenson, Dan., d, 84; *v. Johnson,* 10.
Bricklayer, 133.
Bricks, 22, 51, 70; overseers of, 19.
Bridges, mentioned, presented, etc., Assiscunke, 195, 329; Chesterfield, Crofts, Croswicks, 189; Cropwell, 187; Darwin, 91; Eversham, 343; Farr's, 152; Hancock's, 83, 87, 152, 233; London, 11, 49, 54, 80, 170; Long's, 99, 129, 317; Mattacopenny, 129, 160, 190, 232; Mill Creek, 92, 99, 149, 343; Mulberry, 187; Pennsauken, 92; Ricketts', 145; Shabacunck, 225; Yorkshire, 11, 30, 83, 88, 129, 160, 164, 220, 224, 227; tax for, at "the Point," 182.
Brightwen, Wm., Q, 1, 121; d, 14; gj, 4-101; p, 14, 41; pj, 19-67; *v. Bywater,* 113.
Brock, Thos., A, i, 98; w, 75; *v. Foulk,* 221; *v. Heesom,* 124; *v. Scholey,* 113; *v. Syddall,* 124.
Bromeley, Jacob, 216; w, 218.
Brooks, Jno., Q??, gj, 317, 325; oh, 322.
Brown, Abr., sr., Q, A 1702, gj, 219, 231, 310; i, 228; *v. French,* 216; *v. West,* 236.
Brown, Abr., jr., Q, 253; gj, 206, 318; pj, 220-281.
Brown, Eliz. (Cook), p, 260; w, 265, 267.
Brown, Jno., Q, 26-34, 115, 145, 238-299; c, 93-98; d, 48; gj, 48-176, 246-316; pj, 23-67, 115, 185, 203; w, 179.
Brown, Jos., Q??, d, 16; pj, 43; *v. Hoult,* 22.
Brown, Nich., Q, xxxvi, 340; gj, 334; i, 243, 249; r, 334; tl, 311; *et ux. v. Webley,* 260.
Brown, Preserve, Q, pj, 298.
Brown, Sam., Q, d, 318.
Brown, Wm., cp, 207; i, 271; sv, 207; *v. Allen,* 211; *v. Craft,* 214.
Brunsley, Luke, w, 51.
Bryan, Thos., Q, 237, 259, 287; c, 281; gj, 123, 227-270; pj, 157, 195, 265.
Bryerly, Jno., 258; c, 201-219; gj, 192, 212; i, 177; oh, 176; pj, 198-265; w, 185.
Budd, Jas., Q, 44-72, 114, 174; j, 45-69; *v. Randall,* 48.
Budd, Jno., Q, lii, 64, 78, 94; c, 49; d, 103, 174; gj, 54-112; oh, 131, 154; pj, 23-136; w, 43, 85, 114; *v. Biddle,* 131; *v. Staples,* 333.
Budd, Mary, w, 51.
Budd, Susannah, Q, cp, 43.
Budd, Thos., Q, xxvii, xxx, xxxiii, lii, 1-67, 116, 124; j, 12-23; pj, 2, 49-74; w, 24; *v. Chamnis,* 121; *v. Cole,* 66; *v. Newbold,* 81; *et al. v. Petty,* 14-23; *v. Pickering,* 21; *v. Pumphary,* 20, 45; *v. Salfert,* 81; *v. Yeo,* 39.
Budd, Wm., Q, A 1702, 144, 148, 259, 319, 340; c, 159-181; gj, 40-145; i, 271; j, 292-342; oh, 228; pj, 19-193; w, 22, 24, 175, 233; *v. Potts,* 41, 42.
Budd, Wm., jr., A 1702, 312, 340; gj, 336; pj, 311.
Buddin, Josh., 206.
Buddin, Wm., 206.
Buffin, Mich., Q, 144; c, 115; gj, 82-320; his creek 253; i, 20, 34; oh, 185; pj, 153-209; r, 23.
Bullock, Jno., c, 330; d, 299; pj, 294.
Bunting, Job, Q, pj, 196.
Bunting, Jno., Q, 237; gj, 40-258; oh, 93; pj, 51-270; w, 209; *v. Gilbert,* 260.
Bunting, Sam., Q, gj, 145-270; oh, 122, 131; pj, 117-199; w, 51.

INDEX

Burcham, Henry, Q, 232; c, 159; gj, 141, 154, 293, 316; pj, 185, 186, 324.
Burcham, Jas., Q, gj, 301.
Burden. *See* Borden.
Burden, Symon, 37; i, 40.
Burgess of Burlington, 193, 203, 213, 217, 220, 222, 241, 253.
Burgesse, Anth., 72; i, 82.
Burgesse, Rich., d, 16; *v. Dove*, 59; *v. Hoult*, 16.
Burgin, Jos., d, 100; w, 75; *v. Greene*, 101; *v. Newbold*, 128; *v. Wood*, 74.
Burgis, Sam., c, 331.
Burlace, Jno., gj, 342.
Burley, Elias, gj, 141; pj, 123.
Burling, Jno., Q, gj, 130; pj, 95, 96.
Burlington, "Highstreet" in, 129; inhabitants presented, 91; Island of, 87; monthly courts at, 49; Port of, 183; settlement of, xxv ff.; streets, rubbish in, 164; town landing, 91.
"Burnt," 65.
Burnt in hand, 263, 272.
Burr, Henry, Q, 144, 237; c, 261; gj, 164-316; pj, 198.
Burre, Jno., Q, pj, 23.
Burris, Jno., *v. Hall*, 333.
Burroughs, Sam., Q, 187, 342.
Burrows, Edw., w, 182.
Burt, Rich., gj, 301.
Burton. *See* Borton.
Bustill (Bustin), Wm., A, xxxix, 208, 287, 335; c, 176, 184, 228, 247; cp, 340; gj, 82, 190-227, 306; j, 325-342; pj, 153, 209-317; *et ux. v. Horsman*, 89-94.
Butcher, Anne, Q, w, 89.
Butcher, Edw., w, 90.
Butcher, Gabriel, Q?, 89.
Butcher, Jno., Q, 67, 79, 217; c, 49, 65; d, 216; gj, 32-226, 297; oh, 131, 150; pj, 33, 171-250.
Butcher, Rob., d, 121.
Butcher, Thos., Q, 91; c, 111; gj, 56-98; pj, 102-128.
Byles, Chas., Q?, pj, 181.
Byllynge, Edw., Q, xvi, xxxii-xxxiv, 28, 47, 48, 59.
Bywater, Gervas, 121; d, 113, 116.

Callman, Alex., w, 18.
Calowe, Jno., Q, lii, 144; d, 113; gj, 112-142; pj, 129, 159; w, 84, 104, 119; *v. Lovejoy*, 113; *v. Tuelie*, 171; *v. Wright*, 132.
Cambell, Benj., i, 271.
Camrone, Dan., sv, 197.
Canoe, Indian, 62, 75.
Cantrill, Rich., d. 240.
Cantwell, Sheriff Edm., xxi ff., xxx.
Cape May, 49, 97, 104, 111, 114; court, li.
Capital punishment, Quaker aversion to, liv.
Carelton, Wm., 28.
Carlile, Abr., i, 223-226.

Carlyn, Jno., pj, 324.
Carman, Caleb, li, cp, 46, 54; and sons, i, 82, 97.
Carman, Jno., cp, 46, 54.
Carpenter (occupation), 278, 312.
Carpenter, Lewis, w, 78.
Carpenter, Sam., Q, 26, 28.
Carter, Jno., c, 62.
Carter, Jno., of E. J., 18.
Carter, Rob., *v. Allen et ux.*, 24, 45.
Carter, Wm., *v. Hawkins*, 189.
Carteret, Sir Geo., xv.
Carteret, Gov. Philip, 25, 26, 67.
Cary, Shershaw, *v. Allen*, 324.
Case. *See* Actions.
Cassoone, Jno., i, 130.
Cattle, 44, 68, 90, 184, 236.
Caving (Caluin), Rich., d, 275, 285; i, 252.
Cedar Swamp, 187.
Cemetery, 144, 293.
Cerkett. *See* Surkett.
Cessation of process, 320, 329.
Chaffen, Jno., Q, j, 12-16.
Chamberlaine, Mary, w, 118.
Chambers, Jno., A?, w, 306.
Chamneys, Edw., xxii.
Chamnis, Eliz., d, 103, 121; i, 102.
Chamnis, Jno., 103, 121; d, 60-71; gj, 51; i, 74; pj, 49-62; *v. Cornish*, 44.
Champion, Jno., *v. Jacobs*, 10; *v. Roberts*, 10.
Champion, Math., Q, c, 185; gj, 180-330; pj, 136-270; w, 223; *v. Martineau*, 278.
Channders, Thos., 62; w, 52.
Chapman, Jno., Q, gj, 92.
Chapman, Rob., Q, 250; gj, 148-191; 306; pj, 203, 233, 298.
Chapman, Thos., w, 177.
Charles, Symon, Q, 115; a, 100, 113; gj, 51-69; oh, 49; pj, 48-136.
Cheesley, Walter, i, 18.
Cheshire, Jno., Q, gj, 180-308; pj, 193, 241.
Chester, 93; boundaries, 187.
Chesterfield Creek, 149.
Chesterfield twp., 30, 227; boundaries, 92. *See* Cropwell.
Children, abuse of, 47.
Chinton, Rob., d, 54.
Chissell, Alice, i, 295-307.
Chore, Enoch, Q, 17, 66.
Cider, 210.
Clark, Anne, *v. Dewsbury*, 42.
Clark, Benj., d, 183.
Clark, Jno., 303, 307, 329; c, 212; gj, 40; i, 327; w, 308.
Clark, Thos., A, xlvi; a, 230-341; c, 213, 219; d, 265; i, 304; pj, 257; w, 158, 230; *v. Leonard*, 249; *v. Peares*, 155.
Clark, Wm., Q, xxvii; c, 122, 131; gj, 157, 182; pj, 42-59, 190; w, 2.

INDEX

Clayton, Jno., Q, gj, 308.
Clayton, Math., 69, 213; pj, 98.
Clayton, Wm., Q, 14; *v. Jannings*, 330.
Clement, Edw., sv, w, 8.
Clerk of court, xli, 236.
Cleverly, Sarah, w, 268.
Cleverley, Thos., 252; d, 199; i, 44; r, 248; w, 154, 180, 199, 268.
Cliffe, Sam., Q, w, 9-13; *v. Olive*, 2.
Clinton, Eliz., sv?, i, 71.
Clough, Jno., d, 233; gj, 208; i, 252.
Coates, Rich., d, 10; w, 15, 22.
Coates, Sam., Q, 232; c, 281; gj, 310; i, 271; r, 266.
Cock (Cox), Grinla, i, 322-323.
Cock (Cox), Mouns, 294, 298; c, 247; d, 191, 225, 244, 277, 289; i, 218, 295-298, 322, 334; r, 335.
Cock, Peter, i, 295.
Coddrington, Thos., *v. Cole*, 139.
Cohanzey, 6.
Coleman, Anderson, d, 14.
Coleman, Lassy, 25; d, 16.
Coleman, Thos., 303-308; gj, 240.
Coles, Mary, i, 294, 295.
Coles, Rob., d, 139, 216; i, 130; *v. Baker*, 131; *v. Woodward*, 139.
Coles, Sam., Q, xxvii, xxx, xliii, 1, 28, 99; d, 4, 10, 21; gj, 51; pj, 54; w, 52; *v. Allen*, 21; *v. Cornish*, 102, 112; *v. Cornish and Sherwin*, 100; *v. Evans*, 33; *v. Tradway*, 8.
Coles, Sam., Q?, gj, 253, 297.
Coles, Wm., 314; cp, 40; d, 50, 66, 80, 99; i, 295, 317-325; pj, 69; w, 150; *v. Test*, 222; *v. Vanderlinden*, 83.
Collector, of port, 183.
Collector of taxes, 228, 258, 259, 340. See Taxes.
Collins, Fran., Q, xxvii, 19, 29, 71, 88, 115, 287; d, 320; gj, 180, 186, 246; j, 23-62; pj, 11-20, 195, 198.
Commission to inspect accounts, 112.
Commission of peace, read, 269, 310, 312, 318.
Commissioners, xxviii-xxxi, 1, 2, 5, 7, 44.
Common law, 220.
Concessions, xxviii; election according to, xxx; freeholders and inhabitants to sign, 8.
Conoroe, Isaac, Q, 162; c, 307; d, 171; *v. Jenings*, 222.
Conoroe, Jacob, 162, 165.
Conoroe, Sarah, w, 268.
Constable, 26, 62, 65, 81, 88, 92, 95, 111, 114, 115; attestation of, 6, 66; chosen by town, 212, 261, 321; contempt by, 303, 314; contempt of, 8, 34, 53, 55, 207, 298, 301; continued, 98, 201, 213; fined, 336; fined for non-appearance, 98, 152, 155, 176-181, 212, 301, 314, 321, 325; method of choice, xli; neglect of office, 271; Quakers as, liv; refusal to serve, 180, 303, 337; reports of, 184; stifles king's evidence, 262; substitute, 191, chosen by court, 300, hired,

159; terms of, 98, 116; to attend court in rotation, 168; to collect taxes, 146; volunteer, 261.
"Constablry." See Township.
Continuance of case, 191, 195, 214, 216, 217, 264.
Contract, "out of doors" (oral?), ignored in arbitration, 70.
Cook, Arthur, Q, 17; w, 83; *and Co. v. Bowman*, 53; *and Co. v. Cole*, 50.
Cook, Henry, c, 330; gj, 292, 318, 338, 339.
Cook, Jno., Q, 158; d, 233.
Cook, Thos., 260.
Cooper (occupation), 109, 110, 230, 242, 312.
Cooper, Dan., Q, w, 52.
Cooper, Jos., Q, 326; w, 52.
Cooper, Wm., Q, xii, 1, 8, 30, 240; cp, 51; oh, 30; pj, 1-11.
Cooper, Wm., jr., Q, 46.
Cooper's Creek, 63.
Cooperthwait, Jacob, c. 216.
Cooperthwait, Jno., Q, 187, 342; c, 216-247; gj, 270, 306.
Cooperthwait, Jos., 306.
Cooperthwait, Sarah, Q, w, 306.
Cordery, Wm., w, 266.
Cornbury, Lord, g, xxxvii-xxxviii, 294; ordinance establishing courts, xlvii.
Cornish, Jno., 99, 152; d, 14, 44, 61, 100-151; pj, 72; *v. Hunloke*, 116; *v. Newbold*, 103; *v. Sherwin*, 129, 153.
Coroner, coroner's inquest, 71, 95, 166, 206, 213, 299; substitutes for sheriff, 303-315.
Cottrell, Javes, d, 192.
Council, 18, 19.
Counsel denied, 138.
County, meeting of, 99, 102.
Court, abuse or contempt of, 20, 46, 55, 57, 70, 83, 101, 164, 165, 260, 293, 301, 339; charges, 61, 62, 210, 231, 240, 269; sold for, 127; common pleas, pleas, 93-100, 169-343; disturbing, 70; form of opening, 48; monthly, 49; officers, 112, pay of, 205, 210; president of, 299; private, 122, 141, 156, 291, 299, 336; Provincial, see Appeals; quarterly, quarterly sessions, sessions, 50-342; special, xlvii, 35, 41, 43, 59, 66, 67, 69, 72, 81, 88, 126, 135, 179, 184, 195, 197; special session, 63; record book, 228, 292; rules, 94, 115, 133, 312, 341, 344.
Courthouse, building, repairing, 83, 87, 117, 130, 157, 168, 201, 304, 335. See also Prison.
Courts of West Jersey, organization of, xl ff.; Quaker control of, li; under Cornbury, xlviii; under Duke of York, xxix.
Cowgill, Jno., Q, cp, 108.
Cowgill, Ralph, Q, w, 294; *v. Pumphary*, 310.
Coxe, Dr. Dan., xi, xxxiv, xxxv, 103-116, 134, 172, 179; d, 107-120, 143; g, 74.
Coxe, Col. Dan., A, xxxix; j, 338, 342.
Cozens, Jacob, 10.

INDEX

Crafford, Jno., d, 155; *v. Devell*, 155.
Creek, Jas., 64; gj, 88; w, 82; *v. Peachee*, 94-97.
Creek, Philip, pj, 24, 32.
Crewcorne, xxxi.
Crimes, adultery, l, 235, 253, 261, 332; assault, battery, 26, 49, 69, 249, 294, 338; *vi et armis*, 97; bastardy, 69, 70, 71, 248, 252, 261, 271, 295, 303-311, 319-323 (and *cf.* fornication); breach of the peace, 26-29, 32, 92, 199, 303, 334; buggery, 142-148, 302-309; burglary, 88; cattle, hogs, horses, unlawful killing or marking, stealing, 51-54, 59-60, 118, 185, 292, 298, 303, 308, 334; coin, clipping, 206-209, 254, 267; concealing felon, 304; contempt or abuse of authority, *see* Constable, Court, Government, Justices, Roads, Sheriff; counterfeiting, 272; disorderly house, 192, 267, 325; "felony," 1, 35, 60, 262, 272, 304; forfeiture, 139; forgery, 71, 74, 75; fornication, 123, 127, 177, 226, 261, 271, 332, 341; antenuptial, 123, 129, 177, 183, 234; with Negress, 156 (and *cf.* bastardy); homicide, 56, 95; by misadventure, 139; immorality, cohabiting, 18, 72, 136, 162, 168, 177, 182, 222-226, 254, 266, 295; incest, 72, 117, 123, 261; infanticide, xlv, 69, 166; land, entering on another's, and cutting corn, 20, 141; murder, xlv, 56, 113; perjury, 58, 65, 193, 213, 298; rape, 55, 75, 314; riot, 20, 141, 253; Sabbath breaking, 206-211, 212, 218; search, unlawful, 217; ship, defrauding owners of, 35-41; seizure of, 97; silver, melting and selling, 83-87; stealing, 1, 11, 35, 51, 63-65, 71, 83, 126, 183, 204, 218, 224, 225, 252, 272, 338; receiving stolen goods, 224; stocks, breaking, 4; whale, stealing, 46, 83-84, 87. *See also*, Drunkenness, Games, Liquor, Negroes, Profanity, Roads, Servants, Slander, Timber, Wife. *See also*, xlviii-xlix.
Cripps, Jno., Q, xi, xxvii, 1, 8, 30, 61, 71, 73, 132, 144-147, 190; d, 8; j, 12-18; oh, 19; pj, 1-8; tl, 3, 19; w, 53, 54; *v. Allen*, 13; *v. Coates*, 10; *v. Leeds*, 9; *v. Potts*, 20; *v. Smith*, 10; *v. Wright*, 9.
Cripps, Nath., Q, 121-147, 233-243, 300; cp, 229; gj, 166, 181, 270-313; i, 82, 112, 141; pj, 137-199; w, 190, 250; *v. Clarke*, 183; *v. Pickering*, 132, 143; *v. Pickering etc.*, 154; *v. Stacy et al.*, 147.
Cripps, Theophila, Q?, 190, 227.
Croft, Jas., sr., Q?, A 1704, 144, 189, 213, 259; c, 150; d, 165; gj, 142-253; i, 228; oh, 176; pj, 130, 212, 236.
Croft, Jas., jr., Q, 224, 340.
Croft, Thos., c, 337; d, 214, 333; gj, 325; w, 165; *v. Brown*, 211.
Cropp, Jno., d, 244.
Cropwell, *alias* Chesterfield, 150.
Crosby, Jno., Q, 128, 232; gj, 56, 180, 253; i, 91; oh, 93; pj, 49-136.

Crosse, Jos., Q??, xli, 258; d, 181; gj, 253; pj, 198; s, 226, 231.
Crosse, Thos., 220.
Crosswicks, 164; Creek, 30, 92, 282.
Crues, Wm., 72; d, 116, 125; pj, 70; *v. Senior*, 81; *v. Throp*, 80; *v. West*, 99.
Cryer, court, 175.
Curso, Jno., d, 205.
Curtis, Abigail, 221.
Curtis, Anne, 221.
Curtis, David, Q, 253; pj, 250.
Curtis, Geo., *v. Wells and Wells*, 249, 259.
Curtis, Jno., Q, 31, 121, 144; c, 131; gj, 52, 117; j, 167-184; oh, 150; pj, 98, 153; w, 84, 178; *v. Heathcote*, 84.
Curtis, Jon., i, 252, 314; pj, 209; w, 221; *v. Butcher*, 216.
Curtis, Sarah, w, 12.
Curtis, Thos., Q, 208, 253, 259; gj, 184-231, 330; pj, 21, 60, 270; w, 230.
Curvon, Paule, 26.
Cutcher, Jno., 150.

Daile, Peter, Q, 81; pj, 81.
Dalboe, Peter, 26.
Dalboe, Woolley, 26.
Dane, Jno., gj, 337.
Dane, Wm., pj, 311.
Danford, Sam., Q, w, 268.
Darwin River, 91.
Davenport, Fran., Q, xxxvi, xxxviii, 29-32, 61, 165, 175, 192; cp. 54; gj, 115; j, 32-61, 136-203, 226-291; pj, 69; w, 167.
Davis, And., i, 177.
Davis, Byall, c, 292; gj, 292.
Davis, Eldad, i, 311.
Davis, Elnathan, c, 261.
Davis, Evan, i, 46; r, 54.
Davis, Jon., 205, 335, 336, 340; c, 247; d, 269; gj, 208, 292, 306.
Davis, Jon., jr., gj, 301; oh, 313.
Davis, Mary, i, 177.
Davis, Rich., d, 62, 131; w, 43.
Davis, Sam., 338.
Davison, Jno., d, 48.
Dawson, Anth., 216; w, 218.
Dawson, Jno., gj, 339.
Day, Jno., Q, 31; 115; gj, 32-176, 234-253, 306-330; oh, 49, 331; pj, 19-157.
Day, Stephen, 187; c, 191; pj, 117, 188; *v. Williams*, 170.
Deacon, Geo., Q, xxxviii, lii, 221; d, 231; gj, 182; j, 54, 206-226.
Dean, Dan., w, 322.
Dean, Wm., 232; d, 189, 189; i, 252; pj, 294; *v. Cluft*, 233; *v. Rush*, 153.
Debt, imprisonment for, xlix, 184; working out, 125. *See also*, Actions.

INDEX

Decow, Eliz., w, 127.
Decow, Isaac, Q, 232; c, 213, 219; d, 143; gj, 334; oh, 185, 331; pj, 199, 265, 324; w, 207; *v. Hargrave*, 184; *v. Leonard*, 243.
Decow, Jacob, Q?, 248, 253, 314; gj, 334; oh, 313; pj, 223, 229; *v. Andrews*, 221.
Decow, Jos., Q?, gj, 292.
Decow, Susanna, Q, w, 127.
Deeds, recording of, 7; book to be rebound, 234.
Defamation. *See* Slander.
Delaware, Appoquinimink Creek, 36; New Castle, xiii, xxi-xxiv, xxix, 106; Sussex, 43; Wilmington, xiii.
Delayre, Anth., d, 100.
Dell, Eliz., p, 216.
Dell, Rich., A, d, 189, 192; *et ux. v. Basnet*, 216; *v. Wells*, 212.
Dennis, Jno., cp, 84; w, 87.
Departing province, notice of, 207.
Derickson, Woolley, 25-27.
Devell, Benj., d, 155.
Devonish, Bernard, Q, xxvii, 1, 61, 63, 91; d, 131; gj, 43-54; pj, 3-62; w, 45, 50, 101; *v. Ingram*, 74.
Devonish, Jos., Q, gj, 316, 321.
Dewilde, Jno., d, 113.
Dewsbury, Joan, d, 237, 245.
Dewsbury, Jno., Q, 1, 237; d, 10, 42, 211, 236; pj, 23-32.
Dickinson, Wm., 272.
Dicks, Hector, *v. Righton*, 131, 148.
Dimsdale, Jno., 78.
Dimsdale, Rob., Q, 39, 300; j, 25-45; pj, 23.
Distress, 2, 176, 331; for rent, 222.
Dixi, Capt., 109.
Dixson, Jno., 232; c, 319.
Doctors, names of, *see* D. Coxe, Lanchard, T. Peachee, J. Robards, D. Wills; sued for incompetency, 230.
Dominicy, Bonaventer, sv?, 162; *v. Newbold*, 131.
Doson, Jno., c, 300-309; d, 333; i, 312-320.
Doughty, Edw., d, 96.
Douglas, Geo., sv, 197.
Douglas, Nath., 144; c, 150; d, 170; gj, 141-195; pj, 115-176; w, 89, 230.
Douglas, Thos., 121, 144, 208, 212, 259, 340; c, 185; d, 186, 214; gj, 101-330; oh, 271; pj, 142-212; w, 84, 102, 121, 172, 173, 177.
Dove, Rob., d, 59.
Drewitt, Morgan, *v. Linzey*, 16.
Driver, Mary, i, 72.
Drowned, 23, 206.
Drunkenness, drinking, 26, 165, 263, 325; fined for, 29, 92.
Dubrois, Jno., 112, 113; d, 103; w, 109, 114; *v. Cox*, 120; *v. Dewilde*, 113; *v. Perdriau et al.*, 104; *v. Tatham*, 120.

Duff, Jas., r, 334.
Duke of York, government of, in West Jersey, xiii, xxi ff., xxviii ff.; grant of New Jersey by, xv, xxxi.
Dummer, Martha (Wearing), d, 224; i, 224, 226; tl, 213, 220; w, 231; *v. Fisher*, 335; *v. Nightingall*, 335; *v. Reading*, 224; *v. Skeen*, 325.
Dummer, Rob., d, 224; i, 224; tl, 229.
Dunbar, Euphane, cp, 266; i, 271.
Duncks, Wm., d, 15; *v. Lee and Matlock*, 10.
Dungan, Clement, 201.
Dungworth, Rich., Q, 1.
Durham, Rob., 119; d, 16, 96; w, 9, 15, 93; *v. Wood*, 16.
Dutch, in Delaware River valley, xiii.
Dutchmen, 68.

Eare, Rich. *See* Ayers.
Earmarks, 2, 3n., 80, 119, 196.
Earle, Wm., Q, gj, 310, 316.
East Jersey, 67, 136, 174, 191, 192; Elizabethtown, 18; Freehold, 241; Monmouth, 236; Shrewsbury, 80, 260.
Eberad, Capt. Isaiah, 106; w, 107.
Edridge, Jno., xviii ff., xxxii.
Edwards, Rob., d, 335; gj, 269; i, 292; oh, 331; r, 253, 298, 313, 315.
Edwards, Wm., w, 43.
Eglinton, Edw., *v. Matson*, 54-58.
Eight Mile Run, 205.
Eldridge, Ezekiel, 87.
Eldridge, Jon., Q, 1, 19, 182, 187, 342; c, 159; d, 14; gj, 308-338; oh, 313; pj, 98, 196-236; w, 13, 306.
Elkinton, Geo., Q, 93, 232, 287; gj, 92-313; pj, 42-311; sv, x.
Elkinton, Mary, Q, w, 95.
Ellis, Thos., Q, 1; pj, 3.
Ellis, Wm., 144, 178; c, 122; d, 61; gj, 98; pj, 61.
Ellison, Rich., c, 247; gj, 339; i, 252; pj, 185-206; w, 308.
Elton, Anth., xxvii, lii, 62, 115, 127, 247, 259; gj, 69-265; j, 206-226; oh, 111; pj, 123-166; w, 158, 190; *et ux. v. Hancock*, 120.
Elton, Eliz., p, 120; *v. Fisher and Markett*, 329.
Elton, Susannah, *v. Hollinshead*, 194.
Elton, Thos., w, 180.
Elton, widow, 182, 187.
Ely, Jno., Q?, 285; gj, 339; oh, 337.
Ely, Josh., Q, lii, 247; c, 49, 62; cp, 212; d, 234, 284; gj, 95, 186; i, 224; j, 206-234; oh, 150; pj, 166, 193; w, 191.
Emley, Mary, i, 123.
Emley, Thos., Q, 312; d, 276.
Emley, Wm., Q, xxxviii, xli, lii, 1-3, 30, 32, 78, 91, 170, 247, 259, 282, 340; c, 307, 310; cr, 213; gj, 181, 188, 270; i, 115, 123; j, 19-130, 206-218; pj, 198; s, 5; w, 21, 250.

INDEX

England, committee in, 156; going to 169, 199, 250; letter from, 257; vessel's clearance from, 183.
England, Dan., Q, xxxvi, 54, 121, 211; a, 237; d, 19, 35, 200, 206, 214-226; gj, 63-92, 164; i, 82-112, 130; pj, 73, 184; *v. Dewsbury,* 211, 236; *v. Pyne,* 90; *v. Salter,* 24.
Engle, Jno., Q?, gj, 317; w, 306.
Engle, Rob., 182, 187; c, 122-155; gj, 70-184; pj, 70.
English, Jos., Q??, 208; c, 191, 201; gj, 281; pj, 180, 186; w, 266.
Equity, appeal to, asked, 181.
Erickson. *See* Ponyon.
Escape, out of court, 58-60; from sheriff, 151, 243.
Esopus (Soapas), 296.
Esquire (title), 74, 89, 98, 148, etc.
Evans, Thos., Q, c, 111; gj, 98, 123, 297.
Evans, Wm., Q, 70, 187, 259, 342; d, 33; gj, 157, 240-316; oh, 185; pj, 16-82, 153-198; w, 306.
Evarett, Edw., 10, 14, 29; *v. Stubbs,* 10.
Eversham, 93; boundaries, 187; vale of, 122.
Eves, Thos., sr., Q, xxvii, 1, 149, 247, 259; c, 159, 319; gj, 234-308; pj, 3, 149-203, 265-317; s, 9; w, 193, 268.
Eves, Thos., jr., Q, gj, 337; pj, 281.
Evidences. *See* Witnesses.
Execution, 20, 41, 44, 45, 50, 59, 94, 148, 153, 181, 202, 244, 245, 289, 290, 296; against estate, 236; goods, 124; money in executors' hands, 59; realty, 50; appraisal, 135, 148, 246; denied to plaintiff, 233, 243; form of, 239, 241; method of, 128; renewal, 124; returns of, 97, 123, 128, 140, 151, 181, 212, 243, 246, 260; sale and satisfaction by sale, 135, 148, 153, 181, 218.
Ewer, Mary, Q, *v. Test,* 202.

Fairman, Thos., Q, 145; p, 237.
Falconbridge. *See* Jacobson.
Falls [Trenton], 17, 30, 35, 70, 76, 77, 116, 136, 282.
False imprisonment. *See* Actions.
Farnsworth, Jno., Q, gj, 321.
Farnsworth, Thos., Q, xxvii, 19, 31, 92; c, 114; gj, 51; pj, 112, 118.
Farr, Elias, Q, xi, xxvii, 31, 81, 98, 110; a, 165; j, 15-90.
Farr, Sarah, d, 216.
Farr, widow, 152.
Farrington, Jos., Q, 102; *v. Delayre,* 100.
Farrow. *See* Pharoe.
Fearman, Jon., d, 223.
Fees, xlii; court, 9, 112; amounts paid, 165, 315; cryer's, 152; half, for jury, 74; remitted, 184, 325; to constable, 317.
Fenimore, Rich., Q, lii, 19, 149, 215, 254, 340; c, 176, 180; d, 161, 178; gj, 145-316; oh, 150; pj, 8-270; *v. French,* 151-155.
Fenimore, Wm., c, 292, 300; gj, 318; i, 228; w, 298.
Fenton, Eleazer, 31, 36, 49, 115, 173, 315; d, 83-93; gj, 48-152; i, 129; oh, 74, 122; pj, 8-229; w, 37, 120; *v. Budd,* 103.
Fenton, Eliz., A, i, 129.
Fenton, Thos., Q, 248.
Fenwick, Major Jno., Q, x, xv ff.
Fenwick's Colony, xiv ff., xxxi.
Ferry, 62, 96, 266, 268, 307.
Field, Ambrose, Q, gj, 306.
Field, Benj., Q, 247, 259, 318; gj, 171-261.
Fire hazard in Burlington, 91.
Fisher, Edw., d, 335; i, 298-303; w, 304.
Fisher, Jno., d, 329.
Fisher, Wm., A, 210-231, 296; cp, 263, 267; d, 130; gj, 198-219; i, 252; s, xxxviii, xli, liii, 298-303; w, 304; *v. Farr,* 216; *v. Henry,* 272, 290; *v. Richardson and Gardiner,* 299.
Fisk, Casper, 29; d, 20; pj, 32; w, 33.
Five Mile Run, 205.
Fleckna, Jno., 81, 121; d, 94, 116; i, 82, 112, p, 43; pj, 88; r, 42; w, 71, 103, 124, 125; *v. Smith,* 94; *and Johnson v. Rush,* 165.
Fleetwood, Wm., Q, gj, 45; i, 71.
Folkes, Thos., sr., Q, xxvii-xxix, 31, 61, 189, 196, 237; c, 88, 95; gj, 95; pj, 60; w, 311.
Folkes, Thos., jr., Q, 247; c, 176, 184; gj, 117-265; i, 303-311; oh, 150; pj, 136, 229.
Folwell, Nath., Q?, gj, 338, 339.
Foodstuffs, 114, 127, 150.
Forcible entry. *See* Actions.
Ford, Rich., i, 88.
Forfeiture of goods, 139.
Forsyth, Mat., Q, gj, 192, 226; pj, 181, 241.
Fortune-telling, 76.
Foster, Wm., Q, 237; c, 261; gj, 145-219, 308-334; oh, 313; pj, 95, 96, 183, 206.
Foulk, *alias* Owen, Jno., d, 221.
Fowler, Thos., i, 42.
Fox, Geo., Q, xv, xxxiii.
Fox, Jon., 165; gj, 63, 69; pj, 81; w, 77.
Frampton, Eliz., Q, 225.
Frampton, Sarah, Q, 225.
Frampton, Thos., Q, 225.
Frampton, Wm., Q, 26, 29, 131, 225; w, 59.
France, Fred., w, 36.
Francis, Rich., d, 155; i, 212; w, 173; *v. Pumphray,* 315.
Fredrickson, Fred., 1, 28; pj, 12; w, 33.
Freeholders and inhabitants, list of, 1; and proprietors, meeting of, 30.
French, Chas., Q, c, 247; d, 221, 330; gj, 297, 321; pj, 270; w, 161.
French, Jno., i, 271; w, 196.
French, Rich., Q, 215, 253, 259; c, 292-306; d,

356 INDEX

French, Rich. (*Continued*)
216; gj, 191-313; i, 209; oh, 228; pj, 181; w, 209.
French, Thos., Q, 63, 71, 150, 187, 259, 324; c, 122, 150, 292; d, 70, 96, 124, 151, 191; gj, 32-321; i, 57; oh, 111; pj, 12-131; w, 33; *v. Basnett*, 49; *v. Biddle*, 46; *v. Finimore*, 161; *v. Leeds*, 15; *v. Leeds et al.*, 178.
French, Thos., jr., Q?, gj, 195; pj, 203; w, 161, 197.
French people, 104, 114.
Fretwell, Nath., gj, 310.
Fretwell, Peter, Q, xxxvi, 32, 188-242, 305; c, 150; cp, 158; gj, 129; j, 167-251; oh, 111, 160; pj, 96-164; w, 93, 230; *v. Stephens*, 83.
Fretwell, Sam., Q, 339; c, 337; i, 271; pj, 293.
Fryer, Anth., Q, 238; c, 337; d, 196; pj, 270, 294; w, 194.
Fryley, Mary, i, 163, 223-267; w, 254.
Fryley, Wm., 111, 148, 235, 253; d, 103, 104, 131, 157; gj, 128-154; pj, 137, 142; sv, 82; w, 111; *v. Heesom*, 103; *v. Hunloke*, 111; *v. Pears*, 155; *et ux. v. Port*, 153; *v. Rowell*, 100-103.
Fryor, Anth., Q?, w, 70.
Fuller, Wm., i, 271.
Fullwood, Jno., 32.
Furley, Dan., d, 12; sv, 11.
Furnis, Ben., Q, w, 334.
Furnis, Jno., c, 81, 95; w, 33.
Furnis, Sam., Q, xli, 128, 246, 264, 314-340; c, 111; d, 211; gj, 69-186; i, 193; j, 240-291; oh, 131, 154; pj, 64-184, 324; w, 140, 147, 188, 231, 257; *v. Fryley*, 157; *v. Powell et ux.*, 258.

Gabitas, Wm., Q, 327, 335; cp, 340; d, 258; gj, 270-334; *v. Scattergood*, 276.
Gallais, Samson, 104, 108.
Games, unlawful, 228; gaming house, 325.
Gannington, Rob., Q, sv, 240.
Gano, Rob., *v. Tradway*, 54.
Gardiner, Dan., 250; w, 294.
Gardiner, Jno., Q, 160; gj, 123-136; pj, 142-159; w, 162; *v. Righton*, 124.
Gardiner, Thos., Q, 11, 23, 50, 151; c, 1; cp, 42, 43; gj, 74-129; j, 19-69, 145-171; pj, 8, 72-115; w, 35; *v. Cornish*, 14; *v. Pumphary*, 80.
Gardiner, Thos., jr., Q, 195, 242, 251, 327; a, 202; d, 214, 218, 299, 305; gj, 43; j, 251-291; ka, 226-269; pj, 59; w, 230, 257, 261, 290.
Garner, Eliz., w, 15.
Garrett, Chas., r, 281.
Garrett, Jno., Q?, gj, 297; pj, 293.
Garrett, Thos., Q, gj, 297; pj, 229.
Garwood, Jane.
Garwood, Jno., Q, 219; d, 279; gj, 258.
Garwood, Thos., Q, gj, 320, 330; pj, 250; w, 165.
Gaskill (Gaskins), Edw., Q, gj, 252, 297, 316.

Gaskins (Gaskill), Josias, Q, gj, 313.
Gaunt, Ananias, Q, 208; gj, 82-316; oh, 131, 150; pj, 67, 93.
Gentleman (title), xi, 98, 145, 178, 221, 327, etc.
Gibbs, Isaac, Q, gj, 261-316; pj, 233, 235.
Gibbs, Jno., Q??, d, 139.
Gibbs, Rich., Q, 253.
Gibson, Lydia, d, 35.
Gibson, Sam., Q, 229, 260, 287; c, 228, 247; d, 35, 330; gj, 253-306.
Gilbert, Jane, 314; w, 313.
Gilbert, Jno., Q??, d, 116, 260.
Gilbert, Sam., 314.
Gilbert, Sarah, 272; w, 271.
Gilberthorp, Thos., Q, 189; c, 122; gj, 92-234; oh, 150, 313; pj, 23-281.
Gill, Wm., 126; d, 121, 156; tl, 96.
Gillett, Jno., 108; p, 113; w, 105-109.
Gladwin, Thos., Q, 57, 72, 264; c, 49, 65; gj, 72-164; pj, 18-142; w, 56; *v. Rawle*, 170.
Glassum, Henry, w, 132.
Gleave, Geo., sr., 187, 245, 265; d, 214, 267; oh, 176, 185; w, 194, 196.
Gleave, Geo., jr., A, 252; i, 271, 304; r, 266; w, 196.
Gleave, Henry, a, 253.
Gleave, Isabella, d, 267.
Glenn, Alex., 23.
Gloucester Co., xxvii, 200; court, xii, l.
Godfrey, Benj., p, 111; w, 105-109.
Godling, Sam., 339.
Goforth, Geo., 31; d, 100-104, 113; pj, 70.
Goldsmith, Geo., 46.
Goldy, Eliz., d, 312.
Goldy, Sam., d, 312; gj, 330, 336; op, 331.
Goods, lists of, 35, 38, 64, 126.
Gosling, Jno., Q, 30, 37, 39, 194; gj, 32; j, 19-41; pj, 33; w, 43.
Gosling, Jno., jr., Q, 194; gj, 297, 337; pj, 317.
Gosling, Mary, Q, 64.
Government, contempt of, 57, 102; in Fenwick's Colony, xx, xxiv; in West Jersey, xxx ff.; not acknowledging, 219, 220, 241.
Governor, charge to grand jury, 247; defamation of, 220, 241; orders cessation of process, 319; process referred to, 186; removes justice, 251; scire facias from, 236; submits to, 183.
Grange, Mat., Q, gj, 191.
Grant, Mary, cp, 223; d, 231.
Grasberry, Moses, w, 200.
Graves, Thos., Q?, *v. Hoult*, 21.
Gravesend, 109.
Gray, Jno., d, 48.
Green, Edw., 59.
Green, Geo., c, 336; r, 248.
Green, Hannah, 248.
Green, Henry, 222-225; w, 265; *v. Richards*, 222.
Green, Jno., d, 101-162; w, 88.

INDEX

Green, Katharine, w, 56.
Green, Peter, d, 165.
Green, Sam., 340.
Green, Thos., d, 192, 193, 202; gj, 208; w, 56.
Green, Wm., 340; gj, 292; oh, 337; op, 331.
Griffis, Fran., i, 18.
Griffin, Jno. See Griffith.
Griffith, Alex., A, xxxviii; a, 293-344; j, 305; ka, 292-341; *v. Boys*, 318; *v. Bullock*, 299; *v. Harriot*, 318; *v. Kible*, 310; *v. Paul*, 333; *v. Willis*, 333; *v. Wood*, 333.
Griffith, Alice, d, 75.
Griffith, Jno., cp, 26-29.
Groome, Peter, d, 188, 191; i, 136, 162, 177; *v. Wright*, 188.
Groome, Sam., 18.
Grubb, Henry, Q, xli, 44, 61, 63, 246, 256, 260; cp, 14-23; d, 181; gj, 63-176; ka, 180; oh, 150; p, 14; pj, 11-185; r, 249; s, 269-291; t, 159-241, 295; tl, 92, 126, 154, 190, 220; w, 22, 86, 126; *v. Abbot*, 74, 81; *v. England*, 35; *v. Fisher*, 130; *v. Lillies*, 80; *v. Milner*, 83; *v. Pearce*, 45; *v. Phillips*, 184; *v. Stanbanck*, 80.
Grubb, Mary, Q, 64; w, 56.
Guardian, accounting, 242; chosen, 158, 159, 162, 168, 175, 190, 194, 201, 227; discharged, 254.
Guest, Geo., Q, *v. Willis*, 16.
Guest, Wm., *v. Blake*, 99; *v. Hoult*, 20; *v. Satterthwait*, 100.
Guy, Bridgett, Q, 78; *v. Williams*, 202.
Guy, Rich., Q, xxii, xxiii, xxviii, 5, 30, 78, 104; gj, 101; j, 48-89; w, 67.

Hackney, Wm., Q, d, 305; gj, 269, 292, 330; i, 309; oh, 313, 334; pj, 259, 298; r, 304.
Haddgard, Jas., sv, 200.
Haines, Jno., Q, 182, 187, 340; c, 114, 150; gj, 82, 98, 180, 234, 316, 338; pj, 43, 112-203; w, 45.
Haines, Rich., Q, 187, 343; c, 202; gj, 159, 297; pj, 193, 265; w, 69.
Haines, Thos., Q, 300; gj, 201, 270, 293; pj, 149.
Haines, Wm., Q, gj, 313.
Hall, Dan., Q, d, 330.
Hall, Peter, d, 333.
Hambley. See Tomkins.
Hamilton, And., 241; cp, 200; g, xxxiv ff., 166-190, 240-291; judicial reform under, xliv-xlvi; p, 200, 205.
Hammell, Jno., A, 238, 287, 314; d, 195; gj, 188-306; p, 197, 206, 303; w, 316.
Hance, Capt. See Monse.
[Hance?], Fred., 28.
Hance, Jno., 10, 28; r, 8; w, 33.
Hancock, Godfrey, sr., Q??, xxvii, 1, 31, 36, 61, 63, 68, 94, 118; d, 23, 48, 81, 83; gj, 32-82; oh, 30; p, 84; pj, 2-73; w, 9.

Hancock, Godfrey, jr., Q??, 49, 95; d, 60, 63, 81.
Hancock, Jno., Q, 224, 240; gj, 325; oh, 228; pj, 176-206; w, 172.
Hancock, Mary, Q??, 149, 152, 164, 209; d, 96, 120; i, 228; tl, 240; w, 119; *v. Pumphrey*, 113, 310.
Hancock, Rich., xxiv.
Hancock, Sary, Q?, w, 322.
Hancock, Tim., Q, 30; gj, 157-308; pj, 317; w, 33.
Hancock, Wm., xxv.
Hands, Shamgar, w, 138.
Harden, Magdalen, cp, 313.
Hardin, Benj., gj, 292, 339; i, 306.
Hardin, Rebecca, i, 306.
Harding, Mark, 234.
Harding, Martin, *v. Ely and Price*, 234.
Harding, Thos., Q, xxvii, 61, 80, 149, 247; gj, 43-252; oh, 131, 228; pj, 1-201; w, 193.
Hargrave, Isaac, 134; d, 103, 126, 184; w, 120; *v. Pumphary*, 84.
Hargrave, Jno., d, 103.
Harriott, Jno., Q, pj, 72, 98.
Harriott, Sam., Q, d, 96, 318; gj, 115-182; j, 181-184; oh, 111; pj, 72-161; w, 140, 162.
Harrison, Jas., Q, xi, xxvii; *v. Allen*, 51.
Harrison, Jno., 331, 342; r, 319, 329.
Harrison, Peter, Q?, 31.
Harrison, Rich., Q, gj, 148; pj, 212, 223; w, 53.
Hart, Jno., Q??, gj, 301-325; oh, 313; p, 237.
Hartley, Anne, 121; cp, 117; sv, 302.
Hartley, Eliz., 118, 122.
Hartshorne, Rich., 151.
Harvey, Peter, Q??, gj, 82-171; pj, 61-148.
Harwood, Sam., 190.
Hascor, Wm., Q, gj, 157, 292; oh, 313; pj, 93, 145, 188, 317.
Hat on, in court, 164; while taking attestation, 293, 299.
Hatchley, Martha, d, 153.
Hatchley, Thos., d, 153.
Hawkins, Jno., d, 189.
Hawkins, Roger, Q, 1.
Hay, 154, 161.
Heath, And., 258; d, 318; gj, 223, 310-340; i, 261, 303-308, 323; oh, 228; pj, 233; r, 264; tl, 311; *v. Smith*, 333.
Heath, Joan, sv?, i, 69.
Heath, Jno., *v. Crosse*, 181.
Heathcote, Geo., d, 155.
Heathcote, Jno., d, 84.
Hedge, Sam., xxii.
Heesom, Jno., d, 100-124, 157, 170, 175; *v. Blake*, 113.
Helme, Israel, 26, 34; gj, 54; r, 9.
Helmsley, Jos., xi, xxvii, xxviii, 13; d, 44.
Henton, Mary, 341.
Henry, Jno., 296; d, 263-290; *and Wright v. Chamnis*, 60.

Heritage, Jos., Q, c, 319; gj, 252, 301; oh, 228; w, 306.
Heritage, Rich., Q, pj, 51, 52.
Herman, Casparus, xxx, 37, 40.
Heron, Jos., d, 221.
Heston, Zeb., Q, c, 307-317.
Hewlings, Abr., Q to 1698, A 1702, 149, 197, 254, 259, 340; c, 122, 201-215; d, 178; gj, 281-318; oh, 160; pj, 60, 180-298; w, 178, 197, 210; *v. French*, 191.
Hewlings, Ann, i, 307.
Hewlings, Jacob, 306, 340; gj, 325, 343.
Hewlings, Wm., Q, A 1702, xi, xxvii, xxxix, lii, 247, 259, 340; gj, 69, 157-190; j, 212-218, 292-327; oh, 122-160; pj, 2, 11, 98, 128, 196, 198; w, 161, 178.
Hewling's Point, 164, 177.
Hickman, Jno., d, 153.
Hickman, Rob., A, 229; d, 293.
Hickman, Thos., *v. Hickman*, 293.
Hickson, Wm., 31, 258; c, 176, 184; gj, 159-206, 310; pj, 74, 136, 142.
Higgins, Eliakim, 93; d, 157; pj, 82, 95, 96, 102; w, 74.
Higgins, Wm., w, 22.
Highways. *See* Roads.
Hilbourne, Thos., 151.
Hill, Eliz., Q, w, 254.
Hill, Jas., Q, xli, 19, 44, 126, 154, 211; a, 110; c, 35; d, 91, 97, 147, 151, 162; pj, 18-72; s, 60, 145-171; w, 56-156; *v. Crues*, 125; *v. Matson*, 60; *v. Richards*, 171; *v. Tuely*, 90.
Hill, Seth, Q. 152, 260; c, 185; d, 116; gj, 117-246; i, 254-267, 295; pj, 311; w, 90, 181, 199; *v. Neve*, 259.
Hill, Wm., d, 113.
Hillards, Wm., 1.
Hilliard, Jno., Q??, 232; c, 81-98; gj, 74, 166; pj, 73-241; w, 231.
Hixon, Benj., i, 323; w, 321.
Hod[   ], Thos., 1.
Hodg[   ], Wm., 1.
Hodgkins, Rob., 1.
Hodgkins, Stephen, 294.
Hoeman, Andreas, 26, 27.
Hoemanson, Mattis, 26.
Hogdon, Jobe, 340; oh, 337.
Hogs, killing, 8, 52, 185, 194, 196; stealing, 51-54; unlawful marking, 292-296, 334-337; unringed, in Burlington, 87, 91.
Holbrook, Jno., d, 343, 344.
Holgate, Rob., cp, 32.
Hollinshead, Jno., Q, xxxvi, 1-242; a, 90; c, 206; d, 124, 214-250; gj, 32-129; j, 181-203; p, 103, 116, 216; pj, 8-168; tl, 3; w, 97, 209; *v. Abbott*, 48; *v. Allen*, 63; *v. Bartlemews*, 8; *v. Fryley et al.*, 131; *v. Gill*, 121; *v. Hill*, 97; *v. Jacobs*, 44; *v. Pumphary and Hunloke*, 80, 83; *v. Rush*, 153; *v. Stubbs*, 10; *v. Thrumball*, 35; *v. Warren*, 16; *v. Williams*, 81; *v. Wright*, 14.
Hollinshead, Jno., jr., Q, 233-271; c, 337, 338; d, 194; gj, 253-313; pj, 191; w, 190, 194, 249, 334; *v. Gleave et ux.*, 267.
Hollinshead, Wm., Q, 187, 233, 242; c, 185; gj, 292, 313; pj, 259-311; w, 196, 249.
Hollwell, ——, 174.
Holt, Benj., gj, 63-89; oh, 88; pj, 54-96; w, 82.
Holt, Martin, 82; d, 16-23; gj, 54, 56; pj, 43, 59; *v. Burgesse*, 16.
Holton [Hooton?], Thos., pj, 297.
Hoofe, Powell, c, 292, 306; gj, 336.
Hooper, Abr., *v. Rush*, 162.
Hooton, Jno., Q, xi, xxvii, 1, 30, 31, 61, 145, 151; gj, 51, 69; pj, 16, 60, 74.
Hooton, Thos., Q, xi, xxvii, 323; c, 261; d, 196; gj, 123, 251; i, 326; pj, 14, 201, 257, 317; w, 194, 306, 321.
Hopewell twp., 227.
Hopman, Hance, 25, 26; c, 25.
Hopper, Rob., 104; d, 90.
Horner, Fran., Q?, w, 250.
Horner, Isaac, Q, 115, 144, 237; c, 150; d, 269; gj, 310-334; pj, 61-235; w, 145, 147; *v. Scholey*, 80.
Horner, Jno., Q, 31; cp, 199; gj, 136; oh, 159; pj, 51; *v. Bainbridge*, 197.
Horner, Josh., Q, gj, 214.
Horner, Mary, Q??, i, 303.
Horses, 2, 33, 120, 132, 171; marking, 118, 303, 308; shooting, 298.
Horsman, Marmaduke, Q?, 31; c, 191-247; d, 89-94; gj, 166; pj, 171-212; w, 10.
Horsman, Mary, w, 52, 54.
Horton, Thos., 187.
Hosier, Rob., c, 337.
Hough, Thos., Q?, 247.
Houghton, Sam., Q, 81; gj, 72, 88; pj, 69-157; w, 78, 133.
House, frame of, pulled down, 62; searching without warrant, 217.
Howell, Dan., 56, 97, 340; d, 83; i, 51; *v. Ashton*, 54.
Howell, Mordecai, 56, 200; i, 51; w, 141; *v. Howell*, 83; *v. Smith*, 131.
Howell, Philip, d, 336.
Howell, Thos., xxvii, 28, 52, 97; d, 45; oh, 30.
Howton, Lawrence, r, 334.
Howton, Thos., Q?, i, 326-330; w, 322.
Huddy, Chas., xli, 318, 336, 337.
Huddy, Hugh, A, xxxix, xli, 252, 269, 270, 291; j, 338, 342; s, 318; w, 317; *v. Fuller*, 333; *v. Heath*, 318; *and Hunloke v. Midgeley*, 280, 288; *and Hunloke v. Moone*, 283; *v. Pumphary*, 315.
Hudson, Abimilech, 126; d, 103-121, 185, 258; p, 116; *v. Boyes*, 113.

INDEX

359

Hudson, Jno., Q, 238, 247, 259; c, 191, 292; gj, 203, 261, 308; oh, 313; pj, 281.
Hudson, Priscilla, 126, 143.
Hudson, Rob., Q, 96, 149; gj, 44, 117-188; p, 159; tl, 190.
Hue and cry, 136, 328.
Huff, Joan, *v. Heesom*, 100; *v. Milner*, 83; *v. Smith*, 80.
Huffe, Mich., *v. Parker*, 60; *v. Pearson*, 44.
Hugg, Jno., Q, 28, 52; *v. Silver*, 181.
Hugg, Jno., jr., Q, *v. Silver*, 178.
Huggins, Alice, 64.
Hughes, Humphrey, i, 223, 224.
Humfreys, Alex., s, 47.
Humphries, Josh., Q, 66, 69, 115, 154, 203, 247, 343; c, 111; d, 153; gj, 56-336; i, 95; oh, 313; pj, 89-183, 281; w, 342.
Humphries, Walter, Q, xi, 66; gj, 184, 201; pj, 176.
Hunloke, Edw., xi, xxxv, xli, xlvi, li, 83-130, 222, 280, 283, 296; a, 67, 104, 134; clerk, 231-265; collector, 183, 200; cp, 98, 200; d, 80, 83, 103, 111, 116, 126, 197; g, 145-156; gj, 63; i, 69, 101; j, 69-186, 251; p, 200, 205; w, 86, 188, 231; wife of, 78; *v. Allen*, 94; *v. Bibb*, 265; *v. Blake*, 100; *v. Bowden*, 83; *v. Bowman*, 150; *v. Clark*, 265; *v. Fleckna*, 94; *v. Fryley*, 103, 148, 151; *v. Glave*, 214; *v. Goforth*, 100; *v. Hamell*, 195; *v. Hancock*, 96; *v. Hargrave*, 103-128; *v. Heesom*, 111; *v. Hill*, 91-99, 147, 151; *v. Huntley*, 110; *v. Joosten*, 189; *v. Langford*, 238, 245; *v. Ogborn*, 269; *v. Pidcock*, 180; *v. Pumphary*, 80, 81; *v. Salfert*, 81; *v. Senior*, 147; *v. Smith*, 94; *v. Solly*, 185; *v. Styles*, 143; *v. Tatham*, 206; *v. Terrett*, 96; *v. Wheeler*, 197.
Hunloke, Margaret, A, xxxv; p, 280, 283.
Hunt, Jon., op, 331.
Hunt, Ralph, 225, 329, 340; c, 191; gj, 234, 300, 306; i, 192; j, 226; oh, 212; pj, 190-223; tl, 235; w, 206.
Hunt, Rob., Q, gj, 337.
Hunt, Sam., 225; gj, 223, 292, 336.
Hunt, Wm., Q, 28, 259; c, 191; gj, 44-168, 293-334; pj, 56-70, 176-250; *v. Pumphary*, 80; *v. Renshawe*, 44.
Hunter, Elleanor, w, 29.
Hunter, Rich., xxv, xxvii.
Hunter, Wm., 61; pj, 60; *v. Oldale*, 49.
Huntley, Wm., d, 110, 162; sv, 82; w, 74.
Husband and wife, separation, 129, 163, 168.
Hutcheson, Eliz., cp, 75.
Hutcheson, Geo., Q, xi, xxvii, 32-77, 106-114, 155, 157; d, 69, 172, 179; gj, 128; j, 45-69; *v. Allen*, 49; *v. Steward*, 130.
Hutcheson, Jno., Q, 220, 247, 285; d, 216, 274, 290; gj, 195-246; pj, 193.
Hutcheson, Jos., Q, r, 92; *v. Sheepey*, 83.

Hutcheson, Joyce, 285.
Hutcheson, Martha, 76.
Hutcheson, Rob., gj, 145; i, 155.
Hutchins, Hugh, Q, 253; c, 307; d, 207; pj, 212; *v. Cleverly*, 199; *v. Huntley*, 162.
Hutchinson, Thos., xi, xxvii, 16, 91, 172, 179; gj, 95; p, 59; *v. Hopper*, 90.

Ible, Nath., Q, gj, 40.
Ignoramus, 136; not a full legal discharge, 259.
Illiteracy, 115; marks, 6, 232, 245, 285, 290, 304.
Indian, 34, 46, 62, 68, 166, 204, 218, 307; belt, 186; line, 92; servants, 125, 200; town, Coerxing, 343. *See* Liquor.
Indians: Indoweys, 125; King Charles, cp, 294; Nummy, 47; Peter, 200; Shocollawanghon, 34.
Indictments, 11, 15, 16, 19, 21, 32, 40, 43, 44, 46, 48, 51, 54, 55, 56, 58, 84, 102, 117, 129, 130, 136, 168, 182, 203, 232, 241, 254, 293, 294, 295, 311, 323, 334, 343; copy, furnished, if paid for, 292; quashed, 185. *See also*, Presentments.
Inducto, Jos., gj, 334.
Information, 83, 199.
Ingoldesby, Lt. Gov. Rich., A, 314, 341.
Ingram, Jno., Q?, d, 74; gj, 63; i, 18; p, 96; w, 95; *v. French*, 70; *v. Senior*, 96.
Inheritance, divided, 162.
Inian, Jno., w, 174; *v. Wilobe*, 100.
Inians, Mrs. Mary, w, 174.
Inquests, civil, 70, 72, 138, 206, 236, 237, 238, 258, 286, 297, 312, 315; coroner's, 72, 95, 167, 212; forms of writ, 286; of return, 287, 288.
Inskipp, Jno., Q, 340; c, 307, 319.
Interest, at 6%, 99.
Interpreter, 108.
Ireton, Dugglas, w, 166.
Ireton, Obadiah, 166, 248; c, 292-303; d, 103, 128; gj, 206, 308; pj, 203-311; r, 299; sv, 102; w, 309.
Irish boys, 227.
Isley, Fran., pj, 72.
Ithell, Jno., Q, 28, 44; d, 81; *v. Bishop and Browne*, 48.

Jackson, Jno., i, 228.
Jacobs, Henry, 1, 8, 36, 61, 68; d, 10, 35, 44, 216; pj, 11; *v. Cook*, 233; *v. Wills and Stacy*, 3.
Jacobson, Henry, *v. Bowman*, 120; *v. Revell*, 121; *v. Wright*, 121.
James, Duke of York. *See* Duke of York. King, xxxiii.
Jarvis, Fran., 210.
Jeanes, Wm., i, 43.
Jegou, Peter, 67, 68, 120; d, 23; *v. Anderson*, 34.
Jenings, Henry, xxv.
Jenings, Jno., d, 222; *v. Newbold*, 103.
Jenings, Jon., *v. Cantrill*, 240.

INDEX

Jenings, Peter, gj, 72; pj, 88; r, 42; tl, 92; w, 74, 85, 88, 101; *v. Cornish*, 116; *and Flockna v. Newman*, 43.

Jenings, Sam., Q, xii, xxvii, xxxvi, xxxviii, liv, 5, 8, 25-28, 78, 144, 321, 327; g, xxxii, 9-23; i, 220; w, 147; *v. Andrews*, 250, 260; *v. Dell*, 192; *v. Moon*, 282; *v. Morgan*, 244; *v. Smith*, 276, 287; *v. Stephens*, 10; *v. Vaus*, 184; *and Commissioners v. Wheeler*, 9.

Jenkins, ——, 31.

Jennings, Edw., d, 330.

Jennings, Jno., w, 307.

Jenson, Chas., 25.

Jenson, Mons, 25.

Jewell, Capt. Jno., A, xxxv, xli, lii, 210, 291; j, 208-226; w, 174; *v. Gardiner*, 214.

Jobson, Mich., a, 293.

Johnson, Abigaell, w, 137.

Johnson, Benj., 137.

Johnson, Clause, cp, 69.

Johnson, Derick, cp, 69.

Johnson, Elias, 10.

Johnson, Fran., 113, 115.

Johnson, Henry, 139; c, 139; cp, 136; w, 87.

Johnson, Jas., p, 165.

Johnson, Jno., Q, d, 10; w, 69.

Johnson, Jon., cp, 338.

Johnson, Kath., w, 137.

Johnson, Oliver, w, 107, 110.

Jones, Benj., Q, 208; gj, 220, 261; pj, 206.

Jones, Chas., and Co., p, 43.

Jones, David, gj, 310.

Jones, Griffith, Q, *v. Potts*, 41, 45, 49.

Jones, Henry, r, 8.

Jones, Jno., Q, d, 139, 175; *v. Cox*, 277; *v. Price*, 305.

Jones, Stephen, *v. Jones*, 175.

Jonson, Peter, 25.

Jooston, Jno., d, 189; *and Hammell v. Hunloke*, 197.

Joris[?], Cor., 68.

Joyner, Jno., 186, 210, 264; gj, 129, 142; pj, 118, 145, 166; w, 132, 167-173; *v. Fryley*, 104.

Joyner, Jno., jr., *v. Duglis*, 264.

Judgments, 29, 34, 43, 44, 50, 58, 59, 65, 70, 82, 103, 119, 120, 147, 150, 156, 158, 160, 161, 165, 167, 172, 175, 178, 179, 181, 186, 187, 194, 196, 202, 211, 221, 222, 224, 225, 231, 233, 237, 239, 242, 243, 244, 250, 252, 256, 260, 264, 269, 278, 280, 298, 299; arrest of (new evidence), 21; by confession, 39, 90, 230, 260; by default, 12, 31, 147, 156, 171, 174, 184, 207, 216, 218, 220, 244, 251, 257, 258, 260, 265, 275, 276, 277, 312, 336; *nihil dicit*, 39, 196; misnomer, 115; no cause of action, 236; non suit, 45, 49, 84, 104, 115, 124, 153, 186, 197, 224, 234, 258, 269, 312, 324; instead of continuance by court, 23.

Judicial records, of pre-Quaker West Jersey, xiv.

Jurors, excused, 295; fined for not appearing, 42, 95, 98, 142, etc.; "no freeholder," 317; paid, 205, 210, 218; refuse to serve, 142, 171 (member Assembly); refuse to take attestation, 182; refuse to take oath, 339-341; "too young," 70; withdrawn before verdict, 9.

Jury, lxii, 1, 2, 9, 11, 12, 15, 16, 18-22, 24, 25, 33, 41-43, 49, 50, 60, 67, 69, 72, 73, 81, 93, 96, 118, 132, 133, 141, 147, 153, 173, 174, 181, 184, 200, 229, 250, 257; challenge to, 57, 173; exceptions against jurors, 118, 137; findings on personal knowledge of jurors, 115, 156; grand, 32, 39, 40, 43, 44, 48, 51, 54-56, 58, 61, 63-65, 69, 70, 72, 74, 82, 86, 88, 89, 92, 95, 98, 101, 115, 117, 118, 123, 128, 129, 130, 136, 141, 142, 145, 148, 152, 154, 157, 159, 164, 166, 168, 171, 176, 180-182, 184, 186, 188-192, 195, 198, 199, 201-203, 206, 208, 212, 214, 215, 218, 219, 223, 224, 226, 229, 231, 234, 241, 246, 251, 252, 253, 258, 261, 265, 269, 270, 271, 281, 292, 293, 295, 297, 299, 300, 303, 304, 306, 308, 310, 313, 316-320, 325, 330, 333, 334, 336, 337, 339, 342; audits accounts, 234; to keep minute book, 234; life and death, 166; of enquiry, 237, 238, 243, 265, 275, 277, 287, 288; petty or traverse, 32, 40, 48, 49, 51, 52, 54-56, 57, 62, 64, 70, 72, 74, 75, 82, 88, 89, 95, 98, 101, 115, 118, 123, 128-130, 139, 142, 145, 148, 152, 154, 157, 159, 164, 168, 171, 176, 180, 183, 185, 188-191, 195, 196, 199, 201, 206, 208-210, 212, 214, 216, 220, 223, 233, 235, 241, 259, 265, 270, 281, 292, 293, 297, 298, 303, 308, 309, 311, 317, 324, 328; Quakers and non-Quakers on, liii; recommendations to court, 58; to lay out a road, 143, 164, 177, 189; to raise a tax, 188; waiver of trial by, 85. *See also*, Grand jury.

Justices, abuse of, 43, 53, 207, 226, 263, 341; fined for non-attendance, 12, 156; form of attestation, 146; leave bench, 134, 158; Quaker and non-Quaker, li-liii; removed, 251.

Kea (Key), Jno., Q, 29; gj, 51.

Keen, Jonas, 1, 3, 10, 28; gj, 148; pj, 11, 12.

Keen, Mouns, gj, 325.

Keene, Fred., c, 201; gj, 184.

Keene, Jno., i, 43.

Keich, Elias, pj, 130.

Keith, George, lii.

Kemble. *See* Kimball.

Kemp, Edw., gj, 337-340.

Kendall, Geo., i, 303; w, 294.

Kendall, Jno., 301.

Kendall, Susannah, w, 294.

Kendall, Thos., Q, 70, 281, 321, 324; c, 65; gj, 130-212; pj, 32, 115-195, 324; t, 156, 161, 209, 215; tl, 126, 154, 190, 223; w, 126; *and Wills v. Pope*, 169.

Kendrick, Mary, i, 272, 282.

INDEX

Kerby, Recompence, Q?, gj, 219; pj, 294.
Kible, Jno., Q??, xli, liii; d, 310.
Kilcop, Eliz., Q?, v. Pricket, 207.
Kimball, Benj., 189; i, 228; and Kemble v. Kemble, 209, 218, 243.
Kimball, Edw., p, 209, 218, 243; v. Kemble, 244.
Kimball, Sam., 149; d, 209, 218, 243, 244; gj, 123, 330; pj, 199, 236; v. Dean, 189.
Kimsey, Thos., sr., 316.
Kimsey, Thos., jr., i, 322; r, 316.
King, Fred., pj, 193.
King, Hermannus, Q, gj, 231-337; pj, 250.
King, Jno., Q, gj, 306; w, 59.
King, The, et al. v. England, 199.
King's prosecutor, Attorney general, 56, 95, 138, 142, 152, 167, 176, 180, 190, 199, 204, 226-269, 296, 301, 332, 341.
Kinsey, Eliz., Q, v. Cole, 4.
Kinsey, Jno., Q; xxvii-xxix, 1, 72; gj, 72; pj, 4, 64, 88.
Kirkbride, Jos., Q, 293.
Knapp, Moses, i, 331; w, 307.
Knight, Jos., Q?, cp, 83; d, 61; w, 22; v. Milner, 60; v. Wheatley, 20.
Knowles, Peter, w, 256.

Ladd, Jno., Q, w, 52.
Lamb, Jacob, Q, c, 319; gj, 252, 297; i, 307; r, 187.
Lambert, Betty, Q?, 76.
Lambert, Geo., w, 56.
Lambert, Jno., Q, xi, xxvii, 1, 32, 198, 304; c, 261; cp, 20; gj, 44, 95, 231, 334; oh, 122, 131; pj, 2, 16, 48, 241, 317; t, 184.
Lambert, Thos., Q, xi, xxvii, 1-8, 32, 76, 91, 156, 200, 302; gj, 44, 184; j, 74-154, 231; pj, 1-13, 259; w, 78, 116.
Lancaster, Edw., w, 120.
Lanchard, Dr., 108.
Land, 16, 25, 34; cutting timber on, 34, 46, 49; holders, lists of, 25-32; levied on for debt, 24, 50, 94, 148, 153, 260; meadow, 17, 42; purchased from Indians, 68, 115; refusal to record deed, 193; servants', 7, 14, 102; survey, 8, 11, 35, 154, 190; title, 3, 22, 25, 46, 49, 67, 119, 170, 178, 207, 211, 237; caveat against recording, 44, 63, 71, 134, 162, 165, 187; defamation of, 116, 216.
Lane, Bernard, Q, 232, 233; c, 122; cp, 229; gj, 115, 164, 206; pj, 154-233, 324; sv, 61; v. Chamnis, 69; v. Pears, 207; v. Reeves, 185.
Langford, Ebenezer, xxxv; d, 238, 245.
Langford, Jno., xxxv, 116, 122; d, 238, 245; pj, 59.
Langstaff, Bethel, cp, 29.
Langstaff, Jno., A, 208, 232; gj, 98, 180, 186; oh, 185; pj, 82, 166, 199.
Langstaff, Moses, A?, c, 213-228; i, 252.
Lanning, Jno., 225.

Lanning, Rob., 225, 340; c, 319; pj, 303.
Larceny. See Stealing, *under* Crimes.
Laswell, Wm., 32; d, 20, 24.
Launce, Thos., w, 37.
Law, criminal, under Quakers, xlviii.
Law books cited, 135.
Lawdell, Jno., i, 232.
Lawrance, And., 109; d, 104, 114; p, 107.
Lawrance, Mary, d, 104.
Lawrence, Geo., w, 55.
Lawrence, Marcus, 29; v. Fish, 20.
Lawrence, Noah, r, 314; w, 313.
Lawrence, Rich., 26, 28; j, 54; v. Warner, 42.
Lawrence, Wm., sr., Q??, d, 131.
Lawrenson, Johannes, 225; gj, 208, 223, 270.
Lawrie, Gawen, Q, xvii, 128.
Lawrie, Mary, d, 128.
Lawrison, Peter, 97.
Laws, made *ad terrorem*, 167; to be read, 15; read, 188; require trial by jury, 107.
Lawson. See Matson.
Lawson, Powell, d, 20.
Lawyers, professional, xlii.
Layton, Jas., 222, 296.
Leaming and Spicer, *Grants*, ix.
Leather, searchers, 19; tanning, 140.
Lebake, Isaiah, w, 104.
Lee, Francis, w, 306.
Lee, Jno., pj, 183.
Lee, Wm., d, 10; v. Allen, 20.
Leeds, Dan., Q, A 1702, xi, xii, xxxviii, lii, 30, 31, 100, 115, 154, 162, 221; c, 88-98; cp, 296; d, 9, 16, 178, 231; gj, 32-215; j, 146-342; p, 170; pj, 8-82; surveyor, 6-13, 67; w, 50, 151, 161, 185, 193, 233; v. Hall and French, 330; v. Ithell, 81; v. Moon et al., 221; v. Stacy, 128.
Leeds, Jno., d, 189.
Leeds, Mary, w, 194.
Legrave, Jehosaphat, pj, 72.
Leonard, Sam., cp, 63; d, 243, 249.
Lespine, Peter, d, 114; p, 107; w, 105.
Lessa (Leza) Point, xxix, 43, 67-68, 81, 119.
Levally, Lewis, 181; c, 300; w, 230, 231, 298; v. Dugglas, 170; v. Smallwood, 113.
Levally, Mary, i, 298.
Levincole, Sam., pj, 281.
Libel. See Actions.
Lillies, David, d, 80, 81; w, 106, 114; v. Pumphary, 84.
Linzey, Dan., 25, 34, 46; d, 16; v. Lawson, 20.
Lippincott, Freedom, Q, 36, 45, 71, 149; c, 93, 95; gj, 32-98, 176; oh, 176; pj, 33, 82, 181; v. French, 124.
Lippincott, Judith, Q, w, 321.
Lippincott, Restore, Q, 227; gj, 166, 198, 234, 320; pj, 176.
Lippincott, Sam., Q, gj, 293-337; pj, 241; w, 322.
Lippincott, Thos., Q, 343.

Liquor selling, 2, 9, 95, 101, 125, 155, 163, 192, 196, 218, 228, 262, 267; to Indians, xxx, xxxi, 2, 3, 45, 69, 84, 101, 125, 209.
Litchfield, Thos., a, 44; d, 42.
Lloyd, David, Q, 171; a, 229, 238.
Locker, Alex., c, 330; gj, 292-310.
Log house for prison, 11.
London, 51, 179.
London Tenth, 50.
Long, Jno., 31, 129; d, 209; pj, 42, 98.
Long, Peter, w, 141.
Lotter, Wm., d, 20.
Love, Priscilla, Q, w, 175.
Love, Rich., Q, c, 65; gj, 51-195; pj, 40-176.
Lovejoy, Wm., l; d, 113; i, 182; pj, 81.
Lovett, Jon., Q, pj, 270.
Lovett, Sam., Q, 1; gj, 32, 48; pj, 1-24, 98.
Lovett, Sam., Q??, op, 331; pj, 324.
Low, Henry, r, 252; *v. Conoroe*, 171.
Lowther, Geo., 322; a, 324.
Loyd, Howell, d, 16.
Lucas, Augustus, d, 104.
Lucas, Dan., 105; d, 104; w, 108, 109.
Lucas, Nich., Q, xvii.
Lucas, Rob., Q, gj, 293; pj, 311.
Lunacy, jury, 61.
Lundy, Rich., Q, i, 58.

MacCay, Dan., sv, 227.
Machiver, Jno., w, 87.
Mackintosh, Wm., c, 292-304.
Maclamere v. Gust, 341.
Maidenhead twp., 191, 204, 208, 219, 225.
Malherbe, Nich., d, 114; p, 107; w, 105; *v. Cox*, 107.
Malicious prosecution, 58.
Malpractice. *See* Actions.
Malster, Wm., xxii-xxv.
Mann, Thos., d, 84; *v. Hancock*, 84.
Manhers, Jno., Q??, cp, 302-309; *v. Abbott*, 312.
Mansfield twp., 30; boundaries, 92.
Marcellus, Joris, 68.
Margorem, Henry, Q?, 327.
Markett. *See* Murkett.
Market place, 44.
Markham, Gov. Wm., 10-11, 200, 230, 242.
Marlow, Henry, A, gj, 281.
Marrell, Wm., gj, 301.
Marriage, certificate, 266; clandestine, 229; pretended, 18.
Marriott, Isaac, Q, xli, 50, 142, 148; d, 48; gj, 43-195; pj, 8-54, 130; w, 160, 161; *v. Dell*, 189; *v. Heeson*, 170; *and Sutton v. Negro Will*, 151.
Marriott, Isaac, jr., Q?, 229, 232, 246; s, 258, 261; *v. Cauin*, 275, 286; *v. Garwood*, 279.
Marsh, Sarah, w, 138.
Marshall, Bewley, d, 221.

Marshall, Dan., Q??, gj, 166.
Marshall, Edw., i, 83.
Marshall, Jas., Q, 64, 72, 104, 106, 112, 127; gj, 63; j, 69-169; *v. Fryley*, 157; *v. Newbold*, 111, 143; *v. Senior*, 81; *v. Wheeler*, 103.
Martin, Jas., Q, j, 72.
Martin, Jno., Q, d, 318.
Martin, Rich., d, 94.
Martineau, Nich., A, 109, 139, 340; d, 114, 278; gj, 261, 318, 334; i, 130, 295; p, 107; pj, 154-303; w, 106, 138, 175, 296.
Maryland, 169, 183, 266; Baltimore Co., 39; Treadhaven Creek, Great Choptank River, 90.
Mashon, Henry, c, 330, 336.
Mason, Mary, d, 318.
Mason, Jno., Q??, d, 318; gj, 157.
Masters, Geo., *v. Bassnett*, 59.
Masters and servants: apprentices, 34, 186, 218, 230, 248, 294, 312, 328; servants, 20, 61, 64, 82, 88, 95, 111, 126, 162, 248, 302; abuse of, 15, 268; bound, 200, 240; complaints against, 102, 257; complaints by, 12, 14, 24, 34, 62, 95, 102, 109-114, 207; dealer in (Trent), 197-201; runaway, 11, 152; sold as, for court charges, 127, 163, 167, 252, 282; time fixed by court, 65, 197-201, 215, 218, 227. *See also*, Indians, Land.
Matchett, Isaac, w, 106.
Mathews, Chas., pj, 324.
Mathews, R., 28.
Mathews, Sam., 225; c, 88, 138; w, 87.
Matlack, Wm., Q, 30, 187; c, 185; d, 10-14; gj, 157-336; pj, 74, 117, 270; sv, x.
Mathews, Thos., Q, 28, 30, 34, 49, 87; cp, 45; d, 21, 48; gj, 54; oh, 19; pj, 23-43.
Matinicunck Island, 68.
Matson (*alias* Lawson), Neales, 25-28.
Matson, Peter, d, 54.
Mauger, Jas., p, 113.
Maynard, Wm., 210.
Meach, Thos., cp, 183.
Meadow, 3, 17, 42, 44, 144, 161.
"Meadowe, great," 93.
Meales, Geo., *v. Jacobs*, 35.
Mecarty, Dan., 222, 223; i, 224.
Medcolfe, Mat., 52.
Menor, Wm., d, 214; *v. Perkins*, 210.
Merchants, 39, 43, 83, 103, 180, 205, 238, 275, 276, 284, 289.
Meredith, Jno., 221; gj, 168; pj, 183-229.
Merial, Wm., c, 311.
Meshall, Henry, gj, 301.
Mew, Rich., Q?, 145.
Middleton, Jno., Q, pj, 317; w, 268.
Middleton, Thos., Q, c, 281, 307; gj, 265; *v. Allison*, 257.
Midgley, Thos., d, 280, 288.
Midgley, Vesulah, a, 281.

INDEX 363

Mifflin, Jno., Q, i, 1.
Milbourn, Jno., Q?, 188.
Miles, Mich., i, 338.
Militia Act, 314.
Mill, 15, 120, 123, 141, 149, 205, 215, 225, 227, 248, 253, 304, 343.
Mill Creek, 92, 220, 232, (or Thomas Evans's Run), 343.
Millard, Chas., c, 261, 270, 330; gj, 212; i, 51; pj, 303; w, 54.
Miller (occupation), 120.
Miller, Math., a, 165; *v. Rush*, 170.
Mills, Ann, jr., *v. Craft*, 333.
Mills, Jno., c, 213, 219.
Milner, Ralph, d, 60.
Milner, Thos., Q, d, 83.
Minderman, Bartholomew, gj, 166-184; pj, 184; *v. Bibb and Duggles*, 186.
Minutes, transcribed by succeeding clerk, 265, 291.
Miscegenation, 156, 256.
Mittimus, 14, 18, 20, 27, 208, 219, 252, 259.
Moll, Jno., 36, 257; i, 40.
Mompesson, Roger, xlvii.
Monckhouse, Wm., w, 120.
Money, bits, 331, 332; Boston, English, 21; dollars, 308; pieces of eight, 199, 223, 228, 338; rates, 7.
Monjoy, Jas., w, 104.
Monro, Jannett, sv, 166; i, 152, 166.
Monse, Capt. Hance, 1, 3, 28, 185.
Monseur, Peter, d, 185.
Montgault, Eliz., d, 104.
Moon, Jasper, Q, d, 221.
Moon, Jonas, Q, d, 221-283; w, 256.
More, Benj., sv, 65.
Moore, Benj., Q, 182, 238; gj, 69, 316; oh, 228; pj, 159, 257.
Moore, Benj., jr., Q?, gj, 203.
Moore, Jno., 189, 292; a, 312; c, 281, 292; gj, 212, 223, 310-339; oh, 228; pj, 229, 250; tl, 282.
Moore, Rich., d, 130, 143; w, 119.
Morehouse, Bryan, 31.
Morgon, Griffith, r, 299; w, 322.
Morley, Henry, c, 331; w, 154.
Morrell, Gilbert, 139.
Morrell, Judith, d, 139; *v. Rotchford*, 139, 157.
Morris, Anth., Q, 49; gj, 40, 44; pj, 21-43.
Morris, Anth., of Phila., 107, 210.
Morris, Lawrence, Q, 72, 142, 148, 165; c, 49, 65; gj, 130-181; i, 91, 209; oh, 228; p, 121; pj, 153-188; *v. Hudson*, 103; *v. Martin*, 94; *and Cripps v. Crafford*, 155.
Morrow, Peter, r, 328.
Mortgage on land, 124.
Moss, Thos., pj, 191.
Mosse, Eliz., 18.

Mott, Justice, 238.
Mott, Wm., *v. Gibson*, 330.
Mount Pleasant, 144.
Moÿe, Jas., cp, 108; w, 109.
Mulberry Creek, 182.
Munion, Thos., i, 292, 321.
Murfin, Jno., Q, 32; gj, 336; pj, 236, 270.
Murfin, Rob., Q, xxvii, 1, 32, 91; gj, 74, 152, 159; pj, 9, 112, 136.
Murkett, Jno., c, 319; d, 329.
Muse, Benj., c, 292.
Mus, Jno., 245.
Myers, Mary, sr., Q?, d, 170; w, 142.
Myers, Mary, jr., w, 142.
Myers, Jos., Q?, w, 302, 309.
Myers, Wm., Q?, 61, 94; j, 69-117; pj, 32-69; w, 56, 60, 62; *v. Doughty*, 96.
Myers, Wm., *v. Oldal*, 330.

Naylor, Jno., d, 60.
Neals "of Upland," *v. Coleman*, 16.
Nealson, Anth., 26.
Negroes, 51, 156, 209; abuse of, 56, 268; attached, 169; attempted suicide of, 268; tax on, 157; trial of, 142.
Negroes: Caser, i, 338; Harry, i, 142, 148; Jack, 268; Mingo, i, 256; r, 255; Peter, r, 329; Phillis, 156; Sarah, 186; Will, d, 151; w, 223.
Neve, Jno., cp, 254, 256; d, 259; i, 222-267; *v. Oldale*, 211.
Nevill, Jas., Q, xxii-xxv, 6.
New York, xxiii, 86, 97, 263, 273.
Newberry, Benj., 100.
Newbie, Hannah, Q, 28, 34.
Newbie, Mark, Q, 34.
Newbold, Ann, Q?, 314.
Newbold, Jno., 17; i, 20; pj, 8, 15; r, 23.
Newbold, Josh., Q, A 1702, xxxviii f., lii; d, 81-143; gj, 136-171; j, 215-234, 292-330; pj, 166-206; w, 74; *v. Oldale*, 119-141; *v. Revell*, 121; *v. Snape*, 103; *v. Wood*, 110.
Newbold, Mich., Q?, A 1702, xi, xxvii, xxxix, lii, 31, 93; oh, 111; pj, 56; *v. Allen*, 103.
Newbold, Mich., jr., Q?, A?, 215, 314; gj, 152; i, 20; j, 206-223, 292-338; pj, 166-235; w, 172, 177; *v. Greene*, 165.
Newman, Jno., A?, d, 24, 43; i, 26-29, 42, 43.
Newton, 63.
Nicholls, Sam., *v. Monseur*, 185.
Nicholson, Geo., xxvii.
Nightingall, Symon, d, 335.
Nihil dicit, 39, 196.
Northampton River (*alias* Rancocas Creek), 17, 93, 96, 144, 168, 300.
Northampton twp., 93; boundaries, 144.
Nottingham, 69, 91, 92; boundaries, 92.
Nuisance, presented, 164.

Oath, administered, 233, 298, 307; false, 298; Quaker practice concerning, xlv. *See* Attestation.
Ogbourn, Jane, w, 160.
Ogbourn, Jno., sr., 185, 208; c, 159; d, 90, 248, 269; gj, 63-339; oh, 313; p, 90; pj, 42, 129-298; w, 119; *v. Blowers*, 48; *v. Goldy et ux.*, 312; *v. Hollinshead*, 214, 233, 245, 250.
Ogbourn, Jno., jr., Q??, 232, 340; gj, 318, 330; i, 190, 252; pj, 199, 223, 229; *v. Hutchins*, 207; *v. Prickett*, 192.
Ogbourn, Sam., 160; c, 122; gj, 142, 154; pj, 69-164.
Ogbourn, Wm., 232; c, 307-316; gj, 212, 261, 325; oh, 337; pj, 294.
Oldale, Lemuel, cp, 253.
[Oldale], Mary, 122.
Oldale, Sam., A, 1, 31, 121; cp, 329; d, 49, 96, 119, 211, 330; gj, 72, 98; i, 117; w, 67; *v. Fretwell and Furnis*, 211; *v. Moore*, 130.
Oldman's Creek, 6, 7, 25.
Ollive, Thos., Q, xi, xxvii-xxix, 1-8, 33, 90, 115, 149, 150, 178, 193; a, 90; cp, 35, 44; d, 3, 10; g, xxxiii, 24-48; j, 12-23; pj, 11, 49; w, 12, 60; *v. Potts*, 42; *v. Smith*, 124; *and Hollinshead v. Ogbourne*, 90; —— *v. Hargrave and Hunloke*, 103-147; —— *v. Pumphary*, 90-94.
Oneanickon, 75.
Ong, Jacob, Q, 206.
Ordinary. *See* Tavern.
Otter, Jno., Q, cp, 34.
Outhout, Fopp, j, xxii, xxiv, xxx.
Overton, Sam., Q, 203, 259, 282; c, 185, 191; gj, 159, 208; pj, 115, 136.
Overton, Thos., gj, 208.
Owen. *See* Foulke.
Owen, Griffith, 230.
Owen, Rich., 215.
Oyer and Terminer, Court of, xlv, 166, 342.

Packer, chosen, 148, 242.
Packing, 186.
Page, Wm., 258.
Paine, Jno., Q, 149; c, 49, 65, 228, 247; d, 153; gj, 32-198; pj, 8-250; w, 193; *et ux. v. Deacon and Leeds*, 231.
Paine, Jno., Q?, gj, 313.
Paine, Nath., Q, gj, 252, 297; pj, 236.
Pain, Wm., w, 231.
Palmer, Thos., Q?, pj, 1.
Pancoast, Jane, 221.
Pancoast, Jno., Q, 32, 93, 115; gj, 56, 98, 101; oh, 74; p, 115; pj, 12-117.
Pancoast, Jno., Q??, gj, 203; pj, 220; w, 221.
Pancoast, Jos., Q, 253; c, 247; gj, 292, 337; pj, 229.
Pancoast, Wm., Q, d, 221.
Pankhurst, Jno., Q, pj, 8.
Papist, 209, 211.
Parker, Geo., Q, 232; c, 185; gj, 201, 231; pj, 82-208; tl, 229; w, 188.
Parker, Henry, cp, 49; d, 48, 60; *v. Cornish*, 61; *v. Davis*, 62; *v. England*, 19; *v. Naylor*, 60; *v. Pearsey*, 60; *v. Wright*, 60-66.
Parker, Jno., 60; *v. Bassnett*, 59; *v. Ward*, 260.
Parker, Jos., Q, 319; c, 307-316; gj, 240-295.
Parker, Wm., Q, c, 191-219; gj, 293, 316; pj, 233.
Parks, Fran., 253.
Parks, Jno., c, 307; pj, 311.
Parks, Roger, Q, A 1702, xxxix, lii, 31; gj, 92-206; j, 297-310; oh, 185; pj, 115.
Parks, Wm., Q?, pj, 294.
Parqenett, Peter, A, *v. Brown*, 318.
Parties, excrs. as defts., as pltfs., *see* Administration of estates; pltf.-heir, 131.
Pateman, Edw., *v. Hackney*, 305.
Patrick, Henry, cp, 42.
Pattison, Jno., 32.
Paul, Jas., d, 333.
Peace, attested, 263; breach of, 26, 130, 199, 249, 263, 303, 334.
Peachee, widow, Q, 149.
Peachee, Mary, 163, 169; i, 123.
Peachee, Dr. Thos., 154, 169; d, 94-98; gj, 136; i, 123, 163; w, 173; *v. Jones*, 139; *v. Potts*, 185; *v. Senior et ux.*, 130.
Peachee, Thos., Q 1700, A 1704, 254; c, 261, 270; pj, 303; w, 307.
Peachee, Wm., Q, xi, xxvii, 1, 3, 178, 193; gj, 40-48; j, 45; oh, 27; pj, 2-52; w, 56.
Peake, Jno., w, 36.
Pears, Eliz., w, 255.
Pears, Jno., d, 131, 155, 157, 207, 269; pj, 137; w, 255; *v. Heathcote*, 155; *v. Hill*, 162.
Pearse, Rich., Q, r, 326.
Pearson, Rob., A, 32, 272; c, 95, 98, 159; d, 44-61; gj, 159-270; oh, 159; pj, 93-235.
Pearson, Rob., 340; c, 330; gj, 325; w, 302, 309.
Pearson, Thos, xi, xxvii; d, 59.
Peck, Jno., i, 83; sv, 88.
Penford, John, Q, xxvii-xxix.
Penn, Wm., Q, x, xvi, xx, xxxvii, 25.
Pennsauken Creek, 92, 93, 96, 124, 342.
Pennsylvania, 35, 175, 183, 307; Bristol, 328; Bucks Co., 115, 291; Philadelphia, 37, 97, 106, 107, 158, 210, 238, 257, 283, 289, 294.
Penston, Anne, i, l, 182.
Penston, Stephen, 182.
Penston, Thos., w, 182.
Penton, Wm., xxiii-xxv.
Perdriau, Eliz., d, 104.
Perdriau, Peter, d, 104-114; *et al. v. Cox*, 107.
Pereys, Sam., d, 192; *v. Verier*, 186, 193.
Perkins, Isaac, A, 210, 213; w, 307.
Perkins, Jacob, sr., A, 213, 215; c, 185, 331, 336;

INDEX

d, 210; gj, 171, 208, 294; i, 176; pj, 181, 303; r, 259; *v. Menard*, 214.
Perkins, Jacob, jr., c, 337; d, 202; w, 306.
Perkins, widow, Q??, 14, 17.
Peters, Thos., Q?, w, 132.
Peterson, Hance, 26, 27.
Peterson, Jno., d, 207.
Peterson, Peter, 3.
Pettit, Mary, 218.
Pettit, Moses, gj, 206, 325; i, 192-196, 323.
Pettit, Nath., 258; gj, 184, 208, 292; i, 192-196, 262, 267; pj, 212; tl, 218.
Pettit, Nath., jr., i, 303.
Petty, Jno., Q, 1, 186, 218; cp, 182; d, 14-23; gj, 154, 297, 299; i, 14-23; pj, 137-180, 257; w, 173; *v. Horner*, 269.
Petty, Jno., jr., 248.
Petty, Wm., sr., Q, 287; pj, 265.
Petty, Wm., jr., Q?, cp, 257; gj, 330.
Peyrard, Jas., 108; w, 105, 109; *et al. v. Cox*, 113; *v. Perdriau*, 107.
Pharoe, Gervas, Q, gj, 191-281; oh, 185, 228; pj, 185.
Pharoe, Jas., Q, 1, 32, gj, 74; pj, 2.
Phillips, Phillip, gj, 292.
Phillips, Theophilus, 205, 225, 329; c, 228, 247, 261; j, 334; pj, 191.
Phillips, Thos., d, 184.
Pickering, Chas., 86, 144, 147; a, 87; d, 21, 44, 132, 154; *et al. v. Snoden*, 120, 145; *v. Tatham*, 120.
Pickering, Wm., *v. Reap*, 24.
Pidgeon, Jos., *v. Cock*, 244, 289; *v. Marshall*, 221.
Pinfold, to be built, 92.
Pinnick, Roger, i, 42.
Pirate, suspected, 229.
Pitchforward, Wm., i, 141.
Plea *in absentia*, rejected, 243.
Pleading, 259, 299; amendments, 238; answer, form of, 238; cross action, 195, 196; declaration, defective, 187; filing, 344; form, 272-274, 277, 280; quashed, 224, 233; demurrer, 296, 299; no consideration, 250; pleas, informality of, 172; order to plead (surety), 299; overruled, 259; satisfaction, 199.
Pledger, Jno., xxii.
Poinsett, Jno., r, 168, 328; w, 173, 231, 263; *v. Howell*, 336.
Ponyon, *alias* Erickson, Peter, 25-27, 46; *v. Mathews*, 48.
Poops, Henry, i, 339, 341.
Poor, 233, 296, 322, 327; overseers, 323, 331.
Pope, Henry, 108; d, 155, 169; w, 124, 125, 199; *v. Austin*, 162.
Pope, Jos., Q, xxvii, 61, 64, 88, 91, 134, 175; c, 65; gj, 63-89; pj, 59-96; *v. Beck*, 80; *v. Hancock*, 81.

Pope, Nath., Q, 151, 175; op, 331; pj, 324.
Port, Jno., d, 153; *v. Wheat*, 156.
Porter, Geo., Q, xxvii, 67; w, 29; *v. Biddle*, 178.
Pottash family, 322.
Pottery, 51.
Potts, Anne, i, 64; w, 238.
Potts, Thos., Q?, xxxix, 1, 65, 82, 224, 340; c, 191, 319-330; cp, 46; d, 3, 20-44; gj, 51-212; pj, 40-191, 259; tl, 19; w, 119, 132; *v. Litchfield*, 42.
Potts, Thos., jr., Q, gj, 208, 219; pj, 229; *v. Ashmore*, 216; *v. Simmons*, 211.
Pound, Jno., cp, 136; d, 139.
Powell, Jno., Q, c, 337; cp, 203; gj, 293; pj, 209, 241.
Powell, Mary, d, 258.
Powell, Rob., Q, xxvii, 1, 253; d, 258, 265; gj, 40; pj, 1-21, 212.
Powell, Wm., w, 268.
Powne, Jno., d, 146; i, 130.
Powson, Jno., 176; d, 156, 178.
Presentment, 72, 80, 83, 88, 91, 92, 99, 102, 115, 117, 121, 123, 124, 129, 130, 136, 145, 148, 152, 155, 162, 163, 164, 166, 168, 177, 180, 188, 190, 192, 199, 209, 218, 220, 223, 224, 228, 229, 234, 235, 248, 252, 253, 255, 261, 262, 263, 264, 266, 271, 272, 282, 293, 295, 298, 299, 300, 303, 304, 307, 309, 310, 314, 317, 319, 322, 323, 325-328, 330, 331, 332.
Price, Dan., d, 234.
Price, Jas., 340; d, 305; gj, 223; pj, 236.
Price, Mary, Q?, w, 322.
Price, Rees, Q?, pj, 317; sv, 215; w, 306, 322.
Price, Thos., *v. Brown*, 318.
Prickett, Anne, w, 173.
Prickett, Jno., 328.
Prickett, Josiah, 328; c, 176; d, 192; i, 188; r, 191; w, 173; *v. Fearman*, 223.
Prickett, Zach., Q, 328, 343; d, 207; gj, 297; pj, 257.
Prison, xlviii, 127, 184, 264, 309; attack on, 252; breaking, 272; committed to, 208, 263; insufficiency of, 297, 332; lack of, 72, 80, 102, 117, 136; order to build, 11, 92; tax for, 129, 146, 304.
Privateers, 223.
Procedure, civil, *see* Appeals, Pleading, Witnesses, Writs; criminal, counsel not allowed, 138; self-incrimination, 151; *see also* Punishments.
Profanity, 65, 108, 304.
Pryor, Joanna, Q, *v. Parker*, 48.
Pumphrey, Marcy, 294.
Pumphrey, Walter, Q, 8, 14, 36, 82, 111; d, 20-113; gj, 51; i, 69, 83; pj, 1-69; w, 40; *v. Antram*, 34; *v. Bowman*, 49-54; *v. Brightwen*, 14; *v. Browne*, 16; *v. Gibsons*, 35; *v. Hancock*, 48; *v. Marriott*, 48; *v. Wheeler*, 84.
Pumphrey, Walter, d, 310-315, 333; r, 294, 298.

Punishments: branding, 338; ear cut off, 75; fine, 4, 9, 14, 15, 19, 20, 25, 26, 29, 30, 32, 44, 49, 52, 55, 58-60, 83, 85, 87, 91, 92, 101, 118, 127, 156, 164, 177, 183, 192, 193, 196, 211, 217, 223, 242, 262, 271, 294, 299, 303, 308, 311, 312, 314, 322, 323, 326, 329-333, 338; governor asked to remit, 196; governor to receive, 193; not paid, 9, 84; refusal to pay, 14, 56; remitted, 114, 155, 163, 177, 213, 226, 340; upon townships, 152; hanging, 143; imprisonment, 80; pillory, 65, 74, 102, 125; restitution, double, 41; fourfold, 35, 39, 63, 65, 71, 252, 263, 272, 338; remitted, 119, 127; retraction, public, 86, 293, 297, 315; whipping, 18, 129, 256, 332; at cart's tail, 11, 43, 53, 55, 71, 73, 79, 118, 156, 160, 186, 224.
Pyne, Jon., d, 90.
Pyner, Edw., w, 46.

Quakers, aversion to litigation, xii; burying ground, 293; fines, 314; general meeting, 132; migration to New Jersey, x; purchase of West Jersey, xvi; refuse to swear, 341.
Quicksall, Wm., Q, c, 201-219; gj, 182; oh, 331; pj, 190.
Quietus, 264.
Quit by proclamation, 29, 59, 117.

Radford, Sam., c, 336.
Rambo, Peter, sr., 26.
Rame, Eliz., 104, 110; d, 114; p, 107.
Ramsdell, Rich., w, 15.
Rancocas Creek, 3, 16, 154, 168, 343; Ferry, 266. See also Northampton River.
Randall, Edw., d, 48-51.
Randolph, Edw., xxxv.
Rangers chosen, 45, 49.
Raper, Thos., Q, xli, 72, 248; c, 81, 95; gj, 63-261; oh, 176; pj, 54-181; s, 269-290.
Rapp, Moses, c, 292.
Ratcliffe, Jno., d, 175.
Rawle, Fran., Q, d, 170.
Rawson, Jno., v. Jannings, 330.
Rawood, Alice, Q, i, 123.
Read, Chas., Q, pj, 48-142; w, 140.
Read, Jas., d, 99; v. Rudroe, 202.
Reading, Jno., 44, 340; pj, 54.
Reap, Sam., d, 20-24, 35.
Recognizances, 9, 42, 43, 54, 70, 85, 187, 281; discharged, 299, 300, 308, 317, 320, 327, 337; for tavern licenses, 154, 190, 193, 213, 220; forfeited, 58, 306; to appear, 203, 208, 222, 223, 243, 248, 249, 252, 254-256, 258, 259, 264, 266, 271, 298, 299, 304, 309, 313-315, 324, 327, 329, 334, 342; to keep peace, 267, 329.
Records, Nath., 253; c, 159, 176; w, 178.
Records, public, copies purchasable, 292.
Red Hill, 317.

Redbank, 46.
Redwood, Abr., v. Heron, 221.
Reeves, Anne, i, 203.
Reeves, Jno., 175, 203; i, 44, 327; r, 328.
Reeves, Susanna, sv?, i, 64, 160, 163.
Reeves, Walter, 45, 80, 162; c, 131, 150; d, 23, 185; gj, 129; v. Biddle, 157; v. Howell, 45; v. Humphries, 153; v. Payne, 153; v. Wright, 23.
Reeves, Walter, c, 331.
Register, commission, 6.
Renavein, Anth., 109, 110; d, 114; p, 107.
Renshawe, Jno., d, 44, 96.
Renshaw, Thos., 222; gj, 195; i, 252; pj, 185-203; r, 328.
Replevin, 94.
Resnier, Peter, 192, 211, 237; c, 185; gj, 180, 192; pj, 154-195; w, 105-114; v. Cox, 143; v. Curso, 205; v. England, 206, 214-226; v. Powne, 146.
Restitution. See Punishments.
Revell, Thos., A, xxxv-xxxix, 30, 35, 39, 81, 144, 149, 177, 194; a, 44, 236-257; clerk, 1-26, 154; i, 304; j, 157-226, 292-342; ka, 176; p, 221; w, 68-192; v. Allen, 318; v. Cocks, 225; v. Collings, 320; v. Cornish, 151; v. Heesom, 100; v. Hill, 116; v. Lasswell, 24; v. Potts, 42; v. Powson, 156; and Hancock v. Mann, 84.
Revell, Thos., cp, 46; d, 96, 121; i, 20; r, 23; sv, 20; w, 119; v. Allen, 66; v. Griffith, 75.
Richards, Jeremiah, 28, 30.
Richards, Nath., c, 292, 298.
Richards, Phillice, 72.
Richards, Philip, 170; cp, 97; d, 171; v. Slade, 100.
Richards, Wm., d, 222; pj, 303; r, 271, 301.
Richardson, Ann, 328.
Richardson, Jno., Q, i, 303.
Richardson, Sam., Q, d, 299.
Ricketts, Nath., 145; gj, 201; pj, 130.
Ridgway, Rich., Q, xxxi, xxxviii, 35, 185; gj, 182, 226, 297, 338; i, 311; j, 234-281; pj, 166; w, 206.
Ridgway, Rich., jr., Q, gj, 324; pj, 294.
Ridgway, Thos., Q, 232; gj, 281, 293, 317; pj, 241.
Rigg, Rob., c, 111; d, 131; gj, 88, 92.
Righton, Sabella, w, 140.
Righton, Wm., Q?, 141; d, 124, 131, 162, 175; gj, 115-188; j, 145-159; oh, 122-148; w, 250; v. Harriott, 96; v. Heesom, 175; v. Sheepey, 129.
Righton, Wm., jr., 183; d, 205; w, 133.
River hazardous, 264.
Roads, altering, 186, 227; assessment for, 19; bridle way, 282; county to meet for repair of, 99; dispute over, 208, 219; laid out or to be laid out, 96, 99, 115, etc.; obstructing, 124, 211; overseers, contempt of, 30, continued, 322, 337; fined, 322, names of, 19, 49, 65, etc.,

INDEX

presented, 130, 155, removed, 321, terms of, 116, to be chosen, 27, 212; presented, lack of repair, 80, 136, 152, 220, 229, 316, 317; work on, neglect or refusal, 27, 30, 61, 148, 271.
Robards, Dr. John, A, i, 234; *v. Steward*, 216; *v. Tatham*, 230.
Roberts, Dorothy, 267; i, 248, 261.
Roberts, Edw., 301; d, 100.
Roberts, Jno., Q, 1, 30; c, 95, 98; d, 10; gj, 32, 123-168; pj, 9-93; w, 22, 33.
Roberts, Jon., gj, 310.
Roberts, Sarah, Q, w, 306.
Roberts, Thos., 222, 225; d, 236.
Robinson (Robeson), Andrew, Q?, xxvii, j, 53-67, 145; *et ux. v. Lawrie*, 128.
Robinson, Chas., d, 115-124.
Robinson, Jas., d, 336.
Robinson, Patrick, 106, 112.
Rockhill, Edw., Q, 65, 149, 161, 168, 175; c, 122; gj, 64-316; pj, 69-270.
Rodman, Jno., Q?, 230.
Rodman, Thos., Q?, 187.
Roe, Henry, i, 252.
Rogers, Mary, Q?, w, 301.
Rogers, Jno., Q, 1, 32; c, 111; gj, 166, 201; pj, 2-118.
Rogers, Jno., A, gj, 306.
Rogers, Wm., *v. Smith*, 333.
Rotchford, Dennis, Q, d, 139, 157; *v. Morrell*, 139.
Rowe, Jos., 221; *v. Towle*, 257.
Rowell, Geo., d, 100.
Rowland, Jno., Q, *v. Holbrook*, 343.
Rowland, Sam., 200.
Royden, Wm., xxvii, 29; pj, 62, 67.
Rudroe, Jno., A?, xxxix, 340; c, 261, 269; d, 202; gj, 206; i, 141; j, 315-336; oh, 122, 131, 150, 160; pj, 149, 190; w, 182, 298; *v. Jones*, 175.
Rumsey, Eliz., 295.
Rumsey, Jno., A, 294, 295.
Rumsey, Rich., 272.
Runnion, Thos., gj, 219.
Rush, Jno., Q, d, 153-170; gj, 166.
Russell, Rich., 29; w, 55; *v. Goforth*, 104, 113.
Russell, Thos., cp, 113, 115; i, 102.

Sabbath, breaking, 206-211, 212, 218.
Saddler, 280.
Sadler, Jno., r, 313.
Sailor, 40; runaway, taken up, 14.
St. Mary's Church, xxxix, lii.
St. Pink. *See* Assinpink.
Salaway, Mr., 107.
Sale, public, 123, 124, 128, 242, 298.
Salem, xviii, 6, 36, 49, 93; court at, xxiii-xxv, xlv, lxix.
Salfert, Rob., d, 81.
Salsbury, Eliz., w, 72, 73.
Salt, 107.
Salter, Anna, 19, 28, 120, 132, 143, 145, 147, 237, 245; d, 24, 89.
Salter, Henry, xxv.
Sand Hill, 232.
Sanford, Wm., 186, 218.
Satterthwait, Jas., Q, xxxvi; c, 95, 98, 202-220; d, 100; gj, 88-166; i, 49; pj, 48-154; w, 69; *v. Hierton*, 103.
Satterthwait, Wm., Q, gj, 130, 265; i, 49; pj, 98, 203.
Saunderlands, Jas., 25.
Saunders, Jno., Q, sv, 34.
Say, Wm., Q, 101; sv, 62.
Scattergood, Benj., Q, 253; gj, 297, 330.
Scattergood, Jos., Q, d, 276; gj, 253, 306; p, 258, 269; pj, 208, 317; *v. Pears*, 207.
Scattergood, Thos., sr., Q, gj, 95, 112, 182; pj, 128, 149, 171.
Scattergood, Thos., jr., Q, 232; c, 202, 213; gj, 198-269; pj, 190, 250, 324; w, 230.
Scholey, Jno., Q, 232, 261, 271; pj, 208.
Scholey, Rebecca Bennett, Q, i, 261, 271.
Scholey, Rob., Q, xxxi, 32; gj, 74; pj, 9-13.
Scholey, Sam., d, 100, 113.
Scholey, Thos., Q, xxxi, 32, 92; d, 80; gj, 92, 253, 337; oh, 288; pj, 43-201.
Scholey, Wm., Q??, A 1702/3, gj, 310.
Scotch servants, 197-201.
Scott, Benj., Q, xxvii, xxviii, 161; d, 10-13; j, 12, 14; oh, 19; *v. Furley*, 12; *v. Ollive*, 10.
Scott, Hannah, Q, 218.
Scott, Henry, A, 232, 238; c, 319, 327; gj, 306, 318; *v. Smith*, 344.
Scott, Jno., Q, 149, 197, 247; c, 131; gj, 176, 240, 246; pj, 137; *v. Perkins*, 202.
Scott, Martin, Q?, 200, 238; gj, 258.
Scrivener, 39.
Scusdouck, Eliz., 328.
Seal, 251.
Search, illegal, xxxvi.
Sena, Thurla, cp, 73.
Senior, Abr., 79, 125, 250; d, 81-147; gj, 72-154; pj, 54-145; tl, 92, 126, 154; w, 199; *v. Boyer*, 113; *v. Burgin*, 100; *v. Coles*, 99; *v. Francis*, 155; *v. Goforth*, 100; *v. Heesom*, 100; *v. Hickman*, 153; *v. Pope*, 155, 162; *v. Ratcliffe*, 175; *v. Renshaw*, 96; *v. Salfert*, 81; *v. Scholey*, 100, 113; *v. Sheepey*, 170; *v. Slade*, 162; *v. Smallwood*, 121; *v. Vaus*, 184; *v. Whitty*, 133.
Senior, Mary, 125; d, 130.
Servants, servitude. *See* Masters and servants.
Shabbacunck, 227.
Sharman, Thos., 32.
Sharp, Hugh, Q, 340; gj, 293, 318.
Sharp, Jno., Q, 70, 182, 187; gj, 70, 152, 186, 240, 338; pj, 180-198.
Sharp, Rachel, Q, w, 306.

Sharp, Thos., Q, 28; w, 182.
Sharp, Mr., of Md., 266.
Shaw, Jno., i, 136.
Sheepey, Chas., d, 83, 129, 170, 199, 245; i, 75; *v. Righton,* 121.
Sheriff, attestation, 5; committed, 301; contempt of, 45, 176, 263; deputy or under, 47; draws jury, 275; escape from, 148, 177; fined, 49, 55; list of, xli; return to execution, 246; sued, 162; to pay charges, 192; unlawful execution, 49.
Sherwin, Jas., 63, 99, 187; c, 159; d, 100, 129, 157; gj, 63, 164, 188, 219; pj, 69, 159, 206; w, 196.
Shinglefield, Thos., 248.
Shinn, Clement, 1; *v. Woolverton,* 162.
Shinn, Geo., Q, gj, 70; i, 34.
Shinn, Jas., Q, 227, 237; gj, 293, 320; i, 271.
Shinn, Jno., sr., Q, 1, 31, 115, 219; c, 65; gj, 40-112, 240; oh, 19, 228; pj, 2-164; *v. Arnold,* 16; *v. Righton,* 162.
Shinn, Jno., jr., Q, 45, 49; gj, 101-318; pj, 61-241.
Shinn, Thos., Q, gj, 70, 164; pj, 93, 98.
Ship, building, 107; information against, 199; seized, 183; wreck, 39, 97.
Shippen, Edw., Q, 258; *et ux. v. Basnett,* 194.
Shrieve, Caleb, Q, 253; gj, 253, 297, 337; oh, 331; pj, 281.
Sife, Henry, d, 62.
Silver, Arch., Q?, w, 22.
Silver, Jas., Q?, 72.
Silver, Jno., Q??, d, 178, 181.
Simmons, Randolph, d, 211.
Singleton, Thos., 30.
Six Mile Run, 205, 225.
Skeen, Rob., d, 325.
Skene, Alex., cp, 168.
Skene, Jno., Q, 101, 115; cp, 98; d, 102; g, xxxiii, 47-89; j, xxxiv, 19, 92-112; *v. Knight,* 61.
Skene, Mary, w, 85.
Skene, widow, 144.
Slade, Edw., 64; d, 98-162; w, 89.
Slaiter, Geo., sv, 198.
Slander, scandal, defamation, 4, 8, 13, 24, 58, 60-65, 83, 86, 98, 100, 104, 113, 132, 139, 145, 153, 160, 170, 174, 183, 193, 209, 222, 256, 268, 273, 292, 297, 324-330, 333. See Actions.
Slaves. *See* Negroes, Indians.
Sloop, 23, 36, 86, 97, 106, 107, 109.
Slow, Jno., *alias* Stanton, i, 252.
Small, Rob., d, 336.
Smallwood, Jos., d, 113-121; *v. Hierton,* 128.
Smalwell, Jno., 332.
Smalwell, Mary, i, 332.
Smith, And., Q?, A 1702, 1, 32; gj, 141-148, 270; oh, 176; pj, 115; w, 182; *v. Oldale,* 96.
Smith, And., w, 311.
Smith, Armstrong, *v. Robinson,* 336.

Smith, Chas., d, 333.
Smith, Dan., Q, 154, 327; gj, 164-318; pj, 195-324; w, 262.
Smith, Edw., d, 94, 124; *v. Gilbert,* 116; *v. Goforth,* 103.
Smith, Eliz., cp, 155.
Smith, Emanuell, Q, 217, 254, 340; d, 214; gj, 318, 334; i, 206; pj, 220-324; r, 208, 305, 308; w, 143.
Smith, Geo., Q?, c, 93-98; gj, 129-234; pj, 74-188.
Smith, Isaac, 72; gj, 88.
Smith, Jasper, 225; c, 307-317; gj, 292; pj, 223.
Smith, Jno., Q, d, 96; gj, 63, 74; i, 69; pj, 72, 88; w, 37; of Salem, xxii.
Smith, Jno., Q, c, 319; d, 276, 287; gj, 261, 297; r, 313; w, 250; *v. Edwards,* 335.
Smith, Jos., Q, 225, 232, 238; c, 261-270; gj, 227, 253, 320; oh, 228; pj, 203.
Smith, Mat., cp, 155; d, 10.
Smith, Rich., Q, 238; gj, 265, 269.
Smith, Sam., Q, d, 344.
Smith, Seth, Q, 1, 30; pj, 11-81; *v. Allen,* 16; *v. Hancock,* 60-64; *v. Reap,* 24.
Smith, Thos., Q, 205, 225; c, 336; d, 131; gj, 219; oh, 212; pj, 223, 241, 270; w, 311.
Smith, Wm., 103; d, 80, 94.
Smith, Wm., d, 318; *v. Stacy,* 318.
Smithy, 57.
Smout, Edw., *v. Cropp,* 244.
Snape, Jno., Q?, 259, 287; c, 201-218; gj, 145-293.
Snead, Wm., Q, d, 96.
Snowden, Anne, Q, w, 12.
Snowden, Chris., 95; cp, 98, 296; d, 116; gj, 101; i, 130; ka, 56; pj, 54, 61; s, 296; t, 101, 125, 133; tl, 92; w, 103; *v. Cornish,* 124; *v. Gardiner,* 218; *v. Heesom,* 124; *v. Hollinshead,* 124; *v. Senior,* 125, 127; *v. Sheepey,* 199, 245.
Snowden, Jno., Q, 1, 31, 147; c, 49-62; d, 120; gj, 142; pj, 9, 54; *v. Ellis,* 61.
Snowden, Thos., gj, 43.
Snowden, Wm., xi, xxvii, 145.
Solly, Stephen, d, 184, 185.
Songhurst, Jno., Q, 26.
Sonmans, Peter, j, 342.
South, Thos., w, 254.
Spencer, Chas., c, 307; w, 268.
Spencer, Fran., w, 268.
Spencer, Wm., 258; c, 281; gj, 310; pj, 233, 250; r, 248.
Spicer, Jacob, Q?, *v. Biddle,* 169.
Spinning, 233.
Springfield, 205, 208, 227; boundaries, 93.
Stacy, Eliz., Q, w, 36.
Stacy, Henry, Q?, xxvii, 28, 31, 165; j, 19; pj, 12-15.
Stacy, Jno., Q, 36.
Stacy, Mahlon, Q, xi, xxvii, xxxi, xxxvi, 1-5,

32, 91, 129, 134, 205, 225, 227; d, 128, 172, 179; j, 16-271; w, 129, 238; *v. Brenson*, 84; *v. Tunneclift*, 157.
Stacy, Mahlon, jr., oh, 331.
Stacy, Rebecca, Q, d, 318; *v. Smith*, 318.
Stacy, Rob., Q, xi, xxviii, 1-8, 29-30, 61, 147; d, 3, 147; gj, 63; j, 12-82; oh, 49; pj, 23-64; w, 49, 67; *v. Jegou*, 23; *v. Slade*, 100; *v. Stephenson et ux.*, 42; *et al. v. Dewsberry*, 237, 245.
Stacy, Sam., 128, 144, 181, 225; gj, 112; *v. Croft*, 165; *v. Snoden et al.*, 116.
Stanbanck, Jno., d, 14; i, 55; *v. Woodhouse*, 14.
Stanbury, Nathan [of Phila.], Q, 255, 266.
Staniland, Hugh, 32, 69; pj, 93; tl, 92.
Stanley, Wm., Q, a, 81; gj, 63, 72; pj, 69, 81; w, 81.
Stanton. *See* Slow.
Staples, Jno., d, 333.
Staples, Thos., Q??, gj, 338; oh, 331.
Starr, Rich., w, 87.
Staves, 90.
Stayner, Wm., Q, pj, 69.
Steele's Branch, 44.
Steelman, Chas., 298, 337.
Stephens, Fran., d, 10, 83; *v. Allen*, 10; *v. Scott*, 10; *v. Whittaker*, 10.
Stephens, Jno., 126, 127; d, 44.
Stephenson, Jon., d, 42.
Stephenson, Mary, d, 42.
Stevens, Anne, sv, i, 248, 252.
Stevens, Rob., c, 337; w, 268.
Stevenson, Wm., Q, gj, 258.
Steward, Alex., Q, 208, 223; 232; c, 292; d, 130; gj, 252; pj, 199; sv, 102; wife of, i, 224; *v. Grant*, 231; *v. Hancock*, 96.
Steward, Edm., 31, 208, 227; d, 216; gj, 89-212; pj, 73-311; w, 93, 172, 182; *v. Beswick*, 12; *v. Boarton*, 13; *v. Long*, 209; *v. Wills*, 9.
Steward, Jos., Q, cp, 225; gj, 231; pj, 259; *v. Roberts*, 236.
Steward, Saunder's, wife, 126.
Stiles, Priscilla, p, 97.
Stiles, Rob., sr., c, 281; d, 143; gj, 325; i, 141; pj, 51, 52, 297; *et ux. v. Hill*, 97.
Stiles, Rob., jr., cp, 141.
Stillman, Chas., gj, 325.
Stocks, 4, 125.
Stockton, Job, Q, gj, 281.
Stockton, Jno., c, 261-271; gj, 208, 310, 330; pj, 236, 257; w, 160.
Stockton, Jos., w, 160.
Stockton, Rich., Q, pj, 166, 196.
Stokes, Jno., Q, xxvii; gj, 320.
Stokes, Thos., Q, 232, 238; c, 122; gj, 32-98, 199, 313; oh, 228; pj, 8-82, 183, 190; w, 12; *v. Petty*, 12.
Stones, Jos., Q, 32.
Story, Jno., 90.

Stout, Jon., 315; gj, 301.
Strayner, Wm., pj, 73.
Stubbs, Jos., 10; d, 10.
Suderick, Josiah, Q?, gj, 313.
Sugar, 199.
Suicide, attempted, 268.
Suillavan, Turolas, gj, 192; w, 194.
Summons, delivered by sheriff through keyhole, 236.
Surkett, Jno., Q, gj, 301, 313.
Surveyor, 170, 178; attestation, 6; fees, 7; to lay out tenths, 11.
Surveys, approved, 182, 190.
Sutton, Dan., A, 217; c, 131; cp, 185; gj, 117-339; p, 151; pj, 112-206; r, 252; w, 294; *v. Chamnis*, 103; *v. Decow*, 143; *v. Wills*, 296; *and Morris v. Hudson*, 121.
Sweatnam, Eliz., cp, 191.
Swedes, in Delaware River valley, xiii, xiv.
Syddall, Ralph, d, 124.
Sykes, Nath., sv, 7.
Sykes, Sam., Q, 77.
Sykes, widow, Q, 92.
Symonds, Roger, i, 18, 19.

Talbot, Rev. Jno., A, 293.
Talbot, Wm., of Pa., w, 307.
Talbot, Wm., of the Ferry, w, 307.
Tannhouse Run, 170.
Tantum, Jno., Q, 237; gj, 265-336; pj, 229.
Tatham, Dorothy, 229.
Tatham, Eliz., *v. Basse*, 240.
Tatham, Jno., xxxv, li, 105, 113, 114, 192, 229, 240; a, 116, 211, 214; d, 120, 187, 206, 230; gj, 95; i, 224; j, 145-222; pj, 137; w, 190; *v. Beck*, 178; *v. Budd*, 174; *v. Dubrois*, 103; *v. Gibbs and Allen*, 139; *v. Green*, 193; *v. Hatchley*, 153; *v. Hudson*, 185; *v. Perdriau et al.*, 114; *v. Salter*, 89; *v. Solly*, 184; *v. Wood*, 116; *and Leeds v. Myers*, 170.
Tatham, Jno., jr., 231.
Tavern, bad order in, 101; license forfeited, 229; licenses, 3, 19, 27, 92, 96, 125, 154, 184, 190, 193, 202, 203, 213, 218, 220, 223, 229, 235, 282, 302, 311; no license, 192.
Tax, refusal to pay, xxxvii.
Taxes, 19, 122, 129, 146, 149, 151, 152, 157, 168, 176, 177, 182, 185, 188, 189, 202-205, 213-219, 228, 232, 234, 235, 246, 251, 258, 304, 329, 335-339.
Taylor, Edw., xxvii, 7.
Taylor, Geo., w, 106, 109.
Taylor, Isaac, 230.
Taylor, Sam., Q, xxvii, 52, 237; c, 247; d, 251; gj, 112-208, 301, 313; oh, 159, 313; pj, 95, 229-265.
Taylor, Thos., *v. Watson*, 43.
Temple, Abr., 317; d, 313; oh, 313; r, 341.

Terrett, Sam., A, a, 274; c, 191; d, 96; pj, 212; w, 99.
Terry, Thos., 30; i, 42; w, 120.
Test, Jno., lii, 2, 106, 215; d, 202; j, 206-226; pj, 201; *v. French,* 221.
Testimony, 266; before coroner's jury, 167; by deposition, 172-175, 210, 231, 238, 250, 255, 257, 307; perpetuation of, 54, 82. See also, Witnesses.
Thackeray, Thos., Q, 28; j, 52.
Thatcher, Bartholomew, i, 303.
Theakes, Jno., 31.
Thievery. See Actions.
Thomas, Mich., *v. Gardner,* 96.
Thompson, Jas., c, 331; gj, 338, 339.
Thompson, Jno., Q, 5.
Thorne, Jno., Q?, 340.
Thorpe, Zebulun, 36.
Throp, Jno., d, 80; w, 87.
Thrumball, Sam., d, 21, 35; *v. Stephens,* 10.
Timber, felling, 34, 43, 45, 46, 49, 68, 93; float of, 209.
Tindall, Rich., xxv.
Tindall, Thos., 32, 259, 340; c, 150, 261, 269, 281; gj, 166-223, 301-325; oh, 229; pj, 153-196, 311.
Tobacco, 181.
Toe, Jno., 18.
Toll, over mill dam, 149.
Tomkins, Eliz. (Hambley), 242.
Tomkins, Josh., Q, 227, 242.
Tomlinson, Jno., Q, 185; gj, 152, 190; pj, 82-183; w, 76; *v. Sheepey,* 83.
Tompkins, Anth., 86; cp, 40.
Tompkins, widow, 86.
Tonkan (Thomkins), Jno., A, 237, 272, 309; c, 131, 150, 152; cp, 160; gj, 168-226, 330, 339; pj, 209; w, 185.
Towle, Eliz., 257.
Towle, Jno., d, 257.
Towle, Percivall, Q, xxvii, 30, 31, 115; gj, 43, 95, 117; oh, 93, 122; pj, 41, 115; *et al. v. Robeson,* 115.
Towle, widow, 144, 149.
Town, laying out of, 47.
Town, township meeting, 130, 149, 154, 164, 187, 204-205, 219, 282.
Townsend, Grace, *v. Watts,* 305.
Townships, boundaries, 92, 187, 294, 343; clerk, 282; may lay out highways, 122; organized, 191.
Toy, Elias, 290; c, 150-157; cp, 295, 298; gj, 148, 192, 325; w, 306.
Toy, Fred., r, 295, 298.
Trade, regulation of, 183, 199, 200.
Treadway, Henry, Q?, l, 1, 26, 28; d, 8, 54; i, 32, 72; r, 73.
Treasurer, 188, 192, 195, 201, 202, 205, 206, 210, 219, 220, 228, 229, 234, 340.
Tregidgon, Nich., sv, 152.

Trenoweth, Ralph, pj, 82.
Trent, Jas., 197.
Trespass. See Actions.
Trial, without jury, 107.
Trover. See Actions.
Tuckness, Henry, i, 295.
Tuely, Jno., d, 24, 90, 171; gj, 310-336; i, 63; pj, 208, 311.
Tunneclift, Fran., d, 157.
Turner, Mary, cp, 152.
Turner, Rob., Q, 28, 45, 46, 63; j, 25, 27; *v. Cocke,* 191.
Turner, Wm., i, 152.
Twyn, Rob., 101.
Twyning, Wm., i, 11.

Underhill, Hannah, 331; i, 319.
Underhill, Jno., 31, 253.
Upland, Court of, xxix, xxxi, 68.
Ustason, Hance (Jas.), 25; *v. Coleman,* 14.

Vagabonds, 95.
Van de Grift, Leonard, w, 210.
Van der Grift, Nich., w, 210.
Vanderhoyden, Matthias, cp, 40; w, 37.
Van Standt, Cor., *v. Peterson,* 207.
Vanhist, Reneir, *v. Leeds,* 189.
Vaus, Sam., sr., 185, 208, 212; pj, 206.
Vaus, Sam., jr., d, 184.
Vaus, Thos., i, 209; pj, 297.
Venables, Frances, 261.
Venereal disease. See "Burnt."
Verdict, sealed, 79, 119, 141, 172, 175; special, 33, 86.
Verier, Jas., d, 186; gj, 269.

Wade, Edw., Q, xxiii-xxv.
Wade, Nath., cp, 306.
Wade, Rob., Q, *v. Helmsley,* 44.
Wages, 70, 74, 114, 121, 133, 207.
Wakefield, Thos., pj, 317.
Walbridge, And., i, 180.
Walden, Roger, i, 35.
Walker, Jno., Q, a, 20; cp, 42; w, 24; *v. Reap,* 23, 35.
Walker, Jno., gj, 325.
Walker, Sarah, w, 24.
Wallis, Thos., 30, 187, 215, 326; c, 111; gj, 191; pj, 168-196, 270.
Walter, Hance, w, 55.
Walter, Maudlin, cp, 55.
Walton, Dan., Q?, 28, 30.
Wampum, 36, 125, 126.
Ward, Geo., Q?, 16.
Ward, Howard, w, 72.
Ward, Capt. Jno., A, 259, 340; cr, 305; d, 260; i, 304; *v. Holbrook,* 344; *v. Pumphary,* 333.
Wardell, Wm., i, 156, 234, 303.
Warden, Eliakim, gj, 269.

INDEX

Warner, Edm., xviii ff; xxxii; d, 16.
Warner, Wm., Q, xxvii, 26, 28; d, 42.
Warrant, 46, 53, 59, 80, 84, 112, 121, 207, 212, 249, 256, 261; search without, 217, 264; to bring in prisoner, 266.
Warren, Jno., Q, c, 191; gj, 130-334; pj, 159-190; w, 185.
Warwin, Eph., i, 4.
Warwin, Jno., pj, 102.
Wasse, Jas., xx, xxiii.
Watson, Ann, Q, w, 302.
Watson, Isaac, Q, c, 212, 292; gj, 281-336; oh, 313.
Watson, Jno., Q, pj, 233.
Watson, Luke, d, 43.
Watson, Mat., Q, 16, 31, 228, 234; c, 185; gj, 171-330; pj, 49-270.
Watson, Wm., Q, 91, 189; c, 159, 319-325; gj, 101.
Watts, Wm., d, 305.
Wayt, Wm., i, 20; r, 23.
Wearing. *See* Dummer.
Wearne, Jno., gj, 82-181; pj, 157.
Web, Isaac, d, 277.
Webley, Thos., 136; d, 260.
Weds, Jos., 52.
Weights and measures, 19, 148, 340.
Wellingborough, 93.
Wellingborough twp. v. Chester twp., 327.
Welch, Jos., Q, gj, 297; *v. Pumphary*, 315.
Welch, Wm., xxxiii.
Wells, Edm., 213; d, 249; gj, 270, 301; pj, 220, 223.
Wells, Henry, c, 281; d, 249, 259, 318; *v. Powell*, 265.
Wells [Wills?], Jno., jr., gj, 269.
Wells, Thos., d, 212.
Wessells, Gerrardus, *v. Litchfield*, 44.
West, Jno., 260.
West, Jon., 232, 248; c, 176; d, 99; i, 69, 82, 136; pj, 154, 210; w, 174; *v. Pumphary*, 74; *et ux. v. Pound*, 139.
West, Mary, i, 136; p, 139; w, 174.
West, Nath., 30, 201; gj, 69-181; pj, 51-129.
West, Nath., jr., 201.
West, Wm., d, 236.
West Jersey Society, xxxiv-xxxvii, 221, 227.
Westland, Nath., A, xxxviii f., lii, 335; d, 221, 341; j, 159-226, 292-320; *v. Wills*, 205.
Weston, Anth., *v. Roberts*, 100.
Weston, Abr., 47.
Wetherill, Chris., Q, xli, 72, 134, 151; c, 81, 95; gj, 40-292; i, 209; oh, 176; pj, 23-324; s, 234-260.
Wetherill, Jno., Q, 304; c, 261-270; gj, 320, 338; pj, 303; r, 298, 299; w, 268, 271, 304; *v. Martin*, 318.
Wetherill, Thos., Q, 242; c, 281; gj, 334; oh, 313, 321; pj, 257, 324; r, 327; w, 262; *v. Wills*, 229.
Whales, 47, 83, 87, 106.

Wheat, Benj., Q, xli, 19, 191, 227, 229, 237, 287; d, 156; gj, 310; i, 46; ka, 199; pj, 14-270; s, 46-49; w, 238; *v. Heathcote*, 113.
Wheat, Mary, Q, w, 271.
Wheatly, Caleb, Q, c, 228, 247; w, 302, 309.
Wheatly, Sarah, Q?, w, 302.
Wheatly, Thos., 14; d, 20.
Wheeler, Gilbert, xxxi, 84; d, 84, 103, 114; i, 9.
Wheeler, Rob., Q, A 1702, xxxviii f., lii, 101, 232, 264, 340; c, 131; d, 197; gj, 130-206; j, 234-336; pj, 112-233; *v. Atkins*, 207; *v. Greene*, 131; *v. Hutcheson*, 216; *v. Jacob*, 216; *v. Perrett*, 192; *v. Tatham*, 197.
Wheelwright brothers, 30.
White, Amos, Q?, 101.
White, Chris., Q?, gj, 54.
White, Eliz., w, 265, 267.
White, Jas., Q, c, 122; gj, 88, 154.
White, Jno., Q, xli, 8, 10, 68; a, 9; s, 12-16; *v. Laswell*, 20; *v. Reap*, 20; *v. Stubbs*, 10.
White, Jno., a, 124, 134.
White, Jos., A, 186, 242, 255; gj, 199, 226, 318; pj, 191, 212.
White, Peter, Q, c, 247; pj, 233.
White, Thos., d, 34.
Whitehead, Benj., Q, 63; *v. Sife*, 62.
Whitfield, Rich., Q, p, 237.
Whittaker, Rich., d, 10.
Whitten, Sarah, Q, w, 127.
Whitty, Wm., d, 133.
Wickam, Geo., sv, 257.
Wife, abuse of, 177, 248; complains against husband, 152; deserted, 126; entertaining another man's, 228; no husband, 95; runaway, 18; separation from husband, 163, 169.
Wild, Jas., c, 331; gj, 308.
Wilkins, Jno., pj, 303.
Wilkins, Thos., Q, 187; c, 191; gj, 317, 338; pj, 191-297; w, 342.
Wilkinson, Jno., 340.
Wilkinson, Thos., Q, 209; cp, 35; gj, 152, 246; w, 33, 194, 197.
Will, 162, 179; read in court, 97, 120; suit for legacy, 120.
Willcocks, Rob., i, 262.
Willgoose, Rich., c, 292, 307.
Willhouse, Geo., gj, 152.
Williams, Mary, *v. Dorson*, 333.
Williams, Rob.[?], 333.
Williams, Thos., Q, 271; d, 81, 170; gj, 171-195; i, 130, 261; pj, 164, 176; w, 180.
Willis, Geo., A, 232,305; d, 333; gj, 261, 318, 339; t, 242, 292-343; tl, 190, 220; w. 241.
Willis, Jno., gj, 72.
Willis, Sam., d, 9, 14-16; *v. Allens*, 10; *v. Dewsbury*, 10.
Willocks, Geo., r, 342.
Wills, Dan., sr., Q, xi, xii, xxvii-xxix, xxxvi, 1-158; a, 35; cp, 118; cr, 146, 167; d, 3-4; j, 25-

INDEX

Wills, Dan., sr. (*Continued*)
198; ka, 95; oh, 19, 27, 30; pj, 15, 18; w, 2-161; *v. Chinton*, 54; *v. Grubb*, 181; *v. Hill*, 113; *v. Snead*, 96.
Wills, Dan., jr., Q, 247; c, 247; d, 296; gj, 181, 240, 297; pj, 32-270; *v. Higgins*, 157.
Wills, Jas., Q, liv, 1, 72, 81, 96, 128, 148, 224-246; d, 205, 229; gj, 40-164; i, 56; oh, 88, 160; p, 169; pj, 18-188; w, 69; *v. Burden*, 100.
Wills, Jno., Q, 96, 187, 242, 247, 343; c, 49, 65; gj, 115-180, 292, 336; j, 226-281; oh, 159, 176, 185, 313, 321; pj, 32-195, 311, 324; w, 44, 342; *v. Pumphray*, 330.
Wills, Sam., d, 9; pj, 9.
Wilobe, Wm., *alias* Mathias Barkstead, d, 100.
Wilsford, Jno., Q, c, 88, 95; gj, 136, 159, 176; oh, 159; pj, 89, 115; w, 129.
Wilson, Rob., Q, 16, 31; c, 95, 98; gj, 95, 152, 159, 240; pj, 49, 74.
Wilson, Stephen, Q, c, 228, 247.
Wilson, Thos., Q?, 227; c, 330; gj, 208, 227; op, 331.
Wingerworth Point, 153.
Winn, Thos., Q, 26.
Winn, Wm., w, 51.
Witness, 13, 15, 18, 21-24, 29, 33, 36-40, 45, 49-57, 59-68, 71, 73-79, 81-82, 84-90, 93, 97, 99, 101-111, 114, 116-121, 124-127, 129, 132-133, 137-138, 140, 142-143, 145, 151, 154, 155, 158, 160-162, 165-167, 170-180, 193-194, 196-197, 199-200, 204, 210, 221, 230-231, 233, 241, 249, 250, 254-257, 262, 263, 266-269, 296, 298, 302, 306, 308-309; attested, 40-334 *passim*; fined for not appearing, 182; offered, incompetent to testify, 33, 125; refuses attestation, 151, 233; sworn, 137, 310, 230, 233, 294-316 *passim*; testimony read, 24, 53, 54, 59, 68, 90, 106, 108, 140, 150, 165, 173-175, 231, 255, 257, 260, 266. *See also*, Attestation, Oath, Perjury, Testimony.
Wolverton, Chas., Q, d, 162; oh, 313; pj, 220, 324; *v. Greene*, 162.
Wolves, etc., act for destroying, 149, 152, 339.
Women, jury of, 78.
Wood, Henry, Q, 28.
Wood, Isaac, Q, d, 333.
Wood, Jno., Q, xxvii, 1, 26, 28, 31; d, 16, 116; j, 72; pj, 11, 54; w, 73; *v. Durham*, 16; *v. Hancock*, 23.
Wood, Jno., of Pa., i, 115.
Wood, Jon´., Q, pj, 51.
Wood, Jos., d, 74; *v. Cole*, 216.
Wood, Peter, Q?, gj, 293.
Wood, Thos., A, 1, 31; c, 6; gj, 115, 152, 223; pj, 74, 89, 196.
Wood, Wm., Q, xxxviii, 36, 187, 192, 196; a, 198; c, 159; d, 110; gj, 45, 82, 101, 231-337; i, 292, 297; pj, 42, 57, 130-188, 250; w, 102, 118,

185; *v. Greene*, 202; *v. Greene and Atkins*, 192.
Woodhealth, Henry, d, 336.
Woodhouse, Ant., Q, 1, 31; d, 14; gj, 51; pj, 9; w, 10; *v. Stanbanck*, 14.
Woodhouse, Jno., Q??, 1.
Woodnut, Rich., Q, gj, 70; pj, 43, 59.
Woodrof, Simon, c, 292, 301.
Woodward, Ant., Q, 190; c, 191; *v. Taylor*, 251.
Woolcott, Peter, Q, pj, 88.
Woolman, Jno., Q, xxvii, 115; c, 65; gj, 43-325; oh, 122, 131, 150; pj, 54-201.
Woolman, Jon., gj, 310.
Woolston, Hance, 25.
Woolston, Hanna, Q, 240.
Woolston, Jno., sr., Q, 31, 49, 115, 144, 161; c, 6; d, 3; gj, 48-115; i, 252; oh, 19, 30, 122, 130; pj, 1-123; w, 33-193.
Woolston, Jno., jr., Q??, 65, 340; c, 228, 247; cp, 64; gj, 159, 203, 330; i, 20; pj, 181, 188, 208; r, 23; w, 307.
Work out debt, 35.
Worlidge, Jno., j, 156.
Worth, Jos., Q, 205.
Wright, Alice, i, 319.
Wright, Anne, i, 51, 136, 162, 177.
Wright, Benj., c, 307, 316, 317; gj, 306; p, 318.
Wright, Hugh, *v. Ely*, 284; *v. Embly*, 276.
Wright, Jon., Q, gj, 334, 340.
Wright, Josh., Q, xxvii, 30, 32; c, 1; gj, 98, 231, 246; i, 115; oh, 93; pj, 21, 121, 201; w, 132.
Wright, Rich., 340; gj, 334; oh, 331.
Wright, Sam., Q?, 1, 32; gj, 92; pj, 1.
Wright, Thos., Q?, xxvii, 1, 31-68, 168-231; a, 60; d, 9, 14, 23, 60, 121, 132, 188; gj, 92, 141; i, 115, 118, 188, 190; pj, 1-16, 82, 223; *v. Bowman*, 13; *v. Calowe*, 113; *v. Cripps*, 8; *v. Duncks*, 15; *v. Eldridge*, 14; *v. Fenton*, 83-93; *v. Greene*, 131, 143; *v. Groome*, 188; *v. Hutcheson*, 69; *v. Moore*, 143; *v. Reeves*, 23; *v. Tatham*, 187.
Writs, capias, *non est inventus*, 191, 205, 215; *fieri facias* (forms), 288-290; filing of, 94; new process refused, 147; *scire facias*, 236; summons, 26. *See also*, Inquests.

Yearnens, Erick, xxi.
Yeo, Jno., 67; d, 39.
Yeoman, 271, 277, 283, etc.
York, Mary, p, 224.
York, Thos., d, 236; *et ux. v. Wearing and Dummer*, 224.
Young, Jno., sv, 201.
Young, Nich., d, 24.
Young, Rob., Q, 31; gj, 48, 56; oh, 49; pj, 19-67; *v. Adye*, 14.

Zane, Rob., Q, 288; c, cp, 32.

www.ingramcontent.com/pod-product-compliance
Lightning Source LLC
Chambersburg PA
CBHW071235300426
44116CB00008B/1050